Critical Issues in Education
Dialogues and Dialectics

Ninth Edition

JACK L. NELSON
Rutgers University

STUART B. PALONSKY
University of Missouri

MARY ROSE MCCARTHY
Pace University

WAVELAND

PRESS, INC.

Long Grove, Illinois

For information about this book, contact:
Waveland Press, Inc.
4180 IL Route 83, Suite 101
Long Grove, IL 60047-9580
(847) 634-0081
info@waveland.com
www.waveland.com

Cover image by valiakaka (Shutterstock.com)

Contents

PART ONE
Whose Interests Should Schools Serve?
Justice and Equity   35

PART TWO
What Should Be Taught?
Knowledge and Literacy   177

PART THREE
The School Community
Individuals and Environments 271

Introduction

This Ninth Edition of *Critical Issues in Education* explores a variety of contemporary issues surrounding education and schooling. Each chapter contains two opposing views, original essays incorporating evidence, pointed opinion, and supported argument.

The terrain of education is rugged and rocky, with few clear paths and conflicting road signs. Advocates on each side think they know where they are going and how to get there. Valid information and ideas may appear on each route, but wise long-term choices depend on examination and evaluation. The goal is education that improves life for individuals and society—getting there requires critical thinking and the continual revision of learning. The trip is worthy.

Issues and Education

Education is controversial. Ask an assortment of relatives and friends what they think of American schools and be ready to hear arguments. You might think that sex, politics, and religion are the main hot topics for debate and that discussing schooling is tranquil and bland—but education ranks high on the list of strongly held beliefs and equally strong contrary views. Underlying social issues and ideological views are often reflected in arguments about education. Divergent views in society on sex, politics, religion, and multiple other social issues can be mirrored in school controversies; for example:

- *Politics*: Includes debates between conservative and liberal views on curriculum content, textbooks, speakers, school symbols, school governance, student and teacher rights, state and federal policies, school finance, and school reforms.
- *Religion*: Continuing arguments about religious bias in school policies and practices, private and public education, teaching materials and curriculum; school prayer and religion classes; and religious and nonreligious school groups and activities.
- *Sex*: Such controversial topics as sex education, gender bias, LGBTQ treatment, sexual assault protection, abortion information, social media use, student dress, and ideas about moral conduct.

In this second decade of the twenty-first century, the topic of education remains significant, and critical to society, the nation, and the globe.

For over 300 years, people on this continent have agreed that education is important, but have disagreed over how it should be controlled, financed, organized, conducted, and evaluated. Over two centuries ago, a very young United States was debating whether to establish free and compulsory education, arguing over who should be educated, who should pay, and what should be taught. We now have mass public education with private alternatives, but many of the same arguments continue about schools.

Some say that schools are ineffective and wasteful, with poor teachers, weak programs of study, and low standards. Others view their schools, despite severely limited resources, as remarkably good, with excellent teachers, high-quality programs, and expanding opportunities. Debates over education stimulate us to rethink our positions and, we hope, review and update our information and evaluate our sources. Education is controversial and stimulating.

We invite you to enjoy consideration of various persistent educational issues by examining divergent evidence, views, and arguments. Educational and social issues are usually presented in print and in other media from a single view, often partisan. This can sterilize the issue or just render true believers. Using critical thinking to consider the evidence and reasoning from opposing views can provide a richer, fuller understanding of the issue and more substantial support for your resulting view.

Information like student test scores, school finance decisions, and school activities may seem noncontroversial, but these can hide undercurrents of dissent about the role and value of testing, unequal access, disparate wealth and schooling, and factors like the role of race, gender, and culture. Schools are not treated equally in the United States, nor are students and teachers. Below the surface of apparently neutral and descriptive school news articles and media outlets lie many pervasive controversies that deserve attention.

Organization of the Book

We begin with Chapter 1, which is an introductory chapter presenting background for the study of education and for critical thinking about issues. The text is then divided into three parts. Each part explores a major theme:

- Part One: Whose Interests Should Schools Serve?: Justice and Equity
- Part Two: What Should Be Taught? Knowledge and Literacy
- Part Three: The School Community: Individuals and Environments

These broad themes are exemplified by several multifaceted topics that illustrate some of the political and social debates that occur in the United States. We have selected topics to show the dichotomy of viewpoints found in society and education. Each chapter includes two essays expressing divergent positions on a specific issue. They do not exhaust all possible positions; you are encouraged to explore further.

Acknowledgments

We are indebted to many, including our own teachers and our students, other teachers and students we have met, readers of previous editions, critics of education, writers, and speakers.

We are specifically indebted to colleagues who reviewed this and previous editions. Those who reviewed the manuscript of this edition, given us good criticism as the work progressed, or provided provocative ideas to challenge us along the way are:

James Daly, Seton Hall University; Scot Danforth, Chapman University; William Fernekes, Rutgers University; William Gaudelli, Lehigh University; Valerie Pang, San Diego State University; Nancy Patterson, Bowling Green State University; Al Schleicher, San Diego State University; William Stanley, Monmouth University; John Vernon, Consultant, Carlsbad, California; Mark Vollmer, Senior Consultant, Inspire-Pro, Brisbane, Australia; Barbara Vollmer, Information Management, Moggill, Australia; and Burt Weltman, William Paterson College.

We appreciate the encouragement and support of Neil Rowe from Waveland Press, who recommended this revision. We specifically acknowledge the extraordinary editorial work of Diane Evans. Diane's talent for excellent detailed editing, important critique and questions, clear and superior recommendations on writing and book design, and constructive continuing commentary has improved our work and this edition. Diane, despite workplace and office restrictions in response to the Covid-19 pandemic, kept a steady pace and positive tone.

We owe special thanks to Gwen, Nancy, and Ken for their support, enthusiasm, and criticism when needed.

This edition is dedicated to multiple generations of our families:

Barbara, Mark, Kim, Steve, Robert, Mary Catherine, Jonathan

Meg, Kel, Jordan, Warwick, Jasmyn, Olwyn, Megan, Conall, and Edward

Skyler, Ava, Olivia, Georgia, and Nate

and all generations of students and teachers who are at the center of critical studies of education in this twenty-first century.

Jack L. Nelson
Stuart B. Palonsky
Mary Rose McCarthy

About the Authors

JACK L. NELSON is Distinguished Professor Emeritus, Rutgers University, Graduate School of Education. His BA in social sciences is from the University of Denver; MA from California State University, Los Angeles; and doctorate from the University of Southern California. He taught in elementary and secondary schools in California and was a professor at California State University, Los Angeles, the University of Buffalo, and for 30 years at Rutgers. In the United States, he served as a visiting scholar at the University of California, Berkeley; Stanford University; the University of Colorado; Colgate University; the City University of New York; and the University of Washington. He was a visiting scholar for several years at Cambridge University in England and at Jordanhill College in Scotland. In Australia, he was a visiting scholar at the University of Sydney, Curtin University, Edith Cowan University, and the University of Queensland. *Critical Issues in Education* is his seventeenth book, and he is the author of almost 200 journal articles, chapters, and reviews. He has awards from the American Association of University Professors and the National Council for the Social Studies and is listed in *Contemporary Authors* and *Who's Who in America*.

STUART B. PALONSKY is Professor Emeritus of Education and Adjunct Professor of Honors Humanities at the University of Missouri. He was graduated from the State University of New York, Oneonta and Michigan State University. A former high school social studies teacher in New York and New Jersey, Palonsky taught reading and English to speakers of other languages while serving in the U.S. Army. His publications include the book *900 Shows a Year: A Look at Teaching from the Teacher's Side of the Desk*, an ethnographic account of high school teaching. Between 1991 and 2011, Palonsky was the director of MU's Honors College. Palonsky and Nelson were colleagues at Rutgers University and played tennis regularly, if not well.

MARY ROSE MCCARTHY received her PhD from the State University of New York, Buffalo in the social foundations of education with a concentration in the history of education. While at Buffalo, she was a presidential fellow and a member of the Buffalo Research Institute on Teacher Education. She was an Associate Professor in the School of Education at Pace University. Her research includes historical studies and contemporary issues. She has been secondary school teacher and administrator, director of a work cooperative for guests at a Catholic Worker House of Hospitality, and a family life educator for parents of at-risk children. Her publications include works on women's education, history of teacher education, students with disabilities, inclusive education, and desegregation of schools. Her current research interests include special education law and contemporary educational reform.

Critical Issues and Critical Thinking

A healthy democracy would demand an education that teaches its future citizens to think critically about their civic associations.

—Deane (2016)

Education is what remains after one has forgotten what one has learned in school.

—Attributed to Albert Einstein, who claims it was stated by a "wit"

The function of education is to teach one to think intensively and to think critically.

—King, Jr. (1947)

Education as Critical

Education is a dominant interest of individuals, families, communities, states, nations, and the globe. It is crucial—for development, for preservation, and for progress. Cognitive scientist Steven Pinker (2018) describes the importance of education:

> Studies of the effects of education confirm that educated people really are more enlightened . . . less racist, sexist, xenophobic, homophobic, and authoritarian. . . . They place a higher value on imagination, independence, and free speech. . . . [T]he growth of education—and its first dividend, literacy—is a flagship of human progress. (p. 235)

Education as an essential element of human progress is a feature of a broad and deep literature, theoretical and practical. From philosophers to politicians, economists to real estate agents, sociologists to parents, there is an agreement that education is important to people and populations. The Global Partnership for Education (2020), a partnership formed among developed and nearly 70 developing nations, identifies education as "a vital human right" playing a "key role in human, social and economic development." Lutz (2010), citing research for the Royal Society of England, summarizes: "almost universally more educated people are in better health and are more productive." Improvement in education attainment is the single most important driver of economic growth and among the most important determinants of health and agricultural production in the world. Goal 4 (Quality Education) of the 2030 Agenda for Sustainable Development states that education is the "foundation to creating sustainable development" (United Nations, 2015). Muhammad-Bande, President of the UN General Assembly, notes that education develops "analytical, inventive, and critical thinking capabilities in human beings"; also, he warns about the immense global challenge to provide and improve education, especially for underdeveloped nations and for refugees (UN News, 2020).

The multiple social roles of education cause extensive and continuing growth of schooling worldwide. Basic education is now standard in virtually all nations and most have increasing lengths of schooling. Almost 80 million more children are in primary schools across the globe (Global Partnership for Education, 2020). As of 2000, about 53% of the world's working age population had completed secondary schooling; by 2010 it was 59%, by 2020, 65%, and by 2030 it will be over 70% (Lutz, 2010; Roser and Ortiz-Ospina, 2019). In the United States in the 1970s, about 50% of adults had completed high school; currently about 90% have that level of schooling. Bachelor's degrees were earned by 11% in 1970 in the United States; today, almost 35% have those degrees (U.S. Census Bureau, 2019). The clear trend is more and better schooling for more people.

In these first decades of the twenty-first century, education has become more important around the world. Roser and Ortiz-Ospina (2019) find a dramatic correlation between increased attainment of education and the development of democratic governments around the world. Schools for children of the elite have existed since ancient times, but mass education in schools is a recent, twentieth century, global phenomenon. Mass schooling has become dominant worldwide as democracy has become a significant global trend in governments. Global education and human rights education are in the forefront of civilizing purposes of schooling (Fernekes, 2016; Gaudelli, 2016; UNESCO, 2019; Global Partnership for Education, 2020; UN News 2020).

The idea that education is critical to each person and to society is not startling. But it is a healthy reminder of the significance of this field and the necessity for continuous examination of educational goals, challenges, successes, and failures. The importance of education is the reason for intense disputes over its purposes, its nature, its quality, and its practice. The positive side of education bodes well for civilization, but there is a negative side.

Education for Freedom or Domination

Education is basic as an agent for personal and social progress, but it can also be an agent of control, domination, restriction, and social regression. Dictatorships demand education that spreads conformity and discipline under centralized control. During the 1930s and 1940s, in Germany the Nazi government reshaped school structure, curriculum, teacher education and employment, teaching materials, and school environments to provide unitary knowledge and belief in the party and those in charge. Nazi book burning publicly destroyed books considered anti-Nazi, which were usually written by Jewish, liberal, and socialist authors. Nonconformist teachers were fired and replaced by those who accepted the doctrine. The subjects taught promoted Nazi views of the world, science, arts, history, and culture (Kandel, 1935; Shirer, 1960; Pine, 2010).

China's "Cultural Revolution" from 1962 to 1976 used students as a Red Guard army to force obedience to Mao Zedong and Chinese Communism and the destruction of old-world capitalism. Among the student actions was to harass and berate some of their teachers, in some cases tearing out their hair and beating them. Re-education was implemented by required indoctrination classes, and by moving elite and educated city dwellers out to farms for labor (Dikotter, 2016). North Korea offers a current example where its national education program centers on idolatry, false history, and hatred of the United States and Western ideas. Classes worshipping Supreme Leader Kim-Il-Sung, Great Leader Kim Jong-Il, Anti-Japanese Heroine, Mother Kim Jong Suk, and Socialist Morality are mandatory in each school grade (Kim, 2017).

Education is also used to stifle and control specific segments of national populations. In the United States, the slavery system denied formal education to slave children on the grounds that schooling might lead to uprisings and demands for freedom. Long after the abolition of slavery, we have racial school segregation that commits African-American children to poorer facilities, budgets, teaching materials, and general support, thereby keeping them in a lower status socially and economically (Woodson, 1915; Genovese, 1976; Williams, 2005; Mervosh, 2019). For Native American children, U.S. government policy from 1819 until 1970 was to separate them from their families for placement in boarding schools, which were often run by churches. The argument for this practice was that the schools would "civilize" them, assimilate them, and Christianize them, resulting in an eradication of Indian cultures. Robert Kennedy, speaking at the Native American reservation at Window Rock, Arizona, in 1967, reviewed the history of mandated Indian boarding schools and said: "I believe this disgrace should last no longer. The Indian must have the power to shape his own education" (quoted in Guthman and Allen, 2018, p. 353). In 1970, Native American parents gained the right to deny such separation (Lynch, 2016; Ellwood, 2017; Wong, 2019). The lack of self-determination by native tribes is a continuing issue not only in education, but in many other significant areas, including their land, tribal rights and broken treaties, and encroachment by development and relocation (Gilio-Whitaker, 2019). Canada and Australia had similar historic mandates for their native populations to be sent to residential schools for forced assimilation into "Western culture." Canada's program ended in 1946, and Canada apologized in 2008; Australia's ended in the 1970s (Zalcman, 2016). Currently, China is engaged in a mass forced re-education program for Muslim communities, with Muslim children separated from parents and forced into what *Forbes* magazine terms "prison-like schools" (Doffman, 2019). The program is called "transformation-through-education" designed to prevent "extremism" and "terrorism" (Amnesty International, 2018; Standish, 2019).

Opposing ideologies find education to be a valuable agency for repression or extension of freedom. Dictatorships use the education system as a form of miseducation in order to control the general public, or selected portions of the public; but miseducation of the public can happen in a democracy. Garforth (1980) points out: "Undoubtedly, democracy at its best is a great educative force, but . . . it is not immune from dishonesty, corruption, and the betrayal of truth" (p. 20). Democratization requires mass schooling and critical literacy (Torres, 2002). A strong democracy requires a critical citizenry, a public capable of engaging in critical thinking. Critical citizens depend on critical education (Norris, 1999; Winthrop, 2000; Giroux, 2004; Schweber, 2012; Agosto, 2018).

Thomas Jefferson's point that a civilized nation cannot be ignorant and also free undergirds democratic educational commitments (Lipscomb and Bergh, 1903–04). This direct relation of education to freedom and civilization is commonly noted by Western philosophers from Socrates, Plato, and Aristotle through John Locke, Bertrand Russell, John Dewey, Israel Sheffler, Michel Foucault, and Nel Noddings (Siegel, 2010; Noddings, 2015).

John Dewey (1944), the most notable philosopher of the twentieth century, describes a relationship between education and democracy:

> Since a democratic society repudiates the principle of external authority, it must find a substitute in voluntary disposition and interest; these can be created only by education. One of the fundamental problems of education in and for a democratic society is set by the conflict of a nationalistic and a wider social aim. (pp. 87, 97)

Dewey describes a problem still evident. Nationalistic views appear in schools and educational materials worldwide. Every nation desires loyal citizens who know their nation's positive history, patriotic symbols, and traditions. School environments, textbooks, celebrations, and expectations include nationalistic orientations, and may hide examples of national embarrassment. Schools are seen as nation-building, not nation-criticizing, agencies. American schools in session fly a U.S. flag, national symbols are displayed, and students are expected to recite the Pledge of Allegiance and know something positive about their government and patriotic holidays (Nelson, 1971, 1976; Siebers, 2018). Radford (2020) quotes John Stuart Mill's warning that government schools are "a contrivance for moulding people to be like one another," and Mencken's observation that they are to "train a standardized citizenry" and put down dissent. Radford concludes, however, that American public schools educate far better than that—with critical thinking at the center of most. Some nations require obedience to a nationalistic ethos, providing severe penalties for dissenters. Others give a nationalistic slant in schools, but recognize that informed dissent is patriotic and critical thinking is in the national interest.

Education and Schooling; Limits on Critical Thinking

Education, of course, is far more than what goes on in school. But schools are usually at the center of public arguments about education because schools are the social organizations that take on the formalized task of educating. In colonial America, schools were mainly for the wealthy male elites; most people received their education at home and outside of schools (Bailyn, 1960; Cremin, 1970). Today some reluctant students might prefer that alternative, but that is not an option available to many. For the reluctant ones, school may even be an impediment to education—it interferes with their learning about life. They become educated despite school. For the vast majority, school is a generally positive environment and they recognize its purposes and values.

In addition to schools, there are many other locations for education. We are also educated:

- through observation and mimicry, trial and error;
- by listening, reading, watching, feeling, smelling, tasting;
- by comparing, contrasting, challenging, rethinking, testing;
- in families, among friends and enemies, indoors and out;
- in institutions—i.e., schools, camps, training, sports, prisons, hospitals; and
- in organizations, corporations, as employers and employees, and just living.

Formal learning, for most of us, occurs in school and school-like settings. Society expects schools to provide the central learning location for academic knowledge. In the Middle Ages, the academic subjects for elite education in universities were the seven liberal arts: the Trivium included grammar (language), rhetoric (persuasion) and dialectic (logic), and the Quadrivium included arithmetic (numbers), geometry (space), astronomy (stars), and music (proportion) (Winterer, 2002). Academic subjects are commonly described now as science, history, arts, math, social sciences, languages, and other variations of contemporary knowledge.

A main purpose for the original liberal arts and their current counterparts is the intellectual development of students. Today schools are expected to do far more than teach the organizing structures and traditional methods of study in the separate subjects, but many schools and teachers find themselves caught with time limits and testing demands that can hamper intellectual development. Intellectual learning incorporates the use of skeptical and questioning attitudes and skills, as well as examination of ideas; it includes critical thinking, creative interpretation, and being unlimited by subject-field discipline boundaries (Gouldner, 1979; Barber, 1998; Jacoby, 2008; Pinker, 2018).

Subject-field content is relatively easy to test by standardized exams, providing measurable and comparable results. Over the past half century, large portions of the public demanded schools provide quantifiable evidence of student learnings and school comparisons. Current school activity centers on costly, large-scale, and time-consuming standardized testing. In-school and private test preparation programs consume time, attention, and funds. The process can overwhelm other schoolwork. Open intellectual examination of evidence and argument is difficult to fit into the tight schedule of a standard curriculum, test preparation, and testing. A legitimate test of critical thinking has proven impossible so far, so comparative data are not likely in that realm. Critical thinking takes time, resources, and energy—and it is not testable.

In addition, many people are threatened by having students engage in open and skeptical examination of ideas. That activity can involve controversial topics that challenge traditional values, parental beliefs, and general perceptions of traditional education. Protests, privately to school officials and publicly in meetings and to the media, can produce censorship and political restrictions that limit schools, teachers, and students in their exercise of intellectual freedom.

Education as Controversial

It is easy to agree with some people and disagree with others about nearly everything, from trivial to important subjects. Broccoli? Best colors? Athletic teams? Beauty? The environment? Life? Given its importance, it is easy to find people who disagree strongly about a variety of issues involving schools and education. If you like arguments, you will love the study of education. Few topics elicit more disagreement or have as much at stake for our future. Even if you don't like arguments, your life and our society are influenced by the debates over education and the resulting decisions. Debates over education show up in school reform ideas and efforts to convince others about such issues as: how schools should be organized, who should be in which schools and for what purposes, what should be taught and to which students, who should do that teaching and how, who should be in charge, how should it be financed, how should it be evaluated, what should be done about deviations, and related questions.

Strident school debates involve deeply held views from politics to religion. If school was inconsequential, it would not be worthy of intense, long-lived disputes. But education is not a trivial pursuit. Strong opinions define many controversial topics, but schooling is unusual because few controversial topics have so many personally experienced experts. School is one social institution that virtually all people have experienced for long periods, and most have opinions about it.

Current controversies about schools and schooling include the increasing role of the federal government in school policy, school shootings and violence, measuring school and teacher quality, the relative value of charter and public schools, privatization and corporatization, teacher unions and contracts, student bullies and discipline, what is taught and how, and a host of local and state issues that arise on an almost daily basis. Several chapters in this book cover these topics. All of them exist within the context of a social environment that includes philosophic, political, economic, sociological, psychological, historic, and cultural debates.

SOCIAL CONTEXT OF SCHOOL

A society that does not pay enough attention to schooling suffers; it is on a downhill slope, as is the society or community that restricts education to recitation of conformist beliefs and permits no challenges (Pinker, 2018). The form, function, and practice of education are key elements in either the positive development or negative decline in the future movement toward improving civilization. Those lacking fundamental knowledge and skills experience social, economic, political, and personal inequality. People who can't read, write, or calculate adequately bear a heavy burden in daily existence. Beyond that minimum, people who without the skills to discriminate fact from fantasy and reasoned argument from dogmatic opinion are subject to manipulation and domination unsuited to free people in a democracy. No society stands still; education is an engine up or down.

Joseph Stiglitz (2019), Nobel Prize-winning economist, comments:

> All Americans want their children to live up to their potential, and that requires providing them with the best education that fits their talents, needs, and desires. Unfortunately, our education system has not kept up with the times . . . deficiencies in our education system exacerbate the intergenerational transmission of advantage—rather than, as public education once did, acting as the most important leveling force in our society. (p. 219)

Stiglitz identifies a prime purpose for education to help realize individual human potential in a social context, as he notes a critical issue that confronts that effort. Equal opportunity and social justice are central values in the United States, but achieving those ideals is a continuing struggle, with many backward lurches and failures (Milanovic, 2020). Among the core purposes of education in this nation are the same values—equal opportunity and social justice. Stiglitz (2019) points to the education system as the major actor in this social struggle, making the problem of unequal advantage transmitted through the generations worse. But he credits schools for once being the "most important leveling force in our society."

Funding Education: A Measure of Equity and Social Justice

Few disagree with Stiglitz on parental interest in the education of their children. You may agree or disagree with his idea that the current education system "exacerbates" the social problem of inequity, or that schools should serve as the main social-leveling force. His interpretation of educational purposes and practices in the process of improving equality and justice will be applauded by some, rejected by others. Nick Hanauer (2019), an entrepreneur and venture capitalist, changed his mind about blaming poverty and inequality on a "failing education system." He, Bill Gates, Alice Walton, and other philanthropists originally thought the cure was charter schools. Instead, he argues now that we should change the economic system to pay workers better, increase taxes on the wealthy, and "do everything we can to improve our public schools." This will reinvigorate the middle class and public education (Hanauer, 2019).

Fierce battles, from the seventeenth century forward, about public, free, and universal education in the United States were often predicated on the idea that education can be such a force for equality (Dewey, 1916; Curti, 1935; Warner et al., 1944; Smiley and Diekhoff, 1959; Dormina et al., 2017; Startz, 2019). Those battles continue; efforts to dismantle public education in favor of private are an example. Legal scholar Justin Driver (2018) analyzes Supreme Court cases, showing schools are among the most important subjects of arguments over constitutional expectations of equality. The U.S. Constitution does not specify education, allowing states to control it. That places it as a topic of intense legal debate regarding issues of federal-state relations and constitutional standards of equality and justice. A clear statement on this is the *Brown v. Board of Education* (1954) unanimous decision by the Supreme Court holding racial segregation in public schools to be unconstitutional. This decision, using the Fourteenth Amendment on equal protections, overturned the 1896 Supreme Court decision in *Plessy v. Ferguson*, which had allowed states to continue segregation if the separate schools were otherwise equal. The *Brown* decision is a landmark in the civil rights movement, though racial and other segregation in schools remains a thorny problem in many states over 65 years later (Bromley, 2020; Making Caring Common Project, 2020; Startz, 2020).

State constitutions provide for free, equal, or equivalent education across the state. State laws govern schools, funding, and accounting. This structure has not produced equity in funding. States vary significantly. New York, Connecticut, and New Jersey currently each spend between $20,000 and $23,000 per student, while Utah, Arizona, and Mississippi each spend between $7,500 and $9,000 per student. Within states, school districts and individual schools are also highly unequal in available funds. Some improvements have occurred in school funding equity in some states, but significant disparities remain. In nearly half the states, affluent schools get more funds from state and local sources than do poorer districts (Barshay, 2018; Martin et al., 2018; Morgan and Amerikaner, 2018; SchoolFunding.Info, 2019).

Lawsuits based on state constitutional requirements for equity in providing public education have occurred in 46 states over the past 50 years. Some states have had a succession of such suits, and many states have had to change funding formulae. Yet inequities remain between, within, and among states and their school districts. The standard pattern of school funding sources across the United States allows considerable variation at several levels. Those variations are linked to social and political contexts and to their impact on individuals and communities. Catherine Lhamon (2018), Chairperson of the U.S. Commission on Civil Rights, stated the following in a report on unequal funding for education:

> Quality education is critical to prepare students to be contributing members of a democratic society and competitive workers in a global economy. . . . [V]ast funding inequities in our state public education systems factor significantly in rendering the education available to millions of American public school students profoundly unequal.

Unequal school funding has links to racial and socioeconomic discrimination; consider the following *Washington Post* (2019) headline: "$23 Billion Racial Funding Gap for Schools." Funding disparities can also be reflected in housing issues. Segregation is seen by the public as very negative, but the practice continues (Bomster, 2020). The problem of segregation may appear structural—selection of housing and neighborhood simply fits unequal school funding naturally—but Rothstein (2017) dispels that idea with overwhelming evidence on government control of housing segregation by law, regulation, zoning, and related policies, such as placing schools in locations that attract primarily African Americans and "avoid 'proximity to white districts.'" Local house prices usually correlate with ratings of school quality, a reflection of relative neighborhood wealth, school funding, and racial composition. Unequal school funding and access expand the racial divide despite the 1954 *Brown v. Board of Education* decision that outlawed that discrimination. Parents support integrated schools, but when given the choice, choose segregated schools for their children (Making Caring Common Project, 2020).

Other forms of prejudice and discrimination are also related to inequitable funding of education. Native Americans, women, LGBTQ students, Asians, and immigrants have all experienced serious discrimination from unequal educational access and opportunities, and many still suffer (Nelson and Pang, 2014). Especially hard hit are low-income communities, families, and students. Negative effects from schools that have far less in resources than other public schools continue. Michelle Chen (2018) explains the de facto "punishment" of poor kids as a result of unequal funds for schools. More comprehensive information is contained in the well-documented evidence provided by Bruce Baker (2018), which demonstrates how these inequities harm the poor, minorities, and society.

Large inequalities in school funding directly affect what students receive in such areas as: recruitment and retention of quality teachers, teacher-student ratios, administrative and other school support systems, teaching materials, curriculum development, facilities and maintenance, student activities, and equipment. In addition, there are long-term educational, economic, social, and emotional effects of schools that suffer severe financial handicaps in relation to others. For example, it creates disparities in the availability and amount of student counseling, drop-out and graduation rates, admission to colleges and select vocational programs, lifetime job potential and income, health, personal sense of well-being, and informed understandings of economic and political topics. Thus, equitable personal participation in society is, in some form, dependent on equitable school funding. Educational inequalities exacerbate social injustice and provide highly disparate opportunities for students, opportunities that affect their personal life and social quality. These effects have lasting impact.

The long history of inequities in educational funding is strong and compelling. Disputes have developed over possible interpretations of related data and what actions should be taken (DeAngelis, 2017; Garcia and Weiss, 2017). What causes inequities, how should educational costs be covered, who should benefit and in what ways, and how should funds be collected and distributed are topics that elicit strong diverse opinions. Some of the remedies proposed include privatizing schools, changing school funding from a property tax to a general tax—or no tax, limiting various forms of schooling to certain students, denying or supporting teaching unions, cutting school staff and activities, and increasing technology to replace teachers and buildings. Each of these views offers some evidence and reasoning, and all have potential consequences.

Inequality in financing education, school by school and state by state, is a fundamental issue that restricts our commitment to social justice and a democracy based on a well-educated populace. Chapter 3, Financing Schools: Equity or Privilege, provides two divergent views, with evidence and argument, on this important topic. Should school funding and educational policy be under state or federal control?

Politics and Federal-State Interests in Schools

The role of the federal government in education is an issue with a long history and it is related to issues of equal funding. Education is considered a federal interest but is a state responsibility and a local activity. These guiding principles are a reflection of America's history of battles over state and federal rights, going back to the American Revolution, the Articles of Confederation, the U.S. Constitution, and a string of Supreme Court decisions. The nature and quality of the federal interest in education continues to be the subject of intense political debates.

Glenn Beck (2014), conservative political commentator, radio host, and television producer, states one position:

> We wouldn't think of letting the government tell us where to live, what kind of car to drive or what to eat for dinner. But . . . Americans bought into the idea that the government has the authority to tell us where we must send our children to school. . . . On one side is the complete nationalization of education. . . . (p. xii)

Robert Reich (2018), former Secretary of Labor and Professor of Public Policy, University of California, Berkeley, has a different view:

> This sense of common good also embraces public education. . . . Education is a public good that builds the capacity of a nation to wisely govern itself, and promotes equal opportunity. . . . Without an educated populace, a common good cannot even be discerned. . . . [Horace] Mann believed it important that public schools educate all children together, "in common." (pp. 33, 176)

These two viewpoints illustrate the divide between what is considered federal government interference and what is seen as the federal government acting in the public good. These differences are also seen amid the political context of the history of the U.S. Department of Education.

The Department of Education was originally created in 1867 as a noncabinet-level agency. Among the arguments presented for the establishment of the department was that federal control of education could help develop loyalty to the national government. Federal control, of course, was a threat to the existing state control and local operation of schools. Therefore, the department's charge was limited to the collection and dissemination of information about schools. One year later, the controversy caused a demotion from Department of Education to Office of Education, and placement under the Department of the Interior. At that time it had only 4 employees and a budget of $15,000.

In 1939, it was moved to the Federal Security Agency. It was upgraded to cabinet level in 1952 as part of the Department of Health, Education, and Welfare. In 1979, Democratic President Jimmy Carter advocated for a separate Department of Education, but many Republicans considered that unconstitutional and an intrusion on state affairs. The National Education Association supported the idea of a separate department, but the American Federation of Teachers opposed it. In October 1979, the Department of Education Organization Act (Public Law 96-88) was passed, creating a cabinet-level Department of Education.

During the 1980 presidential campaign, Republican candidate Ronald Reagan called for its elimination. Along with Reagan's election, Republicans regained control of the Senate. The federal education budget was significantly reduced under Reagan's administration, but Reagan could not get legislation to actually abolish the department. However, by 1984, the Republican platform dropped the idea of department elimination. In 1987, Republican George H. W. Bush campaigned to be the "education president," and the resulting Republican Congress increased federal funding and control.

In 2000, the Liberty Caucus of the Republican Party passed a resolution to abolish the department. However, Republican President George W. Bush supported and signed the No Child Left Behind Act of 2001, which significantly increased federal funding for schools, standardized testing, and created national standards. The results from implementing these objectives stimulated protests over federal control and excessive rigidity. Responding to criticism of a heavy hand by the federal government on student testing and teacher evaluation, President Barack Obama (Democrat) obtained passage of bills that funded the Race to the Top Program and the 2015 Every Student Succeeds Act. This act shifted some controls from the federal government to the states, but kept testing and scores as evaluative criteria.

In 2017, one Republican congressman introduced a bill to abolish the department. Arguments over control and finance continue, despite the fact that the federal contribution of funds for education constitute only about 8% of the total school funding in the United States. The average state contribution, from general taxes, is 45%, and local funds, mostly from property taxes, provide 37% of school funding. These sources are often supplemented by local fundraisers, foundations, and grants. As a result, wealthier states, school districts, and individual schools have advantages.

Federal legislation, such as the Elementary and Secondary Education Act of 1965, and other laws and regulations have expanded the federal government's role in education and its funding. These laws often offer carrots of funds and sticks of penalties to prod school districts and states to change school policies and operations. They set national standards and accountability, increase testing, and challenge traditional ways of schools. Critics contend that these laws have not produced remarkable improvements in schools, or in student achievements, and that they:

- Do not address the gross underfunding of schools;
- Misevaluate education by excessive reliance on testing;
- Restrict local curriculum decision making;
- Unnecessarily punish schools for social problems, like poverty;
- Force teachers and students into conformity;
- Ignore critical thinking; and
- Expand federal intervention into a state's responsibilities.

(See American Federation of Teachers, 2005; National Education Association, 2006; Sunderman, 2006; McKenzie, 2007; Ravitch, 2007, 2010, 2020; Nichols and Berliner, 2008; Spring, 2008.)

School funding and federal-state relations are two long term battlegrounds for general school issues. There are also issues that have developed more recently and have distinct qualities that require new ways to address them.

School Shootings Exemplify Another Controversy

Among the controversies that plague education and illustrate federal-state disputes are the rash of school shootings and what can be done to stop them. In the United States, shootings in schools have become standard news with tragic local consequences and national repercussions. Shootings are deeply personal and deeply social; they threaten individual safety and freedom as well as threaten social stability and security (Lerner, 2019). This topic is among our struggles for the future, and about justice in society (Deane, 2019).

School shootings are a relatively recent national phenomenon. The earliest available data show just one shooting of one student by another in the whole decade of the 1840s. Reports in the 1890s show only two shootings resulting in 14 deaths over that 10-year period. In the 50 years between 1900 and 1950, the average number of school shootings in each decade was 27, with an average of 11 deaths over each 10 years. From 1950 to 2000, the average number of shootings per decade was 60, with an average of 44 deaths, including the shooting at Columbine High School in Littleton, Colorado, which alone took 66 lives. Since 2000, shootings at Sandy Hook Elementary School in Newtown, Connecticut, and Marjory Stoneman Douglas High School in Parkland, Florida, have made head-shaking headlines. The average number of shootings each decade of the twenty-first century is 95 shootings accompanied by 80 deaths. At least 41 states have had school shootings in recent years, and some states have had several (K–12 School Shooting Database, 2019).

School shootings are not the product of a foreign-controlled terrorist plot or police-assisted suicide attempts. School shooting data, since 1970, show that over 60% of shooters are students from the same school. Students from rival schools are less than 1% of shooters, and teachers account for only 1% of all shooters. About 65% of the shootings are the result of specific victims being targeted, 28% result from an escalation of a disagreement, about 18% are gang related, and 3% are reported from bullying (K–12 School Shooting Database, 2019).

Virtually everyone agrees that shooting innocent children, teachers, and school staff members is a tragedy, but disagreements are virulent over the causes and the cures. Disputes about school shootings and other school violence often fall along political and social divides, which also leads to different proposed solutions. Some come from state legislative action on guns and schools, some from federal efforts, and some from advocacy groups. Some states have tried to pass laws to limit gun ownership, others want to arm teachers and school staff. Attempts to address shootings in schools reflect differing views on the extent and limits of gun rights under the Second Amendment and conflicts over public safety and protection of children.

The debate over preventing more incidences of gun violence in schools can be difficult to navigate. Some, including religious organizations, argue for more morality training and religious instruction in schools. Some propose increased funding for mental health programs and stronger student support systems. Some propose more gun controls, stricter gun sales requirements, bans on assault weapons, and legal gun-free zones. A specific issue that surrounds school shootings includes the easy availability of guns, which can provide a dramatic way for students who experience severe resentments, feelings of inferiority, mental health issues, or bullying to strike back. One response to this dilemma is to advocate stricter gun controls and an increased effort on mental health conditions and antibullying programs. An opposing viewpoint claims that guns are not the cause of violence; instead, it is due to inadequate school security, a decline in family values, a lack of religion in schools, pornography, and violent media. Responses to these types of issues also include armed officers in schools, metal detectors, single entries to schools, allowing students with arms, digital surveillance, and controls on social media.

The school shooting controversy is local, national, social, and educational. It generates just as much debate and shifts in policies as topics such as unequal funding of education and battles between the federal government and states over control of education. These battles stimulate critics of schools and schooling and create recommendations for reform.

A Tradition of School Criticism and Reform

Cycles of criticism and reform in education are not new (Cuban, 2003). We have had educational reform advocates for so long that it is impossible to identify their beginnings. Perhaps the first educational reformer, a member of some prehistoric group, rose up to protest that children were not learning the basic skills, hunting and gathering, as he had. Some of the bashed skulls lying about prehistoric sites are probably the results of arguments over education.

For more than 3,000 years, human societies have recognized the value of education—and argued about what the goal of schooling should be and how to achieve it (Ulich, 1954). One of the two accusations leveled against Socrates in the indictment that brought him to trial and his subsequent suicide was "corruption of the young." Socrates may have paid the ultimate price for being an educational reformer in a political setting that was not ready for his reforms. From the intensity and vigor of public debate over schooling (a debate that has continued in Western society at least since the time of Socrates), one would expect either dramatic changes in schools or their abolition in favor of an alternative structure. One critic has proposed the abolition of schools (Illich, 1971). Others have proposed revolutionary changes (Sinclair, 1924; Rafferty, 1968; Apple, 1990). Most changes have been moderate, however, and no radical attempts have succeeded. We hold widely disparate views on what societal and educational changes we need to make, and some resist them all. Historian David Tyack (1991), discussing the intertwining of school reform with social reform, says, "For over a century and a half, Americans have translated their cultural anxieties and hopes into demands for educational reform."

Distributing knowledge and providing opportunity are commonly accepted ideals, but controversies arise over what knowledge we should distribute, which children should get which opportunities, and who should be making these decisions. Shifts in criticism and efforts at reform are common in U.S. educational history (Cremin, 1961; Welter, 1962; Karier, 1967; Tyack, 1967; Katz, 1971; Ravitch, 2000, 2010; Cuban, 2003; Ross and Gibson, 2006). Some critics change their views. For example, controversial playwright David Mamet (2011) espoused generally liberal ideas, but became highly critical of liberalism and the "liberal media." He thinks education goes too far in teaching multiculturalism, diversity, social justice, and sex education—topics that are "simply none of their business" (p. 201). Diane Ravitch, a high-level officer in the Department of Education in the 1990s, was a notable critic of progressive education ideas. She now publicly and actively opposes much of the traditionalist reform of the recent past and its unfortunate results in schools (Ravitch, 2000, 2010, 2020). Traditional and progressive reform agendas differ, and schools respond by moving very gradually in one direction with a few widely publicized examples of reform and then await the next movement.

School Reform in Early Twentieth-Century America

The United States has a long tradition of innovation in education, stemming from its pioneer role in providing mass education at public expense. There are some major failures in this history, most notably the lack of equal educational opportunities for African Americans, Native Americans, women, immigrants, and those of lower income.

Beginning in the nineteenth century, American schools were expected to blend immigrants into the American mainstream through compulsory education on such subjects as English, American history, and civics. A history of racism, sexism, and ethnic prejudice was commonly ignored in American social life and schools while we labored under the myth that everyone shared a happy society and its members should all talk, think, and form values the same way. Schools were a primary social agency to meld students from divergent cultural backgrounds into the American ideal, which, unsurprisingly, exhibited European, white, and male characteristics and values. The English language and belief in the superiority of Western literature, history, politics, and economics dominated schools. Schools were key institutions in "Americanizing" generations of immigrants.

In the early twentieth century, urbanization and industrialization created the need for different forms of school services. Large numbers of children from the working classes were in schools in urban areas, and the traditional classical curriculum, teaching methods, and leisure-class approach stumbled. Extensive development of vocational and technical courses was the most dominant change in schooling before World War I, as school activities broadened to include medical exams, health instruction, free lunch programs, schools open during vacation periods for working parents, and other community services. These reforms fit the evolving sense of social progressivism (Jacoby, 2008). The progressive education movement, from about 1920 to World War II, incorporated severe criticisms of traditional schooling ideas and such practices as corporal punishment, rigid discipline, rote memorization and drill, stress on the classics, and high failure rates.

Progressives advocated engaging in practical experiences and projects, community activities, study of controversial topics, practicing democracy in the schools, and study of social problems. Schools became more open to students of all classes, and the curriculum moved from more esoteric studies to include courses with social applications, such as home economics, business and vocational education, current events, health, sociology, sex education, and consumer math.

During the first half of the twentieth century, sporadic criticisms of progressive thought appeared, but a traditionalist reform movement gained strength, once near the end of the Depression and again following World War II. Graham (1967), summarizing the shift, states,

> Sometime between 1919 and 1955 the phrase "progressive education" shifted from a term of praise to one of opprobrium. To the American public of 1919, progressive education meant all that was good in education; thirty-five years later nearly all the ills in American education were blamed on it. (p. 145)

Gurney Chambers (1969) notes that after the 1929 stock market crash, education came under attack: "Teachers were rebuked for their complacency and inertia, and progressive schools, surprisingly enough, were blamed for the increasing crime and divorce rates and political corruption" (pp. 142–143).

Jacoby (2008), writing about the history of anti-intellectualism in America, states,

> Ironically, the denigration of professional educators did not really take hold until the middle of the twentieth century . . . in the eighteenth and nineteenth centuries . . . the hiring of a schoolteacher was one of the two fundamental markers of civilization in frontier communities (the other being the presence of a minister). (p. xvi)

CYCLES OF EDUCATIONAL REFORM AFTER WORLD WAR II

Attacks on schools increased in intensity and frequency during the late 1940s and 1950s. The great school debates of this time involved many issues that extend into the twenty-first century. Church-state issues, including school prayer and religious education, gained significance. Racial issues, such as the landmark Supreme Court decision in *Brown v. Board of Education* (1954) and forced busing, became another focus of school controversy. Rapidly increasing tax burdens to pay for new schools and teachers required by the baby boom aroused protests. Rising expectations for education were driven by the thousands of veterans who went to college on the GI Bill. Curricular issues, including disputes over how to teach reading and improve test scores in math, science, English, and history, filled the news.

The "red scare" in the McCarthy period produced rampant public fear of creeping communistic influence in American life and suspicions that schools were breeding grounds for "communal" and progressive thought. For many, there was simply a lingering sense that schools were not doing their job. Two books illustrate the criticisms of this period: Albert Lynd's (1950) *Quackery in the Public Schools* and Arthur Bestor's (1953) *Educational Wastelands*. Each attacked progressive education and the "educationists" who advocated for the "felt needs" of children as they ignored traditional classical academics. Clarence Karier (1985) notes, "The educationist who spoke out for 'progressive education' and 'life adjustment education' appeared increasingly out of place in the postwar, cold war period" (p. 238).

Other U.S. institutions also assessed progressive education. The Ford Foundation made education a focal point. Grants were made to the Educational Testing Service to improve measures of student performance on academic subjects. The Carnegie Foundation asked James Bryant Conant, former president of Harvard, to study public education. Public criticism of the academic failures of American schools was popular. The Soviet launch of *Sputnik* in 1957, ahead of the United States, gave new focus for educational reform. *Sputnik* was a highly visible catalyst for conservative critics, who blamed the permissiveness of progressive education as a main reason the United States was not competitive.

EXCELLENCE AND ITS DISCONTENTS: POST-*SPUTNIK*

Post-*Sputnik* reform included the reinstitution of rigor, discipline, traditional subject teaching, and testable standards. Excellence, ill defined and excessively used, shows up in many reports and statements. Gardner's (1958) *The Pursuit of Excellence:*

Education and the Future of America is one illustration. Another term common in media treatment is *mediocrity*, a threat suggested in the title of Mortimer Smith's (1954) book *The Diminished Mind: A Study of Planned Mediocrity in Our Public Schools.*

Conant's (1958) report, *The American High School Today,* was, however, a moderate book proposing a standard secondary school curriculum, tracking by ability group, special courses for gifted students, improvements in English composition, better counseling, and other recommendations. Federal funds for reform were increased in the late 1950s and early 1960s. The National Defense Education Act responded to the idea that *Sputnik* showed vulnerability and that schools were important to "national defense." Funds provided grants to university scholars in the subject fields of science, math, foreign languages, social studies, and English to develop better K–12 teaching, and encouraged projects to make the curriculum "teacher-proof" to stop classroom teachers from teaching it incorrectly. The education of teachers also received its share of criticism, with blasts at teachers' colleges, the progressive techniques they advocated, and the quality of students going into teaching. The antiprogressives showed force. This all sounds hauntingly familiar to those who read current educational criticism of schools and teachers.

As conservative educational ideas gained support and school practice turned back to standards and "rigor," then criticism from the left began to emerge. Liberal criticism responded to the rote memorization, excessive testing, lockstep schooling, and increased school dropout and failure rates that began to characterize schools. Paul Goodman, George Dennison, Edgar Z. Friedenberg, A. S. Neill in England, Nat Hentoff, John Holt, Herbert Kohl, and Jonathan Kozol attacked schools for their sterility, bureaucracy, boredom, lack of creativity, rigidity, powerlessness of students and teachers, and inadequacy in educating disadvantaged youth. Holt (1964) stated,

> Most children in school fail. . . . They fail because they are afraid, bored, and confused . . . bored because the things they are given and told to do in school are so trivial, so dull, and make such limited and narrow demands on the wide spectrum of their intelligence, capabilities, and talents. . . . Schools should be a place where children learn what they want to know, instead of what we think they ought to know. (pp. xiii, xiv, 174)

Liberal reform in the 1960s rebelled against conservative authoritarianism and the dehumanization of schools. Reforms included open education, nongraded schools, more student freedom, more electives, less reliance on standardized tests, abolition of dress codes and rigid rules, and more teacher-student equality. The Vietnam War and demonstrations spurred the politics that stimulated much of the late 1960s educational reform literature.

Multicultural education was not on the educational agenda in early America because mass schooling was supposed to produce a melting pot where various cultural strands were blended into the "new American." The civil rights movement in the 1950s and 1960s showed that the melting pot thesis about American society was a myth. This led to other approaches to diversity and unity. One was separatism, where each major subcultural group would go its own way with separate social and school structures. Another was an effort to reconstitute a form of the melting pot by enforcing integration in such institutions as housing, restaurants, and schools. Integration efforts often led to resegregation by white flight and establishment of private all-white academies. Multicultural education, which aimed to recognize positive contributions of a variety of national, racial, ethnic, gender, and other groups to American life, developed as a way to recognize both diversity and unity.

Multicultural efforts intended to correct a century of schooling featuring white male American or European heroes from middle and upper social classes. African American, Latino, and women authors began to show up on lists of standard readings in English classes. Societal contributions of Native Americans, blacks, Chicanos, and females were added to history and civics books. Equal physical education opportunities for boys and girls, compensatory education for the disadvantaged, and programs featuring minority and women role models developed. We have, however, expanded education as a means for developing democracy and offering some social mobility. We may not realize these ambitions, and our real intentions may be less altruistic (Katz, 1968). But idealization of democratic reform through education is an American tradition.

TRADITIONALISM REVISITED; CRITICAL THEORY EMERGES: THE 1980S AND INTO THE TWENTY-FIRST CENTURY

A key word repeated in the reforms of the 1960s and 1980s was "excellence." Remarkable similarities in language and rationales applied during both periods of school reform were used to advocate a return to traditional education, with additions in advancing technology and the needs of business. The term appears less often in twenty-first century school criticism, but still conveys the concept of rigor in academic learning with measurable results—a usage formed in the criticisms of the 1960s and 1980s.

In the early 1980s, reports of falling SAT and ACT scores, drug abuse, vandalism, and chaos in schools increased. Nervousness about international competition, resurgence of business and technology as dominant features of society, and questions about shifting morality and values provided a political setting that blamed schools for inadequacies. President Reagan appointed the National Commission on Excellence in Education (1983), which produced a highly political document, *A Nation at Risk*, that claimed that there was a "rising tide of mediocrity" in schools. Ensuing public debate produced a flurry of legislation to develop "excellence" by increasing the competitive nature of schooling and testable standards.

Student protests of the 1960s had disappeared; a negative reaction set in. "Yuppies" (young upwardly mobile professionals) emerged as role models in the 1980s, embracing careerism and corporate fashion. Public perception of disarray in morality, the American family, and schools were popular issues for discussion. Anticommunism declined as a major influence on conservative education reform as the Soviet Union collapsed. The War on Drugs and character/moral education filled in. Schools took blame for social ills and loss of "traditional values" and were expected to respond by suddenly becoming academically excellent and moralistic in training.

Foundations and individual critics again examined schools. Generally conservative reports appeared from the Twentieth Century Fund (1983), the College Entrance Examination Board (1983), and the National Science Foundation (1983) as well as Mortimer Adler's (1982) *The Paideia Proposal*. Ernest Boyer's (1983) moderate *High*

School for the Carnegie Foundation was popular. More liberal works included John Goodlad's (1983) *A Place Called School* and Theodore Sizer's (1984) *Horace's Compromise.*

School reforms in the 1980s, dominated by mainstream conservative thought, included standardization, more testing, a return to basics, implanting patriotic values, increased regulation, more homework, less student freedom, dress codes and socially acceptable behavior for students and teachers, stricter discipline, and measurable teacher accountability (Bastian et al., 1985; Presseisen, 1985; Giroux, 1988).

States increased school financing until the 1990s recession, and state officials enacted new school regulations and claimed credit for educational change (National Governors' Association, 1986; Barton and Coley, 1990; Webster and McMillin, 1991). In the main, jawboning by the federal government and increased regulatory activity in the states produced little in the way of dramatic change. Most underlying social problems—poverty, family disruption, discrimination, and economic imbalance—worsened during the 1980s. In the 1990s, educational criticism and reform shifted from state regulation and test score worries to more diverse views of the national influence on local schools, school choice, curriculum control, at-risk students, restructuring schools for school-based management, teacher empowerment, parental involvement, and shared decision making. These ideas are potentially conflicting, some leading to increased centralization and others leading to increased decentralization.

From a liberal/progressive view, schools are defective because they are too standardized, excessively competitive, and too factory-like. Students are measured and sorted in an assembly-line atmosphere where social class, gender, and race determine which students get which treatments. Teachers are deprofessionalized and treated as servile workers. Critical thinking is punished; one kind of curriculum or classroom instruction fits all. Creativity and joy are excluded from the school lexicon because education is supposed to be hard, dreary, boring work (Purpel, 1989; Fisher, 1991; Nathan, 1991; Sacks, 1999; Wraga, 2001; Schoenfeld, 2002; McLaren, 2014). Making schools active, pleasant, student oriented, critical, and sensitive to social problems is the reform they advocate.

The "culture wars" spread into the schools. Replacing traditional canons of literature and social thought with modern multicultural material is one example. Finn (1990b) and Ravitch (1990), as officials of the Department of Education, argued for traditional content emphasizing unified American views rather than diverse views from segments of society. The Organization of American Historians, however, supported teaching non-Western culture and diversity in schools (Winkler, 1991). Camille Paglia (1990), arguing against feminist positions, says that her work "accepts the canonical Western tradition and rejects the modernist idea that culture has collapsed into meaningless fragments" (p. xii). Stanford University's faculty debated whether to substitute modern literature for traditional in its basic course; New York State social studies curriculum revision for multicultural content aroused a firestorm when English-only resolutions were adopted by state legislatures. Other arguments over multicultural education linked it with politically correct speech in schools (D'Souza, 1991; Winkler, 1991; Banks, 1995). However, in this case, the idea of protecting civility in schools by limiting racist, sexist, and other derogatory language was in conflict with free speech, causing additional debate.

Results of 1980s and 1990s reform efforts have been mixed. No clear evidence shows reforms significantly changed education (Giroux, 1989; Finn, 1990a; *U.S. News and World Report*, 1990; Darling-Hammond, 1991; Fiske, 1991; Moynihan, 1991; Safire, 1991; *New York Times,* 1992). Ideological chasms are clear among the analysts.

David Berliner and Bruce Biddle (1995), using test scores, international school finance data, and other indicators, demonstrate that school critics are mistaken or uninformed. Critics' assertions that student achievement and teacher quality have declined and schools are failing society are "errant nonsense" (p. 13). Berliner and Biddle conclude: "American education has recently been subjected to an unwarranted, vigorous, and damaging attack—a Manufactured Crisis . . . the major claims of the attack turn out to have been myths; the Manufactured Crisis was revealed as a Big Lie" (p. 343).

Applying critical theory to education, long a philosophic interest, became popular with cogent critiques of the elite and corporate roots of proposed school reforms and the development of critical pedagogy as an applied response for teachers (Giroux, 1988, 1997, 2004; Apple, 1990, 1999; Stanley, 1992, 2001; Aronowitz and Giroux, 1993; Young, 1998; Murphy and Fleming, 2010). Another current avenue of critique of standard education is the domination of one cultural strand (male, heterosexual, white Anglo-Saxon) to the exclusion, severe limitation, or misrepresentation of others, e.g., African American, Hispanic, Asian, Native, Women, and LGBTQ. This domination in schooling shows up in teachers and teacher education, curriculum, textbooks and materials, and classroom discourse. It is under criticism in general research, in multicultural education, in the media, and in critical race theory (Chandler, 2015; Taylor, 2016; Botts, 2019).

Conservative school reform was the main influence on schooling in the United States at the end of the twentieth century. Proposals and action for school change included academically tougher schools, vouchers, charter schools, rigorous standards and more testing, more discipline, privatized management, and training in moral behavior (Will, 2019).

THE TWENTY-FIRST CENTURY

Liberal and radical ideas for schools have not disappeared (Fullen, 2000; Bracey, 2002b; Giroux, 2004). Teacher empowerment, academic freedom, student rights, limiting testing, providing student choice, and active social criticism and participation are ideas percolating in school reform to come. Reconstructionist ideas placing schools at the center of social change have not been entirely forgotten in the current surge of literature on schools and reform. William Stanley (1992, 2001) rethinks social reconstructionism and examines key ideas from the critical pedagogy movement to offer educational possibilities for the twenty-first century. Critical pedagogy offers a focus on practical reasoning providing critical examination of social issues and stimulating positive social action.

Humans have long argued about what children should learn, how they should behave, and who should teach them. Basic subjects like reading and mathematics are often at the eye of the hurricane because of their importance in the ongoing lives of students and their future prospects. Reading is the focus of debates over phonics and whole language instruction, though often it is a more ideological and political issue than merely finding the best way to teach (Coles, 2003; National Education Policy Center, 2020). Arguments over the best approaches to mathematical literacy have included "civil rights" questions (Moses and Cobb, 2001) as well as competing ideologies in curricular reform that Schoenfeld (2002) claims "gave rise to the math wars and catalyzed the existence of what is in essence a neo-conservative back-to-basics movement. This way lies madness" (p. 22). Nearly all subject fields have experienced the same problems in finding stability in seas of change that are dependent on ideological and political contexts. They present a bewildering array of educational ideas, from left-wing, right-wing, moderate, and radical positions.

Academic, intellectual, practical, moral, and behavioral responsibilities are multiple foci of schools. Ethical, physical, and emotional development of children as well as safety, health, and civility are also among school responsibilities. Schools take on such social problems as drugs, sexual mores, incivility, bullying, and crime. For these and other broad responsibilities of schools, one proposal is to make schools even more the centers of their communities by being open all year, seven days a week, early morning to late night (Strike, 2004; Children's Aid, 2020).

A continuing issue involves the use and abuse of technology, artificial intelligence, robotics, and facial recognition for security in schools (Oppenheimer, 2003; McKenzie, 2019; Alba, 2020). The search for knowledge develops faster and more comprehensive systems of communication, travel, and research—which then require faster and more comprehensive systems of education to comprehend and extend that knowledge. Doheny-Farina (1996) claims that "face-to-face teaching will be only for the well-to-do" and that "the virtualization of school removes it from the fabric of the local community" (pp. 108, 117). Educational theorist Michael Apple (1994) shows how distance learning de-skills teachers, making them switch-turners and simple conduits for other people's ideas and procedures, destroying a central characteristic of democratic education (Bromley and Apple, 2002). Robotic classrooms and facial recognition technology threaten critical thinking and privacy, among other issues.

Other contemporary topics include: STEM programs to bring students, especially females, into scientific fields; charter schools; drop out and graduation rates, length of school day and year; improving teacher quality and work conditions; teacher tenure; and student rights. Each of these, and others, offer ideas for examining evidence and engaging in debate.

The Changing Focus of Reforms and Debates

In the early twenty-first century, public debate over education changed from a primary focus on crisis, hand-wringing, and blaming teachers to arguments over ways to increase financial support and equity, smaller classes, excessive testing, and better facilities and teachers. Bashing schools and teachers has been partially replaced by a public affirmation that the future of schools and of society are intertwined. Serious disagreements, of course, continue on most school topics, and we still get teacher bashing on occasion. The politics of bashing benefits politicians seeking an issue. Schools are an excellent target. This means more attention is paid to school failures than to school successes. The general tenor of the debates have shifted from castigation and condemnation to diverse proposals for funding, accountability, standards, and specific corrective action. Economic problems may derail most reforms, and there are still sharply negative criticisms of the current state of schooling, but more moderate voices are present. Nocera (2011) summarizes the situation: "Demonizing teachers for the failures of poor students, and pretending that reforming the schools is all that is needed, as the reformers tend to do, is both misguided and counterproductive" (p. A25).

Reform movements rise and fall. Van Schoales (2019) claims that the education reform movement of the early twenty-first century is over. He argues that top-down requirements from federal and state governments, which included "inspiration, edicts, and coercion," have had mixed results, if any. He proposes a new reform movement (without it having to bear such a title) that argues for bringing school improvement efforts back to the teacher, student, and administration in local schools. Philanthropic efforts to reform schools have gone awry; they are often based on business models, view public schools and teachers as problems to be manipulated, and see outside agencies and political figures as the ones able to "turn schools around." However, these philanthropic efforts can fail, and the public schools are damaged as a result (Russakoff, 2015). Decreasing negative criticism of schools might suggest that school reforms in the past 30 years have been successful, but that would be a misreading of reality. Ravitch (2020) shows how the old education reform movement is dead.

During the 1980s, schools were deemed to be a "rising tide of mediocrity" that put the nation at risk. Analyses of school data from 1980 to 2010 indicate that schools were not as bad as portrayed (Berliner and Biddle, 1995; Bracey, 1998, 2002a, 2002b; Lemann, 2010; Berliner and Glass, 2014). Ravitch (2010, 2020) shows how much of the reform movement went in the wrong direction. Biddle and Glass (2014) claim, with evidence, that "A war is raging for the hearts and minds of Americans. At stake is the nearly 200-year-old institution of the nation's public schools" (p. xi). They then document the myths and lies that are the threat. Extremely negative school criticism has had an impact on the public's perception of public schools, which now has about 50% rating them unsatisfactory (Gallup, 2019). Surprisingly, even with negative national publicity about schools, local public schools actually rate very high, with over 70% giving their local school ratings of totally satisfied or satisfied, and just 10% totally dissatisfied (Gallup, 2019). There is a disconnect between what the public reads abut schools across the nation and how they see the schools nearby. Schools, in general, are rated higher than many other institutions of American society.

Although polls continue to show general public support of local schools, most of us can identify one or more areas needing correction. Impatient or burned-out teachers, cloddish administrators, frazzled counselors, and outdated textbooks and curricula are examples. Most of us know the virtues as well as the warts and blemishes of schools from our direct personal experience. Some critics propose quick and simplistic reforms to improve schools. Fortunately, most people understand that change in schooling is more complex and that potential consequences of change need more thought.

Reformers also see schools as part of the cure, that schools can solve major social problems, such as racism, sexism, automobile accidents, AIDS, teenage pregnancy, and drugs. Reforms have not been especially productive in student achievement, curing social ills, intellectual development, or student and public happiness about schools. Yet the arguments over reform have helped air ideological and political baggage that weighs on the reforms.

Educational Criticism and Democratic Vitality

Critics of schools are easy to find. People are not bashful about noting school problems; but they do disagree over what is wrong, who is responsible, and what should be done to change schools. Of all social institutions in a democracy, the school should be the most ready for examination; education rests on critical assessment and reassessment. That does not mean that all criticism is justified, or even useful. Some of it is simplistic, mean-spirited, or wrong-headedly arrogant. But much of it is thoughtful and cogent. Although some unjustified criticism can be detrimental to education in a democracy, free and open debate can permit the best ideas to percolate, to be developed and revised, and to be evaluated (DeWiel, 2000; Hess, 2011; Will, 2019).

Over the long haul, schooling has improved, and civilization has been served by the debates over education. More people get more education of a better quality across the world now than in previous generations. Despite periodic lapses and declines, the global movement toward increased and improved schooling for more students continues. Debate forces us to reconsider ideas about schooling and increase our sophistication about schools and society.

Democratic vitality and educational criticism are good companions. Democracy, as Thomas Jefferson so wisely noted, requires an enlightened public and free dissent. Education is the primary means to enlightenment and to thoughtful dissent. It follows that schools would be among those fundamental social institutions under continuing public criticism in a society striving to improve its democracy. Bertrand Russell (1928) noted that education is basic to democracy: "It is in itself desirable to be able to read and write . . . an ignorant population is a disgrace to a civilized country, and . . . democracy is impossible without education" (p. 128).

Both democratic vitality and educational criticism require open expression of diverse ideas, yet both are based on an optimistic sense of unity of purpose. Diverse ideas and criticism provide necessary tests of our ideas. Criticism can appear to be negative, pessimistic, or cynical, but these are not its only forms. Informed skepticism, the purpose for this book, offers a more optimistic view without becoming like Pollyanna. Diverse ideas are sought because we think, optimistically, that education can be improved. Unity of purpose suggests a basic agreement on values, the criteria against which to judge diverse ideas. Diverse ideas provide vitality and opportunity for progress, but they can be chaotic and irrational. Conservative thinker George Will (2019) noted that critical thinking and "relentless criticism" are not equivalent (p. 387).

CRITICAL THINKING, DIALOGUE, AND DIALECTICS

Questions about schooling stimulate a variety of potential and often competing answers, but there is no single set of clear and uncontested resolutions. Life would be easier (although less interesting) if we had single and simple answers to all of our problems. But critical social issues are usually too complex to be adequately resolved by easy or absolute solutions. In fact, simple answers often create new problems or merely cause the problems they were supposed to solve to rise again. Research shows that problem-based learning is a rich and comprehensive way to gain understanding, whether or not clear answers emerge. For many, it is far better than lecture-based education (Wirkala and Kuhn, 2011; Brookfield, 2012).

Quick, easy, and absolute resolutions are readily available in contemporary society. Talk shows, editorials, websites, chat rooms, and coffee shops are among the places where we can find clear and forceful presentations, and fake news, about our serious problems, including educational issues. These answers may appear simple, clear, and dynamic—but often will be contradictory, competing, or inconsistent. And fake news can create confusion and distraction (International Federation of Library Associations and Institutions, 2020). Significant debates over complicated human issues such as sex, politics, and religion are engaging partly because they usually are not subject to quick and easy resolution.

Assessment should rely on the type and quality of evidence and argument presented for its support. That is consistent with Pinker's (2018) view that reasoning is the "foremost" of ideas for understanding the human condition and seeking progress; when coupled with science, by which he means the development and use of evidence-based knowledge, this is critical thinking—a skeptical look at conventional wisdom, superstition, and competing opinion and the reasoned examination of available accurate information and logic. Critical social and educational issues and opposing views of their proper resolution deserve critical thinking.

A proper skepticism and critical thinking are the friends of wisdom. Critical thinking, the main process and goal of education, involves at least the following:

- Recognition that an important issue deserves considered judgment;
- Thoughtful formulation of good questions;
- A search for possible answers and evaluating pertinent evidence;
- Consideration of alternative views and competing evidence; and
- Drawing of tentative conclusions that are acceptable until another question or a better answer arises.

Critical thinking is far more difficult—and significantly more important—than just finding answers (Emerson et al., 2002; Kincheloe and Weil, 2004; Shermer, 2011). The search for knowledge goes well beyond puzzle pages with answers printed upside down at the bottom or reporting back to a teacher what an encyclopedia says. Dialogue and dialectics can help.

DIALOGUE AND DIALECTIC REASONING

Reasoned dialogue calls for listening, understanding evidence, and assessing the quality of sources and persuasiveness of the arguments (McCabe, 2000; Audi, 2001). Dialectic reasoning, the examination of opposing ideas to develop a creative and superior idea, is a level beyond dialogue (Farrar, 2000; Sciabarra, 2000). Both are practices of critical thinking. Dialogue and dialectic are dynamic, interactive, and optimistic. They are optimistic since they take the stance that things can and should be improved. Arguments are not the only way to reason. Intuition, reading, and contemplation are perfectly suitable ways to discover testable knowledge; they should be subject to reasoned evidence to confirm or deny the results.

Arguments easily can dissolve into shouting matches or even fistfights. Whether arguments are trivial or significant, they can be heated and unthinking. It is easy to recognize the merits of our own position, and we are not always eager to admit the virtues of others. Arguments about important topics, however, should not devolve into shouting or personal attack. Knowledge and social improvement depend on rational and civil argument: "Disagreement is a key element of communal deliberations" (Makau and Marty, 2001, p. 7). Active democracy requires it (Gutmann and Thompson, 1996, 2004; Hess, 2002; Zurn, 2007). Good arguments can be thoughtful and reasoned, a dialogue between two different points of view—or dialectic reasoning with opposing views.

Dialogue incorporates civil discussion to gain understanding. Dialogue calls for two persons or two ideas—we can have dialogue with ourselves, but we need at least two ideas. Monologues, to others or ourselves, can be valuable for gaining ideas; most textbooks operate as monologues, presenting one view. But dialogue is more dynamic and more challenging. Not all dialogue, however, is civil and productive. It can operate at the lowest level, used to browbeat others into agreement, as in a kind of Socratic attack. Noddings (2015) notes, "Socrates himself taught by engaging others in dialogue . . . he dominates the dialogue and leads the listeners . . . forcing his listeners gently and not so gently to see the errors in their thinking" (pp. 3, 5). But reasoned dialogue involves active consideration of a different view and interest in interaction (Mercer, 2008; National Coalition for Dialogue and Deliberation, 2008).

Dialectic reasoning uses disputes and divergent opinions to arrive at a better idea. Dialectic occurs when you pit one argument (thesis) against another (antithesis) in an effort to develop a synthesis superior to either (see Figure 1.1). It is an inquiry into important issues that identifies the main points, important evidence, and logical arguments used by each of at least two divergent views on an issue. This requires critical examination of the evidence and arguments on each side of a dispute, granting each side some credibility. A synthesis from one level of dialectic reasoning can become a new thesis at a more sophisticated level, and the process of inquiry continues to spiral (Adler, 1927; Cooper, 1967; Rychlak, 1976; Noddings, 2015; Blumenfeld-Jones, 2004). True inquiry is lifelong.

The purpose for dialectic reasoning between competing ideas is not to defeat one and accept the other but rather to search for an improved idea. Dialectic reasoning is not merely the search to certify one side as a winner or to find a political compromise, especially a compromise that pleases neither side very well. It is a search for a higher level of idea that accommodates or incorporates the most important points in the thesis and antithesis. Sciabarra (2000) describes the dialectic process as follows:

> Dialectical method is neither dualistic nor monistic. A thinker who employs a dialectic method embraces neither a pole nor the middle of a duality of extremes. Rather, the dialectical method anchors the thinker to both camps.
>
> The dialectic thinker refuses to recognize these camps as mutually exclusive or apparent opposites. . . . He or she strives to uncover the common roots of apparent opposites [and] presents an integrated alternative. (p. 16)

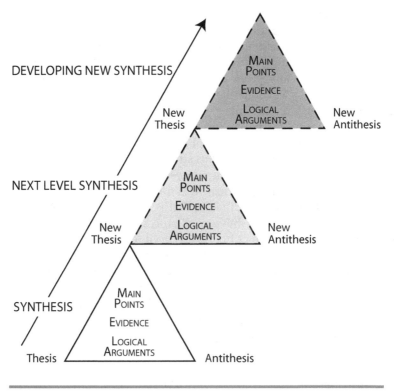

Figure 1.1 Dialectic Reasoning: A Simplified Diagram

For a simple example on a complicated topic: many early philosophers considered individual freedom and social freedom as opposites (Marcuse, 1960). One could enjoy individual freedom only by trampling on social freedoms, and a society could exert its freedom only by limiting the freedom of individuals. One was a thesis, the other its antithesis—apparently opposite views. A synthesis develops as both freedoms are considered necessary to modern civilization and to individuals, using the view that individual freedoms are best maintained in a free society. Without society, humans have no freedom in practice; there is no freedom in mere survival. Without individual freedoms, society cannot be free in practice; the range of individual freedom depends on agreement with other individuals in a social contract requiring essential equality, a system of laws, and rational thinking.

Philosophers have used the idea of dialectics in many different ways; it has justified opposite radical conclusions like absolute social control, as in forms of Marxism, or absolute individualism and against society, as in some of the libertarian ideas of Ayn Rand (Sciabarra, 1999). But Aristotle, the moderate philosopher who initiated Western political philosophy, could be considered the father of dialectic reasoning. He saw dialectic and rhetoric as mutually supportive arts, with dialectic the logical means for developing arguments and rhetoric the means of persuasion, speaking, or writing that uses the results of dialectic reasoning. Aristotle favored the dialectic because it required examining serious questions from many different positions.

The dialectic approach assumes that society and its institutions can and should be improved and that examining diverse ideas is productive. Many issues can't resolve well into a synthesis at any given time, but that does not denigrate the dialectic approach as a good way to comprehend and critically examine opposing positions. Dialectic reasoning may require more energy than you think necessary for some of the educational issues in this book, and dialogue will be perfectly satisfactory. The dialectic process, though, is a valuable tool for considering knotty social problems. It offers a means for depersonalizing various strongly held opinions to strive for a common good in improving schools (van Emeren and Grootendorst, 2003; Caranfa, 2004). As with most educative practices, it is not the finding of predetermined right answers but rather the process of thinking that is most important. A right answer is good for solving a single problem, but a good process is useful for many problems.

Dialogues and dialectics don't necessarily lead to truth; they can merely repeat errors and bias. Thus, we advocate a healthy, informed skepticism in examining these disputes. In the ancient Greek tradition, skepticism was to raise questions about reasons, evidence, and arguments (Sim, 1999; Wright, 2001; Shermer, 2011). Skepticism is not simply doubt, despair, or cynicism; it is intelligent inquiry. Without skepticism, we easily can fall into "complacent self-deception and dogmatism"; with it, we can "effectively advance the frontiers of inquiry and knowledge," applying this knowledge to "practical life, ethics, and politics" (Kurtz, 1992, p. 9). Dialogues and dialectics on educational issues, with prudent skepticism, are thoughtful forms of inquiry (McLaren and Houston, 2004; Van Luchene, 2004).

Welcome to the Study of Education as a Set of Critical Issues

The basis for this book is that:

- Education is necessary for individual and social progress;
- There is general public agreement on personal and social values of education;
- Critical issues in education produce differing views about realizing its potential; and
- Critical thinking, examining evidence and reasoning, is vital to our democracy.

The Ninth Edition has been divided into three parts. The introduction for each part frames selected educational issues in social and individual contexts. The chapters in each part then deal with specific topics and offer evidence and arguments from two divergent views. The views expressed aren't always exactly opposing, but they represent publicly expressed ideas about how schooling could be improved. Contrasting these views in terms of evidence presented and logic of each argument can stimulate a realistic dialogue or dialectic, offering an opportunity to examine issues as they occur in human discourse. Divergent essays sometimes will use the same data or same published works to make opposing cases, but they usually will offer evidence from widely separate literatures.

What we teach in schools is a distillation of traditions, myths, ideals, and morality in addition to what is considered true, accurate, consistent, and reasoned. There is a tension among those rationales that reflects social and intellectual beliefs and expectations. Schools mirror deep social conflicts between church and state, nation and citizen, autonomy and control, unity and diversity, freedom and restraint, and the individual and standardization. Divergent views of social values, the nature of knowledge, and the core purposes of education are intertwined in the politics of education.

The next decades of the twenty-first century may be placid or turbulent for schools, a period of recuperation from the latest round of reforms or a new set of attacks. Even in placidity, however, educational issues are sure to arise, cause alarm, and inflame passions. Some of the issues raised will spawn elements of new school reforms, and some will lead to school improvement; nearly all will be disputed. It is a worthy pursuit.

REFERENCES

Adler, M. (1927). *Dialectic.* New York: Harcourt Brace.

———— (1982). *The Paideia Proposal.* New York: Macmillan.

Agosto, D. E., ed. (2018). *Information Literacy in the Age of Fake News.* Denver, CO: ABC-CLIO, LLC.

Alba, D. (2020, February 6). "Facial Recognition Moves into a New Front: Schools." *New York Times.*

American Federation of Teachers (2005, May 19). *NCLB: Let's Get It Right.* Washington, DC: American Federation of Teachers.

Amnesty International (2018, September 24). Up to One Million Detained in China's Mass "Re-Education" Drive (amnesty.org/en/latest/news/2018/09/china-up-to-one-million-detained).

Apple, M. (1990). *Ideology and Curriculum* (2nd ed.). London: Routledge.

———— (1994). "Computers and the Deskilling of Teachers." *CPSR Newsletter* 12(2):3.

———— (1999). *Power, Meaning and Identity.* New York: P. Lang.

Aronowitz, S., and Giroux, H. (1993). *Education Still Under Siege* (2nd ed.). Westport, CT: Bergin and Garvey.

Audi, R. (2001). *The Architecture of Reason.* Oxford: Oxford University Press.

Bailyn, B. (1960). *Education in the Forming of American Society.* Chapel Hill: University of North Carolina Press.

Baker, B. D. (2018). *Educational Inequality in School Finance: Why Money Matters for America's Students.* Cambridge, MA: Harvard Education Press.

Banks, J. A. (1995). "The Historical Reconstruction of Knowledge about Race: Implications for Transformative Teaching." *Educational Researcher* 24:15–25.

Barber, B. (1998). *Intellectual Pursuits.* Lanham, MD: Rowman & Littlefield.

Barshay, J. (2018, July 9). "In 6 States, School Districts With the Neediest Students Get Less Money Than the Wealthiest." *The Hechinger Report.*

Barton, P. E., & Coley, R. J. (1990). *The Education Reform Decade.* ETS Policy Information Center Report. Princeton, NJ: Educational Testing Service.

Bastian, A., Fruchter, N., Gittell, M., Greer, C., and Haskins, K. (1985). *Choosing Equality: The Case for Democratic Schooling.* San Francisco: New World Foundation.

Beck, G. (2014). *Control.* New York: Mercury Radio Arts.

Berliner, D., and Biddle, B. J. (1995). *The Manufactured Crisis: Myths, Fraud, and the Attack on America's Public Schools.* Reading, MA: Addison-Wesley.

Berliner, D., and Glass, G. V. (2014). *50 Myths and Lies that Threaten America's Public Schools: The Real Crisis in Education.* New York: Teachers College Press.

Bestor, A. (1953). *Educational Wastelands.* Urbana: University of Illinois Press.

Blumenfeld-Jones, D. (2004). "The Hope of a Critical Ethics." *Educational Theory* 54(3):263–279.

Bomster, M. W. (2020, January 7). "It is One of the Most Fraught Words in Education." *Education Week.*

Botts, J. (2019, May 3). "ABCs of LGBTQ History is Mandated for More U.S. Public Schools." *Reuters.*

Boyer, E. (1983). *High School.* New York: Harper and Row.

Bracey, G. (1998). "The Eighth Bracey Report on the Condition of Public Education." *Kappan* 80(2):112–131.

———— (2002a). "The Twelfth Bracey Report on the Condition of Public Education." *Kappan* 84(2):135–150.

———— (2002b). *The War Against America's Public Schools.* Boston: Allyn and Bacon.

Bromley, A. E. (2020, March). Historian Compares Today's Protests to Civil Rights Movement of '50s and '60s. Q&A, *UVA Today* (news.virginia.edu).

Bromley, H., and Apple, M., eds. (2002). *Education/Technology/Power.* Albany: State University of New York Press.

Brookfield, S. D. (2012). *Teaching for Critical Thinking.* San Francisco: Jossey-Bass.

Brown v. Board of Education of Topeka, Shawnee County, Kansas, et al. (1954). 347 U.S. 483.

Caranfa, A. (2004). "Silence as the Foundation of Learning." *Educational Theory* 54(2):211–230.

Chambers, G. (1969, January). "Educational Essentialism Thirty Years After." *School and Society.*

Chandler, P. (2015). *Doing Race in Social Studies.* Charlotte, NC: Information Age Publishers.

Chen, M. (2018, May 11). "How Unequal School Funding Punishes Poor Kids." *The Nation.*

Children's Aid (2020). National Center for Community Schools (nccs.org).

Coles, G. (2003). *Reading the Naked Truth.* Portsmouth, NH: Heinemann.

College Entrance Examination Board (1983). *Academic Preparation for College.* New York: College Board.

Conant, J. B. (1958). *The American High School Today.* New York: McGraw-Hill.

Cooper, D., ed. (1967). *To Free a Generation: The Dialectics of Liberalism.* New York: Collier.

Cremin, L. (1961). *The Transformation of the School.* New York: Random House.

———— (1970). *American Education: The Colonial Experience.* New York: Harper and Row.

Cuban, L. (2003, November). "The Great Reappraisal of Public Education." *American Journal of Education* 110:3–31.

Curti, M. (1935). *The Social Ideas of American Educators.* New York: Scribner's Sons.

Darling-Hammond, L. (1991). "Achieving Our Goals: Superficial or Structural Reforms?" *Kappan* 72:286–295.

Deane, S. (2016). The Education of Tyrants. In H. Reid and L. Tanasi, eds., *Philosopher Kings and Tragic Heroes.* Sioux City, IA: Parnassus Press.

———— (2019). Gun Violence and Democratic Education in America. *Oxford Research Encyclopedia of Education.* Oxford Press.

DeAngelis, C. (2017, November 19). Government is Not the Solution to Educational Inequality. Foundation for Economic Education (fee.org/articles/government-is-not-the-solution-to-educational-inequality).

Dewey, J. (1916, 1944). *Democracy and Education.* New York: Macmillan.

DeWiel, B. (2000). *Democracy: A History of Ideas.* Vancouver, British Columbia: UBC Press.

Dikotter, F. (2016). *The Cultural Revolution.* London: Bloomsbury.

Doffman, Z. (2019, July 5). "Xinjiang Forcing Thousands of Muslim Children into 'Prison-like' Schools." *Forbes.*

Doheny-Farina, S. (1996). *The Wired Neighborhood.* New Haven, CT: Yale University Press.

Dormina, T., Penner, A., and Penner, E. (2017). "Categorical Inequality: Schools as Sorting Machines." *Annual Review of Sociology* 43:311–331.

Driver, J. (2018). *The Schoolhouse Gate: Public Education, The Supreme Court, and the Battle for the American Mind.* New York: Pantheon.

D'Souza, D. (1991). *Illiberal Education: The Politics of Race and Sex on Campus.* New York: Free Press.

Ellwood, L. (2017, September 3). "Native American Students Face Ongoing Crises in Education." *Indian Country Today.*

Emerson, J. D., Boes, L., and Mosteller, F. (2002). Critical Thinking in College Students. In M. A. Fitzgerald, M. Orey, R. Maribe Branch, eds., *Educational Media and Technology Yearbook.* Englewood, CO: Libraries Unlimited.

Farrar, R. C. (2000). *Sartrean Dialectics.* Lanham, MD: Lexington Books.

Fernekes, W. (2016). "Global Citizenship Education and Human Rights Education." *Journal of International Social Studies* 6(2):34–57.

Finn, C. (1990a). "The Biggest Reform of All." *Kappan* 71:584–593.

——— (1990b). "Why Can't Our Colleges Convey Our Diverse Culture's Unifying Themes?" *Chronicle of Higher Education* 36.

Fisher, E. (1991). "What Really Counts in Schools?" *Educational Leadership* 48:10–15.

Fiske, E. B. (1991). *Smart Schools, Smart Kids.* New York: Simon and Schuster.

Fullen, M. (2000). "Three Stories of Education Reform." *Kappan* 83:581–584.

Gallup (2019, July 1). Education (news.gallup.com).

Garcia, E., and Weiss, E. (2017, September 27). Education Inequalities at the School Starting Gate. Economic Policy Institute (epi.org/publication/education-inequalities-at-the-school-starting-gate).

Gardner, J. (1958). *The Pursuit of Excellence: Education and the Future of America.* New York: Rockefeller Brothers Fund.

Garforth, F. W. (1980). *Educative Democracy: John Stuart Mill on Education in Society.* Oxford: Oxford University Press.

Gaudelli, W. (2016). *Global Citizenship Education.* New York: Routledge.

Genovese, E. (1976). *Roll, Jordan, Roll.* New York: Vintage Books.

Gilio-Whitaker, D. (2019). *As Long as Grass Grows: The Indigenous Fight for Environmental Justice, from Colonization to Standing Rock.* Boston: Beacon Press.

Giroux, H. (1988). *Schooling and the Struggle for Public Life.* Granby, MA: Bergin and Garvey.

——— (1989). "Rethinking Educational Reform in the Age of George Bush." *Kappan* 70:728–730.

——— (1997). *Pedagogy and the Politics of Hope.* New York: Routledge.

——— (2004). "Critical Pedagogy and the Postmodern/Modern Divide." *Teacher Education Quarterly* 37(1):31–47.

Global Partnership for Education (2020, February 10). globalpartnership.org.

Goodlad, J. I. (1983). A *Place Called School: Prospects for the Future.* New York: McGraw-Hill.

Gouldner, A. (1979). *The Future of Intellectuals and the Rise of the New Class.* New York: Seabury Press.

Graham, P. A. (1967). *Progressive Education: From Arcady to Academe.* New York: Teachers College Press.

Guthman, E. O., and Allen, C. R., eds. (2018). *RFK: His Words for Our Times.* New York: William Morrow.

Gutmann, A., and Thompson, D. (1996). *Democracy and Disagreement.* Cambridge, MA: Harvard University Press.

——— (2004). *Why Deliberative Democracy?* Princeton, NJ: Princeton University Press.

Hanauer, N. (2019, July). "Education Isn't Enough." *The Atlantic.*

Hess, D. G. (2002). "Discussing Controversial Public Issues in Secondary Social Studies Classrooms." *Theory and Research in Social Education* 30(1):10–41.

——— (2011). "Discussions That Drive Democracy." *Educational Leadership* 69(1):69–73.

Holt, J. (1964). *How Children Fail.* New York: Pitman.

Illich, I. (1971). *Deschooling Society.* New York: Harper and Row.

International Federation of Library Associations and Institutions (2020, January 8). How to Spot Fake News (ifla.org/publications/node/11174).

Jacoby, S. (2008). *The Age of American Unreason.* New York: Pantheon.

K–12 School Shooting Database (2019). Monterey, CA: Naval Postgraduate School Center for Homeland Defense and Security (chds.us/ssdb).

Kandel, I. L. (1935, November). "Education in Nazi Germany." *Annals of the American Academy of Political and Social Sciences* 182:153–163.

Karier, C. (1967). *Man, Society, and Education.* Chicago: Scott, Foresman.

——— (1985). Retrospective One. In A. Bestor, ed., *Educational Wastelands* (2nd ed.). Urbana: University of Illinois Press.

Katz, M. (1968). *The Irony of Early School Reform.* Cambridge, MA: Harvard University Press.

——— (1971). *Class, Bureaucracy, and Schools: The Illusion of Educational Change in America.* New York: Praeger.

Kim, J. H. (2017, February 23). "Inside North Korea's Education System." *Foreign Policy News.*

Kincheloe, J. L., and Weil, D., eds. (2004). *Critical Thinking and Learning.* Westport, CT: Greenwood Press.

King, Jr., M. L. (1947). The Purpose of Education. *The Papers of Martin Luther King, Jr.,* Vol. 1: Called to Serve, January 1929–June 1951. The Martin Luther King, Jr. Research and Education Institute, Stanford University.

Kurtz, P. (1992). *The New Skepticism.* Buffalo, NY: Prometheus Books.

Lemann, N. (2010, September 27). "Comment: Schoolwork." *The New Yorker.*

Lerner, S. (2019). *Parkland Speaks.* New York: Crown Books.

Lhamon, C. E. (2018, January 2). Letter of Transmittal. *Public Education Funding Inequity in an Era of Increasing Concentration of Poverty and Resegregation.* Washington, DC: U.S. Commission on Civil Rights.

Lipscomb, A., and Bergh, A. E., eds. (1903–04). *The Writings of Thomas Jefferson* (14:384). Washington, DC: Thomas Jefferson Memorial Association of the United States.

Lutz, W. (2010, September 27). Dimensions of Global Population Projections. *Philosophical Transactions of the Royal Society B: Biological Sciences.*

Lynch, M. (2016, September 2). "The Sobering History of Native American Education in the 19th Century." *The Edvocate.*

Lynd, A. (1950). *Quackery in the Public Schools.* Boston: Little, Brown.

Makau, J. M., and Marty, D. L. (2001). *Cooperative Argumentation: A Model for Deliberative Community.* Long Grove, IL: Waveland Press.

Making Caring Common Project (2020, January). Do Parents Really Want School Integration? Harvard Graduate School of Education (gse.harvard.edu/news/20/01/do-parents-really-want-school-integration).

Mamet, D. (2011). *The Secret Knowledge.* New York: Sentinel.

Marcuse, H. (1960). *Reason and Revolution.* Boston: Beacon Press.

Martin, C., Boser, U., Benner, M., & Baffour, P. (2018, November 13). A Quality Approach to School Funding: Lessons Learned from School Finance Legislation. Center for American Progress.

McCabe, M. M. (2000). *Plato and His Predecessors.* Cambridge: Cambridge University Press.

McKenzie, J. (2007, May). "The Last Word." *No Child Left* 5(5).

——— (2019, May). "Are Technologies Making Us Smarter? Wiser? More Compassionate?" *From Now On* 29(5).

McLaren, P. (2014). *Life in Schools: An Introduction to Critical Pedagogy in the Foundations of Education* (6th ed.). New York: CRC Press.

McLaren, P., and Houston, D. (2004). "Revolutionary Ecologies." *Educational Studies* 36(1):27–45.

Mercer, N. (2008). "The Seeds of Time: Why Classroom Dialogue Needs a Temporal Analysis." *Journal of the Learning Sciences* 17(1):33–59.

Mervosh, S. (2019, February 27). "How Much Wealthier Are White School Districts Than Non-White Ones?" *New York Times.*

Milanovic, B. (2020, January/February). "The Clash of Capitalisms." *Foreign Affairs* 99(1).

Morgan, I., & Amerikaner, A. (2018). *Funding Gaps 2018.* The Education Trust (edtrust.org/resource/funding-gaps-2018).

Moses, R., and Cobb, C. E. (2001). *Radical Equations: Math Literacy and Civil Rights.* Boston: Beacon Press.

Moynihan, D. P. (1991, Winter). "Educational Goals and Political Plans." *The Public Interest* 32–49.

Murphy, M., and Fleming, T. (2010). *Habermas, Critical Theory and Education.* New York: Routledge.

Nathan, J. (1991). "Toward Educational Change and Economic Justice: An Interview with Herbert Kohl." *Kappan* 72:678–681.

National Coalition for Dialogue and Deliberation (2008). National Coalition for Dialogue and Deliberation Online Newsletter (ncdd.org).

National Commission on Excellence in Education (1983). *A Nation at Risk.* Washington, DC: U.S. Government Printing Office.

National Education Association (2006, February). Independent Commission on NCLB. News Release.

National Education Policy Center and Education Deans for Justice and Equity (2020, March). *Policy Statement on the "Science of Reading."* Boulder, CO: National Education Policy Center.

National Governors' Association (1986). *Time for Results: The Governors' 1991 Report on Education.* Washington, DC: National Governors' Association.

National Science Foundation (1983). *Educating Americans for the 21st Century.* Washington, DC: National Science Foundation.

Nelson, J. (1971). Nationalistic Education and the Free Man. In R. P. Fairfield, ed., *Humanistic Frontiers in American Education.* Englewood Cliffs, NJ: Prentice Hall.

——— (1976). "Nationalistic versus Global Education." *Theory and Research in Social Education* 4(1):33–50.

Nelson, J., and Pang, V. (2014). Prejudice, Racism, and the Social Studies Curriculum. In E. W. Ross, ed., *The Social Studies Curriculum* (4th ed., pp. 203–225). Albany: State University of New York Press.

New York Times (1992, January 5). Education Life. Special Supplement.

Nichols, S. L., and Berliner, D. C. (2008). "Testing the Joy Out of Learning." *Educational Leadership* 65(6):14–18.

Nocera, J. (2011, April 26). "The Limits of School Reform." *New York Times.*

Noddings, N. (2015). *Philosophy of Education* (4th ed.). Boulder, CO: Westview Press.

Norris, P., ed. (1999). *Critical Citizens.* New York: Oxford University Press.

Oppenheimer, T. (2003). *The Flickering Mind.* New York: Random House.

Paglia, C. (1990). *Sexual Personae.* New Haven, CT: Yale University Press.

Pine, L. (2010). *Education in Nazi Germany.* Oxford: Berg.

Pinker, S. (2018). *Enlightenment Now: The Case for Reason, Science, Humanism, and Progress.* New York: Penguin.

Presseisen, B. (1985). *Unlearned Lessons.* Philadelphia: Falmer Press.

Purpel, D. (1989). *The Moral and Spiritual Crisis in Education: A Curriculum for Justice and Compassion in Education.* Granby, MA: Bergin and Garvey.

Radford, B. (2020, January/February). "Is America a Sheeple Factory?" *Skeptical Inquirer* 44(1).

Rafferty, M. (1968). *Max Rafferty on Education.* New York: Devon Adair.

Ravitch, D. (1990). "Multiculturalism: E Pluribus Plures." *American Scholar* 59:337–354.

———— (2000). *Left Back: A Century of Battles over School Reform*. New York: Simon and Schuster.

———— (2007, October 3). "Get Congress Out of the Classroom." *New York Times*.

———— (2010). *The Death and Life of the Great American School System*. New York: Basic Books.

———— (2020). *Slaying Goliath*. New York: Alfred A. Knopf.

Reich, R. (2018). *The Common Good*. New York: Alfred A. Knopf.

Roser, M., and Ortiz-Ospina, E. (2019). Global Education. Our World in Data (ourworldindata.org). University of Oxford.

Ross, E. W., and Gibson, R., eds. (2006). *Neoliberalism and Educational Reform*. Cresskill, NJ: Hampton Press.

Rothstein, R. (2017). *The Color of Law*. New York: Liveright.

Russakoff, D. (2015). *The Prize: Who's in Charge of America's Schools?* Boston: Houghton Mifflin.

Russell, B. (1928). *Sceptical Essays*. London: George Allen and Unwin.

Rychlak, J. F., ed. (1976). *Dialectic*. Basel: Karger.

Sacks, P. (1999). *Standardized Minds*. Cambridge, MA: Perseus Books.

Safire, W. (1991, April 25). "Abandon the Pony Express." *New York Times*.

Schoales, V. (2019, January 25). "Education Reform as We Know It Is Over." *Education Week*.

Schoenfeld, A. H. (2002). "Making Mathematics Work for All Children." *Educational Researcher* 31:13–25.

SchoolFunding.Info (2020). Center for Educational Equity. Teachers College, Columbia University (centerforeducationalequity.org).

Schweber, H. H. (2012). *Democracy and Authenticity*. New York: Cambridge University Press.

Sciabarra, C. M. (1999). *Ayn Rand: The Russian Radical*. University Park: Pennsylvania State University Press.

———— (2000). *Total Freedom: Toward Dialectical Libertarianism*. University Park: Pennsylvania State University Press.

Shermer, M. (2011). *The Believing Brain*. New York: Times Books, Henry Holt.

Shirer, W. W. (1960). *Rise and Fall of the Third Reich*. New York: Simon and Schuster.

Siebers, H. (2018). "Are Education and Nationalism a Happy Marriage?" *British Journal of Sociology of Education* 40(1):33–49.

Siegel, H., ed. (2010). *Oxford Handbook on Philosophy of Education*. New York: Oxford University Press.

Sim, M. (1999). *From Puzzles to Principles*. Lanham, MD: Lexington Books.

Sinclair, U. (1924). *The Goslings*. Pasadena, CA: Sinclair.

Sizer, T. (1984). *Horace's Compromise: The Dilemma of the American High School*. Boston: Houghton Mifflin.

Smiley, M. B., and Diekhoff, J. (1959). *Prologue to Teaching*. New York: Oxford University Press.

Smith, M. (1954). *The Diminished Mind: A Study of Planned Mediocrity in Our Public Schools*. New York: Regnery.

Spring, J. (2008). No Child Left Behind as Political Fraud. In H. L. Johnson and A. Salz, eds., *What Is Authentic Educational Reform?* New York: Lawrence Erlbaum.

Standish, R. (2019, March 1). "China's Expanding War on Islam." *Washington Post*.

Stanley, W. B. (1992). *Education for Utopia: Social Reconstructionism and Critical Pedagogy in the Postmodern Era*. Albany: State University of New York Press.

————, ed. (2001). *Social Studies Research for the 21st Century*. Greenwich, CT: Information Age Publishers.

Startz, D. (2019, January 15). Equal Opportunity in American Education. Brown Center Chalkboard. Brookings Institution.

———— (2020, January 20). The Achievement Gap in Education: Racial Segregation versus Segregation by Poverty. Brown Center Chalkboard. Brookings Institution.

Stiglitz, J. (2019). *People, Power, and Profits*. New York: W.W. Norton.

Strike, K. A. (2004, May). "Community, the Missing Element of School Reform." *American Journal of Education* 110:215–232.

Sunderman, G. L. (2006, February). The Unraveling of No Child Left Behind. Report. Civil Rights Project of Harvard University (civilrightsproject.harvard.edu).

Taylor, A. (2016, March 8). "The Undeniable Sexism in Textbooks Designed for the World's Children." *Washington Post.*

Torres, C. A. (2002). "Globalization, Education, and Citizenship." *American Educational Research Journal* 39(2):363–378.

Twentieth Century Fund (1983). *Making the Grade.* New York: Twentieth Century Fund.

Tyack, D. (1967). *Turning Points in American Educational History.* Waltham, MA: Blaisdell.

——— (1991). "Public School Reform: Policy Talk and Institutional Practice." *American Journal of Education* 100:1–19.

Ulich, R. (1954). *Three Thousand Years of Educational Wisdom* (2nd ed.). Cambridge, MA: Harvard University Press.

UNESCO. (2019, August 29). Education is Transformative (unesco.org).

United Nations. (2015). 2030 Agenda for Sustainable Development (sustainabledevelopment.un.org/post2015/transformingourworld).

UN News (2020, January 24). The Drive for Quality Education Worldwide Faces "Mammoth Challenges" (news.un.org/en/story/2020/01/1055961).

U.S. Census Bureau. (2019, February 21). Educational Attainment in the United States: 2018.

U.S. News and World Report (1990, February 26). "The Keys to School Reform." 108:50–53.

van Emeren, F. H., and Grootendorst, R. (2003). "A Pragma-Dialectical Procedure for a Critical Discussion." *Argumentation* 17(4):365–386.

Van Luchene, S. R. (2004). "Rekindling the Dialogue: Education according to Plato and Dewey." *Academe* 90(3):54–57.

Warner, M. L., Havighurst, R. J., and Loeb, M. (1944). *Who Shall Be Educated?* New York: Harper.

Washington Post (2019, February 26). "$23 Billion Racial Funding Gap for Schools."

Webster, W. E., and McMillin, I. D. (1991). "A Report on Calls for Secondary School Reform in the United States." *NASSP Bulletin* 75:77–83.

Welter, R. (1962). *Popular Education and Democratic Thought in America.* New York: Columbia University Press.

Will, G. F. (2019). *The Conservative Sensibility.* New York: Hachette Books.

Williams, H. A. (2005). *Self-Taught.* Chapel Hill: University of North Carolina Press.

Winkler, K. (1991). "Organization of American Historians Backs Teaching of Non-Western Culture and Diversity in Schools." *Chronicle of Higher Education* 37:5–8.

Winterer, C. (2002). *The Culture of Classicism.* Baltimore, MD: Johns Hopkins Press.

Winthrop, N. (2000). *Democratic Theory as Public Philosophy.* Sydney: Ashgate.

Wirkala, C., and Kuhn, D. (2011). "Problem-Based Learning in K–12 Education: Is It Effective and How Does It Achieve Its Effects?" *American Educational Research Journal* 48(5):1,157–1,186.

Woodson, C. G. (1915). *The Education of the Negro Prior to 1861.* New York: G. P. Putnam.

Wong, A. (2019, March 5). "The Schools That Tried—but Failed—to Make Native Americans Obsolete." *The Atlantic.*

Wraga, W. (2001). "Left Out: The Villainization of Progressive Education in the United States." *Educational Researcher* 30:7.

Wright, L. (2001). *Critical Thinking.* New York: Oxford University Press.

Young, M. F. D. (1998). *The Curriculum of the Future.* London: Routledge.

Zalcman, D. (2016, July 17). Signs of Your Identity: Forced Assimilation Education for Indigenous Youth. Pulitzer Center on Crisis Reporting.

Zurn, C. F. (2007). *Deliberative Democracy and the Institutions of Judicial Review.* Cambridge: Cambridge University Press.

Whose Interests Should Schools Serve?
Justice and Equity

About Part One: Chapters 2 through 7 each focus on a topic that has competing basic interests, as well as divergent views, involving issues of justice and equity. These are two excellent criteria to use when comparing views on education. The topics covered include:

- Chapter 2: Charter schools and vouchers
- Chapter 3: School financing
- Chapter 4: Privatization and corporatization
- Chapter 5: Religion and public schooling
- Chapter 6: Gender equity
- Chapter 7: Immigration

Justice and Equity: Sounds Good to Me

Justice and equity sound simple enough as fundamental elements in a democratic, free society—even within a family, organization, school, or personal relationships. Justice is a forming idea for nearly all political theory, law, ethics, and human relations. Equity is concerned with the fair or proportional distribution of common goods. Justice and equity are based on socially agreed values and principles, legal and moral traditions, political and economic situations, time periods and geographic locations, social and individual conditions, and the eye of the beholder. In other words, they are conditioned by where you happen to be, when, who you are, and what you think. These are not just fuzzy, ill-defined concepts. They have been specifically defined many times and places in laws, traditions, rewards, and penalties in society. Democratic—and nondemocratic—societies vary in how they define and operationalize justice and equity. Redefinition is a regular occurrence.

The U.S. Declaration of Independence and Constitution define core values of the nation: liberty, equality, and democracy. However, prior to several amendments, the Constitution allowed only white, property-holding males to vote. Women, Native Americans, freed and bound slaves, and those without property were denied protection for equality or justice. Despite a series of constitutional amendments and judicial decisions that expanded and modernized our definition and practice of justice and equality, residual negative consequences still exist after almost 250 years.

The treatment of women across the globe is an example of disparate ideas of justice and equity in time and place. Historic and regional conditions, influenced by cultural traditions, keep women from freedom, power, and economic status, and make them subject to violence without recourse (American Civil Liberties Union, 2020; Oxfam International, 2020; Peace Corps, 2020). Massive gender inequities in health care, physical and mental treatment, power and wealth, family structure, and legal status in many nations and regions are documented by Lopez-Claros and Nakhjavani (2018). A striking example is Malala Yousafzai, the youngest Nobel Peace Prize Laureate. Banned from Pakistan schools by the Taliban, she became a vocal advocate for schooling for girls, was shot and survived, and became an international symbol and a leading figure in educational activism (Yousafzai, 2013).

Gender is only one area where ideals of justice and equity are tested. Underrepresented people of many groups suffer similar limits, by legal restriction and discrimination. Shores et al. (2020) review research showing socioeconomic and segregation differences between black and white students are "strikingly consistent predictors" of large gaps in educational outcomes and school disciplinary actions, holding back in grade level, classification as special education or gifted and talented, and Advanced Placement courses taken. Devlin (2018) documents the courageous bravery of school age African American girls who were the first to integrate southern U.S. schools after the 1954 *Brown* decision, a decision that corrected over 175 years of legal discrimination. This landmark in educational justice and equity law has yet to be fulfilled, and is still under threat, in American schools (Green, 2020). Asian Americans also have suffered legal discrimination with social repercussions. The first anti-immigration law was the Chinese Exclusion Act of 1882 and the government-forced internment of Japanese American citizens during World War II are prime example of legal restrictions. In these cases, the essential rationale was fear, not justice and equity (Lee, 2015; Inouye, 2016; Asia Society, 2019). Native Americans still struggle (Woodard, 2018; Gilio-Whitaker, 2019), as do Hispanics (Lopez et al., 2018), other racial groups (Horowitz et al., 2019), and religious groups (Masci, 2019).

Protest demonstrations can raise issues of injustice and inequality. An antislavery protest occurred in Germantown, Pennsylvania, in 1688. British rule and unequal taxation protests led to the U.S. Revolution. Racial discrimination protests by those seeking abolition of slavery surrounded the Civil War. African American justice movements and civil rights campaigns occurred throughout the twentieth century, including marches led by Martin Luther King, Jr. and others. In 2020, a series of demonstrations in response to police brutality against people of color, exemplified by daily, massive, national, and international demonstrations, followed the release a video on social media of the death of George Floyd at police hands. Women's rights movements can be traced to efforts in England before 1800; protests for women's suffrage date from the 1840s. Throughout the twentieth century and into the twenty-first, securing health and reproductive rights for women have been prevalent. Other examples of justice and equality protests relate to LGBTQ issues, gun control, the environment, wars, immigrants, and human rights. These protests pose challenges and opportunities in the redefinition of contemporary justice and equity.

Protests are not always successful in improving justice and equity, even if progress is made it often takes years and decades. Many protests ultimately have enormous impacts on laws, conditions, and human interactions. But some fail completely or turn the public against them. Some result in violence, destruction, and death; some are forgotten quickly, and some are largely ignored.

Inequities not only damage those that are underrepresented, they also damage the progress as a society toward an improved civilization and human rights. Discrimination issues have been addressed through legislation and regulation; civil rights laws in the 1960s made it illegal to discriminate because of race, color, religion, national origin, or gender. Growing awareness of other discrimination categories, like age and disability, has increased as cases develop and the public becomes better informed. In the United States, social progress, however slowly, has ensued. Restricting the full democratic participation of segments of the population is an issue of justice and equity. Education is a significant social agency to address such issues.

Fairness and Social Justice

The concept of fairness is essential to our ideas of justice. Legitimacy, in a democracy, is the granting of authority to government by the people, a form of social contract. Consent of the governed continues to be a widely held belief (Rawls, 2005). We accept decisions, even if we don't like them, when we feel that the procedure is fair and in the public interest. Unfairness, even the perception of it, breeds discontent in politics, business, personal relations, and schools.

Two types of justice are procedural and social. Procedural justice involves legal and judicial frameworks, including crime and punishment as well as systems for resolving disputes. According to Stuart Hampshire (2000), "fairness in procedures for resolving conflicts is the fundamental kind of fairness" (p. 4). Identifying and then burning witches at the stake was justice at one time; schoolmarms using a rod to punish misbehaving students was considered school justice. Prison for debtors was the law once; today, misdemeanors like possessing marijuana or trespassing may mean jail, depending on the state and the economic and cultural status of the accused (Natapoff, 2018). The death penalty is uncivilized and unjust in some nations; others use it routinely, and is often dependent on the social status of the accused (Platt, 2018).

Procedural fairness may result in unequal conditions. Divorcing parents who fight over custody of one child are unlikely to achieve equal condition. Selecting the Teacher of the Year may incorporate a fair procedure with impartial judging, but results are unequal. Equity does not require equality, but it does expect a process to be fair. Most of our notions of equality in the United States are procedural, equal treatment under the law, not equal results.

Some special treatment is based on equity, humanity, or prior injustices. The Americans with Disabilities Act required access to public buildings for people with disabilities. Affirmative action programs are an effort to make up for previous discrimination. Improved funding for special education, the Head Start Program, school lunches for low-income families, and special school treatment of minority or immigrant children are also examples. Justice can be served when some people are given special treatment based on significant social or ethical principles (Rawls, 1971, 1999, 2001).

Presumably, special public school programs for gifted and talented students could be justified by establishing the ethical condition that those students use their gifts to make appropriate artistic, intellectual, or other contributions back to the school and to society. Using Rawlsian theory on distributive justice, McKenzie (1984) studied school programs for gifted and talented students, concluding that the actual operation of these programs was undemocratic and unfair because there was no provision for those specially treated students to use their talents to give back to the school and society.

Social justice covers myriad personal and social relationship arrangements, often without the formality of law, but sometimes testable by law. How parents treat their children can be seen as just or unjust, depending on cultural traditions, social sensibilities, and family history. The UN Universal Declaration of Human Rights states criteria for the quality of justice in nations, but has no legal status, relying instead on ethics, honor, or shame for compliance. Ornstein (2017) succinctly portrays the development of social justice from barbarian times, "life was brutal and short, void of human rights or justice," to civilization in various contemporary forms, including the United States, where "equality, opportunity, and mobility" are ideals, but a work in progress. Human Rights Watch (2020) includes education as a major topic in its regular reports on global human rights conditions.

Characteristics of justice and equity differ by the nature of the government. Aristotle (1981), earliest of Western political philosophers, described the main categories of constitutional government, differing in virtue by whose interests they pursue.

1. A single ruler (monarchy or dictatorship) is good when it is benevolent, serving the interests of the people; but it is tyranny when it serves itself at the expense of the people.

2. Rule by a small group (aristocracy) is good when it consists of the best and brightest citizens and serves all, but an oligarchy is deficient when it serves its own interests.

3. A broadly based government (polity) is good when it serves the whole society, but democracy is not when it becomes anarchy or mob rule.

Many variants on these basic forms have occurred since Aristotle's time, and we have not exhausted the possibilities. The nature of justice follows the form: What is fair and equitable in a dictatorship depends on the views of one; in oligarchies the small group in charge decides; in representative democracies the elected representatives make the determinations. In each form the function of the constitution can act to limit or expand those decisions. Justice in practice may not coincide with existing theory (Miller, 1999; Rawls, 1999; Young, 2011; Frankfurt, 2015). Education is one area where justice and equity exist in theory and practice. Schools teach theoretic ideas of justice and equity, while both are seen in practice by teachers, students, and school staff on a regular basis in rules, punishments, rewards, conditions, and procedures.

Competing Interests

We all have interests, and we are in groups that have interests. We want good things for ourselves, our families, our friends, our associations, and our society. We may also want negative consequences for our enemies, our competitors, and others who oppose our interests. We like to hear that our nation's writers, scientists, athletes, actors, students, or workers have won awards in international competitions. We are dismayed by reports that our children's test scores are lower than scores in other neighborhoods or nations. We compete with a family down the street or some obnoxious cousin, and we want our interests to be successful. There are, of course, times when our personal interests and family or group interests are in opposition, as in arguments over who should get the family car, what kind of career to pursue, or whether to support a war. Tracking students into separate curriculums for college preparation, vocational training, and special education produces similar issues of justice and equity; college admission procedures are another prime example of those issues.

Legally or socially justified discrimination against races, religions, tribes, nationalities, sexual orientation, and other human identities also occur across the globe, including the United States. Competing interests, through politics, wealth, and ideology, determine the main structures for judging what is just and what is equitable. Differing views of what constitutes a just or equitable system are the subject of an extensive literature in politics, economics, sociology, ideology, and democracy (Rawls, 1971, 2001, 2005; Kitching, 2001; Little, 2002; Mitzman, 2003; Barry, 2005; Bowles et al., 2005; Kolm, 2005; Sandel, 2010).

Self-Interest

Ayn Rand (1943, 1997) advocated rampant self-interest, claiming that selfishness is a virtue and arguing against altruism. A softer but similar approach is that of Anthony Downs (1957), suggesting enlightened self-interest in the marketplace, with no damage intended for others and a sense of social responsibility. That can still create serious conflicts as individual or group interests compete for scarce resources. Scrooge and the robber barons illustrate one kind of historic self-interest, with corruption and exploitation, that continues into the twenty-first century (Josephson, 1934; Beatty, 2007; Frasier, 2015).

Individual interests need not be ruthless and irresponsible. Altruism is one form of socially beneficial self-interest. "Do unto others as you would have them do unto you," the Golden Rule, is a principle shared by virtually every culture in the world. Teachers recognize that their self-interest is served by having happy and successful students. There are, of course, many selfless people who devote their lives to helping others—Mother Teresa and Martin Luther King, Jr. come to mind. They have personal interests but are not absorbed with their own welfare.

Social Interests

Beyond individual interests are group interests, and these can be very competitive. "Special interests" is now a term of derision in politics, used to label politicians and policies we don't like. Yet we all belong to various special interest groups by our own or our family's occupations, geographic area, hobbies, charities, travel, religion, shopping, educational pursuits, and nearly all other endeavors. Obviously, these interests do not always coincide. We would like lower taxes but appreciate public benefits such as roads, police, clean parks, and schools. We prefer a healthy environment but like products that come from chemicals, plastics, and other pollution-producing manufacturers. We join or support groups that advocate those ideas we share, even if at times we act in a manner that is not internally consistent.

Then there are national interests. Our stated policy, whether under a Democratic or Republican administration, is to defend national interests in international affairs—trade, borders, war, terrorism, and so on. Not remarkably, every nation places its national interests as foremost, though clearly the definition and delineation of national interest differs. National interest has been one of the fuels of war, genocide, militarism, border vigilantism, isolation, denial of human rights, trade restrictions, and international posturing (Bandy and Smith, 2005; Herbert, 2005; Pavola and Lowe, 2005). It also has been a fuel for peace, international understanding, freedom, trade agreements, charity, economic development, and the protection of human rights (Nelson and Green, 1980; Hahnel, 2005). Our use of language shows interests at work: the term "Axis of Evil" was used to identify nations and groups our government considered threatening, "Manifest Destiny" was invoked to cover the invasion of Native American territory in the West, and the "war on terrorism" is used as grounds for changing accepted patterns of civil rights and civil liberties.

Social interests also involve general safety and welfare, the environment, health, education, security, transportation, communication, freedom, and order. These topics concern people across such political boundaries as cities, states, and nations. Residents of cities, suburbs, and rural areas are interested in safe highways and airports and good hospitals and schools—these are public interests, whether the social institutions are privately or publicly operated. The public also has a stake in how these quality-of-life areas are handled; many are government controlled and operated, some are government regulated but privately operated, and some are privately controlled and operated with little governmental oversight.

Schooling is one of the most important of those broad public concerns in the United States. Laws govern nearly all forms of schooling to include required attendance, financing, staff credentials, curriculum, and operational requirements. Most school-age students in the United States attend public schools, controlled and operated by state governments; about 15% of students are in private schooling, including independent schools, religiously affiliated schools, trade schools, and homeschooling. Other schooling options include publicly funded vouchers, public and private charter schools, homeschooling, and privatized public school operations.

Schools serve many constituencies: students, parents, teachers, administrators, government, commerce, media, special interest groups, historic educational practices, philosophies, and laws. These can be competitive interests with divergent agendas based on politics, economics, social conscience, and ideology. Individuals and groups differ in their power, their wealth, and the rationales they present.

INTERESTS, POLITICS, AND IDEOLOGIES

Our interests are incorporated in and modified by ideologies (e.g., liberal, conservative, radical, reactionary). Ideologies are used to explain and justify the preferred society (Jacoby, 2005), include assumptions about human nature (Shils, 1968), provide criteria for judging human life and society (Lane, 1962), and offer self-identification (Erikson, 1960). All of us have ideologies (Wetherly, 2017). But ideological labels do not identify each of us or our views. They are broad categories that represent relatively coherent structures of attitudes, values, and beliefs. Ideological debates can be fiery, passionate, and not always reasonable, realistic, or precise (Hofstadter, 1965).

Ideological labels can change in application, creating confusion, and people can have conservative ideas on one topic and liberal ideas on another. Governmental regulation, free trade, abortion, universal health care, climate change, public schools, and gay marriage illustrate such topics. Most ideological terms are, however, in common use and, if defined and applied clearly, can be used to examine social and educational issues in any time period.

Political ideologies can be viewed as if on a spectrum, with moderate positions in the center and radical positions placed on either end (see Figure 1). In the United States, the political spectrum is spanned by the ideological left and the ideological right. The radical right and radical left are found on opposite ends of the spectrum, followed by conservatives and liberals, respectively. Moderate views of each ideology are found near the center (Freeden, 1998; White, 2011; see also the *Journal of Political Ideologies*).

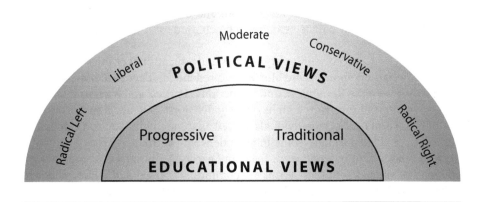

Figure 1   A Spectrum of Political and Educational Views

Liberalism, Liberals, Conservatives, and Radicals: Confusion

Continuing disputes about justice and equity as they apply to individual and social rights are among the grand debates in democratic history and philosophy (Nozick, 1974; Sandel, 1998; Valentyne, 2003; Barry, 2005; Hahnel, 2005; Rawls, 2005; Charen, 2012; Posner and Weyl, 2018). These disputes revolve around disparate opinions about the relative rights of individuals and of society and how equity among those rights should be determined. Liberalism, a belief in freedom and equality, is the dominant political philosophy among Western democracies (de Ruggiero, 1927; Noddings, 1995; Klosko, 2000; Richardson, 2001; Kolm, 2005; Krugman, 2009). According to Shapiro (1958), "What has characterized liberalism at all times is its unshaken belief in the necessity of freedom to achieve every desirable aim. . . . Equality is another fundamental liberal principle" (pp. 10, 11). This dual belief separates the philosophy of modern Western nations from some other political ideas, such as divine right of kings, aristocracy by birth and social class, or theocratic rule.

In the United States and other Western democracies, we don't argue for a return to colonial period theocratic governments, European feudal dictatorships, or politically powerful monarchies. We do argue about the relative weight that should be given to individual freedoms and social constraints (Dahl, 1999; Reisman, 1999; Geuss, 2001; Henderson, 2001; Fuentes, 2005; Goodhart, 2017). Berlin (1969) points out that

> Liberty is not the only goal . . . if others are deprived of it . . . then I do not want it for myself. . . . To avoid glaring inequality or widespread misery I am ready to sacrifice some, or all, of my freedom; I may do so willingly and freely: but it is freedom that I am giving up for the sake of justice or equality. (p. 125)

In the main, both conservatives and liberals in the United States support the basic ideas of democratic freedoms and equality—tenets of traditional liberalism (Dewey, 1930; Lippman, 1934; Russell, 1955; Gutman, 1999; Gill, 2001; Tomasi, 2001; Rawls, 2005). The major differences between conservatives and liberals revolve around what are the best definitions or criteria for freedom and equality, what is the best balance between them, how that balance can best be achieved, and how each is served in a specific situation.

Confusing trends in contemporary politics and educational politics occur as political boundaries and definitions are blurred and redefined. There are basic ideological differences between the Republican and Democratic Parties, and each party has developed its own internal spectrum with its own subdivisions. But labels such as conservative and liberal don't stick on individuals as well as some might like; some people may prefer to be considered to have some independence from the party they are identified with. And others want independence from any party. Definitions of conservative and liberal may be slippery, but these terms are commonly applied and widely understood to refer to two distinct ideologies. We continue, despite the confusions, to use conservative and liberal labels to identify ideas, issues, and various people with certain viewpoints. Because of our readiness to do this, teachers can help students use critical thinking to understand and interpret various ideas and disputes in an educational setting (Nelson, 1990, 2003, 2010).

Contemporary political disputes between conservatives and liberals occur over questions of balance and process, and they spill over into our debates on lawmaking, court proceedings, and schooling. Conservatives, in general, want to limit governmental interference in individual freedom; liberals generally want to ensure individual rights by governmental regulation. Yet, liberals tend to support more individual freedom and conservatives tend to want to regulate and limit views of sexuality, patriotism, politics, and economics. Conservatives argue for unregulated rights of individuals to own guns, liberals for governmental regulation of gun ownership. On school topics, liberals tend to support more individual freedom for students and teachers to examine controversial topics, to join unions, to protest, and to criticize. Conservatives tend to support government-imposed standards, school and teacher accountability, socially acceptable student behavior, privatizing education, and restrictions on what topics can be studied.

More deeply discordant ideological roots, including a variety of radical positions on what a society and its schools should be, run beyond the liberal and conservative dialogue. Radical critiques influence the general debate by providing extreme positions, allowing liberals and conservatives to take more popular positions in the center. Radical ideas tend to have limited credibility in mainstream discussions, but liberals and conservatives draw from those ideas in proposing reforms. Radical ideas contain the seeds for longer term and more significant change. For example, when kings and queens were presumed to rule by divine right, democracy was a radical view. In a dictatorship, individual freedom is radical. Critical positions often appear first in the radical literature, then filter into the liberal and conservative rhetoric (Nelson et al., 1972; Dahl, 1999; Simhony and Weinstein, 2001). Once this rhetoric takes hold, then changes in the mainstream or moderate positions can ensue. In a political debate, neoconservative and neoliberal views are a rethinking of conservative or liberal ideas (DeMuth and Kristol, 1995; Piper, 1997; Dahl, 1999; Newey, 2001; Richardson, 2001).

Individual and Social Rights

One of the major struggles in determining justice in a democracy lies in finding a suitable balance between the rights of individuals and communities. This struggle has many titles but often is described as an ideological battle between individualism and communitarianism. These ideologies compete in their emphases, and in their more extreme versions offer a dialectic.

The radical right wing, composed of reactionaries or libertarians, advocates individual freedoms with the least restraint possible. As Nozick (1974) phrases it,

> Individuals have rights, and there are things no person or group may do to them. . . . [A] minimal state, limited to the narrow functions of protection against force, theft, fraud, enforcement of contracts . . . is justified; that any more extensive state will violate persons' rights not to be forced to do certain things, and is unjustified. (p. ix)

In addition to an antistate position, libertarians convey a strong procapitalism view, relatively unfettered entrepreneurship, and private enterprise. Excessive governmental control is assumed to kill individual initiative. Government, to libertarians, is an unfortunate development that has grown too large and too encompassing—stifling individual freedoms (Jonescu, 2012). They contend that initiative, entrepreneurship, and ambition will suffer when the welfare state takes over and destroys personal freedom.

Far right libertarians want to severely limit government, abolish regulation, taxation, and public financing. They would eliminate Social Security, Medicare, the IRS, welfare, public education, and the right of government to take property under eminent domain; libertarians aim at "nothing short of the privatization of social existence" (Newman, 1984, p. 162). Their view is that a free enterprise, market-determined economy with natural competitiveness provides the most efficient system; the best for each and the best for all. Not all libertarians share the view that all government is harmful; some recognize a need for a limited role in mediating disputes, regulating commerce in basic human needs, and protecting society (Boaz, 2019).

Radical left-wing advocates argue for egalitarian answers to the excesses of individualism. They see a breakdown of social values, family structures, social responsibilities, shared interests, and collective purposes that constitute a decent society. Unbridled individualism poses, they contend, clear and negative repercussions in charitable works, public welfare, public services, and public education—the major contributions to our civilization. Greed and self-absorption promote antigovernment attacks that undermine public confidence and lead to debilitating and discriminatory competitiveness, destruction of protections for the environment, health, and consumers, elimination of other public regulatory needs, increased privatization, and suspicion of others. Excessive individualism also appears in efforts to maintain a social hierarchy based on birth, wealth, and historical status. Individualism is not usually advocated by members of the social class at the bottom. A premise of individualists is that those who have should continue to have. Egalitarian answers, in opposition, include progressive taxation and redistribution of wealth, expansion of equal opportunities, affirmative action, and such programs as national health care, Head Start, and safety net welfare.

Communitarians, like libertarians, come in various stripes. Their major critique involves greed and social corruption of unregulated capitalism and the selfishness and self-centeredness that accompanies excessive individualism. Community, they argue, is our social glue. Some critiques separate individualism from individuality; self over others versus all have worth.

John Dewey (1916, 1930, 1933) developed the concept that individual differences and individual learning are consistent with real education as a social process. He writes of a broader set of conflicts:

> There can be no conflict between the individual and the social. For both of these terms refer to pure abstractions. What do exist are conflicts between some individuals and some arrangements in social life; between groups and classes of individuals; between nations and races; between old traditions embedded in institutions and new ways of thinking and acting which spring from those few individuals who attack what is socially accepted. (quoted in Ratner, 1939, p. 435)

Communitarians don't always ignore or denigrate the value of individuals; they advocate a balance between individual liberty and social needs for common purposes—balancing rights and order (Sandel, 1998, 2010). Amitai Etzioni (1996) notes a major shift from "traditional" social order by edict, authoritarian rule, and rigid control to increasing individual rights.

Ideological Roots of School Disputes

Competing ideas with differing expectations for schools include freedom and equality, public and private, individual and society, the masses and the elites, unity and diversity, and the religious and the secular. Dualisms are useful as mental constructions to assist in making a choice or using dialectic reasoning to find a new synthesis. They can assist in reasoned dialogue about competing interests and ideologies. Dualisms are false in that they don't exhaust the possible ideas, they are not in complete isolation from each other, and they don't usually require a pristine choice of one over the other. Dualisms allow consideration of potentially good and bad consequences. Schooling is one public activity where such dualisms occur with frequency. Schools engage in developing individuals and the society, teaching traditions and developing futures, and promoting and questioning existing values.

Each ideology provides different views of schooling, from advocating abolition of public schools to using public schools for social criticism and the overthrow of oppression. The importance of education in society is reflected in controversies surrounding divergent ideological positions and the interests they represent.

Radical right-wing ideas about schooling are not uniform; they come from different special interest groups. Some promote teaching fundamentalist religious dogma. Some seek to censor teaching materials dealing with sex, socialism, atheism, or anything they think is anti-American. And some want to undercut publicly supported schools in favor of elite schooling for a select group of students. Right-wing groups have attacked secular humanism, feminism, abortion rights, sex education, global education, and values education in schools.

Radical educational ideologies from the right include the following views:

Libertarians: "Get government off our backs and out of our schools."
Abolitionists: "Abolish public schooling."
Extreme elitists: "Schooling for the best only; the rest into the work pool."

The radical left wing also offers a critical view of schools. Some see education as the way for the masses to uncover the evils of capitalism and the corporate state. Some propose education as the means for revolution, opening all the institutions of society to criticism. Left-wing groups have attacked business-sponsored teaching materials, religious dogma in public schools, tracking, discrimination, social control, and education for patriotic obedience.

Radical left-wing views include the following:

Liberationists: "Liberate students from oppressive forces in school and society."
Reconstructionists: "Use schools to criticize and remake society."
Extreme egalitarians: "Abolish all privilege or distinction."

Conservative, liberal, and radical views of society and education provide different rationales for criticism of schools and different proposals for reform. They are general frameworks that underlie individual and group discontent with schools. Radical views are important because they present stark and clearly defined differences between egalitarian and elitist ideologies. However, conservative and liberal ideas govern most reform movements because of their general popularity and immense influence over media and government. Liberals, conservatives, and radicals differ in their views of which mainstream position has the schools in its grip (Aronowitz and Giroux, 1983).

From Elite to Mass Education:
Exercise in Defining Justice and Equity

In education, fundamental goals and general practices have varied during different times and in different locations. Primitive education was dedicated to survival and continuing rituals and life patterns established by elders. Ancient schooling was devoted largely to inculcation of religious learnings. In Athens, philosophic and contemplative schooling supplanted religious training, while Spartan education was heavily committed to the military life. Roman schooling was more practical than philosophic and intended for developing strong loyalty and citizenship. Spiritual ideas predominated in schools of the Middle Ages, a preparation for the afterlife. The Renaissance brought different goals for schools—enlightenment, development of human capacities, and individual creativity. For most of this time, formal schooling was for elites and families of religious, social, and political leaders. The main schooling arguments concerned the preparation of society's leaders, and whether it should focus on either a strict learning of traditional roles, rituals, and concepts of knowledge (or contemplation of the good) or enlightenment and more flexible learnings.

Mass education arose as democracy developed, was fostered especially in schooling in the United States from the mid-nineteenth century, and has now spread throughout the industrialized world. Schooling for all developed some different educational goals under differing ideologies: basic literacy and numeracy, social control, civic responsibility, loyalty and patriotism, vocational and home training, character and values development, health and safety knowledge, human relationships, self-reliance and realization, and solving problems. Schooling also shifted toward more secular, scientific, and technological goals. Consistent with the evolution in democratic political concepts, ideas about schooling shifted from a focus on basic literacy and social control to broader intellectual development and increased interest in individuality.

Newer developments in educational ideas challenged established purposes and practices in schools and posed interesting questions on the relation of individuals to their societies and important issues of justice and equity (Barton et al., 2020). What dimensions of justice and equity should be expected in schools and classrooms? How should schools address justice and equity regarding individual choice, racism, gender, class, wealth, and religion? What interests are at stake? Competing answers to these questions show disparate interests.

We would like to include in this volume all viewpoints on each educational issue, but that is an obvious impossibility. We have, therefore, limited each chapter to two distinct positions about the topic covered to stress the dialogue or dialectic quality of the issue. These positions draw from liberal-progressive ideas, from conservative-traditional, and from radical critiques from the left or right. Additional references to conservative, liberal, and radical literature are included, and we encourage exploration of these highly divergent views.

REFERENCES

American Civil Liberties Union (2020, February 10). Women's Rights (aclu.org/issues/womens-rights).

Aristotle (1981). *The Politics.* Trans. by T. A. Sinclair. London: Penguin Books.

Aronowitz, S., and Giroux, H. (1983). *Education Under Siege.* South Hadley, MA: Bergin and Garvey.

Asia Society (2019, July 25). Asian-Americans Then and Now: Linking Past to Present (asiasociety.org/education/asian-americans-then-and-now).

Bandy, J., and Smith, J. (2005). *Coalitions across Borders.* Lanham, MD: Rowman & Littlefield.

Barry, B. (2005). *Why Social Justice Matters.* Cambridge: Polity.

Barton, A. C., Tan, E., and Birmingham, D. J. (2020, January 15). "Rethinking High-Leverage Practices in Justice-Oriented Ways." *Journal of Teacher Education.*

Beatty, J. (2007). *Age of Betrayal.* New York: Knopf.

Berlin, I. (1969). *Four Essays on Liberty.* Oxford: Oxford University Press.

Boaz, D. (2019, April 12). Key Concepts of Libertarianism. Commentary. CATO Institute (cato.org/publications/commentary/key-concepts-libertarianism).

Bowles, S., Gintis, H., and Gross, M. O. (2005). *Unequal Chances.* Princeton, NJ: Princeton University Press.

Charen, M. (2012, March 16). "Is Liberalism Immoral?" *National Review* Online.

Dahl, G. (1999). *Radical Conservatism and the Future of Politics.* London: Sage.

DeMuth, C., and Kristol, W. (1995). *The Neoconservative Imagination.* Washington, DC: AEI Press.

de Ruggiero, G. (1927). *The History of European Liberalism.* Trans. by R. G. Collingwood. Boston: Beacon Press.

Devlin, R. (2018). *A Girl Stands at the Door.* New York: Hachette Books.

Dewey, J. (1916). *Democracy and Education.* New York: Macmillan.

——— (1930). *Individualism Old and New.* New York: Minton, Balch, and Co.

——— (1933). *How We Think.* Boston: D. C. Heath.

Downs, A. (1957). *An Economic Theory of Democracy.* New York: Harper/Addison Wesley.

Erikson, E. H. (1960). *Childhood and Society.* New York: W. W. Norton.

Etzioni, A. (1996). *The New Golden Rule.* New York: Basic Books.

Frankfurt, H. (2015). *On Equality.* Princeton: Princeton University Press.

Frasier, S. (2015). *The Age of Acquiescence.* New York: Little, Brown.

Freeden, M. (1998). *Ideologies and Political Theory.* Oxford: Oxford University Press.

Fuentes, C. (2005). *This I Believe.* New York: Random House.

Geuss, R. (2001). *History and Illusion in Politics.* Cambridge: Cambridge University Press.

Gill, E. R. (2001). *Becoming Free: Autonomy and Diversity in the Liberal Polity.* Lawrence: University Press of Kansas.

Gilio-Whitaker, D. (2019). *As Long as Grass Grows.* Boston: Beacon Press.

Goodhart, D. (2017). *The Road to Somewhere.* London: C. Hurst & Co.

Green, P. (2020, January 20). "Suitts: Overturning *Brown* and the Segregationist Legacy of the Modern School Choice Movement." *Forbes.*

Gutman, A. (1999). *Democratic Education.* Princeton, NJ: Princeton University Press.

Hahnel, R. (2005). *Economic Justice and Democracy.* New York: Routledge.

Hampshire, S. (2000). *Justice Is Conflict.* Princeton, NJ: Princeton University Press.

Henderson, D. (2001). *Anti-Liberalism 2000.* London: Institute of Economic Affairs.

Herbert, B. (2005). *Promises Betrayed.* New York: New York Times Books.

Hofstadter, R. (1965). *The Paranoid Style in American Politics.* New York: Vintage Books.

Horowitz, J. M., Brow, A., and Cox, K. (2019, April 9). Views of Racial Inequality. Race in America 2019. Pew Research Center (pewsocialtrends.org/2019/04/09/views-of-racial-inequality).

Human Rights Watch (2020, February 12). *"My Teacher Said I Had a Disease"*: *Barriers to the Right to Education for LGBT Youth in Vietnam*. Amsterdam: Human Rights Watch.

Inouye, K. M. (2016). *The Long Afterlife of Nikkei Wartime Incarceration*. Stanford, CA: Stanford University Press.

Jacoby, R. (2005). *Picture Imperfect: Utopian Thought for an Anti-Utopian Age*. New York: Columbia University Press.

Jonescu, D. (2012, March 30). On Restoring American Individualism. American Thinker (americanthinker.com/articles/2012/03/on_restoring_american_individualism.html).

Josephson, M. (1934). *The Robber Barons*. New York: Harcourt, Brace.

Kitching, G. (2001). *Seeking Social Justice through Globalization*. University Park: Pennsylvania State University Press.

Klosko, G. (2000). *Democratic Procedures and Liberal Consensus*. New York: Oxford University Press.

Kolm, S-C. (2005). *Macrojustice: The Political Economy of Fairness*. Cambridge: Cambridge University Press.

Krugman, P. (2009). *The Conscience of a Liberal*. London: Penguin Books.

Lane, R. E. (1962). *Political Ideology*. New York: The Free Press of Glencoe.

Lee, E. (2015). *The Making of Asian America: A History*. New York: Simon and Schuster.

Lippman, W. (1934). *The Method of Freedom*. New York: Macmillan.

Little, I. M. D. (2002). *Ethics, Economics, and Politics*. Oxford: Oxford University Press.

Lopez, M. H., Gonzalez-Barberra, A., and Krogstad, J. M. (2018, October 25). Latinos and Discrimination. Pew Research Center (pewresearch.org/hispanic/2018/10/25/latinos-and-discrimination).

Lopez-Claros, A., and Nakhjavani, B. (2018). *Equality for Women = Prosperity for All*. New York: St. Martin's Press.

Masci, D. (2019, May 17). Many Americans See Religious Discrimination in the U.S.—Especially against Muslims. Pew Research Center (pewresearch.org/fact-tank/2019/05/17/many-americans-see-religious-discrimination-in-u-s-especially-against-muslims).

McKenzie, J. (1984). A Study of the Relative Democratic Nature of Gifted Education Programs in New Jersey. Unpublished dissertation, Rutgers University.

Miller, D. (1999). *Principles of Social Justice*. Cambridge, MA: Harvard University Press.

Mitzman, A. (2003). *Prometheus Revisited: The Quest for Global Justice in the Twenty-First Century*. Amherst: University of Massachusetts Press.

Natapoff, A. (2018). *Punishment Without Crime*. New York: Basic Books.

Nelson, J. (1990). The Significance of and Rationale for Academic Freedom. In A. Ochoa, ed., *Academic Freedom to Teach and to Learn*. Washington, DC: National Education Association.

———— (2003). "Academic Freedom, Academic Integrity, and Teacher Education." *Teacher Education Quarterly* 30(1):65–72.

———— (2010). "The Need for Courage in American Schools." *Social Education* 74(6):298–303.

Nelson, J., Carlson, K., and Linton, T. (1972). *Radical Ideas and the Schools*. New York: Holt, Rinehart and Winston.

Nelson, J., and Green, V. (1980). *International Human Rights*. Stanfordville, NY: Coleman.

Newey, G. (2001). *After Politics*. New York: Palgrave.

Newman, S. L. (1984). *Liberalism at Wit's End*. Ithaca, NY: Cornell University Press.

Noddings, N. (1995). *Philosophy of Education*. Boulder, CO: Westview Press.

Nozick, R. (1974). *Anarchy, State, and Utopia*. New York: Basic Books.

Ornstein, A. (2017). "Social Justice." *Society* 54:541–548.

Oxfam International (2020, January 20). Gender Justice and Women's Rights (oxfam.org).

Pavola, J., and Lowe, I., eds. (2005). *Environmental Values in a Globalizing World*. New York: Routledge.

Peace Corps (2020, February 10). Global Issues (peacecorps.gov).

Piper, J. R. (1997). *Ideologies and Institutions.* New York: Rowman & Littlefield.

Platt, T. (2018). *Beyond These Walls: Rethinking Crime and Punishment in the United States.* New York: St. Martin's Press.

Posner, E., and Weyl, G. (2018). *Radical Markets: Uprooting Capitalism and Democracy for a Just Society.* Princeton, NJ: Princeton University Press.

Rand, A. (1943). *The Fountainhead.* New York: New American Library.

———— (1997). *The Journals of Ayn Rand.* Ed. by D. Harriman. New York: Dutton.

Ratner, J. (1939). *Intelligence in the Modern World: John Dewey's Philosophy.* New York: Random House.

Rawls, J. (1971). *A Theory of Justice.* Cambridge, MA: Harvard University Press.

———— (1999). *The Law of Peoples.* Cambridge, MA: Harvard University Press.

———— (2001). *Justice as Fairness.* Ed. by E. Kelly. Cambridge, MA: Harvard University Press.

———— (2005). *Political Liberalism* (Expanded Ed.). New York: Columbia University Press.

Reisman, D. (1999). *Conservative Capitalism.* New York: St. Martin's Press.

Richardson, J. L. (2001). *Contending Liberalisms in World Politics.* Boulder, CO: Lynne Rienner.

Russell, B. (1955). *Authority and the Individual.* London: Allen and Unwin.

Sandel, M. (1998). *Liberalism and the Limits of Justice* (2nd ed.). Cambridge: Cambridge University Press.

———— (2010). *Justice: What Is the Right Thing to Do?* New York: Farrar, Straus and Giroux.

Shapiro, J. S. (1958). *Liberalism: Its Meaning and History.* New York: D. Van Nostrand.

Shils, E. (1968). The Concept of Ideology. In D. Sills, ed., *The International Encyclopedia of the Social Sciences.* New York: Macmillan.

Shores, K., Kim, H. E., and Still, M. (2020, January 23). "Categorical Inequality in Black and White." *American Educational Research Journal* (OnlineFirst).

Simhony, A., and Weinstein, D. (2001). *The New Liberalism.* Cambridge: Cambridge University Press.

Tomasi, J. (2001). *Liberalism Beyond Justice.* Princeton, NJ: Princeton University Press.

Valentyne, P., ed. (2003). *Equality and Justice* (vols. 1–6). New York: Routledge.

Wetherly, P. (2017). *Political Ideologies.* Oxford: Oxford University Press.

White, J. (2011). "Left and Right as Political Resources." *Journal of Political Ideologies* 16(2):123–144.

Woodard, S. (2018). *American Apartheid: The Native American Struggle for Self-Determination and Inclusion.* New York: IG Publications.

Young, I. M. (2011). *Responsibility for Justice.* New York: Oxford University Press.

Yousafzai, M. (2013). *I Am Malala.* New York: Little, Brown, and Co.

Family Choice in Education

Public Interest or Private Good

2

Is family choice of schools
in the public interest?

Position 1:   Choice Improves Opportunities for Individual Students

---

School choice is about a fundamental right for parents to have access to the educational environment that serves their children best. . . . Parents should have a wide range of high-quality schools or educational options to choose from—be it traditional public schools, public charter schools, private schools, or virtual learning. Private school choice, through scholarship tax credit programs, vouchers, education savings accounts, and individual tuition tax credits, gives students, including those from low-income families or those with special needs, the opportunity to receive tuition to attend a private school that meets their needs immediately.

—American Federation for Children (2019)

Why Educational Choice Is Needed

If your children attended a school in which most students scored below the state average on standardized tests, what could you do? What if they were enrolled in a school with few certified teachers, overcrowded classrooms, few computers, little lab equipment, and not enough books or other supplies? Could you find a way to get them the education they need? If you were unhappy with your child's school because the curriculum was not rigorous enough or because it violated your beliefs and values, could you remedy the situation? Depending on a family's income, your options could be even more limited.

Dissatisfied families can work to correct problems in their children's public schools. Doing so, however, often involves a long, cumbersome process of political action—meeting with teachers and principals, attending school board meetings, working on committees, and being an active presence in a school. Time and energy commitments usually are more than most parents can make, and risk of failure and frustration is high. Even when these efforts are successful, the resulting changes may come too late for the students whose parents initially tried to make them. Students are in a particular grade for only one year. Schools often cannot modify programs or policies that quickly. Although working for long-term change is an option, it is a choice that doesn't meet the most immediate needs of parents and children.

Families with enough money can decide to send their children to expensive, nonsectarian private schools. Their budget can absorb the cost of this decision even as the parents continue paying taxes to support public schools. Additionally, because there are only a limited number of such schools, attending them may mean that students must live away from their families for long periods. This disruption of family life for the sake of a child's education is not often an attractive option for parents or young people, even when the family can afford it. Instead of increasing parental influence in children's lives, this choice weakens it. Private schools remain options only for the wealthiest families since the tuition costs run into the tens of thousands of dollars per child.

Parents with more limited financial resources can choose to send their children to less expensive and more accessible private schools affiliated with religious organizations (McDonald and Schultz, 2019). In fact, of the 32,460 private schools in the United States, 66% have connections to a religious group (Broughman et al., 2019). However, this choice is still of limited help. Many families are not comfortable with the differences between their religious beliefs and those of the organization sponsoring the school. In times of economic distress, tuition may become too much of a burden for the family budget to bear.

Indeed, if a family has no surplus funds in its budget, the option of any kind of private school is not available. Most poor children attend urban or rural public schools, where achievement lags behind their peers in suburban schools, particularly for children of color and English language learners (de Brey et al., 2019). Many African American and Latino parents are deeply concerned about the quality of their children's education and support school choice programs (Peterson et al., 2017). However, the organization of public education hinders families in their efforts to provide their children with the advantages of a good education.

In order to maintain a high level of local control over schools, districts were established on the basis of geography—meaning that cities, towns, villages, or any part of those municipalities can become school districts. That way, local branches of government, most often school boards, could be elected by and held responsible to residents of the areas the schools serve. In practice, however, these forms of governance have become less responsive to dissatisfied parents and limit educational opportunity. For example, once a district is established, students are assigned to schools on the basis of where they live within and among those districts. The dividing lines are firmly maintained. Moving from school to school within a district often is difficult; moving from district to district (unless the family changes its residence) is almost impossible. Assigning students to schools on the basis of their residence minimizes parents' choice about the school their children can attend. Families' financial resources, not their commitments to their children, determine the amount of educational choice they have.

Families are not the only ones concerned about education. Other people have expertise to contribute in deciding what kind of schools and programs will best serve children and our society. Educators have access to research about academic programs that ensure success for children having difficulties with traditional ways of teaching and learning. Health professionals have suggestions about issues affecting children's physical and emotional well-being and how those concerns can be addressed in schools. Businesspeople can offer advice and support to schools in preparing young people for their future in an ever more demanding job market. However, while parental authority with regard to children is not unlimited in this country, it is generally the most significant factor in determining most aspects of a child's life. Ultimately, all families should be able to be the final decision makers about *their* child's education, not just those who have achieved a certain level of economic success. Americans increasingly support the idea that families should be able to choose the school their children attend (Peterson et al., 2017). Public policy has responded to the need for a marketplace of school choices for families by creating multiple options. Among them are choices within the public school system, on its "borders," and in private schools. In each case, public monies provide the necessary funding.

Options for Parents and Children

Open Enrollment Schools

Within the public school system, districts have adopted "open enrollment" or "choice" policies that allow families to research, visit, and apply to a number of schools they believe will best serve their children. Geography is no longer a barrier to educational options; districts provide transportation to whatever school the child attends. When they look over the landscape of schools from which they can choose, parents find large, comprehensive schools; schools linked and responsive to neighborhoods; small schools that provide individualized attention; and magnet schools with specialized curricula, designed to attract and serve particular groups of students. In addition, some states and the District of Columbia have created options that allow taxpayer monies to be turned over to private schools in the form of vouchers. Eighteen states provide substantial tax credits for corporations and individuals that provide students in low-performing districts with scholarships to private schools. Charter schools are other publicly funded choices. They operate on the edges of the public school district—within the borders and under the jurisdiction of some regulations but freed from rules that prevent public schools from serving all children well.

Choice policies within public school systems have been tried on a limited basis. Except for Alabama, Maryland, Illinois, and North Carolina, all states have enacted some type of "open enrollment" policy. However, only 28 states' policies actually require schools within districts or districts within states to participate in open enrollment. Of those, only 23 require "interdistrict" open enrollment polices that mandate districts to accept students from outside their geographic boundaries. In general, the option is available only to students from some low-performing schools, from schools with "distressed facilities," or from schools that are farther away from their homes than the school in the receiving district. Even when open enrollment is mandatory, districts have significant leeway in creating and implementing criteria for acceptance. "Intradistrict" open enrollment, the opportunity to attend a nonneighborhood school, is available in 34 states but mandatory in only 19 (Education Commission of the States, 2018; U.S. Department of Education, 2018b). Some intradistrict open enrollment allows students from low-performing schools or persistently dangerous schools to attend higher performing ones within the district. Usually, the transfer is dependent on space availability and other criteria the district creates.

Other forms of open enrollment allow students to choose among many options within a district. In New York City, for example, a student can list up to 12 elementary schools that he or she would like to attend. Students are accepted into one school, and about 69% receive their first choice and 83% receive an offer to one of the top three choices (Mosle and Park, 2019). For high school applicants, 45% are accepted into their first choice and 75% into one of their top three (Gould, 2019). Nationwide, other large districts are providing intradistrict transfers and enrollment options for families, and in the process they are addressing issues of concern such as transportation, parents' access to information, and funding that can limit the success of open enrollment (Boston Public Schools, 2018; Education Commission of the States, 2018; Denver Public Schools, 2019).

Magnet Schools

In the 1970s, some districts used "magnet schools" to draw students from all across a district as part of their efforts toward racial desegregation. They remain vibrant learning centers in many cities and represent the second largest sector of choice schools in the United States (Snyder et al., 2018a). A magnet school is

> a public elementary school, public secondary school, public elementary education center, or public secondary education center that offers a special curriculum capable of attracting substantial numbers of students of different racial backgrounds. Magnet schools offer a wide range of distinctive education programs. Some emphasize academic subjects such as math, science, technology, language immersion, visual and performing arts, or humanities. Others use specific instructional approaches, such as Montessori methods, or approaches found in international baccalaureate programs or early college programs. (U.S. Department of Education, 2018a)

The magnet school approach to choice enables families to match school specialties with students' interests. Almost 3,200 magnets operate in the United States and serve approximately 2.5 million students, most of them in elementary schools (Snyder et al., 2018a). Studies have shown that young people who attend magnet schools experience less segregated environments and achieve more academic success than do their counterparts in traditional public schools in the same cities. Magnet schools are an increasingly popular choice for urban parents who want their children to have the advantages provided by a diverse student body in which there are high expectations for academic success (Ayscue et al., 2017). Students who attend magnet schools perceive them as providing better preparation for college and careers, and increasing their chances for academic and economic success (Kumah-Abiwu, 2019).

Vouchers

Vouchers transfer taxpayer dollars directly to families to allow them to pay for the educational program they believe will be most beneficial for their child. Milton Friedman, an economist who first proposed vouchers 50 years ago, believed that the idea would work best if each family received an amount of money equal to their school district's per pupil expenditure (Logan, 2018). Additional subsidies would be provided for children with special needs. Ideally, there would be no restriction against parents' adding their own money to what they received from the government to pay for more expensive schools—and there would be no restriction on what type of school a family could choose.

In the early 1990s, experiments with vouchers began with privately funded programs. The largest, the Children's Scholarship Fund, sponsors nearly 26,000 children across the country. However, these programs cannot keep pace with the applications from parents who want to provide their children with the benefits of a private school education (Children's Scholarship Fund, 2018).

Puerto Rico, Arkansas, Florida, Georgia, Indiana, Louisiana, Maine, Maryland, Mississippi, New Hampshire, North Carolina, Ohio, Oklahoma, Tennessee, Utah, Vermont, Wisconsin, and the District of Columbia have publicly funded voucher programs. In most, but not all, states, students must meet eligibility requirements to receive state funding to attend a private school. In others, the state pays only for students with disabilities to attend nonpublic schools of their choice. In Ohio, students can also receive vouchers if they have previously attended or are assigned to attend a low performing school. Because it set its eligibility requirements loosely enough to enable more students to qualify, Indiana is the state with the largest number of participants; over 36,000 children receive funding. Milwaukee, Wisconsin, which has a district with the oldest voucher program, provides assistance to more than 26,000 students, mostly in religiously affiliated private schools (EdChoice, 2019; Education Commission of the States, 2019a). The schools meet state health and safety standards and regulations and agree to use random selection processes in admitting voucher students.

Seventeen states support private school education with public funds by granting tax credits to corporations or individuals who donate to approved and regulated nonprofit scholarship funds. States generally set limits on the amount of tax credits to be given in any year and scholarship funds must be distributed to students with true financial need (Education Commission of the States, 2019c).

Support for vouchers is growing in part because of an advantage they have over other choice programs (Henderson et al., 2020). They allow parents to select schools that not only match their children's academic interests but also conform to the family's values. It is difficult, for example, for young Muslims to find space within their schools where they can meet their obligation to pray; if they cannot, they must leave school on Fridays, their holy day, to attend services at their mosques. Both Muslims and Jews sometimes find it difficult to obtain food in public school cafeterias that meets their dietary laws (Calder, 2019; Islamic Networks Group, 2019). Voucher programs allow parents to remove their children from schools that violate their religious beliefs and place them in schools that allow them to exercise the constitutionally guaranteed freedom to practice their religion.

Critics of vouchers question the use of taxpayer dollars to educate children in schools affiliated with religious groups. Some of their concern is rooted in their understanding of the First Amendment's prohibition against governmental support of religion. Beginning in the 1940s, the Supreme Court began to enforce the ban by creating standards that limited states and municipalities' relationships to religious institutions, establishing a greater distance between church and state than had previously existed. However, the Court has also held that many government policies benefiting religious groups *are* constitutional. For example, tax exemption for churches and religious schools, tax deductions of contributions to religious charities, tax credits for tuition paid to religious schools, transportation for children to those schools, and police or fire protection of religious institutions have all been declared legal. Even more closely related to the question of school choice, the GI Bill, Pell grants, federally subsidized student loans, and state tuition assistance programs for college students have not been declared unconstitutional even though some money from those programs has gone to schools directly affiliated with religious groups.

The Court has established a policy of "neutrality" with regard to such funding. If a program provides benefits to individuals according to neutral guidelines and the individuals use those benefits for a service provided by a religious group, the wall between church and state has not been violated. The government is not supporting a religious institution; individuals are doing so through private decisions (*Mueller v. Allen*, 1983; *Witters v. Washington Department of Services for the Blind*, 1986; *Zobrest v. Catalina Foothills School District*, 1993; *Agostini v. Felton*, 1997). Using that reasoning, the justices ruled in 2002 in *Zelman v. Simmons-Harris* that a Cleveland voucher program was legal. In *Arizona Christian School Tuition Organization v. Winn* (2011), the Court ruled that taxpayers lacked standing to sue the state for providing tax credits to people who donate to a fund that supports scholarships to religiously affiliated private schools, allowing the state to continue to offer such tax credits. However, the Court indicated that it is open to considering the matter in more suitable cases.

Another concern about using taxpayer dollars to provide funds for private education is the potential for discriminatory admissions policies in nonpublic schools. Opponents suggest that religious schools, for example, will be able to refuse admission to young people who are not members of the religious organizations with which the schools are affiliated. They also argue that private schools will be able to refuse students with conditions that create special educational needs. While it is certainly justified to worry about unfair admissions practices, current laws already protect young people from arbitrary discrimination. For example, most scholars agree that the Civil Rights Act prohibition against states' discrimination of citizens based on ethnicity would prevent state-provided vouchers from being used in private schools that denied access based on race or national origin (Mead and Eckes, 2018; Berner, 2019). Private schools are allowed to consider religion in admission decisions; however, state funded voucher systems can and have been constructed to require schools accepting public money to admit students regardless of their religious beliefs (Petrilli, 2017). In addition, Title IX of the Elementary and Secondary Education Act, which prohibits discrimination on the basis of sex in institutions receiving federal funds, exempts religious institutions if the application of the provision would violate core tenets of the organization's beliefs. States also are free to create regulations for schools in which publicly funded vouchers can be used and those rules can include clauses preventing discrimination on the basis of gender and sexual orientation.

Voucher opponents also raise objections based on their fear that parents could use taxpayer funds to send children to schools affiliated with organizations whose beliefs violate American values. At times, their concerns seem exaggerated and based more on opposition to the principle of choice than on any real danger that groups such as the Ku Klux Klan or Muslim extremists would found voucher-funded schools (Shakeel and Wolf, 2017). Laws already exist to prevent anyone in the United States, including school teachers and administrators, from advocating illegal activities (Berner, 2019).

Just because government would not be running schools funded through voucher payments, it does not necessary follow that there could be no oversight of such schools. Student progress could be monitored. Many private schools already participate in state accountability systems. These oversight systems could be modeled on European "inspectorates" and modified to America's needs to ensure that a return to the monopoly of government-run schools was unnecessary (Shakeel, 2018).

Charter Schools

Charter schools are another option that is increasingly available to parents who want to ensure that their children receive an education designed to help them achieve academic and economic success. Charter schools are relatively autonomous of local school district control—they are able to choose their own governing boards, hire and terminate teachers without meeting union contracts or state certification requirements, design and deliver innovative curricula, and use instructional techniques that meet individual students' needs. In exchange for the increased autonomy, charter schools are held accountable for student performance and are subject to closure if they are found to be unsuccessful (Miron, 2017). The first charter school opened in 1992; almost 30 years later, there were over 7,000 schools serving 3 million children— approximately 6% of all public school students (Snyder et al., 2018a).

Charter schools receive per pupil funding from the state and/or local school district, but for a variety of reasons, on average, they receive approximately 27% less money than traditional public schools (DeAngelis et al., 2018). Fortunately, charter schools are able to raise additional funds through donations from individuals or corporations. In fact, many large foundations have given millions of dollars to charter schools. For example, Doris and Donald Fisher, founders of the Gap clothing store chain, have given more than $70 million to the Knowledge is Power Program, known more commonly as KIPP schools (Warner, 2018). The Walton family, owners of Walmart, has contributed over $407 million to charter schools and over $1 billion to programs that create and support choice (Walton Family Foundation, 2019). These extra funds make it possible for charters to offer longer days than traditional public schools do, to provide students with extra academic support, and to offer activities that make them competitive with more privileged peers. Charter schools are also eligible for grants from the federal government, which have totaled more than $3.3 billion in the last 25 years (U.S. Department of Education, Office of Innovation and Improvement, 2015).

Most charter schools are free-standing and operate independently (National Alliance for Public Charter Schools, 2019). Within the charter school sector, nonprofit charter management organizations (CMOs) or networks have been developed. Among the most successful are KIPP, which has more than 240 schools, and Uncommon Schools, whose network includes more than 50. The schools operated by these CMOs are college preparatory and serve students in low-income urban neighborhoods. KIPP schools describe themselves as characterized by "a commitment to excellence, and a belief in helping children develop the academic and character strengths they need to succeed in college, lead choice-filled lives, and build a better tomorrow for themselves, for their communities, for us all" (KIPP Foundation, 2019a). They are built on four principles including high expectations, a focus on character development, effective teaching and leadership, and a physically and emotionally safe environment (KIPP, 2019b). Uncommon Schools describe themselves as having "three goals in mind: [that] every student feels truly loved and cared for, learning is both rigorous and joyful, and students are prepared for success in college and beyond" (Uncommon Schools, 2019b).

Mindful that one of the intended consequences of the increased freedom afforded charter schools was that they would serve as incubators for new and more effective educational practices, Uncommon Schools (2019a) has become a leader in professional development for educators across the spectrum of schools. While not all CMOs are alike in every respect, they do share the core vision of KIPP and Uncommon Schools—that economic hardship should not prevent young people from obtaining an education that will help them achieve personal success.

In addition, about 12% of charter schools are operated by for-profit education management organizations (EMOs). The schools themselves are nonprofits but they contract with EMOs to operate the schools. Whether they are run independently, by nonprofit CMOs, or by for-profit EMOs, all charter schools must meet the same standards set by the state. They must be open to all students, charge no tuition, and meet the same accountability standards as traditional public schools.

Studies of student achievement in charter schools demonstrate great variability in the impact that charters have on student progress. When the studies are disaggregated, however, they reveal that some charters are much more successful than the traditional public schools that students would have attended. Some are particularly effective in urban areas and in lessening differences in educational outcomes between racial, ethnic, and socioeconomic subgroups (Pendergrass and Kern, 2017).

Home and Virtual Schooling

Home schooling and virtual, or online, schooling are two additional options for families who want to provide children with an education that matches their families' values and the children's needs. Home schooling is parent-led home-based education. Virtual schooling is a form of schooling that uses online computers, the Internet, or other web-based methods through which children complete an organized set of courses or grades. Approximately two million children are home schooled in the United States. Study after study has shown that these students scored, on average, in the 65th to 80th percentile on standardized academic tests. The average for public school students was the 50th percentile (Ray, 2018). Home schooling is legal in all 50 states with each state setting its own regulations; some states have home school statutes while others consider students to be attending "private schools" established by their parents (Home School Legal Defense Association, 2019).

Virtual K–12 schooling takes many forms. It can be the only form of education a child experiences or it can be used to supplement in-person schooling at home or in public and private schools. Twenty states allow virtual charter schools (Education Commission of the States, 2019b). Thirty-two states allow fully funded online schools that serve approximately 320,000 students (Digital Learning Collaborative, 2019).

Home schooling and virtual schooling allow families to take advantage of a diverse marketplace of educational opportunities.

School Choice Unlocks the Power of the Free Market

The founders of the modern American educational system believed that it was innovative and necessary to have government provide schools for the country's children, organize their curriculum, certify that teachers were qualified, and deliver services like career counseling and extracurricular activities. However, the governmental monopoly on schools has, over time, become ineffective and costly. A greater reliance on a market-like structure that allows choice can promote freedom and improve education. When there is a monopoly and only governments run publicly funded schools, families are forced to choose them—if only because the other options are so costly. Allowing—and funding—choices other than traditional schools provides more Americans with freedom to seek out the kind of education they believe is right for their children and to share in the competitive advantages enjoyed by people whose wealth made those choices possible in the past. Choice improves education because when public schools are no longer guaranteed "customers," they face competition, and that competition serves as an incentive to improve.

Every American deserves to achieve as much as they are willing to work for. Family choice of schools releases the power of the market to help ensure that they do.

Choice Limits Public Schools' Ability to Achieve Social Goals

In a government like ours, each individual must think of the welfare of the State, as well as of the welfare of his own family, and, therefore, of the children of others as well as his own. It becomes, then, a momentous question, whether the children in our schools are educated in reference to themselves and their private interests only, or with a regard to the great social duties and prerogatives that await them.

—Mann (1843, p. 64)

Public Schools and the Common Good

Americans accepted the idea of the "common school" in the mid-nineteenth century because they became convinced that a publicly funded and publicly governed educational system would achieve desirable social goals and maximize individual opportunity. Public schools would be an efficient and democratic way to prepare citizens—men and women—who had the knowledge and habits needed for self-governance of the new nation. Young people from all socioeconomic backgrounds would be prepared to vote and serve on juries; to behave responsibly toward government, property, and the rights of others; and to be honest and productive workers. They would learn tolerance and respect for the diverse people and different points of view in the country (Good and Braden, 2000). Americans were willing to hand over hard-earned money to the government in the form of school taxes because they believed that public education would return "profits" to every member of society, not just to schoolchildren and their families. In return for public funding of public schools, decisions about the cost, staffing, and curricula would be made through the electoral and representative processes characteristic of public life. For more than 150 years, elected school boards or other forms of local governments have managed schools. If people disagreed with decisions by these elected officials, they elected others. Because taxpayers had the right to make choices about schools, they continued to support an educational system that was open to all American children and served as a beacon for immigrants who wanted their children to have better lives.

The right of some individuals to opt out of that system was guaranteed: private schools remained an option. Some were affiliated with religious groups; some were not. They were, and remain, relatively free of public oversight. In exchange, they have, until very recently, been ineligible to receive public monies. Now, proponents of some types of school choice want to cancel the social contract that has existed between Americans and their government with regard to schools. They advocate an allocation of public funds to multiple types of schools and argue that a pluralistic society requires a pluralistic education system similar to ones found in other liberal democracies around the world. However, they also reject the rigorous oversight of schools that monitoring the use of public funds requires and which is found in other countries (Berner, 2019). Individual families, they argue, should be able to choose how to use their share of the tax revenue set aside for education regardless of whether the philosophies, policies, or curricula of those choices are consistent with the social goals that were the basis of the original arguments for the use of public funds for schooling. Indeed, the idea of choices that provide families with the ability to choose schools whose religious, political, and social beliefs match their own is a key component in marketing school choice. Almost every method of providing funding for private schools is defended, at least in part, on those grounds and parental satisfaction is the most cited positive effect of using public funds for private education (EdChoice, 2019).

To advocates the use of tax dollars for education is not seen as a way to achieve the "common good." Instead, its purpose is the "private good" of individual children and their families. If education is seen as a commodity to be obtained rather than a service to be provided, support for a "marketplace" where competing providers would offer that "product" makes sense to those who see the forces of the free market as the best way to guarantee individual freedom. However, the market model of publicly funded education has serious flaws that limit the ability of the electorate to direct school policy, to oversee the use of funding, and to ensure equal access to schools. Long-standing social problems are not addressed by family choice: schools remain segregated, and differences in achievement among rich and poor; white, black, and Latino; and male and female are not corrected. In fact, the educational marketplace acts pretty much the way most free markets do—people with money, information, the "right" social class, ethnicity, gender, and powerful personal connections have access to "better" goods. A hierarchy among products emerges, and existing social injustices are perpetuated. Most importantly, the needs of the national community are sacrificed to the desires of the lucky few. No one would argue that public schools in the United States are perfect. However, when school choice is designed to serve "consumers" or "customers" it undercuts the single most powerful justification for utilizing common funds for education.

Choice and Integration

Family choice policies have been used by racial isolationists (vouchers for all-white private schools in the post-*Brown* South) and by integrationists (urban magnet schools). Since the Court ruled against the use of choice to support segregated schools, choice proponents have argued that creating attractive options for parents will help integrate American education. There is a consensus of educational research that there are long- and short-term benefits from attending racially integrated schools. Desegregated schools are more likely to have experienced and racially diverse teachers and offer students access to greater educational resources (Frankenberg, 2017; Johnson, 2019). In desegregated schools, the racial achievement gap is lessened and dropout rates are reduced. Students of color who attend desegregated schools have higher educational attainment and intergenerational mobility than their peers who attend segregated ones (Mickelson, 2015). In addition, integrated schools provide experiences that are essential for social cohesion and the well-being of multiracial democracies (Mickelson and Nkomo, 2012).

Supporters of vouchers and state-funded scholarship programs have suggested that because private schools, especially urban Catholic schools, draw from larger geographic areas, they will be able to attract more diverse student populations than public schools that reflect residential segregation. In general, urban private schools serve a larger percentage of white students than public schools in the same city. Public funding would make it possible for more minority parents, disproportionately represented among the poor, to choose private schools, resulting in greater integration within the private schools. However, recent studies indicate that publicly funding attendance at private schools has not resulted in greater integration in private schools (Egalite et al., 2017; Levy, 2018). Over two-thirds of private school students are white (Broughman et al., 2019). In Indiana, which has the most generous state-funded financial aid programs for private school attendance, almost 60% of students who participated were white and more than a third attended suburban, rural, or small town schools. Fewer than half had ever attended an Indiana public school (Indiana Department of Education, 2019).

Charter schools also appear to do little to remedy racial and ethnic segregation. Charters are more racially segregated than the districts from which students come (Synder, 2018a). In New York City, if students had to attend their neighborhood schools, the system would be less segregated than it is in the current environment, which is rich with choices and charter schools (Mader et al., 2018). Even magnet schools appear to have lost their ability to lessen racial isolation. As more and more school districts are released from court-ordered school desegregation plans, fewer white parents are choosing to send their children to those schools (Snyder et al., 2018b).

Supporters of family choice ignore how race and class prejudice affect the marketplace they are trying to create. First, the ability to take part in choice programs is dependent on whether families have access to information about their options and whether the need for transportation to schools is met. If school districts do not provide outreach and transportation to all families, children attending "schools of choice" are in more segregated environments than they would have been if they had stayed in schools in their geographically based attendance zones (Ellison and Aloe, 2018; Mader et al., 2018). White parents often measure school quality by the "qualities" of the students and believe that the classmates who are white and middle class make the best companions for their children (Billingham and Hunt, 2016). Research and experience has shown that there is a "tipping point"—a demographic profile at which white parents leave a school or district. Early studies indicated that once the black enrollment in a school or district reaches approximately 30%, white enrollment decreases (Gulosino and d'Entremont, 2011). More recent ones suggest that the economic status of students affects family decisions about what schools children will attend almost as much as race does (Caetano and Mahesri, 2017). Most schools of choice do not attempt to balance enrollments based on race, ethnicity, or poverty levels, and there has been disincentive from the federal government to do so. Cities and states do not create policies and procedures that positively influence racial or economic integration (Frankenberg et al., 2019). Consequently, market forces take over, and schools of choice reflect the racial prejudices of society. Nothing in uncontrolled choice plans diminishes these social realities (Buchanan, 2018).

In addition to segregation by race, school choice encourages other forms of isolation. Data indicate that there are fewer English language learners or students with disabilities in charter schools than in comparable traditional public schools (Mader et al., 2018; Prothero, 2018). Furthermore, the religious affiliation of many schools participating in voucher programs and the conversion of some religious schools to charters also pose problems. They protect families' desires that children participate in their traditions at the expense of the social goal of broadening young peoples' horizons and helping them take their place in an increasingly diverse society (Mead and Eckes, 2018). Sectarian schools do not prepare young people adequately enough to meet society's goals and, therefore, are not worthy of public funding.

Choice and Academic Achievement

Proponents of family choice in education argue that public schools, especially those that serve poor children, no longer enable their students to learn and excel academically to a level that will prepare them for college and the labor force. They believe that the competition created by an array of educational choices will result in improved outcomes not only in schools of choice but also in the traditional public schools that are challenged by them. However, the promise seems to be unfulfilled.

The outcomes of voucher programs that allow children to attend private schools at public expense have been studied for many years. Previous research on the differences between private and public schools demonstrated that private school students do have slightly higher academic achievement than their public school counterparts. However, that same research indicates that most differences between students can be attributed to factors beyond the schools' control, including parents' educational attainment and their income. In the past, researchers showed that the "private school effect"—the amount of the difference in achievement between public and private school students that can be attributed to attending private school—is very small indeed (Coleman et al., 1982; Hoffer, 2000). Newer studies about using public funds to help students attend private schools show very mixed results. As Berner (2017) argues, "The bottom line: while the presence of diverse, state-supported private schools can be beneficial to students, there is nothing inevitable about their success."

Early research on the largest voucher programs—in Milwaukee, Cleveland, and Washington, DC—demonstrated that attending a private school does not in and of itself guarantee higher academic achievement. More recent evaluations have found little or no difference in voucher public school students' performances; some studies have even found negative effects. In Indiana there was no effect on students' achievement in English Language Arts and a negative effect on math achievement (Waddington and Berends, 2018). In Washington, DC, although students attending private schools using vouchers did have marginally higher reading scores, the most disadvantaged students have not shown test score gains statistically different from their peers in traditional public schools. Similar outcomes were found in Ohio and Louisiana

(Dynarski and Nichols, 2017). Calls to expand voucher or scholarship programs seem incongruous in light of evidence that they may be having a negative impact on the very criteria they are meant to improve.

Findings about student achievement in charter schools are less consistent. One of the largest early projects included approximately 65% of charters across the country. The study found that of charter school students, 17% had higher results than comparable traditional public schools students, 37% had significantly worse results, and 46% had average growth no different from students in traditional public schools (Center for Research on Education Outcomes, 2015). There are over 60 additional studies that provide evidence of charter schools' impact on student achievement. Their conclusions are that, in general, charter schools perform at levels similar to those of traditional public schools but that the performance level differs widely among charter schools. When charters are viewed nationally or at the state level, they appear to have less impact than traditional public schools; when a small number of schools are studied, the results tend to be more positive in charter schools (National Conference of State Legislatures, 2019). Those charters that are most successful have the financial resources to provide longer school days and school years, multiple instances of testing students, and additional pay for high-performing teachers, all of which at least one study acknowledged as being correlated with the schools' positive results (Center for Research on Education Outcomes, 2015).

Charter school advocates argue that they receive less state and federal funding than traditional public schools—by as much as 20%—and that they "do more with less." However, the differences in resources among schools of choice and between those schools and traditional public schools have several sources. State funding formulae are very complicated, but, in general, schools with needier students receive a larger share of state and federal educational dollars. One reason why charters receive less money is that they serve fewer of the neediest students, particularly students with disabilities. In addition, charter schools are not required to provide transportation or food (although some do). Those schools that do not provide those services do not receive the subsidies that public schools, which are mandated to provide them, do (Miron et al., 2015).

Charters are able, however, to supplement their public dollars with private ones—and they do so. One study found that some charters receive private funds exceeding $10,000 per pupil more than traditional public schools receive and $10,000 more than the less philanthropically "popular" charter schools (Baker and Ferris, 2011). Private foundations have given half a billion dollars since 2006, primarily to the large charter networks (*Philanthropy News Digest*, 2018). Charter schools are also eligible for large federal grants to help them expand. In 2019, KIPP and IDEA, two of the largest charter networks, received over $200 million and the federal budget included an additional $240 million for charter school development (Greene, 2018; Barnum, 2019). It appears that rather than creating greater equity in the resources available to all children's education, the charter school movement is re-creating the hierarchy of schools in the traditional public sector, establishing a system of "have" and "have-not" schools. And they are doing so while not providing the academic gains they promised.

Choice and Public Accountability

Choice proponents want to sidestep the democratic decision-making process when it comes to schooling. They dislike the compromises it demands with regard to policies and curricula, perhaps because compromises require everyone to "give in and give up" on some issues. Advocates of family choice argue that allowing free market forces to operate with regard to education will safeguard families from unwanted loss of their freedom to educate their children as they see fit. In actuality, it allows them to avoid participation in dialogues with other citizens that enable the creation of shared societal values, which are vital for maintaining a viable democracy.

For example, most charter school laws and voucher programs do not require that those schools be responsible for the protection of all students' rights, including those of students with disabilities. Schools in choice programs can operate with what would be for traditional public schools discriminatory admissions policies. Religious schools, those for which students most often receive vouchers, can use the religious commitments of parents as admissions criteria, adopt textbooks in all subjects that support the beliefs of their denomination, require all students to participate in religious instruction, and hire and fire teachers on the basis of their commitments to the faith communities' beliefs. Disciplinary practices in voucher and charter schools are subject to less public scrutiny than in traditional public schools (Mead and Eckes, 2018).

Voucher and charter schools' fiscal accountability is less rigorous as well. The lack of fiscal accountability for public funds results in several major concerns. Public expenditures intended to provide educational services to children is being used for personal or business financial gains for some charter operators, resulting in inefficiencies and waste. Charter school management companies are, in some cases, making profits from lucrative management fees, rents, and government incentives. Because the laws regarding disclosure of charter school financial information are inadequate, illegal, unethical, or inappropriate policies and practices do not come to light without investigations (Baker and Miron, 2015).

Current accountability systems focus on test scores and relieve choice schools of the need to be answerable for their fiscal, admissions, discipline, and curricular policies. Of even more consequence is the fact that they are not held responsible for their contribution to societal goals even though they operate with public funds. Schools that answer only its "consumers"—families and students—are called "private" because they provide private goods and use only private funds. When Americans began to use public funds to pay for schooling, they called those schools "common" because they served the common good. It is time to return to that concept.

FOR DISCUSSION

1. The Supreme Court has ruled that providing parents with governmental funds to pay for their children's education is constitutional even if they use the money to pay for tuition at a school sponsored by a religious organization. How can you reconcile that ruling with the constitutional guarantee of the separation of church and state?

2. Sponsors of family choice have argued that allowing schools to become part of "free market" competition is the only way to improve the quality of public education in the United States. Do you agree with the idea of allowing market forces to operate on schools? Are there any characteristics of the free market system that would prevent competition among schools from achieving the goal of equality?

   Does freedom of choice alone guarantee that all consumers have an equal chance in the marketplace? Do other protections need to be in place?

3. Imagine that a voucher program has been created in your state and that you have been asked to create the "accountability" regulations for private schools receiving such payments. Create a set of rules and develop a "white paper" explaining your rationale.

4. Design a proposal for a charter school you'd like to create. Explain the mission of the school, its organizational structure, and the ways it would differ from a traditional public school. Investigate your state and local school district's regulations concerning charter schools and be sure your proposal complies with those rules.

References

Agostini v. Felton (1997). 522 U.S. 803.

American Federation for Children (2019). School Choice in America (federationforchildren.org/school-choice-america).

Arizona Christian School Tuition Organization v. Winn 563 (2011). U.S. 125.

Ayscue, J., Levy, R., Siegel-Hawley, G., and Woodward, B. (2017). *Choices Worth Making: Creating, Sustaining, and Expanding Diverse Magnet Schools.* Los Angeles: The Civil Rights Project.

Baker, B. D., and Ferris, R. (2011). *Adding Up the Spending: Fiscal Disparities and Philanthropy among New York City Charter Schools.* Boulder, CO: National Education Policy Center.

Baker, B. D., and Miron, G. (2015). *The Business of Charter Schooling.* Boulder, CO: National Education Policy Center.

Barnum, M. (2019, April 22). Charter Networks KIPP and IDEA Win Big Federal Grants to Fund Ambitious Growth Plans. Chalkbeat (chalkbeat.org/posts/us/2019/04/18/charter-networks-kipp-and-idea-win-big-federal-grants-to-fund-ambitious-growth-plans).

Berner, A. (2017). Expanding Access to Non-Public Schools: A Research and Policy Review. Johns Hopkins School of Education. Institute for Educational Policy (edpolicy.education.jhu.edu/wp-content/uploads/2017/05/SchoolChoicemastheadFINAL.pdf).

———— (2019). *The Case for Educational Pluralism in the U.S.* New York: Manhattan Institute (media4.manhattan-institute.org/sites/default/files/R-0719-ARB.pdf).

Billingham, C., and Hunt, M. (2016). "School Racial Composition and Parental Choice: New Evidence on the Preferences of White Parents in the United States." *Sociology of Education* 89(2):99–117.

Boston Public Schools (2018). Discover Boston Public Schools. Choice and Registration Guide (bostonpublicschools.org/cms/lib/MA01906464/Centricity/Domain/2242/DiscoverBPS%2018%20English_online.pdf).

Broughman, S. P., Kincel, B., and Peterson, J. (2019). *Characteristics of Private Schools in the United States: Results from the 2017–2018 Private School Universe Survey First Look* (NCES 201971). Washington, DC: U.S. Department of Education, National Center for Education Statistics.

Buchanan, N. (2018). School Choice: The Impact of Ethnicity, Race, Diversity, and Inclusion. In R. Fox and N. Buchanan, eds., *The Wiley Handbook of School Choice* (pp. 517–531). Chichester, West Sussex, UK: Wiley-Blackwell.

Caetano, G., and Mahesri, V. (2017). "School Segregation and the Identification of Tipping Behavior." *Journal of Public Economics* 148:115–135.

Calder, R. (2019, May 19). "DOE Slacking on Jewish, Muslim Dietary Options at Schools: Councilman." *New York Post.*

Center for Research on Education Outcomes (2015). *Urban Charter School Study Report on 41 Regions.* Palo Alto, CA: Center for Research on Education Outcomes, Stanford University

Children's Scholarship Fund (2018). Why CSF: A Brief Overview (scholarshipfund.org/drupal1/?q=why-csf).

Coleman, J., Hoffer, T., and Kilgore, S. (1982). *High School Achievement.* New York: Basic Books.

de Brey, C., Musu, L., McFarland, J., Wilkinson-Flicker, S., Diliberti, M., Zhang, A., Branstet-ter, C., and Wang, X. (2019). *Status and Trends in the Education of Racial and Ethnic Groups 2018* (NCES 2019-038). Washington, DC: National Center for Education Statistics, U.S. Department of Education.

DeAngelis, C., Wolf, P., Maloney, L., and May, J. (2018). *Charter School Funding: (More) Inequity in the City.* School Choice Demonstration Project, Department of Education Reform, University of Arkansas.

Denver Public Schools (2019). 2019–20 Great Schools Enrollment Guide. Elementary (schoolchoice.dpsk12.org/wp-content/uploads/2018/11/DPS_EnrollmentGuide19-20_Elementary_English_WEB.pdf).

Digital Learning Collaborative (2019). Snapshot 2019: A Review of K–12 Online, Blended, and Digital Learning (evergreenedgroup.com/keeping-pace-reports).

Dynarski, S., and Nichols, A. (2017, July 13). "More Findings about School Vouchers and Test Scores, and They Are Still Negative." *Evidence Speaks Reports* 2(18). Washington, DC: Brookings Institution.

EdChoice (2019, April 11). *The 123s of School Choice: What the Research Says about Private School Choice Programs in America* (edchoice.org/research/the-123s-of-school-choice).

Education Commission of the States (2018). Open Enrollment 50 State Report—All Data Points (ecs.force.com/mbdata/mbquest4NE?rep=OE1805).

——— (2019a). 50 State Comparison: Vouchers (ecs.org/50-state-comparison-vouchers).

——— (2019b). Does State Law Explicitly Allow Virtual Charter Schools? (ecs.force.com/mbdata/mbquestNB2C?rep=CS1724).

——— (2019c). Overview of Scholarship Tax Credit Programs (ecs.org/wp-content/uploads/An-Overview-of-Scholarship-Tax-Credits).

Egalite, A., Mills, J., and Wolf, P. (2017). "The Impact of Targeted School Vouchers on Racial Stratification in Louisiana." *Education and Urban Society* 49(3):271–296.

Ellison, S., and Aloe, A. (2018). "Strategic Thinkers and Positioned Choices: Parental Decision Making in Urban School Choice." *Educational Policy* 33(7).

Frankenberg, E. (2017). "Assessing Segregation under a New Generation of Choice Policies." *American Educational Research Journal* 54(1S):219S–250S.

Frankenberg, E., Ee, J., Ayscue, J., and Orfield, G. (2019). *Harming our Common Future: America's Segregated Schools 65 Years after* Brown. Los Angeles: UCLA Civil Rights Project.

Good, T., and Braden, J. (2000). *The Great School Debate: Choice, Vouchers and Charters.* Mahwah, NJ: Lawrence Erlbaum.

Gould, J. (2019, March 18). "Latest Specialized High School Acceptance Rates Still Don't Reflect NYC's Diversity." *Gothamist.*

Greene, P. (2018, August 13). "How to Profit from Your Non-Profit Charter School." *Forbes.*

Gulosino, C., and d'Entremont, C. (2011) "Circles of Influence: An Analysis of Charter School Location and Racial Patterns at Varying Geographic Scales." *Educational Policy Analysis Archives* 19(8). https://doi.org/10.14507/epaa.v19n8.2011

Henderson, M., Houston, D., Peterson, P., and West, M. (2020, Winter). "Education Next—Program on Education Policy and Governance—Survey 2019." *Education Next* 20(1).

Hoffer, T. (2000). Catholic School Attendance and Student Achievement: A Review and Extension of the Research. In J. Youniss and J. Convey, eds., *Catholic Schools at the Crossroads*. New York: Teachers College Press.

Home School Legal Defense Association (2019). Home School Laws in Your State (hslda.org/content/laws).

Indiana Department of Education (2019). *Choice Scholarship Program Annual Report* (doe.in.gov/sites/default/files/choice/2018-2019-choice-scholarship-program-report-final-040219.pdf).

Islamic Networks Group (2019). Religious Practices of Muslim Students in Public Schools (ing.org/religious-practices-muslim-students-public-schools).

Johnson, R. (2019). *Children of the Dream.* New York: Basic Books & the Russell Sage Foundation Press.

KIPP Foundation (2019a). Network (kipp.org/schools/structure).

——— (2019b). Our Approach (kipp.org/approach).

Kumah-Abiwu, F. (2019, March 6). "Urban Education and Academic Success: The Case of High Achieving Black Males." *Urban Education.* doi:10.1177/0042085919835284

Levy, M. (2018). *Washington, D.C.'s Voucher Program: Civil Rights Implications.* Los Angeles: UCLA Civil Rights Project.

Logan, S. (2018). "A Historical and Political Look at the Modern School Choice Movement." *International Journal of Educational Reform* 7(1):2–21.

Mader, M., Hemphill, C., and Abbas, Q. (2018). *The Paradox of Choice: How School Choice Divides New York City Elementary Schools.* New York: The New School Center for New York City Affairs.

Mann, H. (1843). *Sixth Annual Report of the Secretary of the Board of Education.* Boston: Dutton and Wentworth.

McDonald, D., and Schultz, M. (2019). *United States Catholic Elementary and Secondary Schools 2010–2012: The Annual Statistical Report on Schools, Enrollment, and Staffing.* Washington, D.C.: National Catholic Education Association.

Mead, J., and Eckes, S. (2018). *How School Privatization Opens the Door for Discrimination.* Boulder, CO: National Education Policy Center.

Mickelson, R. A. (2015). "The Cumulative Disadvantages of First- and Second-Generation Segregation for Middle School Achievement." *American Educational Research Journal* 52:657–692.

Mickelson, R. A., and Nkomo, M. (2012). "Integrated Schooling, Life Course Outcomes, and Social Cohesion in Multiethnic Democratic Societies." *Review of Research in Education* 36(1):197–238.

Miron, G. (2017). Description and Brief History of Charter Schools. In R. Fox and N. Buchanan, eds., *Wiley Handbook of School Choice* (pp. 224–236). Chichester, West Sussex, UK: Wiley-Blackwell.

Miron, G., Mathis, W., and Welner, K. (2015). Review of *Separating Fact & Fiction: What You Need to Know about Charter Schools.* Boulder, CO: National Education Policy Center (nepc.colorado.edu/thinktank/review-separating-fact-and-fiction).

Mosle, S., and Park, S. (2019, March 28). Happy, Frustrated, or Wait-Listed: New York City Families Get Kindergarten Offers. Chalkbeat (chalkbeat.org/posts/ny/2019/03/28/kindergarten-offer-placement-letters-new-york-city-2019).

Mueller v. Allen (1983). 463 U.S. 388.

National Alliance for Public Charter Schools (2019). Are Charter Schools For-Profit? (publiccharters.org/latest-news/2019/01/16/are-charter-schools-profit).

National Conference of State Legislatures (2019). Charter School Research and Report (ncsl.org/research/education/charter-schools-research-and-report.aspx).

Pendergrass, S., and Kern, N. (2017). The Case for Charters. In R. Fox and N. Buchanan, eds., *The Wiley Handbook of School Choice* (pp. 237–252). Chichester, West Sussex, UK: Wiley-Blackwell.

Peterson, P., Henderson, M. B., West, M. R., and Barrows, S. (2017, Winter). "Ten-Year Trends in Public Opinion from the *EdNext* Poll." *Education Next* 8–28.

Petrilli, M. (2017, June 5). Are Private Schools Allowed to Discriminate? *Education Next* (educationnext.org/private-schools-allowed-discriminate).

Philanthropy News Digest (2018, July 23). "Billionaires Fueling Charter School Movement, Shaping State Policy."

Prothero, A. (2018, December 20). Charter Schools More Likely to Ignore Special Education Applicants, Study Finds. Blog. Charters & Choice. *Education Week* (blogs.edweek.org/edweek/charterschoice/2018/12/charter_schools_more_likely_to_ignore_special_education_applicants.html).

Ray, B. (2018). A Description and Brief History of Home Schooling in America. In R. Fox and N. Buchanan, eds., *The Wiley Handbook of School Choice* (pp. 327–343). Chichester, West Sussex, UK: Wiley-Blackwell.

Shakeel, M. D. (2018). "Islamic Schooling in the Cultural West: A Systematic Review of the Issues Concerning School Choice." *Religions* 9, 392. https://doi.org/10.3390/rel9120392

Shakeel, M. D., and Wolf, P. (2017). *Does Private Islamic Schooling Promote Terrorism? An Analysis of the Educational Background of Successful American Homegrown Terrorists* (Working Paper No. 2017-20). Fayetteville: University of Arkansas, Department of Education Reform.

Snyder, T., de Brey, C., and Dillow, S. (2018a). Table 216.20. Number and Enrollment of Public Elementary and Secondary Schools, by School Level, Type, and Charter, Magnet, and Virtual Status: Selected Years, 1990–91 through 2016–17. *Digest of Education Statistics* (https://nces.ed.gov/programs/digest/d18/tables/dt18_216.20.asp). Washington, DC: Department of Education, National Center for Education Statistics.

——— (2018b). Table 216.30. Number and Percentage Distribution of Public Elementary and Secondary Students and Schools, by Traditional or Charter School Status and Selected Characteristics: Selected Years, 2000–01 through 2016–17. *Digest of Education Statistics* (nces.ed.gov/programs/digest/d18/tables/dt18_216.30.asp?current=yes). Washington, DC: Department of Education, National Center for Education Statistics.

Uncommon Schools (2019a). Educator Resources and Workshops (uncommonschools.org/books-workshops).

——— (2019b). An Uncommon School Day (uncommonschools.org/the-student-experience).

U.S. Department of Education (2018a). Magnet School Assistance Program (ed.gov/programs/magnet/index.html).

——— (2018b). State Education Reforms (SER), Table 4.2 (nces.ed.gov/programs/statereform/tab4_2.asp).

U.S. Department of Education, Office of Innovation and Improvement (2015, December). The U.S. Department of Education's Charter Schools Program Overview (ed.gov/programs/charter/cspdata.pdf).

Waddington, R. J., and Berends, M. (2018). "Impact of the Indiana Choice Scholarship Program: Achievement Effects for Students in Upper Elementary and Middle School." *Journal of Policy Analysis and Management.* https://doi.org/10.1002/pam

Walton Family Foundation (2019). 2020 K–12 Education Strategic Plan (waltonfamilyfoundation.org/our-work/k-12-education).

Warner, J. (2018, November 1). "Doris Fisher: Down the Dark Money Rabbit Hole." *Capital & Main* (capitalandmain.com/doris-fisher-down-the-dark-money-rabbit-hole-1101).

Witters v. Washington Department of Services for the Blind (1986). 474 U.S. 481.

Zobrest v. Catalina Foothills School District (1993). 509 U.S. 1.

Financing Schools

Equity or Privilege

3

Should government
educational spending e
within and among schoo

P1: Equitable educational Spending is a matter of justice

Position 1: Equitable Educationa

P2: Privileged educational Spending is necessary in a free market economy

The path to our mutual well-being is built on
opportunity begins with an equitable, purpos
schools to support high-quality teaching for each and every child.

—Darling-Hammond (2019)

Some Consequences of Inequitable School Funding

In 1991, Jonathan Kozol described the "savage inequalities" American children faced in public schools. Ten years later, activists around the country were still uncovering similar conditions (Campaign for Fiscal Equity, 2001; Oakes, 2002). Almost 30 years later, differences among schools within a state or among schools within a district remain because of how we finance public education and allocate those funds. The shocking disparities among school facilities and resources constitute unequal educational opportunities for our young people. A fundamental injustice is built in to the way we finance public schools (EdBuild, 2019).

The conditions of underfunded schools make the best argument for why changes in school financing are necessary. For the most part, those children in the United States whom fate has placed in middle- or upper-class families attend schools that are well equipped, safe, and clean. They have science labs and necessary supplies for conducting experiments. They have access to up-to-date technology, which often is housed in libraries well stocked with reference materials. Their textbooks are new and, more importantly, each student has one. The schools of the "lucky" have art rooms and gyms, pools and playing fields, and auditoriums and music rooms. When these districts spend money to improve facilities, the funds go to changes—such as new science labs or computer equipment—intended to enhance learning directly (Jimenez, 2019).

In the urban schools that are attended by children from the poorest families, conditions are dramatically different. The buildings are overcrowded; almost half hold classes in temporary buildings (U.S. Department of Education, 2019a). Researchers from Harvard's School of Public Health have found unambiguous evidence that the quality of the school building impacts student health, thinking, and performance (Allen, 2017). Cities need to build new schools to replace out-of-date facilities, create additions to current buildings to house science and computer labs, upgrade heating and cooling facilities, repair plumbing and roofs, paint classrooms, replace lockers and boilers, and update security and technology systems (Build U.S. Schools, 2018; Jimenez, 2019).

In most other nations, the national government—not the state, province, city, or town—provides most school funding. In the United States, the federal government provides less than 10%. As a result, students depend on state and local governments to pay for their schools. States contribute about 40% of monies spent on schools. States like New Jersey, New York, Connecticut, and Rhode Island spend two or three times as much per student as Utah, Mississippi, Louisiana, and Tennessee do. The gap between the highest and lowest funded states has increased in the last decade (Baker et al., 2018; Darling-Hammond, 2019).

Intrastate differences also account for differences in the type of education students receive. For example, in New York State, combined state and local funding is almost 20% less for children in districts where at least 30% live in poverty than in the state as a whole. "In fact, most states do not provide enough funding for their highest poverty children to achieve average outcomes. In some states, the funding disparity for the most vulnerable students exceeds $10,000 per pupil" (Baker et al., 2018, p. 28). "Overwhelmingly white school districts received $23 billion more than predominantly nonwhite school districts in state and local funding in 2016, despite serving roughly the same number of children" (EdBuild, 2019).

Causes of Inequitable School Funding

American public schools have long been a beacon of hope for the residents of this country. From the early 1800s, education offered the promise of social mobility and equal opportunity. When reformers encouraged taxpayers to accept the responsibility of paying for schools, they promised that by doing so, they would be providing young people with the chance to increase their own wealth and that of the nation as a whole. Tax dollars spent on schools would help to eliminate the potential for conflict between rich and poor by decreasing the numbers of the poor. Horace Mann expressed the belief this way: "Education, then, beyond all other devices of human origin, is the great equalizer of the conditions of men—the balance-wheel of the social machinery" (quoted in Cremin, 1957, p. 87).

Although many Americans came to believe that education should not be a luxury that only the wealthy could afford, they worried about how publicly funded schools would be controlled. As compromises built into the Constitution suggest, having secured their independence from England, Americans in the early republican period wanted to limit the power of centralized governments. In establishing public schools, they did not want local communities to lose control over what children would learn and who would teach them. States authorized local governments to impose property taxes on their citizens and to use those funds for the support of schools. Because these revenues came from local communities rather than state or federal governments, primary control of schools remained with municipalities themselves. Through elected boards of education, the community maintained control of the curriculum, hiring of teachers, and allocation of funding. Despite the growing oversight of schools by state agencies and the centralization of teacher preparation (and sometimes curricula), nineteenth-century Americans were reassured local funding guaranteed that ultimate control of their schools would remain in their hands (Tyack, 1974; Katz, 1975; Urban and Wagoner, 2008).

This system remained in place, essentially unchanged, until the 1930s. During the Depression, cities, towns, and villages faced tremendous financial difficulties. School districts across the country had trouble meeting payrolls and maintaining their buildings. State-level financial contributions more than doubled for public education between 1930 and 1950 (Mackey, 1998). That percentage has continued to increase. Currently, states contribute about 47% of school districts' revenue. Local funding is about 45%. A small contribution from federal tax dollars (roughly 8%) makes up the remainder (U.S. Census Bureau, 2019).

So, if states are providing almost half of school districts' resources, why do disparities among districts still exist? Can't states provide enough money to equalize the resources available to each child regardless of his or her parents' income? To a certain extent, states' contribution to school funding has helped lessen the differences among schools (Baker et al., 2018; Darling-Hammond, 2019). However, continued reliance on local property taxes to fund almost half of a district's budget still leads to large disparities in the amount of money available to educate students. Here's how it happens.

A local school district is authorized to levy property taxes and, through their votes, citizens have some voice in the rate at which they will be taxed. Let's imagine two districts—one urban and one suburban—that adopt the same property tax rate of 2%. In the suburban community, District A, the total value of property that can be taxed averages out to be $250,000 per child enrolled in the district's schools. In the inner-city community, District B, the property tax base is $50,000 per pupil. When taxpayers in each community pay the same rate, 2%, District A raises $5,000 to spend on each student in its schools. District B raises only $1,000. To achieve equality with District A in the amount they could spend on their children's education, taxpayers in District B would have to agree to a tax rate of 10%. When you consider that most taxpayers in District B have dramatically lower incomes than those in District A, you can see how much of a hardship such a high tax rate would be. People who already are poor would be forced to pay a much higher percentage of their income to fund their schools than their wealthier neighbors do. The higher rates of taxes in District B would make it less attractive to home owners and business owners.

Despite the sacrifices involved in creating such higher tax rates, that is what many urban and rural school districts have been forced to do. However, political and economic realities put a ceiling on how much they could raise the tax rate and how much of the funds could be allocated to school expenses. As a result, even though residents of those communities pay a higher share of their income to fund their schools, they never raise enough money to equal the resources available to schools in wealthier communities. This pattern creates fundamental inequalities of educational opportunity in the United States. In those states that rely most heavily on property taxes for educational funding, the disparity between revenues available for students in high- and low-poverty schools is the greatest (Baker et al., 2018; Education Trust, 2018).

Legal Challenges to Inequitable School Financing

Since 2000, court cases in at least 36 states challenged school funding inequities. All states' constitutions guarantee public education in some form. The U.S. Constitution does not guarantee the right to a publicly funded education but it does guarantee that everyone living in the United States is entitled to equal protection under whatever laws a state does enact. So, if a state guarantees a "sound" or "efficient" or "appropriate" education, it must see that every child's right to that education is protected. Courts have held states accountable to those constitutional obligations by mandating states to provide adequate schooling for all their children. In addition, the courts ensure that the Fourteenth Amendment is safeguarded despite economic differences among students and their families.

The earliest school funding equity case established *fiscal neutrality* as the litmus test for the constitutionality of school financing in various states (*Serrano v. Priest,* 1971). States were ordered to reduce disparities among districts by providing low-wealth communities with additional funds or tax relief as long as the municipality made a good faith effort to contribute to its schools. The goal was a fairly straightforward, dollar-for-dollar equality of school expenditures across districts; it was easily measured, if not so easily achieved. However, other court decisions pointed us toward more complex and, ultimately, more just definitions of equity when the term is applied to school funding.

These later cases changed the criteria from *fiscal neutrality* to *adequacy.* A consensus definition of what constitutes an "adequate" education emerged from state court rulings. Simply put an adequate education is one that prepares students to be capable voters and jurors and to be able to compete effectively in the economy. To meet those goals schools must develop literacy and oral fluency in English; mathematical and scientific knowledge; a fundamental understanding of geography, history, and political and economic systems; critical thinking skills; social and communication skills; and sufficient intellectual or vocational skills to move forward in educational or employment settings. To develop such knowledge and skills, schools need teachers and administrators qualified to provide academic instruction and to create a safe and orderly learning environment; adequate school facilities; appropriate class sizes; supplemental and remedial programs for students from high-poverty backgrounds, students with disabilities, and English language learners; and resources such as textbooks, libraries, laboratories, and computers.

With this definition of an adequate education in hand, plaintiffs argued that it actually cost more to provide some children with the same educational opportunities and outcomes as other children. What is adequate funding depends on the needs of students and the historic, social, and political contexts that have shaped their schools. Advocates insisted that schools and districts whose populations include more poor, disabled, or non-English-speaking students were entitled to greater financial assistance to achieve the same results as their wealthier, nondisabled, and English-speaking peers. Such a funding model had long been utilized to meet the needs of students with disabilities and that precedent was applicable to other children with special needs. Translating those differences in need into funding formulas is called "costing out."

A variety of costing-out methods have been used around the country. Some states have relied on the judgment of experienced educators, some on educational researchers. Others have built on an analysis of the resources that successful school districts have and determined how much it would cost to replicate those resources in less successful schools. The most successful processes of determining adequacy in school funding—those that are approved by the courts—appear to share some characteristics regardless of the specific method they use. These characteristics are: carefully articulated outcomes or goals, rigorous attention to the needs of poor, disabled, and non-English-speaking students, minimizing the political manipulation of the process, and maintaining a high degree of openness and public engagement in the process (Rebell, 2007). Whatever process is used, once a state has determined the basic cost of providing a sound education, it can, in theory, guarantee every student that amount of funding and then provide additional resources to those districts that serve large numbers of poor, disabled, or non-English-speaking students.

Adequacy litigation has had some success in reducing inequity in school financing. Eleven states' funding formulas provide greater funding to high-poverty districts than to low-poverty ones. Seventeen states give more revenue to wealthier districts than to poorer ones. Twenty states have systems that provide essentially the same amount of funding to school districts regardless of the needs of students (Baker et al., 2018). However, it is only through federal funding targeted to poor students that high-needs districts' resources come close to matching those of lower-needs districts (Chingos and Blagg, 2017). On average, even when all revenue sources are included high-poverty districts receive 3.5% less funding than low-poverty ones (Cornman et al., 2019).

Equitable School Funding and Outcomes

Money does matter when it comes to education. Despite early studies emphasizing the influence of nonschool factors, such as family background and neighborhood environment (Coleman, 1966; Hanushek, 1996), growing evidence shows that student achievement is affected by the amount of money schools spend on their education. A new model of research has emerged that links spending to student outcomes. These studies separate the influence of family and other external factors from school spending. The results provide more focused and reliable information. For example, one project found that a 10% increase in per pupil spending each year for all 12 years of public school leads to 0.31 more completed years of education, about 7% higher wages, and a 3.2 percentage point reduction in the annual incidence of adult poverty. They also found that the effects are more pronounced for children from low-income families (Jackson, 2018). Another found that, when state financing reform resulted in a 12% increase in funding for high-poverty districts, graduation rates went up between 7 and 12% (Candelaria and Shores, 2019).

Once a state has created clear and rigorous standards and provided adequate funding, schools can implement the type of changes that improve student outcomes. They can create small classes, employ experienced teachers and administrators, buy textbooks and materials, and repair and maintain facilities (Lafortune et al., 2016; Darling-Hammond, 2019; Knight, 2019; Reuben, 2019). Lack of funding means schools cannot improve or maintain educational opportunities by making technology available, reduce class size, or increase salaries to attract better teachers (Baker et al., 2016).

Centralized School Funding

It is clear that differences in local communities' abilities to raise revenue through property taxes means that overreliance on mixed funding streams, those that combine state and local revenue, for schools will always result in unfair disparities among schools. The courts have attempted to remedy the injustice by creating new obligations for the states to ensure that all districts within their borders have the income to provide adequate education for all. However, these remedies cannot fully correct the problem. What is needed instead is a radical rethinking of school funding.

Equality would be better served if the states had access to all tax dollars collected to support education and could distribute them "unequally." That is, if the amount of money currently being collected through property taxes could go to the state instead of to local governments, then each district—and each school—could receive the amount of money that is determined to be needed to provide "adequate" education for its children. Districts with more educationally needy students—English language learners, young people with disabilities, or children living in poverty—would receive higher per pupil allotments. Providing schools with resources that were matched to the needs of their students and preventing wealthier communities from creating greater advantages for their children would, for the first time in American history, really ensure that the conditions of a child's birth did not determine his or her educational opportunities.

Of course, adequate oversight by federal, state, and local government would be needed to ensure that resources were being spent appropriately and honestly; such accountability is difficult but not impossible to achieve. The requirement to meet rigorous academic standards in order to receive federal funding is already pressuring states to create such systems. However, convincing residents of affluent communities to support state-based systems of school funding will not be easy. Many people justify the mixed revenue stream approach to school finance precisely because they allow more affluent communities to create better-resourced and more effective schools. They resent efforts made by government to equalize opportunity. They argue that such efforts unfairly penalize hardworking people who have achieved a measure of success through their own labor and sacrifice and reward people who have not worked as hard and who have come to expect handouts (Rosenthal and Rothman, 2017). These attitudes play out in a special way with regard to property taxes. Connected as they are to the value of the homes they have struggled to provide for their families, property taxes represent, for many people, an investment in their children's future. They believe taxes should be used for their own school districts and not applied to those of children whose parents are unwilling to support education in their locality. They attribute their ability to afford more expensive homes and higher property taxes solely to their hard work and ignore advantages race and socioeconomic status of their own parents may have given them. Consciously or unconsciously, they appear to want to maintain the advantages afforded to their children when they came into the world, even if doing so means other children are seriously disadvantaged. Correct or not, however, these attitudes are translated into powerful political forces when citizens who hold them exercise their right to vote. They result in opposition to proposals that school funding be centralized at the state or federal level.

The reasons to centralize funding for school districts are compelling. Equity in school finance is a matter of justice. The courts have ruled that all children in this country have constitutionally guaranteed rights to equal treatment. Clearly, they are currently not receiving that protection under the present system of paying for schools. Issues of individual freedom, local control, and over involvement by government in our daily lives certainly deserve consideration. They do not, however, automatically outweigh the rights of all children to receive an education that will empower them to be competent to take up their duties as citizens, members of society, and workers. Centralizing the funding for public schools will ensure that all children in a state have the resources they need to meet that state's learning standards regardless of where they live or their families' socioeconomic status. Every other educational funding formula is designed to maintain the privilege of wealthier families at the expense of the rights of less affluent ones.

Position 2:   Privileged Educational Spending
Is Necessary in a Free Market Economy

The concept of local control is grounded in a philosophy of government premised on the belief that the individuals and institutions closest to the students and most knowledgeable about a school—and most invested in the welfare and success of its educators, students, and communities—are best suited to making important decisions about its operation, leadership, staffing, academics, teaching, and improvement.

—Great Schools Partnership (2016)

Those suggesting that we provide equal funding for all American public schools in an attempt to ensure equal opportunity for children are well meaning but misguided. They demonstrate a concern for justice for some but almost completely ignore the rights of others. Most states currently use a foundation grant type of education funding. The state determines the minimum amount that should be spend on each student's schooling. School districts are required to set school tax rates, based on the value of property in their communities and the capability of citizens to pay. If the resulting local funds don't rise to the minimum amount, the state provides aid to bring districts' funding to that level. Wealthier districts are free to raise more local revenue and to spend more than the minimum amount on their children's education (Chingos and Blagg, 2017). In the concern to provide what they call equal educational opportunity for children, some policy makers advocate for the elimination of local funding for schools in favor of a centralized state system. Such a system would ignore taxpayers' right to exercise the maximum possible control over the use of their money. It would deny those footing the bill the opportunity to see that their funds are spent efficiently, wisely, and honestly. It would dismiss strong reasons for allowing parents and other taxpayers to support their own children's schools to the full extent of their ability. It would also make it more difficult to support the academic achievement of more capable students who are likely to make significant returns on public funds spent on their education.

The Connection between School Finances and Academic Achievement

Those who support centralized educational funding schemes believe that we should allow federal or state governments to collect taxes and distribute them unequally among all school districts. That is, they believe that in order to compensate for what parents are unable or unwilling to provide for their children, taxpayers should provide greater funding for poor children, those who are English language learners, and those who are disabled. They argue that these students need and deserve more public resources than those students whose backgrounds better prepared them for school success. It sounds as if the plan has possibilities for addressing the persistent problem of underachievement by students from low socioeconomic backgrounds. However, in over four decades, scholars have been unable to demonstrate conclusively that spending in schools can make up for what is missing in homes and communities.

The first of these research efforts, the famous "Coleman study," took place in the mid-1960s. It was the era of President Johnson's War on Poverty, and many Americans were convinced that schools could be a primary tool in winning that battle. James Coleman and his colleagues conducted a large-scale national survey of thousands of schools. They calculated the resources that they assumed would be connected to student achievement—teacher education and experience, number of books in the library, laboratory equipment, and so on. In other words, they counted the things that money can buy. The results were surprising, even to them. They concluded that a school's material resources had little effect on student achievement. Instead, they found that "family background differences account for much more variance in achievements than do school differences" (Coleman, 1966, p. 73). "In fact, virtually all subsequent analyses have included measures of family background (education, family structure, and so forth) and have found them to be a significant explanation of achievement differences" (Hanushek, 2016). For example, poverty increases the likelihood that families will become more mobile and children will have to change schools. Homes may be crowded with few quiet spaces for study or homework. Poor children are more likely to come to school hungry or malnourished, to be in poor health, and to live with adults who are under emotional stress. Mothers and fathers living in poverty are not able to prepare young people for challenges they will face in schools. They do not have money to buy books or computers; they cannot take them to concerts. They have so many other problems and demands on their time that they cannot give children the attention they need to grow and develop. No matter how much money is spent on education, it cannot make up completely for all that poverty denies children (Egalite, 2016; Hanushek et al., 2019).

Let's face it—if more money led to better academic performance, we would have it by now. In the last three decades of the twentieth century, we spent more money for each child's education than almost any other industrialized nation (Organization for Economic Cooperation and Development, 2019). In the last 10 years alone, spending on education has risen 22% nationally (in constant dollars) and by 35% in high poverty schools (U.S. Department of Education, 2019b). However, some children are still less successful than others. It may simply be that family situations cannot be overcome by spending more money in schools. Taxpayers have a right to insist that their hard-earned money be spent in the most efficient way possible. Instead of diverting other people's money to schools with large numbers of failing students, a wiser use of public funds would include providing poor children and their families with social services they need to create better lives (Egalite, 2016).

We need to change the realities of their homes and neighborhoods if children are going to be able to take advantage of what schools have to offer. We should channel tax dollars to fight crime, provide recreational facilities, and create jobs rather than waste money on schools; we should ensure that every child has adequate health care—both physical and mental—and lives in a safe home and neighborhood. Only then will they come to school ready to learn. Spending money to solve their economic and social problems directly will be a better choice than putting more money into school districts that are often corrupt and mismanaged (Dryfoos and Maguire, 2019).

Historical Misuse of Public Funds in Urban School Districts

Urban schools have long been used to better the lives of some city residents at the expense of children's education. Urban school districts historically were a source of patronage jobs that politicians could hand out in exchange for votes. Members of various ethnic communities have, in their turn, assumed control of the districts and provided salaries to members of their constituencies—sometimes without requiring work in return (Connors, 1971). "The history of patronage is a method by which city residents without access to other political and economic resources have taken care of themselves and their friends" (Anyon, 1997, p. 159). Thirty years ago, one critic charged that in a city in the Northeast, "the political patronage has been so widespread that those filling district positions of responsibility have no idea of their actual duties. Positions were created to be filled by cronies. Routine hiring, evaluating and record keeping were not only bypassed but not even expected" (Morris, 1989, p. 18).

There is evidence that little has changed. In many school districts, patronage jobs have resulted in bloated bureaucracies that eat up funds that could be used to meet students' needs. Employees within these bureaucracies are sometimes involved in corrupt and illegal activities. Administrators and employees in large urban districts have been accused of taking bribes, diverting public funds for their private use, or using them for purposes for which they were not originally intended (Ross, 2015; Huntsberry, 2018; Stein, 2018; Maddison, 2019). Any scheme to centralize state funding to schools would have to ensure that new monies did not create more ineffective administrative positions in these districts. In addition, oversight procedures would need to be in place to prevent misappropriation of new funds.

As part of their legacy of providing patronage jobs, urban schools also employ a large number of paraprofessionals. These jobs are an excellent source of income for local community members. Cafeteria workers, teachers' aides, attendance assistants, special education aides, bus drivers, transportation aides, and sentries are all positions that ordinarily require no education beyond high school. They are jobs that members of the neighborhoods around the schools seek out. Getting one's name on "the list" is often a matter of *who*, not *what*, you know. In many cities, these paraprofessionals have unionized and command far higher wages in the school system than they would be able to earn in similar private sector jobs.

In the past, teachers who were hired in urban schools were often better "connected" than "prepared." Union contracts protect underqualified teachers who entered the system under preexisting patronage arrangements under the guise of "seniority" privileges, which often prevent principals from hiring less experienced but more committed teachers. The problem is magnified when money becomes tight and layoffs are required. Less effective teachers maintain their jobs, while more effective, newly hired ones lose theirs (Adely, 2018).

Those who demand, in the name of justice, that hardworking taxpayers provide more funds to these mismanaged districts need to rethink their priorities. No such increases in funding should take place until appropriate personnel, accounting, and management policies and practices are in place. Fairness to those paying the bills demands no less. No taxpayer should be asked to sacrifice to provide opportunities for "fat cats" to get richer by skimming money from school budgets or providing jobs for those who keep them in power. School finance equalization plans would do just that.

The Consequences of Equalizing School Finance

LOWER STUDENT ACHIEVEMENT

Those who propose we equalize funding at the state or federal level seem oblivious to what happens when such attempts are made. The "equalizers" have been successful in some states, often with disastrous results. There are two options for creating equalization plans for school spending. The financing can be "leveled up" or "leveled down." In leveling up, the state funds all schools at the same per pupil rate as the wealthiest districts. In leveling down, all schools receive a per pupil amount equivalent to that being spent in middle class or poorer districts in the state. In most leveling-down schemes, a limit is placed on what a district can spend above the state subsidy. Leveling up is an expensive proposition. It requires an increase in taxes across a state; people pay higher taxes, but only a few of them see increased services to their communities as a result of those rate hikes. Therefore, leveling-up schemes are unpopular and rarely are implemented fully.

In 1971, the California Supreme Court heard the first legal challenge to differences in school financing. In that case, *Serrano v. Priest*, the court held that inequalities in district per pupil funding violated the equal protection clauses of the state and federal constitution. Those who supported equalization of school spending believed they had won a victory. They assumed that the changes resulting from the court order would improve education for all of California's students. They were wrong. Taxpayers revolted against any plan to increase state taxes in order to equalize school spending (Fischel, 1989, 1996). They passed Proposition 13, which placed a "cap" on taxes and effectively limited funds for all California districts. The result of the highly complex and centralized process was that schools educating high-poverty students received only $13 more per student than their counterparts serving wealthier students (Timar and Roza, 2008). Adjustments were made to the distribution formula in 2013 with the goal of increasing aid to students in high-needs districts and increasing local control over the use of funds. The Local Control Funding Formula (LCFF) gives each district a set amount for each student. Districts then receive an additional 20% for each high-need student. Districts serving higher than average numbers of high-need students receive even more funding (Public Policy Institute of California, 2019). Despite claims that centralizing the funding of their schools would improve their academic chances, California's students are performing below national averages on the National Assessment of Educational Progress (2019) in mathematics and reading.

Despite the enthusiasm of some supporters, only two states, Vermont and Hawaii, actually fund schools in a centralized way. Each provides almost 90% of the revenue to schools. Vermont's students scored significantly above average on the National Assessment of Educational Progress (2019), but Hawaii's scored lower or at the average. In other words, funding schools almost exclusively at the state level is no guarantee that academic achievement will improve.

DECREASES IN LOCAL SUPPORT

Research into other instances of equalization attempts shows that court-ordered increases in state financial support for schools often were accompanied by decreases in local support. In other words, schools did not experience a real increase in resources. Municipalities sometimes saw the increased state aid as an opportunity to reduce the local tax burden on residents instead of a chance to provide better schools for their children (Driscoll and Salmon, 2008). These decisions made sense politically and economically for those cities and towns. They also reflected the antagonism often generated by decisions imposed on people by judges. It is not only local financial support for schools that suffers as a result of centralizing finance. When the state exercises a high degree of control over schools' funding, it necessarily means that local parents and residents have less control. Parents and neighbors can find this alienating. They are less likely to be involved in schools if they feel they have no real power over educational decisions. They are also less likely to make the additional contributions of time and material resources if they have little say in how those commodities are used. No school district can afford to lose the support of parents who are most interested in their children's school success. Parental involvement in their children's education is one of the best predictors of positive academic outcomes (Waterford.org, 2019).

Loss of Local Control

One of the most unique aspects of the U.S. school system is the fact that schools historically have been designed to meet the needs of individual areas. In the late nineteenth and early twentieth centuries, for example, different courses of study were taught in rural schools than in urban ones. Each local school district, working with concerned members of the community, was able to create schools that met its children's needs (Cremin, 1961). Schools were able to hire and fire teachers and could do so on the basis of criteria established locally. A teacher needed to live up to an individual community's standards, not just ones created by some state bureaucrats with little or no sense of the municipality's needs or values.

Even in the late twentieth century, local control of schools remained an important aspect of their governance. Taxpayers could accept or reject school boards' proposed budgets. They could elect or throw out of office school board members. In doing so, they ensured that their ideas for their children's education would be carried out in the schools. In addition, taxpayers could select those elected officials who set property tax rates for funding schools and thus could work to see that their tax burden would not be unduly high. Because most people in a town, city, or village had attended a local school or had children who did, interest in a local school district was high. The added dimension of locally controlling school funding increased taxpayers' involvement in the schools. People are willing to pay if they can see that their money is being spent on something of value and that they have something to say about what constitutes that value.

When school funding is centralized—when states take over most of the task of paying for education—taxpayers lose a substantial amount of the control over the schools for which they are paying. When local control is lost, administrators' flexibility is also sacrificed. Local school and civic leaders can no longer respond effectively to the needs of their community and their students. For example, some schools may want after-school programs, others may want to provide very small classes, and still others may want to create accelerated programs. When funding is centralized and its distribution mandated by the state, programmatic decisions no longer belong to local communities. In fact, local control has been recognized as so important that California, a state with a very centralized funding system, returned a significant amount of authority to districts in the LCFF (Public Policy Institute of California, 2019).

Good Schools Are a Reward for Hard Work

Whether proponents of centralized educational funding like it or not, we live in a capitalist society. We have an economic system that thrives on full and fair competition among businesses and workers. If you produce a product or provide a service that members of society value, you are more highly rewarded than those who do not. It is a system that has created a standard of living in the United States that is the envy of the rest of the world. We provide safety nets for those who cannot participate in the free market; we do so even for the children of those who will not take part.

However, one reason this economy works so well is because people can enjoy the fruits of their labor. Those who "crack the system" and figure out what the public will buy can reap monetary rewards that they then can translate into assets, one of the most cherished of which is a home. One of the factors that most influence home buyers is the opportunity to provide better schools and safer neighborhoods for their children. In turn, the quality of schools is an important factor in determining the market value of a home. Equalizing funding for schools and ensuring that all students receive the same advantages will remove one of the primary reasons why one house is worth more than another.

The American economic system is based on competition and on the idea that some things are "better" than others. These perceived advantages provide an incentive for most Americans to work hard and save and spend their money. If we centralize school spending and equalize the education children receive, we remove one of the greatest incentives for adults to make sacrifices of time and money that this economy requires. It may not seem "fair," but, in general, the system works, and it is foolish to think about making dramatic changes to it.

Kozol (2006) lamented the fact that children in poorer school districts perceive the differences between their schools and those in wealthier districts. He suggested that this awareness makes young people bitter and that as a result they eventually drop out of the competition that is at the heart of the American economic system. There is, however, another way of looking at the children's awareness. We can see it as the same kind of knowledge that has propelled so many others in this country to work harder than they ever imagined possible. We can see it as providing the same kind of motivation possessed by the pioneers who crossed this country in search of a better life. Some who currently live in municipalities that provide more resources for their schools started out in neighborhoods such as those that Kozol and others describe. Their hard work, determination, and perseverance enabled them to provide a better life for their children. We should not assume that today's young people are incapable of the same kind of effort and success. We need to hold out the promise of rewards for the kind of behavior that most benefits this society. Equalizing school funding takes away one of the primary reasons people choose to act in ways that will build up this great country. We cannot risk the consequences of removing that motivation.

FOR DISCUSSION

1. Research your own state. Have there been lawsuits pursuing equity in educational funding? What were the arguments, pro and con? What were the courts' decisions? Have they been implemented? What have been the results?

2. Some proposals for reducing school financial inequity rely on a shift from property tax revenue to sales tax revenue. Discuss the pros and cons of such a shift. Remember to consider questions such as the reliability of each revenue source in times of economic difficulty.

3. Consider how increased state contributions to school districts may affect local control of schools. Research your own state's policies with regard to the level of independence that school districts have in the areas of curriculum, testing, personnel, and length of the school year.

4. For a moment, turn the whole question of school financing on its head and consider whether governments have the right to tax citizens to pay for schools. Discuss whether such taxation violates individual rights of those citizens who do not have children in public schools. In doing so, you might try to support the argument that only parents have the right and obligation to provide their children with an education they deem appropriate and that government has no right to interfere in their decisions. What might be some effects on the country of implementing such a school financing policy?

REFERENCES

Adely, H. (2018, December 12). "Last in, First Out Policy Protecting NJ Teachers with Seniority Will Stay Put." *North Jersey Record.*

Allen, J. G. (2017). *Foundations for Student Success: How School Buildings Influence Student Health, Thinking and Performance.* Cambridge, MA: Harvard T.H. Chan School of Public Health, Harvard Center for Health and the Global Environment.

Anyon, J. (1997). *Ghetto Schooling.* New York: Teachers College Press.

Baker, B., Farrie, D., and Sciarra, D. (2016). *Mind the Gap.* Princeton: Educational Testing Service.

——— (2018). *Is School Funding Fair? A National Report Card.* Newark, NJ: Education Law Center.

Build U.S. Schools (2018). *Education Equity Requires Modern School Facilities.* Washington, DC: 21st Century School Fund.

Campaign for Fiscal Equity (2001). *Special Report: The Trial Court's Decision. In Evidence: Policy Reports from the CFE Trial.* New York: Campaign for Fiscal Equity.

Candelaria, C., and Shores, K. (2019). "Court-Ordered Finance Reforms in the Adequacy Era: Heterogeneous Causal Effects and Sensitivity." *Education Finance and Policy* 14(1). https://doi.org/10.1162/edfp_a_00236

Chingos, M., and Blagg, K. (2017). *Making Sense of State School Funding Policy.* Washington, DC: Urban Institute.

Coleman, J. (1966). *Equality of Educational Opportunity.* Washington, DC: U.S. Department of Health, Education, and Welfare, Office of Education.

Connors, R. (1971). *A Cycle of Power: The Career of Jersey City Mayor Frank Hague.* Metuchen, NJ: Scarecrow Press.

Cornman, S. Q., Ampadu, O., Wheeler, S., Hanak, K., and Zhou, L. (2019). *Revenues and Expenditures for Public Elementary and Secondary School Districts: School Year 2015–16 (Fiscal Year 2016)* (NCES 2019-303). Washington, DC: National Center for Education Statistics.

Cremin, L., ed. (1957). *The Republic and the School: Horace Mann on the Education of Free Men.* New York: Teachers College Press.

Cremin, L. (1961). *The Transformation of the School: Progressivism in American Education 1876–1957.* New York: Random House.

Darling-Hammond, L. (2019). *Investing for Student Success: Lessons from State School Finance Reforms.* Palo Alto, CA: Learning Policy Institute.

Driscoll, L., and Salmon, R. (2008). "How Increased State Equalization Aid Resulted in Greater Disparities: An Unexpected Consequence for the Commonwealth of Virginia." *Journal of Educational Finance* 33(3):238–261.

Dryfoos, J., and Maguire, S. (2019). *Inside Full-Service Community Schools.* New York: Simon and Shuster.

EdBuild (2019). $23 Billion (edbuild.org/content/23-billion).

Education Trust (2018). *Funding Gaps, 2018.* Washington, DC: Education Trust.

Egalite, A. (2016). "How Family Background Influences Student Achievement." *Education Next* 16(2).

Fischel, W. (1989, December). "Did *Serrano* Cause Proposition 13?" *National Tax Journal* 42(4):465–473.

——— (1996). "How *Serrano* Caused Proposition 13." *Journal of Law and Politics* 12:607–645.

Great Schools Partnership (2016). Glossary of Education Reform (edglossary.org/local-control).

Hanushek, E. (1996). School Resources and Student Performances. In G. Burtless, ed., *Does Money Matter? The Effect of School Resources on Student Achievement and Adult Success* Washington, DC: Brookings Institution.

——— (2016). "What Matters for Student Achievement?" *Education Next* 16(2).

Hanushek, E., Peterson, P., Talpey, L., and Woessmann, L. (2019, March). *The Unwavering SES Achievement Gap: Trends in U.S. Student Performance* (NBER Working Paper No. 25648). Cambridge, MA: National Bureau of Economic Research.

Huntsberry, W. (2018, August 20). "A Small Pot of School Funds Is Regularly Mismanaged and Sometimes Abused." *Voice of San Diego.*

Jackson, K. (2018, December 10). Does School Spending Matter? The New Literature on an Old Question. Presented at the Bronfenbrenner Center for Translational Research Conference (works.bepress.com/c_kirabo_jackson/38).

Jimenez, L. (2019). The Case for Federal Funding for School Infrastructure. Center for American Progress (cdn.americanprogress.org/content/uploads/2019/02/11124042/School-Infrastructure1.pdf).

Katz, M. (1975). *Class, Bureaucracy and Schools: The Illusion of Educational Change in America.* New York: Praeger.

Knight, D. (2019). "Are School Districts Allocating Resources Equitably? The Every Student Succeeds Act, Teacher Experience Gaps, and Equitable Resource Allocation." *Educational Policy* 33(4):615–649. https://doi.org/10.1177/0895904817719523

Kozol, J. (1991). *Savage Inequalities.* New York: Harper.

——— (2006, January). "Jonathan Kozol Takes on the World." *District Administration.*

Lafortune, J., Rothstein, J., and Schanzenbach, D. (2016). *School Finance Reform and the Distribution of Student Achievement* (IRLE Working Paper No. 100-16). Cambridge, MA: National Bureau of Economic Research.

Mackey, S. (1998). "The School Money Puzzle." *Government Finance Review* 2:39–42.

Maddison, T. (2019, January 16). Financial Mismanagement of San Diego Schools Hurt Students the Most. Blog. Transparent California (blog.transparentcalifornia.com/2019/01/16/financial-mismanagement-of-san-diego-school-hurts-students-the-most).

Morris, G. (1989). "The Blackboard Jungle Revisited." *National Review* 41(8):18–19.

National Assessment of Educational Progress (2019). Highlights from the 2017 Assessments. The Nation's Report Card (nationsreportcard.gov/reading_math_2017_highlights).

Oakes, J. (2002). *Education Inadequacy, Inequality, and Failed State Policy: A Synthesis of Expert Reports Prepared for* Williams v. State of California. Los Angeles, UCLA Institute for Democracy, Education, and Access.

Organization for Economic Cooperation and Development (2019). *Education at a Glance 2019: OECD Indicators.* Paris: OECD Publishing. https://doi.org/10.1787/f8d7880d-en

Public Policy Institute of California (2019). *Financing California's Public Schools.* San Francisco: Public Policy Institute of California.

Rebell, M. (2007). "Professional Rigor, Public Engagement and Judicial Review: A Proposal for Enhancing the Validity of Education Adequacy Studies." *Teachers College Record* 109(6):1,303–1,373.

Reuben, K. (2019, June 12). School Funding in New York State: Does the Current Formula Ensure Access for Students of Color? Testimony before New York State Advisory Committee to the U.S. Commission on Civil Rights. Washington, DC: Urban Institute.

Rosenthal, H., and Rothman, D. (2017). *What Do We Owe Each Other?* New York: Routledge. https://doi.org/10.4324/9781351298445

Ross, T. (2015, January 20). "Where School Dollars Go to Waste." *The Atlantic.*

Serrano v. Priest (1971). 5 Cal. 3d 584.

Stein, P. (2018, April 14). "D.C. is Misspending Millions Intended to Help the City's Poorest Students." *Washington Post.*

Timar, T., and Roza, M. (2008, April 18). A False Dilemma: Should Decisions about Education Resource Use Be Made at the State or Local Level? Paper presented at the University of California, Davis Center for Applied Policy in Education Symposium, Davis, CA.

Tyack, D. (1974). *The One Best System: A History of American Urban Education.* Cambridge, MA: Harvard University Press.

Urban, W., and Wagoner, J. (2008). *American Education: A History* (4th ed.). New York: McGraw-Hill.

U.S. Census Bureau (2019). 2017 Public Elementary-Secondary Education Finance Data (census.gov/data/tables/2017/econ/school-finances/secondary-education-finance.html).

U.S. Department of Education (2019a). Table 217.10. Functional age of public schools' main instructional buildings and percentage of schools with permanent and portable (temporary) buildings, by selected school characteristics and condition of permanent and portable buildings: 2012. *Digest of Educational Statistics* (nces.ed.gov/programs/digest/d17/tables/dt17_217.10.asp). Washington, DC: National Center for Educational Statistics.

——— (2019b). Table 236.15. Current expenditures and current expenditures per pupil in public elementary and secondary schools: 1989–90 through 2028–29. *Digest of Educational Statistics* (nces.ed.gov/programs/digest/d18/tables/dt18_236.15.asp?current=yes). Washington, DC: National Center for Educational Statistics.

Waterford.org (2019). How Parent Involvement Leads to Student Success (waterford.org/education/how-parent-involvment-leads-to-student-success).

Privatization, Commercialization, and the Business of School

Complementing or Competing Interests

4

Should schools be more like business?

Position 1: Improving Education by Privatizing and Corporate Support

---

Privatization as a moral ideal reflects the ideal of voluntarily providing goods and services. The problem with public provision is that citizens do not consent to it.

—Flanagan (2019)

Ultimately, I believe the best education policy is no education policy at all: the separation of school and state.

—Caplan (2018)

Privatization Is Just Applying Good Business Sense

Privatization is the process of transferring functions performed by the government to private enterprise (Lewis, 2019). Historically, in the United States many services like roads, bridges, water supplies, and public safety were privately initiated, built, developed, and operated. Businesses conducted society's main work. During the nineteenth century, with an expanding population and land for development, the scale of activity grew and there was a shift toward increasing government operations using taxpayer funds. Government replaced many private enterprises and took on the mantle of public welfare. The government saw its role as interpreter of the social interest, but it lost track of individual rights, what America's founders often called natural rights (Gottlieb, 2016). Those rights, according to the Declaration of Independence, include "Life, Liberty, and the pursuit of Happiness." In order "to secure these rights, Governments are instituted among men." It is not to create or dispense them. The actions of government to "secure" rights legitimately includes national security, public safety, and the creation of legal structures needed to interpret and protect those rights; there are no other requirements for government.

George Will (2019), tracing the political history of the founding of America, states: "The case for limited government is grounded in the empirical evidence that human beings have something in common—human nature—but are nevertheless incorrigibly different in capacities and aspirations . . . government cannot hope to provide happiness to all" (pp. 8, 14). He argues that government gains a monopoly on the power to enforce "education and other sources of norms by which society is regulated" (p. 14), however, simply being able to wield that power does not make it reasonable or just.

Big government has replaced private enterprise in many facets of public life, bringing along the problems of bureaucracy, such as excessive expenses, lack of competition, "free rider" welfare issues, political infighting, low efficiency, and low quality of performance. This litany of defects has caused a rethinking of public services. Private businesses, on the other hand, have to engage in competitive markets and have to improve efficiency and productivity while providing improved quality and customer service. Mounting evidence of better outcomes as a result of business approaches compared to governmental inadequacies has pushed the public toward the movement to privatize.

We suffer from government deficiencies in many public spheres—incompetence, irrational rules, corruption, delay, frustration, denial without reason, poor maintenance, service disruption, long lines for service, and more. There is little remedy because there is no competition. Private enterprise survives in competitive situations, providing quality with lower costs. Business successes are partly derived from limiting bureaucratic bloat, cutting the "free rider" problem by tailoring services to individual and family needs, and circumventing political interference (Desperio, 2018; Hodge, 2018; Lewis, 2019). Dunkelberg (2018) states: "even in a democracy, there is a 'tyrant' that can exercise despotic power if left unchecked—the government: federal, state and local. . . . History has proven that governments cannot deliver the success that an unfettered economy can" (p. 1).

Massive expansion of governmental powers over public life is a larger context for this issue. Galles (2019) makes the point: "Over the years, Americans' power to make their own decisions has been increasingly displaced by governments." Government overreach and overregulation stifle individual liberty, private enterprise, and innovation. The cost of government in the United States is about 25% of all goods and serviced produced each year (Sumner, 2020). There is insufficient space here to fully explore this broad topic, but government overreach and high cost frame this discussion of the value of privatization, in education and society.

Privatization programs have assisted all levels of government in performing their functions better, with less taxpayer cost. The complete privatization of a service, such as in building and operating private prison systems or community fire safety, is one form. Other forms include outsourcing or contracting for selected goods and services, as in police car maintenance, trash hauling, or food service at public facilities. Public-private partnerships are another way to capitalize on the values of private enterprise while maintaining the public interest and function. In addition, many government agencies have utilized corporate sponsorship or support for special projects, facilities, or events. Public education is one important area where private experience and talent can be used to great public advantage.

Privatization and Education

Milton Friedman (1955), one of the most important economists of the twentieth century and advisor to President Reagan, points out: "the administration of schools is neither required by the financing of education, nor justifiable in its own right in a predominantly free enterprise society." This idea is evolving as the public recognizes the difference between public finance of a social interest, the education of youth, and government management. Betsy DeVos, Secretary of Education in President Trump's administration, strongly advocates using public funds to increase school choice through charter schools, vouchers, and related programs. The Libertarian Party (2020) platform warns that government-mandated "one-size-fits-all education" restricts our children. They call for the separation of education and the state because government schools can indoctrinate and "interfere with the free choice of individuals." Education should be a free market (Republican Views, 2016).

Schools, students, parents, and taxpayers gain when business ideas and competition are encouraged in education. Privatizing schools (or many of their services) and engaging corporations directly in school matters are two good ways to improve American education (Snell, 2011; Gilroy, 2012; Heimer, 2018; Business Roundtable, 2019). Public schools have an unfortunate history of waste, inefficiency, duplication, and poor performance related to their primary purpose: educate young people. Friedman (1980) noted that "the threat to public schools arises from their defects, not their accomplishments." Privatization can benefit schools by bringing the efficiency and effectiveness of private enterprise to bear on school organization and operation. Business management has become highly sophisticated and outcome directed. A business that is not well organized, clear in its work, devoted to meeting the needs of its customers, and keeping up with competition is destined to fail. Public schools can fail to educate, but administrators and teachers keep their positions and the taxpayers foot the bill.

Public schools are prime candidates for privatization. They are one of the most tax-costly, bloated, and inefficient enterprises of government. They are also largely monopolistic but have not consistently produced sound education (*The Economist,* 2005; Caplan, 2018). For these and other reasons, public education has not fulfilled its social purpose—providing high-quality education at reasonable cost. With no competition and traditional inefficiency, public schools are the major burden on and frustration for local taxpayers. Privatization offers market efficiency, accountability, professional design, and choice (Lipana, 2011).

Reasons for the Privatization of American Public Schools

IMPROVING SCHOOLS FOR OUR CHILDREN

The most important reason to privatize schools is to benefit our children. They deserve the best schools we can provide. Bureaucracy created for government-operated schools overwhelms local budgets and does not respond to complaints. Privatization increases accountability, making school staff responsible for performance that benefits children. Accountability, a keystone of private enterprise, offers a way to clearly identify problems and reward good performance in schools. Private enterprise sets specific goals and measures how well they are met; schools need that also. Schools that work will be rewarded; those that don't will be changed or closed.

PROVIDING DEMOCRATIC CHOICE—BREAKING THE PUBLIC SCHOOL MONOPOLY

Privatizing schools offers choices to parents concerned about their children's education. School choice is certainly in the best interest of children and their parents, but it also forces schools to compete to attract students and financial support. The public schools have had a monopoly for far too long and suffer from lack of competition. Privatization can bring customer satisfaction and state-of-the-art efficiency to such schools. Studies show K–12 private programs and other programs work (K12, Inc., 2012). Public schools do not welcome privatization, and their unions continue to fight it (Snell, 2005; *The Economist,* 2005; Carroll, 2019).

INCREASING PRODUCTIVITY IN EDUCATION

Privatizing increases productivity in public schools, where productivity has not changed for a century. Public schools operate as they did when our grandparents were students. Expensive, labor-intensive schools sap local and state finances. Improvements in technology and communications revolutionized U.S. businesses and provide manifold increases in productivity. But public schools have not changed. Most school administrators have an education background and lack the business background needed to develop and implement sound strategic planning, efficient resource use, accountability control, and effective management. Public schools lack interest in improving productivity (Hentschke et al., 2004).

MEETING GLOBAL COMPETITION

International competition requires the United States to remain at the cutting edge of innovation or suffer future decline. As democracy and capitalism increase across the globe, privatization continues to be a strong movement in public life. Government-run operations show weaknesses that private enterprise can overcome. Worldwide, leaders recognize private enterprise as the key vehicle for improving citizens' lives while making government more efficient with available funds and resources—a movement toward private operation of a variety of public services. Schools are increasingly undergoing privatization in many nations. England and New Zealand provide excellent examples of this process.

A Variety of Approaches to Privatization: Charter Schools to Food Operations

Complete privatization offers some distinct advantages, but there are many ways to provide private enterprise solutions to public education, improve learning. and cut costs. Charter schools, private and public, are usually not subject to some of the bureaucratic regulations that have kept the public school establishment so entrenched and so costly. These schools may establish teacher accountability without tenure requirements, develop a curriculum without contending with state mandates, and organize classes and provide instruction without meeting some of the trivial regulations that have petrified public education.

Another approach is outsourcing school management; with this approach, school districts can hold private managers accountable for student learning. Entire public school districts can operate under a multiyear contract specifying performance standards and allowing the board to fire managers with 90 days notice. Rigorous contracts control performance for general management: hiring and evaluating staff, developing curriculum, evaluating students, communicating with parents and the community, and providing custodial and ancillary maintenance. Other selected management services that are too costly or too cumbersome to handle under public control, like payroll and accounting services, are increasingly outsourced. Educational management organizations, similar to health maintenance organizations, are emerging to improve schools. Sylvan Learning Systems, Nobel Learning Communities, Edison Learning, and Knowledge Universe are examples of competent private management of education.

Some school services are well suited to private contracting. Many schools find that contracting with popular fast-food companies, such as McDonald's and Pizza Hut, to provide school lunch service is more cost effective, more acceptable to students, and sometimes more nutritious than the standard school cafeteria food. Outsourcing, a form of privatization of school services, has been working well for years in many schools (Shuls, 2016). The twenty-first century will see expansion of many forms of school privatization as the public recognizes its benefits.

Corporate Involvement in Schools

Privatization may be an excellent idea, but difficult politics remain until the public becomes better informed and schools more responsive. Another business-related approach that benefits schools occurs when corporations and local businesses provide funds and political support for needed facilities and services and by advocating for improvements in schools. Corporations are often eager to help with finances and materials, offering educational programs for school and social leaders, engaging in community, regional, and national efforts in school reform, sponsoring activities, and providing large-scale funds for schools. Business interests go far beyond simply financial sponsorship or privatizing some activities of public schools. Privatization offers a direct way to improve schools; corporate support offers encouragement and assistance in helping schools improve on their own.

The health and vitality of our economy and our society depend on schools. Businesspeople understand this principle. For many years, corporations and local businesses have been among the strongest supporters of education. Business enterprises provide substantial financial contributions, internships and scholarships, guest speakers and teaching materials, advisers and consultants, fund-raising assistance, and employment for parents, students, and other taxpayers. Leaders of the business community recognize the significant benefits that good schools offer, and they are active advocates of improvements in education. The strength of the U.S. society lies in the fortuitous combination of democracy and capitalism. Free enterprise is basic to releasing the entrepreneurial spirit in humans; entrepreneurs built and developed this nation. The free marketplace for which the United States has become respected globally requires continual improvement—that directly incorporates education. Schools are key to the future development of the American economy (Business Roundtable, 2008).

Our success causes many other nations to emulate American entrepreneurship. That is complimentary, but it is also a challenge. The breakdown of most communist countries at the end of the 1980s illustrates the flawed nature of socialism. The death of communism has given the twenty-first century a world of competing capitalist nations. This new scenario requires even more U.S. commitment to an education-business partnership. Schooling that will maintain our leadership in international business competition is a top priority. With or without privatization, business must enter into new and more intertwined partnerships with schools to ensure that the United States keeps its competitive edge in global markets.

Business Interest in Partnerships with Schools

A competitive incentive for schools develops when businesses propose ideas and provide a source of funds. Businesspeople and school administrators have a joint interest in good schools. Business leaders are in the forefront of efforts to reform schools (Aaron et al., 2003; Business Roundtable, 2010, 2019). The Business Roundtable strongly supports high standards, accountability, and efficiency in education and participates in various school reform activities and initiatives (businessroundtable.org). The Roundtable is composed of chief executive officers from 200 prominent corporations that are the leading businesses in virtually all segments of the economy. They employ about 34 million people and are an influential group with educational interests (Koebler, 2011; *Philanthropy News Digest*, 2011). Corporate-sponsored school activities focus on such diverse areas as academic instructional improvement, career awareness, civic and character education, drug abuse prevention, dropout prevention, and programs for the disadvantaged. The new Workforce Partnership Initiative intends to close the "workforce skills gap" by strengthening school and training pipeline programs (Heimer, 2018).

Public-private partnerships work well also. Almost all member corporations of the Business Roundtable belong to school partnerships for educational improvement.

The Workforce Partnership Initiative of the Roundtable is an example. Education World (2020) notes multiple partnership examples at the local level. The Boston Compact established a partnership between Boston's schools and the Boston Private Industry Council (bostonpic.org). Businesses promised students jobs if the schools were able to raise test scores and decrease dropout rates. This alliance has provided jobs for over 1,000 graduates, and reading and math scores have improved.

Through such partnerships, business leaders can come into the schools to teach, to talk with students, and to help teachers and guidance counselors develop programs to improve student skills and attitudes. Students can visit places of employment and gain understanding of the economy and business interests and concerns. Partnerships can establish work-study arrangements for students, produce teaching materials, and provide financial support for all aspects of schooling from teacher seminars to improving school technology and career guidance. Many businesses participate in Adopt-a-School programs that enrich the school's ability to prepare students for employment. Other businesses invite teachers to visit, provide summer employment and other opportunities for teachers to learn about their operations, and prepare free teaching materials. Business-to-school financial support by direct grants, special project sponsorship, advertising in school media, discounted purchase arrangements, equipment and resource acquisition, and a variety of other avenues provides much-needed money for school uses (Weldon, 2011; Bladgett, 2016; McFadden, 2016).

Corporations help schools in key areas because they recognize the value of helping students reach their full potential. This is not a new role for business leadership; business-education relations have a long and positive history (Mann, 1987). These contributions include cash, services, sympathy, and assistance in political and economic coalitions. There are many varieties of school-business partnerships; the most effective ones provide for mutual respect and participation, with each partner satisfied with the results (Daniels Fund, 2008; Hann, 2008).

Education and the Changing Nature of Employment in the United States

Prominent changes in the nature of employment in American society have had major implications for schools. Historically, the shift was from agricultural to manufacturing jobs; now the shift is from manufacturing to service and information. In the short space of the last 50 years, the proportion of farmers and farm workers has declined from almost 20% of the workforce to only 3%; manufacturing jobs have declined from about 32 to 27% of total employment, whereas service jobs have increased from about 53 to 69%. The service sector has grown primarily in social and producer services (e.g., health and medical technology) rather than in personal services (e.g., hairdressing or domestic work) or distributive services (e.g., sales and delivery). The most prominent change has been in the kinds of jobs available. White-collar jobs rose from about 45% of the labor force in 1940 to over 70% by the mid-1980s and is predicted to be about 85% by 2020 (U.S. Census Bureau, 2011; Baker and Buffie, 2017).

In educational terms, this means that students need more and better schooling. Many agricultural jobs no longer demand just sheer physical labor but involve technical work that requires strong academic skills. White-collar jobs typically require increased education (Tyszko, 2019). Women, although subjected to a history of lower average earnings, and currently earning only about 80% of the income of men for equivalent work, are increasingly using education to improve their incomes. Women with bachelor's degrees or more increased average inflation-adjusted income by 34% between 1979 and 2018, while the average income of men with the same education level increased by 11% (U.S. Bureau of Labor Statistics, 2019).

In early U.S. history, basic literacy had inherent value; it had no special relation to people's work requirements. When most citizens lived rural, agricultural lives, reading, writing, and calculating were nice to know but not necessary for securing and keeping employment. Even in those times, however, obvious links existed between education and employment. A study conducted in 1867 by the Commonwealth of Pennsylvania, for example, showed that income was related directly to literacy: those who could not read earned an average of $36 per month, those who could read but were otherwise poorly educated earned an average of $52 a month, and those who were well educated earned an average of $90 a month (Soltow and Stevens, 1981). Current data show the average annual range of income per year for those with less than a high school education is $18,000 to $24,000; with high school graduation the average is $24,000 to $80,000; and with a BA degree it is $40,000 to $128,000 (U.S. Bureau of Labor Statistics, 2019).

There is a correlation between education and income, between education and national development, and between education and "the good life." Nations with the highest levels of education also have the highest levels of wealth, innovation, and achievement (Isaak, 2005). Social class and occupational experience are also influential in employment status, but education has the greatest effect. Literacy for business purposes does not mean just proficiency in reading and writing. It means a set of values related to work.

Consumers and Schools

In addition to the business interest in education for developing the economy and preparing good employees for good jobs, there is an obvious interest in schools as a location of consumers. Consumers, of course, are one of the driving forces of our economy. It is not only the earnings of retail stores that rise and fall according to consumer choices. Manufacturers of electronics, clothing, appliances, and vehicles, as well as their suppliers of raw materials, are also subject to consumer selections. Banks and other financial institutions, gas and oil companies, house construction and repair agencies, food producers and suppliers, entertainment industries, and other consumer-driven corporations exist and change because of what people buy.

Consumer confidence is one of the major indicators of economic activity, one closely examined by Wall Street firms and market watchers worldwide. We are a consumer society. A free market gives us competition that provides choices among quality, prices, and variety. An important part of the economic process in a consumer society is getting information to the consumer about new or improved products and services, places to obtain them, reminders about trade names, and ways to obtain competitive prices or opportunities. This is a place for corporate notices, news releases, advertising, and other uses of media to convey information. Although we may complain at times about some advertising, we recognize that much of the information that ads contain is valuable. Through advertising, we learn of innovations, modifications, and opportunities that make our lives easier or happier. We can find better prices, products, and services for things we want. We can find standards against which we can measure products and services. Advertising provides us with important ideas and information that are necessary to our roles as consumers. The marketplace adjusts according to the decisions made by consumers; advertising adjusts according to the market and how consumers respond to ads.

Consumer life does not stop at the school door. After all, students are consumers, and they influence consumer decisions in families. They deserve to know about products and services available. The school setting is an appropriate location for some of that information. Schools employ teachers and administrators to develop curricula and classroom practices designed to help students gain an adequate understanding of life. Student life outside of school involves advertising and commerce. Schools should provide education that reflects society, and societies depend on commerce. Businesses know that children and adolescents are a very significant segment of buyers, among the most important in many areas of retail purchases. Within this context, the provision of corporate-sponsored school material offers information for students, and it gives financial support for schools. Students can learn from the material, and schools are relieved from the extra burden of paying for it.

Business Approaches to School Operation

Schools could also benefit from the use of business models in school organization and operation. Schools are often inefficient. If U.S. industry had been as stultified as schools, it would have failed long ago. In fact, those businesses that have not updated and improved their efficiency and productivity have failed; private enterprise cannot survive stagnation. Yet, we have protected our schools from this necessary competition.

Improved technology and productivity could increase school efficiency considerably. For example, if innovative technologies come into play, the teacher could present more interesting material to larger groups in less time, individual students could work more extensively on computers under the general guidance of the teacher or a teacher's aide, the school day and curriculum could be more varied, parents could get up-to-date information on their child's progress, early warning systems could limit student failures, and teachers could identify their own and their students' peak performance data. Schools would be organized very differently, but that is what we need. Businesses are constantly reorganizing to achieve better productivity because competition demands it.

Another businesslike approach that could bring great benefits to schools is in the use of incentives and rewards for good performance. Currently, schools pay teachers on the basis of nineteenth-century ideas that all teachers are the same and that only increased experience should provide increased income. This levels down the performance of many teachers and schools to the lowest common denominator. There is no incentive for individual teachers to perform in a superior manner. With teacher pay based on performance, the most talented teachers will get better salaries, and other teachers will have a very good reason to start measuring up. That would make the salaries of the best teachers competitive with salaries of other professionals and would attract more topflight college graduates into teaching.

School administration is a place to bring incentives for performance also. Often, administrator salaries are limited by job title, and excellent performance is rewarded only by having to change jobs. One idea would be to tie administrator income to accountability standards. When administrators lead their schools forward to better student achievement, they get increased income through bonuses or other rewards.

Business thinking can help education in other areas. School buildings are often large, inefficiently utilized, and costly to build and maintain. In districts where student enrollment has declined, expensive school buildings have been sold, destroyed, or renovated at great public financial loss. Some school buildings are used less than half the year and then for only one-third of the day. The practice of issuing bonds has passed the debt for building these behemoths on to future generations. Many small schools, with separate buildings and school staffs, could be reorganized into less costly regional districts if we applied business concepts. Individual school districts purchase millions of dollars' worth of books, equipment, and teaching materials at high cost when a coordinated effort could decrease such expense considerably. Businesses have shown that they can train large numbers of employees by using video and computer systems, lectures, programmed materials, self-study, and other devices that do not consume the high levels of precious human resources that schools use. Furthermore, this training occurs in facilities used extensively for the whole of each year.

Obstacles to Privatization of Schools

When people understand that, for less cost, they can have better service and more accountability, they quickly become supporters of the shift to private operation. Other, more difficult obstacles remain. Public employee labor unions lobby against privatization of public services—obviously there is an issue of self-interest. Teacher unions have been particularly active opposing school privatization and are among the largest, best financed, and most active organizations in state legislatures. Many state legislators fear their power.

Government bureaucracies also present obstacles to private enterprise since bureaucracies may lose some of their power. The public education bureaucracy built a massive fortress of regulations. It is the Internal Revenue Service of the school business. Businesspeople know that there may be no more important work in American society than the improvement of schools. Good schools are simply good business.

Educational Improvement—A Private and Public Goal

This is not a time for schools to continue their course—it is a time to change schools, and business-proven techniques can effect the changes. The structure of business based on a competitive marketplace has withstood the most severe tests of war, depression, and dislocation. We need to introduce contemporary business management—management concerned with improved efficiency and productivity—into education. And we need to offer privatization of schools or many of their services as a competitive challenge to a public monopoly.

It is a social and educational necessity that we reorder our schools to give students solid grounding in academic skills and good, positive workplace values. It is an economic necessity that we reorganize school operations to more closely approximate good business practices. All in all, business has much to offer education, much more than just providing money for school projects (Oravitz, 1999; Aaron et al., 2003; Weldon, 2011). Financial support alone cannot confront the crisis in education. Developing basic and advanced skills, improving workplace attitudes and values, increasing the productivity of U.S. business, enhancing our competitive stance in international markets, and making schools more efficient are goals that business and the schools share. For the good of our young people and for our future as a nation, we need to encourage privatization and strong alliances with business to reach these shared goals.

Position 2:   Public Schools Should Be Public

Public education is not broken. It is not failing or declining. The diagnosis is wrong, and the solutions of the corporate reformers are wrong. . . . The transfer of public funds to private management and the creation of thousands of deregulated, unsupervised, and unaccountable schools have opened the public coffers to profiteering, fraud, and exploitation. . . . Stop the mindless attacks on the education profession.

—Ravitch (2020, pp. 4, 9)

The road necessarily traveled to achieve freedom and equality in the United States leads directly through public education.

—Rooks (2017, p. 1)

The idea that private operation of public services is superior is a socially destructive myth (Krugman, 2011, 2012; Nealon, 2012; Eisen, 2018; Ravitch, 2020). Schrag (1999) points out that "the pattern in our society is toward withdrawal from community into private, gated enclaves with private security, private recreational facilities, private everything, even as the public facilities deteriorate." Self-serving myths—promoted in the corporate world and corporate-oriented mass media—are that private enterprise offers superior services, efficiency, competition, and management. That is not demonstrated in fact, and obscures larger social issues. Cohen (2016) summarizes a long history of privatization, as an ideological and political idea, becoming a corporate "grab for gold" in the public trough.

Is Privatization Better or Just Privateering?

Privateering is the wartime practice of getting government approval to commit hostile acts against enemy ships on the seas; acts such as stealing the enemy's cargo and establishing dominance over an area made this practice a kind of government-sponsored piracy. Often, privateers were pirates and returned to piracy when government contracts ended. It is a term that, with minor modification, could be used to describe some forms of privatization today. The government, with lobbyist pressure, provides public funds to private enterprises to do the government's work, often without oversight or control equivalent to that required of regular government agencies.

Privatization can make things far worse for a democratic society (Krugman, 2002; Levin, 2006; Knight and Schwartzberg, 2019). Dickinson (2018) states: "Privatization profoundly unsettles the structure of democratic governance . . . privatization complicates . . . our mechanisms for transparency and democratic deliberation" (pp. 37, 47). Similarly, Harel (2018) says: "massive privatization erodes shared responsibility and . . . threatens political engagement" (p. 69). These problems arise in many forms of privatization, war-making, peacekeeping, national and local security, police, and a host of other public services and responsibilities (Freeman and Minow, 2009; Hagedon, 2014; Cameron, 2017).

Prison privatization provides one continuing example of the negative results of privatization. Eisen's (2018) comprehensive study outlines a history of using prisoners for profit: prior to the American Revolution, prisoners were "commodities." British merchant marines earned money transporting debtors and other prisoners to the colonies; "bed-brokers" during the 1990s were paid a fee for filling private prison beds. In the twenty-first century private prisons are big business: the government pays about $23,000 per inmate. CoreCivic, the largest operator of private prisons, had revenues in 2000 of about $280 million; in 2017 it was reported at $1.7 billion, with over 70 lobbyists employed. In addition, "there is no evidence that they actually save taxpayers any money" (Vittert, 2018). The Sentencing Project (2018) also points out that the evidence does not support the claim that for-profit prisons are more cost-efficient. Private prisons handle 70% of immigrant detainment as well as about 10% of all those convicted of crimes in the United States. But private is not better. Eisen (2018) notes that current prisoner recidivism rates have not declined, despite privatization promises 35 years ago. Private prisons have no incentive to rehabilitate prisoners and lots of incentive to keep prison populations high. Eisen says: "America's experiment with private prisons has largely failed. The industry is simply not transparent and their operating contracts do not hold them accountable" (p. 238).

Not only is the complete privatization of a prison costly and inefficient, when private operators provide only segments of prison services, it is profitable for them, but it is not cost-saving for the public and sometimes results in much lower quality.

Requarth (2019) notes some privatized prisons had spoiled foods delivered, kept food improperly, and maintained vermin-infested kitchens. The privatization record does not support claims of improving efficiency or quality.

Prison privatization is only one example. Wedel (2009) discusses privatization of government services in many areas, including: information, procurement and contract management, defense, technology, housing, health, energy, environment, foreign aid, economic reform, and foreign policy. She discusses the limited oversight or control, hidden arrangements, overlapping bureaucracies, lack of transparency, and manipulation of resources that identify privatization across the gamut of governmental responsibilities. The subtitle of her book is instructive: "How the World's New Power Brokers Undermine Democracy, Government, and the Free Market." That is not a positive future for public education if privatized in this democracy.

Social Purposes and Private Goals

In a capitalistic democracy, some activities fit private enterprise and some deserve public operation and oversight. Kozol finds no evidence that "a competitive free market, unrestricted, without a strong counterpoise within the public sector will ever dispense decent medical care, sanitation, transportation, or education to the people" (quoted in Rethinking Schools, 1998). The fundamental social purposes of public education in a democracy must be the center point of any debate over privatization. Public and private operation of schools must be measured against the broad social purposes of schooling. Is public or private control more likely to move us toward fulfilling those large social purposes (Giroux, 2012)? Molnar (2017) concludes: "Policies based on the 'market' as a principle of social organization have wrought havoc with a founding principle of American democracy."

Despite a century-long tradition of excellent public service in difficult social and financial conditions, public schools have been subjected to a relentlessly negative campaign during the past three decades. The long-term campaign of demonizing public schools is coupled with a clamor to privatize them; this has stifled the more significant debate on social purposes. Ironically, the privatization myth protects private enterprise from similar attacks for its many failures and its significant threat to democracy.

The history of private enterprise—with its questionable ethics, cavalier treatment of employees and the public, financial manipulation of the political process, and escapes into bankruptcy or taxpayer bailout when in trouble—goes unmentioned in reporting and in public discourse on privatization. Much support for privatization of public schools revolves around shallow advertising that capitalizes on negative images of public schools, unsupported claims of potential cost savings, and a paternalistic aura that corporations know best. The evidence does not support the claims. For-profit schools do not have innovative practices, curriculum, or management programs (Kaplan, 1996; Zollers and Ramanathan, 1998; Pizzuro, 2011; Smith, 2011). They make a profit, but don't improve education (Krugman, 2012).

In certain situations and under strict and open public regulation and school district supervision, it is reasonable to provide some aspects of public services, such as food service in school lunchrooms, through private contracts. But wholesale privatizing of schools, where a private corporation controls the management, curriculum, and instructional decisions of a whole school or school district, is an extremely hazardous approach to dealing with public services. In areas as important to society's future as education, privatizing may destroy the soul of democratic life (Saltman, 2000; Bracey, 2001; Sudetic, 2001).

Among the most compelling statements for public education in a democratic society is John Dewey's (1916) *Democracy and Education*. In recent years, leading political theorists and education scholars have reiterated the significance of public education to democracy (Gutmann, 1999, 2008; Saltman, 2000; Kadlec, 2007; Ravitch, 2010, 2013, 2020).

The goals of improving justice, equality, and freedom are central to the idea of a public school, but not to private enterprise. We have a long way to go in public education to meet these high standards; minorities and women have not had equal opportunities or freedom in schools. But we are improving significantly in this area, and we continue to pursue those goals in public education. Privatizing, with its attendant emphasis on cutting costs and improving test scores, is less likely to expand opportunities for the weakest or most disadvantaged.

Free, critical study of social problems may not be a goal in corporation-operated schools. Open examination of controversial topics, necessary in democratic society, may conflict with corporate agendas. How many corporations encourage criticism, especially public criticism, of their purposes and practices? Saltman (2000, 2005, 2012) condemns the utter commercialization of public education as a major threat to democracy. Ravitch (2020) shows how privatization of public education was defective, and why it has failed the public. Dayton and Glickman (1994) point clearly to one aspect of the threat:

> A fundamental problem with the privatization movement is that it views public education as merely another individual entitlement and ignores the vital public interests served by common public schools. Public education is democratically controlled by the elected representatives of the People. Ultimately it is the People who decide how public education funds are expended. Privatization systems use public funds, but limit public control. Allowing private control of public funds circumvents the democratic control and interests of the People. (p. 82)

Privatizing Public Education for Profit

The privatization of education in the United States provides no solid evidence of superior performance, higher quality, lower costs, or better management. Evidence actually demonstrates the opposite. When Edison Schools was the largest of private corporations running schools, they could produce no substantial data of improvements in academic performance by students (Miron and Applegate, 2000; Bracey, 2002, 2008; Henriques and Steinberg, 2002a, 2002b; Holloway, 2002; American Federation of Teachers, 2003; Lubienski and Lubienski, 2004; Ratchford, 2005; Molnar et al., 2010). Edison, founded in 1992, was to be the prime example of the new school privatization trend that would take over, claiming to improve schools, eliminate the public monopoly, and make money for investors. Independent research on student achievement showed poor comparative results for Edison, and over the course of about 10 years, almost 30 public school districts in 14 states canceled privatization contracts with Edison. In 2008, Philadelphia schools cancelled Edison's contract for lack of improvement.

Investors thought Edison would make them money because of "business-based" models. Edison stock traded for four years with only one profitable quarter and the share price fell from $40 to 14 cents per share. The Securities and Exchange Commission found Edison failed to disclose a problem with 40% ($150 million) of its finances. Edison went private in 2003, senior management was replaced, its name was changed to Edison Learning Corporation, and its focus changed from managing schools to "partnering" with schools for some services like tutoring and testing (Henriques and Steinberg, 2002b; Mathews, 2002; Quart, 2003; Moberg, 2004; Saltman, 2005, 2012; Parents Advocating School Accountability, 2009). The new company charges colleges a finder's fee to deliver students to them—a business with revenues around $100 million and seen as an investment for profit, not necessarily for education (Markman, 2019).

Levin (2006), an economist who directs the Center for the Study of Privatization in Education at Columbia University, summarizes research on private operation of public schools:

> Studies of EMOs [for-profit educational management organizations, like Edison Schools] have found greater administration costs than comparable public schools. EMO contracts have also been more costly than funding received by similar public school sites. Moreover, there is little evidence that EMO-run schools outperform public schools with similar students. (pp. 11, 12)

Outsourcing also has public and educational defects. Hoopes (2019) shows some unfortunate results from public school outsourcing of selected services when school districts "jettison" staff to avoid rising health and pension costs: "the real winner in the equation appears to not be students, teachers or parents, but private equity funds." Sometimes there are other motives at work; Rosales (2017) reports a school board member who emailed: "We must outsource busing and break this union at any cost." State data showed the union drivers were actually less costly, lived locally, had children in the schools, and voted. Strauss (2013) notes that public schools in middle-class or upper-class suburbs do not outsource food, transport, or educational services; that occurs almost entirely in poor and underserved communities.

Corporations, simply because they exist, are not better than public agencies in providing public benefits, but many are better at public relations. Enron, Bank of America, Lehman Brothers, Wells Fargo Bank, and subprime mortgage bundlers are good examples of private enterprise at work. Ethical considerations are not foremost. Privatizing public schools might handsomely reward a school CEO, some insiders, and private equity managers, but it can also penalize teachers, staff, students, parents, and others—then walk away from the schools with little responsibility.

Charter Schools and Privatization

Charter schools have public funding, but are operated independently, with less governmental oversight. They are a form of privatization of public assets. Uncritical reporting by mass media on charter schools describes them as innovations to improve education but hides their lack of academic performance and actual cost. A Stanford University (2009) research study found that while 17% of charters had student achievement scores better than comparable public schools, 40% of the charters showed no improvement, and 37% had significantly worse scores than traditional public schools. Teacher satisfaction also suffers; studies show that teachers in charter schools are 132% more likely to leave than are teachers in public schools (Stuit and Smith, 2009). Some charter schools, relieved from many state regulations, have serious problems in finances, student achievement, and operations. A Brookings Institution Brown Center (2002) report on American education, examining academic achievement in charter schools in 10 states from 1999 to 2001, concludes that "in a nutshell, charter schools performed about one-quarter standard deviation below comparable regular public schools on these three years of state tests" (p. 1). Shortsighted goals of higher test scores and saving money are insufficient reasons for privatizing, even if private schools could ensure these results. Of course, they can't. Short-term test score improvement has been shown to be the result of manipulation, not superior schooling.

Privatizing schools is not improvement or progress, just another avenue for private wealth to gain more control (Arsen and Ni, 2012; Giroux, 2012; Krugman, 2012; Saltman, 2012; Ward, 2012; Boninger et al., 2019). Further, some privatization through charter school programs has demonstrated corruption, theft, and poor management at levels that would not be tolerated if they were under the same requirements as regular public schools; a minimum of $216 million was reported lost through fraud, waste, abuse, and mismanagement (Center for Popular Democracy, 2016). Ravitch (2018) identified a litany of arguments against charter schools, including: they are more segregated than public schools; they drain public school money (the National Labor Relations Board ruled they are private corporations, not public schools); and one operator—Electronic Classroom of Tomorrow—collected $1 billion from taxpayers of Ohio then declared bankruptcy after 8 years and the lowest graduation rate (20%) in the United States. One of the largest private operators—K12—was established by Michael Milken, the junk bond king of recent times, and the antiunion Walton family is the largest supporter of charter schools. We Are Teachers (2017) finds other reasons teachers may not prefer charters: Teachers in charter schools work a longer school year, 210 days compared with 180 days at public schools, and charters often have lower salaries. Charter teachers work longer days, as much as 12 hours compared with 8 to 9 for public. Most charters are nonunion; teachers can't bargain for better salaries or conditions. Extracurricular activity work at charters is usually without extra pay. Charters are not required to employ state certified teachers or be accredited by state agencies.

Privatization is not the only business-oriented issue for schools. Commercialization continues to overtake public education.

Kids as Commodities, Schools as Agents

The commercialization of education is one of the most unfortunate developments in modern society. Schools and corporations may share some general social interests, but they have incompatible goals. The major purpose of corporations is to make profits for shareholders and executives; corporations are not concerned with social well-being unless that stance happens to suit their profit-seeking purpose. The major purpose for schooling, however, *is* social well-being; schools are social institutions intended to transmit and expand knowledge and to develop critical thinking.

Corporate strategy in regard to schools is to see students as commodities and schools as advertising agents. The pattern of this work is to offer inducements to have schools become partners in endeavors that bear direct or subtle business imprints. These endeavors are not always as obvious as teaching materials and school television programs that display company logos or school stadiums named after corporate sponsors (Lewin, 2006; Weissman, 2007). Some sponsored resources involve "free enterprise" educational programs or corporate speakers on environmental or governmental policies. Others involve efforts to improve the basic work skills and work ethics of students—future employees. Seldom does corporate sponsorship come with no strings or only with a proviso that schools stimulate creative or critical thinking.

Companies are necessarily interested in self-preservation and expansion of market share. Corporation efforts in schools reflect their interest in the pursuit of commercial enterprise (Apple, 2004; Boninger and Molnar, 2007; Saltman, 2012). Schooling, however, is too important to leave to corporations. But, sadly, as David Korten (2001) states: "Corporations are now moving aggressively to colonize the second major institution of cultural reproduction, the schools" (p. 157).

Among the most educationally dysfunctional results of commercialization is the negative impact on critical thinking. According to the annual report *Schoolhouse Commercialization Trends*, "Advertising first creates or amplifies adolescents' insecurities, and, then, literally sells them a 'solution' in the form of a product that cannot solve the problem it created" (Molnar et al., 2011, p. 2). Another annual report documents the kinds of harms brought to schools when commercialization takes place, including the following areas (Boninger et al., 2017):

1. Appropriating public school space, as in putting a company name on a school library, buses, or stadium.

2. Exclusive agreements, as in only having Coke products available or only Russell Athletic gear for teams.

3. Sponsored programs, activities, or teaching materials, as in a Hot Wheels sponsorship to teach a STEM class using that product.

4. Fundraising, as in McTeacher Nights when McDonald's contributes a small amount of profit to schools when teachers promote it.

5. Digital marketing, as in "personalized learning" requiring certain computer skills and sponsored programs, and the collection of personalized data on students.

Some commercializing contains explicit contradictions between what is taught in schools and what is advertised there: eat healthy foods, but the school only offers unhealthy foods in vending machines. Education is compromised by commercial activities when classes are suspended for assemblies sponsored by a corporation. Critical thinking is suppressed when students are asked to accept claims of commercial sponsors without criticism or challenge.

Extensive Evidence of Commercialization

Commercial Alert, sponsored by Public Citizen, organized to stop commercialization of public space, including the exploitation of "captive audiences of school children for commercial gain." The Campaign for a Commercial-Free Childhood also shares this interest. And the Commercialism in Education Research Unit of the National Education Policy Center conducts studies on these activities. These efforts deserve more public and school district attention.

A Government Accountability Office report found some 200 schools had exclusionary contracts with soda bottling companies, providing funds for schools in return for restricting sales of on-campus soda to one corporation (Hays, 2000; Fege, 2008). One school in Georgia actually suspended a student who wore a T-shirt with a Pepsi logo on the school's "Coke Day" (Hertz, 2001). Another place for corporate intrusion on schools when school funding is desired is in selling the right to name schools and school facilities. "Naming" of school facilities and events for corporate dollars now includes more than a building. There is advertising on school buses and school rooftops, sponsorship of school proms, and corporate names on principals' offices, science labs, libraries, cafeterias, and parts of athletic fields (Lewin, 2006; Flowers, 2008; Quinlan, 2016) (edufundingpartners.com).

Corporate-sponsored teaching material is another area where schools are seen as agents of one view. Some teaching materials provided by oil and coal companies suggest that they are environmentally friendly (Korten, 2001; Hightower, 2011; Boninger et al., 2017). Corporate sponsorship means that students are offered material that intends to stimulate purchases of certain products and also supports corporate views of environmental, social, economic, and governmental actions. The corporate message and orientation come across even when the material does not overtly pressure for consumer purchases. These materials treat students as:

1. Consumers who need to buy some product, service, or viewpoint.

2. Potential workers required to be punctual, to have good "work habits," to show deference to management, and to refrain from critical thought.

3. Citizens whose opinions and future votes should be probusiness.

Corporate materials for classroom use are expanding throughout all aspects of schools (Hertz, 2001; Korten, 2001; Hartman, 2002; Court, 2003; Fege, 2008; Commercial Alert, 2011; Ball, 2012; Boninger et al., 2017).

Field trips are an example of this creeping commercialization. Field trips to museums, art galleries, botanical gardens, and fire stations are intended for cultural and civic educational purposes, and to broaden horizons. Now commercialized trips go to stores like Petco, A&P or Albertsons supermarkets, and automobile agencies. San Diego schools schedule over 75 such commercial field trips during the school year (Parmet, 2005). Field Trip Factory organizes and offers such trips to schools (Cullen, 2004). They provide "permission slips" and claim to help "meet national learning standards" (fieldtripfactory.com).

Even report cards get a commercial spin. One district sent out report cards in envelopes printed by McDonald's that recommend a "Happy Meal" to reward good grades (Deardorff, 2007). Weissman (2007) says, "Marketers can't seem to stop thinking about the spectacular marketing opportunity afforded by schools" (p. 1).

The digital age brought computer forms of "personalized learning" to schools, along with commercial interest. "Personalizing" is an older concept, using workbooks, programmed texts, and online courses, but it is expanding under an umbrella of large-scale funding from foundations and high-tech corporate support. It threatens to "disable teachers," "outsource education to programmers," forfeit student privacy, and socialize students to uncritically accept commercial views (Boninger et al., 2019).

School Reform and Business Interests

Reform movements in education often target lower-income groups on the pretext of making them "fit for work and for citizenship." Schools tell students to be obedient, punctual, frugal, neat, respectful, patriotic, and content with their lot in life. The work ethic, drawing from Puritan views, is of great value to industrialists who desire uncomplaining and diligent workers. This ethic has become the school ethic in many locations. An opposing view is that of social responsibility: human rights, dignity, and democratic citizenship are more important than profit. Education for democratic participation, in the pursuit of justice and equality, is in the rhetoric of school literature but may not be acted on in all schools—because that would be bad for business.

This disparity in school purposes—preparing students to be obedient workers versus participating as thinking, equal citizens—is an historic issue in school reform. Upton Sinclair's (1922) *The Goose-Step* detailed industrialists determining college educational policies and selecting professors at important U.S. institutions. Sinclair (1924) then studied public schools, publishing *The Goslings*, showing heavy-handed school control by business leaders: "The purpose of this book is to show you how the 'invisible government' of Big Business which controls the rest of America has taken over the charge of your children" (p. ix).

Callahan's (1962) significant history of early twentieth century education found: "the most powerful force was industrialism . . . business ideology was spread continuously into the bloodstream of American life. . . . It was . . . quite natural for Americans, when reforming the schools, to apply business methods" (pp. 1, 5). Finkelstein's (1984) study also shows: "contemporary reformers evoke historic specters of public schools as crucibles in which to forge uniform Americans and disciplined industrial laborers" (pp. 276–277). Things may have gotten much worse since Sinclair, Callahan, and Finkelstein wrote about schools and business. Their conclusions coincide with evidence today (Court, 2003; Berger, 2004; Saltman, 2005, 2012; Commercial Alert, 2011; Mayer, 2016; Boninger et al., 2019).

The business influence is costly for education and society because it substitutes efficiency for effectiveness and limits students and teachers. Cost control can mean the sacrifice of high-quality schooling for all. Schools are influenced by a corporate value system with its factory mentality: students treated as objects on school assembly lines; conformity and standardization through excessive testing; teachers treated as

laborers with poor pay and bad treatment; hierarchical structure of school organization; and penny-pinching financing.

Corporate Language and Human Capital

This hidden curriculum of business has been successful. We are more concerned
with efficiency than effectiveness, with capital than with minds, with investment than
with progress, with accountability than with intellect, and with management than
with creativity. The human capital concept is a good example of this extension of
business orientation into education and society. The human capital view of the world
sees people as equivalent to property that can be exploited for commercial benefit or
profit. One consequence of this business school approach to education is that individuals begin to think of themselves as "maximizers of their own expected utility"
(Shiller, 2005). This leads to complete selfishness, with people engaged in calculations
of ways to turn all situations to their advantage, and little concern for others.

This human capital orientation can lead to a decline in civic involvement and
shared concern. Court (2003) describes it: "The individual's growing commercial relationship with the corporation has coincided with the individual's shrinking social relationship to the civic community and to other individuals" (p. 113). Another
consequence is the differentiation between management and worker. Management
decides the skills and attitudes and provides them to workers. Education, then, is actually training. Students are commodities and the school is a processing plant. Schools
weed out those who don't "fit," who cause trouble, who challenge authority, who
make critical evaluations, and who are not business oriented. Employees who are considered "creative" or "independent" are given low ratings (Henwood, 2003).

Students are not commodities or uncritical consumers, and schools should not be
business agents. Corporate altruistic rhetoric about supporting schools is clouded by
their self-interest in profit. Corporations would like taxpayers to pay for the education
they want their employees to have. Businesses will serve their own interests if they can
gain control of the schools, but schools exist for society's benefit. Privatization's myths
need exposure.

Exposing the Myths of Privatization

Myths about privatization include the ideas that privatization is:
- Efficient, so it can save tax money while providing quality services.
- Market driven, so it is responsive to the consumer.
- Performance based, rewarding the productive and cutting out the incompetent.

MYTH: EFFICIENCY

Efficiency is a means, not a goal; the mere act of being efficient is inadequate as a
rationale for social policy. Profit motives define efficiency as a cost-saving way to

increase corporate income. "Efficient" manufacturing creates toxic waste, workplace accidents, worker health problems, overproduction, and waste. Social costs are seldom calculated and the public often subsidizes the private sector through corporation-friendly tax and resource policies. Large homes, expensive cars, servants, yachts, exclusive clubs, private planes, and legal and financial assistance typify those who gain the most from "efficient" private enterprise. These are not expectations from public school educators. Effectiveness is more important than efficiency.

Myth: Market Driven and Consumer Responsive

The current economy does not provide a free and open market. Giant corporations, monopolistic trusts, special interest legislation, weak regulatory agencies, and business-protective practices skew the market to control prices and services. Lobbying, graft, buyouts, control of regulating authorities, and an "old boys' network" combine to deny newcomers equal marketplace opportunity and consumer protection. Even bankruptcy law has shifted to favor businesses over individuals. Consumer responsiveness is another myth. Marketing is a high priority in business to increase profits, not to satisfy customers.

Myth: The Performance-Based Corporation, Rewarding Merit, and Cutting Incompetence

Another myth about private enterprise is that it is rigorous about performance, expecting increased productivity and eliminating incompetence. But performance, in business terms, is merely selling more products at less cost with more profit. This goal has little to do with quality. CEOs whose corporations underperform may still receive large salary increases. Incompetence at high levels is permitted or causes an exit with a golden parachute.

Education Is for Civilizing, Not Privatizing

Critical examination of business values and practices, in terms of social justice and human ethics, is important. The current situation, in which business controls schools, needs to be inverted to one where education influences business values and practices, encouraging responsibility and enlightenment. This is education in its proper role, improving society by examining various social institutions, including business. That would improve education and business. Private enterprise has virtues and advocates, but it can cause severe economic and social disparity among people and it carries a history of exploitation. Similarly, public enterprise offers virtues and has supporters but creates tax burdens and opens itself to bureaucratic bungling. Each sector serves different needs of individuals and society at large. Increasing the proportion controlled by the private sector comes at a cost to the public.

Schools often teach what business wants them to teach. We need to return to the civilizing purposes of schooling—justice and ethics. The school should be the place where commercialization and corporatization are critically examined, not merely imposed. Bakan (2011) states that "our current failure to provide stronger protection of children in the face of corporate-caused harm reveals a sickness in our societal soul." Children's welfare, especially in schools, is undermined by corporate interests.

Business has a grasping and greedy history, whereas education serves higher purposes. Among the schools' most positive goals is to enable students to improve society by knowledge, increasing justice, and expanding social ethics to incorporate a stronger concern for others. This ensures the future of American democracy. It is a significant challenge for schools; privatization and commercialization do not serve those ends. For a democracy, the cost of privatizing public education is too high.

FOR DISCUSSION

1. Table 4.1 shows categories and examples of government services that are candidates for privatization.

Table 4.1   Government Services and Privatization

Category of Service	Example Activities for Privatization
Defense	Military support, training
Health	Public hospitals, FDA operations
Transportation	Airports, Amtrak, urban mass transit
Recreation	Parks service, public land development
Justice	Crime control, prisons
Communication	Public radio, monitoring airwaves
Taxes	Collection enforcement, Internal Revenue Service audits

   a. What are the advantages and disadvantages of privatization in regard to each of the examples?

   b. What criteria should be used to determine the advantages and disadvantages?

   c. How do these criteria fit in a discussion of privatizing schools?

   d. Who should be empowered to make the decisions about privatization?

2. *Dialogue Ideas:* Even if we find that it costs more to educate children under private operations, this clearly would show the public the need to better finance schools. Either way, it benefits education. What are the implications of this position?

3. In your local schools, ask to examine teaching materials. Look for educational value and business bias. Check the use of television, computers, schoolbook covers, and other media or materials along the same lines. Inquire about sponsorship of school activities, publications, and extracurricular events. Ask about private contracting of school services: the costs and the value. Prepare an analysis of the positive and negative effects of privatization and commercialization at the local level on schools.

4. Bill Gates delivered the keynote address at the National Summit on High Schools. The conference was sponsored by Achieve, Inc., an organization created by state governors and business leaders to improve school standards and achievement so that graduates are prepared for "college, careers, and citizenship" (achieve.org).

Gates suggested that American public schools are obsolete and that America is falling behind in developing "knowledge workers."

Philip Kovacs (2005) argues that the underlying reason for Gates's view is corporatization. He comments that "raising standards" is tied to corporate interests in obedient workers, that information technology outsources for cheaper labor no matter the quality of American schools, and that active citizenship may conflict with corporate interests because citizens may question why corporations have so much influence.

    a. Select one of these positions or propose a different position on this topic and present an argument to support it. Provide school examples to illustrate the position you select. Discuss the results in class.

    b. How would you define "knowledge workers"? Does teaching fit? Does librarianship? Does automobile repair? Does orthopedic surgeon? What criteria are useful in making this definition? Is this corporatization of schools?

5. Do you recall examples of commercialization at schools you attended? Were they generally positive, or supportive of the school's mission? Or were they generally negative, distracting from the school's mission?

6. What school policies would you recommend for use in considering proposals from businesses for sponsorship, partnerships, or other activities in schools?

REFERENCES

Aaron, H., Lindsay, J., and Nivola, P., eds. (2003). *Agenda for the Nation.* Washington, DC: Brookings Institution Press.

American Federation of Teachers (2003). *AFT Report on Edison Schools Finds Achievement Worse Than Edison Claims.* Washington, DC: American Federation of Teachers.

Apple, M. (2004). *Ideology and Curriculum* (3rd ed.). New York: Routledge.

Arsen, D., and Ni, Y. (2012, March). *Is Administration Leaner in Charter Schools?* National Center for the Study of Privatization in Education, Columbia University.

Bakan, J. (2011, August 22). "The Kids Are Not All Right." *New York Times*, A19.

Baker, D., and Buffie, N. (2017, February 22). The Decline of Blue Collar Jobs. Center for Economic and Policy Research.

Ball, S. J. (2012). *Global Education Inc.* New York: Routledge.

Berger, A. A. (2004). *Ads, Fads, and Consumer Culture* (2nd ed.). Lanham, MD: Rowman & Littlefield.

Bladgett, K. (2016, Fall/Winter). "School-Business Partnerships." *School Community Journal* 26(2).

Boninger, F., and Molnar, A. (2007). *Adrift: Tenth Annual Report on Schoolhouse Commercialism Trends.* Boulder, CO: National Education Policy Center, University of Colorado.

Boninger, F., Molnar, A., and Murray, K. (2017, August 15). *Asleep at the Switch: Schoolhouse Commercialism, Student Privacy, and the Failure of Policymaking.* Boulder, CO: National Education Policy Center, University of Colorado.

Boninger, F., Molnar, A., and Saldana, C. (2019). *Personalized Learning and the Digital Privatization of Curriculum and Teaching.* Boulder, CO: National Education Policy Center, University of Colorado.

Bracey, G. (2001). *The War against America's Public Schools: Privatizing Schools, Commercializing Education.* Boston: Allyn and Bacon.

———— (2002). "The 12th Bracey Report on the Condition of Public Education." *Kappan* 84(2):135–150.

———— (2008, January 30). "Who's Out to Get Public Education?" *Huffington Post.*

Brown Center (2002). *Annual Report on Education in the United States Charter Schools.* Washington, DC: Brookings Institution.

Business Roundtable (2008, February). Prospering Together (businessroundtable.org).

———— (2010, December 8). Road Map for Growth (businessroundtable.com).

———— (2019, February 5). Open Letter to President Trump and Members of the 116th Congress (businessroundtable.org).

Callahan, R. (1962). *Education and the Cult of Efficiency.* Chicago: University of Chicago Press.

Cameron, L. (2017). *The Privatization of Peacekeeping.* Cambridge, UK: Cambridge University Press.

Caplan, B. (2018). *The Case Against Education: Why the Education System is a Waste of Time and Money.* Princeton: Princeton University Press.

Carroll, C. (2019, January 20). "Los Angeles Teachers Strike for an End to Privatization." *Socialist Alternative.*

Center for Popular Democracy (2016, April 31). Charter School Vulnerabilities to Waste, Fraud and Abuse (populardemocracy.org).

Cohen, D. (2016). The History of Privatization. TPM Features (talkingpointsmemo.com).

Commercial Alert (2011). Home page (commercialalert.org).

Court, J. (2003). *Corporateering.* New York: Putnam.

Cullen, L. T. (2004, June 28). "Brand Name Field Trips." *Time.*

Daniels Fund (2008). School Business Partnerships (danielsfund.org).

Dayton, J., and Glickman, C. D. (1994). "American Constitutional Democracy." *Peabody Journal of Education* 69:62–80.

Deardorff, J. (2007, December 16). "Fast Food Gets Its Greasy Hands on Report Cards." *Chicago Tribune.*

Desperio, G. (2018, November 12). What Are Some of the Arguments in Favor of Privatizing Public Goods? (investopedia.com).

Dewey, J. (1916). *Democracy and Education.* New York: Macmillan.

Dickinson, L. A. (2018). In Defense of Accountability as a Lens to Perceive Privatization's Problems. In J. Knight and M. Schwartzberg, eds., *Privatization.* New York: New York University Press.

Dunkelberg, W. (2018, June 6). "Economic Freedom is Essential to Democracy." *Forbes.*

Education World (2020, April 8). School-Business Partnerships That Work (educationworld.com).

Eisen, L-B. (2018). *Inside Private Prisons.* New York: Columbia University Press.

Fege, A. (2008, June). Commercialization of Schools. Campaign for a Commercial-Free Childhood (commercialfreechildhood.org).

Finkelstein, B. (1984). "Education and the Retreat from Democracy in the United States, 1979–1980." *Teachers College Record* 86:276–282.

Flanagan, J. (2019). Coercion and Privatization. In J. Knight and M. Schwartzberg, eds., *Privatization.* New York: New York University Press.

Flowers, L. F. (2008, January 26). "Naming Rights May Provide Districts with Funding." *Morning News* (Northwestern Arkansas).

Freeman, J., and Minow, M., eds. (2009). *Government by Contract.* Cambridge, MA: Harvard University Press.

Friedman, M. (1955). The Role of Government in Education. In R. A. Solo, ed., *Economics and the Public Interest.* New Brunswick, NJ: Rutgers University Press.

———— (1980). *Free to Choose.* New York: Harcourt.

Galles, G. M. (2019, January 19). Vices Are Not Crimes. Foundation for Economic Education (fee.org).

Gilroy, L. (2012, April 3). Teachable Moment: Yonkers Evaluating Private Finance for $1.7 Billion K–12 School Modernization Program. Reason Foundation (reason.org).

Giroux, H. A. (2012). *Education and the Crisis of Public Values.* New York: Peter Lang.

Gottlieb, H. (2016). *The Dream of Reason*. New York: W. W. Norton.

Gutmann, A. (1999). *Democratic Education* (2nd ed.). Princeton, NJ: Princeton University Press.

——— (2008). Educating for Individual Freedom and Democratic Citizenship. In H. Siegel (ed.), *Oxford Handbook of Philosophy of Education*. Oxford: Oxford University Press.

Hagedon, A. (2014). *The Invisible Soldiers*. New York: Simon and Schuster.

Hann, L. W. (2008, April). Profit and Loss in School Business Partnerships (districtadministration.com).

Harel, A. (2018). Why Privatization Matters: The Democratic Case against Privatization. In J. Knight and M. Schwartzberg, eds., *Privatization*. New York: New York University Press.

Hartman, T. (2002). *Unequal Protection: The Rise of Corporate Dominance and the Theft of Human Rights*. New York: Rodale Press.

Hays, C. (2000, September 14). "Commercialism in U.S. Schools Is Examined in New Report." *New York Times*.

Heimer, M. (2018, June 22). "Here's How Some of America's Biggest Companies Plan to Shake Up Worker Training." *Fortune*.

Henriques, D. B., and Steinberg, J. (2002a, May 15). "Operator of Public Schools in Settlement with SEC." *New York Times*.

——— (2002b, May 14). "Woes for Company Running Schools." *New York Times*.

Hentschke, G., Oschman, S., and Snell, L. (2004). "The Rise of Education Management Organizations." *Privatization Watch* 28(7):13.

Henwood, D. (2003). *After the New Economy*. New York: New Press.

Hertz, N. (2001). *The Silent Takeover: Global Capitalism and the Death of Democracy*. New York: Free Press.

Hightower, J. (2011, June 16). Big Coal Buys Access to 4th Graders. Hightower Report (jimhightower.com).

Hodge, G. A. (2018). *Privatization: An International Review of Performance*. New York: Routledge.

Holloway, J. H. (2002). "Research Link: For Profit Schools." *Education Leadership* 59(7):84–85.

Hoopes, Z. (2019, March 17). "Outsourced." *The Sentinel*.

Isaak, R. (2005). *The Globalization Gap*. New York: Prentice Hall.

K12, Inc. (2012, April). K–12 Produces Results (k12.com).

Kadlec, A. (2007). *Dewey's Critical Pragmatism*. Lanham, MD: Rowman & Littlefield.

Kaplan, G. (1996). "Profits R Us." *Kappan* 78:K1–K12.

Knight, J., and Schwartzberg, M., eds. (2019). *Privatization*. New York: New York University Press.

Koebler, J. (2011, June 1). "Major Corporations Promote STEM Education." *U.S. News and World Report*.

Korten, D. C. (2001). *When Corporations Rule the World*. San Francisco: Berrett-Koehler.

Kovacs, P. (2005). Bill Gates and the Corporatization of American "Public" Schools. Common Dreams (commondreams.org).

Krugman, P. (2002, November 19). "Victors and Spoils." *New York Times*.

——— (2011, July 25). "Messing with Medicare." *New York Times*, A21.

——— (2012, March 25). "Lobbyists, Guns and Money." *New York Times*.

Levin, H. (2006, January). Why Is Educational Entrepreneurship So Difficult? Unpublished paper. National Center for the Study of Privatization in Education, Teachers College, Columbia University.

Lewin, T. (2006, January 26). "In Public Schools, the Name Game as a Donor Lure." *New York Times*.

Lewis, M. (2019, August 18). What is Privatization of Public Services—Definition, Pros and Cons. Money Crashers (moneycrashers.com).

Libertarian Party (2020, February 6). Education (lp.org).

Lipana, J. (2011, June 12). Save Education, Privatize Government Schools. American Thinker (americanthinker.com).

Lubienski, C., and Lubienski, S. J. (2004). *Re-Examining a Primary Premise of Market Theory.* New York: National Center for the Study of Privatization in Education, Teachers College, Columbia University.

Mann, D. (1987). "Business Involvement and Public School Improvement, Part 2." *Kappan* 69:228–232.

Markman, J. D. (2019, December 31). "How to Play It." *Forbes.*

Mathews, J. (2002, May 31). "Putting For-Profit Company to the Test." *Washington Post.*

Mayer, J. (2016). *Dark Money.* New York: Doubleday.

McFadden, J. (2016, December 28). 7 Big Companies Giving Back to Schools in Big Ways. We Are Teachers (weareteachers.com).

Miron, G., and Applegate, B. (2000). *An Evaluation of Student Achievement in Edison Schools Opened in 1995 and 1996.* Kalamazoo: Evaluation Center, Western Michigan University.

Moberg, D. (2004). "How Edison Survived." *The Nation* 278(10).

Molnar, A. (2017, March 1). *Dismantling Public Education: Turning Ideology into Gold.* Boulder, CO: National Education Policy Center, University of Colorado.

Molnar, A., Boninger, F., and Fogarty, J. (2011, November). *The Educational Cost of Schoolhouse Commercialization: The Fourteenth Annual Report on Schoolhouse Commercialism Trends.* Boulder, CO: National Education Policy Center, University of Colorado.

Molnar, A., Miron, G., and Urschel, J. (2010). *Profiles of For Profit Education Management Organizations: 2009–2010.* Boulder, CO: National Education Policy Center, University of Colorado. www.nepc.colorado.edu.

Nealon, J. T. (2012). *Post-Postmodernism, or, The Cultural Logic of Just-in-Time Capitalism.* Stanford: Stanford University Press.

Oravitz, J. V. (1999). "Why Can't Schools Be Operated the Way Businesses Are?" *Education Digest* 64(6):15–17.

Parents Advocating School Accountability (2009, November). Canceled Contracts (pasaf.org).

Parmet, S. (2005, May 2). "Reading, Writing and Retail Tours." *San Diego Union-Tribune.*

Philanthropy News Digest (2011, July 19). "Corporations Pledge $118 Million to Improve Education."

Pizzuro, S. (2011, June 20). Plan to Privatize New Jersey's Schools Reveals a Flawed Outcome (newjerseynewsroom.com).

Quart, A. (2003). *Branded: The Buying and Selling of Teenagers.* New York: Basic Books.

Quinlan, C. (2016, October 3). Corporations are Taking Advantage of Our Underfunded Public Schools. ThinkProgress (thinkprogress.org).

Ratchford, W. (2005, September/October). "Going Public with Schools Privatization." *The Abell Report* 18(3).

Ravitch, D. (2010). *The Death and Life of the Great American Public Schools.* New York: Basic Books.

———— (2013). *Reign of Error: The Hoax of the Privatization Movement and the Danger to America's Public Schools.* New York: Knopf.

———— (2018, June 22). "Charter Schools Damage Public Education." *Washington Post*, opinion.

———— (2020). *Slaying Goliath.* New York: Alfred A Knopf.

Republican Views (2016, January 16). Libertarian Views on Education (republicanviews.org).

Requarth, T. (2019, May 13). "How Private Equity is Turning Pubic Prisons into Big Profits." *The Nation.*

Rethinking Schools (1998). The Market Is Not the Answer: An Interview with Jonathan Kozol (rethinkingschools.org).

Rooks, N. (2017). *Cutting School: Privatization, Segregation, and the End of Public Education.* New York: The New Press.

Rosales, J. (2017, September 19). "In Fight Against Outsourcing, Flipping a School Board Makes the Difference." *NEA Today.*

Saltman, K. J. (2000). *Collateral Damage: Corporatizing Public Schools—A Threat to Democracy.* Lanham, MD: Rowman & Littlefield.

——— (2005). *The Edison Schools: Corporate Schooling and the Assault on Public Education.* New York: Routledge.

——— (2012). *The Failure of Corporate School Reform.* Boulder, CO: Paradigm.

Schrag, P. (1999, January 8). "Private Affluence and Public Squalor." *San Diego Union-Tribune.*

Shiller, R. J. (2005, February 8). "How Wall Street Learns to Look the Other Way." *New York Times.*

Shuls, J. V. (2016, July 15). Outsourcing Public Education. Show-Me Institute (showmeinstitute.org).

Sinclair, U. (1922). *The Goose-Step.* Pasadena, CA: Sinclair.

——— (1924). *The Goslings.* Pasadena, CA: Sinclair.

Smith, G. (2011, May 8). "Privatization Effort for School Buses Cost State More, Study Says." *The State* (South Carolina).

Snell, L. (2005). "Unions Try to Discredit Education Outsourcing." *Privatization Watch* 29(1):12–13.

——— (2011). *Annual Privatization Report 2010: Education.* Los Angeles: Reason Foundation.

Soltow, L., and Stevens, E. (1981). *The Rise of Literacy and the Common School in the United States: A Socioeconomic Analysis to 1870.* Chicago: University of Chicago Press.

Stanford University (2009). *Research on Educational Outcomes.* Stanford, CA: Center for Research on Educational Outcomes.

Strauss, V. (2013, January 5). "The Dangers of 'Outsourcing' Public Education." *Washington Post.*

Stuit, D. A., and Smith, T. (2009). *Teacher Turnover in Charter Schools.* Nashville: National Center on School Choice, Vanderbilt University.

Sudetic, C. (2001). "Reading, Writing, and Revenue." *Mother Jones* 26(3):84–95.

Sumner, S. (2020, May 10). Big Government Is Not the Solution; It's the Problem. The Library of Economics and Liberty (econlib.org).

The Economist (2005). "The Missing Rungs in the Ladder." 376(8435):17.

The Sentencing Project (2018, July 17). Capitalizing on Mass Incarceration (sentencingproject.org).

Tyszko, J. A. (2019, July 11). Upskilling, the Future of Work, and the Coming Agile Workforce. U. S. Chamber of Commerce Foundation.

U.S. Bureau of Labor Statistics (2019, November). *Highlights of Women's Earnings in 2018* (Report 1083). Washington, DC: U.S. Bureau of Labor Statistics.

U.S. Census Bureau (2007). *Employment, Work Experience, and Earnings by Age and Education.* Table 1. Washington, DC: Government Printing Office.

——— (2011). *Statistical Abstract of the United States.* Table 702. Washington, DC: Government Printing Office.

Vittert, L. (2018, December 19). The Cold Hard Facts about America's Private Prison System. Fox News (foxnews.com).

Ward, S. C. (2012). *Neoliberalism and the Global Restructuring of Knowledge and Education.* New York: Routledge.

We Are Teachers (2017, October 25). Teaching in Charter School vs. Public School (weareteachers.com).

Wedel, J. R. (2009). *Shadow Elite.* New York: Basic Books.

Weissman, R. (2007, May 25). "Resisting the Commercialization of Public Schools." *CounterPunch.*

Weldon, T. (2011, July 5). "Creating Effective Business-Education Partnerships." *Council of State Governments Newsletter.*

Will, G. (2019). *The Conservative Sensibility.* New York: Hachette.

Zollers, N., and Ramanathan, A. (1998). "For-Profit Charter Schools and Students with Disabilities." *Kappan* 80(4):297–315.

Religion and Public Schools

Free Expression or Separation

How do schools balance freedom of religious expression and the separation of church and state?

5

Position 1:   Freedom of Religious Expression
                Must Be Protected in Public Schools

Congress shall make no law respecting an establishment of religion or prohibiting the free exercise thereof. . . .

—U.S. Constitution, First Amendment

Take out a dollar bill. Turn it over to the back. What do you see when you look beneath the heading "The United States of America"? Printed on the dollar, as on every other denomination of American paper currency, is the motto "In God We Trust." Will we soon have to add the phrase "Except in Public Schools"? Students, public school teachers, and administrators who attempt to discuss the God on whom Americans supposedly rely face disciplinary action and lawsuits. Court decisions and pressure from special interest groups have whittled away at religious freedom in schools. This situation can be remedied, and full freedom of religious expression can be restored to all citizens in America's public schools without violating the Constitution. Public schools can protect the basic human right of religious liberty and still maintain the separation of church and state.

The First Amendment

The First Amendment to the Constitution was carefully crafted by the founding fathers to protect what they considered "unalienable rights" of American citizens. They wanted to protect their countrymen's right to practice the religion of their choice without fear. Aware of British history, they knew that one of the greatest impediments to religious freedom was state support of one denomination. To these early Americans, breaking away from England meant, among other things, putting an end to religious conflicts. Therefore, they believed prohibiting governmental support for any individual faith was the best policy for their new republic (Meacham, 2007; Hall, 2019).

To protect religious freedom, the founders included two clauses in the First Amendment. The first, called the Establishment Clause, decrees that religions and the state should be kept separate so that no religion has more rights than any other. The second clause, the Free Exercise Clause, prevents the government from limiting Americans' expression of religious beliefs in ways that seem right to them. Reading these two clauses carefully is important in understanding that current attempts to banish religion from public schools violate the founders' intention.

The Establishment Clause says, "Congress shall make no law respecting *an* establishment of religion." Many people, when referring to the clause, quote it incorrectly as saying, "Congress shall make no law respecting *the* establishment of religion." The difference is crucial. The first—and accurate—reading clearly shows the intent was to prevent any one religious denomination from receiving governmental support or protection not available to all others. In fact, one of James Madison's original drafts of the religious section of the amendment said, "The civil rights of none shall be abridged on account of religious belief or worship, nor shall any national religion be established" (quoted in Robb, 1985, p. 7). His purposes were clear. Governmental support of any one religion or domination was prohibited because it would negatively affect individuals' freedom of religious expression. The fact that many states already had done exactly that added a sense of urgency to the task of the Constitutional Convention. Madison and others wanted to prevent a repeat of the religious wars in England that resulted from royal support of different Christian denominations (Meacham, 2007; Hall, 2019).

The founding fathers had no intention of barring all mention of God from American public life—almost all professed belief in God, although many did not identify themselves as members of any religious denomination. They routinely began assemblies with prayers for guidance and inspiration. They asked God's blessing on themselves and their countrymen in their foundational documents. Their language in such settings went beyond the traditional words used in different denominations. They spoke of a God who had created all and maintained the world, a God who was bigger than the claims of any individual group of believers (Meacham, 2007).

For most of American history, the Supreme Court did not interfere in state laws regarding religious practices in schools (Batte, 2008). Any act on the part of government supporting one religious denomination at the expense of others was considered unconstitutional. Any act of the government limiting an individual's right to free expression of his or her religious beliefs was equally illegitimate. Recently, however, the balance between the needs expressed in the two clauses has been reinterpreted.

The Supreme Court and Religion in Public Schools

Contemporary court decisions have emphasized the Establishment Clause to the detriment of the Free Exercise Clause. The trend began in a decision that, on the surface, appeared to support religious freedom. In 1947 in *Everson v. Board of Education*, the Supreme Court ruled that using state funds to reimburse parents for the cost of transporting children to religious schools did not violate the Establishment Clause. However, in writing the majority opinion, Judge Hugo Black interpreted that section of the First Amendment in a way that ignored its text. Black wrote that the Establishment Clause created "a complete separation between the state and religion" (*Everson v. Board of Education*, 1947). This interpretation was based on a letter Jefferson wrote 10 years after ratification of the First Amendment in which he made his famous "wall of separation" statement. It reads, in part,

> I contemplate with sovereign reverence that act of the whole American people which declared that their legislature should "make no law respecting an establishment of religion, or prohibiting the free exercise thereof," thus building a wall of separation between Church and State. (quoted in Koch and Peden, 1944, p. 307)

Those using this statement of Jefferson's to limit individual freedom of religious expression would do well to read the rest of the quote. He writes,

> Adhering to this expression of the supreme will of the nation in behalf of the *rights of conscience*, I shall see with sincere satisfaction the progress of those sentiments which tend to restore to man all his natural rights, convinced he has no natural right in opposition to his social duties. (quoted in Koch and Peden, 1944, p. 307)

Clearly, Jefferson's words about the strict separation between church and state were meant not to limit individual rights but rather to argue against the possibility that any one religious sect would become a "national religion" through government efforts. When understood in this light, Jefferson's "wall" should be seen as the protector of freedom of religious expression (Chadsey, 2007; Waldman, 2009). Instead, it has been used to remove religion from public schools in ways that neither he nor the other founders of this nation intended. Over 60 Supreme Court cases have followed, relying on the interpretation offered by Justice Black in *Everson*. One by one, they have created a legal legacy that violates the intentions of our founders.

In *McCollum v. Board of Education* (1948), the Supreme Court ruled sectarian religious leaders were constitutionally forbidden from conducting voluntary, optional religious instruction in school buildings. Some years later, the Court held in *Engel v. Vitale* (1962) and *Abington Township School District v. Schempp* (1963) that neither classroom prayer nor Bible readings were constitutional even when students had the option of being excused from participation. Building on the misinterpretation of the Establishment Clause as presented by Justice Black in *Engel*, the Court took the serious step of defining governmental acts to accommodate religious freedom that could be deemed constitutional. In doing so, however, the Court created such narrow parameters that, since *Lemon v. Kurtzman* (1971), almost no religious practices in school have been declared constitutional. The "Lemon test," as the policy has come to be known, consists of three standards that must be met if the action of a school district can be established as protecting religious freedom rather than endorsing religious practices. To be constitutional, a policy or activity supported by a school must (1) have a secular purpose, (2) not have the effect of advancing or inhibiting religion, and (3) avoid excessive entanglement between government and religion (*ACLU Legal Bulletin*,

1996). Applying the Lemon test in other cases has resulted in even more limitations on religious practices in schools.

For example, in *Stone v. Graham* (1980), the Court declared that a state law requiring public schools to post the Ten Commandments was unconstitutional. *Wallace v. Jaffree* (1985) struck down a state law requiring a moment of meditation or silent prayer. In *Lee v. Weisman* (1992), the Court ruled that, even when offered by a private individual with no formal connection to the school or government, prayer during a public school graduation ceremony is unconstitutional. Apparently, asking students to bow their heads, remain silent, and show respect during such a prayer violates the rights of students who do not believe in God. They are, according to the Court, compelled to participate, and in so insisting on their participation, the school is "conveying a message that religion or a particular religious belief is favored or preferred" over unbelief (*County of Allegheny v. American Civil Liberties Union, Greater Pittsburgh Chapter*, 1989).

Finally, in *Santa Fe Independent School District v. Jane Doe* (2000), the Court ruled that student-led prayer at football games was unconstitutional. Even though participation in such games is purely voluntary, the fact that the school district sponsors and pays for the games makes them governmental actions. So, prayers at the games also are government-supported activities that must pass the Lemon test. The Court says that they are not legal because there is no secular purpose for the prayers. They have the effect of advancing religion because they will be "perceived by adherents . . . as an endorsement, and by nonadherents as a disapproval, of their individual religious choices" (*School District of the City of Grand Rapids v. Ball*, 1985). In 2002, a federal court ruled that the phrase "under God" in the Pledge of Allegiance also fails the Lemon test (*Newdow v. U.S. Congress*, 2002).

Consequently, students are prevented from leading prayers at high school graduation ceremonies even when members of the senior class want to include such devotions. Student athletes are forbidden from praying at sporting events even in their own locker rooms. School board meetings cannot be opened with prayer or a moment of silent meditation. Teachers cannot discuss their own religious experiences with children, even if they believe that their religion commands them to do so. They cannot use such expressions as "God bless you" in communications with students or parents. Children cannot read Bible stories to classmates as part of oral communication lessons, nor can they express religious beliefs during a class presentation. In addition, they should not expect to see drawings they've made of religious figures or symbols hanging on the walls of their classrooms or schools. Bibles may not be distributed in public schools during regular operating hours. Teachers and students may not celebrate the religious aspects of such holidays as Thanksgiving, Christmas, or Easter (Pregent and Walker, 2018).

History of Religion in American Education

Banishing religion from all but the most innocuous aspects of U.S. public school life is truly ironic. The very first schools in the English colonies that would become the United States were instituted for religious reasons. The leaders of the Pilgrims, living in the Massachusetts Bay Colony, passed a law establishing schools that would teach children to read their Bibles. Their literacy would protect them from "that ould deluder, Satan."

In the early days of the Republic, American schools were, for the most part, privately funded, and religious practices considered an essential part of the curriculum. Early public schools taught religion from a perspective shared with others influenced by the Enlightenment. For them, a shared belief in God was necessary to create the moral discipline required for living in a democratic society (McConnell, 2000). The *McGuffey Readers*, the most popular textbooks for most of the nineteenth century, built on a presumption that Americans shared a belief in God in order to teach children what behaviors were expected of them. Concern for the needs and rights of others, honesty, and perseverance despite difficulties were presented as the responsibility of all God's children in America. "It was almost universally accepted that American democracy drew its strength from the general conviction that there was a divine power, the author of the rights of man defined in America's first political document" (McCluskey, 1967, p. 237). Children were taught that each citizen derived his or her rights from their Almighty Father and that no human being had the right to take away those rights. In that era, most Americans believed the majority could, on the basis of their religious beliefs, determine basic community norms, including the place of religion in the public school curriculum and activities (McCarthy, 1983, p. 7). "Nonsectarian did not mean nonreligious. . . . Nondenominational Christianity was assumed to be 'nonsectarian'" (McConnell, 2000, pp. 1,263–1,264). Protestant Christian beliefs and practices were incorporated into public schools. Teachers led children in daily prayer. The Bible, usually the King James Version, was read in schools. Religious holidays were celebrated (Goodman and Lesnick, 2001). State laws not only permitted such practices but also mandated them (McCarthy, 1983). So what happened?

The loss of balance between protecting both clauses of the First Amendment's statements on religion began in the first half of the nineteenth century. Immigrant children from Ireland, Germany, and, later, Italy and Eastern Europe swelled American public school enrollment, especially between 1840 and 1924. Most of these children were Catholics. Catholic religious leaders objected to what they saw as the Protestant character of religion being taught in public schools. They did not understand that the religious dimensions of public school life actually were designed to help their children become part of American life (Goodman and Lesnick, 2001; Fessenden, 2005). Their leaders protested strenuously and began a campaign to create schools that socialized children to their own religious beliefs (Sanders, 1977; Tozer et al., 2002). To many Protestant Americans, these early immigrants seemed to reject becoming part of the very country to which they had turned as a refuge from political and economic oppression (Fessenden, 2005).

Despite the conflict, several factors made compromise possible. Immigrants perceived that public education would contribute to their social mobility. Native-born citizens believed that schools would Americanize the newcomers. To achieve both ends, schools made reasonable accommodations. Some districts eliminated Bible readings altogether to end the Catholics' objections to using the Protestant version of the scriptures (Wright, 1999; Fessenden, 2005).

A kind of neutrality among religious denominations was maintained in public schools that preserved the freedom of students and teachers to exercise their religious freedom (Goodman and Lesnick, 2001). Prayers were offered in "theistic" rather than "Christian" language, and holidays from both traditions were celebrated. Catholics and Jews who could not make this accommodation sent their children to schools in which their own beliefs could be practiced more freely (Sanders, 1977; Zeldin, 1986). As some historians see it, by the end of the nineteenth century, sectarian religious practices had been eliminated from public schools. However, schools were still faithful to the project of assimilating children, especially immigrant children, into the American way of life, which included belief in God.

In the last half of the twentieth century, public schools were faced with new challenges to that Americanization obligation. Immigrant children from nonbiblical faith traditions began to appear in public schools. Among those who believe in God or seek divine assistance, compromises on language and practices have been achievable. For example, many schools have found ways to accommodate Muslim students' religious obligation to pray five times during the day or fast during Ramadan. In other instances, dress code regulations have been modified to allow students to dress according to the norms of their religious traditions (Chavez, 2017; Liberatore, 2017).

However, in the last 60 years, the delicate balance required to enforce both clauses of the First Amendment has been upset by the growth of a more secular belief system. The United States, like many other Western countries, saw an expansion of agnostic, atheistic, and antireligious philosophies. Those who shared these beliefs were concerned about what they perceived to be the vulnerability of children in schools. They worried that schools, by openly supporting free expression of religious beliefs—indeed by mandating them in some cases—were creating situations in which young people were being taught that religious beliefs were normative. They argued that such tacit approval of religious faith would pressure young people to profess such beliefs themselves without being given the opportunity to evaluate them.

Most Americans—approximately 80%—believe in God (Pew Research Center, 2018). Only a very small number of Americans totally reject the existence of a divine being. However, that very vocal and powerful minority brought many of the lawsuits that have had such negative effects on the free exercise of religion by students and teachers (*McCollum v. Board of Education*, 1948; *Zorach v. Clauson*, 1952; *Engel v. Vitale*, 1962; *Abington Township School District v. Schempp*, 1963; and *Murray v. Curlett*, 1963). These "nonbelievers" actually have a belief system that is derived from the secularization of liberal political thought. For secularists, investigation rather than religious teachings is the source of answers to important human questions (Council for Secular Humanism, 2011). Even the Supreme Court has affirmed that secular humanism is a religious belief and that the rights of those who share that belief to practice their religion are protected by the Free Exercise Clause of the First Amendment (*Torcaso v. Watkins*, 1961; *United States v. Seeger*, 1965).

Most Americans who believe in God have come to accept that sectarian religious education is no longer possible in American public schools. Nonbelievers, however, want to impose their ideology in schools in ways that closely resemble the sectarian projects of nineteenth-century school reformers. They argue their beliefs actually are neutral regarding religion. In many ways, however, they are hostile to it. They contend that any expression of belief in God is unconstitutional in public settings because, by being exposed to such activities, their children are coerced into accepting the beliefs from which they spring. In most cases, the Supreme Court has accepted their arguments. The result is that the most privileged belief system in public schools is secularism. The rulings against common prayer, moments of silence, and celebrations of religious holidays in schools give privilege to secular beliefs.

Of course, such a policy clearly is unconstitutional. Several Supreme Court justices have explained what neutrality with regard to religion in public schools really means. Writing in *Everson v. Board of Education* (1947), Hugo Black stated, "State power is no more to be used so as to handicap religions than it is to favor them." In *Abington Township School District v. Schempp* (1963), Tom Clark wrote, "The state may not establish a 'religion of secularism' in the sense of affirmatively opposing or showing hostility to religion, thus 'preferring those who believe in no religion over those who do believe'" (p. 225). In *Lynch v. Donnelly* (1984), Sandra Day O'Connor argued, "What is crucial is that the government practice not have the effect of communicating a message of endorsement or disapproval of religion" (p. 692). It would seem that these warnings were ignored. The public school environment has increasingly become hostile to believers, limiting their freedom of expression while allowing secularists and nonbelievers license to incorporate their beliefs into the curricula. In doing so, the role of religious belief in American culture has been overlooked (Gateways to Better Education, 2019).

Religion and American Culture

While U.S. laws have prevented the establishment of a state sect, religious belief has influenced its culture. From its beginnings, America has been a nation that integrated political and religious understandings of the value of human life and the nature of freedom. According to Supreme Court Justice Anton Scalia, the secular model of the relationship between church and state, requiring that religion be strictly excluded from the public forum, "is not, and never was, the model adopted by America" (*McCreary County v. ACLU*, 2005, p. 74).

As Scalia and others argue, religion has contributed and continues to contribute to the culture of the United States in positive ways. For example, a democracy requires moral citizens who are able to practice self-restraint, put the needs of others above their own interests, and sacrifice for the sake of the common good. Americans have seen religion as one of the most significant teachers of that kind of morality (*McCreary County v. ACLU*, 2005). In fact, our history—distant and recent—demonstrates that the government has affirmed society's belief in God to strengthen us in difficulty, to guide us in perplexity, to comfort us in sorrow, and to express gratitude for the benefits of our shared life. "Historical practices thus demonstrate that there is a distance between the acknowledgement of a single Creator and the establishment of religion" (*McCreary County v. ACLU*, 2005, p. 89). A small minority of believers in impersonal gods, polytheists, and atheists may feel excluded when God is called on in public settings. However, as long as they are not coerced into joining in the invocation, their rights to private belief are maintained (Ali and Lakhani, 2017).

In fact, "public expressions of religion even hold out the possibility of enabling religious minorities to participate fully in the American public sphere." If we allow the public acknowledgment and celebration of religious holidays, we enable Jewish, Hindu, Buddhist, and Muslim traditions to become part of a traditionally Christian culture. In doing so, we validate the "sense of belonging" in a greater number of citizens and may generate more national loyalty from them (Ali and Lakhani, 2017).

Curricular Consequences

Integrating religion in U.S. public life and culture is an admittedly difficult and delicate process. Chief Justice William Rehnquist has suggested that in doing so, the courts must be like Janus, the Roman god who was depicted with two faces looking in opposite directions. "One face looks toward the strong role played by religion and religious tradition throughout our Nation's history. . . . The other face looks toward the principle that governmental intervention in religious matters can itself endanger religious freedom" (*Van Orden v. Perry*, 2005, p. 11). Public schools no longer balance these two aspects of the First Amendment. The perspectives of religious believers have almost been eliminated from public school curricula. In general, fear of controversy has led textbook publishers to neglect the study of religious influences on thought or historical events.

In fact, antagonism to religious approaches exists in most subjects. One of the most serious examples of this conflict takes place daily in science classes when students study the origin of life. Any perspective that does not support the Darwinian theory of natural selection is at best ignored and at worst ridiculed. Evolution is presented as fact even though there is convincing evidence that randomness and material forces alone cannot explain the complexity of the world in which we live.

The theory of intelligent design is a scientific approach to the origins of life that presents such a challenge to the theory of evolution (Dembski and Wells, 2007; Gordon and Dembski, 2011). Opponents of intelligent design fail to distinguish intelligent design science from creationism—the belief that the universe was created in six days as described in the book of Genesis in the Hebrew Bible. However, intelligent design is rooted in the principles of science, not religion. For example, biochemist Michael Behe (2007) argues that natural selection cannot explain "irreducibly complex systems"— systems composed of a variety of parts that interact with one another to carry out the system's task. In systems like the flagella of bacteria, the flow of proteins in cells, and the mechanisms that cause blood to clot, the removal of any one part causes the whole to stop working. The theory of evolution argues that these systems were produced by a series of small changes to prior systems, taking place in succession. However, that is impossible because if an irreducibly complex system were missing any one of its parts, it would simply not work. There would be no system from which the new one could evolve. Similarly, no known scientific "law" can explain the specific sequence of the four nucleotide bases found in DNA. William Dembski has established a reliable scientific method for identifying designed objects or systems from those that result from chance or the laws of nature (Dembski and Wells, 2007). Even theorists who accept evolution have acknowledged that many organisms seem to be the result of an intelligence beyond the organism itself—an intelligence with a purpose. Some of the most honest among them questioned their own theories (Buell, 2007; Gray et al., 2010). However, the law prevents teachers from presenting students with opportunities to hear about this alternative to the theory of evolution (*McLean v. Arkansas Board of Education*, 1982; *Edwards v. Aguillard*, 1987; *Webster v. New Lenox School District*, 1990; *LeVake v. Independent School District 656 et al.*, 2000; *Kitzmiller v. Dover*, 2008).

Some school districts have been blocked by federal courts from alerting students to the theoretical nature of evolution. Cobb County, Georgia, was prevented from placing stickers on science books advising students that material about evolution should be studied and considered critically (Selman Injunction, 2005). Although the Cobb County plan represented a good-faith effort to provide quality education without violating the Constitution, those who objected and won in court prevented a compromise that accommodated both believers and nonbelievers. They imposed a solution that favored nonbelief. In fact, Louisiana and Tennessee are the only states to pass laws that allow school districts to help students think critically about evolution by using supplemental materials to do so, and its efforts are under constant attack by secular humanists (Khazan, 2019; Masci, 2019).

Health classes are also sites where governmental neutrality toward belief and nonbelief has not been maintained. Students, regardless of their religious beliefs, are compelled to hear presentations about abortion, premarital sex, homosexuality, and masturbation. Despite research showing the efficacy of abstinence only sex education programs, they are being tossed aside in favor of ones that are silent on the rich Western tradition of philosophical and religious thinking about moral issues (Jemmott et al., 2010; Santos and Phillips, 2011). Only about one-third of federal funding for teen sex education is for abstinence only programs (Kaiser Family Foundation, 2018).

The First Amendment religious clauses clearly establish two duties for government regarding freedom of religion. Government must not favor one religion over others and must not prevent citizens from expressing their religious beliefs. The founders assumed that religion would have a vital place in the private and public lives of Americans. When courts ignored that fundamental reality and the historic role of religion by requiring governmental neutrality between belief and nonbelief, they created an unsolvable problem. In protecting a minority of students from hearing religious speech that is "offensive" to them, they have provided inadequately for the rights of students who are religious.

> In a country of many diverse traditions and perspectives—some religious, some secular—neutrality cannot be achieved by assuming that one set of beliefs is publicly more acceptable than another . . . religious citizens and religious ideas can contribute to the commonwealth along with everyone and everything else. (McConnell, 2000, p. 1,264)

Certain practices, such as prayer in public gatherings or reference to God in discussions of moral issues, are part of a long-standing American tradition and have enjoyed historical acceptance. If administrators, teachers, and students ensure that no one is coerced to participate in such activities or accept the beliefs on which they are based, the First Amendment can be protected in public schools to a greater degree than it currently is.

Position 2:   The Separation of Church and State
               Must Be Maintained in Public Schools

The Civil Rights of none shall be abridged on account of religious belief or worship,
nor shall any national religion be established, nor shall the full and equal rights of
conscience be in any manner, or on any pretence, infringed.

> —James Madison (original wording of the First Amendment;
> Annals of Congress 434, June 8, 1789)

To hear members of the religious right complain, you'd think that all religious
expression had been totally banned in American public schools. Actually, teachers
and students enjoy a great deal of freedom to engage in religious speech and practices.
The U.S. Department of Education's (2020) Guidance on Constitutionally Protected
Prayer and Religious Expression in Public Elementary and Secondary Schools
reminded school officials that "the First Amendment requires public school officials
to show neither favoritism toward nor hostility against religious expression, such as
prayer" (p. 3,263). Some teachers' and administrators' actions are prohibited in
school: leading classes in prayer, reading devotionally from the Bible, persuading or
compelling students to participate in prayer or other religious activities, and including
prayer at school-sponsored events. However, the document also contains an impressive list of students' rights, including reading scriptures, saying grace before meals,
and discussing religious views in informal settings such as cafeterias and hallways.
Students may also speak to and try to persuade other students about religious topics,
participate in prayerful gatherings before and after school, and express their religious
beliefs in homework, artwork, and other written and oral assignments—as long as
their beliefs cannot be attributed to the school. Their prayer groups or religious clubs
must be given the same right to use school facilities as is extended to other extracurricular groups. They can be dismissed for off-premise religious instruction and excused
briefly from class to enable them to fulfill religious obligations such as prayer. A
school can limit these expressions of free speech only to the same degree it limits other
comparable words or activities. So, for example, students have the right to distribute
religious literature, hold prayer gatherings on school grounds, and discuss their religious beliefs to the same extent that they could engage in similar activities on comparable topics—such as politics or social issues. School districts across the country have
created policies to ensure that students can meet their personal religious obligations
(Pregent and Walker, 2018; Russo, 2018). Four in ten American public high school
students say that they see other students praying before school sporting events; half
see other young people wearing religious clothing or jewelry; and a quarter see their
peers inviting one another to religious youth groups or religious services (Pew
Research Center, 2019).

Sounds good, doesn't it? It appears that students who want to engage in religious
activities or speak about their faith have lots of freedom to do so. It sounds fair and

reasonable—an all-American compromise that respects every student's right to religious liberty. So what's the problem?

Some believers want to break down the separation between church and state. They think that schools ought to sponsor religious activities and coerce students to attend those events. For example, they believe that school officials should be able to organize or mandate prayer at graduation ceremonies or, alternatively, to organize religious "baccalaureate" ceremonies for graduates, their friends, and their families. They believe that it should be acceptable for teachers or principals to encourage students to participate in prayer gatherings before or after school, want teachers to be able to speak openly about their own religious beliefs in classroom settings, and advocate celebrating religious aspects of holidays in school. Their demands violate the First Amendment's prohibition against support of religion by the government.

Establishing Religion in Public Schools

Supporters who argue for greater freedom of religious expression in schools argue that they want the same protection for believers as for nonbelievers. There is evidence, however, that their real intent is to reestablish Christianity as a state-sponsored religion. Members of the religious right often suggest that public schools promote amoral values, are antireligious, and threaten the health and well-being of Christian children and youth. Some leaders have gone so far as to suggest that parents remove their children from public schools, establish Christian alternatives, or home school (Hasson and Farnan, 2018; Ruse, 2019). Others see public schools as "gardens to cultivate" in the effort to promote their religious beliefs. For example, members of the group Gateways to Better Education "envision public schools as learning communities enriched by the appropriate and lawful expression of Christian values and ideas, and educators teaching about the contribution Christians and Christianity have made and continue to make to America and the world." The group calls on educators to become "Campus Partners" in the effort, provides curricular resources for teachers, and offers materials to begin a local campaign to restore celebrations of religious holidays to schools (Gateways to Better Education, 2019).

"Good News Clubs," organized by the Child Evangelism Foundation, are tools that believers hope to use to create these witnesses. At the club meetings, children sing hymns, memorize scripture verses, and act out Bible stories. Since 2001, with the blessings of the Supreme Court, they have been able to meet in public schools after classes (*Good News Club v. Milford Central School*, 2001). Leaders have also demanded that administrators allow them to use official school communications to advertise their meetings, and, in cases where secular groups have been allowed to advertise sports clubs or child care centers, the courts have ruled that the religious groups be given the same access to "customers." Other evangelical organizations have come to public schools to offer what they bill as motivational speakers, sometimes intentionally omitting the religious content of their presentations until they arrive at schools. In other cases, they have promoted events during school sponsored presentations at schools without making the religious nature of the events clear to parents (Mildrum, 2018).

Another result of the *Good News Club* decision is that many schools have opened their buildings to churches that are looking for rent-free worship spaces. Since most schools are busy with activities, including sports, except for Sunday, Christian groups are most often the beneficiaries of this policy. For example, over 60 public schools in New York City provide rent-free homes for mostly evangelical Christian congregations (Stewart, 2011). Fortunately, in an appeal of this policy, the federal Second Circuit Court ruled that the *Good News Club* decision did not require the city to continue to do so. The decision affirmed that the Department of Education had a strong basis to believe "that allowing the religious services to be conducted in schools could be seen as the kind of endorsement of religion that violated the First Amendment's establishment clause" (Weiser, 2011).

Not satisfied with their gains, Christian leaders campaign to include Bible study in public school curriculum itself. Groups like the National Council on Bible Curriculum in Public Schools (NCBCPS) distribute course syllabi in school districts around the country, claiming that they "convey the content of the Bible as compared to literature and history" (Ridenour, 2019). However, the curriculum "strongly reflect conservative Protestant presuppositions . . . and claims that the Bible was the primary inspiration for the Founding Fathers and is thus the basis of the American political and legal systems. . . . Its not-so-subtle message is that 'real' Americans are socially and theologically conservative Christians" (Chancey, 2018, p. 278). Despite sustained political pressure—and lawsuits—to remove the curriculum from schools and prevent even more districts from implementing it, the NCBCPS claims that it has been used in 3,500 high schools in 41 states. Over 650,000 students have taken the course, for credit during school hours. An electronic version of the curriculum has been introduced, making it even easier and less expensive for districts to adopt (Ridenour, 2019). Other Bible courses have similar problems. They present the Bible as a source of personal and social moral inspiration and downplay the ways it has been used to justify oppression or violence. In many ways, these efforts mimic the "nonsectarian" Bible instruction in nineteenth century public schools (Chancey, 2018).

Another way that some religious believers have attempted to ensure that public schools endorse their religious beliefs is by regulating sex education. Because their religious beliefs prohibit sexual intercourse outside of marriage, groups like Focus on the Family, Concerned Women for America, and the American Family Association oppose education about birth control or sexually transmitted infections. As a result of heavy lobbying from the Christian right, from 1996 to 2010 the federal government provided funding for sex education programs only to school districts that have "abstinence only" sex education. The regulations governing these programs ensured that the beliefs of certain religious groups are embodied in the programs. For example, they required that students be taught that a mutually monogamous relationship in the context of marriage is the expected standard for human sexual activity and that sexual activity outside marriage is likely to have harmful physical or psychological effects. Heterosexuality was also considered the norm, and efforts to address sexual orientation were condemned as part of "the homosexual agenda" (Society for Adolescent Medicine, 2006). The "standards" embedded in abstinence only programs are rooted in *some* Americans' religious faith. Federal government funding of only those programs that adhered to these standards constituted a governmental stamp of approval for a particular set of religious beliefs and violated the First Amendment. New regulations were issued to provide funding for programs that go beyond abstinence and allow students to explore the topic in an atmosphere of religious and intellectual freedom. Funding became available for evidence-based programs that "educate adolescents on both abstinence and contraception to prevent pregnancy and sexually transmitted infections" (National Campaign to Prevent Teen and Unwanted Pregnancy, 2011). However, the federal government is once again increasing funding for abstinence only programs.

The pressure by some believers to privilege one type of program that reflects a certain set of religious values includes a threat to young Americans' health. Although 29 states and the District of Columbia mandate sex education, only 20 states require that the content include information about birth control. Twenty-nine require that abstinence be stressed. Nineteen require that instruction on the importance of engaging in sexual activity only within marriage be provided. Ten states and Washington, DC require inclusive content with regard to sexual orientation. In seven states students receive only negative information about homosexuality and positive information about heterosexuality or discriminatory views of sexual orientation (Guttmacher Institute, 2019).

The Creationism/Intelligent Design Debate

Similar efforts to infuse a particular religious perspective into public school curricula have taken place with regard to science courses. The theory of evolution is one of the most important contributions ever made to our understanding of the connections between all living things and is fundamental to genetics, biochemistry, physiology, and ecology. "Biological evolution is one of the most important ideas of modern science. Evolution is supported by abundant evidence from many different fields of scientific investigation. It underlies the modern biological sciences, including the biomedical sciences, and has applications in many other scientific and engineering disciplines" (National Academy of Sciences, 2008, p. 47). An earth science or biology course that does not include evolution shortchanges students.

> Science and technology are so pervasive in modern society that students increasingly need a sound education in the core concepts, applications, and implications of science. Because evolution has and will continue to serve as a critical foundation of the biomedical and life sciences, helping students learn about and understand the scientific evidence, mechanisms, and implications of evolution are fundamental to a high-quality science education. (National Academy of Sciences, 2008, p. 47)

Yet, after 80 years, the teaching of evolution is being disputed once more in school districts across the country. Some people are convinced that unless the "theory" of evolution is challenged in science classes, then the state is violating their right to religious liberty and perpetuating intellectual fraud. What is going on?

Some people object to the teaching of evolution because they believe that the world was created 6,000 years ago by a divine being acting purposefully. Beginning with the Scopes trial in 1925, creationists have attempted to protect their children from what they see as the evil influences of the teaching of evolution. Consequently, they have lobbied to have textbooks removed from schools if authors do not give "equal time" to creationism and convinced legislators and departments of education to remove evolution from state science standards that strongly influence the curriculum taught in public schools. They have had all mention of evolution removed from statewide tests, thus giving school districts the green light to ignore the topic in their classes without fear that students will suffer.

However, the courts repudiated their efforts (*Edwards v. Aguillard*, 1987). So creationists repackaged their argument and attempted to seize the intellectual high ground. Instead of lobbying for creationism, they now argue for "intelligent design" theory and want schools to present it to students as an alternative to natural selection—despite the lack of scientific evidence to support their ideas. They argue that science teachers should be required to suggest that it is quite possible that the process of evolution is the work of an "intelligent designer." That is, they want students to be taught that the existence of God is supported by scientific evidence. However, the "antievolutionary" forces would have to redefine science in order to justify that claim.

"The formal scientific definition of theory is quite different from the everyday meaning of the word. It refers to a comprehensive explanation of some aspect of nature that is supported by a vast body of evidence" (National Academy of Sciences, 2008, p. 11). In *McLean v. Arkansas Board of Education* (1982), the Supreme Court noted five characteristics of science: "(1) It is guided by natural law; (2) It has to be explanatory by reference to natural law; (3) It is testable against the empirical world; (4) Its conclusions are tentative; (5) It is falsifiable." Neither creationism nor intelligent design meets such criteria. The "scientific" explanation for creationism, that the universe came into being from "nothingness," cannot be explained in reference to natural law, does not establish its own scientific hypotheses, and is neither testable nor falsifiable. Similarly, intelligent design's claim that there is a plan for the universe does not lead to predictions that are testable or to results that can be verified or reproduced. It is not rooted in natural law but explains the origins of life with reference to a supernatural force. Creationism and intelligent design are, in fact, religious beliefs, and their claims don't need to be tested in order to be accepted as *religious* truths. A person can accept on faith any explanation he or she chooses for the origin of the world or the relationships between its living things. People can draw on statements based on revelation or religious authority. They can take great comfort from such faith and can be profoundly inspired by its explanations. They can study different expressions of those beliefs, comparing and contrasting them—sifting among them for the one that is most convincing. But what they can't do is call them "science."

In contrast, evolution is an explanation for the facts that have been collected through the scientific tools of observation and experimentation. Scientific knowledge consists of explanations that are derived from confirmable evidence. The theory of evolution has been built up through facts, such as "the presence and/or absence of particular fossils in particular strata of the geological column. From these confirmed observations we develop an explanation, an inference, that what explains all of these facts is that species have had histories, and that descent with modification has taken place" (Scott, 2001, p. 6). The theory of evolution has been supported by so much observation and experimentation that scientists are confident there is no new evidence that is likely to contradict it. Scientists no longer debate whether evolution has taken place because the data from experimentation and observation are too strong (National Academies of Sciences, Engineering, and Medicine, 2019).

Nevertheless, supporters of intelligent design portray themselves as victims of discrimination, unable to exercise their First Amendment free speech rights. They create slogans such as "Teach the controversy" and "Go where the evidence leads." They argue for fairness, tolerance for diversity, individual choice, and opposition to censorship, which are powerful arguments in a society committed to those core values. The problem is that there is no controversy, at least no scientific controversy. Instead, adherents of one faith tradition are attempting to alter school curricula and teaching methods because they cannot be reconciled with their religious beliefs. And they are making gains despite the court decisions declaring the teaching of creationism and intelligent design to be violations of the First Amendment. Louisiana and Tennessee have passed laws requiring that evolution be a topic of critical investigation, logical analysis, and open and objective discussion and allowing the use of supplementary materials, including those produced by organizations and authors with a distinctly religious point of view (Khazan, 2019; Masci, 2019). A study of high school biology teachers has shown that between 12 and 16% are creationist in orientation—"one in eight reported that they teach creationism or intelligent design in a positive light" (Berkman and Plutzer, 2015). In addition, the topic of evolution has become so controversial that it appears that teachers are reluctant to address it scientifically. Students reported that evolution was addressed superficially most often and that a religiously based critique of the theory was frequently part of the instruction (Khazan, 2019).

Lately, supporters of intelligent design have avoided any mention of religious motivations or intentions in their efforts to limit the teaching of evolution. They have created what some scholars call "mini-intelligent design." They no longer argue that the intelligent designer must be supernatural. They know that the Supreme Court has ruled that mention of a creator in public schools violates the separation of church and state. So they stick with arguments that adaptations in organisms "scientifically" prove the poverty of evolution as an explanatory theory and hope that Americans, whose own science education has often been limited, will be impressed and lobby for "fairness" (Meyer, 2019).

What's the Big Deal?

What's wrong with majority rule in regard to curriculum and religious practices in public schools? Sixty percent of Americans support daily prayer in public schools, 75% support prayer at school sponsored events, and 40% believe that the creation story in Genesis is literally true (Riffkin, 2014; Brenan, 2019). What's the harm in bringing those beliefs into public schools? Some argue that America is a nation founded by men with Judeo-Christian beliefs and that religion provides a moral compass for individuals and society. Public prayer and other rituals serve "in the only ways reasonably possible, the legitimate secular purposes of solemnizing public occasions, expressing confidence in the future, and encouraging the recognition of what is worthy of appreciation in society" (*Lynch v. Donnelly*, 1984, p. 693). Only a few people object to them, and in schools no one is forced to participate; they can remain silent while others pray. Why should most citizens be denied their preferences because they would offend a minority of non-Christians or nonbelievers?

While it might prove satisfying in the short term, breaking down the barrier between religion and the state in schools—even in the name of majority rule—is in no one's best interests. It hurts individuals by making full acceptance as a member of the school community dependent on sharing the majority's religious beliefs. Further harm is done by minimizing the complexity of American history at the expense of supporting—or establishing—a more sectarian "truth." Finally, taking down the wall between church and state undermines religion because in the effort to make language, symbols, and practices acceptable to all, they become so bland that they lose all spiritual meaning. As Justice Alito noted, "With sufficient time, religiously expressive monuments, symbols and practices can become embedded features of a community's landscape and identity. The community may come to value them without necessarily embracing their religious roots" (*American Legion v. American Humanist Association*, 2019, p. 177).

When the separation of church and state is violated in schools—for example, by a prayer at a graduation ceremony or a football game or by the introduction of creationist arguments in a science class—students receive the message that belief is favored over nonbelief. So, young people who are atheists or members of nonmonotheistic traditions are plunged into crises of conscience by these school practices. They must either risk their acceptance in the school community or take part in religious activities with which they do not agree (Dupper et al., 2015).

The Establishment Clause was meant to prevent the development of such dilemmas in public spheres. Under its protection, religious belief or nonbelief should be irrelevant in one's ability to participate fully in schooling. Even though members of the majority find the practices untroubling, the situation upsets the delicate balance between individual and collective rights that the Constitution preserves.

Violating the separation of religion and state in schools also harms society. Favoring the beliefs of one religious tradition over others or belief over disbelief creates tensions that pose a threat to the cohesiveness of our very pluralistic society. For example, when "nonsectarian" prayers are said at school events, they reflect the Judeo-Christian tradition. Members of nonmajority religious groups get the message that their beliefs are not really "American"—they are both overlooked and excluded (Chancey, 2018). The result is a society in which individuals and groups are assigned social status on the basis of how closely their beliefs adhere to the preferred religion. That kind of social stratification can have serious results. Jews, Hindus, Muslims, Sikhs, other non-Christians, and nonbelievers may isolate themselves from public schools if they feel their rights are not protected in them. That separation could exacerbate differences and cause resentments and misunderstandings. We can look into the past—recent and ancient—and discover the harm that such divisiveness has caused. The struggles of Shiite and Sunni Muslims in Iraq and Protestant and Catholic Christians in Ireland are but two recent examples. In each case, one group's religious beliefs and practices were sanctioned by the government; members of that group enjoyed social and economic privileges that members of the other did not. The results were tragic for both societies.

Although believers argue that religion exerts a good influence by encouraging people to act morally, that opinion overlooks historical reality. Religion has been used to justify slavery, war, terrorism, imperialism, and genocide. Systems of belief suggesting that they have answers to every question can threaten fundamental aspects of democracy. When government endorses religious belief, it limits the necessarily critical discourse about the impact of faith on culture. In fact, research shows that governmental support for religion makes it more difficult for people to adapt to changes in their society. By establishing one set of beliefs or customs as emblematic of the nation, "citizens see religious newcomers as a threat to their way of life and react with animosity to their practices and demands" (Hebling and Traunmuller, 2016). When the wall between church and state is maintained, however, citizens see less to lose from newcomers—whether they are members of nondominant religious communities or atheists. The separation of church and state maintains tolerance and accommodation within a society despite changing demographics.

FOR DISCUSSION

1. The National Academy of Sciences (NAS) has argued that creationism does not meet the criteria for a scientific theory. Investigate the NAS definition further and determine whether creation scientists could gather facts that would support their theory regarding the origin of life on earth and what type of evidence they would need. Can you find other definitions of scientific knowledge that might be expansive enough to include creation science?

2. The courts have ruled that teachers may not communicate their own religious beliefs to students. What do you think is the basis for those rulings? Research other legal limitations that have been placed on teachers' individual freedoms. Do they reflect society's attempt to balance the rights of individuals and needs of a democratic society? Do you agree with the way that balance has been achieved? What would you do differently?

3. Read or watch a film or video version of *Inherit the Wind*, the dramatization of the Scopes trial. Research the actual event as well. What role did the historical and geographical setting play in the case? Would the case have been brought to court in a different location—even during the same period? Speculate on whether geographic differences might exist today regarding the question of religious freedom in public schools. What implications might these differences have for those entering the teaching profession? On what grounds would you base your guesses? How could you verify your thesis?

4. The U.S. Department of Education has issued guidelines for religious expression in public schools. Using those guidelines, take the role of a school superintendent and prepare a set of rules for your school district. Assume that they will need to be approved by your school board and create an explanation for each of the regulations you propose.

REFERENCES

Abington Township School District v. Schempp (1963). 374 U.S. 203.

ACLU Legal Bulletin (1996). The Establishment Clause and Public Schools (aclu.org.issues/religion/pr3.html).

Ali, S., and Lakhani, Z. (2017, February 6). Schools Should Recognize non-Christian Holidays. MeteaMedia (meteamedia.org/8650/opinions/the-cry-for-more-schools-to-recognize-other-religious-holidays-is-on-the-rise).

American Legion v. American Humanist Association (2019). 588 U.S. ___.

Batte, S. (2008). School Prayer Decisions. The Constitutional Principle: Separation of Church and State (members.tripod.com/candst/pray2a.htm).

Behe, M. (2007). *The Edge of Evolution: The Search for the Limits of Darwinism.* New York: Free Press.

Berkman, M., and Plutzer, E. (2015, March). "Enablers of Doubt: How Future Teachers Learn to Negotiate the Evolution Wars in Their Classrooms." *ANNALS of the American Academy of Political and Social Science* 658:253–270.

Brenan, M. (2019, July 26). 40% of Americans Believe in Creationism. Gallup (news.gallup.com/poll/261680/americans-believe-creationism.aspx).

Buell, J. (2007). Preface. In W. Dembski and J. Wells, eds., *The Design of Life: Discovering Signs of Intelligence in Biological Systems.* Dallas: Foundation for Thought and Ethics.

Chadsey, M. (2007). "Thomas Jefferson and the Establishment Clause." *Akron Law Review* 40:623.

Chancey, M. (2018). "The Bible and Public Schools." In M. Waggoner and N. Walker, eds., *The Oxford Handbook of Religion and American Education* (pp. 271–282). New York: Oxford University Press.

Chavez, S. (2017, March 28). "Prayer Rooms Are One Way Public Schools Accommodate Students and Freedom of Religion." *Houston Public Media* (houstonpublicmedia.org/articles/news/education-news/2017/03/28/193467/prayer-rooms-are-just-one-way-public-schools-accommodate-students-and-religious-freedom).

Council for Secular Humanism (2011). What Is Secular Humanism? (secularhumanism.org/index. php?section=main&page=what_is_).

County of Allegheny v. American Civil Liberties Union, Greater Pittsburgh Chapter (1989). 492 U.S. 573.

Dembski, W., and Wells, J. (2007). *The Design of Life: Discovering Signs of Intelligence in Biological Systems.* Dallas: Foundation for Thought and Ethics.

Dupper, D., Forrest-Bank, S., and Lowry-Carusillo, A. (2015). "Experiences of Religious Minorities in Public School Settings." *Children & Schools* 37(1):37–45. https://doi.org/10.1093/cs/cdu029

Edwards v. Aguillard (1987). 482 U.S. 578.

Engel v. Vitale (1962). 370 U.S. 421.

Everson v. Board of Education (1947). 330 U.S. 855.

Fessenden, T. (2005). "The 19th Century Bible Wars and the Separation of Church and State." *Church History* 74(5):784–811.

Free Inquiry (2019). "What is Secular Humanism?" *Free Inquiry* (secularhumanism.org/what-is-secular-humanism).

Gateways to Better Education (2019). What We Do (gogateways.org).

Good News Club v. Milford Central School (2001). 533 U.S. 98.

Goodman, J., and Lesnick, H. (2001). *The Moral Stake in Education.* New York: Longman.

Gordon, B., and Dembski, W., eds. (2011). *The Nature of Nature: Examining the Role of Naturalism in Science.* Wilmington, DE: Intercollegiate Studies Institute.

Gray, M., Lukes, J., Archibald, J., Keeling, P., and Doolittle, W. (2010). "Cell Biology. Irremediable Complexity?" *Science* 330(6006):920–921.

Guttmacher Institute (2019). State Laws and Policies: Sex and HIV Education (guttmacher.org/state-policy/explore/sex-and-hiv-education).

Hall, M. (2019). "America's Founders, Religious Liberty, and the Common Good." *University of St. Thomas Law Journal* 15(3):642–661.

Hasson, M., and Farnan, T. (2018). *Get Out Now: Why You Should Pull Your Child from Public School Before It's Too Late*. Washington, DC: Gateway Publications.

Hebling, M., and Traunmuller, R. (2016). "How State Support of Religion Shapes Attitudes Toward Muslim Immigrants: New Evidence From a SubNational Comparison." *Comparative Political Studies* 49(3):391–424.

Jemmott, J., Jemmott, R., and Fong, G. (2010). "Efficacy of a Theory-Based Abstinence Only Intervention over 24 Months: A Randomized Controlled Trial with Young Adolescents." *Archives of Pediatric and Adolescent Medicine* 164(2):152–159.

Khazan, O. (2019, September 19). "I Was Never Taught where Humans Came From." *The Atlantic.*

Kaiser Family Foundation (2018). Abstinence Education Programs: Definition, Funding, and Impact on Teen Sexual Behavior (kff.org/womens-health-policy/fact-sheet/abstinence-education-programs-definition-funding-and-impact-on-teen-sexual-behavior).

Kitzmiller v. Dover (2005). 400 F. Supp. 2d 707.

Koch, A., and Peden, W. (1944). *The Life and Selected Writings of Thomas Jefferson*. New York: Random House.

Lee v. Weisman (1992). 505 U.S. 577.

Lemon v. Kurtzman (1971). 403 U.S. 602.

LeVake v. Independent School District 656 et al. (2000). 625 N.W.2d 502.

Liberatore, W. (2017, May 25). "Shenendehowa Offers Muslim Students Prayer Room During Ramadan." *Times Union.*

Lynch v. Donnelly (1984). 465 U.S. 668.

Masci, D. (2019, February 6). Darwin in America. Pew Research Center (pewforum.org/essay/darwin-in-america).

McCarthy, M. (1983). *A Delicate Balance: Church, State and the Schools*. Bloomington, IN: Phi Delta Kappan Educational Foundation.

McCluskey, N. (1967). The New Secularity and the Requirements of Pluralism. In T. Sizer, ed., *Religion and Public Education*. Boston: Houghton Mifflin.

McCollum v. Board of Education (1948). 333 U.S. 203.

McConnell, M. (2000). "Religion and Constitutional Rights: Why Is Religious Liberty the 'First Freedom'?" *Cardozo Law Review* 21:1,243.

McCreary County v. ACLU (2005). 545 U.S. 844.

McGaughy, L. (2018, September 14). "Texas Board Votes to Eliminate Hillary Clinton, Helen Keller from History Curriculum." *Dallas Morning News.*

McLean v. Arkansas Board of Education (1982). 529 F. Supp. 1255.

Meacham, J. (2007). *American Gospel: God, the Founding Fathers and the Birth of a Nation*. New York: Random House.

Meyer, S. (2019). Evolution: Bacteria to Beethoven. Discovery Institute (discovery.org/v/evolution-bacteria-to-beethoven).

Mildrum, G. (2018, February 1). "Effingham Parents Confused about Creationism Event." *Shelbyville Daily Union.*

Murray v. Curlett (1963). 371 U.S. 944.

National Academies of Sciences, Engineering, and Medicine (2019). Is Evolution a Theory or a Fact? (nas.edu/evolution/TheoryOrFact.html).

National Campaign to Prevent Teen and Unwanted Pregnancy (2011). Personal Responsibility Education Program (thenationalcampaign.org/federalfunding/ prep.aspx).

Newdow v. U.S. Congress (2002). 293 F. 3d. 597; 328 F.3d 466.

Pew Research Center (2018, April 25). When Americans Say They Believe in God, What Do They Mean? (pewforum.org/2018/04/25/when-americans-say-they-believe-in-god-what-do-they-mean).

———— (2019). For a Lot of American Teens, Religion Is a Regular Part of the Public School Day (pewforum.org/2019/10/03/for-a-lot-of-american-teens-religion-is-a-regular-part-of-the-public-school-day).

Pregent, K., and Walker, N. (2018). Religious Expression in Public Schools. In M. Waggoner and N. Walker, eds., *The Oxford Handbook of Religion and American Education* (pp. 244–258). New York: Oxford University Press.

Ridenour, E. (2019). It's Coming Back and It's Our Constitutional Right. National Council on Bible Curriculum in Public Schools (bibleinschools.net).

Riffkin, R. (2014). In U.S., Support for Daily Prayer in Schools Dips Slightly. Gallup (news.gallup.com/poll/177401/support-daily-prayer-schools-dips-slightly.aspx).

Robb, S. (1985). *In Defense of School Prayer*. Santa Ana, CA: Parca.

Ruse, C. (2019). Get Your Kids Out of Government Schools, Right Now, Today. Family Research Council (frc.org/op-eds/get-your-kids-out-of-government-schools-right-now-today).

Russo, C. (2018). Extracurricular Activities and Access. In M. Waggoner and N. Walker, eds., *The Oxford Handbook of Religion and American Education* (pp. 283–294). New York: Oxford University Press.

Sanders, J. (1977). *Education of an Urban Minority*. New York: Oxford University Press.

Santa Fe Independent School District v. Jane Doe (2000). 530 U.S. 290.

Santos, F., and Phillips, A. (2011, August 10). "Sex Education Again a Must in City Schools." *New York Times*, A1.

School District of the City of Grand Rapids v. Ball (1985). 437 U.S. 373.

Selman Injunction (2005). *Selman v. Cobb County School District*, Civ. No 1 02-CV 2325-CC, 005. U.S. Dist LEXIS 432.

Scott, E. (2001). Dealing with Anti-Evolutionism. National Center for Science Education (ncseweb.org/resources).

Society for Adolescent Medicine (2006). "Abstinence-Only Education Policies and Programs: A Position Paper of the Society for Adolescent Medicine." *Journal of Adolescent Health* 38:83–87.

Stewart, K. (2011, June 12). "Separation of Church and School." *New York Times*.

Stone v. Graham (1980). 449 U.S. 39.

Torcaso v. Watkins (1961). 367 U.S. 488.

Tozer, S., Violas, P., and Senese, G. (2002). *School and Society*. New York: McGraw-Hill.

United States v. Seeger (1965). 380 U.S. 163.

U.S. Department of Education (2020, January 16). Guidance on Constitutionally Protected Prayer and Religious Expression in Public Elementary and Secondary Schools (34 CFR; 85 FR 3257). *Federal Register* 3,257–3,272.

Van Orden v. Perry (2005). 545 U.S. 677.

Waldman, S. (2009). *Founding Faith: How Our Founding Father Forged a Radical New Approach to Religious Liberty*. New York: Random House.

Wallace v. Jaffree (1985). 472 U.S. 38.

Webster v. New Lenox School District (1990). 917 F. 2nd 1004.

Weiser, B. (2011, June 3). "Court Lets City Restrict Church Use of Schools." *New York Times*.

Wright, E. (1999). "Religion in American Education: A Historical View." *Phi Delta Kappan* 81(1):17–20.

Zeldin, M. (1986). A Century Later and Worlds Apart: American Reform Jews and the Public School-Private School Dilemma, 1870–1970. Paper presented at the annual meeting of the American Educational Research Association, San Francisco, CA.

Zorach v. Clauson (1952). 343 U.S. 306.

Gender Equality in Schools

Eliminating Discrimination or Accommodating Difference

6

Should schools or classrooms separate students by gender or sexual identities?

Position 1:   Inclusive Schools Prevent Discrimination

Schools are a primary site of young people's lives, where they explore and enact their sexualities and genders. In schools, students' emotional, intellectual, and social lives expand as they enter relationships with people outside their families and neighborhoods. They claim gendered, sexual, and racialized identities, interests, and selves; challenge and reproduce social inequalities; and imagine how to belong to the communities they make and remake with their peers. These imaginings are stunted by inequalities that compromise schools' promise to offer all students a place to value themselves and others.

—Gilbert et al. (2018, p. 166)

The ongoing struggle for civil rights in the United States has included efforts to end gender discrimination in public schools. The attempt to ensure equal educational access, opportunity, and achievement has focused primarily on the rights of women, whose limited opportunities in schools have contributed to inequality in career choices and lifetime earnings. Issues regarding educational equity for men and women still remain to be addressed. Additional concerns have emerged regarding educational opportunities and outcomes of students whose gender and sexual identities challenge traditional categories. Some recent responses to these concerns have been single-sex schools and classes. In some cases, these efforts were sincere attempts to meet young people's needs. In others, they represent efforts to impose particular religious and moral beliefs about gender on publicly funded school communities. Whatever the motivation for single-sex settings, they segregate young people from one another. Public schools were created to prepare citizens for a democratic republic. Among the skills they need to acquire is the ability to defend the rights of all people—

not only those whose backgrounds or beliefs or physical characteristics place them in the majority. Segregated educational settings—no matter how well intentioned—can never serve that purpose.

Traditional Gender Roles and Education

Although publicly funded schools in the United States have historically been coeducational, discrimination has been present. Colonial Christianity required each believer, male or female, to be able to read and interpret the scriptures. So most boys and girls were taught to read and do basic arithmetic. Boys, who were expected to work in the public sphere, were allowed to pursue more education. Girls, who were expected to perform private religious and domestic duties, were denied similar schooling (Tyack and Hansot, 1992; Urban and Wagoner, 2008; Tozer et al., 2012; Spring, 2018).

After the American Revolution, gender roles were rooted in a political, not religious, ideology. Men were expected to be moral neighbors, informed voters, and responsible businessmen. Schooling was designed to help boys develop "manly" virtues (obedience to authority, respect for the rights of others, an appreciation of "fair play") and provide opportunities to develop skills in literacy, natural science, history, and mathematics (Tozer et al., 2012). Women were expected to provide homes in which their sons and daughters learned to be responsible citizens and in which their husbands could find respite from the cares of the world (Tyack and Hansot, 1992). As the system of publicly funded schools developed during the nineteenth century, Americans in general supported gender equity in access (Kaestle, 1983; Tyack and Hansot, 1992). By the middle of the nineteenth century coeducational elementary schools had become the country's norm (Tyack and Hansot, 1992; Sklar, 1993).

Equality of access and opportunity in secondary education was more contentious (Tyack and Hansot, 1992). By the early nineteenth century, upper- and middle-class boys increasingly went beyond elementary school, attending "grammar" schools that prepared them for college or for occupations such as business, surveying, and teaching (Tozer et al., 2012). Pioneers such as Catharine Beecher, Emma Willard, and Mary Lyon argued that the country's well-being required women to extend their duties as "Republican mothers" by taking their "natural" aptitude for teaching into schools. As a result of their arguments and their fund-raising, private "academies" for women opened, allowing girls to continue their educations to prepare for careers as teachers and, eventually, nurses. By the early twentieth century, the academies were replaced by public high schools that admitted boys and girls on a relatively equal footing (Rury, 1991; Tyack and Hansot, 1992; Urban and Wagoner, 2008; Spring, 2018). The belief that both men and women had some role in public life resulted in greater equity in schooling.

However, even as equality of access to high schools improved, gender stereotypes once again resulted in limited opportunities. During the Progressive Era (1870 to 1930), girls were tracked into programs preparing them to be teachers, nurses, secretaries, receptionists, and clerks. Their participation in academic courses that prepared students for college, decreased (Rury, 1991). Gender-based high school programs persisted, with the result that although more women than men completed high school between 1940 and 1965, fewer women than men earned college degrees in that same period (U.S. Census Bureau, 2011). Few women had the opportunity to pursue education preparing them for professions. The right to work in law, business, medicine, and ministry belonged almost exclusively to men (Horowitz, 1984; Solomon, 1986; Tozer et al., 2012).

The 1960s saw a renewed commitment to the equality of educational opportunity for men and women. Advocates argued that the differences between men and women actually were more social than biological (Miller, 1976; Chodorow, 1978; Gilligan, 1982; Segal, 1990; Connell, 1995). Scholars investigated the policies, practices, curriculum, and student-teacher interactions in schools for explanations for differences in school achievement between boys and girls and reported many gender inequities (U.S. Department of Health, Education, and Welfare, 1978; Sadker and Sadker, 1982, 1994; Mac an Ghaill, 1994). They discovered the preferential treatment boys received with regard to teacher attention, counseling, athletics, extracurricular activities, and financial aid (Frazier and Sadker, 1973; Howe, 1984; Biklen and Pollard, 1993; Sadker and Sadker, 1994; American Association of University Women, 1995). Activists linked educational gender discrimination to the larger civil rights movement, arguing that gender discrimination was a violation of the Fourteenth Amendment, depriving women of the "unalienable rights" named by the Declaration of Independence and guaranteed by the Constitution.

In 1972, Title IX of the Education Amendments Act was passed to ban discrimination on the basis of sex in *any* educational program or activity receiving federal financial assistance. In 1974, the Women's Educational Equity Act (WEEA) funded programs that promoted gender equity in schools, including the development of nondiscriminatory curricula, resources, and standardized tests (U.S. Department of Education, 2011b). Title IX provided the framework for ending gender discrimination; WEEA provided the financial assistance that enable schools to do so. Together, they resulted in progress toward equity in academic achievement as identified by standardized test scores, course taking, participation in sports and extracurricular activities, and college degrees.

In 2017, census figures showed that, among Americans 25 years old or older, approximately 35% of both men and women had bachelor's or graduate degrees. Among younger people (ages 25 to 29), women's attainment actually surpassed that of men. Forty-one percent of women had bachelor's degrees or higher, compared with 33% of men. As Figure 6.1 shows, women's attainment took a jump immediately after the passage of Title IX. Ten years later they were earning degrees at the same rate as men (U.S. Census Bureau, 2019). As Table 6.1 shows, the increase in degrees awarded to women in fields of study that historically have been dominated by men is even more dramatic since Title IX took effect.

These remarkable developments resulted, at least in part, from efforts to end discriminatory practices in elementary and secondary schools. Girls adjusted their high school course-taking patterns, making them better prepared to enter college and previously male-dominated professions. Girls and boys now take advanced science and mathematics courses at almost equal rates. Nineteen percent of both boys and girls now complete calculus and 36% take physics. As they have taken more math courses, girls' scores on the twelfth grade NAEP mathematics test have increased and now equal those of their male counterparts (National Science Board, 2018).

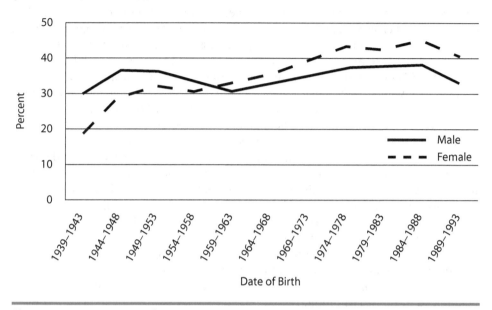

Figure 6.1   Percentage of Americans 25 Years or Older with a Bachelor's Degree or Above by Gender (U.S. Census Bureau, 2019)

Table 6.1 Percentage of Bachelor's and Graduate Degrees Conferred on Women in Selected Fields of Study		
	1970 (%)	**2017 (%)**
Bachelor's Degree		
Engineering	0.7	22
Agriculture	4.1	53
Business	9.0	47
Physical Science	13.6	40
Graduate Degree		
Law (LLB, JD)	5.4	50
Medicine (MD)	8.4	47
Dentistry (DDS, DDM)	0.9	48
Computer Science (PhD)	1.9	22
Engineering (PhD)	0.7	24
Physical Sciences (PhD)	5.4	32
Business (MBA)	1.6	50

Source: Snyder et al. (2019).

Title IX and Athletics

The provisions of Title IX legislation have been applied most noticeably to athletics. Although some gender differences remain with regard to resources, females' participation in scholastic programs has dramatically increased. In 1972, approximately 30,000 women participated in college or university sports programs; almost 50 years later, approximately 287,000 did. Prior to Title IX, athletic scholarships for women were virtually nonexistent. Women now receive 46% of the financial aid given to athletes (U.S. Department of Education, 2011a; U.S. Department of Education, 2019a). Before 1972, approximately 300,000 girls played high school sports; now, there are approximately 3.5 million (National Federation of State High School Associations, 2019).

Women who take part in sports are less likely to develop heart diseases, osteoporosis, and breast cancer over the course of their lives. They are less likely to become obese (Tucker Center for Research on Girls and Women in Sport, 2018). Female high school athletes are three times more likely than other girls to do better in school and get their diploma. They have higher grades and do better in science and math courses. They are less likely to smoke, do drugs, engage in sexual activity, or become pregnant (Zarrett et al., 2018).

There has been a backlash to these changes. Schools have played the "blame" game. Funding expensive, and revenue producing, male sports such as football and basketball can stretch athletic budgets to the breaking point. Then, to make ends meet, colleges and universities cut smaller men's teams and point the finger at the necessity of funding women's programs due to Title IX and not the costs associated with the marquee sports. Yet nothing in the law requires that men's teams be cut. In fact, under Title IX, men's opportunities to participate in school athletics, the number of them doing so, and the budgets for their sports have all increased (U.S. Department of Education, 2019a).

Other Forms of Sexual Discrimination in Schools

Despite backlashes and challenges, the laws that have protected women's educational rights have been effective. Now, educational gender equality faces new challenges. Bullying, sexual harassment, and sexual assault particularly threaten girls, students whose sexual orientation is not or appears not to be heterosexual, and those whose gender identities fall outside the traditional binary of male and female. According to the Supreme Court, Title IX requires school districts to prevent or respond to sexual harassment that is pervasive and severe enough to "prevent students from receiving the benefits of their public education" (*Davis v. Monroe County Board of Education*, 1999). However, school districts have been negligent in fulfilling this responsibility (Grant et al., 2019; Kingkade, 2019). Over 80% of students in middle and high school report that they have experienced sexual harassment and 96% have witnessed sexual harassment in schools (American Association of University Women, 2011; Lichty and

Campbell, 2012). Yet, the Office of Civil Rights in the Department of Education claimed that they received only 87,000 allegations of harassment based on gender or sexual orientation (U.S. Department of Education, 2019c). Furthermore, 79% of grade 7 to 12 schools reported zero incidents of sexual harassment and 94% reported zero incidents of sexual assault on the School Survey of Crime and Safety (Musu et al., 2019). Girls were the victims in two-thirds of the reports of sexual harassment made to the Office of Civil Rights (U.S. Department of Education, 2019b). Nearly 14% report having skipped school in order to avoid being harassed (Chaudhry and Tucker, 2018).

The majority of lesbian, gay, bisexual, transgendered, and questioning (LGBTQ) high school students develop as healthy teenagers. What is remarkable is that they do so even though schools often are hostile environments for them. In a nationwide survey, 98.5% of LGBTQ students reported they had heard "gay" used in a negative way (e.g., "that's so gay") at school. Seventy percent of LGBTQ students experienced verbal harassment based on sexual orientation, 59% based on gender expression, and 53% based on gender. More than a quarter reported being pushed or shoved and 12% were assaulted (punched, kicked, injured with a weapon). More than half were sexually harassed and almost half experienced cyberbullying. Fifty-seven percent of students reported hearing homophobic remarks and almost three-quarters reported negative remarks from teachers or other school staff (Kosciw et al., 2018).

Transgendered youths reported particular difficulties with school staff who refuse to accept the students' preferred gender identities: 42% of them had been prevented from using their preferred name or pronoun. Almost half had been required to use a bathroom or locker room of the sex on their birth certificates (Kosciw et al., 2018).

In-school victimization of LGBTQ young people has costly consequences. It is linked to absenteeism, disciplinary problems, and health risks such as drug use, alcoholism, depression, and attempted suicide, which occur at higher rates in the LGBTQ population than among their heterosexual peers (Aragon et al., 2014). Absenteeism and disciplinary problems create a greater likelihood that a student may drop out (Russell et al., 2010).

New Challenges to Ending Discrimination

Policies allowing publicly funded single-sex education would appear to run counter to Title IX and other civil rights laws. For example, in 1996, the Supreme Court declared that state funding of single-sex schools was unconstitutional (*United States v. Virginia*, 1996). However, in 2004, the Department of Education issued new regulations that permitted single-sex schools and classes in publicly funded schools and imposed few limitations on such projects. In 2006, the department invited and encouraged school districts to create single-gender classes and schools. The Department of Education continues to allow them under Title IX as long as students of the other gender have access to "a substantially equal single-sex school or coeducational school" (U.S. Department of Education, 2014). Two decades ago, there were only four single-gender public schools in the country; today, there are almost 300 and over 400 that have at least some single-gender classes (Mitchell, 2017).

Arguments supporting single-sex education generally point to particular weaknesses in the academic achievement of one gender or another. In fact, no review of single-sex education has shown that the setting alone improves academic outcomes. Most studies show that factors other than gender explain whatever academic advantages may occur in single-sex settings. Analysis of outcomes reveal that students entering such settings often were already outperforming their peers academically and that less successful students transfer out before graduation, skewing the data. Single-sex schools tend to be smaller and have more personal relationships among school community members and teaching strategies that allow students to be more active learners. In addition, parents have made a "pro-academic choice" by sending children to single-sex schools. When those factors are included, the single-sex advantage disappears. Enthusiasm for gender-segregated settings appears to be predicated not on science but on bias-sampled anecdotal evidence (Halpern et al., 2011; Pahlke et al., 2014).

Since they cannot prove the effectiveness of single-sex education, proponents have simply provided reasons why it *should* work—arguments based on a pseudoscience of gender differences (Sax, 2006, 2007; Gurian, 2007a, 2007b; Halpern et al., 2011). Aside from the facts that girls' brains finish growing sooner than boys' brains do and that the volumes of boys' brain are, on average, larger than those of girls, neuroscientists have found very few gender-related differences in children's brains. Neither of these two differences is related to how or how much either gender learns. Even the differences in how gender affects the way brains work—sound sensitivity, memory, and activation—are not significant enough to indicate that children should be educated differently (Halpern et al., 2011). Thus far, research has not found a "definitive neural signature of gender" (Williams, 2018).

Support for single-sex educational settings are based on dubious science and unproven benefits. On the other hand, there are solid arguments against gender segregation. Segregation based on gender or sexual identity fosters belief in significant behavioral or ability differences when none or only superficial ones exist. It reinforces gender stereotyping behavior among students and teachers and limits the range of socially acceptable ways of being male or female (American Council for CoEducational Schooling, 2011). It emphasizes binary gender identities and ignores the growing science on the fluidity of gender. It risks making transgender and gender-nonconforming students "incompatible with the core mission of single-sex education" and cause them to "experience intense psychological pressure trying to locate themselves within the binary on which single-sex programs are largely based" (Benham et al., 2019, p. 535). Even when the segregation is "chosen," such as in "gay-safe" Harvey Milk High School in New York City and Alliance High School in Milwaukee or in the online Global Village School, it can contribute to the isolation of youth from their peers. As Barnett and Rivers (2012) argue, "There is a veritable mountain of evidence, growing every day, that the single-sex classroom is not a magic bullet to save American education. And scant evidence that it heightens the academic achievement of girls and boys."

Inclusive Schools

The U.S. Department of Education (2020) recently reaffirmed that

> Every school and every school leader has a responsibility to protect all students and ensure every child is respected and can learn in an accepting environment. Title IX protects all students, including LGBTQ students, from sex discrimination. Title IX encompasses discrimination based on a student's failure to conform to stereotyped notions of masculinity and femininity.

The label "coeducational" is no longer appropriate for schools in which gender is viewed as fluid, not binary. Instead, schools that promote understanding among students about gender and sexual orientation and enforce bans against sexually based verbal or physical harassment and assault can be called "gender-inclusive." They provide an atmosphere in which all students can thrive. The students, teachers, administrators, families, and communities of gender-inclusive schools "recognize that gender impacts all students, interrupt binary notions of gender, acknowledge and account for gender diversity, question limited portrayals of gender, support students' self-reflection, and teach empathy and respect" (Gender Spectrum, 2019).

An additional approach to gender and sexual orientation is the creation of a gay-straight alliance (GSA). GSA's and similar student-initiated groups addressing LGBTQ issues can play an important role in promoting safer schools and creating more welcoming learning environments. In schools with GSAs, students and staff report positive environments for all students.

The benefits of gender-inclusive schools are many. Three, in particular, stand out. First, research has shown that LGBTQ students experience less harassment or assault and are more likely to stay in school and achieve academically (Russell et al., 2009; Sadowski, 2017; Kosciw et al., 2018). Second, children who are supported in their explorations of gender-expansive identities have notably lower rates of psychopathology than questioning children who are forced to live out decisions about their gender that were made for them at birth (Olson et al., 2016). Third, inclusive schools address gender-based harassment through systemic change. Sex education curriculum no longer silences the reality of LGBTQ lives. Administrative policies allow transgendered students to change their names and gender on official documents. Gay-straight student alliances and similar student-initiated groups addressing LGBTQ issues are fully accepted (Sadowski, 2017; Gilbert et al., 2018).

Ironically, some who advocate segregating young people based on gender actually want to reinforce existing gender roles and heterosexism and ignore the violence that has historically supported them. Creating and maintaining educational policies and settings where gender discrimination is not tolerated, that have zero tolerance and serious consequences for sexually based verbal or physical violence, and that are safe spaces where young citizens unlearn the prejudice of the past are the best ways to protect all young people and create a safer future.

Position 2:   Single-Sex Schools and
              Classrooms Accommodate Differences

It appears that parents and students are not waiting for more studies to be conducted or for long-ranging debates about gender-based brain differences to be settled. Parents and students are looking for the educational environment that will give them the best chance of success in a complex world, and an increasing number are finding that the best educational environment may be one without the opposite sex.

—Chen (2017)

Gendered Experiences in Schools

All children in America have equal access to public education, from kindergarten to graduate school, regardless of gender. However, rigid policies that require all students to attend the *same* school, regardless of gender, actually limit opportunities for students. There is ample evidence that boys and girls do not learn nor experience school in the same way. Making legitimate accommodations to those differences by creating single-sex educational settings opens up new opportunities and results in improved outcomes.

The opposition to single-sex schools and classrooms is ironic. The recent generation-long effort to eliminate discrimination from schools began with analyses of the way gender affected students' educational experiences. Researchers found that preschool boys played with tools, simple machines, balls, and blocks much more often than girls (American Association of University Women, 1995). Teachers encouraged boys to be assertive and independent, discouraged girls from taking risks, and rewarded them for being timid, cooperative, and quiet (Tozer et al., 2012).

In elementary schools, teachers worked with boys more often and gave them more attention and affection than they provided girls (Sadker and Sadker, 1994). By the time they got to middle school, girls were struggling with messages about their academic competency and had become tentative about speaking up in class (Brown and Gilligan, 1993). By high school, boys were more likely to take higher level math, science, and computer classes.

Researchers found that coeducational settings posed pitfalls for boys too. They faced peer pressure to take part in sports, and their masculinity was judged on their ability to compete. They encouraged one another to engage in drug and alcohol use and other risky behaviors. Expressions of emotion were mocked (Kindlon and Thompson, 1999; Pollack, 1999). Acting as if they had power through posturing and violence was rewarded. Interest in "feminine" things, such as reading and the arts, was ridiculed (Kimmel, 2000).

Textbooks contributed to sex discrimination in schools by not deeply challenging traditional understandings of gender. Curricular materials did not affirm differences between members of the same gender or integrate the experiences, needs, and interests of both sexes in their material (American Association of University Women, 1995). Vocational education programs reflected and reproduced traditional gender expectations.

Finally, researchers found schools discriminated against young women who were pregnant or parenting, doing little to accommodate their special needs. Few schedules were adjusted to allow for the extra time mothers might need to transport their babies to child care. Even fewer provided such centers on-site. These young women were more likely to drop out of school than other female students (U.S. Department of Education, 2011b).

While more recent research indicates some improvement in the most blatant forms of gender discrimination in schools, serious problems still exist. For example, teachers still rate girls' math skills lower than those of boys unless they perceive girls as working harder and behaving better than similarly achieving boys. The gender gap in math achievement tends to grow during elementary school and teachers' differential ratings of boys and girls account for about half of that growth (Robinson-Cimpian et al., 2014). If teachers thought differently about their gender biases, the achievement gap might not exist.

The research has made a compelling case over time that boys and girls have different experiences in schools—and that each group is shortchanged because of gender discrimination.

Title IX Does Not Mandate One-Size-Fits-All Education

During the 1970s, feminists and other civil rights advocates tried to equate racism and sexism. They lobbied for passage of an Equal Rights Amendment (ERA) that would have prohibited all discrimination on the basis of gender. However, the decade-long national debate on the ERA made it clear to most Americans that treating people differently based on their gender was far different from discriminating on the basis of race. They understood that it sometimes was necessary to make legitimate distinctions between the genders in order to serve the best interests of women and their children.

After 1977, no state legislature could be persuaded to ratify the amendment. By 1982, even the most ardent feminists declared the effort to pass the ERA to be at an end.

However, in 1972, Congress passed Title IX, which required more equitable distribution of educational resources and opportunities among males and females. It prohibited discrimination in recruitment, admissions, counseling, financial assistance, sex-based harassment, treatment of pregnant and parenting students, discipline, and employment.

As originally interpreted, Title IX was applied to coeducational schools, outlawing publicly funded single-sex educational settings altogether. However, when No Child Left Behind mandated the disaggregation of educational achievement data on the basis of gender, the gaps between male and female outcomes identified anecdotally became verified. As practitioners sought ways to address the gaps, they turned to the idea of single-sex education, long a practice in private education. The Department of Education agreed that publicly funded single-sex classes and schools were worth trying. New regulations were issued, declaring that Title IX does allow single-sex education under certain conditions. If districts can identify an important objective, and can demonstrate that the single-sex nature of the class is related to achieving that objective, a single-sex setting is allowed. Schools must ensure that enrollment is completely voluntary, offer a substantially equal coed class, offer single-sex classes equally to male and female students, and avoid gender discrimination in faculty assignments (U.S. Department of Education, 2014).

Perhaps the most well-known example of how Title IX allows gender specific opportunities is its application to school sports. Title IX requires that women and men be provided equitable opportunities to participate in sports and that athletic scholarship funds are distributed to female and male student athletes in proportion to their participation in sports. It requires equal treatment of male and female athletes with regard to recruitment, coaching, scheduling, tutoring, facilities, equipment, and medical, housing, dining, and other support services. "Title IX does not require the creation of mirror image programs. Males and females can participate in different sports according to their respective interests and abilities. Thus, broad variations in the type and number of sports opportunities offered to each gender are permitted." The law allows for separate and equitable programs for each gender (National Collegiate Athletic Association, 2020).

When Title IX has been applied in rational and thoughtful ways, the consequence has been a more just educational system. However, when it has been used as an ideological tool to remedy all past wrongs against one gender or another, it results in a less fair system.

For example, early efforts of the "gender police" to engineer textbooks resulted in the imposition of gender quotas on examples and illustrations and bans on words like "actress," "heroine," "brotherhood," and "forefathers." Portraying men and women in jobs or activities or expressing emotions traditionally associated with their gender were censored (Ravitch, 2003). Those who proposed changes to textbooks may have begun with the laudable aim of creating an equal playing field for girls and boys by opening their minds to possibilities that transcended traditional gender roles. They overcompensated however and their efforts were discounted as "political correctness."

One of the most absurd consequence of efforts to eliminate all discrepancies in treatment of boys and girls in schools is their effect on school dress codes. The language of dress codes that connect violations with a student's gender have been challenged across the country. According to the most rigid interpretations, districts can make no distinctions between males and females with regard to clothing, jewelry, or makeup. Language that uses the criteria that girls should refrain from dressing in ways that distracts boys is labeled as "victim blaming" (Bates, 2015; Barrett, 2018; Jones, 2018). Surely, creating equality of educational opportunity for male and female students does not require the creation of policies that equate sameness with fairness or ignore biology.

Another example of overreach in the use of Title IX can be found in policies and practices regarding sexual harassment. With regard to Title IX, sexual harassment is defined as "unwelcome conduct on the basis of sex that is so severe, pervasive, and objectively offensive that it effectively denies a person equal access to the school's education program or activity" (*Federal Register*, 2018). In response to pressure from the federal government—and in attempts to better respond to victims—colleges, universities, and school districts adopted policies and procedures that created problems of their own. Definitions of sexual harassment were unclear and applied arbitrarily. Differences among situations were ignored; policies left no room to evaluate facts in context. Complainants often felt revictimized by the process and dissatisfied with the result. Alleged perpetrators were often denied due process. The lives of both survivors and accused were destroyed. "Definitions of sexual wrongdoing became overly broad . . . and unfair to all parties, and squandered the legitimacy of the system" (Bartholet et al., 2017). Title IX is meant to provide equal access to educational benefits for all students. When its application is based on a "one-size-fits-all approach," it fails in its primary mission.

Why Single-Sex Settings Are Necessary

There is certainly no denying that biological differences between males and females really exist. Women conceive, gestate, give birth, and suckle new members of the human race. Men do not. But reproductive differences are only one way in which men and women are not the same. Male and female brains also differ. Scientists have known for more than a hundred years that men's brains are larger than women's. Some studies have indicated that men's brain structures allowed them to perform better than women when attempting visual or spatial tasks. According to that research, women's brain structures help them do better than men on verbal or language-oriented tasks (Burman et al., 2008). In single-sex settings it is possible to utilize the knowledge of these differences in the development of curriculum, instruction, and assessment practices. Meeting the particular needs of one gender can be the focus of everyone's efforts.

Recent studies indicate that what a community teaches its members, explicitly or implicitly, about gender roles also plays a key role in creating cognitive abilities. Even at a young age, a child's acceptance of stereotypes of what a person of a particular sex is good at is more predictive of their cognitive abilities than gender itself (Bian et al., 2017; McGeown and Warhurst, 2019). Schools and teachers must be responsive to the stereotypes children have internalized if children are going to have equal educational opportunities. In many cases, challenging those ideas can expand students' sense of competency and open possibilities for their futures.

In other situations, single-sex settings expand educational opportunities because they accommodate a religious or ethnic community's beliefs about interactions between males and females. Some groups believe that contact between males and females in public spaces should be limited to preserve the dignity and well-being of both genders and to eliminate any fear about sexual harassment or assault. Creating separate schools for each gender means that, without violating a family's right to freely exercise their religion, all students can access public resources for education.

Why Single-Sex Settings Are Effective

Single-sex classes and schools are not discriminatory—they are necessary accommodations that produce real and significant results. For many years, only those children whose families could afford private schools were able to experience the benefits of single-sex schools. Now, there is no impediment in federal education law to prevent all children from gaining the advantages all girl or all boy schools offer.

Single-sex schools present students with alternatives to gender stereotypes and, more important, with spaces in which it is safe to challenge them. For example, in single-sex schools, girls are encouraged to work hard, discover what kinds of efforts are successful for them, and develop time management, leadership, and problem-solving skills. None of those abilities are considered "unwomanly." So, they can come to believe that they have tremendous control over the course of their lives, work in nontraditional jobs, and still see themselves as "feminine." Teachers and administrators also expand the definition of acceptable gender behavior for girls in most single-sex schools. Students see women teaching subjects such as chemistry, physics, and advanced mathematics that traditionally have not been considered "feminine." Research has shown that the benefits to girls of single-sex education include greater academic engagement, higher SAT scores, more interest in graduate education, academic self-confidence (especially in math and engineering), and a stronger predisposition to extracurricular and political engagement (Piehl, 2018).

Research on the effects of single-sex settings on boys provides some evidence that in such spaces, traditional male gender roles are challenged. There is a greater range in the definitions of masculinity in schools for boys than in coeducational ones. So, many boys and young men take part in activities traditionally defined as "feminine," such as the arts and community service (Excellence Charter School, 2008; National Association for Single-Sex Public Education, 2011). In addition, there is evidence that single-sex schools for boys, particularly where the faculty is also male, provide opportunities for them to experience teaching and learning that is relational in nature. Research increasingly shows that boys, no matter how much they have internalized stereotypes of masculinity, are unlikely to be successful in schools without caring and supportive relationships with teachers (Reichert and Hawley, 2014; Brooms, 2017). Teachers who are effective in creating those relationships reach out, identify boys' unique needs, acknowledge and craft teaching around students' interests and talents, reveal their own vulnerability and personal experiences in professional ways, and participate appropriately with students in school-related activities (Reichert and Hawley, 2014; Nelson, 2016). Black and Latino male students demonstrate particular appreciation for single-sex schools in which their definitions of themselves as "hardworking, motivated, funny and being a leader" are respected. Such schools support young people's definition of success, which includes doing well in school as well as financial security and family stability (Howard et al., 2019).

By revealing the multiple ways in which masculinity and femininity can be expressed, single-sex educational settings can also respond to young people's questions about their gender identities. Expanding young people's experiences of the multiple ways it is possible to act, think, or feel as a male or female can allow them to embrace their gender rather than feeling that their only option is to reject their bodies (Focus on the Family, 2018). Single-sex schools can give students the opportunity to escape "outside expectations that never quite fit into place" and find a "holistic unity" among the many aspects of themselves (Greene, 2019). Children should have the right to discover who they are without having adults making decisions for them, forcing them into gender categories—whether binary or expansive. Single-sex settings can provide safe places for them to do so.

While there has been little research about the effectiveness of single-sex settings for lesbian, gay, or bisexual students, studies about their experiences in other educational settings provide hints about possibilities. For example, Michael Sadowski's (2017) work on the creation of safe schools suggests that even though efforts are necessary, they are not sufficient to ensure that LGBTQ students actually have a sense of security. For example, when rainbow stickers on doors proclaim those rooms as "safe spaces," do they send negative messages about the relative security of other places in the building? If only some people in the school are members of a GSA, does that mean nonmembers should be feared? Gilbert and her colleagues (2019) suggest that "thick friendships" provide an alternative way of supporting young people's sexuality *and* learning. Friendships are intermediate kinds of relationships, neither familial nor sexual in nature. Residing in what they call an "ethics of discomfort," educators and students can address possibilities that come with forging friendships with members of the same gender, regardless of their sexual orientation. These relationships are sustaining, significant, and powerful and allow people to take part in dialogue with one another. In doing so, participants come to hear and know one another, aware of the differences among their experiences and the complexities of each person's life. A single-sex setting, whose guiding philosophy included such friendships, could be a place where the traditional curricula is explored and even bigger questions could be asked. Such settings could be "young people's greatest defense against the impulse common among adults, educators, and researchers to imagine and craft interventions into young people's lives" (Gilbert et al., 2019, p. 421).

Educational gender inequity remains a fact of life in American schools. It will continue to do so until educators are allowed to create settings addressing the total process by which gender differences in schools are produced. Coeducational settings tend to reproduce society's dominant gender prescriptions. By refusing to permit educators to create settings that resist those stereotypes, we pressure students to conform to them. What is needed is a commitment to make public education better able to meet the needs of all the students it serves. Young people deserve nothing less than having an equal right to education that recognizes the complexity of the problem of gender.

FOR DISCUSSION

1. Although the positions in this chapter allude to the effects that race, class, and ethnicity might have on an individual's creation of his or her gender identity, they do not discuss those effects in any detail. Consider how the other facets of a person's identity or situation in life might affect the choices they make about how much or how little to conform to various forms of masculinity or femininity. That is, does a

person's race, class, or gender affect how free people feel they are able to deviate from gender stereotypes?

2. Access information about gender differences in test scores from your state's department of education. In light of the discussions in this chapter, how do you explain such differences? How do you explain the fact that there appears to be little variance among gender differences from one racial/ethnic group to another? What does that suggest to you about ways to remedy gender inequity?

3. Research your college or university's athletic program. Does it seem to be in compliance with Title IX regulations? Have any male teams been cut to achieve "proportionality"? Interview male and female athletes and coaches to get their views on gender issues in the program and to determine for yourself if any discrimination exists.

4. Interview friends or classmates who attended single-sex high schools. How do their experiences confirm or refute the arguments made in the chapter?

REFERENCES

American Association of University Women (1995). *How Schools Shortchange Girls.* New York: Marlowe.
———— (2011). *Crossing the Line: Sexual Harassment at School.* Washington, DC: American Association of University Women.
American Council for CoEducational Schooling (2011). Evidence-Based Answers. Arizona State University, T. Denny Sanford School of Social and Family Dynamics (thesanfordschool.asu.edu/acces/evidence-based-answers).
Aragon, S, Poteat, P., Espelage, D., and Koenig, B. (2014). "The Influence of Peer Victimization on Educational Outcomes for LGBTQ and Non-LGBTQ High School Students." *Journal of LGBTQ Youth* (11)1. https://doi.org/10.1080/19361653.2014.840761
Barnett, R., and Rivers, C. (2012, February 17). "Why Science Doesn't Support Single-Sex Classes." *Education Week* (edweek.org/ew/articles/2012/02/17/21barnett.h31.html).
Barrett, K. (2018, July 24). "When Dress Codes Discriminate." *NEA Today* (neatoday.org/2018/07/24/when-school-dress-codes-discriminate).
Bartholet, E., Gertner, N., Halley, J., and Suk-Gersen, J. (2017, August 21). Fairness for All Students under Title IX (nrs.harvard.edu/urn-3:HUL.InstRepos:33789434).
Bates, L. (2015, May 22). "How School Dress Codes Shame Girls and Perpetuate Rape Culture." *Time* (time.com/3892965/everydaysexism-school-dress-codes-rape-culture).
Benham, N., Desai, M., Freeman, M., Kutzner, T. and Srivastav, K., eds. (2019). "Single-Sex Education." *Georgetown Journal of Gender and the Law* 20(2):509–540.
Bian, L., Leslie, S., and Cimpian, A. (2017). "Gender Stereotypes about Intellectual Ability Emerge Early and Influence Children's Interests." *Science* 355(6323):389–391.
Biklen, S., and Pollard, D., eds. (1993). *Gender and Education.* Yearbook of the National Society for the Study of Education. Chicago: National Society for the Study of Education.
Brooms, D. (2017). "Black Otherfathering in the Educational Experiences of Black Males in a Single-Sex Urban High School." *Teachers College Record* 119(1):1–46.
Brown, L., and Gilligan, C. (1993). *Meeting at the Crossroads.* Cambridge, MA: Harvard University Press.
Burman, D., Bitan, T., and Booth, J. (2008). "Sex Differences in Neural Processing of Language among Children." *Neuropsychologia* 46(5):1,349–1,362.

Chaudhry, N., and Tucker, J. (2018). *Let Her Learn: Stopping School Pushout*. Washington DC: National Women's Law Center.

Chen, G. (2017). Why Single-Sex Public Schools are Growing in Popularity. Public School Review (publicschoolreview.com/blog/why-single-sex-public-schools-are-growing-in-popularity).

Chodorow, N. (1978). *The Reproduction of Mothering*. Berkley: University of California Press.

Connell, R. (1995). *Masculinities*. Berkeley: University of California Press.

Davis v. Monroe County Board of Education (1999). 526 U.S. 629.

Excellence Charter School (2008). Our Program (uncommonschools.org/ecs/aboutUs/programAndValues.html).

Federal Register (2018). Nondiscrimination on the Basis of Sex in Education Programs or Activities Receiving Federal Financial Assistance. A Proposed Rule by the Education Department. 34 CFR Part 106, 61462.

Focus on the Family (2018). Our Position on Transgenderism (focusonthefamily.com/get-help/transgenderism-our-position).

Frazier, N., and Sadker, M. (1973). *Sexism in School and Society*. New York: Harper & Row.

Gender Spectrum (2019). Framework for Gender Inclusive Schools (genderspectrum.org/resources/education-2/#more-424).

Gilbert, J., Fields, J., Mamo, L., and Lesko, N. (2018). "Intimate Possibilities: The Beyond Bullying Project and Stories of LGBTQ Sexuality and Gender in U.S. Schools." *Harvard Educational Review* 88(2):163–183.

——— (2019). "Tending toward Friendship: LGBTQ Sexualities in U.S. Schools." *Sexualities* 22(1).

Gilligan, C. (1982). *In a Different Voice: Psychological Theory and Women's Development*. Cambridge, MA: Harvard University Press.

Grant, B-J. E., Wilkerson, S., Pelton, D., Cosby, A., and Henschel, M. (2019). "Title IX and School Employee Sexual Misconduct: How K–12 Schools Respond in the Wake of an Incident." *Educational Administration Quarterly* 55(5):841–866. https://doi.org/10.1177/0013161X19838030

Greene, C. (2019, May 24). It Should Be Illegal to Give Children Transgender Hormones and Surgery. The Federalist (thefederalist.com/2019/10/24/it-should-be-illegal-to-give-children-transgender-hormones-and-surgery).

Gurian, M. (2007a). *The Minds of Boys: Saving Our Sons from Falling Behind in School and Life*. New York: Jossey-Bass.

——— (2007b). *Nurture the Nature*. New York: Jossey-Bass.

Halpern, D., Eliot, L., Bigler, R., Fabes, R., Hanish, L., Hyde, J., Liben, L., and Martin, C. (2011). "The Pseudo-Science of Single-Sex Schooling." *Science* 333(6050):1,706–1,707.

Horowitz, H. (1984). *Alma Mater*. New York: Knopf.

Howard, T., Woodward, B., Navarro, O., Huerta, A., Haro, B., and Watson, K. (2019). "Renaming the Narrative, Reclaiming Their Humanity: Black and Latino Males' Descriptions of Success." *Teachers College Record* 121(5):1–32.

Howe, F. (1984). *Myths of Coeducation: Selected Essays*. Bloomington: Indiana University Press.

Jones, S. (2018, August 31). "Do School Dress Codes Discriminate against Girls?" *Education Week* (edweek.org/ew/articles/2018/09/05/do-school-dress-codes-discrimate-against-girls.html).

Kaestle, C. (1983). *Pillars of the Republic: Common Schools and American Society 1780–1860*. New York: Hill & Wang.

Kimmel, M. (2000, November 1). "What About the Boys?" *WEER Digest*, 1–2, 7–8.

Kindlon, D., and Thompson, M. (1999). *Raising Cain: Protecting the Emotional Life of Boys*. New York: Ballantine.

Kingkade, T. (2019, April 24). New Documents Show Trump Administration Has Confronted Dozens of School Districts across the Country for Mishandling Sexual Assault Cases. The 74 million.org (the74million.org).

Kosciw, J., Greytak, E., Diaz, E., and Bartkiewicz, M. (2018). *2017 National School Climate Survey: The Experiences of Lesbian, Gay, Bisexual and Transgender Youth in Our Nation's Schools.* New York: GLSEN.

Lichty, L., and Campbell, R. (2012). "Targets and Witnesses: Middle School Students' Sexual Harassment Experiences." *Journal of Early Adolescence* 32:414–430.

Mac an Ghaill, M. (1994). *The Making of Men: Masculinities, Sexualities and Schooling.* Buckingham, UK: Open University Press.

McGeown, S., and Warhurst, A. (2019). "Sex Differences in Education: Exploring Children's Gender Identity." *Educational Psychology* 40(1):103–119. https://doi.org/10.1080/01443410.2019.1640349

Miller, J. (1976). *Toward a New Psychology of Women.* Boston: Beacon Press.

Mitchell, C. (2017, November 15). Single-Sex Education in Five Charts (edweek.org/ew/section/multimedia/single-gender-public-schools-in-5-charts.html).

Musu, L., Zhang, A., Wang, K., Zhang, J., and Oudekerk, B. (2019). *Indicators of School Crime and Safety: 2018* (NCES 2019-047/NCJ 252571). Washington, DC: National Center for Education Statistics, U.S. Department of Education and Bureau of Justice Statistics, Office of Justice Programs, U.S. Department of Justice.

National Association for Single-Sex Public Education (2011). Single-Sex Schools/Single-Sex Classes: What's the Difference (singlesexschools.org/schools-schools.htm).

National Collegiate Athletic Association (2020). Title IX Frequently Asked Questions (ncaa.org/about/resources/inclusion/title-ix-frequently-asked-questions#benifit).

National Federation of State High School Associations (2019). 2017–18 High School Athletics Participation Survey (nfhs.org/media/1020205/2017-18_hs_participation_survey.pdf).

National Science Board (2018). *Science and Engineering Indicators 2018* (NSB-2018-1). Alexandria, VA: National Science Foundation.

Nelson, J. (2016). "Relational Teaching with Black Boys: Strategies for Learning at a Single-Sex Middle School for Boys of Color." *Teachers College Record* 118(6):1–30.

Olson, K., Durwood, L., DeMeules, M., and McLaughlin, K. (2016). "Mental Health of Transgender Children Who Are Supported in Their Identities." *Pediatrics* 137(3):1–10.

Pahlke, E., Hyde, J. S., & Allison, C. M. (2014). "The Effects of Single-Sex Compared with Coeducational Schooling on Students' Performance and Attitudes: A Meta-Analysis." *Psychological Bulletin* 140(4):1,042–1,072.

Piehl, T. (2018). *Fostering Academic and Social Engagement: An Investigation into the Effects of All-Girls Education in the Transition to University.* Higher Education Research Institute at University of California, Los Angeles.

Pollack, W. (1999). *Real Boys.* New York: Dimensions.

Ravitch, D. (2003). *The Language Police: How Pressure Groups Restrict What Students Learn.* New York: Alfred A. Knopf.

Reichert, M., and Hawley, R. (2014). *I Can Learn from You: Boys as Relational Learners.* Cambridge, MA: Harvard Education Press.

Robinson-Cimpian, J., Lubienski, S., Ganley, C., and Copur-Gencturk, Y. (2014). "Teachers' Perceptions of Students' Mathematics Proficiency May Exacerbate Early Gender Achievement Gaps." *Developmental Psychology* 50(4):1,262–1,281.

Rury, J. (1991). *Education and Women's Work.* Albany: State University of New York Press.

Russell, S., Muraco, A., Subramaniam, A., and Lamb, C. (2009). "Youth Empowerment and High School Gay-Straight Alliances." *Journal of Youth and Adolescence* 38:891–903.

Russell, S., Ryan, C., Toomey, R., Diaz, R., and Sanchez, J. (2010). "Lesbian, Gay, Bisexual, and Transgender Adolescent School Victimization: Implications for Young Adult Health and Adjustment." *Journal of School Health* 81(5):223–230.

Sadker, M., and Sadker, D. (1982). *Sex Equity Handbook for Schools.* New York: Longman.

——— (1994). *Failing at Fairness: How Schools Cheat Girls.* New York: Touchstone.

Sadowski, M. (2017). *Safe is Not Enough: Better Schools for LGBTQ Students*. Cambridge, MA: Harvard Education Press.

Sax, L. (2006). *Why Gender Matters: What Parents and Teachers Need to Know about the Emerging Science of Sex Differences*. New York: Broadway.

——— (2007). *Boys Adrift: The Five Factors Driving the Growing Epidemic of Unmotivated Boys and Underachieving Young Men*. New York: Basic Books.

Segal, L. (1990). *Slow Motion: Changing Masculinities, Changing Men*. London: Virago.

Sklar, K. (1993). "The Schooling of Girls and Changing Community Values in Massachusetts Towns 1750–1820." *History of Education Quarterly* 33(4):511–542.

Snyder, T., de Brey, C., and Dillow, S. (2019). *Digest of Education Statistics 2018* (NCES 2020-009). Washington, DC: National Center for Education Statistics, Institute of Education Sciences, U.S. Department of Education.

Solomon, B. (1986). *In the Company of Educated Women*. New Haven, CT: Yale University Press.

Spring, J. (2018). *The American School from the Puritans to the Trump Era*. New York: Routledge.

Tozer, S., Senese, G., and Violas, P. (2012). *School and Society: Historical and Contemporary Perspectives* (7th ed.). New York: McGraw-Hill.

Tucker Center for Research on Girls and Women in Sport (2018). *The 2018 Tucker Center Research Report, Developing Physically Active Girls: An Evidence-Based Multidisciplinary Approach*. Minneapolis: Tucker Center for Research on Girls and Women in Sport, University of Minnesota.

Tyack, D., and Hansot, E. (1992). *Learning Together: A History of Coeducation in American Public Schools*. New York: Russell Sage Foundation.

United States v. Virginia (1996). 518 U.S. 515, 533.

Urban, W., and Wagoner, J. (2008). *American Education: A History*. New York: Routledge.

U.S. Census Bureau (2011). Educational Attainment of the Population 25 Years and Older by Selected Characteristics (census.gov/hhes/socdemo/education/data/cps/2010/tables.html).

——— (2019). Educational Attainment of the Population 25 Years and Older by Selected Characteristics (census.gov/data/tables/2018/demo/education-attainment/cps-detailed-tables.html).

U.S. Department of Education (2011a). *Equity in Athletics Disclosure Act Survey Results*. Washington, DC: Office of Postsecondary Education.

——— (2011b). Women's Educational Equity (ed.gov/programs/equity/index.html).

——— (2014). *Questions and Answers on Title IX and Single-Sex Elementary and Secondary Classes and Extracurricular Activities*. Washington, DC: Office of Civil Rights.

——— (2019a). *Equity in Athletics Disclosure Act Survey Results*. Washington, DC: Office of Postsecondary Education.

——— (2019b). Resources for LGBTQ Students. Washington, DC: Office of Civil Rights (ed.gov/about/offices/list/ocr/lgbt.html).

——— (2019c). *School Climate and Safety*. Washington, DC: Office of Civil Rights (ed.gov/about/offices/list/ocr/docs/school-climate-and-safety.pdf).

——— (2020). Resources for LGBTQ Students. Washington, DC: Office of Civil Rights (ed.gov/about/offices/list/ocr/lgbt.html).

U.S. Department of Health, Education and Welfare (1978). *Taking Sexism Out of Education: The National Project on Women in Education*. Washington, DC: U.S. Department of Health, Education and Welfare.

Williams, S. (2018, February 28). "Are the Brains of Transgender People Different from Cisgendered?" *The Scientist* (the-scientist.com/features/are-the-brains-of-transgender-people-different-from-those-of-cisgender-people-30027).

Zarrett, N., Veliz, P., & Sabo, D. (2018). *Teen Sport in America: Why Participation Matters*. East Meadow, NY: Women's Sports Foundation.

Immigrants and the Schools

Unfair Burden or Business as Usual

7

What responsibilities should schools have for immigrants?

Position 1:   Schools Must Help New Immigrants

For children, the immigrant experience begins at school . . . assimilation into American culture does not happen purely through osmosis. Schools play a key role in this process.

—Wicks and Kimball Johnson (2018)

Human migrations across this continent have taken place throughout history . . . historical constructs of nations, laws, and inequality impel people to migrate to places of relative safety. What would make parents send their children on a dangerous and life-threatening journey . . . to a hostile foreign land?

—Mayers and Freedman (2019)

We are all descendants of immigrants. Some Native American tribes disagree, but available evidence indicates that all Americans arrived by immigration. Archaeology, anthropology, and genetics studies find the first modern humans, after Neanderthals, emigrated from Africa between 50,000 and 80,000 years ago (Sutton, 2016). There is a current academic dispute about timing and potential evidence (Zimmer, 2017), but the main point is that we are the product of immigration. Migration is human history (Migration Data Portal, 2020; United Nations, 2020).

Nation-states evolved, making the establishment of geographic borders and citizenship consequential. Migration across national boundaries became a national and international concern. Emigration can be a problem for nations that lose populations because of conditions like famine, war, ethnic cleansing, economic disorder, or climate change. Nations need people to sustain their society. Immigration is a problem when governments or significant portions of nations feel threatened by all or specific immigrants. Nationalism and protectionism are now dominant interests of govern-ments (Lepore, 2019). Citizenship, as historian Jill Lepore (2018a) eloquently writes, has been a question since America's founding, especially for women, blacks, Native Americans, immigrants, and others. Citizenship restrictions, border protection by walls or electronics, trade and economic policies, and other avenues prevent or limit immigration. Globalization and open borders are seen as threats to a history of pro-tected borders and national restrictions (Bremmer, 2018).

Oscar Handlin's (1951) classic history of immigration in America, *The Uprooted: The Epic Story of the Great Migrations That Made the American People*, begins: "Once I thought to write a history of the immigrants in America. Then I discovered that the immigrants were American history." This view, however, is not one that is shared across the nation, or throughout its history. The colonies and the United States have a mixed tradition on immigration, from welcoming to severe restriction. Immigration relatively free from restrictions was the norm, with some religious differences, until the late 1700s. The Naturalization Act of 1790 limited citizenship to "free whites of good character" who had lived here for 2 years. The Alien and Sedition Acts of 1789, which were enacted to address a French threat, allowed deportation of foreigners and raised residency requirements from 5 to 14 years. The Know-Nothing Party, formed in 1848 as the first anti-immigration party, was a response to German and Irish immi-gration. Between 1880 and 1950, laws banned polygamists, prostitutes, the sick and diseased, Chinese, certain categories of criminals, and others; over time, some have been rescinded, others remain. Immigration, as a hot political issue, rises and falls over time. It is also an educational issue, whether it is found in public debate or not. Handlin (1951) saw heredity as the raw material for immigrants, with education and environment as tools for integration or limit. Sizable immigration, legal or illegal, cre-ates educational issues and opportunities.

The so-called "immigration problem" in America, Benton-Cohen (2018) writes, was invented to politicize an increase in immigrants, to fuel a common and politically stoked fear. She traces the work of the U.S. Immigration Commission, also known as the Dillingham Commission, from 1907 to 1911, whose prime leadership included aristocrats and politicians who shared a "passion for imperialism and immigration restriction" (p. 1). The Commission's voluminous report contained 29,000 pages in 41 volumes and was identified by the *New York Times* as all "garbage." But the report was used by Congress to develop policies, like stopping mass immigration, that continue into the twenty-first century, and laws that establish a nationality based quota system, a literacy test, exclusion of Asians, race-oriented policies, a concern for oversupply of unskilled labor, and preventing entry to those with bad habits or personal qualities. Today, immigration is still perceived as a problem, a crisis, a threat—but Handlin (1951) says it is us. Policies and practices now include family separation, raids on businesses and homes, quick deportations, local defensive claims of sanctuary status, and serious questions for the education of migrant children.

Using oral history interviews, Mayers and Freedman (2019) documented the life stories of young refugees from Central America who came to the United States during the 1980s and 1990s. Why did young people migrate from their homes? A partial answer, the authors note, is the Cold War, "when, in the name of fighting Communism, the United States intervened in Central America, overthrowing a democratic regime in Guatemala, and backed right-wing dictatorships in El Salvador, Honduras, and Nicaragua" (p. 2). Following the U.S. overt intervention, over 250,000 people were killed by government forces, many were tortured and injured, and hundreds of thousands were forced to leave these countries. Then, partly because of some CIA behind-the-scenes involvement, drugs and drug gangs became powerful in the region; they continue to dominate in many areas today. Gangs force residents to join, flee, pay extortion, be victimized, or be killed. Prior to the U.S. interventions, "youth migration from Central American was virtually nil" (p. 3). Now, thousands of families with children, and children on their own, come from Central America to the U.S. border, seeking asylum, safety, and a better life.

Senator Jeff Merkley (2019) says that the situation for immigrant children and families seeking asylum in the United States is very difficult because of U.S. government policies and practices. He identifies the child separation policy begun in 2018 as "the most cruel" law. His book, *America Is Better Than This*, cites the United Nations' Universal Declaration of Human Rights and Refugee Convention, which established the rights of people to seek asylum from persecution, along with the U.S. law recognizing these rights. Restrictive procedures and practices make the exercise of these rights very cumbersome for refugees who arrive without adequate resources, legal assistance, and language and cultural differences. Some may not seek asylum, may not succeed in the pursuit of asylum, or may not know of the process and conditions. They become illegal when they enter regardless. Politics change and so do laws; there are obvious differences between legal and illegal immigration, but both types include innocent children coming into a new country.

Providing Schooling for New Immigrants

A U.S. Supreme Court decision in 1982, *Plyler v. Doe*, held that a Texas state law that denied public education for illegal immigrants was unconstitutional under the Equal Protection Clause of the Fourteenth Amendment. Arguing the Texas law was discriminatory and "directed against children," the Court said the children had a right to attend public school. Justice William Brennan, delivering the majority opinion of the Supreme Court, wrote,

> Aliens, even aliens whose presence in this country is unlawful, have long been recognized as "persons" guaranteed due process of law by the Fifth and Fourteenth Amendments. . . . The American people have always regarded education and [the] acquisition of knowledge as matters of extreme importance. . . . [E]ducation provides the basic tools by which individuals might lead economically productive lives to the benefit of all of us. In sum, education has a fundamental role in maintaining the fabric of our society. . . . Denial of education to some isolated group of children poses an affront to one of the goals of the Equal Protection Clause. . . . This law imposes a lifetime of hardship on a discrete class of children not accountable for their disabling status. (*Plyler v. Doe*, 1982)

Plyler remains the law of the land, despite attempts by various states and Congress to reverse its effects. Well-reasoned arguments of the Court notwithstanding, undocumented students are still a vulnerable school population because of their precarious status outside of the school and their struggles with English in the classroom (Rabin et al., 2008). Lepore (2018b) notes the *Plyler* decision is not widely known, but is very significant, especially in the current immigration situation. She cites Justin Driver's (2018) legal analysis that the *Plyler* decision is among the "most egalitarian, momentous, and efficacious constitutional opinions" in the history of the Supreme Court.

The education of immigrant children has always been a function of public schools, and it is a responsibility in today's schools. The children of immigrants—documented or undocumented—have a right to a free, public education. Schleicher (2015), introducing an Organisation for Economic Co-operation and Development document, *Helping Immigrant Students to Succeed at School—and Beyond*, says: "How school systems respond to migration has an enormous impact on the economic and social well-being of all members of the communities." This international body recognizes problems in migrant children's sense of belonging in the school, language barriers, and cultural dissonance. Cordoza (2019) identifies issues for U.S. schools in areas where migrant children live.

1. *Adjustment*. It can take weeks or months to adjust and be minimally comfortable.
2. *Large gaps in schooling*. Academic and skill needs can be extensive.
3. *Social and emotional needs*. Friendships, counseling, empathy, and humanity.
4. *Language and culture differences*. Bilingual teachers and resources; sensitivity.
5. *Fractured family life*. Home visits, family involvement, assistance.
6. *Trauma*. Psychological support, provision for assistance without penalty.
7. *Health*. Medical support, education, nutrition, and exercise.
8. *Special needs*. Extra personnel; bilingual.
9. *Economic*. Financial needs, not only for immigrants, but for schools.

School staffs need pertinent training and assistance for meeting some of these needs. Special personnel may be needed to deal with social, emotional, physical, or academic concerns. Schedules, curriculum, standards, and expectations may need more flexibility to account for language and cultural differences. Facilities and operations may need some revision to accommodate numbers and mattes like health and nutrition support. Implementing good ideas to help immigrant children adapt to a new environment and adjust to school may require additional funds (Jordan, 2019).

Immigration Rates and School Responses

A Brookings Institution report shows the United States experiencing the slowest population growth rate of natural citizens in 80 years (Frey, 2019). Birth rates are declining and age and deaths are increasing. Without immigration, this will be a very serious national issue. Since the turn of the twenty-first century, average natural population growth rates are projected to fall (see Table 7.1).

Record high immigration rates are projected through 2050, when one in five people in the United States is expected to be foreign born (Passel and Cohn, 2008). Without young immigrants, by 2035 we become an older society, with more seniors over 65 than children under 18 (Frey, 2018). We depend on immigration to supply the workforce and maintain economic vitality that is the nation's tradition; otherwise our society can decline. Social Security, Medicare, general social services, highways, construction, and far more are in jeopardy.

Table 7.1 Decade Natural Population Growth Rate and Projections	
2000 to 2010	9.7%
2010 to 2020	7.7%
2020 to 2030	6.8%
2030 to 2040	5.2%
2040 to 2050	4.1%

Source: Frey (2019).

In the late nineteenth and early twentieth centuries, immigrants tended to settle in urban areas, but twenty-first century immigrants are settling in cities, suburbs, and small towns. Schools everywhere are being directly affected by immigration, and teaching students whose primary language is not English is becoming common.

The children of immigrants are transforming American schools by their unprecedented numbers and sheer diversity. About 40% of newcomer children are from Mexico, the largest sender nation. China is second largest, followed by Cuba, India, and the Dominican Republic (Hernandez et al., 2007; Baugh and Witsman, 2017). The level of education and social experience in their home counties varies widely. As one team of researchers notes, "On one end of the spectrum, we find children from middle-class urban backgrounds who have been preparing in their countries since early childhood for high-stakes, competitive exams. . . . In sharp contrast are those children from strife-ridden countries with little or no schooling" (Suarez-Orozco and Suarez-Orozco, 2001, p. 128). The children of immigrants have always made good use of schools to improve themselves and their economic well-being (White and Glick, 2009). Any attempt to deny today's immigrants access to education harms the newcomers and deprives the nation of an educated workforce and important investments in our future.

Cultural and Family Challenges: More Than Language Skills

> Great achievements were the product of [the immigrants'] labors; without their contributions the country could not have taken the form it did. But they paid a heavy price, not only in the painful process of crossing and resettlement but also in the continuous ache of uprootedness. . . . And to the extent that the process succeeded, a widening gulf developed between the immigrants and their children. (Handlin, 1966, pp. xiii, xiv)

Immigration has always been a difficult and stressful experience for newcomer families. Immigrants leave behind friends and familiar ways, and older family members often forfeit esteemed community roles and assume lower social status and lesser-valued employment in the United States. Children of immigrants may struggle in schools as they wrestle with the different culture and unfamiliar language of their new home (Gaytan et al., 2007). Americans have always celebrated the success stories of this nation of immigrants. Today, as in the past, many immigrants do very well in school and life, but many more are at risk of failure. As Suarez-Orozco and Gardner (2003) write, "Our research indicates that while some [children of immigrants] will end up as the beneficiaries of life in the new land, too many others are unable to cope with the global dislocations. As we have come to put it, the life options become Yale or Jail, Princeton or Prison" (p. 44).

Success in schools has always been important to the children of newcomers, but it may be more important today than ever. Doing well in school is essential to economic survival and social integration. Schools can help expand the range of successful options. Schooling is central to the processes by which the children of immigrants are taught to survive and prosper and forge a better life in their new country (Suarez-Orozco et al., 2008). In schools, the children of immigrants learn the skills necessary for academic success. Newcomers also experience schools as cultural sites where they are introduced to the social "rules" of American society, and they meet teachers, typically members of the dominant culture, who help them understand their new country and find their way in it. Experience in schools and greater language facility allow children of immigrants to become culture interpreters for their parents and families. With a foot in each of two worlds, they are called on to mediate the conflicting expectations and experiences of host and heritage cultures while trying to honor both (Adams and Kirova, 2007). They can also suffer if their families are not supportive. Informed teachers, sensitive to immigration issues, can help students navigate between the two worlds.

To benefit the children, their families, and society, schools should develop programs for immigrant families that "resonate with their cultural backgrounds, immigrant experience, and daily lives" (Colon, 2019). Those families should be the center of participation, recognizing their experiences, interests, and knowledge. Participation in family literacy programs are a good start.

Schools should help children of immigrants achieve academically without uprooting them from the traditions of their families. Schools and teachers can help the children of new immigrants preserve their heritage language and culture and maintain their own historical identity while mastering English and the values and skills necessary for economic and social advancement in the United States (Suarez-Orozco and Qin-Hilliard, 2004; Adams and Kirova, 2007; Suarez-Orozco et al., 2008; White and Glick, 2009).

Adjusting to American schooling is no easy matter for many children of immigrants. Multiple social forces influence the academic success of the children of newcomers, including the difficulties associated with the stress of migration, the separations from long-standing cultural traditions, and, for many immigrants, the complex interplay of poverty, racism, social segregation, and identity formation with new cultural rules.

Schools need to take into account the differences between today's immigrants and the immigrants of earlier periods. It is not uncommon to hear immigrant success stories about someone's grandparents who came to America, learned English in night school, and gave up the ways of the "old country" in order to succeed in America. The old model of assimilation—in which immigrants abandoned heritage languages and cultural identity to become part of the "melting pot" of America—has given way to an understanding that many of today's immigrants want to be bilingual and bicultural and will remain "unmeltable." New immigrants are less willing to follow a path that promises success at the expense of depriving themselves and their children of language diversity and cultural history (Salomon, 2010). They argue that success will follow more comfortably by embracing old and new worlds. Speaking more than one language and being at home in more than one culture is a benefit in a multilingual, multicultural world.

Language and Languages

The first census in 1790 shows that half the population of the United States was of English descent, 15% were English speakers from Scotland and Ireland. Dutch, French, and Spanish origin made up about 14%, and 19% were of African heritage (Wiley, 2007). Many people, including enslaved Africans and Native Americans, were uncounted in the first census, and did not speak English as their first language. By 1890, immigrants represented 14.8% of the total U.S. population, and very few of the new arrivals of that time were from English-speaking counties.

American free public education developed in the period between 1830 and 1850, the era of the common school. Schooling at public expense was viewed as broadly beneficial, contributing academic, social, and political value to daily life. Faced with a new and large number of newcomers from Ireland and Germany, advocates of the Common Schools urged the government to provide public-supported education to develop in the new immigrants the language, habits, and values of the old immigrants (Kaestle, 1983). The schools were seen as the most appropriate agency for advancing a common culture.

It was no doubt challenging for nineteenth-century schools to encourage the children of German immigrants to learn English and the children of Irish Catholic immigrants to adopt Protestant values, but today's schools contend with students from everywhere in the world and of every religious belief. Forging a common social and political ideology would be impossible, even if it were desirable. Consider language alone: according to one estimate, within the next several years, over 30% of children in public schools will come from homes with limited English proficiency or where English is not the first language. Although 82% of English language learners (ELLs) in schools come from Spanish-speaking homes, surveys have identified over 350 different first languages spoken among ELLs (NCTE ELL Task Force, 2006, p. 1).

Language Matters

Bilingual speakers outnumber monolingual speakers around the world, and bilingualism is associated with a wide range of cognitive benefits, from better problem-solving skills to improved memory and attention (Adesope et al., 2010). Americans claim to admire bilingualism, a traditional measure of a well-educated person, and typically express envy of anyone who can speak two or more languages. Multilingual job seekers are at an advantage in careers ranging from business to national security. Beyond offering foreign language courses, it is rare for American schools to encourage English-dominant speakers to become proficient in a second language. The unidirectional approach to second-language instruction penalizes students who have limited English proficiency, imposing academic burdens on them not faced by English-dominant speakers. Language instruction of this sort can devalue languages other than English, and the cultures of speakers of other languages (Salomon, 2010).

Bilingual education has been the center of controversy, and it is not surprising that misconceptions have developed about the programs. You may have heard some or all of the following myths about bilingual education:

- Learning two languages, especially during the early childhood years, confuses children and delays the acquisition of English.
- Total English immersion is the most effective way for ELLs to acquire English.
- It divides the United States and discriminates against European languages.
- The public is against it (Espinosa, 2008; Education.com, 2019).

These myths do not stand up to scrutiny. "A generation of research and practice has shown that developing academic skills and knowledge in students' vernacular supports their acquisition of English" (Crawford, 2007, p. 146). Bilingualism is an asset to all children in a multicultural society. Research demonstrates that young children are fully capable of learning two languages (NCTE ELL Task Force, 2006; Espinosa, 2008). Research also finds that instruction in both English and the heritage language can effectively introduce newcomer children to the success patterns in the United States without denigrating the home culture, but the loss of home language has negative consequences for student learning (Adams and Kirova, 2007; Crawford, 2007; Faltis and Coulter, 2008). In addition, 87% of academics support bilingual education (Education.com, 2019).

Dual language immersion (DLI) programs have developed as a solid alternative under some circumstances. Initially, these programs provided at least 50% of school language time devoted to building both literacy skills and content knowledge. Now, there are two forms: (1) 50% of time in each language and (2) a graduated program, where 80 to 90% of time is spent in the student's first language in the earliest grades and is subsequently decreased each school year until each language receives 50% of time by middle school years. Evidence suggests that dual language immersion programs work; they increase students' self-esteem, family cultural heritage, and personal identity—and research shows that learning one language transfers to learning other languages (Rosales, 2018; Muniz, 2019).

Law, Language, and Education

The Bilingual Education Act, also known as Title VII of the Elementary and Secondary Education Amendments of 1967, supported the teaching of English as a second language for ELLs. It also strengthened students' heritage language skills, knowledge of their cultural past, and supported innovative multicultural curricula and multilingual instruction. English is essential for their economic security and social integration, but not at the expense of losing their cultural history and original language.

The No Child Left Behind Act of 2001 set high academic standards through testing and identified historically neglected language-minority learners as needing attention to try to keep them from falling between the cracks of public education. These goals have good intentions, but are heavily reliant on nationally standardized testing and English language facility is stressed as very important (National Association for Bilingual Education, 2007; Solorzano, 2008; Kieffer et al., 2009). The Teachers of English to Speakers of Other Languages (TESOL), concerned about "inappropriate assessment tools" because "a singular test for high-stakes decisions will undermine, rather than promote, the academic success of English language learners," recommended multiple measures to assess and report on the progress of learners, such as curriculum-based, rubric, and holistic assessments. Also, native language skills should be developed alongside English skills (Aronson, 2010, pp. 1–4).

Subject-matter tests in English can produce inaccurate assessments of actual academic ability or performance of ELL students (Kieffer et al., 2009), and the schools they attend could face sanctions. According to Darling-Hammond (2008), "Virtually all schools with significant ELL enrollments will soon be in the 'failing' category. It is hard to see how such an indiscriminate 'accountability' system . . . has anything to do with improving schools." It is a "diversity penalty," requiring "the largest gains from lower-performing schools, although these schools serve needier students and generally have fewer resources than schools serving wealthier students" (p. 164). The 2015 Every Student Succeeds Act (ESSA) provides flexibility for states to determine some testing and standards, but still requires tracking of ELLs on their English skills.

The politics of bilingual education, an offspring of partisan battles over immigration, caused some states to pass English-only laws, and others required separation of ELLs from other students for special English immersion classes, making adjustment to school more difficult. Research has showed unfavorable results for English-only programs in language proficiency and in learning other subjects. State laws are changing toward support of bilingual and bicultural programs again, however, the issue remains politically charged and legal battles continue.

The 1982 *Plyler* decision on public education for undocumented children did not resolve all matters. Since that decision, policies have been implemented in order to address the issues they face. If passed, the Development, Relief, and Education for Alien Minors (DREAM) Act would grant unauthorized youth of good moral character permanent residency status in the United States and open a path to citizenship and economic success not currently available to undocumented youth. DREAM legislation has been introduced in Congress regularly since 2001. In 2012, Deferred Action for Children Arrivals (DACA) was implemented by the Obama administration, protecting some undocumented children by deferring deportation and providing work authorization. It was rescinded in 2017 by the Trump administration, but federal judges have intervened to allow DACA to continue for current and past recipients to renew their status (American Immigration Council, 2019). These acts are in harmony with the positive part of immigration history in the United States and the ways education helps newly arrived immigrants and serves national ends.

Fear Mongering, Myths, and the Needs of the Undocumented

The United States has a checkered history of discouragement and encouragement for immigrants, but we like to think of ourselves as a nation made and improved by them.

Chomsky (2018) identifies many myths about immigration, such as

1. They take our jobs, compete with workers, drive down wages, and avoid taxes.

2. Immigrants are illegal, criminals, drug dealers, terrorists, and worse.

3. They are not learning English and not assimilating, thereby threatening American culture.

4. The American public opposes immigration.

She provides evidence that destroys these myths. Immigrants as a group are not an economic burden. They take low-paying jobs that do not attract native workers and pay at least as much in taxes as the government returns to them in services. Immigrants pay social security, property, sales, and income taxes (Camarota, 2009; Chomsky, 2018). As a group, they work hard, don't take others' jobs, don't have criminal records, are not terrorists, learn English and want to adjust to American life, contribute to the diversity of American culture, come by legal means or desire to be legal, and have the support of the majority of Americans in national polls. Almost 50% of the Fortune 500 corporations were founded by first or second generation immigrants (Hathaway, 2017). Immigration is positive for the American society and economy.

What are some of the reasons for so much anti-immigrant fear and negative comments? Foreign terrorism? Bias against new immigrants or select groups based on religion, color, or national origin? White supremacy rhetoric? Generalized fear of the "other"? Is it also fear mongering for political gain (Benton-Cohen, 2018)? What these reasons elucidate is that fear and negativity toward a particular group can exist due to a multitude of social, cultural, and political beliefs. Asking ourselves why we hold those beliefs is the beginning of a productive conversation of how, as a country, we can confront the policy issues surrounding immigrants.

Education is the traditional key to economic success for all immigrants and education can serve the 10 million unauthorized immigrants now living in the United States. Unauthorized immigrants, roughly 23% of the foreign-born population, need access to schools and school services to enhance their lives, as they are handicapped by their "unauthorized" status. Millions of immigrant children in the United States are at risk of lower educational performance and limited economic futures because of their unauthorized status: "that unauthorized status harms [personal] development, from beginning of life through adolescence and young adulthood, by restricting access to some of the most important pathways to adult well-being and productivity." These pathways begin with the availability of child care and preschools and extend to higher education and subsequent paths to employment (Suarez-Orozco et al., 2011, p. 462).

Immigrants have always needed schools, and the nation has always needed immigrants, prospering from their contributions to the culture and the economy. Schools can assist new immigrants, encourage their aspirations, and help them flourish for the good of the students, the schools, and the nation as a whole. Helping immigrants find their place in America and equipping them with tools necessary to succeed have always been responsibilities of schools.

Position 2:   Bad Policy Overburdens Schools

Public school districts across the United States are suffering under a massive unfunded mandate imposed by the federal government: the requirement to educate millions of illegal aliens, the school age children of illegal aliens, refugees, and legal immigrant children.

—Ferris and Raley (2016)

The number of children from immigrant households in schools is now so high in some areas that it raises profound questions about assimilation . . . immigration has added enormously to the number of public school students who are in poverty and the number who speak a foreign language.

—Camarota et al. (2017)

Uncontrolled Immigration, Illegal Entry, and National Security

Immigration has become, once again, a major concern for the United States. Immigrants overwhelm our borders, stretch our resources, and threaten our culture. The Center for Immigration Studies, a nonprofit, independent research organization, identifies itself as the only one devoted entirely to research and policy studies on the impact of immigration on the United States. Their analysis of data shows that net U.S. immigration, the difference between people leaving and those coming in, will be 46 million by 2060. About 95% of the difference will be from immigration if we continue current policies and practices (and barring other global events that produce even more massive population shifts). As a result, today's total population of 330 million would increase 25% for a total population of 404 million (Camarota and Zeigler, 2019a). The Migration Policy Institute (2006, 2019) estimates an even greater U.S. population by 2060, about 420 million. The United States currently has the third largest population in the world, behind China and India at about 1.3 billion each. Do we want to compete with them in population, largely determined by immigration?

If the United States had an open border policy, who might come? Sussis (2019) analyzed international polling conducted by Gallup, which found that about 158 million people around the world would chose to migrate to the United States if given the opportunity. He also found that chain migration, where immigrants sponsor family members and others to immigrate, has increased in the past decades: in 2000, each new immigrant sponsored an average of 3.5 additional immigrants, about one-third more than the average number sponsored in the 1980s. Chain migration functions as a multiplier; when added to those who would come if they could, the total number of immigrants would boom to over 700 million. With 330 million here now, an added 700 million brings us into the population territories of China and India.

That extreme number is, of course, only an illustration of the statistical possibilities of open borders. Explosive immigration of this magnitude brings to light the issues surrounding the sustainability of such an influx of immigrants. Imagine the kinds of social, political, and economic problems created by that scenario. The additional demands for basics such as food, water, and shelter would be problematic to meet. National security, the environment, government, safety, health, and everyday personal and social life would change in unpredictable ways. Finding additional funds for buildings, teachers, and school materials would be even more difficult than it is now. This extreme projection shows why immigration must be more tightly controlled, seriously limited, or stopped when circumstances necessitate it.

Most projections primarily deal with legal or anticipated legitimate immigration; they usually don't account for secret, smuggled, hidden, or other types of illegal entry. Legal immigration is now at record levels in the United States, and illegal immigration produces large but uncharted numbers. The number of legal and illegal immigrants overwhelms U.S. services at the border and in society in areas like housing, feeding, health care, and general social services, including education.

National Sovereignty, American Culture, Social Issues

Projections of excessive total immigration to the United States with no barriers may be unrealistic but it can focus attention. Realistic projections based on current loose, flexible, or nonexistent barriers that allow surges of illegals and asylum-seekers also show immense numbers in the near future. This suggests a compromising of national sovereignty and a fragmentation of the American culture. Conditions of disunity, social upheaval, interethnic conflict, and economic disorder can occur as the population changes dramatically. It is usually difficult for individual legal immigrants from different cultural backgrounds to adjust to life in a new country. Many American agencies, communities, and local people help in that adjustment process. When additional millions of immigrants arrive, a difficult adjustment is magnified. It swamps agencies, drains local resources and philanthropic interests, and creates serious tensions between the immigrant groups and the broader society.

Newt Gingrich (2008), historian and former Majority Leader of the House, describes the issue in a larger context: "This cultural struggle over the future of America—and the very definition of America—underlies the immigration fight. The gap between the leftist elites and the rest of America could hardly be broader" (p. 129). Inconsistent policies and disparate practices create special problems and expenses for schools with immigrant populations.

One example of this problem is the fact that the average age of immigrants is increasing quickly (Camarota and Zeigler, 2019b). Open immigration advocates claim that we need young immigrants to replenish our aging population and keep the economy moving. But data show the average age of new immigrants in 2000 was 26, and in 2017 was 31. During this same time period, the average age of new immigrants and existing immigrants rose from 39 to 45. The number of immigrants over age 50 nearly doubled, and those over 65 nearly tripled. Instead of replenishing with youth, older immigrants are more likely to be a burden on social services and the economy with shorter work lives, more health needs, and more infrastructure and taxpayer strain. Obtaining increased funding for educating new immigrants will be significantly more difficult when in competition with funding necessary welfare and medical support.

Another issue related to Gingrich's concern about the cultural struggle underlying immigration arguments is exemplified in a recent report on the distribution of population. The U.S. Census projects that the United States will become "minority white" in 2045 (Frey, 2018). This projection has the white population at 49.7%, Hispanic at 24.6%, black at 13.1%, Asian at 7.9%, and multiracial at 3.8%. Frey (2018), a widely respected demographer, notes that projections show that immigration accounts for one-third of the Hispanic increase and three-fourths of the Asian increase. He reports that current existing minority populations are younger than the white population; the combination of immigration and higher birth rates for minority populations account for more minority growth. For those under 18, the "tipping point" for white minority status is right now, for those 18 to 27, the tipping point is about 2027, and for age 60 and over, it comes about 2060 (Frey, 2018). For schools, this may create demands for major adjustments in staffing, curriculum, instruction, funding, and traditional efforts to assimilate these children.

Our national interest rests on providing for American citizens and their security. This includes protections from overwhelming immigration, extensive taxation to cover the costs of immigration, and vulnerability to foreign control, crime, disease, or economic and social disorder. Immigration reduction or stabilization is one avenue for our national policy and practices (Department of Homeland Security, 2019). It should be the focus of Congress and the executive branch of government, along with border security. NumbersUSA (2019) offers sensible suggestions for cutting immigration in half, from 1 million per year to 500,000, by ending chain migration for extended families, stopping the overstaying of visas and visa fraud, reforming birthright citizenship for children of noncitizens, stopping amnesty for illegal entrants, and reducing rewards for illegal immigrants—such as free public education.

Education Problems from Immigration, Legal and Illegal

Pat Buchanan (2006) stated:

> The average immigrant comes to this country much poorer and far less educated than Americans and consumes far more per capita in public services. Economically, immigrants are a net burden on the nation. . . . We are on a treadmill we will never get off if we do not get control of immigration. (pp. 13, 46)

Since 2006, there has been a change in reported education level of immigrants, but there is actually a more negative social impact. Camarota and Zeigler (2018) show that newer immigrants claim higher levels of formal education now, but our society is not better off. The data show that, between 2007 and 2017, immigrant median incomes fell, the rate of poverty is higher, Medicaid use jumped threefold, and the use of food stamp benefits increased 150%. Despite increased reported schooling outside of the United States, immigrants need public assistance.

The relation of new immigrants to schools is complex. Historic, political, legal, and cultural issues surround the question of how immigration influences education. Massive increases in legal and illegal immigration demonstrate our nation's lack of intelligent measures to control, identify, and follow up on recent immigrants and their status, as well as a lack of adequate funding for the additional social services required. Schools did not create these problems, but they bear much of the brunt of the predicament. Educational problems that stem from weak and ineffective immigration policies and practices should be examined within that larger context (Brimelow, 2008).

Education is a significant issue influenced by and influencing immigration. Many immigrants desire our free public education. Education costs can be added to an estimate of the main health and related social services bill at about $113 billion per year, plus other, often hidden costs in the police, court, administration, and transportation costs (Federation for American Immigration Reform [FAIR], 2011, 2016). Questions surround American immigration policies in regard to education. Should schools be responsible—and accountable—for the education of all immigrants, legal and illegal? Should this all be taxpayer financed? Should that include taxpayer-subsidized higher education? Should we place no educational barriers on those who want to enter our nation? Should we be concerned about disparities between the levels of schooling of immigrants, according to the nations from which they come, as compared with levels of U.S. citizens? Should we require demonstrated fluency in English, knowledge of American history and government, and allegiance to America before immigrants are granted permanent status? These questions are politically thorny.

School Responsibilities, Immigrant Needs, and Who Pays

Schools are expected to provide basic knowledge, skills, and corrective educational assistance to immigrant children and also to help Americanize and integrate them into society. That is a major undertaking; if done well, it takes extensive and focused effort. Schools also offer immigrant parents and other foreign-born adults avenues to self-improvement and preparation for citizenship. Immigrants from a variety of nations show wide differences in their educational attainment, skills, attitudes toward American traditions and values, English language fluency, and requirements for public assistance. School responsibilities for new immigrants create multiple problems with corollary extra costs—retraining or finding well-prepared teaching and school staffs, and providing facilities and materials, are examples.

The current source of many immigrants is Latin America. About 45% of immigrants are of Hispanic or Latino origin; 27% are Asian, and about 9% black. School budget costs are borne largely by taxpayers in states and local communities. Only about 8% of local school costs come from federal sources; the rest is state and local taxes. Added costs of immigrant education are not usually covered by supplemental funds. Special teaching, curricular, and staff needs created by an influx of immigrants distract schools from their primary purposes for local citizens, requiring additional care and effort. And immigrants are more likely to need other social services, like school nurses and social workers, draining funds from regular school activities.

More Than Just Money

Poorly controlled immigration gives more than just money problems to schools. English language fluency is a particular problem. English is essential for community relations, self-confidence, jobs, and just getting along in America. Many immigrants have nonexistent or extremely limited English skills and they may not be eager to gain adequate skills. This leads to more estrangement from American society and creates a further drain on social services. Jarzen (2009) argues that "bilingualism, diversity, and multiculturalisms undermine our national identity . . . the current crop of immigrants have failed at successfully becoming Americans."

States have enacted English-only laws; a necessary improvement that should be national legislation along with an immigration policy that favors those fluent in English (see usenglish.org). The percentage of limited English proficiency (LEP) students among immigrants is very high in many states. Nationally, immigrants account for 82% of LEP students (Immigration Counters, 2011; FAIR, 2016). Almost 25% speak a language other than English in the home. Without English and job skills, social welfare protections mean extra costly assistance (Barclay, 2009; Southern Poverty Law Center, 2009). Over 92% of all nations have an official language, we do not. Frustration and public costs increase with multiple language documents, ballots, interpreters, and related social interactions.

A further illustration of this educational problem with immigrants is shown in school dropout rates among immigrant youth. In New York City, that rate is over twice the rate of other residents, and the Mexican immigrant dropout rate is even higher (Semple, 2011). Hispanics born outside of the United States have a high school dropout rate three times the rate of those born here (National Center for Educational Statistics, 2019). These issues are related to language facility, but they also reflect broader questions of immigrant integration. They portend future problems as lesser-educated immigrants find fewer good jobs and pay less in taxes, becoming burdensome on social welfare programs. The proportion of immigrants who have not completed high school is about 27%; that proportion is increasing (Zong et al., 2019).

Regarding assimilation, immigrants from highly diverse cultural, tribal, religious, and economic backgrounds, when mixed in U.S. schools, create conditions for significant misunderstandings, and potentially explosive environments. Differences stimulate the development of school-disruptive behaviors like gangs, bullying, ethnic slurs, extortion, violence, and threats. They also contribute to student segregation by immigrant group, intimidation, and necessarily restrictive school rules with enforcement officers. This is not consistent with the idea of school as a safe place to gain knowledge and develop positive attitudes toward the nation.

Illegals Make the Problems Worse

Long-term problems in immigration policy, implementation, and enforcement create unfair and inadequate conditions, especially with regard to those who come into or stay in the United States illegally. Some illegals are smuggled in, some enter on fraudulent documents, some climb fences or run across fields, and some come legitimately on short-term student or work visas but do not leave when the visa expires. Opportunities for employment and other conditions that make the United States a desirable migration destination, coupled with weak national controls and enforcement of laws, have produced a situation of immigration chaos. We have vast numbers of illegals with resulting public outrage that questions all immigration, legal or not. Human rights, employment, security, economic, taxation, political, and cultural issues arise in this setting.

Efforts to enact legislation to permit illegal immigrants to attend state-funded colleges and universities at low, taxpayer subsidized in-state rates can add to increasing costs. Higher-education budgets are strained and applications for attendance are increasing, so institutions are limiting admissions and raising tuition and fees. Illegal students could be displacing qualified students who are legal residents while adding to budget problems.

Illegal immigration causes higher net costs for schools and other social services than legal immigration. Two-thirds of illegal aliens have not graduated from high school, thus earning less income and contributing less in taxes—while requiring more from U.S. public education and social services. Camarota (2018) shows the net public cost (taxes paid minus cost of social services used by illegal immigrants) to be almost $70,000 over each lifetime, with additional net costs of about $18,000 for each descendant. O'Brien and Raley (2017) summarize the total social costs at $135 billion annually, with taxes paid by illegals at $18 billion, for a net cost of $117 billion at that time. They note that education is the largest taxpayer cost at $46 billion, federal and state level combined, for all services used by illegal immigrants.

Birthright Citizenship

One peculiarity of U.S. immigration policy is the provision for birthright citizenship; the Fourteenth Amendment to the Constitution provides, "All persons born or naturalized in the United States, and subject to the jurisdiction thereof, are citizens of the United States and of the state wherein they reside." This 1868 amendment was designed primarily to provide citizenship to African Americans at the end of the Civil War, but it is now used by illegal immigrants to obtain U.S. citizenship for the children they bear here. For a fee, smugglers offer to get pregnant women into the United States to have a child. These babies are called "anchor babies" because they provide a legal connection to the United States and offer many benefits to the parents from citizenship application assistance, social welfare, and health to education rights. They also provide a means for sympathy and appeals for leniency when the parents are caught and deportation is likely. Only about 17% of the nations of the world have such a birthright citizenship policy (Lacey, 2011).

Records from 2016 show about 790,000 births to immigrants, of which 300,000 were births to illegal immigrants. Of the immigrant births, 23% were on Medicaid, and 31% were uninsured. Births to immigrants in poverty situations were 30% of the total (Camarota et al., 2018). Immigrants are over 13% of the U.S. population, but account for about 25% of the births (*The Economist*, 2017; Radford and Noe-Bustamante, 2019).

Efforts to amend the Fourteenth Amendment or legislation or court decisions to severely limit birthright citizenship have emerged (*The Economist*, 2011). About 40% of citizens favor changing the Constitution to prohibit automatic citizenship for American-born children of illegals. Birthright citizenship has implications for education, including financing the extra costs, language use, parental fear and invisibility, students' legal rights, care for the student if arrest and deportation loom for parents, and others. If passed, a related cost issue for American taxpayers would be the American Dream and Promise Act because it would give a form of permanent residency to children of illegal immigrants and allow them to be eligible for full citizenship.

Immigration Policies: A Study in Turmoil

Immigration is America's great tradition and glory; it is also its great peril. We are a nation founded by immigrants, and we remain prideful of immigrant contributions to culture, industry, technology, and life. Immigration, if it can be intelligently controlled, balanced, and enforced, helps the United States. But we have failed to control it. Policies veer from open door to limited restrictions by nationality and personal history, and then amnesty. And restrictive laws have often not been followed up with serious enforcement and actual control.

Large-scale immigration waves have occurred four times in our history (Leonhardt, 2008). Political reaction to each of the previous great waves—in the 1850s, 1880s, and 1900s—was intense and restrictions ensued. Anti-immigration movements developed as each wave became more threatening to Americans. Laws were passed to limit immigration with modest results in attempts to bring more orderliness to the process.

The United States was concerned about risks in naturalizing immigrants from unfriendly nations too quickly in the 1790s, but until the 1870s, we encouraged immigration as helpful to build society. Then, in 1875, we barred immigration by convicts and prostitutes, adding paupers and "mentally defectives" to the immigrant ban in 1882. Congress passed laws for two decades to require a literacy test of immigrants, but these laws were vetoed by three presidents before Woodrow Wilson's second veto was overridden in 1917 and all adult immigrants had to be able to read in some language. Immigration laws in the 1920s limited annual streams to 150,000, plus immediate families, and imposed a quota system favoring immigrants from northern and western Europe.

These quotas were eliminated in 1965, and later modifications increased the total annual immigrant limits. Immigration reform laws in 1986 tried to restrict illegal immigration by penalizing employers and offering amnesty to some illegals who came forward. Enforcement has been very uneven, in some cases even nonexistent, and illegal immigration expanded to our current estimates of 12 million to 23 million. Legislation in the 1990s increased the annual number of legal immigrants from 270,000 to 675,000 and doubled the number of visas for economic and employment purposes to 140,000 (Meilander, 2001; Cornelius et al., 2004; Morris and McGann, 2007; Leonhardt, 2008). Without adequate and appropriate limits, controls, enforcement, and follow-up on immigration, we are threatened with another chaotic wave of immigration. Any immigration policy should be based on protecting American interests.

America's Great Peril

The peril to America is not from the idea of immigration. We have an immigrant tradition, but that occurred over a long time and a smaller scale. One aspect of the peril is simply the relative size of immigrant groups. The United States has more immigrants than any other nation, about 40 million (Radford, 2019). This is four times the size of the U.S. immigrant population in 1965, when the laws were changed to eliminate quotas. Such large numbers produce dislocations, suspicions, economic uncertainty, and fear among existing citizens. The size of immigrant groups creates difficult assimilation conditions, taxes social services, and undermines local employment arrangements and social conditions.

A second important aspect of the peril to America is the disorderly, disruptive, and potentially dangerous illegal acts of people who come into America without proper authorization or who stay longer than their visas permit. The main threats of unfettered and uncontrolled immigration include: crime, disease, national security, undercutting American workers, dislocation in low-income communities, and overloading social services like health and education.

Between 2000 and 2005, about 4.5 million illegals were caught trying to break in to the United States, and more than 300,000 of them had criminal records (Buchanan, 2006). That is one criminal in every 12 immigrants, and that is only among illegals who were caught. The current immigration issue differs significantly from those in the past in that a large number of immigrants have come illegally or overstayed their visas and have become illegal. We have done little to fully identify these illegal immigrants or to enforce the immigration laws that they have broken. Simply coming over our borders without official permission or overstaying an authorized visa is a crime. Those who intentionally engage in these activities are criminals. It is illegal for good reason. Open access to public schools should not be a reward for illegal activity.

A third aspect of the peril for America by uncontrolled immigration is more esoteric but important: challenges to American values, national unity, social relations, and commonalities of the spirit that define the United States. Finding and nurturing common grounds for social life is a long and often grueling process; it can easily be fractured by competing ideologies from immigrant groups.

Our national security, national integrity, and economy depend on controlling our borders and developing clear and reasoned policies to limit immigration. We welcome immigrants who follow the rules. Most of our immigrant ancestors endured long and difficult journeys to come here. They applied for permission to enter, and those who desired citizenship fulfilled requirements that included good health, a law-abiding history, learning English, and passing a test of American history and government. They understood the needs for national security and border integrity that require laws, rules, and regulations regarding immigration. They desired opportunities and rights that American citizenship provides, and they used their time, energy, intelligence, and commitment to fulfill those requirements. They were often leaving places where those opportunities and rights did not exist.

True, some legal immigrants also had criminal records, serious health problems, or antipathy to American ideals, but they were often weeded out through the application, waiting, educational, and testing processes for citizenship. And we had records for them. Rules and regulations worked in these cases to protect America. Orderly immigration and legitimate educational requirements serve well those who have properly immigrated.

Needed Basic Immigration Policies: Immigration Policy in the National Interest

America needs a thorough and vigilant border protection system as a beginning point. In an age of terrorist threats, fast transportation, and massive population shifts, a sound immigration policy has to start with full control of our borders (Auster, 2003). That can mean fences, electronic monitoring, active and frequent land and air patrols, night-vision imaging, lighting, and similar screening devices. They work (Von Drehle, 2008). It can also mean personal identification that cannot be compromised, coordinated international verification and tracking systems, and speedy deportation arrangements.

We also need improved control over legal entry of visitors, workers, and scholars. This requires complete and verifiable application data, with continuing full information on travel and contact locations for all entrants to improve our ability to find them when their authorized visitation time is nearing completion. Our visa limits must be stringently enforced, with severe and enforced penalties for overstaying without permission.

We need clear and simple federal procedures for immigration and for illegals. Employers and sponsors should be legally responsible for checking positive identification for legality, with verification from government agencies, before employment. We should strengthen all bans on the hiring of illegal immigrants, with serious penalties that increase if the offense is repeated. In the meantime, we should do better enforcement of existing laws governing immigrant employment, identification, and supervision. The European Union passed tougher laws on immigration, with longer detention and easier expulsion (Brothers, 2008).

We must require demonstrated fluency in English as basic to permanent residency or citizenship, and we should provide government information, except for tourist purposes, only in English. A knowledge of American history, government, and economics and agreement with values should also be required of anyone applying for naturalization. At a minimum, we should require at least high school graduation for all adult immigrants.

Our immigration system should primarily focus on improving our nation, followed by humanitarian and other purposes. More intelligent and limited immigration policies are necessary to coordinate our national needs for well-educated people in particular fields. We must cut the sheer numbers of immigrants to ensure the continuation of American values and traditions, and we must encourage the best and brightest of those who want to come to the United States and who have skills that are complementary to our national interests. It is only with intelligent immigration reform and consistent enforcement practices that we can hope to deal with the educational problems that flow from the current immigration situation.

Immigration and education are linked. Lack of control and coordination of immigration creates problems for schools and society. Mass immigration threatens the basic fiber of the nation and overloads the schools. Illegal immigration has exploded, is hidden, and is a peril to our country. Immigration reform is necessary not only for national security and to promote our national interest but also to help schools refocus on their primary purposes for American citizens.

FOR DISCUSSION

1. U.S. population projections, 2000 to 2050, contain the following key points:
   - Almost 20% of the U.S. population in 2050 will be immigrants.
   - The elderly population will increase by more than double, and the working-age group will decline as a percentage of population.
   - Hispanics, currently the largest minority group, will triple in size, becoming about 29% of the population; Asians are also increasing at a fast rate.

   If this develops,
   a. What are the most important positive and negative consequences of these points?
   b. How is education likely to be affected by these changes?
   c. What would you recommend to schools to prepare for each of these potential impacts?
   d. What social, cultural, and economic impacts would you expect from these changes?
   e. How would you change current U.S. immigration policy? Why?
   f. How would your proposals affect educational, social, and economic conditions?
2. One thesis is that the United States needs an expanding younger population to support economic growth and social services in addition to extending cultural development.
   a. What is a reasonable antithesis to this approach?
   b. What evidence supports each view?
   c. Identify the main positive and negative consequences if either thesis becomes public policy.
   d. Describe a viable synthesis of this issue.
   e. How would your proposed synthesis influence education in the United States?

3. Schools are the great Americanizing institution for immigrants.

   a. How well have schools met their role in Americanizing immigrants? What are the failings and successes?

   b. Discuss ways schools should help develop the integration of immigrants into U.S. society.

   c. How should schools deal with immigrant limited English proficiency students?

4. Immigrants who enter the United States without official status or who overstay their visas are classified as illegal or undocumented.

   a. What short- and long-term policies and practices would you propose for them?

   b. How do your proposals fall within American immigration history and social values?

REFERENCES

Adams, L. D., and Kirova, A., eds. (2007). *Global Migration and Education.* Mahwah, NJ: Lawrence Erlbaum.

Adesope, O. O., Lavin, T., Thompson, T., and Ungerleider, C. (2010). "A Systematic Review and Meta-Analysis of the Cognitive Correlates of Bilingualism." *Review of Educational Research* 80(2):207–245.

American Immigration Council (2019, September, 3). The Dream Act, DACA, and Other Policies Designed to Protect Dreamers (americanimmigrationcouncil.org/research/dream-act-daca-and-other-policies-designed-protect-dreamers).

Aronson, R. (2010, May 4). Letter to the Honorable Tom Harkin and the Honorable Mike Enzi, U.S. Senate. Alexandria, VA: TESOL.

Auster, L. (2003). *Erasing America: The Politics of the Borderless Nation.* Raleigh, NC: AIC Foundation.

Barclay, E. (2009, April 21). "Language Barriers Complicate Immigrants' Medical Problems." *Washington Post* and *Kaiser Health News.*

Baugh, R., and Witsman, K. (2017, March). *U.S. Lawful Permanent Residents: 2015.* Washington, DC: U.S. Department of Homeland Security, Office of Immigration Statistics.

Benton-Cohen, K. (2018). *Inventing the Immigration Problem.* Cambridge, MA: Harvard University Press.

Bremmer, I. (2018). *Us vs. Them: The Failure of Globalism.* New York: Portfolio/Penguin.

Brimelow, P. (2008). Mass Immigration and Education (commonsenseonmassimmigration.us?articles/ art-brimelow).

Brothers, C. (2008, June 19). "EU Passes Tough Migrant Measures." *New York Times.*

Buchanan, P. J. (2006). *State of Emergency.* New York: St. Martin's Press.

Camarota, S. A. (2009, November 25). Immigration's Impact on Public Coffers in the United States. Center for Immigration Studies.

——— (2018, October 28). Enforcing Immigration Law is Cost Effective. Center for Immigration Studies.

Camarota, S. A., Griffith, B., and Zeigler, K. (2017, September). Mapping the Impact of Immigration on Public Schools. Center for Immigration Studies.

Camarota, S. A., and Zeigler, K. (2018, April 17). Better Educated, But Not Better Off. Center for Immigration Studies.

——— (2019a, February 4). Projecting the Impact of Immigration on the U.S. Population. Center for Immigration Studies.

——— (2019b, July 1). Immigrants are Coming to America at Older Ages. Center for Immigration Studies.

Camarota, S. A., Zeigler, K., and Richwine, J. (2018, October 9). Births to Legal and Illegal Immigrants in the U.S. Center for Immigration Studies.

Chomsky, A. (2018). *"They Take Our Jobs!"* Boston: Beacon Press.

Colon, I. T. (2019). "How to Bring Immigrant Families Into Schools." *New America Weekly*.

Cordoza, K. (2019, August 9). "How Schools Are Responding to Migrant Children." *Education Week*.

Cornelius, W. A., Takeyuki, T., Martin, P., and Hollifield, J., eds. (2004). *Controlling Immigration*. Stanford, CA: Stanford University Press.

Crawford, J. (2007). Hard Sell: Why Is Bilingual Education So Unpopular with the American Public? In O. Garcia and C. Baker, eds., *Bilingual Education*. Clevedon, UK: Multilingual Matters.

Darling-Hammond, L. (2008). Improving High Schools and the Role of NCLB. In G. L. Sunderman, ed., *Holding NCLB Accountable: Achieving Accountability, Equity and School Reform*. Thousand Oaks, CA: Corwin.

Department of Homeland Security (2019, September 19). Stopping Illegal Immigration and Securing the Border (dhs.gov).

Driver, J. (2018). *The Schoolhouse Gate*. New York: Pantheon.

Education.com (2019, September 23). 10 Issues That Fuel the Bilingual Education Debate (education.com).

Espinosa, L. M. (2008). *Challenging Common Myths about English Language Learners*. New York: Foundation for Child Development.

Faltis, C. J., and Coulter, C. A. (2008). *Teaching English Learners and Immigrant Students in Secondary Schools*. Boston: Allyn and Bacon.

Federation for American Immigration Reform (FAIR) (2011, July 6). Illegal Immigration a $113 Billion a Year Drain on U.S. Taxpayers (fairus.org).

——— (2016, September). The Elephant in the Classroom: Mass Immigration's Impact on Public Schools (fairus.org).

Ferris, M., and Raley, S. (2016, September). What Every Parent and Taxpayer Should Know about Immigration and the Public Education Crisis. Federation for American Immigration Reform (fairus.org).

Frey, W. H. (2018, March 14). The U.S. Will Become Minority White in 2045, Census Projects. Brookings Institution.

——— (2019, April 10). America is Not Full. Its Future Rests with Young Immigrants. Brookings Institution.

Gaytan, F. X., Carhill, A., and Suarez-Orozco, C. (2007). "Understanding and Responding to the Needs of Newcomer Immigrant Youth and Families." *The Prevention Researcher* 14:10–13.

Gingrich, N. (2008). *Real Change*. Washington, DC: Regnery.

Handlin, O. (1951). *The Uprooted: The Epic Story of the Great Migrations That Made the American People*. New York: Grosset and Dunlap.

———, ed. (1966). *Children of the Uprooted*. New York: George Braziller.

Hathaway, I. (2017, December 4). Almost Half of Fortune 500 Companies Were Founded by American Immigrants or Their Children. Brookings Institution (brookings.edu/blog/the-avenue/2017/12/04/almost-half-of-fortune-500-companies-were-founded-by-american-immigrants-or-their-children).

Hernandez, D. J., Denton, N. A., and Macartney, S. E. (2007, April). *Children in Immigrant Families—The U.S. and 50 States: National Origins, Language, and Early Education*. Child Trends and Center for Social and Demographic Analysis, University at Albany, SUNY.

Immigration Counters (2011). Real Time Data (immigrationcounters.com).

Jarzen, M. (2009, March 12). Language Barriers Limit Ability of Immigrants (unlvrebelyell.com).

Jordan, M. (2019, July 9). "Schools Scramble to Handle Thousands of New Migrant Families." *New York Times*.

Kaestle, C. (1983). *Pillars of the Republic: Common Schools and American Society, 1780–1860.* New York: Hill and Wang.

Kieffer, M., Lasaux, N., Rivera, M., and Francis, D. (2009). "Accommodations for English Language Learners Taking Large-Scale Assessments: A Meta-Analysis on Effectiveness and Validity." *Review of Educational Research* 79:1,168–1,201.

Lacey, M. (2011, January 5). "Birthright Citizenship Looms as Next Immigration Battle." *New York Times*, A1.

Leonhardt, D. (2008, March 2). "The Border and the Ballot Box." *New York Times.*

Lepore, J. (2018a). *These Truths.* New York: W.W. Norton.

——— (2018b, September 10). "Is Education a Fundamental Right?" *The New Yorker.*

——— (2019). *This America.* New York: Liveright Publishing.

Mayers, S., and Freedman, J. (2019). *Solito, Solita.* Chicago: Haymarket Books.

Meilander, P. C. (2001). *Toward a Theory of Immigration.* New York: Palgrave.

Merkley, J. (2019). *America Is Better Than This.* New York: Hachette Book Group.

Migration Data Portal (2020, January 2). Migration and Vulnerability (migrationdataportal.org).

Migration Policy Institute (2006). Annual Immigration to the United States: The Real Numbers (migrationinformation.org).

——— (2019, September 30). State Immigration Data Profiles (migrationinformation.org).

Morris, D., and McGann, E. (2007). *Outrage.* New York: HarperCollins.

Muniz, J. (2019, June 3). Promoting Equitable Access to Dual Language Immersion Programs. Blog. New America.

National Association for Bilingual Education (2007). *NABS Principles on the Reauthorization of NCLB.* Washington, DC: National Association for Bilingual Education.

National Center for Education Statistics (2019, October 3). *Trends in High School Dropout and Completion Rates in the United States.* Washington, DC: National Center for Education Statistics.

NCTE ELL Task Force (2006). *NCTE Position Paper on the Role of English Teachers in Educating English Language Learners (ELLs).* Washington, DC: National Council of Teachers of English.

NumbersUSA (2019). Sensible Solutions (numberusa.com).

O'Brien, M., and Raley, S. (2017, September 27). The Fiscal Burden of Illegal Immigration on the United States. Federation for Immigration Reform.

Passel, J. S., and Cohn, D. (2008, February 11). *U.S. Population Projections 2005–2050.* Washington, DC: Pew Research Center.

Plyler v. Doe (1982). 457 U.S. 202 (supreme.justia.com/us/457/202/ case).

Rabin, N., Combs, C., and Gonzalez, N. (2008). "Understanding *Plyler*'s Legacy: Voices from Border Schools." *Journal of Law and Education* 37:15–82.

Radford, J. (2019, June 17). Key Findings about U.S. Immigrants. Washington, DC: Pew Research Center.

Radford, J., and Noe-Bustamante, L. (2019, June 3). Facts on U.S. Immigrants, 2017. Washington, DC: Pew Research Center.

Rosales, J. (2018). "Dual Language Immersion Programs Boost Student Success." *NEA Today.*

Salomon, E. R. C. (2010). *True American: Language, Identity, and the Education of Immigrant Children.* Cambridge, MA: Harvard University Press.

Schleicher, A. (2015). *Helping Immigrant Students to Succeed at School—and Beyond.* Paris: Organisation for Economic Co-operation and Development.

Semple, R. (2011, November 25). "In New York, Mexicans Lag in Education." *New York Times*, A1.

Solorzano, R. W. (2008). "High Stakes Testing: Issues, Implications, and Remedies for English Language Learners." *Review of Educational Research* 78:260–329.

Southern Poverty Law Center (2009, April). Language Barrier (splcenter.org).

Suarez-Orozco, C., Suarez-Orozco, M., and Todorova, I. (2008). *Learning a New Land: Immigrant Students in American Society*. Cambridge, MA: Belknap Press.

Suarez-Orozco, C., Yoshikawa, H. Teranishi, R., and Suarez-Orozco, M. (2011). "Growing up in the Shadows: The Developmental Implications of Unauthorized Status." *Harvard Educational Review* 81:438–472.

Suarez-Orozco, M., and Gardner, H. (2003, October 22). "Educating Billy Wang for the World of Tomorrow." *Education Week* 23(8):34, 44.

Suarez-Orozco, M., and Qin-Hilliard, D. B. (2004). *Globalization: Culture and Education in the New Millennium*. Berkeley: University of California Press.

Suarez-Orozco, M., and Suarez-Orozco, C. (2001). *Children of Immigration*. Cambridge, MA: Harvard University Press.

Sussis, M. (2019, May 8). How Many Would Really Come if the Borders Were Open? Center for Immigration Studies.

Sutton, M. Q. (2016). *A Prehistory of North America*. New York: Routledge.

The Economist (2011, August 19). "Amending the Amendment."

——— (2017, August 30). "Immigrants Boost America's Birth Rate."

United Nations (2020, February 10). Migration (un.org).

Von Drehle, R. O. (2008). "A New Line in the Sand." *Time* 17:28–35.

White, M. J., and Glick, J. E. (2009). *Achieving Anew: How Immigrants Do in American Schools, Jobs, and Neighborhoods*. New York: Russell Sage Foundation.

Wicks, A., and Kimball Johnson, A. (2018, Winter). "For Children the Immigrant Experience Begins in School." *The Catalyst* 9.

Wiley, T. G. (2007). Accessing Language Rights in Education: A Brief History of the U.S. Context. In O. Garcia and C. Baker, eds., *Bilingual Education*. Clevedon, UK: Multilingual Matters.

Zimmer, C. (2017, April 26). "Humans Lived in North America 130,000 Years Ago, Study Claims." *New York Times*.

Zong, J., Batalova, J., and Burrow, M. (2019, March 14). Frequently Requested Statistics on Immigrants and Immigration in the United States. Migration Policy Institute.

PART TWO

What Should Be Taught?
Knowledge and Literacy

About Part Two: Part Two includes controversies over the politics of school and curricular reform. These issues involve divergent views of testing and standards to address academic gaps, which values and character traits should be emphasized in schools, what cultural traditions should prevail, and how or why technology should be a main focus. Topics covered in Part Two include:

- Chapter 8: the academic achievement gap and the standards movement
- Chapter 9: values and character development
- Chapter 10: diversity and multicultural education
- Chapter 11: technology and learning

Each issue involves theoretical and practical concerns: what does it mean to know something, to be literate? How should schools undertake that activity?

Introduction

What should be taught is a political question involving definitions of knowledge and literacy, conditioned on learning and intelligence. According to Stiglitz (2019): "the true source of a country's wealth—and therefore increases in productivity and living standards—is knowledge, learning, and advances in science and technology" (p. 183). Literacy incorporates the ability to comprehend and use knowledge, e.g., math literacy, economic literacy, mechanical literacy, financial literacy, computer literacy, and even vegetable literacy (Madison, 2013). The struggle to control the definition of valued knowledge is inevitably a struggle for power (Cherryholmes, 1978; Sizer, 2004; Moran, 2005; Apple, 2018). Control of what people know is control of their expectations, behavior, and allegiance. Michel Foucault used "power/knowledge" to show they are inextricably related; one is a function of the other (Pollard, 2019; Stanford Encyclopedia of Philosophy, 2018). Decisions on knowledge are necessarily decisions on power. Those decisions can lead in opposite directions: more social egalitarianism or more elitism, more separation or more integration, more ethnocentrism or more globalism.

What should be taught structures curriculum. Traditionally that includes English, math, science, history and social studies, the arts and applied arts, foreign languages, and physical education. Each field has disputes about the nature of knowledge (academic arguments), what should be in schools (curricular arguments), and appropriate school responses to social pressures (social arguments). Beyond teaching subjects, what about teaching creativity (Sparks, 2020)?

Academic arguments occur among specialists in their related fields: Are graphic novels part of the literary canon? Is Keynesian economic theory outdated? Is new biology consistent with evolution? Curricular arguments include applied and professional judgments by school staffs about what should be included, to whom it should be taught, when, and in what sequence. That may sound simple, but K–12 school curricular decisions involve historic and current social arguments, signs of competing social forces, and involve power and politics (Au, 2012; Heller, 2012). Ideologies can limit knowledge and curriculum (Apple, 2004; Laird, 2019). Social arguments about climate change, the value of science, discrimination, patriotism and national identity, church and state, the news media, sex and gender, proper measures of merit, and others are reflected in school curricular arguments and decisions. Whose history, language, science, arts, music, and values should dominate what is taught?

The School Curriculum: Knowledge, Literacy, and Politics

School curriculums reflect prevalent definitions of formal knowledge and literacy. These definitions can conflict—arts versus sciences, practical versus theoretical, and socialization versus independence. The term literate describes those who have and use knowledge considered socially valuable. Schools provide literacy credentials through diplomas, degrees, and certificates. In an age of witchery, a literate person shares the language and values of the sorcerer. Sorcerers enjoyed power and status; their pronouncements became laws and policies. Only a select few were permitted to learn secret rites; most understood their power. When witchcraft was labeled evil, sorcerers were burned. In an age of technology, a literate person shares the language and values of technological value. If artificial intelligence (AI) or artificial general intelligence (AGI) becomes equivalent to human intelligence (Kuhn, 2020), what curriculum results? "Diminished inquisitiveness" may be the result (Kissinger et al., 2019).

Traditional school subjects, based on social expectations, inhabit the curriculum until new topics or arguments arise that successfully challenge that emphasis. Seventeenth-century secondary schools taught all classes in Latin; Greek was also a required subject. Moral philosophy was one subject during colonial times in the United States, religion was the basic subject. Reading was taught to thwart "that ould deluder, Satan" in his quest to keep humans from knowledge as written in the scriptures. *McGuffey Readers* contained moral tales to build character. Some girls were taught to read and write, but not permitted further education so they could stay home to learn homemaking. Boys from affluent families continued schooling at Latin grammar schools; other boys went to work.

African Americans and Native Americans were virtually excluded from all schools, as was accurate information about the history, cultures, traditions, and contributions of these groups and others. Overt and legal racial discrimination was one political reaction to the abolition of slavery. Slaves and the poor had been denied education, so some states used literacy tests to restrict voting rights, denying former slaves, the poor, and recent immigrants. Tyack (1967) quotes a Ku Klux Klan imperial wizard saying, "Ominous statistics proclaim the persistent development of a parasitic mass within our domain. . . . We have taken unto ourselves a Trojan horse crowded with ignorance, illiteracy, and envy" (p. 233).

As the United States developed its democracy and grew in population, religion waned as the primary social and curricular glue; national political interests emerged. After the Revolution, nationalism largely replaced religion. Patriotic literacy, with attendant symbols and rituals, became significant, and nationalism remains strong in U.S. schools. Renewed emphasis on allegiance and patriotic exercises develops each time social values seem threatened (Westheimer, 2007). The "red scare" of the 1920s, McCarthyism in the 1950s, and anticommunist political rhetoric from the 1980s increased curricular emphasis on national history, government, literature, and economics. California, Florida, and New Hampshire, for example, passed school regulations calling for teaching communism as a governmental form, but demanded it be taught negatively as a threat to America (Nelson, 1971).

In the last decades of the twentieth century, political debates and negative claims about schooling led to increased testing; the resulting scores indicated that there were deficiencies in reading and arithmetic. The "Reading Wars" between proponents of teaching phonics (considered conservative) versus the whole word approach (liberal) date back to the 1800s, but surged with a controversial congressional mandate in 2000 (Castles et al., 2018; Strauss, 2018). Wexler (2019a, 2019b) argues that today's reading instruction harms student learning because of the focus on a set of skill drills and rote memorization unrelated to curiosity and knowing things, like science, social studies, and other knowledge fields. An EdWeek (2020) study finds the Reading Wars are not dead and reading teachers may be using conflicting techniques. D'Orio (2020) describes loud critics of "level reading," which uses material that is at the student's reading level rather than a bit above; one calls it "educational malpractice." Other subjects have equivalent battlefields. Elementary schools cut curricular time from science, social studies, the arts, and applied arts to emphasize reading and arithmetic. Math education battles related to standard math, "new math, and new, new math" show efforts to control power by local schools or ivory tower experts (Phillips, 2015). History and social studies are often the most controversial fields in their treatment of topics like patriotism, sectionalism, economics, minorities, religion, and ideology (Sawchuck, 2018). Science versus religion, creationism, and climate change are other battle areas. The arts, sex education, vocations, English, home economics, physical education, and more are also subject to social pressures and curricular debate in the twenty-first century.

International competition in technology and trade threatens Americans today and translates into an increased curricular emphasis on mathematics, science, technological subjects, and foreign languages. Additions like driver's education, physical education, drug education, and character education illustrate curriculum changes as politics redefined school knowledge. Ethnic studies, women's studies, multicultural education, and human rights education illustrate recent knowledge structures in higher education and some K–12 schools. And AI could restructure it all (Klein, 2019). The specific mix of emphases within the curriculum depends on prevailing visions of the "good" individual and the "good" society. Some want individuals to be free, independent, and critical; others advocate behavior modification to ensure social conformity. Some demand prescribed moral values and beliefs; others demand release from moralisms and prescriptions. Some desire respect for authority; others prefer challenges to authority.

Curriculum Control

A central purpose of schooling is to prepare thoughtful citizens and leaders of society. In mass education, the curricular questions revolve around what all members of the society need to know to participate fully and actively. If the powerful class controls education, the essential curricular question is what should members of the ruling class know? Curricular needs of those identified as potential leaders receive special attention. Higher academic tracks and honors programs characterize many modern high schools.

Control of knowledge and the school curriculum is a product of prevailing social goals and social structures. The struggle for control of knowledge parallels social-class differences (Anyon, 1980, 2005; Spring, 1998). Workers get practical knowledge, privileged classes get academic knowledge; both need moral knowledge, but for different purposes. Moral instruction for the masses intends to teach respect for authority, hard work, and frugality. The privileged class is to learn morality for ruling wisely, justly, and with civility.

R. H. Tawney (1964) criticized the elite "public boarding school" tradition in England and advocated improvements in the developing system of free schools for the working classes. The very nature of the elite system was a part of the hidden curriculum, teaching the sons of the wealthy "not in words or of set purpose, but by the mere facts of their environment, that they are members . . . of a privileged group, whose function it will be, on however humble a scale, to direct and command, and to which leadership, influence, and the other prizes of life properly belong" (p. 83). Social class is not the only major factor lying behind curricular decisions. Race, gender, national origin, sexual orientation, and religion are other conditions that influence decisions about which people receive what knowledge in a society. The concept of privilege and the education that privilege brings have been linked to racism and sexism in American and other national histories. Educational discrimination against racial minorities, women, Jews, Catholics, Native Americans, Eskimos, and others is a sorry tradition in a democratic society.

Psychologist Kenneth Clark, whose studies were a significant factor in the Supreme Court decision that found segregated schools unconstitutional (*Brown v. Board of Education*, 1954), put the case clearly:

> The public schools in America's urban ghettos also *reflect* the oppressive damage of racial exclusion. . . . Segregation and inferior education reinforce each other. . . . Children themselves are not fooled by the various euphemisms educators use to disguise educational snobbery. From the earliest grades a child knows when he has been assigned to a level that is considered less than adequate. . . . "The clash of cultures in the classroom" is essentially a class war, a socioeconomic and racial warfare being waged on the battleground of our schools, with middle-class and

middle-class-aspiring teachers provided with a powerful arsenal of half-truths, prejudices, and rationalizations, arrayed against the hopelessly outclassed working-class youngsters. (Clark, 1965, pp. 111–117)

The Hidden Curriculum

The hidden curriculum consists of unexpressed and usually unexamined ideas, values, and behaviors that convey subtle, often unintended things to students (and teachers). A few brief examples illustrate the hidden curriculum at its simplest level. Teachers tell students to be independent and express their own ideas, but they often chastise or punish the student who actually exhibits independence and expresses ideas the teacher doesn't like. In history courses, students hear that justice and equality are basic American rights, yet they see that compliant and well-dressed students earn favored treatment. In school, students are told that plagiarism is an academic sin, then the news shows prominent and award-winning historians (probably quoted in the high school history textbook) who plagiarized from others. Students are told to not smoke by teachers who do. The hidden curriculum is a vast, relatively uncharted domain often much more effective than the formal curriculum in shaping student learning and knowledge.

At a deeper level, discrepancies between what schools say and what schools do may raise a more significant concern about competing ideologies. The hidden curriculum conflicts with the stated purposes of the visible curriculum. The stated curriculum may value diversity; the hidden curriculum expects conformity. The stated curriculum advocates critical thinking; the hidden curriculum supports docility. The visible curriculum emphasizes equal opportunity; the hidden curriculum separates students according to social-class background, gender, race, or other factors. Tinkering with the stated curriculum leaves the powerful hidden curriculum intact. Superficial school reforms do very little to change schooling, and neither mainstream liberals nor conservatives really want much change.

Critical literature examines the hidden curriculum and its ideological bases (see Young, 1970; Cherryholmes, 1978, 1988; Anyon, 1979, 1980; Giroux and Purpel, 1983; Giroux, 1988; Stanley, 1992; Apple, 2000; Aronowitz, 2008; Apple, 2018). From this critical view, the "great debates" about schooling extensively covered in the media and mainstream educational literature are actually narrowly constructed differences between liberals and conservatives. Public debates do not raise ideological concerns about the control of knowledge and its social consequences (Stanley, 1992; Greene, 1994; Ippolito et al., 2008; Au, 2012).

At the surface level, where much school reform debate occurs, a discussion about whether to spend more school time on computers, math, and English and less on the arts and social studies is a comparatively trivial matter; it hides more fundamental disputes about whose interests are served and whose are maligned (Apple, 2018). Shallow arguments about whether the curriculum should stress the basics, provide vocational courses, allow electives, or emphasize American values should lead to deeper, more critical examinations of who controls the school curriculum and consequences of that control. Mainstream discourse hides basic issues, including how knowledge is defined, its social purposes and consequences, whose ideas should prevail in schools, implications for teaching or denying topics, and how knowledge should be measured (Rosenberg, 2002; Raskin, 2004; Rubio and Baert, 2012; Apple, 2018).

Critics wonder if traditional knowledge provides enduring wisdom or promotes social oppression. In opposition to the traditional use of literacy as a tool of the dominant class to separate and control the masses is the idea of literacy as a tool for liberation (Freire and Berthoff, 1987). Paulo Freire, born in one of the most impoverished areas of Brazil, vowed to dedicate his life to the struggle against misery and suffering, and his work led him to define the "culture of silence" that he saw among the disadvantaged.

Freire realized the power of knowledge and recognized that the dominant class used education to keep the culture of silence among the victims—the poor and illiterate. He taught adults to read to liberate them from their imposed silence. As a professor of education in Brazil, he worked to erase illiteracy, and his ideas became widely used in literacy campaigns. Freire, as a threat to the government, was jailed after a military coup in 1964. Forced to leave Brazil, he went to Chile to work with UNESCO, came to the United States, then joined the World Council of Churches in Geneva as head of its educational division. Freire promotes the development of critical consciousness, using communication to expose oppression. Teacher and student are "co-intentional," sharing equally in dialogues on social reality and developing a critical understanding that can liberate them from the culture of silence. Henry Giroux, citing Freire, argues that we need a redefinition of literacy to focus on its critical dimensions. Mass culture via television and electronic media is controlled by dominant economic interests, who create a "technocratic" illiteracy that is a threat to self-perception, critical thought, and democracy.

Intelligence and Learning

Knowledge depends on intelligence; it is only through intelligence that we gain, interpret, and use knowledge. Disputes about intelligence parallel those about knowledge. Psychologist Howard Gardner (1999, 2000, 2003) argues we really have multiple intelligences, not just a single form. He suggests intelligences are actually potentials for people to develop processes to solve problems or create things. They are not completed events, nor clearly observable or testable, and they are relatively independent of each other. Some kinds of intelligence (such as logical-mathematical and linguistic) are useful in satisfying school academic requirements, and others, including musical and bodily-kinesthetic, are more useful in other settings in and out of school. This level of complexity makes "intelligence" testing and other efforts to standardize and measure schooling more difficult, if not impossible. As Gardner (1999) puts it, "intelligence is too important to be left to the intelligence testers" (p. 3).

Similarly, we have multiple literacies and multiple learning processes (Hull and Schultz, 2002; Coiro et al., 2008). Literacy can be defined in many ways (Gee, 1996, 2000; Jetton and Shanahan, 2012). Critical literacy provides a way to use basic school knowledge to identify and correct significant power disparities between haves and have-nots (Freire, 1970; Freire and Macedo, 1987; Comber and Simpson, 2001; National Council of Teachers of English, 2019). Multiple learning processes are obvious to anyone who observes children acquire walking, speaking, reading, creative, and interpretive abilities. This sophisticated concept of multiple intelligences, literacies, and learning processes not only makes definitions of knowledge, intelligence, literacy, and learning very problematic but also raises important questions about school curriculum, national and state standardized testing, and teaching. AI and AGI offer similar questions for curriculum.

Practical, Theoretical, and Moral Schooling

How should schools develop the good individual and the good society? Aristotle (1962) considered the fulfillment of social drives and education as a state activity to provide social unity: "education is therefore the means of making it [the society] a community and giving it unity" (p. 51). In *The Politics,* Aristotle discussed whether schools should teach practical knowledge, moral character, or esoteric ideas. Contemporary curriculum debate continues to raise this and other basic questions. Comprehensive public schools offer some useful applied educational programs, such as reading, music, wood shop, home economics, computer operation, physical education, and vocational training. They also offer the study of theoretical concepts in English, math, social studies, the arts, and science. And schools provide various forms of moral education; students study materials conveying ideas of the good person and the good society and learn from school rules and teachers to be respectful, patriotic, loyal, and honest. The exact mix of these forms of education varies as different reforms become popular and as local communities make changes.

Curricular reforms that were implemented between 1980 and 2010 are seen by many as essentially mechanistic and "top down," that is, the president, governors, legislators, and national commissions told the schools what and how to teach to correct educational ills. Their prescriptions—for increased course requirements, longer school days and school years, more homework, more testing, and force-feeding knowledge to students in factory-like schools—do not prove curative abilities. Most schools teach a relatively standard curriculum. States mandate some courses and keep track of what other states require. Accrediting agencies examine schools periodically and review the curriculum for conformity to some standard. Publishers, aiming at a national market, produce teaching materials for a national curriculum. And school curriculum coordinators and department heads attend national conferences and read journals that stress standard curricular structures. Thus, a broad outline exists for a general national curriculum based on common practices, even though specific curricula in each state differ.

At the start of the second decade of the twenty-first century, external forces still largely determine the formal curriculum in American schools. We have national and state standards, increasing external accountability for student learning, and more complex ideas of socially expected literacy. Since colonial times, the curriculum has evolved from a narrow interest in teaching religious ideals to multiple and often conflicting interests in providing broad knowledge, skills, and values relevant to nearly every aspect of social life. In U.S. schools, the medieval curriculum of "seven liberal arts"—rhetoric, grammar, logic, arithmetic, astronomy, geometry, and music—has given way to a long list of subjects. And the formal curriculum is certainly not all that students are expected to learn in school.

Social Expectations

You won't be surprised that what is taught and what is learned are often different things. We are taught things in many settings; we may not learn those things—but we learn. Teaching is more than telling or testing; learning is more than listening and recalling. According to Pinker (2018):

> Any curriculum will be pedagogically ineffective if it consists of a lecturer yammering . . . or a textbook that students highlight. . . . People understand concepts only when they are forced to think them through, to discuss them with others, and to use them to solve problems. (p. 378)

It is easy to assume that what we were taught is what ought to be taught. That self-congratulatory idea places education as static or backward looking (Ippolito et al., 2008). But ideas of knowledge, intelligence, literacy, and learning change (Dzisah and Etzkowitz, 2012). Schools, from day care to graduate school, determine, examine, convey, question, and modify knowledge. That responsibility is the root of issues surrounding what should be taught. Communicating and questioning knowledge are core purposes of schools and an ever-active process (Coiro et al., 2008). The role of teachers is particularly consequential.

Sloman and Fernbach (2017), in a thought-provoking book about cognitive science, conclude: "A real education includes learning that you don't know certain things (a lot of things) . . . a matter of looking at the frontiers of your knowledge and wondering what is out there beyond the border. It's about asking why" (p. 220). They note that Columbia University has a course entitled "Ignorance," where scientists discuss what they would like to know.

Some people enjoy mathematics. For others, reading history or literature is a great joy. Some like to dissect white rats in biology class, saw wood in shop, or exercise in gym. Others are completely baffled or utterly bored by textbooks and teachers. Different strokes, as they say, for different folks. Are there things that everyone should know? Who should decide the criteria for literacy? Should schools concentrate on subject knowledge of historic and socially approved value or on material encouraging critical thinking and student interest?

These questions suggest the choice is simple; it is not. Complex and changing relationships exist between the kinds of individuals we desire, the society we want to develop, political pressures, and the schooling we provide. These relationships often send conflicting signals to schools, and the conflicts become enshrined in the school curriculum. Society wants students to become self-sufficient individuals—but not too self-sufficient too early so that students have little latitude in deciding what to study until they reach college. We desire a society that is democratic and inspires voluntary loyalty, but we do not trust open inquiry, so we require courses stressing nationalistic patriotism.

The formal curriculum is one of the most visible parts of a school, indicating the relative value that schools put on various forms of knowledge and definitions of intelligence and literacy. There is far more to knowledge and literacy than what schools organize and teach, but schools provide legitimacy to the knowledge they select and teach and credentials to those students who are successful in school. What does it mean to be educated in the twenty-first century?

The chapters of Part Two examine some of the current curriculum disputes that have emerged as part of various reform movements in education. These disputes illustrate the question of what knowledge is most valuable in our society, a question that, in turn, relates to our differing visions of what constitutes the good individual and the good society.

REFERENCES

Anyon, J. (1979). "Ideology and U.S. History Textbooks." *Harvard Educational Review* 7:49–60.

———— (1980). "Social Class and the Hidden Curriculum of Work." *Journal of Education* 162:67–92.

———— (2005). *Radical Possibilities.* New York: Routledge.

Apple, M. (2000). *Official Knowledge.* London: Routledge.

———— (2004). *Ideology and Curriculum* (3rd ed.). New York: Routledge.

———— (2018, November 8). "Critical Curriculum Studies and the Concrete Problems of Curriculum Policy and Practice." *Journal of Curriculum Studies* 50(6).

Aristotle (1962). *The Politics of Aristotle.* Trans. by E. Barker. Oxford: Oxford University Press.

Aronowitz, S. (2008). *Against Schooling: Toward an Education That Matters.* Boulder, CO: Paradigm.

Au, W. (2012). *Critical Curriculum Studies.* New York: Routledge.

Brown v. Board of Education of Topeka, Shawnee County, Kansas, et al. (1954). 74 Sup. Ct. 686.

Castles, A., Rastle, K., and Nation, K. (2018, June 1). "Ending the Reading Wars." *Psychological Science in the Public Interest* 19(1).

Cherryholmes, C. (1978). "Curriculum Design as a Political Act." *Curriculum Inquiry* 10:115–141.

———— (1988). *Power and Criticism: Poststructural Investigations in Education.* New York: Teachers College Press.

Clark, K. (1965). *Dark Ghetto.* New York: Harper and Row.

Coiro, J., Knobel, M., Lankshear, C., and Leu, D. (2008). *The Handbook of Research in New Literacies.* Mahwah, NJ: Lawrence Erlbaum.

Comber, B., and Simpson, A. (2001). *Negotiating Critical Literacies in Classrooms.* Mahwah, NJ: Lawrence Erlbaum.

D'Orio, W. (2020, February). "Reading Levels Unfairly Label Learners, Say Critics." *School Library Journal.*

Dzisah, J., and Etzkowitz, H. (2012). *The Age of Knowledge: The Dynamics of Universities, Knowledge and Society.* Series: Studies in Critical Social Sciences (vol. 37). Boston: Brill.

EdWeek (2020, January 24). *Early Reading Instruction: Results of a National Study.* Bethesda, MD: EdWeek Research Center.

Freire, P. (1970). *Pedagogy of the Oppressed.* Trans. by M. B. Ramos. New York: Herder and Herder.

Freire, P., and Berthoff, D. (1987). *Literacy: Reading and the World.* South Hadley, MA: Bergin and Garvey.

Freire, P., and Macedo, D. (1987). *Literacy.* South Hadley, MA: Bergin and Garvey.

Gardner, H. (1999). *Intelligence Reframed: Multiple Intelligences for the 21st Century.* New York: Basic Books.

———— (2000). *The Disciplined Mind.* New York: Penguin.

———— (2003, April 23). Multiple Intelligences after Twenty Years. Paper presented at the American Educational Research Association Meeting.

Gee, J. P. (1996). *Social Linguistics and Literacies* (2nd ed.). London: Falmer Press.

———— (2000). The New Literacy Studies. In D. Barton, M. Hamilton, and R. Ivanic, eds., *Situated Literacies: Reading and Writing in Context.* London: Routledge.

Giroux, H. (1988). *The Teacher as Intellectual*. South Hadley, MA: Bergin and Garvey.

Giroux, H., and Purpel, D. (1983). *The Hidden Curriculum and Moral Education*. Berkeley, CA: McCutchan.

Greene, M. (1994). "Postmodernism and the Crisis of Representation." *English Education* 26:206–219.

Heller, D. (2012). *Curriculum on the Edge of Survival*. Lanham, MD: Rowman and Littlefield.

Hull, G., and Schultz, K. (2002). *School's Out: Bridging Out-of-School Literacies with Classroom Practice*. New York: Teachers College Press.

Ippolito, J., Steele, J., and Samson, J. (2008). "Introduction: Why Adolescent Literacy Matters Now." *Harvard Education Review* 68(1):1–5.

Jetton, T. L., and Shanahan, C., eds. (2012). *Adolescent Literacy in the Academic Disciplines*. New York: Guilford Press.

Kissinger, H. A., Schmidt, E., and Huttenlocher, D. (2019, August). "The Metamorphosis." *The Atlantic* 324(2).

Klein, A. (2019, August 3). "What Every Educator Needs to Know about Artificial Intelligence." *Education Week*.

Kuhn, J. (2020, February). "The Quest for Human-Level AI." *Fortune*.

Laird, R. K. (2019). *The Politics of Knowledge*. Lanham, MD: Lexington Books.

Madison, D. (2013). *Vegetable Literacy*. Berkeley, CA: Ten Speed Press.

Moran, B. T. (2005). *Distilling Knowledge*. Cambridge, MA: Harvard University Press.

National Council of Teachers of English (2019, March 6). Resolution on English Education for Critical Literacy in Politics and Media. Position Statements.

Nelson, J. (1971). Nationalistic Education and the Free Man. In R. Fairfield, ed., *Humanistic Frontiers in American Education*. Englewood Cliffs, NJ: Prentice-Hall.

Phillips, C. J. (2015, December 3). "The Politics of Math Education." *New York Times*.

Pinker, S. (2018). *Enlightenment Now*. New York: Penguin.

Pollard, C. (2019, August 29). Knowledge and Power—Understanding Foucault. Open Forum (openforum.com.au).

Raskin, M. (2004). *Liberalism: The Genius of American Ideals*. Lanham, MD: Rowman Littlefield.

Rosenberg, J. F. (2002). *Thinking about Knowing*. Oxford: Clarendon Press.

Rubio, F. D., and Baert, P. (2012). *The Politics of Knowledge*. New York: Routledge.

Sawchuck, S. (2018, October 23). "How History Class Divides Us." *Education Week*.

Sizer, T. (2004). *The Red Pencil*. New Haven, CT: Yale University Press.

Sloman. S., and Fernbach, P. (2017). *The Knowledge Illusion*. New York: Riverhead Books.

Sparks, S. D. (2020, February 4). "A Creativity Conundrum." *Education Week*.

Spring, J. (1998). *American Education* (8th ed.). New York: McGraw-Hill.

Stanford Encyclopedia of Philosophy (2018, May 22). Michel Foucault. Center for the Study of Language and Information, Stanford University (plato.stanford.edu).

Stanley, W. (1992). *Education for Utopia: Social Reconstructionism and Critical Pedagogy in the Postmodern Era*. Albany: State University of New York Press.

Stiglitz, J. (2019). *People, Power, and Profits*. New York: W.W. Norton.

Strauss, V. (2018, October 30). "Why the Reading Wars Are a Waste of Time." *Washington Post*.

Tawney, R. H. (1964). *The Radical Tradition*. London: Allen and Unwin.

Tyack, D. (1967). *Turning Points in American Educational History*. Waltham, MA: Blaisdell.

Westheimer, J., ed. (2007). *Pledging Allegiance*. New York: Teachers College Press.

Wexler, N. (2019a). *The Knowledge Gap*. New York: Penguin.

——— (2019b, August). "The Radical Case for Teaching Kids Stuff." *The Atlantic*, 3224(2).

Young, M. F. D., ed. (1970). *Knowledge and Control*. London: Collier-Macmillan.

The Academic Achievement Gap and the Standards Movement

Real Change or Badly Flawed Policy

8

Will the standards-based reform movement reduce differences among the average academic achievements of students in various racial, ethnic, and economic groups?

Position 1: Standards-Based Education Will Reduce the Academic Achievement Gap

---

Most states have spent the past decade overhauling their standards, tests, and accountability systems, and finally committing real resources to capacity-building, especially in the form of curriculum implementation. . . . What's needed isn't to spin the wheel of education policy once again, but to show some patience and commitment—and finish what we started.

—Petrilli (2019b)

The Enduring Achievement Gap

For over 50 years, tests designed to measure academic achievement have documented differences between students of color and their white counterparts. The National Assessment of Educational Progress (NAEP) testing program was established in 1969 "to monitor the academic achievement of nine-, thirteen-, and seventeen-year-olds currently enrolled in school" (Jencks and Phillips, 1998, p. 152). NAEP annually tests 70,000 to 100,000 students in reading, math, science, and writing. It is influential and credible enough to be called "The Nation's Report Card." In the early 1970s, the NAEP demonstrated dramatic differences between the average scores of white students and those of color. In all subjects, across all grade levels, white students outperformed African American and Latino students by 12 to 20% (Campbell et al., 2000). Over 40 years later, differences in average test scores are still present. Asian students outperform the national average scores in both reading and mathematics by approximately 8%. White students' average score is about 10% higher than black students' average in mathematics and reading and about 8% higher than Hispanic students' averages (McFarland et al., 2019).

Other indicators of academic success reveal similar discrepancies. Twelve percent fewer black students graduate from high school than their white peers. The gap between Hispanic and white graduation rates is 9% (McFarland et al., 2018). The college enrollment rate for whites for the last 20 years has been consistently higher than the rate for black and Hispanic young people (McFarland et al., 2019). Black students' rate of completing bachelors' degrees in four years is 21.5%; Hispanic students' rate is 32.5. Forty-six percent of white students graduate in four years (Snyder et al., 2019).

Reconsidering Causes of the Achievement Gap

Clearly, there is no one easy answer to the question of why African American and Latino children continue to have lower scores on standardized tests and generally experience less academic success than white students. The reasons are complex and fluid and probably interact with one another in ways we have yet to understand. It is possible, however, to think of them in two categories: sociocultural and school related.

For most of the last 50 years, educators and policy makers emphasized sociocultural causes, arguing, for example, that racial segregation was mostly to blame for the low levels of achievement among students of color. The Supreme Court prohibited states and local government from racially segregating schools (*Brown v. Board of Education*, 1954). However, court-ordered desegregation did not prevent the continued residential isolation between white people and those of color. Forced integration did not change people's minds and hearts. Schools, like most neighborhoods, remain racially distinct.

In 2007, the Supreme Court noted that there was a kind of racial superiority implicit in the frantic efforts to get children of color into "good" schools—schools whose populations historically had been white. The Court ruled that while diversity and racial isolation are compelling interests for local governments, school districts must tailor desegregation programs narrowly and cannot simply classify every student on the basis of race and assign each of them to a particular school based on that classification (*Parents Involved in Community Schools Inc. v. Seattle School District*, 2007). A single-minded focus on which students should attend particular schools does not ensure that educators or the community will hold all schools accountable for providing equal opportunity and outcomes for every student.

Another social factor that has been blamed for the achievement gap is poverty. Nearly 13 million American children (approximately one in five children) live in poverty (an annual income below $25,094 for a family of four) and half of them are in "extreme poverty" (an annual income of $12,547). A third of black children and over a quarter of Hispanic children live in families whose incomes fall under the federal government's poverty threshold. Only 11% of white children's families and 10% of Asian children's families are poor (McFarland et al., 2019). In the families of nearly two-thirds of poor children at least one adult is working; in one-third, at least one adult is working full-time (Children's Defense Fund, 2019).

There are clear correlations with poor academic outcomes and poverty and racial isolation (Reardon et al., 2019). Three-quarters of black and Hispanic children attend schools that primarily serve poor children. Only a third of white or Asian children attend schools that have similar concentrations of poor children. Children who attend schools serving high poverty students have significantly lower scores on the NAEP than those serving wealthier students (McFarland et al., 2019). They are also less likely to graduate and far less likely to enroll in college immediately after completing high school (McFarland et al., 2018).

There is no question that there are sociocultural factors that correlate with the opportunities and outcome differences among groups of students. However, there is no evidence to support the notion that an individual student of color who is poor and attends a school that is racially and economically isolated cannot excel academically. Moreover, racism and poverty are social, not school-based, problems and are beyond schools' ability to control. What schools can do is to provide sound, rigorous instruction to students regardless of their backgrounds. Standards-based curricula and assessments have proven to be an effective way of doing so.

School-Related Causes of the Academic Achievement Gap

Prior to the implementation of state and national standards-based curricula and assessments, researchers had identified several school-related causes of the academic achievement gap. In many public schools, children of color encountered teachers who had low expectations of them. Teachers did not search aggressively for instructional strategies to help African American or Latino American students who were having difficulty, having already concluded that those children had limited potential. In turn, students of color internalized these low expectations and did not see themselves as capable of succeeding in school (Diamond et al., 2004). Children of color were less likely than their white counterparts to attend schools with experienced teachers, more likely to have teachers without college preparation in subjects they were teaching, and twice as likely to have teachers without state certification (Peske and Haycock, 2006; Clotfelter et al., 2007).

Students of color were more likely than their white peers to attend schools that prepared them for industrial jobs that no longer existed (Haycock, 2003). Students of color were less likely than their white peers to attend schools that offered advanced math and science or be prepared to take advantage of them if such opportunities were presented. They too often had been tracked into "general" or "basic" courses where the curriculum was simplified and teachers covered less material, gave less homework, and rewarded low-level performance with high grades. This failure to take high-level coursework resulted in lower scores on standardized tests and lower likelihood of college enrollment—and so contributed greatly to the achievement gap (Tyson et al., 2007). By opting out or being forced out of the most challenging curriculum, the futures of students of color were being limited.

School districts that serve students of color had high mobility rates. Children routinely moved from one school to another in the district *within* a school year. Yet urban districts did little to respond to that reality. They did not standardize curriculum, textbooks, or instruction. Students who moved found themselves repeating material they had already learned or being challenged to do work for which they had not been prepared. They often lost heart and stopped trying (Smith et al., 2008; Cordes et al., 2019).

Standards-Based Reform and the Achievement Gap

In 1965, Congress passed the Elementary and Secondary Education Act (ESEA) as companion legislation to the Civil Rights Act. ESEA was designed to close achievement gaps between children from low-income households in rural or urban areas and children from suburban middle-class families. It provided Title I funding to districts that served large numbers of low-income children. As President Johnson said when he signed the bill into law, "It represents a major new commitment of the federal government to quality and equality in the schooling that we offer our young people . . . we bridge the gap between helplessness and hope for more than five million educationally deprived children" (Johnson, 1965). Millions of Title I dollars flowed into schools that served black and Latino children.

In the Reagan and Bush administrations of the 1980s, the failures of ESEA's "throw money at the problem" way of addressing school inequality were identified. In 1983, the National Commission on Excellence in Education's report *A Nation at Risk* called public attention to serious deficiencies in schools despite the increase in federal and state spending. Six years later, the Bush administration proposed high national standards and ongoing assessment of student performance and the standards-based reform movement was born. Rather than focusing on the inequality represented by differences in achievement among economic or racial/ethnic groups of children, in its earliest days, the movement's focus was on excellence in school curricula and resources.

It took over 20 years for the federal government to recognize the power of standards-based reform to address the achievement gap. In 2001, No Child Left Behind (NCLB), a reauthorization of the ESEA, supported by large majorities of Democrats and Republicans, was passed. NCLB was specifically designed to use the tools of high standards and rigorous assessment to remedy the achievement gaps among white, Asian, black, and Hispanic students and between children from wealthy and poor families. It required each state to develop its own standards for math, English language arts (ELA), and science and to test students in math and ELA annually in grades 3 through 8. States were required to develop an accountability system to ensure that outcomes were improving in math, ELA, and science. In particular, to demonstrate success in closing the achievement gap, schools had to demonstrate progress for all students. They were held accountable to meet annual objectives for (1) economically disadvantaged students, (2) students from major racial and ethnic groups, (3) students with disabilities, and (4) students with limited English proficiency. The goal was that, in little more than a decade, all students would demonstrate proficiency on state tests. By requiring states to report test scores for multiple subgroups of students, NCLB highlighted the differences in test scores and held states, districts, and schools accountable for achieving greater equity in outcomes.

Race to the Top and Common Core State Standards

By the early 2000s, in compliance with NCLB, every state had developed its own learning standards, with individual definitions of proficiency. However, multiple standards made it impossible to evaluate how well young people from a state or school were prepared for college and a career in comparison with their peers across the country. In 2009, 50 states agreed to participate in the effort to establish rigorous national academic standards that came to be known as the Common Core State Standards (CCSS). The goal was to ensure that every student was ready for college or a career (Common Core State Standards Initiative, 2019). The Common Core ELA Standards were clearer and more rigorous than existing ELA standards in 39 states and the math standards were superior to those in 37 states (Carmichael et al., 2010).

As a voluntarily collaborative effort among the states, the CCSS preserved states' control over elementary and secondary education while making comparisons of student performance, in every subgroup, within and across states, more accurate. The costs of creating and implementing standardized tests were reduced. Students who moved from state to state found greater similarity in curricula and assessment. Students across the country could be confident that they would be equally prepared for college or the workplace (Meador, 2019).

The federal government provided significant incentives to states to adopt the CCSS. In 2010, in the midst of the worst economic downturn since the Great Depression, the Department of Education announced the Race to the Top competition for federal education funding. States that adopted the CCSS had a distinct advantage in the competition, earning almost 15% of the total points available in the grant application, by doing so.

In addition, the performance of students with disabilities and students of color were not meeting the progress required by NCLB and states faced loss of funding. When Congress failed to revise the law, the Department of Education began issuing waivers to states to exempt them from the consequences. Adopting the CCSS was a requirement for the waivers.

Every Student Succeeds Act and Standards

Some critics viewed the "carrot and stick" approach of the Race to the Top as evidence of inappropriate interference of the federal government. The reauthorization of NCLB as the Every Student Succeeds Act (ESSA) (2016) explicitly forbade the Department of Education from attempting "to influence, incentivize, or coerce State adoption of the Common Core State Standards developed under the Common Core State Standards Initiative or any other academic standards common to a significant number of States, or assessments tied to such standard" (p. 1,852).

The law does require that each state adopt "challenging academic standards" in mathematics, ELA, and science; utilize some form of common assessment matched to those standards; and report student performance on those assessments, disaggregated by the subgroups identified by NCLB. States are free to adopt the CCSS, to work collaboratively with other states to revise them and/or adopt those revised versions, or to create new standards of their own. Almost two-thirds of states have adopted new state standards. However, the vast majority of them are based on the CCSS that clarified or reworded concepts and reformatted materials (DeNisco, 2017). Recent analysis has concluded that the closer state standards are aligned with Common Core Standards, the stronger they are (Friedberg et al., 2018).

Standards Support Equity

By requiring that instruction be aligned with state standards that match the Common Core and implemented by well-prepared teachers, states can close the gap between the academic outcomes of students from marginalized and underserved social groups and those of their more privileged peers. Children from middle, upper-middle class, and wealthy backgrounds find their home culture is validated in schools and the curriculum they are taught is aligned with it. For poorer children or those from marginalized groups, the distance between home and school cultures is simply too large to close without explicit instruction. Standards that spell out what students need to know and be able to do and instruction that, step by step, helps them do so remedies one of the most significant school-based causes of the academic achievement gap. The distance between the knowledge and skills that different groups of students bring to school is bridged by the scaffolding provided by standards-based teaching and assessment.

Equity of opportunity and outcomes was a goal in New York State's development of its Next Generation Language Arts Standards. The task force identified practices of lifelong readers and writers. The list included: reading and writing competently for diverse purposes, persevering through complex tasks and texts, analyzing texts, developing vocabulary and background knowledge, and utilizing a variety of strategies. In addition, readers monitor their comprehension and writers strengthen their writing by planning, revising, editing, rewriting, or trying a new approach. The Next Generation Mathematics Standards identify expertise in processes and procedures that enhance opportunities and options for students to shape their futures. Doors open for people who can make sense of problems and persevere in using math to solve them. Reasoning abstractly and quantitatively, constructing viable arguments, critiquing the reasoning of others, modeling with mathematics, and using the correct tools appropriately and precisely are competencies that lead to success in college and the job market. Analysis of these practices and competencies resulted in the identification of a set of necessary skills. Levels of these skills were assigned to each grade. In New York, schools are now mandated to provide students with instruction and activities that help them build those skills in developmentally appropriate ways (New York State Education Department, 2019a).

The accountability components of the standards-based reform movement—common exams aligned with the standards and teacher, school, district, and state report cards that make test results public, and policies that reward professionals whose students are successful—are crucial to its success. Previously underperforming students receive more focused instruction and better resources when their test scores count toward district and teacher evaluations.

Standardized Tests and Standards-Based Reform

Although standardized testing provides the scientific base necessary to support the art of teaching, standardized testing sometimes has a negative connotation. The truth is that standardized tests are designed to provide fair evaluations and a level playing field for all test takers. *Standardized* refers to the fact that the test content and the conditions for test takers are always the same everywhere and that students taking the tests are protected from an evaluator's personal preferences or prejudice. Within the standards-based reform movement, the term also refers to exams that are aligned with the states' rigorous goals for their students. When students take PARCC or Smarter Balanced exams, for example, they are all taking the same tests under the same testing conditions, and they will be compared objectively with students of their age with similar years of schooling.

By using standardized tests, schools can determine one student's command of content and compare that student to others in an objective and fair manner. Schools can also measure an individual teacher's contributions to student learning. Modern information technology enables school officials to assemble good data over time about student achievement and teacher abilities. Standardized tests provide schools and teachers with data to inform answers to questions about curriculum, student learning, and teacher effectiveness.

Moreover, standardized tests also make comparisons among individual and groups of students possible. Disaggregating data by socioeconomic criteria reveals the differences among subgroup performance and allows schools and teachers to address the gaps that Finn and Petrilli (2011) have called "morally unacceptable, socially divisive, and politically unstable" (p. 6). As Slover and Muldoon (2018) argue, this ability can help close the achievement gaps. It prevents states from setting "different performance levels, some higher than others, in effect establishing different targets for what level of academic achievement was expected of students and exacerbating the problem of disparities by Zip code."

Some schools' responses to the high-stakes nature of the standardized tests mandated by NCLB, the breathtakingly swift pace at which tests based on the CCSS were introduced, and the switch from paper to computer-based exams have been frenetic. In particular, parents, students, and teachers reacted negatively to the ways test preparation dominated instructional time and achieving positive results dominated school cultures. A great deal of the criticism was well founded. The reforms of the ESSA were needed.

The law still requires annual testing in math and ELA using exams aligned with states' standards. The results must be disaggregated by subgroups and each group's performance and progress must be reported. However, states may also implement innovative assessments including competency-based, instructionally embedded, interim assessments and summative assessments. States can substitute ACT and SAT scores for high school assessments and demonstrate equal access to college prepara-tory curricula and other indicators of college readiness (U.S. Department of Educa-tion, 2018).

> The inclusion of these indicators thereby strengthens the ability of states to mean-ingfully tackle many of the structural and societal challenges they face in locally relevant ways in an effort to provide statewide access to this type of curriculum to all students. (Cardichon and Darling-Hammond, 2017)

States are "designing assessment systems that better reflect and support the daily work of students and teachers in classrooms" (Olson, 2019, p. 1). They are providing test results more quickly, utilizing end-of-unit (rather than end-of-term) tests and per-formance-based tasks. At the same time, they are providing teachers with more and better information about how to adapt instruction to help students demonstrate mas-tery of the standards (Desimone et al., 2019).

Promising Results from Standards-Based Reforms

While academic achievement differences among socio-culturally defined groups still exist, there is evidence that correlates standards-based reform with positive results. Between 2000 and 2016 the dropout rates among Hispanic students decreased from 28 to 9%, the rate among black students decreased from 13 to 6%, and the rate among white students decreased from 7 to 5%. The white-black gap on the NAEP average on fourth grade reading and math scores narrowed between 1992 and 2017 (Indicators 10 and 11) (de Brey et al., 2019).

In states that adopted rigorous standards, changes were notable. For example, in New York State, in 2001, only 42% of black or Hispanic students scored at the profi-cient level on state exams. Seventy-four percent of white students did. Forty-five per-cent of black students and 49% of Hispanic students were proficient in mathematics, compared to 81% of white students (New York State Education Department, 2003). In 2014, the first year in which statewide learning standards had been fully imple-mented, 38% of white students, 17% of black students, and 19% of Hispanic students were proficient in ELA (New York State Education Department, 2014a). That same year, 45% of white students, 20% of black students, and 19% of Hispanic students were rated proficient in mathematics (New York State Education Department, 2014b). In 2019, 51% of white students, 36% of Hispanics, and 35% of black students were rated proficient in ELA (New York State Education Department, 2019b). That year, 56% of white students, 35% of Hispanics, and 35% of black students were profi-cient in mathematics (New York State Education Department, 2019c). Two things are evident from this data. First, by adopting rigorous standards and assessing them, weaknesses in students' knowledge and skills were revealed. Second, with time, scores improved for all groups of students, with more significant gains for black and His-panic students than for white students. That is, the academic achievement gaps were identified and progress had been made in closing them.

While the media and politicians have presented standards-based reform as simply a series of high-stakes testing, the movement is much more. The nitty-gritty, day-today work of helping students meet high expectations is challenging—but it is the kind of challenge that, if met successfully, will change young people's lives and our collective future. It requires leadership from administrators, commitment from teachers, and deserves support from policy makers and the public.

Position 2: Standards-Based Reform Is Flawed Policy That Will Not Close Achievement Gaps

---

In schools serving low-performing students, the strategy has bordered on obsession, with preparation for reading and math tests crowding out other subject areas. Even at schools that serve high-performing students, the pressure to raise test scores has led administrators to narrow the curriculum and treat teachers as instruments of the bureaucracy. Failure should have been anticipated. Absent from the strategy was any new approach to teaching and learning, except for the unproven assumption that "if you test it, they will learn."

—Wise (2019, p. 10)

Suspicious Origins of the Standards-Based Reform Movement

Advocates of the standards movement argue that they are responding responsibly to a crisis in education identified almost 40 years ago in *A Nation at Risk*. However, the crisis to which they are responding is not the real educational scandal facing America's schools. *A Nation at Risk* fueled the myth of failing schools and paved the way for a conservative agenda that had little to do with making the American *public* school system more equitable for its most underserved students. It is more closely linked with supporters of a market-based educational system, in which the data it produced would provide "consumers" (aka parents and children) with information about "products" (aka schools) (Apple, 1996).

The standards-based reform movement cannot close the academic achievement gaps among racial, ethnic, and economic subgroups of students in the United States. Not on its own, at any rate.

Over the last 50 years, we have developed other and better laws and programs designed to make equal educational opportunity a reality. For example, the courts declared that laws mandating segregation in schools are illegal. Congress enacted legislation creating Head Start, early childhood programs, and Title I, which allocates funds to schools with high concentrations of low-performing students. Some of these programs faced tremendous opposition. It took many legal, political, and social struggles to put them into place. It was a fight well worth having and a legacy that should be preserved.

Integration

The Supreme Court ruled in the landmark case *Brown v. Board of Education* (1954) that laws assigning students to school based on their race were unconstitutional. Segregated schools could never be equal, the Court declared in its unanimous ruling. The struggle to carry out the Court's ruling was difficult—at times even violent. The federal courts' uncompromising commitment in the early desegregation period meant, however, that there was no turning back. All across the country, school districts were forced to comply with desegregation orders. Creative opportunities for all students resulted, including magnet schools whose innovative programs were designed to attract white students to attend integrated schools (Lewis, 1965; Sarratt, 1966; Cecelski, 1994; Taylor, 1998; Orfield, 2001).

The desegregation struggle for Latino Americans was somewhat different. In many parts of the country, their segregation from Anglo students was not based on their "race." The courts had declared them "white." However, states passed laws requiring that all instruction be conducted in English. Although their language skills were not evaluated, Latino children were presumed to be deficient in English and segregated from their Anglo peers. Lawsuits seeking an end to the practice predated the *Brown* decision—*Mendez v. Westminster School District of Orange County et al.* (1946) used a framework that would later be articulated in *Brown* (Wilson, 2003). After *Brown,* in *Cisneros v. Corpus Christi Independent School District* (1970) and in *Keyes v. School District No. 1, Denver, Colorado* (1973), the courts ruled that Latinos could suffer the same kind of discrimination as blacks and were, therefore, eligible to receive the same kind of remedies—namely, desegregated schools.

The early integration era was a period of dramatic changes in the academic achievement gap. Students of color who attended desegregated schools, especially if they began to do so in the early grades, had educational achievement levels one grade higher than they would have attained in a segregated school (Mahard and Crain, 1984). African American and Latino students who attended desegregated schools were less likely to become teenage parents or delinquents. They also were more likely to graduate from high school and to enroll in and be successful in college (Liebman, 1990; Orfield and Eaton, 1996; Orfield, 2001).

Despite its success, integration has become increasingly difficult to maintain. The Supreme Court has ruled that courts can only intervene if segregation is the result of previous governmental policies, not individual choices (*Keyes v. School District No. 1, Denver, Colorado,* 1973). Mandated interdistrict desegregation is not allowed (*Milliken v. Bradley,* 1974). Municipalities cannot protect the gains of the desegregation era by student assignment polices that maintain a racial balance comparable to that of the community—even when the voters and their elected officials deem those policies to be absolutely necessary to providing equal opportunity for every child in their school district (*Meredith v. Jefferson County (Ky.) Board of Education,* 2007; *Parents Involved in Community Schools Inc. v. Seattle School District,* 2007). These decisions resulted in an increase in the number of districts seeking to end court ordered desegregation plans and adopting "color blind" systems of school assignment. Most segregation in public schools today occurs because district boundary lines sort students into separate school systems rather than because laws order them into separate schools within the same system. The number of school district boundaries have increased in the last decade as local areas secede from larger school districts and create their own (Frankenberg et al., 2017). History shows that when the rate of desegregation slows, so does the closing of the black-white achievement gap (Hanushek et al., 2019).

In fall 2015, 30% of all public elementary and secondary students attended schools where students of color were at least 75% of the population. Only 5% of white students attended schools with that population distribution; 60% of black and Latino students did. Eighty percent of white youth attend schools where less than 25% of the students are members of other racial groups (de Brey et al., 2019). Three quarters of black and Latino students attend schools designated as "high poverty," where more than half of the population receive free or reduced lunch. Only one-third of white students attend "high poverty schools" (McFarland et al., 2019). Clearly, racially segregated schools not only isolate students by race or ethnicity, they also concentrate students of color in "high poverty schools, that provide significantly less educational opportunities than schools serving higher-income students" (Reardon et al., 2019, p. 8). It is the inequality of opportunities, not abilities, which result in the academic achievement gap.

Supporters of the standards-based movement have contributed to the acceptance of a narrative that "integration was a failed experiment . . . if our schools remain grossly imbalanced, we just have to live with that, to make that necessary concession to reality" (Johnson, 2019, p. 2), and establish rigorous standards and accountability measures. Careful research has demonstrated the falsehood of the claim "that it is possible to have high quality schools in every neighborhood, regardless of racial or economic composition" (Reardon et al., 2019, p. 2). The claim ignores the facts that even with the reforms of the post NCLB era (that resulted in improvements in high-poverty school resources such as compensatory funding and better prepared and more experienced teachers and administrators), very significant gaps in academic outcomes remain. What likely mattered more than the standards-based reform "were the vastly improving social and economic conditions for our poorest children" (Petrilli, 2019a, p. 28) and a period of enforced racial and, consequently, economic integration.

"Integration is a necessary means to a broader end: equal opportunity" (Johnson, 2019, p. 9). Reviving the commitment to creating schools with racially, ethnically, and economically diverse student populations requires changing people's minds about some cherished beliefs. It will also require political will and power. The claims that education laws and policies are colorblind; that education is an individual benefit and not a societal one; that micro-local control of schools is best all must be challenged. Policy makers in fact have given better-resourced communities "race-neutral, legally sanctioned, and politically persuasive ways" to justify and defend those resources (Siegel-Hawley et al., 2018, p. 651). Researchers have found examples of effective high-poverty schools, but no examples of a district that has closed the racial achievement gap if students of color attend segregated schools with high levels of student poverty. "If it were possible to create equal educational opportunity under conditions of segregation and economic inequality, some community—among the thousands of districts in the country—would have done so. None have. Separate is still unequal" (Reardon et al., 2019, p. 35).

Early Childhood Education

The link between educational opportunities, racial segregation, and poverty starts early in a child's life. Significant racial achievement gaps are present among kindergarteners (Bassok et al. 2016; Reardon and Portilla, 2016). Researchers have demonstrated that early childhood education can help bridge the differences in children based on parental income and education levels, educational resources in the home, and neighborhood conditions (Bassok and Engel, 2019).

Governmental efforts to educate the very youngest children began over 50 years ago when Congress funded Head Start, an innovative program to address the disadvantages poor children faced in becoming "school ready." Since then 36 million children have participated. Today, the program distributes almost $10 billion to over 1,600 Head Start centers. Its mission is "to promote school readiness of children ages birth to five from low-income families by supporting the development of the whole child" (Office of Head Start, 2019). Head Start provides a variety of services, including individualized learning experiences, health and development screening, meals, oral and mental health support, support for families to strengthen parent-child relationships, and ensuring housing stability and financial security.

Since 2000 there has been a dramatic increase in early childhood learning programs created and maintained through the states—between 2002 and 2017, state funding for preschool tripled. There is consensus among researchers that children who attend preschool have stronger academic readiness skills than those who do not. The finding applies to Head Start, state, and other early childhood programs (Bassok and Engel, 2019). Academic readiness gaps among racial, ethnic, and income gaps are all closing somewhat, apparently as a result of increased participation of poor children and those of color in high-quality preschool programs. In addition, gaps in self-control and approaches to learning also declined among racial/ethnic groups.

These successes in early childhood education did not come as a result of the standards-based reform movement. Early childhood educators approached the CCSS and other efforts with immense caution and concern. For example, rather than adopt a set of standards for Head Start programs, they developed a "framework for learning" that "is grounded in a comprehensive body of research about what young children should know and be able to do to succeed in school. It describes how children progress across key areas of learning and development and specifies learning outcomes in these areas" (Early Childhood Learning & Knowledge Center, 2019). Educators and supportive adults use the information to create effective and developmentally appropriate learning experiences. While recognizing that states would develop standards for early childhood education, leaders in the field sought (with a relatively high degree of success) to ensure that early learning standards had meaningful and developmentally appropriate content and outcomes and that implementation and assessment strategies were ethical and appropriate for young children (National Association for the Education of Young Children, 2015). The evidence that achievement gaps are closing for children entering kindergarten and that the effect seems to last through the primary grades validates their approach.

Despite these gains, it is critical that federal, state, and local funding for developmentally appropriate and holistic early childhood education programs increase. If the pace continues at its current rate, it will still take two to three generations to close the gaps among groups of kindergartners (Reardon and Portilla, 2016, p. 12).

Hidden Costs of the Standards-Based Reform Movement

The standards-based reform movement inappropriately brought certain business principles to education. Supporters argued that testing data could be used to provide incentives and punishments for classroom teachers and school administrators.

McNeil (2000) and Horn and Kincheloe (2001) explained the role of business in the Texas standards movement. Ross Perot, a successful businessman with a folksy straight-talking approach, was appointed head of a state commission on education reform. He argued that if something had proved to be effective in business management, it must be good for managing schools as well. Based on his distrust of middle managers in business, who he believed were obstacles to change and supporters of the status quo, Perot placed the blame for Texas's education problems at the doorsteps of school administrators (education's middle managers). Over time, the Texas school reform committee advocated a centralized system of curriculum and assessment that bypassed school administrators. The legislature adopted a micromanagement style and standardized planning, teaching, and assessment. They attempted to "teacher-proof" the curriculum with a checklist for instructors' behaviors and tests of students' minimum skills.

This approach, adopted widely during the height of state involvement in schools during the NCLB era, was ideal for mediocre teachers who liked to teach routine lessons according to a standard sequence and format and who liked not having to think about their work. On the other hand, it drove out more talented teachers who most inspired students, who were creative, who developed lesson plans based on what they knew about their students, and who made a difference in students' lives. They established relationships with students and believed in students and supported them—all behaviors that research has demonstrated are particularly important for black and Latino students. They are the teachers who former Secretary of Education John King (2017) said, "quite literally saved my life. During the period when I lost both parents at an early age, they gave me a haven. They challenged me with high expectations and a rich, well-rounded curriculum; they provided me with hope in a time of despair; they helped me thrive and become the person I am today."

Standards-based reforms that were based on a business model distorted the critical role that teachers play in education. They failed to take into account teachers' ability to encourage or discourage students, to bring out their potential or thwart it, to open students to new worlds of understanding, or to close them off. Using student performance on annual standardized tests was an unfair measure of teacher competency. Linking individual student scores to individual teachers in one school year and basing teachers' job security, promotions, or raises solely on that one indicator made no scientific or mathematical sense. The practice was especially ironic in an era that billed itself as "research based."

Similarly, according to a business model, school success could be measured by test scores and increases in the number of test takers who improve. The emphasis on scores and statewide achievement measures was too narrow a measure for schools. The narrowness of statewide testing fails to capture important dimensions of learning, including social and emotional growth. In addition, such accountability systems did not include measures of a school's importance and contributions to the communities in which they were located, particularly salient for schools in high-poverty neighborhoods.

Recent changes to federal law reflect how fully the business informed standards-based reform movement has been rejected by educators and policy makers (U.S. Department of Education, 2018). The requirement that teacher evaluation be linked solely to student performance on standardized tests has been eliminated. Like teachers, schools must be evaluated with multiple measures. Costly annual tests scores may, and in some states and districts must, be supplemented with additional measures of student performance. Reducing the high-stakes nature of those exams may encourage the most effective teachers to remain in the profession and prevent students from dropping or being pushed out of schools.

Standards Alone Cannot Close the Achievement Gap

The real crisis facing the United States is social, not academic. Children who come to school hungry, poor, or sick are not likely to be helped by more rigorous standards. Children with children of their own and children from abusive homes are unlikely to see their lives improve through statewide accountability plans. The real national risk is more appropriately measured not by test scores but by dropout rates, unemployment statistics, and the juvenile incarceration rate. By itself, the standards-based reform movement will not affect deeper social problems. The standards movement can be thought of as a new kind of discrimination. Under the guise of fairness, offering all students the same curriculum, same forms of instruction, and same objective assessments, students from less wealthy homes with less well-educated parents are denied the education they need. With its emphasis on drill and repetitive practice for standardized tests, the standards movement increased classroom tedium and time spent on numbing routine. High-stakes testing added stress and the threat of failure. The negative impact of standards reform has fallen hardest on poor and minority students.

Everyone wants to improve schools and raise the levels of learning. The problem is not with standards. However, high standards cannot paper over the social problems that accompany students to school every day and cannot close the academic achievement gap.

For Discussion

1. Using the NAEP's Achievement Gaps Dashboard (nationsreportcard.gov/dashboards/achievement_gaps.aspx), research the achievement gaps in your state. Speculate on factors that may influence conditions in your state. Using other sources of information, research and evaluate your state's efforts to close the gaps.

2. Choose two school districts in your state or two schools in the same district that, while geographically close (in the same county, for example), are economically dif-

ferent. Identify how and when the district boundaries or school assignment zones were created.

Compare the data from state report cards on resources such as teacher qualification and experiences, per pupil expenditures, and facilities. Note the demographics of each district—race and ethnicity of the school population, the number of students with disabilities, and the number of students eligible for free and reduced lunch. Then compare achievement indicators such as graduation rate and scores on state testing. What are your observations with regard to the data? What questions do your observations raise?

3. As a result of the constitutional division of legislative authority between the states and the federal government, the United States has developed a system of local rather than national control of education. Other countries have long had national systems of education. Research a country in which schools are centrally controlled. Are national standards and testing part of the system? Do they have achievement gaps among economic and ethnic/racial groups?

REFERENCES

Apple, M. (1996). "Being Popular about National Standards: A Review of National Standards in American Education: A Citizen's Guide." *Education Policy Analysis Archives* 4(10).

Bassok, D., and Engel, M. (2019). "Early Childhood Education at Scale: Lessons from Research for Policy and Practice." *AERA Open* 5(1) https://doi.org/10.1177/2332858419828690

Bassok, D., Finch, J., Lee, R., Reardon, S., and Waldfogel, J. (2016). "Socioeconomic Gaps in Early Childhood Experiences." *AERA Open* 2(3). https://doi.org./10.1177/2332858416653924

Brown v. Board of Education of Topeka, Shawnee County, Kansas, et al. (1954). 347 U.S. 483.

Campbell, J., Hombo, C., and Mazzeo, J. (2000). NAEP 1999 Trends in Academic Progress: Three Decades of Student Performance. National Assessment of Educational Progress (nces.ed.gov/nationsreportcard/pubs/main1999/2000469.asp).

Cardichon, J., and Darling-Hammond, L. (2017). *Advancing Educational Equity for Underserved Youth: How New State Accountability Systems Can Support School Inclusion and Student Success.* Palo Alto, CA: Learning Policy Institute.

Carmichael, S., Wilson, W., Porter-Magee, K., and Martino, G. (2010). *The State of State Standards—and the Common Core—in 2010.* Washington, DC: Thomas B. Fordham Institute.

Cecelski, D. (1994). *Along Freedom Road.* Chapel Hill: University of North Carolina Press.

Children's Defense Fund (2019). *Ending Child Poverty Now.* Washington, DC: Children's Defense Fund.

Cisneros v. Corpus Christi Independent School District (1970). 324 F. Supp. 599 (S.D. Tex.).

Clotfelter, C., Ladd, H., and Vigdor, J. (2007). "Teacher Credentials and Student Achievement." *Economics of Education Review* 26(6):673–682.

Common Core State Standards Initiative (2019). Development Process. About the Standards (corestandards.org/about-the-standards/development-process).

Cordes, S. A., Schwartz, A. E., and Stiefel, L. (2019). "The Effect of Residential Mobility on Student Performance: Evidence from New York City." *American Educational Research Journal* 56(4):1,380–1,411. https://doi.org/10.3102/0002831218822828

de Brey, C., Musu, L., McFarland, J., Wilkinson-Flicker, S., Diliberti, M., Zhang, A., Branstetter, C., and Wang, X. (2019). *Status and Trends in the Education of Racial and Ethnic Groups*

2018 (NCES 2019-038). Washington, DC: U.S. Department of Education, National Center for Education Statistics.

DeNisco, A. (2017, October 9). Common Core No More? New York and 21 Other States Revise or Rename K12 Standards. District Administration (districtadministration.com/common-core-no-more-new-york-and-21-other-states-revise-or-rename-k-12-standards).

Desimone, L., Stornaiuolo, A., Flores, N., Pak, K., Edgerton, A., Nichols, T., Plummer, E., and Porter, A. (2019). "Successes and Challenges of the 'New' College- and Career-Ready Standards: Seven Implementation Trends." *Educational Researcher* 48(3):167–178. https://doi.org/10.3102/0013189X19837239

Diamond, J., Randolph, A., and Spillane, J. (2004). "Teachers' Expectations and Sense of Responsibility for Student Learning: The Implications of School Race, Class, and Organizational Habitus." *Anthropology and Education Quarterly* 35(1):75–98.

Early Childhood Learning & Knowledge Center (2019). Head Start Early Learning Outcomes Framework. U.S. Department of Health and Human Services (eclkc.ohs.acf.hhs.gov/school-readiness/article/head-start-early-learning-outcomes-framework).

Every Student Succeeds Act (2016). PL 114-95 (govinfo.gov/content/pkg/PLAW-114publ95/pdf/PLAW-114publ95.pdf).

Finn, C. E., and Petrilli, M. J. (2011). *ESEA Briefing Book.* Washington, DC: Thomas B. Fordham Institute.

Frankenberg, E., Siegel-Hawley, G., and Diem, S. (2017). Segregation by District Boundary Line: The Fragmentation of Memphis Area Schools. *Educational Researcher* 46(8):449–463. https://doi.org/10.3102/0013189X17732752

Friedberg, S., Barone, D., Belding, J., Chen, A., Dixon, L., Fennell, F., Fisher, D., Frey, N., Howe, R., and Shanahan, T. (2018). *The State of State Standards Post Common Core.* Washington, DC: Thomas B. Fordham Institute.

Hanushek, E., Peterson, P., Talpey, L., and Woessmann, L. (2019) *The Unwavering SES Achievement Gap: Trends in U.S. Student Performance* (NBER Working Paper No. 25648). Cambridge, MA: National Bureau of Economic Research.

Haycock, K. (2003). "A New Core Curriculum for All: Aiming High for Other People's Children." *Thinking K–16* 7(1):1–2.

Horn, R. A., and Kincheloe, J. L., eds. (2001). *American Standards: Quality Education in a Complex World.* New York: Peter Lang.

Jencks, C., and Phillips, M., eds. (1998). *The Black-White Test Score Gap.* Washington, DC: Brookings Institution.

Johnson, L. (1965). Johnson's Remarks on Signing the Elementary and Secondary Education Act. LBJ Presidential Library (lbjlibrary.org/lyndon-baines-johnson/timeline/johnsons-remarks-on-signing-the-elementary-and-secondary-education-act).

Johnson, R. (2019). *Children of the Dream: Why School Integration Works.* New York: Basic Books.

Keyes v. School District No. 1, Denver, Colorado (1973). 413 U.S. 189.

King, J. (2017). "Guest Perspective: U.S. Secretary of Education John B. King, Jr." *Journal of College Access* 3(1).

Lewis, A. (1965). *Portrait of a Decade.* New York: Bantam Books.

Liebman, J. (1990). "Desegregating Politics: All-Out School Desegregation Explained." *Columbia Law Review* 90:1,463.

Mahard, R., and Crain, R. (1984). Research on Minority Achievement in Desegregated Schools. In C. Rossell and W. Hawley, eds., *The Consequences of School Desegregation.* Philadelphia: Temple University Press.

McFarland, J., Cui, J., Rathbun, A., and Holmes, J. (2018). *Trends in High School Dropout and Completion Rates in the United States: 2018* (NCES 2019-117). Washington, DC: U.S. Department of Education, National Center for Education Statistics.

McFarland, J., Hussar, B., Zhang, J., Wang, X., Wang, K., Hein, S., Diliberti, M., Forrest Cataldi, E., Bullock Mann, F., and Barmer, A. (2019). *The Condition of Education 2019* (NCES 2019-144). Washington, DC: U.S. Department of Education, National Center for Education Statistics (nces.ed.gov/pubsearch/pubsinfo.asp?pubid=2019144).

McNeil, L. M. (2000). *Contradictions of Reform: The Educational Costs of Standardized Testing.* New York: Routledge.

Meador, D. (2019). What Are Some Pros and Cons of the Common Core State Standards? ThoughtCo (thoughtco.com/common-core-state-standards-3194603).

Mendez v. Westminster School District of Orange County et al. (1946). 64 F. Supp. 544 (S.D. Cal.).

Meredith v. Jefferson County (Ky.) Board of Education (2007). 127 U.S. 575.

Milliken v. Bradley (1974). 419 U.S. 815.

National Association for the Education of Young Children (2015). *Developmentally Appropriate Practice and the Common Core State Standards: Framing the Issues.* Washington, DC: National Association for the Education of Young Children.

National Commission on Excellence in Education (1983). *A Nation at Risk: The Imperative for Educational Reform.* Washington, DC: U.S. Department of Education.

New York State Education Department (2003). *Overview of Statewide Performance in English Language Arts, Mathematics, and Science and Analysis of Student Subgroup Performance for Public Schools* (data.nysed.gov/files/reportcards/archive/2001-02/overview/800000081568.pdf).

——— (2014a). NY State Grades 3–8 ELA Assessment Data (data.nysed.gov/assessment38.php?subject=ELA&year=2014&state=yes).

——— (2014b). NY State Grades 3–8 Mathematics Assessment Data (data.nysed.gov/assessment38.php?subject=Mathematics&year=2014&state=yes).

——— (2019a). New York State Next Generation Learning Standards (nysed.gov/next-generation-learning-standards).

——— (2019b). NY State Grades 3–8 ELA Assessment Data (data.nysed.gov/assessment38.php?subject=ELA&year=2019&state=yes).

——— (2019c). NY State Grades 3–8 Mathematics Assessment Data (data.nysed.gov/assessment38.php?subject=Mathematics&year=2019&state=yes).

No Child Left Behind (2001). PL 107-110 (ed.gov/nclb).

Office of Head Start (2019). About Head Start. U.S. Department of Health and Human Services (acf.hhs.gov/ohs/about/head-start).

Olson, L. (2019). The New Testing Landscape: State Assessments under ESSA. Future Ed. McCourt School of Public Policy, Georgetown University (future-ed.org/the-new-testing-landscape-state-assessments-under-essa).

Orfield, G. (2001). *Schools More Separate: Consequences of a Decade of Resegregation.* The Civil Rights Project, Harvard University (civilrightsproject.ucla.edu /research/deseg/separate_schools01.php).

Orfield, G., and Eaton, S. (1996). *Dismantling Desegregation.* New York: New Press.

Parents Involved in Community Schools Inc. v. Seattle School District (2007). 127 U.S. 2738.

Peske, H., and Haycock, K. (2006). *Teaching Inequality: How Poor and Minority Students Are Shortchanged on Teacher Quality.* Washington, DC: The Education Trust.

Petrilli, M. (2019a). *Fewer Children Left Behind: Lessons from the Dramatic Achievement Gains of the 1990s and 2000s.* Washington, DC: Thomas B. Fordham Institute.

——— (2019b, September 25). A New Era of Accountability in Education Has Just Barely Begun. Thomas B. Fordham Institute (fordhaminstitute.org/national/commentary/new-era-accountability-education-has-barely-just-begun).

Reardon, S., and Portilla, X. (2016). "Recent Trends in Income, Racial, and Ethnic School Readiness Gaps at Kindergarten Entry." *AERA Open* 2(3):1–18. https://doi.org/10.1177/2332858416657343

Reardon, S., Weathers, E., Fahle, E., Jang, H., and Kalogrides, D. (2019). *Is Separate Still Unequal? New Evidence on School Segregation and Racial Academic Achievement Gaps* (Working Paper No. 19-06). Center for Educational Policy Analysis, Stanford University.

Sarratt, R. (1966). *The Ordeal of Desegregation.* New York: Harper & Row.

Siegel-Hawley, G., Diem, S., and Frankenberg, E. (2018). "The Disintegration of Memphis–Shelby County, Tennessee: School District Secession and Local Control in the 21st Century." *American Educational Research Journal* 55(4):651–692. https://www.doi.org/10.3102/0002831217748880

Slover, L., and Muldoon, L. (2018). How the Common Core Changed Standardized Testing. FutureEd. McCourt School of Public Policy, Georgetown University.

Smith, J., Fien, H., and Paine, S. (2008). "When *Mobility* Disrupts Learning." *Educational Leadership* 65(7):59–63.

Snyder, T., de Brey, C., and Dillow, S. A. (2019). *Digest of Education Statistics 2018* (NCES 2020-009). Washington, DC: U.S. Department of Education, National Center for Education Statistics, Institute of Education Sciences.

Taylor, S. (1998). *Desegregation in Boston and Buffalo.* Albany: State University of New York Press.

Tyson, W., Lee, R., Borman, K., and Hanson, M. (2007). "Science, Technology, Engineering, and Mathematics (STEM) Pathways: High School Science and Math Coursework and Postsecondary Degree Attainment." *Journal of Education for Students Placed at Risk* 12(3):243–270.

U.S. Department of Education (2018). *ESSA Flexibilities* (ed.gov/policy/elsec/leg/essa/essa-flexibilities-document-for-publication.pdf).

Wilson, S. (2003). "*Brown* over 'Other White': Mexican Americans' Legal Arguments and Litigation Strategy in School Desegregation Lawsuits." *Law and History Review* 21(1):145–194.

Wise, A. E. (2019). Toward Equality of Educational Opportunity: What's Most Promising? *Phi Delta Kappan* 100(8):8–13. https://doi.org/10.1177/0031721719846882

Values/Character Education

Traditional or Liberational

Which and whose values should public schools embrace and teach?

9

Position 1: Teach Traditional Values

The results . . . should be a warning sign to liberal activists that wish to inject controversial issues into the classroom. Parents are simply against social engineering in the classroom.

—Sheldon (2011, p. 1)

The Founders believed morality was essential to the well-being of the republic, and that religion was the best way to foster morality. . . . Just as knowledge does not make us wise, so also knowledge does not make us virtuous.

—Scalia (2017, pp. 73, 329)

Traditional Values Can Be Restored to Schools

There is a tight relationship between good families and good schools in a society based on common values. From the perspective of character education, every moment of the school day is a "character moment. . . . Every experience, very interaction . . . has the potential to shape the values and character of a child" (Lickona, 2018, p. xxiii). Efforts to bring schools and society back to their moral base can yield positive results (Institute of Education Sciences, 2007). Although we can differentiate among definitions of values, ethics, morals, and character, school programs bearing labels such as "values education," "ethics education," "moral education," and "character education" often use the same principles, purposes, and general practices. None of these are "value free" or "value neutral." Those titles are covers for the denial of morality.

The best values education programs restore traditional values to schools and students. The Center for the 4th and 5th Rs (Respect and Responsibility) continues the restoring of good character to its historic place at the center of schooling. Leming and Silva (2001) found excellent results in a five-year study on teaching a special Heartwood Ethics Curriculum for Children to fifth graders, including more caring, respectful actions, and fewer disciplinary referrals. Other indicators of success include the increasing number and quality of educational materials available for teachers and parents. Teaching materials are aimed at instilling universal values in students: honor, honesty, truthfulness, kindness, generosity, helpfulness, courage, convictions, justice, respect, freedom, and equality.

Organizations offer assistance, teaching guides, supporting materials, and guidance with conferences and in-school events. Some examples are GoodCharacter.com, Character Counts! (charactercounts.org), Character Education Network (charactered.net), National Center for Youth Issues (ncyi.org), Family Research Council (frc.org), American Family Association (afa.net), Alliance Defending Freedom (adflegal.org), Chalcedon Foundation (chalcedon.edu), Character First (characterfirsteducation.com), and National Character Education Foundation (ncef.org). To illustrate one source, Character.org maintains a database that includes ideas, materials, and descriptions and analyses of various instruments that can be used to assess character education. It also certifies Schools of Character that implement its programs.

Model centers and programs for character education are in a number of states, including North Carolina, California, Iowa, New Mexico, Utah, Connecticut, Maryland, Washington, Missouri, Kentucky, New Jersey, and South Carolina. Centers sponsor programs devoted to creating safe and orderly school environments, encouraging students to take responsibility for their conduct and for others, preventing violence, and reinforcing efforts to curb drug abuse and weapons in school. Character education is developing as one of the most important projects in schools (Thorkildsen and Wallberg, 2004; Nucci and Narvaez, 2008, Lickona, 2018).

What Should Be Taught: Traditional Values as the Focus

Clearly, schools need to rediscover their proper role and function in a moral society. The United States was founded on Judeo–Christian ideals. They form the basis of our concepts of justice and democracy. Schools were established to transmit those values to the young to preserve values and society. Support for traditional values gave early American schools a clarity of purpose and a solid direction. Children did not receive mixed messages about morality and behavior and did not get the impression they could make up and change their values on a whim. Supreme Court Justice Antonin Scalia (2017), citing the writings of our founding fathers on the topic of education, notes that one focus was on the importance of discipline and the rule of law. "The Founders were as interested in teaching virtue as in teaching civics" (p. 69). And Scalia couches that virtue in the "necessity of religion to a successful republic" (p. 71).

We are not born with a set of values, they are all—good and bad—learned. Although we learn values in many places, from many people, and through many media, schools form a particularly significant institution for imparting values. Blackburn (2001) points out that Aristotle "emphasized that it takes education and practice in order to become virtuous" (p. 113). Former Secretary of Education William Bennett (1992) highlights the tradition of common schools as the basis of common values, with leaders of the common school movement coming mainly from people who "saw the schools as upholders of standards of individual morality and small incubators of civic and personal virtue; the founders of the public schools had faith that public education could teach good moral and civic character from a common ground of American values" (p. 58).

Character education should have a prominent focus on traditional values at all levels. In elementary school, reading material should emphasize ideals (Anderson, 1994; O'Sullivan, 2002; Bennett, 2008). Stories of great heroes, personal integrity, resoluteness, loyalty, and productivity should dominate. The main emphasis should be on the positive aspects of U.S. history and literature, showing how individuals working together toward a suitable goal can succeed. Teachers should stress and expect ethical behavior, respect, and consideration (Lickona, 1991, 2004, 2018). Classes should study various religions with the purpose of understanding their common values and how those values apply to life. Providing time in school for children to reflect on personal religious beliefs would be appropriate.

Signs and symbols in school should reinforce American values. Pictures, displays, and assemblies on morality offer students a chance to see how important those values are to society and school. Inviting speakers into classes, showing films, and taking students to see significant monuments to American values are techniques that can help. Teachers can emphasize good values by providing direct instruction on moral precepts and rewarding students for good citizenship.

At the secondary level, emphasis on traditional values should continue with more sophisticated materials and concepts. Literature classes should teach U.S. and foreign literature portraying rewards of moral behavior and negative consequences of immorality. American history classes should express ideals for which we stand and our extraordinary historical achievements. Science courses should feature stories of hard work and perseverance in making scientific discoveries as well as stories of how basic values and religious views have guided many scientists in their work. The arts are a rich place to show values through study of paintings, compositions, sculptures, and other art forms that express the positive aspects of human life under a set of everlasting ideals. Religious music and art can be a part of the curriculum, as can nonreligious art idealizing such values as the golden rule and personal virtue. Vocational subjects afford numerous ways to present good attitudes toward work, family, responsibility, loyalty, decency, and respect. There is no need for a special course on sex education. Family values are for families to teach at home.

Sports are an especially important place in which to reaffirm these same values; numerous professional and college teams pray together before matches, and many players are leading figures in setting high standards of moral conduct. Student honor rolls should cite acts of outstanding school citizenship, and should be prominently displayed, as are athletic trophies. Libraries should feature books and computer programs conveying thoughts and behaviors we encourage.

Teachers should demonstrate strong personal commitments to traditional values with behaviors and lives that exhibit that commitment. Determining a teacher's moral beliefs goes beyond examining his or her college transcripts; the subjects studied may bear little relation to his or her moral conduct. States have an obligation to the public to require high moral standards from those who gain licenses to teach in public schools. Colleges preparing teachers should examine potential students' records and deny entry to those with criminal or morally objectionable backgrounds (e.g., a history of cheating or dishonesty). Applicants for teaching credentials, as is done in law schools and state bar exams, should submit references on their moral character, and should prepare an essay discussing their values. Student teaching and the first years of teaching provide an opportunity to screen young teachers to ensure that they uphold and encourage high moral standards. Such criteria should be clearly and publicly stated; teachers found wanting should find other employment. They should not be where they can influence young people's ideals.

How Schools Destroy Values:
Values Relativism and Moral Obfuscation

Unfortunately, schools are subject to the relativism that underlies much of life today. Relativism in schools reflects the ideas that (1) all values are relative, with none superior; (2) there is no enduring set of ethical standards; and (3) personal character is a matter of individual choice and particular situations. It incorporates situational ethics and egotistical rationalization to justify any values or actions. Relativism keeps such schools and their students adrift in a sea of personal and social temptations.

In many schools, children are taught that values they learn at home or church are simply matters of choice. Teaching relativistic values and morality by questioning students on their values and the values of their parents, as is recommended in "value inquiry," "values clarification," and other value-free school programs, causes children to believe that right and wrong are purely matters of individual opinion. This obscures the traditional moral code and offers no moral guideline for conduct or thought. In some relativistic values programs, teachers may ask children to publicly identify situations when their father or mother was wrong and to present their own view of what the parent should have done. Teachers ask children personal questions about their family lives and private thoughts, and pursue them in class discussion.

In those discussions, children who present their personal opinions with conviction can influence other children, and the teacher is not to intercede. An entire class can agree that tying cans to a cat's tail, euthanizing people who are old or ill, or remaining seated during the salute to the flag may be acceptable behavior. Children also learn to report on their parents and to ridicule those who support traditional values concerning discretion and privacy. Obviously, without clear and consistent standards of acceptable behavior and belief, our society is doomed to ethical destruction. Can one argue seriously that a life of dishonesty and cheating is morally equal to a life of honesty and integrity? How can schools adopt a position of neutrality regarding values and character development? Yet that absurd view is behind values clarification and other relativistic approaches to dealing with values in schools. Students are not provided with sound criteria to weigh right and wrong (Bennett 1992, 2008). Instead, teachers encourage children to determine their own set of values.

Values clarification is also used in behavioral psychology therapy, but that is not the school's business (Selva, 2019). American public schools, echoing moral defects in American popular culture, commonly operate without an ethical compass. Schools, instead, should provide a firm education in ethical principles that help youth sort, analyze, and evaluate behaviors and values expressed in popular culture. This is character education, designed to instill and inspire good character—morally grounded behaviors and attitudes (Lockwood, 2009).

Schools lost this central purpose in a contemporary welter of value-neutral, value-relative, and anything-goes approaches to values education. Formerly, schools were stalwart conveyors of good values and sound character, with exemplary moral modeling by teachers and administrators. That was replaced by an institutional blind eye to values and educator fear that maintaining high standards of morality and ethics for themselves and their students could make them unpopular. Far too many public schools lack a central core of fundamental morals and give students no ethical basis for guidance through life. Instead, secular domination of education mistakenly keeps religious values at bay, while self-absorption becomes a primary focus for students. Education that emphasizes personal freedom, selfishness, and permissiveness contributes to the significant decline in social and family values (Sowell, 1992; Shapiro, 2005). Increased crime and abuse are natural outcomes of schooling that preaches self-indulgence. Inside the classroom, students can gain a deep respect for other people, property, and social traditions. These things matter.

Liberalism and Moral Decline

The liberal view of education—that traditional values don't matter and that students should decide basic value questions for themselves without guidance from educators, religious leaders, or parents—has an eroding effect on the center of American society. Liberalism is a culprit; in education, it does significant damage to American morality (Bork, 1996; Charen, 2004; Hannity, 2004; Frank, 2005; Savage, 2005, 2017; Coulter, 2007, 2015; Sowell, 2007; Pirro, 2019). Common values of civility, manners, and courtesies once dominant in the United States have given way to values of greed, destruction, consumption, distrust of authority, and anti-religion. This erosion has been the companion of permissive attitudes fostered in schools since progressive education concepts enveloped schools in the 1930s. Family values have declined in the face of a long-term educational philosophy based on individualism and libertine lifestyles (Gallagher, 2005; Shapiro, 2005; Family Research Council, 2020). Evidence of moral disaster surrounds us: extraordinarily high divorce rates, child and spouse abuse, lack of ethics in business and government, drug and alcohol addiction, out-of-control teenage pregnancy rates, excessive reliance on child care outside the home, acceptance of immorality on television and in the arts, cheating scandals, bullying, and explosive violence in schools (Jacobs, 2004; Barter and Berridge, 2011; Hamburger et al., 2011).

Attacks on American family values have appeared under the banners of "diversity," "multiculturalism," and "sexual orientation." These banners bear the root idea of moral relativism, that all views are equally valid in the classroom—from killing by euthanasia or abortion to gay and lesbian advocacy. It destroys traditional values and substitutes amorality or immorality as a guide to life. Even in this, there is rank logical inconsistency in the advocacy of value neutrality by many liberals. While claiming that no values are more important than any others, liberal advocates still propose a set of special interests that they claim deserve special treatment in classrooms and textbooks: minorities, women, disabled, gay, and lesbian (Charen, 2004; Gallagher, 2005; Savage, 2005; Pirro, 2019). This special treatment constitutes a set of values they consider more important. Further, they accept mercy killings, abortions, and homosexuality as examples of perfectly acceptable topics of study and conduct, while praying in school is not. This is hypocrisy. Radical approaches to education have weakened values.

Lickona (1991, 2004) outlines the kinds of problems that demonstrate a decline in values among youth. He includes violence, vandalism, bad language, sexual promiscuity, peer cruelty, stealing, and cheating. He links this decline to a series of factors, including the following:

- Darwinism and the relativistic view that springs from it.
- A philosophy of pseudoscientific logical positivism that separates "facts" from "values."
- Personalism, emphasizing individual rights over social responsibilities and moral authority.
- Pluralism, suggesting multiple values and raising a question of which ones we should teach.
- Secularization, which falsely separates church and state and offers no religious guidance.

Confusing Values in the Current Curriculum

School curriculum and textbooks currently present a wide array of relativistic values that only confuse children. Secular humanism, relativism, and liberalism are not defined as school subjects, and schools offer no courses with those titles. Instead, these insidious ideas filter into nearly all courses and often go unrecognized, even by teachers. Because no specific curriculum stresses traditional morals and values, teachers and courses easily present differing views, leading students to believe that there are no eternal or universal values, only personal ones. If courses and teachers do not attest to a common core of morality, students are left morally rudderless. This spawns confusion or self-indulgence at best and scorn for morality at worst.

Teaching materials children learn from often are either vapid, without any connection to moral thought and behavior, or confusing, displaying multiple values of supposedly equal weight. Current school reading materials include trash directing attention to the values of the worst elements of society and adult stories well beyond children's moral development. In civics and history, the focus is on political power, not virtue. Children are taught how to manipulate others and how interest groups get their way. History texts are bland and noncommittal about basic values, treating religion with disdain. Sex education instruction assumes that students will be promiscuous and can't exercise abstinence and responsibility (Shapiro, 2005). Science ignores religious views and substitutes "value-free" ideas; any scientific experiment is okay. Instead of protecting and encouraging innocence, schools savage and debase it.

Results of this permissive and selfish education are apparent. We are subject to increasing abuse in contemporary life. A startling increase in child abuse is so prevalent that we now have 24-hour telephone hotlines to report it. Spousal abuse is another item almost daily in newspapers. Animal abuse is so common it no longer makes news. And sex and drug abuse have become epidemic. Bullying and antipatriotic actions in schools are among the signals that value-free morality has its consequences (Barter and Berridge, 2011; Hamburger et al., 2011).

Other abuses currently abound. We abuse our ideals, respect, heroes, national honor, and religious base. Political and business leaders abuse the public trust through cheating and corruption. Young people no longer understand why we fought wars to protect our liberties. Some children refuse to recite the Pledge of Allegiance or to sing the "Star-Spangled Banner." Graffiti covers many of our national monuments and our statues of heroes. Children no longer honor their parents or respect their elders.

An in-depth interview study of young adults across the United States shows the weak level of their moral thinking (Smith, 2011). David Brooks (2011), commenting on this study, noted, "The default position, which most of them came back to again and again, is that moral choices are just a matter of individual taste. 'It's personal,' the respondents typically said, 'It's up to the individual. Who am I to say? . . .'" Smith (2011) found an atmosphere of extreme "moral individualism" or "relativism and nonjudgmentalism" (pp. 1, 2). Another study, surveying over 40,000 high school students in public and private schools, shows that well over half admitted to cheating on tests, about half admitted to lying, and almost one-fourth admitted to stealing (Character Counts, 2011). These examples illustrate the major reason we need a dramatic shift to traditional moral or ethical education, a school program and setting that gives a compass to young people for judging good and bad and acting to enhance the good.

Schools Are Rooted in Moral Values

Schools in America were founded to provide a moral foundation, and they were effective. Colonial schools had as their core a firm commitment to morality, ethics, and traditional values. The first school laws, passed in Massachusetts in 1642 and 1647, mandated that communities provide schooling for young people and that those schools preserve religious and social values. The *New England Primer*, the colonial schoolbook used to teach the alphabet and reading, incorporated moral virtues in its teaching of basic skills. All schoolbooks followed this pattern for many generations. Early Americans clearly recognized the link between a good society and solid religious, family, and school values. Religion continues to be a firm foundation for teaching traditional values and should not be kept out of public school classrooms.

From the *New England Primer* through the *McGuffey Readers*, the content studied in school was consistent with America's traditional values. Originally published in the

1830s, the *McGuffey Readers* have taught children to read using moral tales; they are among the most popular books of all time, and are now in ebook form. We can learn much from the moral stories these old works present. Children learned that it was wrong to misbehave at home, in the community, and at school. They learned the common morality, reading the consequences of those who did not. They gained respect for proper authority in families, churches, society, and school. We need to reject permissiveness and the loss of values of current schools and return to emphasizing moral precepts and proper behavior. The crisis in education has the same origin as the crisis in society: a decline in basic values. Correction in schools is the main avenue to correction in society.

Religion affords a good moral base for young people but isn't the only source of traditional values. Ethical personal behavior also derives from deep-rooted family and social values. The good society depends on citizens who have developed keen concern for others, awareness of personal responsibility, and habits of moderation. Etzioni (1998) argues that values education has broad and deep support among the American public, and he proposes that "we just teach the values that most Americans agree upon" (p. 448).

The obvious decline in values among the young results from a number of factors. Foremost is that schools have forsaken the responsibility to teach solid values, instead substituting highly relativistic opinions that undermine parental and religious authority. Children are taught that all values are equal, so whatever they value is fine. We can't hold children responsible for this rejection of common morality because their natural tendency is to be selfish. Parents must teach children to share and to respect traditional social values. Historically, we relied on schools to reinforce and extend the basic ethical code families, churches, and other religious institutions teach. When parents are unable or refuse to teach children right from wrong, schools usually have supplied this important function. Those who now run the schools have forgotten their history, and people who forget will repeat mistakes of the past.

With current high divorce rates and parental lack of attention to their children's moral development, schools should play an even more significant role in conveying American values to children. In times of family and social stress, schools should exert expanded influence to ensure continuation of our heritage. Many parents grew up during the 1960s and 1970s, when there was a sharp decline in religious participation and a significant increase in immorality. Without the value base provided by strong religious and national traditions, the United States will be in trouble. Schools must assume an increased responsibility for training students in traditional values.

Sommers (1998) demonstrates the link between a host of other school problems and the fact that Johnny can't read, write, or count. "It is also true that Johnny is having difficulty distinguishing right from wrong. . . . Along with illiteracy and innumeracy, we must add deep moral confusion to the list of educational problems" (p. 31). This is a very serious problem that will continue to haunt American society until it is adequately addressed. Hansen (2001) notes, "Studies suggest that teaching is inherently a moral endeavor" (p. 826). Finn (2019) writes: "It is high time we—and our schools—refocus on character building." He argues for a return to religion-based education as done in nonpublic schools.

Morality cannot be escaped by pretending schools are outside its sphere. Schools have lost their moral focus and, thus, their ability to educate youth in the most important of areas—morality. Without a moral focus, other learnings are shallow.

We must restore basic American values to schools and to our young people, and it is possible. But a potential opportunity is n   nough. It is crucial that we move quickly to reinvigorate our school leaders with the   to do it. We are facing a crisis of values in society, and the crisis is reflected in   Our society is extremely vulnerable. Schools must reassume their original   moral teachings.

Position 2:   Liberation through Active Value Inquiry

Never has the practice of thinking critically, reading critically, and developing a sense of engaged and courageous agency been more important. We have a time when free speech, critical inquiry, and democracy itself are under siege . . . ignorance is no longer innocence.

—Giroux (2019)

The great majority of character education programs consist largely of exhortation and directed recitation. . . . Most character education programs also deliver homilies by way of posters, banners, and murals throughout the school. . . . The children are passive receptacles to be filled—objects to be manipulated rather than learners to be engaged.

—Kohn (1997, p. 158)

Values, Moral, Ethical, and Character Education

It is possible, and sometimes necessary, to get very technical about defining terms. Philosophers, linguists, lawyers, teachers, and writers earn reputations and their livings by precise definition of terms—and by arguments over which definitions are superior. Defining values or character education can be confusing because popular definitions differ, sometimes in remarkable ways, and some terms are used interchangeably. Websites, programs, books, and journals focus on these terms: values education, moral education, ethical education, and character education. That does not exhaust possibilities; education for "virtue" was a focus at one time.

There are definitional distinctions, but some agreement in the main purpose—education intending to develop principles, ideas, and behaviors that are considered positive. Generally, morals are found at the deepest level, knowing what is right and what wrong, good and bad. Ethics translates moral precepts into codes of conduct, like "do no harm" for physicians or "be fair" for teachers. Values are ideas drawn from morals and ethics that inform our decisions, like honesty, integrity, and respect.

Character can be seen as the sum of these social positives in an individual, such as, "she exhibits good character," although Cornwall (2005) argues that:

> "Character" is an archaic, quasi-metaphysical term, more related to horoscopes than any scientific concept. It is a term with no agreed upon definition, even among proponents of character education . . . character education is part of an agenda to introduce conservative ideology, alone, into the minds of . . . students.

Schools deal with all such terms, no matter the specific definitions.

Education is not a neutral activity. Schooling is a social construct that reflects the values of society and community. School practice incorporates values: to provide and finance schooling, establish purposes and organization, prescribe attendance and length of studies, set up curricula, fix calendar and time schedules, develop activities, determine standards of performance and their measurement, set school colors and traditions, govern student and teacher behavior, and a wide variety of other matters. We school and are schooled for purposes we consider good and for ideas and behaviors we think valuable (Purpel, 2003; Spring, 2008). It is difficult to contemplate schools without goals, teaching without purpose, and curricula without objectives. Schools are subject to and providers of value-based decisions. Values are also the basis for decisions about the nature of personal and family participation in schooling.

Values, personal or social, are not necessarily well reasoned or even in the best interests of the individual or society. Some are forced or coerced; some hidden, some circumstantial, some from indoctrination, and some wildly inconsistent for schools or individuals. Students, teachers, and parents commonly learn values very different from those stated in school mission statements and other formal documents of purpose and conduct. Cheating, lying, vandalism, theft, bullying, selfishness, profanity, and other categories of behaviors considered socially destructive can be learned in school settings, as well as at home and in other situations.

Students and Values

Students come to school with a collection of beliefs and behaviors, both good and bad; these have been acquired from family, television, friends, and other experiences (Aronowitz, 2008). Students do not come to school as empty moral vessels, waiting for proper values to be poured in. Even primary-grade children have a pretty clear sense of right and wrong; in fact, they are almost too clear in their determination of what is fair and what is not and who should get punished and for what infractions. Lawrence Kohlberg's (1981) studies of stages of moral development show the earliest stage as "preconventional"; children ages 4 to 10 hold rules firmly and absolutely and mainly want to avoid punishment. The highest stages, ones that most people do not achieve, include "universal ethical principles" and involve reasoned and reflective thinking (Cherry, 2019). For young children, there are few gray areas. Try playing a game with young children and see how rules are interpreted. Some adults and some of senior ages also have severely limited tolerance for dissent on their views of morals and values.

A nineteenth century character education book, *Hopes and Helps for the Young of Both Sexes* by G. S. Weaver illustrated Victorian views of morality and the necessity for rigid education to combat sin: "Amusements have dissipated [a child's] mind, stolen his heart, corrupted his manners and morals, eaten up his earnings, made him the child of folly, and the dupe of an insatiable desire for a life of giddiness . . . and more exciting amusements, are more dangerous" (quoted in Oneill, 2019). Another upholder of Victorian virtue claimed to measure the amount of sin in 1915 Kansas City amusements, finding: motion picture shows were 79% good, dance halls were only 23% good, river boats merited just 7.7%, penny arcades came in at 38.5%, and men's only shows rated 0 (Oneill, 2019, p. 215). A common approach to character education was based on fear, control, unreasoned conviction, and dogma. Some of the roots of this absolutistic idea come from social structure and class, some from political effort to control the masses, some from genuine fear for the ruination of the young and future society, some from religion, some patriotism, and some simply tradition. Evidence indicates that actual life in Victorian times was no more pure nor morally superior to that in other times and places, and it was often hypocritical. Life practiced was not the life prescribed.

This is instructive for considering current approaches to education for values, ethics, morals, and character. Traditional values education proclaims that morals, values, and ethics must be inculcated in children to develop their good character. They are authoritarian in orientation and can be highly prescriptive. Some, as in Victorian times, are based on fear and punishment, others on external rewards, and some on social pressure. In the main, codes of conduct promoted in schools are presented as rules and unthoughtfully accepted, rejected, or ignored by students: walk, don't run in the halls; don't interrupt; repeat the flag salute whether or not it is understood; don't plagiarize; treat everyone with respect; honor your parents; don't swear; report students who misbehave; be loyal to school and nation; don't spread rumors or be a bully; and myriad others illustrate the climate. Some of these are grounded in reason and are self-evident or are supported by evidence-based knowledge—it is possible to be hurt or hurt others if you run in the hall; bullies can be physically and emotionally damaging to people. Others are just arbitrary rules.

Nikki Stern (2011), a widow as a result of the September 2001 attacks on the World Trade Center, writes forcefully about dangers inherent in moral authoritarianism: "My experience and observation suggest that people who believe themselves in possession of the truth tend to believe they're also in possession of the moral authority to act on it" (p. 17). Proclaimed moral authority can create troubling actions; similar dangers occur in attempting to impose morality on schoolchildren rather than have them gain a critical understanding of morals, values, and ethical behavior. As Stout (2011) shows, "Emerging evidence suggests that cultural habits of unselfish prosocial behavior . . . are powerful engines for social stability and economic growth. . . . A healthy, productive society cannot rely solely on carrots and sticks" (p. 19). Maturity brings a more sophisticated sense of justice, morality, ethics, and values—much of which is honed among families, friends, media, and such institutions as religion and schools.

Lepore (2018), professor of American history at Harvard, describes the views of Richard Weaver, a 1940s conservative intellectual "whose complaint about modernity was that 'facts' had replaced 'truth.' [Weaver] . . . rejected the idea of machine-driven progress—a view he labeled 'hysterical optimism'—and argued that Western civilization had been in decline for centuries" (p. 554). Among other things, he blamed the printing press and free expression for bad popular habits: "they read mostly that which debauches them" (p. 554). Russell Kirk, another influential conservative intellectual, argues: "The conservative . . . knows that 'civilized society requires order and classes, believes that man has an evil nature and therefore must control his will and appetite' and that 'tradition provides a check on man's anarchic impulse'" (p. 555). This root of some values and character education programs explains their emphasis on restriction, exhortation, penalty, and uncompromising belief.

Critical Values Inquiry

Against that framework is the idea that critical thinking, using evidence and reason, is a sound way to examine values, determine and improve ethical behavior, and develop wise character. This is well within the democratic ideals of enlightenment, civic engagement, free speech, academic freedom, and education. It is also within rational discourse on morality, the right and wrong of beliefs and behaviors that befits contemporary democratic society. Education has a key role in offering a framework for and practice in identifying, examining, reflecting upon, and affirming or changing values. Thoughtful education about values incorporates society's primary ideals expressed and examined by students in a rational, respectful approach. That requires teachers to encourage intelligent and critical examination that reflects the ethical dimensions of education (Giroux, 2004, 2019; Kohn, 2008). It respects student learning and maturity as well as disagreements. Rather than preach morality and goodness, it expects students to develop reasoned appreciation of core civilizing values and correlated ethical behavior.

Good character is a work in progress, exhibited in actions in situations where morals, values, and ethics are tested. Values education should critically examine traditional and contemporary moral ideas and test and refine a set of personal beliefs about ethical conduct. Attempted indoctrination by slogans, moralisms, and dogmatic piety does not meet that high standard and can result in knee-jerk reactions. Examples of unethical and immoral actions by some clergy and corporate executives show that moral righteousness can be spoken by anyone, but moral action requires a higher level of principles and fortitude. Sociologist J. S. Victor (2002) points out, "It is much more useful to offer our children a path to follow than a battery of abstract values . . . a way of thinking rather than a code of rules to follow" (p. 31).

This essay does not favor abandoning the civilizing characteristics of human society, including decency, respect, responsibility, courage, and magnanimity. Indeed, it is the opposite—a plea in favor of values inquiry that offers to empower students to develop and enhance civilization without hypocrisy. We cannot impose traditional values on schoolchildren and not allow criticism of those values. Students, in traditional values indoctrination courses, learn conformity to authority, not thinking. Value inquiry into basic values of civilization will yield stronger, more realistic convictions among students than mere sloganeering and student conformity. Student passivity and obedience allows such moral problems as social injustice and inequality to be ignored. Instead of questioning and acting to improve society, students are expected to sponge up moralisms and be quiet. Greene (1990) argues that moral choice and ethical action should be products of careful and critical thought. That occurs where there is freedom and encouragement for individual students and teachers to engage in such thinking.

The purpose of education is liberation—from ignorance. That is the foundation beneath freedoms from slavery, dictatorship, and domination. Freedom to know underlies the freedom to participate fully in a democracy, enjoy and extend justice and equality, live a healthy and satisfying life, and provide the same opportunities to others. These are all solid values students can critically examine and relate to their own lives. That inquiry requires freedom to question, to think, and to act. Schools that restrict and contort the minds of the young are opposed to that principle; democratic civilization is the victim. Students learn a lot about values by observing the operation of values in the world about them, unreasonably authoritarian schools convey antidemocratic values inconsistent with many basic moral principles in addition to being disrespectful of student intelligence (Kessler, 2000; Kincheloe, 2008; DeLeon and Ross, 2010).

Limits and Opportunities

There are, of course, reasonable limits and conditions to this concept of freedom, as there are to all freedoms. Very young children require guidance and direction in basic good habits. And the small number of people whose development has been arrested at the equivalence of infancy or young childhood may require some caring control for their own safety and well-being over much of their lives. The vast majority of children and school students, however, will mature in intellectual development and reasoned values, progressing beyond fixed habits and views. For this development, students deserve a process of values inquiry that accounts for the age, maturity, experience, and family and cultural conditions of students, as well as the school and community setting. As age and experience increase, natural curiosity and normal schoolwork in literature, science, social studies, and other subjects are likely to raise questions among students about common values. This offers educational opportunity to consider evidence that supports or challenges those values by examination of moral pronouncements within the context of a thoughtfully considered view of right and wrong.

Some families, cultures, school administrators, and communities may be upset at ideas they consider too controversial, and intelligent teachers will be sensitive to such situations in relation to their professional orientation to educate. Teachers and students have academic freedom, but not license to force acceptance of views. Forcing is inconsistent for an advocate of critical thinking and education. Teachers' values should also be subject to rational, evidence-based inquiry. Students and teachers should fully comprehend social mores and values and take responsibility for the consequences of their actions. This means they must understand and reason through moral principles undergirding adequate ethical conduct and values.

Such principles as humanity and human rights, justice, equality, freedom, and civilization deserve considerable rational deliberation in order to be used as standards against which to weigh ethical conduct and values in given situations. Confronted with a choice between rational deliberation and emotional outburst, few thinking students will pick emotion. They want to reason, even as emotion plays some role in their decisions (Smith, 2006; Harris, 2010). Given a choice between freedom and slavery, most will pick freedom—and for good reasons.

Value inquiry involves the thinking through of fundamental moral principles, testing those principles in the cauldron of value conflicts in society and daily life, providing opportunity to rationally criticize, and developing a more consistent set of values and operational ethics (Singer, 2002). This is not blind obedience to authority. Smith (2006) states that Ayn Rand, a right-wing libertarian, had ethical views grounded in rational decision making. Harris (2010), on the liberal side, argues that reason based on evidence, as in science, provides a basis for morality.

Authoritarian institutions have abused their power in the past decades. Dictatorial leaders in government, religion, corporations, schools, and communities have provided plenty of examples of abuse. Some who preach morality, ethics, and responsibility have been found wanting in exactly those areas. Wolfe (2001) points out: "In an age of moral freedom, moral authority has to justify its claims to special insight" (p. 226). Legitimacy and credibility are necessary conditions for sound moral authority (Coles, 1997; Piaget, 1997; Wolfe, 2001). Eisgruber (2002) comments,

> One of the defining characteristics of liberal democracy is that persons must give reasoned justification for the power they seek to exercise; they behave undemocratically insofar as they rely only on personal status or authority . . . the liberal democratic state teaches most powerfully by example, not by sermonizing. (pp. 72, 83)

Principles of liberation and education are well suited to student learning of basic skills and academic knowledge, and are also suited to learning values, ethical conduct, morality, and the development of character. While it may be possible to develop basic skills and rote information in dogmatic and dictatorial schools, that denies the concept of independent thinking necessary to a democracy. It is, therefore, undemocratic to teach academic subjects in that system. Similarly, it is possible to indoctrinate students with values and ethical standards, but that approach is inconsistent with democracy and independent thinking. In addition to being undemocratic, teaching values and ethics in authoritarian settings also is counterproductive. The purpose of values education is to get students to understand, examine, derive, and thoughtfully adopt a set of socially positive values that can be translated into ethical behavior. Authoritarianism is in opposition to that purpose; it requires only blind obedience.

School Decisions about Values Education

The issue is not whether schools should be engaged in values education, since all schools are by their very nature engaged in such a pursuit. Rather, the issue is what values are central to society and schoolwork and how should they best be learned. Teachers, textbooks, and schools all teach some values. Schools can be organized and operate in ways that develop conformity, obedience to external authorities, and passive, docile behavior. Schools also can work to develop thoughtful critics of society's problems, students who are willing to challenge social norms, and pursue continued improvement of humankind into the future (Kohn, 1997, 2008; Purpel, 2003; Anyon et al., 2008; Kidder, 2010; Giroux, 2019). There are many variations on these purposes of either socializing students to conform to social values or liberating them to engage in social improvement.

Much contemporary school activity is devoted to producing docile, passive students who will be unlikely to challenge the status quo or raise questions even in the face of unreasoned authoritarianism. Current materials for teaching values and character in schools often are intended to protect the status quo, make students vessels for conformist behavior, and offer a noncritical perspective. Schools often are successful in this purpose. School life focuses far too much on conformity, placing extreme pressure on all students to think, behave, and view life in the same way. This is hypocritical, since many adult citizens and educators do not adhere to the moralistic standards prescribed, and it destroys our young people's creativity and energy.

In traditional schools, students are force-fed moralisms and value precepts inconsistent with what they see in society. Poorly paid teachers preach honesty while wealthy financiers, bankers, and politicians loot the public. Well-heeled or well-connected people who commit so-called white-collar crimes seldom are punished, although a few may be sent to luxurious detainment centers for brief stays. People from lower social class backgrounds who commit nonviolent crimes can receive long and debilitating sentences. U.S. presidents who engage in questionable ethical behavior are given credibility in some places, as though the behavior is acceptable. These obvious disparities in our concept of justice and in our other values are evident to students. Similar examples of disparity in equality, justice, honesty, and citizenship abound in our national life. Students are well aware of these inequities. A moralistic slogan or required reading in classrooms does not hide the defect.

Mainstream Mystification

Too little in popular educational literature speaks to liberation, opposition to oppressive forces, and improvement of democracy. Most mainstream educational writing raises no questions about the context that schools sit within; the writers seem to accept the conservative purposes of schools and merely urge us to "fine tune" them a bit. Standard educational writing does not examine our schooling system to the depth of its roots, ideologies, and complexities. Instead, teachers and teachers in training read articles on implementing teaching techniques and making slight modifications in curriculum. There is nothing critical in these pieces and no liberation of the mind from strictures of a narrow culture. The dominant concern is to make schools more efficient, mechanical, factory-like, and conformist.

In school, students read mainstream literature, hear mainstream views from teachers and peers, see mainstream films, listen to mainstream speakers, and engage in mainstream extracurricular activities. The school library carries only mainstream periodicals and books. Finding an examination of highly divergent ideas is virtually impossible. When students are not in school, they read the mainstream press, watch mainstream television, and live in families of people who were educated in the same manner. Teachers prepare in colleges where they study mainstream views of their subjects and the profession of teaching. No wonder schools are prime locations for cultural reproduction; they contain no other sources of ideas. To have mainstream ideas broadly represented in schools is certainly not improper, but to suppress critical examination of those ideas and limit students to such a narrow band of ideas is not liberating.

Essentially, those in power in schools guard knowledge that they consider high status and use it to retain power and differentiate themselves from the masses. Although some auto mechanics, for example, must use complex skills and knowledge, it is not considered high-status knowledge. Law and medicine, which also utilize complex skills and knowledge, are considered high status. Apple (1990) notes a relationship between economic structure and high-status knowledge. A capitalist, industrial, technological society values knowledge that most contributes to its continuing development. Math, science, and computer science have demonstrably more financial support than do the arts and humanities. A master's degree in business administration, especially if from a "prestigious" institution, is more valuable than a degree in humanities. Technical subjects, such as math and the sciences, are more easily broken into discrete bits of information and are more easily testable than are the arts and humanities. This leads to easy stratification of students, often along social class lines. The idea of school achievement is to compete well in the "hard" technical subjects where differentiation is easiest to measure. Upper-class students, however, are not in the competition since they are protected and usually do not attend public schools. The upper middle class provides advantages for its children; the working class child struggles to overcome disadvantage.

Liberation Education and Critical Pedagogy: Values Inquiry

Liberation education offers an opportunity to examine social problems and conflicting values. It is linked well with ideas of critical pedagogy, a program to assist teachers to engage students in this examination (Shor, 1987; Burbules and Berk, 1999; Kincheloe, 2008; De Lissovoy, 2010). Liberation education is not a prescribed set of teacher techniques, a specific lesson plan, or a textbook series for schools to adopt. There is no mechanistic or teacher-proof approach that will produce liberation. Critical pedagogy is anything but mechanical and teacher-proof; it is dynamic and teacher oriented. Liberation is the emancipation of students and teachers from the blinders of class-dominated ignorance, conformity, and thought control. Its dynamic quality views students and teachers as active participants in opposing oppression and improving democracy (Giroux, 2004, 2008, 2019). Applied to values, it proposes that students inquire into basic moral concepts, apply them to disparities in society's values, examine alternative views, and arrive at a valid and usable set of ethical guidelines. It is grounded in reason, based on well-examined beliefs. A very popular ethics course at Harvard appropriately includes work on liberation education (ethics.harvard.edu).

Liberation education is complex because the social forces it addresses are complex. The central purpose is to liberate the individual and society and to broadly distribute liberating power (Freire, 1970; Glass, 2001). It requires a set of values, including justice and equality, to serve as ideals in opposition to oppression and authoritarianism as well as a critical understanding of the many cultural crosscurrents in contemporary society and mechanisms of manipulation that hide ideological purposes. Liberation education and critical pedagogy uncover myths and injustices evident in the dominant culture. They also embrace the expectation that the powerless can, through education, develop power. This requires us to recognize that forms of knowledge and schooling are not neutral but are utilized by the dominant culture to secure its power.

Schools must become sites where we examine conflicts of humankind in increasing depth to understand ideological and cultural bases on which societies operate. The purpose is not merely to recognize those conflicts or ideologies but also to engage in actions that constrain oppression and expand personal power. This profound, revolutionary educational concept goes to the heart of what education should be. Schools themselves need to undergo this liberation, and we should take actions to make them more truly democratic. Other social institutions also merit examination and action. Obviously, liberation education, a redundant term, is controversial in contemporary society. Liberated people threaten the traditional docility and passivity that schools now impose.

What Should Be Taught

Liberation education for values inquiry requires us to blend curriculum content with critical pedagogy. We cannot separate what students study from how they study it. This approach to schooling engages students in critical study of the society and its institutions. It also serves the dual purposes of (1) liberating students from blinders that simply reproduce old values that continue such ethical blights as greed, corruption, and inhumanity and (2) liberating society from oppressive manipulation of people by government, corporate, and institutional propaganda (Baker and Heyning, 2004; Yu, 2004; Blau, 2005).

Critical study involves both method and content. It expects an open examination and critique of diverse ideas and sees the human condition as problematic. That places all human activity within the scope of potential curriculum content and makes all activity subject to critical scrutiny through a dynamic form of dialectic reasoning.

Obviously, students cannot examine all things at all times. Thus, selection of topics for study depends on several factors, including what students previously have studied and the depth of those investigations, which contemporary social issues are significant, students' interests and maturity level, and the teacher's knowledge. There is no neatly structured sequence of information that all students must pass through and then forget. Students should examine the nature of knowledge itself. That can lead to liberation. And liberation develops strong character.

Among topics of early and continuing study should be ideologies. Students need to learn how to strip away layers of propaganda and rationalization to examine root causes. Ideology, in its most literal sense, is the study of ideas. Those ideas may be phrased in a language intended for mystification or designed to persuade people. Racism and sexism are not considered acceptable public views in the United States, yet they often lie behind high-sounding pronouncements and policies. Test scores from culturally biased tests are rationalized to segregate students for favored treatment in neutral-sounding nonracist and nonsexist terms, but basic causes and consequences are still racist or sexist. Imperialism is not considered proper in current international relations, but powerful nations do attempt to control others through physical or political-economic means while labeling their actions defensive or even "freedom fighting." Ideological study can help students situate events in historic, economic, and political settings deeper and richer than surface explanations.

FOR DISCUSSION

1. Values and character are two very important dimensions of education. If indoctrination is one view of how values should be imparted—a thesis—and relativistic open inquiry is another—an antithesis—what are some possible school approaches that could represent a synthesis view? How do you justify your proposal?

2. You are asked to recommend members for a local advisory council on values education:

   a. What kinds of people would you select, and how many of each? Why?

   b. What educational background and occupations should be represented?

   c. What groups or agencies should be represented, and in what proportions?

   d. What age, gender, or ethnic categories should be represented, and in what proportions?

   e. What other characteristics would you look for?

   f. What kinds of people would you want to exclude? Why?

3. Paulo Freire, a major advocate of liberation education, claims that traditional teaching is fundamentally "narrative," leaving the subject matter "lifeless and petrified."

   Does this description fit your experience in schools? What evidence can you provide? Criticize Freire's view of this "banking" form of education. Has he properly characterized what happens in schools? Should it happen? What are the social costs of changing to liberation education? What are the costs of not changing? What would be an example of an antithetical position to Freire's?

4. Many agree we should teach values in school but disagree about which values and who makes that choice. Some propose everlasting universal values, others propose utilitarian short-term values, some propose general and vague social values, and still others propose values based on individual or immediate circumstances. What is a reasonable way to determine what kind of values education we should teach in U.S. schools? What possible social consequences can you foresee for the various forms of values education? Who should decide on which values should be taught?

REFERENCES

Anderson, D. (1994). "The Great Tradition." *National Review* 46:56–58.

Anyon, J., Dumas, M., Linville, D., Nolan, K., Perez, M., Tuck, E., and Weiss, J. (2008). *Theory and Educational Research: Toward Critical Social Explanation*. New York: Routledge.

Apple, M. (1990). *Ideology and Curriculum* (2nd ed.). London: Routledge and Kegan Paul.

Aronowitz, S. (2008). *Against Schooling*. Boulder, CO: Paradigm.

Baker, B. M., and Heyning, K. E. (2004). *Dangerous Coagulations? The Uses of Foucault in the Study of Education*. New York: Peter Lang.

Barter, C., and Berridge, D., eds. (2011). *Children Behaving Badly*. Malden, MA: Wiley-Blackwell.

Bennett, W. J. (1992). *The De-Valuing of America*. New York: Summit Books.

———— (2008). *Book of Virtues for Boys and Girls*. New York: Aladdin Paperbacks.

Blackburn, S. (2001). *Being Good*. Oxford: Oxford University Press.

Blau, J. R. (2005). *Human Rights: Beyond the Liberal Vision*. Lanham, MD: Rowman & Littlefield.

Bork, R. (1996). *Slouching toward Gomorrah: Modern Liberalism and American Decline*. New York: Regan Books.

Brooks, D. (2011, September 12). "If It Feels Right. . . ." *New York Times*.

Burbules, N., and Berk, R. (1999). Critical Thinking and Critical Pedagogy. In T. Popkewitz and L. Fendler, eds., *Critical Theories in Education*. New York: Routledge.

Character Counts (2011, September 28). The Ethics of American Youth (charactercounts.org).

Charen, M. (2004). *Do-Gooders: How Liberals Hurt Those They Claim to Help*. New York: Sentinel.

Cherry, K. (2019, September 19). Kohlberg's Theory of Moral Development. Verywell Mind (verywellmind.com).

Coles, R. (1997). *The Moral Intelligence of Children*. New York: Random House.

Cornwall, W. (2005, April). The Problem with Character Education. Patriotism for All (patriotismforall.tekcities.com/character_ed.html).

Coulter, A. (2007). *Godless: The Church of Liberalism*. New York: Three Rivers Press.

———— (2015). *Adios, America*. New York: Regnery.

De Lissovoy, N. (2010). "Rethinking Education and Emancipation." *Harvard Education Review* 80(2):203–220.

DeLeon, A. P., and Ross, E. W. (2010). *Critical Theories, Radical Pedagogies, and Social Education*. Rotterdam, Netherlands: Sense Publications.

Eisgruber, C. L. (2002). How Do Liberal Democracies Teach Values? In S. Macedos and Y. Tamir, eds., *Moral and Political Education*. New York: New York University Press.

Etzioni, A. (1998). "How Not to Discuss Character Education." *Kappan* 79:446–448.

Family Research Council (2020). Parental Rights (frc.org).

Finn, C. E. (2019, January 11). "How to Bring Back Moral Education." *Education Next*.

Frank, J. (2005). *Left Out! How Liberals Helped Reelect George W. Bush*. Monroe, ME: Common Courage Books.

Freire, P. (1970). *Pedagogy of the Oppressed*. New York: Herder and Herder.

Gallagher, M. (2005). *Surrounded by Idiots: Fighting Liberal Lunacy in America*. New York: William Morrow.

Giroux, H. (2004). "Critical Pedagogy and the Postmodern/Modern Divide." *Teacher Education Quarterly* 31(1):31–47.

———— (2008). *Against the Terror of Neoliberalism*. Boulder, CO: Paradigm.

———— (2019, October 14). Interview with H. Giroux on his book *The Terror of the Unforeseen* (published by Los Angeles Review of Books). The Seminary Co-Op Bookstores (semcoop.com).

Glass, R. D. (2001). "On Paulo Freire's Philosophy of Praxis and the Foundations of Liberation Education." *Harvard Education Review* 20(2):15–25.

Greene, M. (1990). "The Passion of the Possible." *Journal of Moral Education* 19:67–76.

Hamburger, M., Basille, K., and Vivolo, A. (2011). *Measuring Bullying Victimization.* Washington, DC: U.S. Government Printing Office.

Hannity, S. (2004). *Deliver Us from Evil: Defeating Terrorism, Despotism, and Liberalism.* New York: Regan Books.

Hansen, D. T. (2001). Teaching as a Moral Activity. In V. Richardson, ed., *Handbook of Research on Teaching* (4th ed.). Washington, DC: American Educational Research Association.

Harris, S. (2010). *The Moral Landscape.* New York: Free Press.

Institute of Education Sciences (2007, June 4). What Works: Character Education. What Works Clearinghouse (ies.ed.gov/ncee/wwc).

Jacobs, J. (2004). *Dark Age Ahead.* New York: Random House.

Kessler, R. (2000). *The Soul of Education.* Alexandria, VA: Association for Supervision and Curriculum Development.

Kidder, R. (2010). *Good Kids, Tough Choices.* San Francisco: Jossey-Bass.

Kincheloe, J. (2008). *Critical Pedagogy Primer.* New York: Peter Lang.

Kohlberg, L. (1981). *Essays on Moral Development.* San Francisco: Harper and Row.

Kohn, A. (1997). The Trouble with Character Education. In A. Molnar, ed., *The Construction of Children's Character.* Chicago: National Society for the Study of Education.

———— (2008, Spring). "Progressive Education: Why It's Hard to Beat, but Also Hard to Find." *Independent School.*

Leming, J., and Silva, D. (2001). A Five Year Follow-Up Evaluation of the Effects of the Heartwood Ethics Curriculum on the Development of Children's Character (character.org).

Lepore, J. (2018). *These Truths: A History of the United States.* New York: W.W. Norton.

Lickona, T. (1991). *Educating for Character.* New York: Bantam.

———— (2004). *Character Matters.* New York: Simon and Schuster.

———— (2018). *How to Raise Kind Kids.* New York: Penguin.

Lockwood, A. (2009). *The Case for Character Education.* New York: Teachers College Press.

Nucci, L., and Narvaez, D. (2008). *Handbook of Moral and Character Education.* Mahwah, NJ: Lawrence Erlbaum.

O'Sullivan, S. (2002). *Character Education through Children's Literature.* Bloomington, IN: Phi Delta Kappa Foundation.

Oneill, T. (2019). *Ungovernable: The Victorian Parent's Guide to Raising Flawless Children.* New York: Hachette Book Group.

Piaget, J. (1997). *The Moral Judgment of the Child.* New York: Free Press.

Pirro, J. (2019). *Radicals, Resistance, and Revenge.* New York: Hachette Book Group.

Purpel, D. (2003). "The Decontextualization of Moral Education." *American Journal of Education* 110(1):89–95.

Savage, M. (2005). *Liberalism is a Mental Disorder.* Nashville: Nelson Current.

———— (2017). *God, Faith, and Reason.* New York: Hachette Book Group.

Scalia, A. (2017). *Scalia Speaks.* New York: Crown Forum.

Selva, J. (2019). Values Clarification (positivepsychology.com).

Shapiro, B. (2005). *Porn Generation: How Social Liberalism Is Corrupting Our Future.* Washington, DC: Regnery.

Sheldon, L. (2011, September 22). Traditional Values Coalition News Release (traditionalvaluescoalition.org).

Shor, I. (1987). *Pedagogy for Liberation.* South Hadley, MA: Bergin and Garvey.

Singer, M. G. (2002). *The Ideal of a Rational Morality.* Oxford: Oxford University Press.

Smith, C. (2011). *Lost in Transition: The Dark Side of Emerging Adulthood.* Oxford: Oxford University Press.

Smith, T. (2006). *Ayn Rand's Normative Ethics.* Cambridge: Cambridge University Press.

Sommers, C. H. (1998). "Are We Living in a Moral Stone Age?" *Current* 403:31–34.

Sowell, T. (1992). "A Dirty War." *Forbes* 150:63.

———— (2007). *Conflict of Visions.* New York: Basic Books.

Spring, J. (2008). *American Education* (13th ed.). Boston: McGraw-Hill.

Stern, N. (2011). "Because I Say So." *The Humanist* 71(5):13–17.

Stout, L. (2011). *Cultivating Conscience: How Good Laws Make Good People.* Princeton, NJ: Princeton University Press.

Thorkildsen, T. A., and Wallberg, H., eds. (2004). *Nurturing Morality.* New York: Kluwer Academic Press.

Victor, J. S. (2002). "Teaching Our Children about Evil." *The Humanist* 62(4):30–32.

Wolfe, A. (2001). *Moral Freedom: The Search for Virtue in a World of Choice.* New York: Norton.

Yu, T. (2004). *In the Name of Morality: Character Education and Political Control.* New York: Peter Lang.

Multicultural Education

Democratic or Divisive

10

Should schools emphasize America's cultural diversity or the shared national culture?

Position 1:   Multiculturalism: Central to a Democratic Education

---

Multiculturalism is a philosophical concept built on the ideas of freedom, justice, equality, equity, and human dignity as acknowledged in various documents, such as the United States Declaration of Independence, the constitutions of South Africa and the United States, and the Universal Declaration of Human Rights adopted by the United Nations.

—National Association for Multicultural Education (2019)

The population of the United States is expected to rise from 332 million in 2020 to 404 million by 2060. According to the U.S. Census Bureau (2018), both the native and foreign-born population will be culturally, racially, and ethnically diverse. Across the country in 2060, 45% of Americans will be non-Hispanic whites; 28% will be of Spanish descent; 22% will be of African descent; and 9% will be of Asian descent. As Figure 10.1 shows, the size of the non-Hispanic white segment of the population is decreasing over time. Over the last hundred years, other segments have been growing because the waves of "old immigrants" from Europe have been replaced by the arrival of "new immigrants" from Asia, India, Africa, Mexico, and South and Central America. No matter what changes take place in immigrant laws over the next generation, there will be more Americans in the future and they will differ from one another more than ever before in history. Because the United States is already a multicultural society and will become even more so in the future, multicultural approaches to education are not an option.

Efforts to address the diversity of American society in public schools have a long history. Schools were sites of Americanization for many European immigrants in the nineteenth century. They were also sites where the language and culture of those

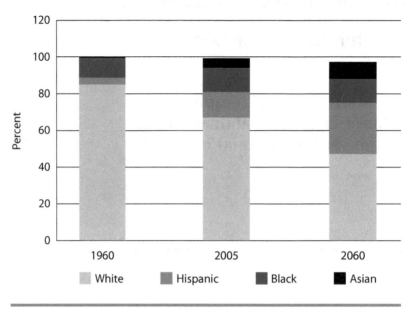

Figure 10.1   Population Percentages by Racial and Ethnic Groups
(1960–2060) (U.S. Census Bureau, 2018)

immigrants were honored and taught. For example, in places with large German-speaking communities in Indiana, Wisconsin, and Pennsylvania, some lessons were taught in German and students used textbooks in that language. The education was what we would now call "dual language" and continued until World War I (Gershon, 2017). When schools were desegregated in the 1960s and 1970s, African Americans and students from other marginalized groups called for curriculum and school culture that was more inclusive and welcoming of them—what they called "multiethnic" education. The movement to "multicultural education" evolved as women, people with disabilities, and members of other minority groups sought their inclusion as well (Sleeter, 2018).

Multicultural education can take many forms. Some scholars in the field, for example, believe that it should focus mainly on the concept of culture and problems resulting from the clash of cultures. They believe that students should examine the conflicting demands of home versus school culture, as well as the conflict between cultures of the powerful and the powerless and unequal treatment afforded certain groups because of race, gender, and sexual preference (Spring, 2017). For other scholars, multiculturalism is less about the study of culture than a vehicle for change. It is the method for critiquing and reforming society that includes political and moral correctives to assist working-class and nonwhite students in attaining social and economic advancement (Giroux, 2015; Kincheloe et al., 2018; Macedo, 2018; Sleeter, 2018).

Some critical multiculturalists consider their approach as a way to challenge "Eurocentric" modes of thinking and as a means to question taken-for-granted assumptions about the nature of knowledge. Other critical multiculturalists see multiculturalism as a remedy for the ills of economic systems (Bailon and De Lissovoy, 2019). According to the National Association for Multicultural Education (2019):

> [Multicultural education] prepares all students to work actively toward structural equality in organizations and institutions by providing the knowledge, dispositions, and skills for the redistribution of power and income among diverse groups. Thus, school curriculum must directly address issues of racism, classism, linguicism, ablism, ageism, heteroism, religious intolerance, and xenophobia.

Nieto and Bode (2018) view multiculturalism as a strategy to confront educational inequality and advance social justice. It is not enough, they argue, that multiculturalism seeks to help students get along, feel better about themselves, and to be more sensitive to one another. "If multicultural education does not tackle the far more thorny questions of [social] stratification and inequity . . . these goals can turn into superficial strategies that only scratch the surface of educational failure" (p. 6).

Conservative multiculturalists accept that contemporary America is made up of people from diverse cultures. However, they argue that equality within that diversity will be achieved through assimilation into a common culture, including its language and values. That culture will itself be modified over time by the contributions of newcomers to it, but a common core will be maintained (Alismail, 2016). Taking a conservative approach to multiculturalism, Glazer (1997) argued that some groups have been denied appropriate recognition. "Multiculturalism is the price America is paying for its inability or unwillingness to incorporate into its society African Americans, in the same way and to the same degree it has incorporated so many groups" (p. 147). Two decades later, David Cameron echoed that assessment when speaking of disaffected young people whose families had emigrated to Great Britain: "We have failed to provide a vision of society to which they feel they want to belong" (quoted in Hardy, 2014).

Although there are many approaches to multiculturalism in schools, the approaches discussed here are elucidated by Banks and McGee-Banks (2020), who write,

> Multiculturalism is an idea, an educational reform movement, and a process whose major goal is to change the structure of educational institutions so that male and female students, exceptional students, and students who are members of diverse racial, ethnic, language, cultural, gender, and religious groups will have an equal opportunity to achieve academically in school. (p. 1)

Banks and McGee-Banks argue that the successful implementation of multicultural curricula requires schools to recognize the multiple dimensions of multicultural education (see Figure 10.2). Schools should not assume that multicultural education is the responsibility only of social studies and language arts teachers. Multiculturalism has to be defined broadly so that everyone in every school discipline can embrace it appropriately.

> **Content Integration:**
> Teachers use examples from many cultures and groups in their teaching.
>
> **Equity Pedagogy:**
> Teachers organize their teaching to encourage the academic success of students from diverse racial, cultural, and social-class groups.
>
> **The Knowledge Construction Process:**
> Teachers help students understand how knowledge is constructed as part of cultural processes.
>
> **Prejudice Reduction:**
> Teachers use materials and methods to modify students' racial attitudes.
>
> **An Empowering School Culture and Social Structure:**
> The school culture is examined and analyzed to empower students from diverse racial, ethnic, and cultural groups.

Figure 10.2   Dimensions of Multicultural Education (Banks and McGee-Banks, 2020, p. 19)

The Best That Is Thought and Known

Multiculturalists agree that people construct knowledge from slightly different perspectives. Everyone brings understandings to events based on their personal and academic experiences and on other interpretive lenses through which they view the world. Women, minorities, and new immigrants, for example, may see the world from a different vantage point than men, majority group members, and long-established American families. Everyone develops separate frames of reference and different perspectives for interpreting the social and political world. No one frame of reference is more "true" than others, and all deserve to be heard and understood. Multiculturalism may be considered as part of the struggle to incorporate a wider range of perspectives into the way we make meanings in school. As Banks (2018) notes, "Individuals who know the world only from their own cultural and ethnic perspectives are denied important parts of the human experience and are culturally and ethnically encapsulated" (p. 3).

Multicultural education provides appropriate representation in the school curriculum to groups previously marginalized or excluded because of gender, class, race, or sexual orientation. Public schools should be places where students hear the stories of many different groups. The curriculum should present the perspectives of women as well as men, the poor as well as rich, and should celebrate the heroism not only of conquering generals but also of those who are victorious in the struggles of everyday life. In a multiculturally reconfigured curriculum, the voices of all Americans find legitimacy and academic consideration (Banks and McGee-Banks, 2020). Multiculturalism is not about pitting one group against others or claiming that any one perspective is more valid or more valued. Multicultural education is about fairness and justice. In the past, schools have done a disservice to students by assuming a single view of truth and ignoring students' need to create their knowledge of the world by considering multiple truths and multiple perspectives. A multicultural society will inevitably have competing views of truth and multiple sources of knowledge.

Different Voices

For almost three decades critics have argued that multiculturalists are bent on destroying not only the schools but the whole of Western civilization. Samuel P. Huntington (1996) castigated multiculturalism as an immediate and dangerous challenge to America's sense of itself. Multiculturalists have "denied the existence of a common American culture and promoted racial, ethnic, and other subnational identities and groupings" (p. 305).

Other traditionalists saw multiculturalism as a threat to national identity, one that would divide the nation. E. D. Hirsch (1987, 1996), for example, tried to convince his readers that the nation would disintegrate unless schools required all students to study a common unifying curriculum. Allan Bloom (1987) warned that multiculturalism posed the threat of cultural relativism, a disease, he says, that regards all values as equally valid and that would likely cause the decline of the West. Another critic of multiculturalism, Diane Ravitch, argued that multiculturalism would lead to the death of education and fragmentation of American society. Ravitch (1987) touted the elementary school curriculum of what she believes was a better time, the first decade of the twentieth century, when children were exposed to a common culture and high expectations:

> Most children read (or listened to) the Greek and Roman myths and folklore from the "oriental nations." . . . The third grade in the public schools of Philadelphia studied "heroes of legend and history," including "Joseph; Moses; David; Ulysses; Alexander; Roland; Alfred the Great; Richard the Lion Hearted; Robert Bruce; William Tell; Joan of Arc; Peter the Great; Florence Nightingale." (p. 8)

This represents a rich literature, to be sure, but, like the canon championed by Huntington, Hirsch, and Bloom, it was skewed toward a white, Western, male orientation. No people of other races were represented in classroom readings during the "good old days," and for women to find their way into the curriculum, they had to either be burned at the stake or pioneer as nurses. The old days were good for only a privileged handful—the high-achieving children of English-speaking families of means. For most others, it was a time of alienation caused by a denial of their ethnic heritages. After 50 years of efforts to make change, progress has been limited. In 2016, only 22% of children's books published had a person of color as the main character and only 13% were written by people of color (Black, 2018). There are consequences to privileging white, male characters in the materials students encounter in school. As Daniel Pels argues,

> Representation is about power. If you're mainly reading books about straight white boys and men, the message you receive is that straight white boys and men are— and should be—at the center of the universe. A steady literary diet of such books risks creating arrogant, self-centered white boys, and it risks telling all others that their stories are just not as worth telling, that they are less important. (quoted in Strauss, 2017)

Multicultural Perspectives

Critics charge that multiculturalists pose a threat to schools and the social cohesion of the country and that they are trying to impose political correctness on all Americans. Take a look at some of the multiculturalist arguments for curriculum change in the schools and decide for yourself.

As noted earlier, multiculturalists are a diverse group that includes feminists, Afrocentrists, social critics, and many people who defy labels but who simply want to transmit the variety of American culture more faithfully to their children. The charge that multiculturalists want to purge the school curriculum of Western culture is simply false. Multiculturalism, as the term is used here, does not require that schools rid the curriculum of all stories of white males and substitute the experiences of women, gays, African Americans, and other exploited and disadvantaged persons. Multiculturalism is not a euphemism for white male bashing or an anti-Western movement. Multiculturalists ask only for a fair share of curricular attention, an honest representation of the poor as well as the powerful, and reasonable treatment of minority as well as majority culture perspectives. Whatever the outcome of the current struggle over cultural representation in the curriculum, the world that American students know already is multicultural. The curriculum must change to reflect this society, or it becomes irrelevant to students' lives (Gay, 2018).

You might think of the multiculturalist reaction against the traditional curriculum as a "victims' revolution," a repudiation of the top-down approach to literature, art, music, and history. It demands change by those discounted and otherwise harmed by traditional approaches to schooling. Multiculturalists ask schools to tell the cultural tale in a way that weaves experiences of the disadvantaged and marginalized into the tapestry of U.S. history. Multiculturalism is a call for fairness and a better representation of the contributions of all Americans. Multiculturalists do not disparage the school's role in developing a cohesive, national identity. At the same time, however, they recognize that schools must ensure *all* students also preserve their individual ethnic, cultural, and economic identities (Nieto and Bode, 2018; Bailon and De Lissovoy, 2019; Banks and McGee-Banks, 2020).

Schools are obligated to teach multiple perspectives in the name of academic fairness and historical accuracy. Few events of significance can be understood considering only one perspective, and viewing any event from diverse, competing viewpoints leads to a fuller, more complete representation of truth. For example, school textbooks typically emphasize the role that nineteenth-century white abolitionists played and discuss how whites struggled to achieve integration in the twentieth century. This is, of course, appropriate; many whites have played and continue to play vital and significant roles in the struggle for social justice. But these same textbooks typically minimize the stories of African American resistance to slavery as well as their efforts to achieve integration and equality (Asante, 1991; King and Swartz, 2015). These omissions alienate young African American students and present an inaccurate picture to their white peers. The story of slavery must be told from many sides, including the perspective of African Americans as agents in their own history and not simply as people who were colonized, enslaved, and freed by others (King and Swartz, 2015). A multiculturally educated person would be able to see the slave trade from the view of the white slave trader as well as from the perspective of the enslaved people. The point is not to replace one group's story with another but rather to tell the whole story more fully. To include women, the poor, and minorities is simply a way to make history richer and more complete. Including reports of the powerless as well as the powerful allows students to examine the historic relationship among race, class, gender, and political power (Sleeter, 2018).

Anyone familiar with schools knows that the most effective way to teach is to make the curriculum relevant to students. Curricula have more meaning when students find characters like themselves in the books they read, and instruction has a better chance of engaging students when the subject matter speaks to their experiences. Exclusion of particular groups of students and their history from the literature alienates students and diminishes academic achievement. Conversely, students who participate in classes in which their cultural heritage and their experiences are included have better attendance, higher GPAs, and are more likely to earn the number of credits needed to graduate (Cabrera et al., 2014; San Pedro, 2015; Dee and Penner, 2017). Uniting a population with diverse cultural backgrounds requires an educational process that includes everyone. Descendants of immigrants from northern and western Europe need to read stories and listen to tales that resonate with their experiences. They also need to learn about the narrative experiences and cultural perspectives of children and families different from their own (Banks and McGee-Banks, 2020). Children of new immigrants from Asia and Latin America need to learn about the lands they left, their new home, and varied neighbors. They must examine their cultural histories and perspectives so that they can better understand how they and their families fit into their new society. The stories told and read in schools must become richer and broader, reflecting the traditions of African Americans, Native Americans, as well as Europeans. Multicultural education reflects the multicultural realities of schoolchildren. Multicultural education is an essential component to a sound basic education, as indispensable as reading, arithmetic, writing, and computer literacy (Nieto and Bode, 2018). Students cannot be considered well educated unless they are able to consider broadly inclusive content and multiple interpretations of events.

Multicultural Curriculum and Citizenship

Critics of multicultural curricula argue that it prevents the creation of a sense of unity among the citizens of a diverse society such as the United States. However, research and our lived experiences disprove them. In fact, children from groups that are racial, ethnic, religious, or linguistic minorities have weak identification with their countries if they believe they are excluded or marginalized within them (Banks, 2017a).

These findings challenge a historical model of cultural assimilation. Proponents of state-funded education in the nineteenth and early twentieth centuries encouraged schools to teach immigrants social behaviors and patriotic rituals designed to encourage "Americanization." For European immigrants socialization toward an Anglo-American model of behavior may not have been very discontinuous with their heritage. Now, the majority of immigrants are from Asia and South America. They are less likely to find resonance in the Anglo-American cultural ideal than those who came to the United States from Ireland, Germany, and Italy.

"To embrace the national civic culture, students from diverse groups must feel that it reflects their experiences, hopes, and dreams. Institutions such as schools cannot marginalize the cultures of individuals and groups and expect them to feel structurally included within the nation and develop a strong allegiance to it" (Banks, 2017b). Schools in the United States have historically been the primary site where citizens are prepared to participate in democracy. A multicultural curriculum contributes to that endeavor. By learning about the religious beliefs, literature, art, music, and history of multiple cultures, students develop knowledge on which they can make informed political decisions. Their exposure to cultures different from their own does not require that students change their beliefs or cultural practices. Instead, the goal of citizenship education that embraces multiculturalism is that students will become able to participate in American democracy in several ways. First, multicultural citizenship education aims to develop knowledge about and respect for the cultural sources of other citizens' behaviors. Second, it endeavors to ensure that students understand the constitutional rights that belong to them and to others. Third, it offers insight into toleration for differences among citizens. Finally, it provides opportunities to develop skills to become politically active and to settle disagreements about rights peacefully (van Waarden, 2017).

While the content of many disciplines address cultural diversity, citizenship education is a special focus of social studies. The National Council for the Social Studies (NCSS) identifies 10 themes that social studies in schools address. The first of these is the study of culture and requires experiences that help students "understand the multiple perspectives that derive from different cultural vantage points." In addition, the standards require instruction in global interdependence and civic ideals and practices (National Council for the Social Studies, 2019). The NCSS (2016) states that the content of such classes "engages students in a comprehensive process of confronting multiple dilemmas, and encourages students to speculate, think critically, and make personal and civic decisions on information from multiple perspectives." The connection between multicultural education and citizenship is embodied in the curriculum of many states.

New York State provides an interesting example of a responsible multicultural curriculum designed to help students develop civic knowledge and skills. In the late 1980s, the New York State commissioner of education invited scholars and curriculum writers to review the appropriateness of the state's K–12 social studies curriculum and recommend any needed changes. The resulting report, *A Curriculum of Inclusion, 1989*, recognized that New York's curriculum was not fairly representing minorities. Although the state had opened its doors to millions of new immigrants, their ways of life, foods, religions, and histories were not found in the curriculum. Instead, the new immigrants were socialized along an "Anglo-American model" (New York State Social Studies Syllabus Review and Development Committee, 1991). The unstated curricular message asked new immigrants to abandon their forebears' cultures and learn to prize the literature, history, traditions, and holidays of the Anglo-American founding fathers. There was no comparable expectation that native-born students learn about the cultures of their peers.

Thirty years later, New York State's social studies curriculum acknowledges the importance of socialization and nationalism for an increasingly diverse population within the context of respect for cultural diversity. According to the curriculum, "The primary purpose of Social Studies is to help young people develop the ability to make informed and reasoned decisions for the public good as citizens of a culturally diverse, democratic society in an interdependent world" (New York State Education Department, 2014, p. 1). The state's learning standards require students to "examine the wide sweep of history from a variety of perspectives" reflecting the broad range of people, their cultures, and beliefs that make up the nation (p. 4). It might be possible to dismiss New York's efforts as the result of its dramatic levels of ethnic complexity and combination of urban, suburban, and rural school districts. However, social studies curriculum that unites understandings of multiculturalism and citizenship can be found in less diverse states as well. In Iowa, for example, sixth graders are required to "identify what makes up a culture and examine how people acquire their cultural beliefs and value systems" (Iowa Department of Education, 2019, p. 26). The curriculum for Utah's required course in American History specifies that students must examine cultural differences among explorers and early settlers, the role of tradition in cultures and communities, and cultural tensions whose resolution produced social change (Utah Education Network, 2017).

Multiculturalism begins by recognizing the cultural diversity of the United States and asks that the school curriculum explore that diversity. Being well educated in a multicultural sense means learning about the histories, literature, and contributions of the varied people who have fashioned the complex tapestry of American life. All students should sample broadly from all the cultures and all the ideas that have contributed to the making of the United States. The multiculturalist does not argue that Eurocentric views are wrong or evil or that all American children should not learn about the European cultural legacy and its impact on the United States. It does argue, however, that it is not the totality of America's legacy. It can be examined critically without jeopardizing the country's unified commitment to the "values that sustain America's democratic republic, such as open-mindedness, engagement, honesty, problem-solving, responsibility, diligence, resilience, empathy, self-control, and cooperation" (Utah Education Network, 2017).

Position 2:   Multiculturalism Is Divisive and Destructive

The overarching priority of American nationalists has to be protecting and fostering the cultural nation, as a source of coherence and belonging and the foundation of our way of life.

—Lowry (2019)

Schools and the Cultural Heritage

For the past 150 years, public schools have had three broad objectives: to educate individual citizens for democratic participation, to encourage individual achievement through academic competition, and to promote, encourage, and teach the values and traditions of the American cultural heritage. "The creation of a common 'American' culture has been a foundational goal of public schools in the U.S. since the birth of the Republic" (Ezzani and King, 2018, p. 115). Any fair assessment would find it difficult to fault the success that schools have had in passing the common culture of the United States to new generations of Americans—immigrants and native-born citizens alike. In doing so, it has supported the development of a healthy nationalism—one that is based on love of country, not on hatred of other nations. That affection has been at the heart of many achievements—achieving independence from England, establishing and preserving a functioning government, expanding the country's boundaries across the continent, defeating foreign powers, assimilating immigrants, and establishing an international network of sovereign and independent countries (Lowry, 2019). The school's role in cultural transmission has been one of brilliant success for well over a century.

Nineteenth-century proponents of public education recognized that the United States was a dynamic nation, with succeeding waves of immigrants changing and invigorating American culture. The new arrivals came from every corner of the world and brought energy, talent, and cultural variation never before gathered in one nation. When they arrived in the United States, they spoke different languages, were of many races, and practiced many religions. What they shared was an eagerness to succeed economically and politically and to learn how to become "American," to fit into a unique, unprecedented cultural amalgam. Public schools provided the tools for that assimilation by teaching English to students and their families and by celebrating holidays that marked national leaders, events, and achievements. In art classes, students created their own testimonies to the country; in music classes, they sang songs that described the nation's history and articulated its vision. Even in coursework in "domestic sciences" they were introduced to standards of housekeeping, personal cleanliness, food, and fashion that matched national values like thrift, hygiene, and hard work.

Nineteenth-century common schools, influenced by Western ideas of philosophic rationalism and humanism, were an expression of optimism about human progress and democratic potential. Advocates of mass public education shared a common belief in education, "an education, moreover, which was neither a privilege of a fortunate few nor a crumb tossed to the poor and lowly, but one which was to be a right of every child in the land" (Meyer, 1957, p. 143). Children of the poor as well as the rich received a public education, and children of immigrants read the same texts and learned the same lore as the children of native-born Americans. The mix of immigrants now coming to the United States is far richer and more diverse than the founders of the common schools could ever have envisioned. The need for schools to transmit the common culture has never been greater. Among the 4.2 million English learners across the United States, over 400 languages are spoken at home (U.S. Department of Education, 2018). In New York City schools alone almost half of the 1.1 million students speak one or more of 170 languages other than English at home (Inside Schools, 2019). While many of them also speak English, and some even do so fluently, their bilingualism reflects extensive participation in a cultural heritage different from the one that unites the country.

In an era of expansive global migration, American public schools also face unique challenges in preparing students for participation in a complex democracy. The United States always has been a haven for those seeking political freedom and political expression. In the nineteenth century, millions of immigrants came to this country, in large measure to enjoy the fruits and accept the burdens of participating in a democratic society. This still is true today, but unlike the immigrants of former times, today's new arrivals typically have had little or no direct experience with democratic traditions. Today's immigrants may want democracy, but when they come from autocratic regimes in Asia and South America, they have had no experience with the responsibilities of democratic living. They are less prepared for assuming a role in a democratic society than any previous generation of immigrants.

Although schools should expose children to the common culture, they need not pretend there is cultural homogeneity or deny individual students' ethnic experiences. Schools are obligated to represent the range of cultural voices—male and female, African American, Asian American, and European American—but these voices must be trained not for solo performances but to be part of a chorus. Schools must encourage individual identification with one central cultural tradition, or the United States might fall prey to the same ethnic tensions undermining the sovereignty of Afghanistan and the nations of Eastern Europe and Africa. Students should learn about the common Western ideals that shaped the United States and bind us together as a nation: democracy, capitalism, and monotheism. "Unless a common purpose binds them together, tribal hostilities will drive them apart. Ethnic and racial conflict, it seems evident, will now replace the conflict of ideologies as the explosive issues of our times" (Schlesinger, 1998, p. 10).

Ethnic Studies

The United States stands to benefit—economically, politically, and socially—from the infusion of talent brought by new immigrants, as it has in the past. Assimilated new immigrants pose no threat to U.S. growth or nationhood. However, the United

States faces a threat from those who demand that public schools give up trying to teach the commonalities of American cultural heritage in favor of teaching a curriculum centering on the mix of cultural backgrounds represented in a given school or community. These programs are labeled "ethnic studies." For example, a high school in Tucson, Arizona, offered a curriculum that emphasized Mexican American heritage; another offered a course in Native American literature. A number of states, including California, Vermont, Oregon, and Connecticut, have a requirement that schools offer ethnic studies courses (Jensen, 2013; San Pedro, 2015; Dee and Penner, 2017).

Ethnic studies courses do not lend support to the unifying and democratic ends that the founders of the common schools envisioned. An early example of an Afrocentrist curriculum proposed to teach African American children about their African cultural roots but not about Western traditions. Its chief proponent argued that majority as well as minority students are disadvantaged by the "monoculturally diseased curriculum" (Asante, 1991, p. 175). A Mexican American studies program in Arizona presented a curriculum based on a pedagogy of oppression that taught that the United States was and is a racist country (Horne, 2007). The Native American studies course attempted to "de-standardize" Western tradition's central role in high school curriculum and prioritize other cultural knowledge (San Pedro, 2015). When Arizona passed House Bill 2281 to prohibit such classes, the language of the bill was clear about the dangers. The legislature banned courses that promote resentment toward a race or class of people; advocate ethnic solidarity instead of the treatment of pupils as individuals; or are designed primarily for pupils of a particular ethnic group (State of Arizona, 2010). The cultural focus of the curriculum is a serious matter, and although petty and irrational arguments exist on all sides, the real issue is the role schools must play in transmitting the common cultural heritage. Schools must teach children that regardless of race, gender, or ethnicity, one can achieve great feats. The public school curriculum should allow all children to believe that they are part of a society that welcomes their participation and encourages their achievements. Schools cannot fulfill their central mission to transmit the common culture if they cater to demands for teaching the perspective of every minority group. Many minority communities from generation to generation—Jews, Catholics, Greeks, Poles, and Japanese—have used private lessons, after school or on weekends, to instill ethnic pride and ethnic continuity in their children. These are valuable goals, but they have never been the public schools' province, nor should they be. Public schools must help young people participate in a common culture that is expansive and inclusive. The best education they can receive is one that speaks primarily to our commonalities and identifies the differences among us as the result of our uniqueness as individuals, not our membership in a particular group. The public school curriculum must not succumb to demands to prize our differences rather than celebrate our common good.

Anticanonical Assaults

Among the greatest absurdities the particularists have produced is their attack on the "canon," denouncing it as racist, sexist, Eurocentric, logocentric, and politically incorrect. Before we put these distortions to rest, a few words about the nature of the canon. The term *canon* (from the Greek word *kanon*, meaning "measuring rod"), which originally referred to the books of the Hebrew and Christian Bibles, meant Holy Scripture as officially recognized by the ecclesiastic authority. Today, it has taken on secular and political meanings. The canon represents, first of all, the major monuments to Western civilization, great ideas embodied in books forming the foundation of our democratic traditions. The "great books" of the Western tradition (e.g., the writings of Plato, Aristotle, Machiavelli, and Marx, to name but a few) have shaped our political thinking, whether we trace our origins to Europe, Africa, or Asia; Homer, Sophocles, George Eliot, and Virginia Woolf inform our sense of literature whether we are male or female. Every major university offers courses in the Western canon, and as the late Alan Bloom (1987) noted, generations of students have enjoyed these works.

> Wherever the Great Books make up a central part of the curriculum, the students are excited and satisfied, feel they are doing something that is independent and fulfilling, getting something from the university they cannot get elsewhere. . . . Their gratitude at learning of Achilles or the categorical imperative is boundless. (p. 344)

The particularists' attack on the canon is new and somewhat surprising. The value of the canon has long been taken for granted as the cornerstone of quality education. As the philosopher John Searle (1990) wrote, educated circles accepted, almost to the point of cliché, that there is a certain Western intellectual tradition that goes from, say, Socrates to Wittgenstein in philosophy and from Homer to James Joyce in literature, and it is essential to the liberal education of young men and women in the United States that they receive some exposure to at least some of the great works in this intellectual tradition; they should, in Matthew Arnold's overquoted words, know the best that is thought and known in the world.

In the past, support for the canon was an article of faith, not belabored or examined at length. People considered these works and the ideas they contained to be of enduring worth, part of a timeless literary judgment—as Samuel Johnson spoke of it—and quite apart from the hurly-burly of politics. Canonical authors were acknowledged representatives of the evolution in the thought of ideas shaping Western civilization. However, in the last 50 years, the canon has been under ongoing attack. Particularists and multiculturalists argue that Western civilization is rooted in a history of imperialism, colonialism, and the oppression of women, slave and serf populations, and ethnic and cultural minorities. They claim that the predominance of Western white males in the literary canon is evidence of their dominating role in the culture (Searle, 1990).

Claims that students from underserved or minority communities need curricula focused solely on the contributions of those groups are misguided and have the potential to limit students' opportunities. As Sowell (2013) argued, "Intellectuals who imagine that they are helping racial or ethnic groups that lag behind by redefining their lags out of existence with multicultural rhetoric are in fact leading them into a blind alley." If students are prevented from reading classics of the Western literary tradition, they are deprived of the chance to develop knowledge that is shared among people who wield influence in this society. If students are not exposed to the giants of

Western political thinking such as Plato, Aristotle, and Machiavelli, they will find it difficult to interact on equal terms with others who attempt to exercise civic power. The anticanonical curriculum underestimates the ability of Western literature's great books to capture the imaginations of majority as well as minority students and the ability of minority students to appreciate those classics. The truths in these works transcend accidents of birth. No curriculum should determine that students' race, ethnicity, gender, or social class should limit what they can learn.

The Common Core Reform Movement and Multiculturalism

During the last 10 years, approximately 42 states adopted some form of the Common Core State Standards for student learning. State standards were required by federal law and the Common Core standards were the result of cooperation in that effort. The Common Core standards have been revised over the years. In their efforts to measure student and teacher achievement, many states relied on tests matched to the standards. Over time, those high-stakes tests have also been changed.

While the standards and tests have been revised, they have not been abandoned completely; nor have the curricular reforms that accompanied the movement. The influence of multiculturalists on those reforms is most clear in the content, or more precisely, the lack of required content presented in the Common Core Standards in English Language Arts. Although its developers lack authority over curricular decisions in any state, the Common Core does present educators with "exemplar texts." The exemplars include canonical texts but offer a dazzling array of "multicultural" or "culturally responsive" examples as well. For example, the suggestions for tenth and eleventh grade literature do include classics like *The Canterbury Tales* and *Hamlet* as well as more modern but influential works like *A Farewell to Arms* and *The Great Gatsby.* Also included in the list are even more recent works such as *The Bluest Eye* and *Dreaming in Cuban* (Common Core State Standards Initiative, 2010). The list might not be so problematic if schools could teach everything, but curriculum is a zero-sum game; that is, if a school adds something, it also must take something out. In the absence of content requirements, teachers could opt out of teaching the classics altogether and still claim to be meeting the Common Core standards.

New York State's efforts to respond to multicultural education activists is illustrative. In New York, curriculum content officially is decided by local districts. However, the long-standing presence of statewide year-end testing in high school has resulted in the state's requirements actually guiding local curricula. Historically, New York State's requirement that high school students study American and British literature for at least four semesters and that one of Shakespeare's plays be read each year ensured that all students were introduced to classics in Western literature. Over time, however, those requirements have been weakened. For example, the P–12 Common Core Learning Standards (New York State Education Department, 2011) referenced a few specific texts that were required at the high school level, including works by Shakespeare. The Next Generation Learning Standards (New York State Education Department, 2019) do not include this specific expectation. The state insists that it is "important, and highly recommended, to include classic works of literature in the classroom, to ensure that all students have a wide range of reading experiences and a rich understanding of the timeless nature of certain classic literary works and how they provide insight into the human experience" (New York State Education Department, 2019). However, they provide few resources to enable teachers to offer students such experiences.

Multiculturalism lumps individuals together inappropriately and without their permission. One critic notes that "Americans now speak of the 'African American community,' the 'Asian American community,' the 'Latino community,' and the 'Native American community' as though these constitute a fully integrated, fully homogenous whole that are fully distinctive and unchangeable" (Welsh, 2008). Multicultural education serves to undermine the school's commitment to forging a single national identity.

> Mexican children newly arrived in American public schools now frequently find themselves in classrooms where they are taught part of the day in Spanish, where they learn more about the achievements of Mayans and Aztecs than about the Puritans, where they are taught to revere Miguel Hidalgo and Emiliano Zapata on the same plane as George Washington or Thomas Jefferson, and to celebrate Cinco de Mayo with more fanfare than the Fourth of July. (Chavez, 2002, p. 387)

The defining experience for Americans has not been ethnicity or sanctification of old cultures. Instead it has been creating a national culture and national identity. Schools should continue to serve the nation by passing on to children elements of the common culture that define the United States and bind its people together. This is not to say schools should be asked to portray the culture as unchangeable or force students to accept it without question. The culture of a nation changes as a reflection of its citizens; U.S. culture will continue to change. School curricula will of necessity expand and sample more broadly from the various influences that have shaped our culture. However, to turn the schools away from Western ideals of democracy, justice, freedom, equality, and opportunity is to renounce the greatest legacy one generation ever bequeathed to the next. No matter who sits in American classrooms—African Americans, Asian Americans, Latin Americans, or European Americans—and no matter what their religion or creed, those students and their nation have been shaped by democratic and intellectual traditions of the Western world, and they had better learn those traditions or risk losing them.

FOR DISCUSSION

1. According to John Searle (1990), the following characteristics define a well-educated person:
   a. The person should know enough of his or her cultural traditions to know how they evolved.
   b. The person should know enough of the natural sciences that he or she is not a stranger in that world.
   c. The person should know enough of how society works to understand the trade cycle, interest, unemployment, and other elements of the political and economic world.

d. The person should know at least one foreign language well enough to read the best literature that culture offers in the original language.

e. The person needs to know enough philosophy to be able to use the tools of logical analysis.

f. The person must be able to write and speak clearly and with candor and rigor.

Do you agree or disagree with Searle's characteristics of a well-educated person? Do you like Searle's approach to defining a well-educated person, or do you prefer the approach of those who assemble long lists of supposedly significant dates, names, and events, such as *Cultural Literacy: What Every American Needs to Know* (Hirsch, 1987) or *Critical Literacy: What Every American Ought to Know* (Provenzo, 2005)? Are there other ways to define a well-educated person?

2. Steinberg and Kincheloe (2001, pp. 3–5) identify five positions in the public discourse about multicultural education. From the following excerpts, do you find yourself more comfortable with one or more of these positions than others? Does your teacher education program adhere more closely to one or more of them?

a. Conservative multiculturalism or monoculturalism position:
   • Believes in the superiority of Western patriarchal culture.
   • Promotes the Western canon as a universal civilizing influence.
   • Targets multiculturalism as the enemy of Western progress.

b. Liberal multiculturalism position:
   • Emphasizes the natural equality and common humanity of individuals from diverse race, class, and gender groups.
   • Argues that inequality results from lack of opportunity.
   • Maintains that problems that individuals from divergent backgrounds face are individual difficulties, not socially structured adversities.

c. Pluralist multiculturalism position:
   • Exoticizes difference and positions it as necessary knowledge for those who compete in a globalized economy.
   • Contends that the curriculum should consist of studies of various divergent groups.
   • Avoids the concept of oppression.

d. Leftist-essential multiculturalism position:
   • Maintains that race, class, and gender categories consist of a set of unchanging priorities (essences).
   • Assumes that only authentically oppressed people can speak about particular issues concerning a specific group.

e. Critical multiculturalism position:
   • Grounds a critical pedagogy that promotes an understanding of how schools/ education work by the exposé of student sorting processes and power's complicity with the curriculum.
   • Makes no pretense of neutrality, as it honors the notion of egalitarianism and elimination of human suffering.
   • Analyzes the way that power shapes consciousness.

3. Diane Ravitch argues that pressure groups from both the left and the right have persuaded textbook publishers to censor the words and ideas children are allowed to read. Ravitch (2003) compiled "A Glossary of Banned Words, Usages, Stereotypes, and Topics" to illustrate some of the "words, usages, stereotypes, and topics banned by major publishers of educational materials and state agencies."

Consider some of the following examples of banned terms that Ravitch uncovered. Does the conscious omission of these terms from textbooks constitute a reasonable or an unreasonable censorship of ideas? Are the terms so offensive that students should be protected from reading them, or is this, as Ravitch claims, a form of censorship and little more than an exercise in "political correctness"?

- Able-bodied (banned as offensive; replace with *person who is nondisabled*)
- Black (banned as adjective meaning "evil")
- Cowboy, cowgirl (banned as sexist; replace with *cowhand*)
- Dwarf (banned as offensive; replace with *person of short stature*)
- Eskimo (banned as inauthentic; replace with Inupiat, Inuit, Yupik, Yuit, or Native Arctic peoples or Innuvialuit; note: Yupik and Yuit are "not interchangeable")
- Fat (banned; replace with *heavy, obese*)
- Indian giver (banned as offensive)
- Slave (replace whenever possible with *enslaved person, worker,* or *laborer*)
- West, Western (banned as Eurocentric when discussing world geography; replace with reference to specific continent or region)
- White (banned as adjective meaning "pure")

REFERENCES

Alismail, H. (2016). "Multicultural Education: Teachers' Perceptions and Preparation." *Journal of Education and Practice* 7(11).

Asante, M. K. (1991). "The Afrocentric Idea in Education." *Journal of Negro Education* 60:170–180.

Bailon, R., and De Lissovoy, N. (2019). "Against Coloniality: Toward an Epistemically Insurgent Curriculum." *Policy Futures in Education* 17(3):355–369.

Banks, J. A., ed. (2017a). *Citizenship Education and Global Migration: Implications for Theory, Research and Teaching*. Washington, DC: American Educational Research Association.

Banks, J. A. (2017b). "Failed Citizenship and Transformative Civic Education." *Educational Researcher* 46(7):366–377.

——— (2018). *An Introduction to Multicultural Education* (6th ed.). New York: Pearson.

Banks, J. A., and C. A. McGee-Banks, eds. (2020). *Multicultural Education: Issues and Perspectives* (10th ed.). Hoboken, NJ: John Wiley and Sons.

Black, D. (2018, April 25). "Reconstructing the Canon." *Harvard Political Review* (harvardpolitics.com/culture/thecanon).

Bloom, A. (1987). *The Closing of the American Mind*. New York: Simon and Schuster.

Cabrera, N. L., Milem, J. F., Jaquette, O., and Marx, R. W. (2014). "Missing the (Student Achievement) Forest for all the (Political) Trees: Empiricism and the Mexican American Studies Controversy in Tucson." *American Educational Research Journal* 51(6):1,084–1,118.

Chavez, L. (2002). The New Politics of Hispanic Assimilation. In A. Thernstrom and S. Thernstrom, eds., *Beyond the Color Line: New Perspectives on Race and Ethnicity in America*. Stanford, CA: Hoover Institution.

Common Core State Standards Initiative (2010). *Common Core State Standards for English Language Arts & Literacy in History/Social Studies, Science, and Technical Subjects*. Appendix B: Text Exemplars and Sample Performance Tasks (corestandards.org/assets/Appendix_B.pdf).

Dee, T., and Penner, E. (2017). "The Causal Effects of Cultural Relevance: Evidence from an Ethnic Studies Curriculum." *American Education Research Journal* 54(1):127–166.

Ezzani, M., and King, K. (2018). "Whose Jihad? Oral History of an American Muslim Educational Leader and U.S. Public Schools." *Journal of Educational Administration and History* 50(2):113–129.

Gay, G. (2018). *Culturally Responsive Teaching: Theory, Research, Practice* (3rd ed.). New York: Teachers College Press.

Gershon, L. (2017, May 9). "When American Schools Banned German Classes." *JSTOR Daily* (daily.jstor.org/when-american-schools-banned-german-classes).

Giroux, H. (2015). *Schooling and the Struggle for Public Life*. New York: Taylor Francis.

Glazer, N. (1997). *We Are All Multiculturalists Now*. Cambridge, MA: Harvard University Press.

Hardy, J. (2014). "Does Multiculturalism Make Society Less Cohesive?" *Political Review* 24(2).

Hirsch, E. D., Jr. (1987). *Cultural Literacy: What Every American Needs to Know*. Boston: Houghton Mifflin.

——— (1996). *The Schools We Need, and Why We Don't Have Them*. New York: Doubleday.

Horne, T. (2007, June 11). An Open Letter to the Citizens of Tucson. State of Arizona, Department of Education (faculty.umb.edu/lawrence_blum/courses/CCT627_10/readings/horne_open_letter_tucson.pdf).

Huntington, S. P. (1996). *The Clash of Civilizations: Remaking of the World Order*. New York: Touchstone.

Inside Schools (2019). English Learners (insideschools.org/insidetools/english-language-learners).

Iowa Department of Education (2019). Iowa Social Studies Standards (iowacore.gov/sites/default/files/k-12_socialstudies_508.pdf).

Jensen, B. (2013). "Chapter Six: Race Erased? Arizona's Ban on Ethnic Studies." *Counterpoints* 445:81–100.

Kincheloe, J., McLaren, P., Steinberg, S., and Monzo, L. (2018). Critical Pedagogy and Qualitative Research. In N. Dinzen and Y. Lincoln, eds., *The Sage Handbook of Qualitative Research* (5th ed.). Thousand Oaks, CA: Sage.

King, J. E., and Swartz, E. E. (2015). *The Afrocentric Praxis of Teaching for Freedom: Connecting Culture to Learning*. New York: Routledge.

Lowry, R. (2019). *The Case for Nationalism*. New York: Broadside Books.

Macedo, D. (2018). *Literacies of Power* (Expanded Ed.). New York: Routledge.

Meyer, A. E. (1957). *An Educational History of the American People*. New York: McGraw-Hill.

National Association for Multicultural Education (2019). Definitions of Multicultural Education (nameorg.org/definitions_of_multicultural_e.php).

National Council for the Social Studies (2016). A Vision of Powerful Teaching and Learning in the Social Studies (socialstudies.org/publications/socialeducation/may-june2016/vision-of-powerful-teaching-and-learning-in-social-studies).

——— (2019). The Themes of Social Studies (socialstudies.org/standards/strands).

New York State Education Department (2011). New York State P–12 Common Core Learning Standards for English Language Arts and Literacy (engageny.org/resource/new-york-state-p-12-common-core-learning-standards-for-english-language-arts-and-literacy).

——— (2014). *New York State K–12 Social Studies Framework: Introduction* (nysed.gov/common/nysed/files/programs/curriculum-instruction/ss-framework-k-12-intro.pdf).

————— (2019). *Next Generation Learning Standards for English Language Arts: FAQ* (nysed.gov/common/nysed/files/programs/curriculum-instruction/nys-next-generation-ela-standards-faqs.pdf).

New York State Social Studies Syllabus Review and Development Committee (1991). *One Nation, Many Peoples: A Declaration of Cultural Independence.* Albany: State Education Department, State University of New York.

Nieto, S., and Bode, P. (2018). *Affirming Diversity: The Sociopolitical Context of Multicultural Education* (7th ed.). Boston: Pearson.

Provenzo, E. F. (2005). *Critical Literacy: What Every American Ought to Know.* Boulder, CO: Paradigm.

Ravitch, D. (1987, December, 4–10). "Tot Sociology, Grade School History." *Current.*

————— (2003). *The Language Police: How Pressure Groups Restrict What Students Learn.* New York: Alfred A. Knopf.

San Pedro, T. (2015). "Silence as Weapons: Transformative Praxis among Native American Students in the Urban Southwest." *Equity & Excellence in Education* 48(4):511–528.

Schlesinger, A. M. (1998). *The Disuniting of America.* New York: Norton.

Searle, J. (1990, December 6). "The Storm over the University." *New York Review of Books,* 34–41.

Sleeter, C. (2018). "Multicultural Education Past, Present, and Future: Struggles for Dialog and Power-Sharing." *International Journal of Multicultural Education* 20(1):5–20.

Sowell, T. (2013, March 12). "Multiculturalism is Counterproductive." *Washington Examiner.*

Spring, J. (2017). *The Intersection of Cultures: Multicultural Education in the United States and the Global Economy* (4th ed.). New York: McGraw-Hill.

State of Arizona (2010). Arizona House Bill 2281. House of Representatives, Forty-Ninth Legislature, Second Regular Session (azleg.gov/legtext/49leg/2r/bills/hb2281s.pdf).

Steinberg, S. R., and Kincheloe, J. L. (2001). Setting the Context for Critical Multi/Interculturalism: The Power Blocs of Class Elitism, White Supremacy, and Patriarchy. In S. R. Steinberg, ed., *Multi/Intercultural Conversations.* New York: Peter Lang.

Strauss, V. (2017, December 11). "Just How Racist is Children's Literature? The Author of 'Was the Cat in the Hat Black?' Explains." *Washington Post.*

U.S. Census Bureau (2018). 2017 National Population Projection Tables (census.gov/data/tables/2017/demo/popproj/2017-summary-tables.html).

U.S. Department of Education (2018). Languages Spoken by English Learners. Office of English Language Acquisition (ncela.ed.gov/files/fast_facts/FastFacts-Languages-Spoken-by-ELs-2018.pdf).

Utah Education Network (2017). Social Studies Core (uen.org/core/socialstudies).

van Waarden, B. A. F. (2017). Teaching for Toleration in Pluralist Liberal Democracies. *Democracy and Education* 25(1).

Welsh, J. F. (2008). *After Multiculturalism: The Politics of Race and the Dialectics of Liberty.* Lanham, MD: Rowman & Littlefield.

Technology and Learning

Enabling or Subverting

11

What technology deserves significant school attention, and who should decide?

Position 1:   Technology Enables Learning

> Human rights to education and development are possible without access to and use of information technologies, but they are much more effective with the technologies.
>
> —Jaeger et al. (2019)

> When computers are integrated into the flow of classroom action, a qualitative transformation occurs regarding the ways teachers teach and students learn.
>
> —Angeli (2008)

Technology is transformative. It changes as it is used, and it changes those who use it. Ideas to improve technology arise as it is used—new technology leads farther, spiraling in speed and complexity. As we employ new tools, like lasers, artificial intelligence, and digital platforms for daily life, we alter our perceptions of technology and our environments. Changes occur in our lives with advances in areas like solar energy, telemedicine, telecommunication, microwaves, and other modern conveniences. Hockfield (2019) describes developing convergence of fields like biology and engineering where viruses make energy, proteins purify water, and life is improved by brain-enabled prosthetic limbs. The human genetic revolution has "monumental potential for good" depending on improving technology and education (Metzl, 2019). Gerstein (2019) writes: "technology has been a central organizing construct throughout the history of humankind. . . . At its core, technology is about solving problems" (pp. 10, 18).

Teaching and learning improve as a result of technology (International Society for Technology in Education, 2008, 2019; Baker, 2012; Collins and Halverson, 2018).

Spiro (2006) argues a revolution is happening, but the pace in schools is too slow; incremental school thinking should be replaced by "principled leaps" (p. 4). He identifies several emerging themes:

- Increasing complexity with cognitive understanding.
- Speeding up the acquisition of experiences.
- Newer ways to comprehend knowledge structures without traditional pedagogy.
- Changing the way people think and getting them to think for themselves.

Technology in schools continues to change from simple devices to more complicated, sophisticated, and engaging environments; from chalkboards and textbooks to interactive media, systems of distance learning, e-learning, virtual schools, cloud computing, 3-D printing, and customized individualized pacing (Rotherham, 2006; Livingston, 2008; Reigeluth, 2011; Villinger, 2012; Paganelli, 2019; Fingal, 2020). From essential reading skills, to the most advanced academic work in all fields, technology is a key tool (Paganelli, 2019; U.S. Department of Education, 2019, 2020). It is not only a subject to be taught, it also is a tool for teaching all fields and a resource for changing education by continued use and modification. Technology demonstrates daily its practical value in classroom instruction, teacher and student research, improved school design and operation, increasing student interest and teacher scope, and interlinking the school and the globe. Inherent in these illustrations is technology's obvious importance to education and to society. It has the potential to completely reconstruct what we normally think of as schooling, learning, and teaching. Digital literacy provides a basis for thinking and doing and improving.

Young people have a direct relation with technology; they are immersed in media, adapt easily to highly mobile technology, and have become multitaskers. "Screenagers" is a term used to describe teenagers who engage with screens (televisions, cell phones, computers, and so on) as their natural habitat and use devices to comprehend and shape their environments. Today, for younger children, "technology is deeply embedded in their lives" (Watson, 2010, p. 29). Pew Research data show that nearly 95% of teenagers have access to a smart phone and over 50% use it on a daily basis; 93% now use the Internet, including 88% of those ages 12 to 13 and 95% of those ages 14 to 17. (Pew Research Center, 2009; Anderson and Jiang, 2018). Social media are a significant form of technology for the young, primarily for online social networking, keeping up with current interests, purchases, and finding information. Edutopia (2019) suggests "There's a Cell Phone in Your Student's Head," reflecting what students are thinking about. Robotics, nanotechnology, genetics, Internet development, and myriad emerging technologies will become integral parts of life for youth of school age (Brockman, 2010; Allenby and Sarewitz, 2011; *Technology Review,* 2011). Compared with older generations, teenagers are "digital natives in a land of digital immigrants" (Rainie, 2006, p. 3). The implications for schools are enormous, as "learning and research tasks will be shaped by their new technoworld" (Rainie, 2006, p. 15; Gonzalez, 2019).

Evidence That Learning from and with Technology Is Beneficial

The significant benefits of technology for education far outweigh issues that might arise from its misuse. A half century of educational research indicated media and technology are highly effective in schools (Reeves, 1998). Johnson and Barker (2002), examining studies of about 100 government-funded educational technology projects, show the positive results from using technology, including improved student outcomes in cognitive knowledge and information access and improved teaching. Ringstaff and Kelly (2002) analyzed findings from a large variety of research studies on the use of technology in learning and teaching, finding substantial improvements in most subjects. Tamin (2011) conducted a meta-analysis of many studies of the impact of technology on learning conducted over a 40-year period and found that using technology in instruction produced gains in student learning over instruction that does not include technology. Gains were better for when technology is used to support the teacher than when technology is used alone. And blended, face-to-face, and online learning environments produced the best results in student learning. Projects involving blended instruction are under way in several large city schools, an applied test of this research work (Schorr and McGriff, 2011). In an update to the National Educational Technology Plan, John King, former Secretary of Education, concluded: "One of the most important aspects of technology in education is its ability to level the field of opportunity for students" (U.S. Department of Education, 2017). This leveling ability is based on the demonstrated value of technology for learning.

Over time, there are consistent demonstrations of the educational value of contemporary technology in schools; students learn from and with it (Strawn, 2011). MIT News (2019) reports an analysis of 126 studies that showed the effectiveness of technology in improving academic achievement, helping individual learners, and developing skills in computer use. The Educational Media and Technology Yearbook publishes updated analyses of research on the effectiveness of technology in schools worldwide (Branch et al., 2019).

The Importance of Technology in Schools

Local, state, and federal governments spend billions to place new technology in schools, and private support adds considerable amounts. The results are remarkable. In 1994, about 35% of public schools had Internet access; by 2005, at least 99% of public schools had access. And the ratio of students to computers has decreased, from 12:1 in 1998 to 5:1 (U.S. Department of Education, 2004, 2019). Gallup's national surveys for the International Society for Technology in Education (Rose et al., 2004) found that 98% of respondents stated that technology should be in the school curriculum. Gallup surveyed students to see technological usage for education (see Table 11.1) and surveyed teachers and administrators about the relative value of technology in the classroom (see Table 11.2).

Not only is study from and with technology of great benefit to students, teachers, and the school curriculum, it also has benefits for society. International competition

Table 11.1	Gallup Survey of Students on Use of Technology for Learning			
	Every Day	**1 to 4 Days/Week**	**Less**	**Never**
Use of digital technology in school	57%	39%	3%	0
Use to learn at home; homework	38%	42%	12%	7%

Source: Calderon and Carlson (2019).

Table 11.2   Gallup Survey of Educators on Relative Value of Technology in Education

Reason for Use	Positive—Great Value (%)
Search for information	90
Create projects	84
Personalize learning	76
Practice lessons	83
Assessment	71
Learn new content	69
Communication	60

Source: Calderon and Carlson (2019).

demands that the United States remain in the forefront of technological innovation and development. Technology permits us to put the best schooling in the hands of all children—rural, suburban, or urban. Children can have access to fine teachers, excellent culture, significant science, and interesting learning (Salpeter, 2008; Villinger, 2012; U.S. Department of Education, 2019).

More Than Just Teacher Gimmicks

Technology in schools is not merely a collection of devices occasionally used by teachers to illustrate a lesson. Educational technology and technological education are basic knowledge that students must have to survive and thrive in our society. Technological knowledge itself is fundamental and should be deeply incorporated into main courses of study in schools (Edutopia, 2011; Paganelli, 2019). Historians of technology show how all human existence has been assisted and improved by technological developments (Gerstein, 2019). Schools engage future generations in learning and should be at the forefront of technological knowledge to improve education and encourage students as intelligent consumers and users. Schools can't be backward, nor have an antitechnology bias. Technological advances are so important we must fully integrate pertinent ones into the central purposes of schooling. The teacher's role changes from "sage on the stage" to "guide on the side," designing and organizing instructional material, facilitating learning, and acting as a knowledgeable and supportive mentor, using technology for actual instruction and assessment as well as record keeping (Reigeluth, 2011; Edutopia, 2019). This requires well prepared and practiced teachers in technology as well as subjects. It suggests a more comprehensive approach to teacher education, to develop and improve practice, conduct scholarship, and communicate about digital technologies in education.

Technology is knowledge, but it can also be a major means to learning and to developing improved knowledge. Technology is one of the knowledge products of human minds; it is useful in conveying that knowledge to others, and it is used in conducting research to improve knowledge. Learning, as well as teaching, is enabled by technology. Integrating technology into instruction seamlessly is an important task for teachers, transforming classrooms and education (King, 2011).

For higher education, Educause continues the Horizon Project of the New Media Consortium, with a large panel of experts from many nations offering ideas on emerging trends in technology education in higher education. The *2020 Horizon Report* discusses technological impacts on student learning, receptiveness of faculty, issues of equity and inclusion, and the expected costs to higher education institutions (Educause, 2020). Among the trends identified are:

- *Adaptive learning*—rethinking courses and curricula to personalize learning.
- *Artificial intelligence, machine learning*—automated chatbots to help students 24 hours a day.
- *Elevating instructional design*—increasing technology use and participation.
- *Open education resources*—available without purchase, royalty, or fees.
- *Extended Reality*—including virtual reality, 3-D, and holography.

Elementary and secondary schools engage in similar frontier efforts using technology to change learning and teaching. The following small sample of the increasing variety of school-oriented websites offer assistance to teachers and students:

- Nearpod (student engagement) (nearpod.com)
- Kahoot! (learning games) (kahoot.com)
- EDpuzzle (videos into lessons) (edpuzzle.com)
- Empatico (connecting students) (empatico.org)
- Makers Empire (3-D game design) (makersempire.com)
- Equity Maps (class discussions) (equitymaps.com)
- Epic! (digital library) (getepic.com)
- Hopscotch (computational thinking) (gethopscotch.com)

This is a mere sample; more are being developed as you read this. *Tech & Learning* magazine is one source for teaching ideas using technology.

Developing Technological Knowledge, Skills, and Attitudes

Technological *knowledge* involves a working understanding of technical and operational language, an understanding of common technological equipment and related software, a grasp of basic scientific and mathematical principles on which technology rests, and an understanding of the history of technology and its impacts on society. It also includes the use of technology to learn: to discover, analyze, test, and comprehend ideas.

Technological *skills* are the techniques useful in efficient and effective operation of various technical devices, from computers and telecommunication equipment to image reproduction and robotics, and the techniques useful in dealing with the results of that work. This incorporates skills used in learning, evaluating, reporting on, and correcting or repairing technological, academic, and creative material. Technological *attitudes* include a curiosity about ideas and knowledge, an awareness of the need for continued technological innovation, an openness to change, a desire to improve technology, and an optimistic sense that recognizes the value of technology to social and individual lives. This functional set of knowledge, skills, and attitudes should be included in the basic education for all students.

In addition to Internet connections, schools with state-of-the-art equipment and teaching materials, a suitable technology curriculum, and teachers well prepared in the use and value of various technologies are a necessity. Schools play a particularly important role in diagnosis, delivery, and development of technological learning. Qualified teachers diagnose the students' technical knowledge and skill in reference to national standards, deliver appropriate learning to improve student mastery, and develop innovative and interesting teaching materials and techniques for continuing improvement. Further, schools must provide a supportive, sustaining environment for technology, assisting teachers and other staff to acquire and improve their skills.

Papert (2002) thinks technology can do the following:

1. Change the whole system of schooling to improve learning and teaching (e.g., show that knowledge is interdisciplinary with no need for separate, compartmentalized subjects and that the learning process has continuity without age segregation).

2. "Mobilize powerful ideas" (e.g., use virtual reality to try things out and offer immediate feedback from multiple sources).

3. Encourage "children to become a driving force for educational change instead of passive recipients" (e.g., students teach along with teachers, and children's curiosity stimulates innovative uses for technology).

Technological knowledge goes beyond basic operations and information to expand and engage students and teachers in redesigning the very nature of schooling and learning. It is transformative. National education standards have a major impact on schools, providing focus for curriculum and instruction and offering accountability to society. Any subject not included in approved national standards is destined to be marginalized in schools. The International Society for Technology in Education offers standards that are the basis for nearly every state's standards documents (iste.org). General standards for technology education are to enable students to become capable users, information seekers, problem solvers, communicators, analyzers, evaluators, and decision makers—thus, informed, responsible, and productive citizens (International Society for Technology in Education, 2019).

Obstacles: Resources, Traditionalism, Fear

Obstacles to adequate technological education are evident, including financing, adequate staffing, suitable curriculum, technological fear, and the traditional slow speed of educational change. Financing is an important issue but must be weighed against the social costs of not preparing students for twenty-first-century technical life. If funds are not provided, we expand the digital divide between the well-to-do and the poor. A 10-year national investment in wiring schools helps to close that divide and Internet access in public schools increases each year, moving from less than one-third of all schools in the mid-1990s to virtually all schools now.

Some teachers fear or are reluctant about technology and are not prepared to properly educate students. This fear can prevent them from exploring its uses and benefits as instructional tools. Fearful teachers often lack adequate preparation. Other reluctant teachers are more comfortable in their traditional roles of standing in front of a class and talking; they often consider technology an irritating distraction. Some are content to use older technologies. Teachers may disparage new computer or telecommunications devices as useful only for "entertainment" or "self-indulgence." Many teachers see laptop computers merely as a "presentation" tool and "marginalize every aspect of the laptop" in their classrooms (Windschitl and Sahl, 2002, p. 197). Teacher-imposed classroom rules often prohibit students from bringing in technological equipment; school rules and parent fear may limit the use of such equipment. McKenzie's (2001, 2019) books are designed to assist schools and teachers in overcoming this obstacle with practical ideas. This can help with parents, also (Rogers-Whitehead, 2020).

Some schools make it difficult for students to get access to various devices, and experimentation is not permitted. School computer rooms are often separated from class work areas, are limited to select students or times, are heavily controlled and monitored, and have too few computers that are often poorly maintained older models with creaky programs. Only certain students get special training on computers. Teachers and administrators often perceive technical equipment as expensive and separate from standard schoolwork. They don't trust the students, and they may be uncomfortable around the equipment themselves. Sometimes they suspect that students are using computers and other equipment inappropriately, as in "surfing" the Internet and finding something interesting. That hardly ties them into the ongoing educational activity in classrooms. This is not a setting that encourages learning from or with technology.

Cyberbullying as a Technology Issue

Cyberbullying is an unfortunate development in technology use and contributes to fear about technology. Bullying has been a school problem for generations, and is covered in another chapter in this book, but digital devices make that cowardly behavior easier, faster, and more secret. Technology is not at fault; it is the fault of certain users. It should be addressed as an issue involving the proper practice of technology and personal safety. Outside or inside schools, it affects students and their education. Cyberbullying has become a major interest of school administrators, educators, and parents. This bullying uses online social media, forums, game rooms, and other sites to spread negative, hurtful, harmful, and false personal rumors about individuals. It has led to depression, anxiety, excess stress, withdrawal, and even suicide among youth.

Efforts to educate students about the dangers of cyberbulling and to help protect from the use of technology for malicious attacks, destruction of reputations, and personal vendettas have had some success (Edutopia, 2011; National Center for Education Statistics, 2019; StopBullying.gov, 2020). Student reports of bullying at school have declined by one-third over the past decade (National Center for Education Statistics, 2019). Many new sources provide insight, examples, and assistance in controlling cyberbulling (Giumetti and Kowalski, 2019; Jones, 2019; Englander, 2020; Gagne, 2020). Fear of cyberbullying should not be the basis for antitechnology ideas or actions in schools. Students should not suffer cyber gaps because of fear that technology can be misused. Instead, schools should undertake appropriate technology and anti-cyberbullying education to better arm students.

Academics and Technology

We need constantly improving math, science, and technology education. This is not only for students who want to go into careers in math, science, and technology; technological knowledge is needed in virtually all contemporary occupations. Long-distance truck drivers, building contractors, salespeople, government employees, lawyers, doctors, travel agents, and farmers use and rely on technological equipment for their work. Homeowners, renters, taxpayers, parents, and voters need technological knowledge.

Technological change happens faster and faster—but not school change (Prensky, 2008a). The time gap between discoveries in science and their application in technology has been shortening at an increasing rate. While it took more than 100 years to transform scientific discoveries about light in the eighteenth century into technology for photography, it took only 65 years between the science behind electric motors and the technology that provided them. For radios, the gap between discovery and technology was about 35 years. From discoveries in atomic theory to technology for atomic weapons, the gap was only six years, and from science to technology on transistors it was only three years (Gleick, 1999).

We have a continuing deficiency in U.S. scientific and technological education. Comparative tests of math and science achievement show American students well behind some European countries and Japan. Math, science, and technology are very significant subjects; the United States should not be behind in these areas. Friedman (2005) noted that one U.S. university tied for seventeenth place, the lowest ranking ever in the 29-year history of an international programming competition, and that no U.S. school had won since 1997. American colleges dominated this competition for years but have been falling behind. He attributes it to a serious lack in math and science education in precollegiate schools.

Developing Technological Proficiency

The United States requires a populace well informed about new technologies, their use, and their social value (Braun, 2007). Technological literacy is the beginning point, and schools are the obvious place to start (Salpeter, 2008). No other institution in society has such broad responsibilities for the development of various literacies—the ability to read, write, speak, understand, and apply information—among the young. Schools have a long, proud tradition of providing a common curriculum in necessary and important learnings: language use, civic responsibility, computation skill, scientific and economic understanding, and appreciation of the arts. Each is a form of literacy, and schools offer the means to student comprehension and use. Technology's increasing significance to human life and societal well-being means schools must ensure basic education from and with technology—providing digital citizenship, to use Edutopia's term (Edutopia, 2008, 2011; Prensky, 2008b; Allenby and Sarewitz, 2011; Lee, 2019).

Education occurs in a variety of locations, under a number of circumstances, at any time, and through uncountable individual interests. Technology is a necessary subject to be taught, and it offers the means and variety to improve and expand all learning for schools. Student research is enhanced via Internet, satellite, laser, and other means. Virtual situations and simulations approximate real life and provide extraordinary learning experiences not available from books and teachers. Distance learning programs allow students to stay at home, sit on a beach, wait in a line, sip some milk and eat cookies, or be anywhere and still be connected for learning. Computer programs exist in all subjects: English literature and grammar, histories of all types, math beyond belief, philosophy, multiple combinations of sciences, any of the arts, foreign language and culture, homemaking and home construction, and any other topic deemed important or interesting. Appreciation for and participation in creative arts is stimulated through use of technologies. Health and physical education can be better designed to suit individual needs and monitored more effectively by teachers with technology.

Not only are available technological options for education more interesting and involving, but they are lower in cost and time than many equivalent educational activities. A trip to Italy to use Italian and see art can be simulated by computer at a far less cost than by plane and tour guide. Designing a building or city is more efficient by computer. Reconstructing historical events is possible and educationally entertaining by computer. Obviously, technology can't fully substitute for real experience, but it is far better than the unreality that typifies standard schooling and is safer and more open to multiple tries and modification than real experience. It allows rapid rethinking with "what-if" possibilities, stretching student thinking and creativity.

Available technology in schooling also is intellectually stimulating, interactive, visually stunning, pleasing in sound, and engaging of mind. It is tuned to individual student interests, tastes, and levels of knowledge—it is customized education that can be reorganized and re-sorted to fit changes in interests or level of understanding. Such education can occur at various times in libraries, on laptops, in centers, at home, by handheld device, and multiple other means at various locations and times. In addition, there is evidence that introduction of technology into classrooms has many other educational benefits, including a significant increase in the potential for learning. Students can gain understanding, via technology, of the most theoretical and most applied knowledge. And that knowledge can be rerun as often as students desire until it is mastered or revised.

Technological progress requires talented people, with solid educations, and substantial resources in funds, facilities, and encouragement. Schooling is the key to continuing scientific achievements. In the past century, expansion of public schooling, a shift toward science and technology, new attitudes among workers and management about technology in the workplace, government encouragement of research and development, improved patent systems, and incentives for innovation helped make America powerful.

There is no better way to assess the future development of American science and technology than by examining our educational system. The future of American enterprise exists in the schools. We can tinker with current technology for short-term improvements, but long-lasting development depends on new generations of scientists, inventors, business leaders, skilled workers, and knowledgeable consumers. If schools falter, we are likely to continue declining in society and in world leadership.

Position 2:   Technology Can Subvert Learning

Even more troubling than the potential threats to our economy and our privacy posed by the new technologies are those posed to our democracy.

—Stiglitz (2019)

We have to find a way to live with seductive technology and make it work to our purposes. This is hard and will take work . . . we have agreed to a series of experiments; robots for children and the elderly, technologies that denigrate and deny privacy, seductive simulations that propose themselves as places to live. . . . We deserve better.

—Turkle (2011, pp. 294, 296)

Technology is the application of science for some practical purpose. Decisions about suitable applications of science and the evaluation of practical purposes, however, require serious scrutiny. Some technologies seem to be just good sense. Safety goggles for welders, testing equipment used to ensure safe blood supplies, staplers, and gummed stamps are examples. But some technologies bring serious problems; technologies are responsible for supplies of crack cocaine, torture machinery, surveillance systems that abrogate civil liberties, and pollution of air and water. We can use weapons technology to protect ourselves and maintain peace or to threaten others in belligerence. Lasers can be used to save lives or to take them.

Technology, however, is not necessarily beneficial. Robotic elimination of workers' jobs, with no adequate and equivalent replacement policies and practices, is bad for society and individuals. It is also bad for an economy that requires extensive consumer participation. Survivors of nuclear testing on Pacific islands during World War II suffered cancers, blood illnesses, other long-term effects, and early death because they were not adequately educated about or protected from "new technology." Excessive "screen time" on digital devices has harmed some people physically with eye and arm ailments, and some with changes in behavioral patterns in such areas as weaker reading in detail, intellectual concentration, and patience (Goldberg, 2020). Engineering new-model humans and building robots to replace people are technologically possible; should they happen simply because they can? Most of us have frustrations while fighting through a maze of menus on a phone call, correcting mistakes because of electronic handling of finance and other matters, checking an apparently simple issue on car maintenance, and dealing with major corporations on electronic subscriptions, updates, service, and operations.

Personal experiences in technology can fuel belligerence. Fox (2004) identifies behaviors variously called tech rage, web rage, or CRAP (computer rage, anxiety, and phobia), including physically attacking a computer, swearing at it, and experiencing frustration, anger, and exasperation. The commonly identified remedy is that "people must, in other words, adapt to the machine" (p. x). But that is not the only answer, probably not even the best answer. Neither is the extreme Luddite response, nor are head-in-the-sand attitudes about all new technology.

Technology can provide many extraordinary benefits to society and individuals, but wholesale adoption of new technology, without skepticism, is of benefit primarily to entrepreneurs, corporations, and advertising companies. As Zuboff (2019) argues, the increasing concentration of power in the hands of technological interests tied to capitalistic pressures leads to surveillance capitalism and the loss of civil liberties and privacy, and results in the control of knowledge. This describes a significant loss of democracy and enlightened education. She points out that a small number of corporations, like Google, Facebook, and Microsoft, can "threaten Western liberal democracies." She does not think that is inevitable, but must be "contested and interrupted." Anderson and Rainie (2020), in a study for the Pew Research Center, find that many tech experts think democracy will be damaged from the use of digital devices to distort reality, alter truth, and damage social institutions during this decade.

Critical Skepticism of Educational Technology Is Wise

Similarly, overreliance on technology to provide knowledge runs risks to freedom in education and democracy. Technology does not automatically or inevitably help learning. In some cases, it can be a detriment, including psychological problems (Rosen, 2012). McKenzie (2019) admonishes schools and teachers who adopt "technology for the sake of technology." Without wise use, technology can be an educational impediment, a distraction (McWilliams, 2019). Neiderman and Zaza (2019) note studies showing technology use can cause a decline in the ability to process and retain information, a decline in academic performance, cognitive overload, and less self-control. Student habituation to cell phones, verging on addiction, infects classrooms and triggers restrictive school policies and practices (Jacobs, 2019).

We need reasoned criteria, solid evidence, and critical skepticism to make adequate judgments about the relative value of technologies. Commercialism, politics, and ideology are commonly the pressures for or against certain technological uses—these forces are not consistent with the reasoned judgment needed. You don't have to be a knee-jerk advocate of technology to show you are modern, and you don't have to be Neanderthal in views against technology to show you resist being dragooned. Good critical judgment based on evidence and logic, along with some healthy skepticism, is pertinent. But that critical judgment is what is often lacking in discussions about technology in education.

Morozov (2011) makes an important point about the overzealous salesmanship and lack of critical thinking behind the advocacy of new technologies: "excessive optimism about what technology has to offer, bordering at times on irrational exuberance, overwhelms even those with superior knowledge of history, society, and politics" (p. 313).

Advocates of technology in schools want students trained to use and love the latest device and do not appreciate critical judgment to question its value. Bromley and Apple (1998) warned early that writing in this area "implicitly assumes that technology is beneficent, sure to bring us a better tomorrow if we simply attend to a little fine-tuning now and then" (p. 3). Technology, in the form of more computer activity, is often treated as an inevitable happening in schools, a type of determinism that leads us to feel helpless to stop or modify expansion (Watson, 2010; Wu, 2010; Cuban, 2011; Bridle, 2018). Pflaum (2004) states: "Test scores would soar, or tests would disappear altogether, as newly engaged, motivated students acquired skills, problem-solving abilities and a newfound thirst for knowledge. That was technology's promise. The reality, so far, has fallen short" (p. 4). Cuban (2011) agrees: "Without a broader vision of the social and civic role that schools perform in a democratic society, our current excessive focus on technology use in schools runs the danger of trivializing our nation's core ideals."

Old and New Technologies: Replace Schools and Teachers?

A theme, sometimes undercurrent, in discussions about technologies and education is that "new" technology will replace schools and teachers. Sir Anthony Seldon, head teacher at an elite English private school, predicts artificially intelligent (AI) machines will take the place of teachers in the next decade, making teachers "little more than classroom assistants" (von Radowitz, 2017) (see Seldon and Abidoye, 2018). AI is a recent addition to the list of teacher replacements. Failed predictions about technology replacing teachers have a long history. The fifteenth century printing press is one example Novak (2014) identified as "15 Technologies That Were Supposed to Change Education Forever." Other examples include: 1900s—electrified books, the Victrola; 1920s—motion pictures, radio, radio books; 1930s—blackboards delivered to a home TV, long-play records; 1940s—TV; 1950s—robot teacher; 1960s—Auto-Tutor, classroom computers; 1970s—the Answer Machine; 1980s—personal robot, homework machine, videophone. Additions could be interactive TV, virtual reality, brain implants, and AI (Walsh, 2018). Technology advocates in earlier times proposed to "revolutionize" classrooms and eliminate teachers by the use of such new technologies as (1) printed textbooks, (2) educational films and filmstrips, (3) school-based radio, (4) classroom television, (5) programmed learning, and (6) computers and online learning (Tyack and Cuban, 2000; Light, 2001; Monke, 2001; Oppenheimer, 2003). Thomas Edison predicted in 1922 that "the motion picture is destined to revolutionize our educational system and that in a few years it will supplant largely, if not entirely, the use of textbooks" (quoted in Lee, 2000, p. 48). Movies have changed much of American life and influenced teaching, but they have not replaced books, libraries, or reading.

Some technological advances have helped schools, but the recurring threat that teachers and schools would be replaced as machines take over has not happened. Even the Tech Edvocate is skeptical of that ever happening: "Let's face it, good teachers will never become obsolete" (Lynch, 2018). Fang (2019) makes the point in *Forbes* magazine that "humans are irreplaceable, but tasks and jobs are automatable." Good teachers, not machines or devices, are the key to good education. Students recognize the value of teacher-mitigated technology: "Teachers are vital to the learning process. Technology is good, but it is not a perfect substitute" (Oblinger and Oblinger, 2005). Teachers have employed technologies in their work for a long time. Teachers invent creative ways to improve their instruction; technologies are often a key ingredient. Useful technologies have been used in schools for centuries, technologies that show value in assisting learning. Writing instruments; printed material; graphics, arts-and-crafts tools, media centers, physical education equipment; and myriad other technological means can help learning. Electronic and digital equipment help teachers organize, conduct, assess, and record instruction.

Commercialism, Salesmanship, and Educational Technology

Most of the effort for significant expansion of technology in schools involves computers and support materials. Presumably, computers improve learning, lower costs, and improve teaching; corporate salesmanship and lobbying are key ingredients. "Revolutionizing" teaching by replacing solid teaching practices for the sake of business interests is not a compelling argument. Computers and other advanced technologies, of course, can be valuable additions to a teacher's toolkit and teachers need to be prepared to find good ways to use them in education.

Education is well suited to technologies that can improve schooling; education is also the most suitable location to raise questions and challenge the use and value of various technologies. But education is also a very large budget item for states and communities, a major target for commercial enterprise. In the United States and Europe, the total educational technology expense is over $100 billion (Editorial Board, 2019). The amount spent per student in the United States ranges from about $140 to $500, showing another digital gap in resources along with raising some serious questions about school spending on technology; in addition, a high proportion of technological school purchases go unused (Christensen, 2019; Vega and Robb, 2019).

The Federal Trade Commission (FTC) now requires teachers who are "ambassadors" for educational technology companies and receive anything in return to disclose that relationship when they endorse those products (*EdWeek*, 2019). It is a big business with a high profit margin. More importantly, the educational return on investment may not be adequate.

The strong commercial interest in having schools adopt a technology-heavy and noncritical school program is evident in corporate support for technology in schools. Problems occur in the corporatization of schooling, technology provides an easy means to make corporations more influential in education by control over machines, software, faculty, and intellectual property.

Corporate control is not likely to lead to critical education. Who benefits? Those already in power gain more, and the rest lose more. More than $5 billion per year is spent for computer technology in classrooms, providing great benefits to tech companies (Landry, 2002; Gabriel 2011). Expensive equipment, programs, and maintenance divert scarce resources from other educational activities. Corporate intrusions into education are abundant, but few have been so successful and so generally supported by government and school officials as the effort to computerize all schools (Bromley and Apple, 1998; Giroux, 2001; Werry, 2002; Oppenheimer, 2003; Leistyna, 2008; Gabriel, 2011). Sofia (2002) states, "The computer is an educational technology that did not arise within the classroom, but was imported into it as a result of vigorous corporate and government efforts to commercialize and eventually domesticate a tool initially developed within military-industrial complexes" (p. 29).

For mass public education, technology often is touted as a way to save money and standardize education. School, of course, is more than a set of taped lectures, an interesting keyboard or mouse activity, some "interactive" homework, and answering questions on a keypad. Technological replacement of schools will be shown, in the long run, to be neither efficient nor effective (Gabriel, 2011). Where students live vast distances from schools, as in Australia's outback or sparsely settled parts of the United States, there is a good reason to provide the highest-quality television and computer courses that can be arranged. Similarly, continuing education for professionals and preliminary classes for students who just want to try out a subject for interest may be good places for electronic schooling. At the precollegiate or collegiate level, well-done distance education takes more resources and money—not less. Large volume and cheaper distance learning may mean that only the rich can afford real schools and real teacher contact; the rest get devices and learning on screens.

Do Computers Improve Learning?

In terms of academic learning, there is little evidence that computers add much. Several current and older studies of the use of technology in education conclude the following: no consistent evidence of increased achievement (Cuban, 2001); "performance in math and reading had suffered significantly" among 175,000 students in 31 nations (MacDonald, 2004); "after hundreds of exhaustive studies, there remains no conclusive proof that technology in the classroom actually helps to teach students," and it hinders learning in some cases (Landry, 2002); a review of studies finds "no discernible effects" in student achievement outcomes for software aimed at teaching math and reading (Gabriel and Richtel, 2011); and an analysis of massive data shows lackluster results in academic achievement for online study (Glass and Welner, 2011). According to McKenzie (2007, 2019), studies that show positive results should be examined carefully, as they are often very short-term and based on limited test data only. There are many others and all studies should be analyzed to see if they are narrowly structured or controlled to show computer advantages without adequate study of comparable noncomputer settings (Wenglinsky, 1998; Cordes and Miller, 2000; Oppenheimer, 2003; Alliance for Childhood, 2004; McKenzie, 2007; Tamin, 2011; Hiltzik, 2012).

Computer technology conveys information to students very quickly, develops skills of machine and program usage, and has excellent visual and auditory features. But it does not encourage questioning or critical examination—certainly not examination of the technology itself. Papert (1993) has reservations about noncritical true believers: "Across the world children have entered a passionate and enduring love affair with the computer. . . . In many cases their zeal has such force that it brings to mind the word *addiction* to the minds of concerned parents" (p. ix). Significant expansion of computers in schools often is accompanied by a blind and mistaken belief in technology and collateral decline in support for the academic work of schools (Cuban, 2011).

Broad integrative learning, beyond acquiring bits of information, can be even less satisfying via computer. Learning involves much more than test-item information easily presented in workbook form. Visuals, narratives, and data may be impressive, but most students find that computer-based education does not expect them to think outside that box. A curriculum based on computers suffers a decline in time for critical thinking, humanities, arts, health, and exercise. An inclination to get the quickest, most efficient right answer that students know is hidden in the program can easily translate into a distaste for intellectual work that requires struggle or time, that uses resources outside the classroom, and that may have no right answer. They lose the richer context of human issues that are not mathematically computable.

School computer use is usually individual and lacks social involvement or ethical considerations (Healy, 1998; Alliance for Childhood, 2004). So-called interactive educational "personal" programs are actually highly programmed and provide a limited set of responses to predictable keyboard or mouse entries, with an air of unreality and superficiality. Imagine learning to play tennis using only the computer and not going outdoors to swing a racket. The same occurs in learning chemistry, biology, physics, and many more subjects by computer without labs or the outdoors for real experience. Learning by machine does not provide the quality of educational experience that a classroom or lab of live students offers in the various questions and interchanges and experiments.

Richtel (2011) notes the irony of a Waldorf School in Silicon Valley, where many high-tech executives and experts send their own children, that has not allowed computers and has no tech-based classrooms. Three-fourths of the students have parents with high-tech connections. And the school also discourages computer and high-tech use at home. Waldorf stresses learning through participatory, creative activities and physical action, claiming computers "inhibit creative thinking, movement and human interaction, and attention spans." Memorization and simplistic, often useless information is anti-intellectualism dressed up in technology and corporate language (Siegel, 2008).

Do Computers Improve Teaching?

A significant problem resulting from the overselling of technology in schools is the deprofessionalization of teachers and a decline in respect for teachers, teaching skill, and the value of academic/professional judgment. This problem is exacerbated by the too easy manipulation of students, teachers, and curriculum as a result of corporate pressures and institutional control of electronic educational sources and testing. If the operation of a machine is all there is to good education, where does that leave teachers at any level? Academic knowledge, teaching experience, instructional theory, and practice will come to mean less, leading to no need for credentialed teachers, no respect for the position, no tenure to protect academic freedom, and no security (Bromley and Apple, 1998; Oppenheimer, 2003).

Erosion of intellectual freedom for teachers and students is a very serious possibility, denying the open pursuit of knowledge because technology substitutes sterilized and canned material that is easily controlled and censorable. A related problem is the question of intellectual property: who has economic and editorial rights to material produced for technology, and who can change it? With increasing technological incursions into schools, administrators are more likely to become like corporate vendors, and teachers will be less likely to make academic decisions about their courses or their students. Teachers will lose instructional freedom and responsibilities for actual education but are likely to remain accountable for any test results and school failures.

There is another, perhaps more important toll on the teaching profession and on educational policy when public perception of good schools focuses more on technology than learning. Even some supporters of technology in education agree that the focus should not be on technology; as McKenzie (2001) notes, "It is wrong-minded and shortsighted to make technology, networking, and connectivity the goal" (p. i). This problem is illustrated by the current craze to get more computers into schools, without providing the well-prepared teachers, effective educational programs, and critical literacy elements that McKenzie and others advocate (Leistyna, 2008; McKenzie, 2019).

Technology and the Schools: The Digital Divide

Uncritical expansion of computer technology in schools spawns social and personal problems. One widely held assumption is that more computers means more democratic technological development. The digital divide, however, has not diminished. It separates high-income people from low, those living in urban or suburban locations from the rural, the young from the old, and the otherwise privileged from those who are not. It is sometimes hidden by the veneer of corporate advertising that implies that their products are necessary for all people for a better life. Bill Gates predicted in 1995 that the Internet would assist rural people to stay in small communities since they would have equal advantage with city dwellers in terms of their access; his foundation provided substantial support to wire and equip many small-town libraries. But evidence suggests new computers may aid the exodus from rural areas as people go online to find jobs in other locations (Egan, 2002).

Schools that can afford it add more technology and frills, and those that can't are separated even further. Another divide in the technological workforce also has an educational component. Most jobs created by technology actually will be low-paid and boring work in such areas as maintenance; fewer jobs will occur in well-paid high-tech positions, and these will require more advanced education. Should schools be responsible for training workers for low-paid, boring corporate jobs and not provide all students with critical thinking skills challenging that system? Education should work to provide equity by enhancing equality of opportunity. The digital divide seems to move schools in the opposite direction. It separates races and classes even more—producing a new class of poor, the technologically illiterate, with increased disparity between managers and workers.

Personal and Social Costs of Excessive Reliance on Technology

Schools are social institutions; they cannot ignore how technologies influence personal and social life. A dependence on technology contains the seeds of narcissism, with individuals losing connections to others' political, economic, social, and personal problems. Social responsibility is ignored in the rush for self-satisfaction. Technology can separate people and soften the reality of human suffering (Turkle, 2011).

Technologies can threaten society and human decency and contain threats to individual freedoms and privacy. Secret surveillance and invisible recording of personal information, buying habits, interests, and contacts with others occur. This capacity is more than just annoying; it abrogates basic rights to personal privacy and against illegal search and places an unnecessary caution on your exercise of rights to free speech, assembly, and association. Technology is used to steal your personal identity, alter your records, confound your credit, and cause you substantial misery and trouble. Further, censorship by electronic screening of material restricts your access to ideas. Whether by commercial, criminal, or governmental action, technological intervention has multiple implications for personal and, thus, school life (Wu, 2010).

In addition to the costs of technology in personal loss of independence, ingenuity, and intellectual stimulation, there are various social costs. When individualism overcomes social responsibility, we lose the contributions many people could have made to improve society. Much new technology fragments people's lives and adds to isolation and alienation. We expect increased speed in everyday life, have lost the patience and focused attention that thoughtful reflection or social interaction require, and have seen dissolution of the family and home setting for maintaining social values and attitudes. Social bonds have deteriorated, and there are increases in violent and technology-based crime, technologically produced drug abuse, and noninvolvement in community affairs. Technology saps the core of culture, it is too great a loss for the limited benefits we receive (Postman, 1992).

Technology has been used to monitor and help clean the environment, but has also created significant threats to the environment and ecosystem, including ozone depletion, various pollutions, and health hazards. Other threats include the possibility of inappropriate cloning and inadequate ethics for technological medical research;

insufficient regulation of gene research; racist, sexist, or humanly degrading content on the Internet; and military development of laser, nuclear, or biological weapons (Talbott, 2008). Other social costs from technology include the multiple health problems associated with it and related costs in life quality, time, energy, and money. For the users of computers and other electronic equipment, we now have unusual muscle and eyestrain problems, headaches, fatigue, crippling hand and arm pain, and the potential of other long-term problems from radiation. Workers in high-tech manufacturing are subject to safety problems from chemical and radiological materials along with many ailments related to that work. In many industries, workers must have so-called protective gear—but the longer-term quality and extent of protection need further study. Gleick (1999) points out, "Modern times have brought certain maladies that might be thought of as diseases of technology: radiation poisoning (Marie Curie's truest legacy); carpal tunnel syndrome (descendant of Scrivener's palsy)" (p. 102). Beyond the examples suggested, there are many other personal and social costs to technology; schools offer the opportunity to consider them in critical examination of technology in society.

The Need for Critical Technological Education

We need *critical* technological education, where serious questions are raised about technologies and their multiple impacts on individuals, society, and schools. The addition of the word *critical* to the idea of technological education changes the concept in basic ways. This phrase connotes an analysis of technology that does not varnish over or ignore important negative implications. Critical technological education means a full examination of issues involving the use and value of technology in schools as well as those issues that arise from technology in the larger society. It expects students to study claims and evidence provided by advocates and opponents and apply supportable criteria derived from civilizing individual and social values (Leistyna, 2008).

A good life is far more than the ability to read manuals and operate new devices, and technological education is more than just recreational or vocational training to use machines. Education is rich and intellectually rewarding, entailing the posing of questions, examination of issues, and search for adequate evidence (Dewey, 1933). These are elements of critical thinking, needed in the study of technology in society and school. Technological issues, both social and educational, are suited to examination in classes because schools exist to help students comprehend and deal with aspects of their environment, and technology has certainly become a major player in all our environments.

This position does not oppose all technologies; it is against the overselling of certain technologies with little critical examination. It also is against development of a school curriculum or school system where technology supplants teachers as a main ingredient. The headlong and uncritical plunge into electronic technology over the past decades has had mixed results. The deprofessionalizing of teachers and runaway computer budgets are examples in schools (Bromley and Apple, 1998; McKenzie, 2019). Has the wonder of technology caused our enchantment with it, or is it just extraordinarily good salesmanship?

Schools should be the best places for students to evaluate these kinds of questions without commercial or ideological interference or influence. The mass media, corporations, and those with strong linkages to technological development cannot be expected to provide both sides of this argument fairly; forces related to the marketplace and ideology limit media and business presentations of negative ideas about the technology they like or in which they have huge investments. The current and future social impact of technology is directly related to the kind of instruction and questioning that goes on in technological education.

Good educators want good schools with students evaluating important ideas. Such teachers also want students to learn, use, and improve their critical thinking. Whether working with students on the study of technology or using technologies in the classroom to explore another topic, responsible teachers recognize the importance of critical thinking on significant ideas and issues. Where technological innovation serves those ends in classrooms, teachers will pursue technologies with relish. But educators realize that educational technologies are not a panacea and do not exist in a social vacuum. There are large-scale issues beyond the classroom use of machines, such as the use, value, and impact of technologies in society. Critical examination of the social context of technological innovation and the instructional use of technologies are both topics of importance to educators.

We should subject technologies to critical examination in terms of education and society. The essential question is this: does a new technology improve or diminish the quality of life for most people? If it does, then we need to ask whether the technology is worth its various costs. Answering those questions involves dealing with many other questions about technology, history, social values, and making choices. We cannot expect students to use and improve their critical thinking if teachers don't think critically themselves about such issues as the role and impact of technologies.

The overpromise and underachievement of computer technology in schools represents a major concern for education, one that goes far beyond financing problems. It includes questions about the nature and quality of learning that results, unfortunate alterations in the culture of schools that deprofessionalize teachers and restrict intellectual freedom, and the corporatization of schools and increases in the digital divide. Critical technological education also provides for full study of multiple personal and social costs of technology.

FOR DISCUSSION

1. *Dialogue Ideas:* Essays in this chapter propose different projections about the possible social and educational consequences of a school curriculum weighted toward technology. Select three examples of current technology in schools and discuss your views of them in terms of: How likely are any of them to occur? Are the potential consequences mostly positive or negative? On what grounds do you determine that they are positive or negative? Do you have some suggestions for enhancing the positives and diminishing negatives?

2. *Dialectic Analysis:* A common definition of technology is science applied to a specific purpose. W. Brian Arthur (2009) notes that it not only serves human purposes

but can also direct and control our lives—including, presumably, addictive tendencies and controlling our behaviors. That tension, a servant or a master, gives pause to many who criticize technology in schools.

Prepare a reasoned position for each side—technology as human directed and technology as directing humans. Using one as a thesis and the other as antithesis, construct a possible synthesis of these positions.

3. Technology, some argue, is neutral—it simply exists. The real question revolves around how the technology is used. Draft a short statement that addresses these questions:

   a. How should schools organize their use of technology?

   b. What are the best criteria for judging the most educational use of technology?

   c. Should technological innovators be free to develop any technology?

   d. Should technology advertising be regulated to prohibit misleading information?

   e. Should education about technology be changed? How?

   Draft a short statement of opposite positions based on the idea that technology is not neutral.

4. Is there a digital divide? What evidence can you find that supports your contention? How do you define it?

   If you find a divide, consider these questions:

   a. What are its characteristics—those identifying elements like social class, race, gender, and age?

   b. What would you propose doing about a divide?

   If you do not find a digital divide, consider these questions:

   c. What criteria and what resources did you use to get evidence?

   d. What policies would you propose to prevent a divide?

5. What would you think if a local school offered programs for students to do the following?

   • Stay away from school for all courses and all years, with school-provided technology.

   • Have an implant to permit instant information transfer to the brain.

   • Get full school credit for Internet game scores.

   • Graduate only if they invent one important technological innovation.

   Using your sense of the development of technological education over the next 30 to 50 years, present your view of a school of the future. Include physical features and curriculum.

REFERENCES

Allenby, B. R., and Sarewitz, D. (2011). "The Accelerating Techno-Human Future." *The Futurist* 45(5).

Alliance for Childhood (2004). *Tech Tonic: Toward a New Literacy of Technology.* College Park, MD: Alliance for Childhood.

Anderson, J., and Rainie, L. (2020, February 21). Many Tech Experts Say Digital Disruptions Will Hurt Democracy. Pew Research Center.

Anderson, M., and Jiang, J. (2018, May 31). Teens, Social Media and Technology, 2018. Pew Research Center.

Angeli, C. (2008). "Distributed Cognition." *Journal of Research on Technology in Education* 40(3):271–297.

Arthur, W. B. (2009). *The Nature of Technology*. New York: Free Press.

Baker, F. W. (2012). Media Literacy in the K–12 Classroom. International Society for Technology in Education (iste.org).

Branch, R. M., Lee, H., and Tseng, S. S., eds. (2019). *Educational Media and Technology Yearbook* (Vol. 42). New York: Springer.

Braun, L. W. (2007). *Teens, Technology, and Literacy*. Westport, CT: Libraries Unlimited.

Bridle, J. (2018). *New Dark Age*. London: Verso.

Brockman, J. (2010). *Future Minds*. Boston: Nicholas Brealey.

Bromley, H., and Apple, M., eds. (1998). *Education / Technology / Power: Computing as a Social Practice*. Albany: State University of New York Press.

Calderon, V. J., and Carlson, M. (2019, September 12). Educators Agree on the Value of Ed Tech. Gallup (gallup.com).

Christensen, D. (2019, May 28). What is the Real Cost of Technology in Education? Classcraft (classcraft.com).

Collins, A., and Halverson, R. (2018). *Rethinking Education in the Age of Technology*. New York: Teachers College Press.

Cordes, C., and Miller, E. (2000). *Fool's Gold: A Critical Look at Computers in Childhood*. College Park, MD: Alliance for Childhood.

Cuban, L. (2001). *Oversold and Underused: Computers in the Classroom*. Cambridge, MA: Harvard University Press.

———— (2011). "Critique of Celebratory Accounts of School Digital Technology." Book review of Neil Selwyn, *Schools and Schooling in the Digital Age*. *Educational Technology* 51(4):49–51.

Dewey, J. (1933). *How We Think*. Lexington, MA: D. C. Heath.

Editorial Board (2019, September 25). Classroom Technology Does Not Make the Grade. Bloomberg Opinion (bloomberg.com/opinion/articles/2019-09-25/classroom-computers-little-benefit-seen-in-test-scores-for-cost).

Educause (2020). *2020 Horizon Report, Teaching and Learning Edition*. Louisville, CO: Educause.

Edutopia (2008, March 16). Why Integrate Technology into the Curriculum? (edutopia.org).

———— (2011). Digital Citizenship and Cyber-Bullying (edutopia.org).

———— (2019). There's a Cell Phone in Your Student's Head (edutopia.org).

EdWeek (2019, November 13). "FTC: Ed-Tech 'Ambassadors' Must Follow Social Media Guidelines" (educationweek.com).

Egan, T. (2002, November 6). "Bill Gates Views What He's Sown in Libraries." *New York Times.*

Englander, E. K. (2020). *25 Myths about Bullying and Cyberbullying*. Hoboken NJ: Wiley-Blackwell.

Fang, K. (2019, April 1). "Will Technology Ever Replace Teachers?" *Forbes.*

Fingal, J. (2020, February 7). Digital Citizenship. International Society for Technology in Education (iste.org).

Fox, N. (2004). *Against the Machine*. Washington, DC: Island Press.

Friedman, T. (2005, May 13). "Americans Are Falling Further Behind." *New York Times.*

Gabriel, T. (2011, April 5). "More Pupils Are Learning Online, Fueling Debate on Quality." *New York Times.*

Gabriel, T., and Richtel, M. (2011, October 9). "Inflating the Report Card." *New York Times*, A1.

Gagne, T. (2020). *Online Shaming and Bullying*. San Diego, CA: ReferencePoint Press.

Gerstein, D. M. (2019). *The Story of Technology*. Amherst, NY: Prometheus Books.

Giroux, H. A. (2001). *Stealing Innocence: Corporate Culture's War on Children.* New York: St. Martin's Press.

Giumetti, G. W., and Kowalski, R. W., eds. (2019). *Cyberbullying in Schools, Workplaces, and Romantic Relationships.* New York: Routledge.

Glass, G. V., and Welner, K. G. (2011, October). *Online K–12 Schooling in the U.S.* National Education Policy Center, University of Colorado Boulder.

Gleick, J. (1999). *Faster: The Acceleration of Just about Everything.* New York: Pantheon.

Goldberg, J. (2020, January/February). "Millennials and Post-Millennials—Dawning of a New Age?" *Skeptical Inquirer* 44(1).

Gonzalez, E. (2019, October 9). The Value of Digital Tools in Science Classes. Edutopia (edutopia.org).

Healy, J. M. (1998). *Failure to Connect: How Computers Affect Our Children's Minds—for Better and Worse.* New York: Simon and Schuster.

Hiltzik, M. (2012, February 4). "Who Really Benefits from Putting High-Tech Gadgets in Classrooms?" *Los Angeles Times.*

Hockfield, S. (2019). *The Age of Living Machines.* New York: W.W. Norton.

International Society for Technology in Education (2008). *Transforming Classroom Practice.* Washington, DC: ISTE.

——— (2019). *National Educational Technology Standards for Teachers.* Washington, DC: ISTE.

Jacobs, T. (2019, June 6). "Computers in the Classroom May Do More Harm Than Good—If They Are Overused." *Pacific Standard.*

Jaeger, P. R., Gorham, U., and Taylor, N. G. (2019). Human Rights and Information Ethics. In J. T. F. Burgess and E. J. M. Knox, eds., *Foundations of Information Ethics.* Chicago: Neal-Schuman.

Johnson, J., and Barker, L. T. (2002). *Assessing the Impact of Technology in Teaching and Learning.* Ann Arbor: Institute for Social Research, University of Michigan.

Jones, E. (2019). *What is Cyberbullying?* New York: Kidhaven.

King, K. P. (2011). "Teaching in an Age of Transformation." *Educational Technology* 51(2):4–10.

Landry, J. (2002). "Is Our Children Learning?" *Red Herring* 116:37–41.

Lee, L. (2000). *Bad Predictions.* Rochester, MI: Elsewhere Press.

——— (2019, September 24). Using Simple Tech Solutions to Drive Mastery-Based Learning. Edutopia (edutopia.org).

Leistyna, P. (2008, Spring). "Introduction: Teaching about and with Alternative Media." *Radical Teacher* 81:3–6.

Light, J. (2001). "Rethinking the Digital Divide." *Harvard Educational Review* 71(4):709–733.

Livingston, P. (2008, May 22). "E-Learning Gets Real." *Technology Learning.*

Lynch, M. (2018, March 1). Why Artificial Intelligence Will Never Replace Teachers. The Tech Edvocate (thetechedvocate.org).

MacDonald, G. J. (2004, December 6). "Contrarian Finding: Computers Are a Drag on Learning." *Christian Science Monitor.*

McKenzie, J. (2001). *Planning Good Change with Technology and Literacy.* Bellingham, WA: FNO Press.

——— (2007). "Digital Nativism, Digital Delusions and Digital Depravation." *From Now On* 17(2).

——— (2019). *Technology for the Sake of Technology.* Boulder, CO: FNO Press.

McWilliams, J. (2019, April 3). "How Should Teachers Deal with Distracting Technology in the Classroom?" *Pacific Standard.*

Metzl, J. (2019). *Hacking Darwin.* Naperville, IL: Sourcebooks.

MIT News (2019, February 26). What 126 Studies Say about Education Technology (news.mit.edu).

Monke, L. (2001). *Breaking Down Digital Walls: Learning to Teach in a Post-Modern World.* Albany: State University of New York Press.

Morozov, E. (2011). *The Net Delusion.* New York: Public Affairs Press.

National Center for Education Statistics (2019, April). Indicators of School Crime and Safety. Indicator 10: Bullying at School and Electronic Bullying (nces.ed.gov/programs/crimeindicators/ind_10.asp).

Neiderman, E., and Zaza, C. (2019, Spring). "A Mixed Blessing." *The Canadian Journal for the Scholarship of Teaching and Learning* 10(1).

Novak, M. (2014, January 14). 15 Technologies That Were Supposed to Change Education Forever. Gizmodo (paleofuture.gizmodo.com).

Oblinger, D. G., and Oblinger, J. L., eds. (2005). *Educating the Net Generation.* Washington, DC: Educause.

Oppenheimer, T. (2003). *The Flickering Mind: The False Promise of Technology in the Classroom and How Learning Can Be Saved.* New York: Random House.

Paganelli, A. (2019). *Power Up Your Read-Alouds.* Santa Barbara, CA: Libraries Unlimited.

Papert, S. (1993). *The Children's Machine: Rethinking School in the Age of the Computer.* New York: Basic Books.

——— (2002). Technology in Schools: To Support the System or Render It Obsolete. Milken Family Foundation (mff.org/edtech).

Pew Research Center (2009). Internet and American Life Project. Washington, DC: Pew Research Center.

Pflaum, W. D. (2004). *The Technology Fix.* Washington, DC: Association for Supervision and Curriculum Development.

Postman, N. (1992). *Technopoly: The Surrender of Culture to Technology.* New York: Knopf.

Prensky, M. (2008a, February). "The True Twenty-First Century Literacy is Programming." *Edutopia.*

——— (2008b, June). "Young Minds, Fast Times." *Edutopia.*

Rainie, L. (2006, March 23). Life Online. Annual Conference of the Public Library Association, Boston, MA.

Reeves, T. C. (1998, February 12). The Impact of Media and Technology in Schools. A Research Report Prepared for the Bertelsmann Foundation (athensacademy.org).

Reigeluth, C. M. (2011). "An Instructional Theory for the Post-Industrial Age." *Educational Technology* 51(5):25–29.

Richtel, M. (2011, October 23). "A Silicon Valley School That Doesn't Compute." *New York Times*, A1.

Ringstaff, C., and Kelly, L. (2002). *The Learning Return on Our Educational Technology Investment: A Review of Findings from Research.* San Francisco: Regional Technology in Education Consortium, WestEd.

Rogers-Whitehead, C. (2020, February 10). How to Empower—Not Scare!—Parents about Technology. International Society for Technology in Education.

Rose, L., Gallup, A., Dugger, W., and Starkweather, K. (2004). *The Second Installment of the ITEA/Gallup Poll and What it Reveals as to How Americans Think about Technology.* Reston, VA: International Technology and Engineering Educators Association.

Rosen, L. D. (2012). *iDisorder.* New York: Palgrave Macmillan.

Rotherham, A. J. (2006, April 7). "Virtual Schools, Real Innovation." *New York Times.*

Salpeter, J. (2008, May 22). "Make Students Info Literate." *Technology and Learning.*

Schorr, J., and McGriff, D. (2011). "Blended Face-to-Face and Online Learning." *Education Next* 11(3):11–17.

Seldon, A., and Abidoye, O. (2018). *The Fourth Education Revolution.* Buckingham, UK, Buckingham University Press.

Siegel, L. (2008). *Against the Machine: Being Human in the Age of the Electronic Mob*. New York: Spiegel and Grau.

Sofia, Z. (2002). The Mythic Machine. In H. Bromley and M. Apple, eds., *Education/Technology/Power*. Albany: State University of New York Press.

Spiro, R. J. (2006, January/February). "The New Gutenberg Revolution." *Educational Technology*, 3–5.

Stiglitz, J. E. (2019*). People, Power, and Profits*. New York: W.W. Norton.

StopBullying.gov (2020). What is Cyberbullying; Cyberbullying Tactics (StopBullying.gov).

Strawn, C. (2011). "Research Windows: What Does the Research Say?" *Learning and Leading* 39(2).

Talbott, S. (2008). *Beyond Biotechnology: The Barren Promise of Genetic Engineering*. Lexington: University Press of Kentucky.

Tamin, R. M. (2011). "What 40 Years of Research Says about the Impact of Technology on Learning." *Review of Educational Research* 81:4–28.

Technology Review (2011). "The Next Generation of Technology" 114(5).

Turkle, S. (2011). *Alone Together: Why We Expect More from Technology and Less from Each Other*. New York: Basic Books.

Tyack, D., and Cuban, L. (2000). Teaching by Machine. In *Jossey-Bass Reader on Technology and Learning*. San Francisco: Jossey-Bass.

U.S. Department of Education (2004, January 7). *Toward a New Golden Age in American Education*. National Education Technology Plan 2004. Washington, DC: U.S. Department of Education, Office of Educational Technology.

——— (2017, January). *Reimagining the Role of Technology in Education: 2017 National Education Technology Plan Update*. Washington, DC: U.S. Department of Education, Office of Educational Technology.

——— (2019, January). Nine Ways Technology Can Boost STEM Learning. Homeroom, Blog of the U.S. Department of Education (blog.ed.gov).

——— (2020, February 22). 2020 National Educational Technology Plan. Office of Educational Technology (tech.ed.gov).

Vega, V., and Robb, M. B. (2019, November). *The Common Sense Census: Inside the 21st-Century Classroom*. San Francisco: Common Sense Media.

Villinger, S. (2012). Get the Most Out of School PCs. Education World (educationworld.com).

von Radowitz, J. (2017, September 11). "Intelligent Machines Will Replace Teachers within 10 Years, Leading Public School Headteacher Predicts." *The Independent*.

Walsh, T. (2018). *Machines That Think*. Buffalo: Prometheus Books.

Watson, R. (2010). *Future Minds*. Boston: Nicholas Brealey.

Wenglinsky, H. (1998). *Does It Compute?* Princeton, NJ: Educational Testing Service.

Werry, C. (2002, Spring). "The Rhetoric of Commercial Online Education." *Radical Teacher* 63.

Windschitl, M., and Sahl, K. (2002). "Tracing Teachers' Use of Technology in a Laptop Computer School." *American Educational Research Journal* 39(1):165–205.

Wu, T. (2010). *The Master Switch*. New York: Alfred A. Knopf.

Zuboff, S. (2019). *The Age of Surveillance Capitalism*. New York: Hachette Book Group.

PART THREE

The School Community
Individuals and Environments

About Part Three: Chapters in this section illustrate dimensions of the school as a community of individuals and considers the settings in which schools operate. Included are issues related to:

- Chapter 12: school discipline
- Chapter 13: bullying in person and by technology
- Chapter 14: treatment of students with special needs
- Chapter 15: teachers and their unions
- Chapter 16: intellectual freedom in schools and society

Public Education and Public Purpose

Chapter 1 argues that educational issues should be examined critically and against a social backdrop. Issues in education may seem to concern only building and classroom matters: curriculum, instruction, learning, and assessment. But the introduction to Part Two claims schools are strongly influenced by social values and politics and the influence flows in both directions. Schools affect society long term by values and knowledge passed on to children.

Schooling is part of the political, cultural, and economic environment of society. Schools and society form a mutually sustaining environment with obvious tensions. This is an ancient theme. About 2,400 years ago, Plato, the "first philosopher of education," simply described the link between society and schools as schools support the state (Warmington and Rouse, 1984). Mishra (2018) notes: "Education is the key to Plato's scheme of a just and virtuous society." Schools are only necessary to secure order, produce consenting citizens, and develop Plato's idea of virtue. Plato viewed democracy as dangerous and beyond the intellectual grasp of most citizens, claiming the masses will not rise above bodily pleasure; a small, select group could rise to the pleasure of honor, and only a few of those are capable of the truest pleasure, the intellect (Curren, 2000). So, farmers will farm, craftsmen build, and philosophers rule. His idea of a just society sacrifices individual liberty and intellectual freedom, advocating censorship to create a "positive" educational and social environment. That plan, he argues, protects a vulnerable class of young citizens from dangerous effects of "inappropriate" information that can harm the individual and undermine the state. Educa-

271

tion, thus, becomes "the most effective ideological apparatus in the hands of the ruling class" (Mishra, 2018).

Plato represents the authoritarian school tradition in which (1) schools serve the interests of rulers; (2) any idea that may harm the state must be excluded from schools; and (3) teachers are obedient servants of the state and have no inherent freedom in teaching. This environment determines relations among teachers, students, administrators, parents, and society. Rulers decide, teachers teach, students learn. Some people in current society might agree.

In contrast, contemporary ideals of democratic society include equal treatment of individuals, justice in relationships among individuals, and critical thinking by citizens (Dewey, 1944; Stitzlein, 2017; Holdo, 2018; Franco, 2019). Those ideals set high standards that are unmet when they are denied, ignored, obstructed, or confused. But those ideals remain as standards and serve to mark progress. The belief that a democracy is not ideal is not a good reason to toss it out without the framework of a better one for the whole society. Plato found no society that could meet his standards for rule by an individual, and no authoritarian government since has met his tests of justice, virtue, and wise rule.

A thoughtful democracy balances the interests of individuals and society. Schools are transactional social institutions in that process: the focus of public disputes and a logical place for thoughtful consideration of social problems. Schooling involves social expectations as well as considering how society can be improved. Unlike Plato, most people in democracies believe in the potential of education for enlightenment and progress. The ongoing struggle to improve democracy creates a more complex and dynamic system than Plato's. Education within that system is also more complex and dynamic, and controversial. Democracy is messy, but worthy.

Politics, Arguments, and Operating School Environments

Arguments over organization and operation of schools lie along a continuum of political thought. This is not to label all critics; it is to draw distinctions among competing narratives in society and education. In thinking about what teaching and education should be, consider the arguments of both the political left and right. Individuals don't fit neatly into each of these categories on each topic. And the specifics of definition for each label change; old-time liberal views may now be conservative, and vice-versa. But the labels are widely used in common discourse, and arise in schooling disputes. Where do you fit along the spectrum of opinion on each issue? What evidence is most convincing? Is there a synthesis?

The left, or liberal, end of the continuum is critical of school discipline policies that limit civil rights and liberties and that fall most heavily on minorities and the poor. Instead of developing punishments, they argue, schools should work to reduce the causes of disorder in schools, and society should address the external environments of discrimination, poverty, and despair. The right, or conservative, end of the continuum is more comfortable with the traditional exercise of authority in the schools, strict school disciplinary practices to maintain an orderly learning environment, and zero-tolerance policies. They think public education has a liberal bias, so they distrust changes that loosen academic rigor or student behavior.

Bullying and violence have become troubling problems facing American educators. Schools, once safe havens from the outside world, now must contend with acts of bullying and violence from within, and shootings, attacks, and cyberbullying from outside. Liberals and conservatives differ on what to do about these issues: liberals want ongoing educational efforts to address internal violence as a matter of personal and school community concern, anger management programs, counseling, and related actions. Conservatives tend toward strict discipline, suspension or expulsion, and similar means. There are differences on shootings also, with one side pushing gun control and the other side wanting armed guards and teachers.

Among educational debate topics is what schools should do with students who are hard to teach. A conservative view is that standards on traditional subject matter are important. Students who are not compliant or don't show ability or interest in learning should be separated. The other side counters that schools should be student-centered, with information and programs organized around their interests, along with encouraging teacher guidance. In 1902, John Dewey characterized the two "sects": (1) organize schools by academic topics that are divided into separate lessons with a set of facts; children proceed step-by-step to master those facts and (2) focus on the needs and interests of the individual child as the purpose of education (Loveless, 2001). Forms of those arguments continue into the twenty-first century.

Similar issues surround students with special needs or exceptional children. Separation for special education and gifted and talented programs is a traditional approach. Inclusion of as many of these students as possible into regular programs is more popular among liberals.

Teachers in School Environments

Teacher rights and responsibilities are another set of controversies. Liberals are sympathetic to teacher empowerment, positive views of unions and union involvement in school reform, and academic freedom for teachers and students. They think school reform failed largely because reformers have a heavy hand and ignore the role teachers should play as professionals with genuine authority in schools. Teachers should be able to assume a responsible role in shaping the purposes of schooling (Aronowitz and Giroux, 1985). One of the most important conditions for education is academic freedom for teachers and students. Critical thinking requires it; so does a free, democratic society.

Conservatives are more skeptical about teacher power, tenure, freedom, and unions, viewing unions as the protectors of incompetent teachers and as unwise meddlers in local school management. Conservatives want some academic freedom to counter what they see as liberal bias, but they want to limit many controversial topics that parents should control (Davis, 2019). They see teachers as employees who should be treated fairly and with respect, but that important educational decisions should be made by those with administrative responsibilities and oversight by parents and boards. The purpose of educational reform, from this view, is to restore and improve excellence in learning common subjects, with measurable results that can be used to evaluate schools and teachers (Hawkins, 2018).

Reforms Reformed

In the educational reform movements of the 1980s, schools were declared to be in crisis, and the nation at risk, because of the poor quality of teaching and learning. Teachers were weighed, measured, and evaluated as lacking quality shown by low student test scores. Teachers were not doing—or were not able to do—the job expected of them. The popular press printed stories of increases in school violence, crime, and the numbers of poorly educated students. Teacher unions were attacked for protecting weak teachers and opposing school reform. The implemented reforms of that time, and subsequent decades, were primarily on the conservative side of the spectrum— standards and testing. Teachers and unions were considered a major part of the problem and not suited to addressing it. One answer was to remove education from teacher hands; another was to privatize schools or set up charters that operated on public education funds or were for-profit.

Reforms failed and things began to change. Ayers et al. (2018) describe 18 myths that evolved then and later. Teachers, their unions, and public education were not the culprits described, and private, for-profit, and charter schools were not succeeding any better, while public school budgets suffered. Ravitch (2020) shows how the reform movement failed the nation. Increasing teacher burdens, more limited freedom, and lack of financial and civic support for public education are the more likely causes of school problems.

Currently, despite teacher strikes in many states, including Oklahoma, Kentucky, Colorado, Arizona, and North Carolina, the public supports teachers and continues to view teachers positively. A poll by Ipsos/*USA Today* found 72% of respondents said teachers made significant and positive impacts on their lives, that 61% would encourage their children to become teachers, and 75% approve of teachers in their local public school (Jackson and Newall, 2018). A *Phi Delta Kappan* poll showed 68% considered teacher salaries too low and 75% support teachers going on strike for better wages (Ferguson, 2018). The conditions of teaching are being revisited as objects of policy reform, and teachers' work has been reopened for debate (Ravitch, 2010; Brill, 2011). Salaries are increasing and work issues, like excessive testing, are under reconsideration.

The Parts and the Whole

Although this book is divided into three parts, the parts are related to each another in important ways. Part One focuses on the interests that schools should serve; the chapters ask you to consider the nature of justice and equity and what they mean for people interested in public education. If justice is about social fairness, with each getting what he or she is due, how is this related to the practical matters of education? The chapters in Part One ask you to examine competing perspectives about the interests schools should serve and ask you to decide which positions seem to you to be the more just and offer greater equity.

Part Two asks what knowledge schools should teach. Those on one side of the debate argue that American society in the twenty-first century has an agreed-on body of knowledge important for all citizens and that should be the core taught in all schools. On the other side is the claim that knowledge depends on perspective. For them, a single or absolute truth does not exist; what we call knowledge is the perspective or interpretations made by various groups and classes of people.

Part Three asks you to consider the human environment of schools, specifically the rights and roles of teachers and whether we can teach all students in public schools. These issues are likely to be related to your positions on the nature of knowledge, the content you believe schools should teach, and ultimately your views of justice and equity. We encourage well-reasoned dialogue and/or dialectic.

As we wrote in Chapter 1, if you like arguments, you'll love the study of education.

REFERENCES

Aronowitz, S., and Giroux, H. A. (1985). *Education under Siege: The Conservative, Liberal, and Radical Debate over Schooling.* South Hadley, MA: Bergin and Garvey.

Ayers, W., Laura, C., and Ayers, R. (2018). *"You Can't Fire the Bad Ones!": And 18 Other Myths about Teachers, Teachers' Unions, and Public Education.* Boston: Beacon Press.

Brill, S. (2011). *Class Warfare: Inside the Fight to Fix America's Schools.* New York: Simon and Schuster.

Curren, R. R. (2000). *Aristotle on the Necessity of Public Education.* Lanham, MD: Rowman & Littlefield.

Davis, M. W. (2019, July 9). "Academic Freedom's Nonsense." *The American Conservative.*

Dewey, J. (1944). *Democracy and Education.* New York: Macmillan.

Ferguson, M. (2018). "Washington View: Public Opinion on Teachers and Teaching." *Phi Delta Kappan* 100(1):40–41.

Franco, J. (2019, July 4). "Henry Giroux: Education Should Not Be Neutral." *Truthout.*

Hawkins, M. (2018, April 6). How Conservatives Would Reform Education. ThoughtCo (thoughtco.com).

Holdo, M. (2018). "The Virtuous, the Critical and the Trustworthy." *Scandinavian Political Studies* 41(1):1–21.

Jackson, C., and Newall, M. (2018, September 12). Most Americans Believe Teachers Have a Big Impact, But Are Paid Unfairly. Ipsos (ipsos.com).

Loveless, T., ed. (2001). *The Great Curriculum Debate: How Should We Teach Reading and Math?* Washington, DC: Brookings Institution.

Mishra, N. (2019, September 17). Plato's Theory of Education (countercurrents.org).

Ravitch, D. (2010). *The Death and Life of the Great American School System: How Testing and Choice Are Undermining Education.* New York: Basic Books.

——— (2020). *Slaying Goliath.* New York: Alfred Knopf.

Stitzlein, S. M. (2017). Education, Change, and Development. Oxford Research Encyclopedias. Education (oxfordre.com/education).

Warmington, E. H., and P. G. Rouse, eds. (1984). *Great Dialogues of Plato.* Trans. by W. H. D. Rouse. New York: Mentor.

Discipline and Justice

Zero Tolerance or Discretionary Practices

12

What concept of justice should govern school and classroom discipline?

Position 1: Zero Tolerance Policies Provide Justice in Public Schools

---

In the end, those kids who receive less than firm, fair, and consistent discipline end up being taught that there are no consequences for inappropriate—and sometimes illegal—behavior as long as it occurs within the grounds of those schools having administrators who are often more worried about keeping their disciplinary and criminal incident reports down for the sake of their own career advancement.

—National School Safety and Security Services (2019)

Why We Need Zero-Tolerance Policies

Every day in American public schools, students and adults face disrespect, disruption, and disorder. Countless minutes and hours that could be used for teaching and learning are lost in classrooms each year as teachers struggle to control unruly students. Zero-tolerance policies ensure that such students can and will be removed from the school setting. They protect the educational rights of the majority of students from being violated by undisciplined classmates. While these policies may at first appear harsh, in fact, they are an important tool for school personnel who seek to carry out their mandate to educate the next generation of responsible American citizens.

Discipline problems in public schools receive substantial attention when the rare but devastating acts of violence take place. However, once the media spotlight dims, the significant but less dramatic difficulties faced by teachers and students in thousands of schools continue. In the most recent government reports about school disruption, 5% of schools reported that verbal abuse of teachers happens at least once a week, and 10% reported that other acts of disrespect for teachers take place as often. In urban schools, the percentages are higher. Ten percent of students in those schools reported that verbal abuse took place once a week, and 15% said that they saw other acts of disrespect that often. Two percent of students nationally and 5% in urban schools reported that widespread disorder in their classrooms happened at least once a week as well (Musu et al., 2019).

Removing disruptive students from class has become a Herculean task in some school districts. For example, the discipline code for New York City schools is over 40 pages long. It includes a "range of possible disciplinary options" that leaves students and, to a large extent, teachers and administrators confused about what happens when a child or adolescent violates an element of the code (New York City Department of Education, 2019). The infractions are categorized in five levels, with a set of possible consequences for each level (see Table 12.1).

There are multiple possible consequences running the gamut from admonishment by school staff to expulsion. Each consequence can be meted out only by the appropriate bureaucrat. As the severity of the infraction increases, the authority to apply any consequence is reserved for personnel farther and farther removed from the student's action—and its impact on the learning environment. For example, a teacher can remove a student from her classroom for disruptive behavior, but only a regional superintendent can suspend a student for longer than five days. Principals who want to suspend a disruptive general education student must follow most of the following steps *every* time:

- Confirm that the teacher who originally removed the student from class has followed the applicable regulations.
- Determine that the student's behavior is so disruptive as to prevent the orderly operation of the school or represents a clear and present danger to the student, other students, or school personnel.
- Inform the student of the charges and evidence against him or her and listen to the student's side of the story.
- Inform the student that he or she is suspended and for how long.
- Notify the parent or guardian to come and pick up the child.
- Reach the parent within 24 hours with a written notice that describes the event and the time and place of the suspension conference (which must be held within five days of the written notice).
- Write a second letter to parents explaining that the student is going to have a suspension conference, describing the alternative instruction arrangements and the hearing process, notifying them that they may bring a translator, and listing the parents' and student's rights to question witnesses at the hearing, be accompanied by advisers (including a lawyer), be returned to school at the end of the suspension, and appeal the process.
- Hold the suspension conference at a time convenient for the parents.
- Reschedule the conference if the parents cancel.
- Prepare and maintain a record of the conference.

Table 12.1   Levels of Infractions and Range of Consequences—New York City Schools

Level	Infraction	Examples	Range of Consequences
1	Uncooperative/ non-compliant behavior	• Failing to wear uniform • Being late to school • Bringing cell phone to school • Making excessive noise • Wearing clothing that disrupts the learning process	Admonition by school staff to removal from classroom to principal suspension
2	Disorderly behavior	• Smoking and gambling • Using profane or obscene language • Lying to school personnel • Leaving school premises • Causing school bus disruptions	Admonition by school staff to removal from classroom to principal suspension
3	Disruptive behavior	• Being insubordinate or disobedient • Using hate speech • Fighting • Stealing • Tampering with school records • Committing vandalism • Entering a school building without authorization • Cheating, plagiarizing	Admonition by school staff to removal from classroom to 30-day regional superintendent's suspension
4	Aggressive or injurious/harmful behavior	• Engaging in intimidation, threats, extortion • Engaging in risky, intimidating, bullying, gang-related, or sexually harassing behavior • Possessing and using illegal drugs or alcohol • Possessing pepper spray or mace, imitation gun, or items that can be used as a weapon • Bullying and cyberbullying	Parent conference to one-year regional superintendent's suspension
5	Seriously dangerous or violent behavior	• Using force against school personnel or students • Arson • Selling drugs • Possessing or using weapons such as firearm, knives, billy clubs, brass knuckles, or explosives	Regional superintendent's suspension or expulsion

- Notify the parents within 10 days whether the suspension was ruled justifiable.
- Notify the parents within 10 days of additional recommendations.
- Respond to the regional superintendent in writing within five days if student appeals the suspension.
- Respond to the chancellor if the student appeals to him (Common Good, 2008).

Disciplining a student with disabilities is even more complicated and time consuming. In that case, a hearing must be held to determine whether the behavior is a "manifestation of the student's disabilities" and if the school somehow failed to provide "appropriate" (and usually very costly) services. If such a determination is made, the administrator's options become even more limited.

Regulations like these limit administrators' effectiveness in almost every school district in the United States. Given these cumbersome processes, many principals simply do not have the time to suspend disruptive students. Instead, the youngsters are returned to classrooms, and the cycle of disrespect and disorder continues. Without zero-tolerance policies that clearly spell out the inevitable consequences for inappropriate school behaviors and give administrators the freedom they need to apply them swiftly and consistently, students who wish to learn and teachers who want to teach are the ones being punished.

Emergence of Zero-Tolerance Policies

Zero tolerance in law enforcement and in school discipline "relies upon the motivation of deterrence to insure that people will make positive decisions. . . . Anti-social behavior, according to this approach, is not tolerated, and both major and minor infractions are punished severely" (Livermore, 2008). In the late 1980s, school districts across the country enacted disciplinary policies that promised "zero tolerance" for the possession of weapons in schools. At the federal level, the concept inspired the 1994 Gun-Free Schools Act (PL 103-227), which mandated a minimum one-year expulsion for a student who brought a gun (and later other weapons) to school. As an amendment to the Elementary and Secondary Education Act, it also required that school districts or states develop disciplinary policies that conformed to the law or else lose federal funding. Over time, the term zero tolerance has come to be applied not only to those infractions for which the consequence is expulsion or suspension. In practice as a school disciplinary method, the zero-tolerance method manifests itself in mandatory suspension and/or expulsion rules for incidences involving weapons, drugs, alcohol, and violence, without investigation into context or intent (Fissel et al., 2019).

States took advantage of the opportunity to create clear and definitive behavioral codes and initiated expulsion for possessing, selling, or using drugs or alcohol and for fighting and threatening students or staff (Skiba, 2000; Casella, 2003; Brownstein, 2010). By 2019, all 50 states and the District of Columbia mandate expulsion for the possession of a firearm on campus. The vast majority of states allow or require students to be suspended for defiant or disruptive behavior, assault or physical harm, and drug use or possession (Education Commission of the States, 2019).

Bullying and cyberbullying have been issues of particular concern in schools. Although there is no consensus on how to define bullying, most people agree that students are bullied when they are exposed repeatedly and over time to negative actions at the hands of one or more other students and when the harassed have difficulty defending themselves against their harassers. Bullying takes many forms, including overt bullying (verbal and physical attacks) and covert bullying (spreading rumors or purposely excluding someone from a group's activities). Bullying often varies by gender. Boys tend to be physically aggressive, while girls are "relationally aggressive," that is, intentionally harming others through gossip, spreading rumors, and excluding them from social contact (Leff et al., 2007). Students who identify as LGBTQ (lesbian, gay, bisexual, transgendered, or questioning) are at greater risk of all forms of bullying than straight-identified youth (Kosciw et al., 2018). Researchers also find that the presence of a few disruptive and aggressive children in class can result in increased aggressiveness among other children (Cornell and Mayer, 2010). Schools cannot afford to ignore bullying. Inaction sends a message to bullies that they have a "right to hurt people," and it tells victims and witnesses that they are "not worth protecting" (Olweus, 2008). That is why discipline policies that have zero tolerance for bullying are vital. As of 2019, all 50 states and the District of Columbia have enacted antibullying laws (U.S. Department of Health and Human Services, 2019).

There is a clear and present danger in America's schools; children live in a society where the media creates "heroes" who are disdainful of legitimate authority and pursue their own interests at the expense of other people's safety. For those characters, revenge and retaliation for real or imagined injuries are justified. When young people accept the values of such role models, there are several results. At worst, they put the lives of others at risk. In less severe cases, they jeopardize the learning process. Since education leads to individual success and provides society with competent citizens and leaders, anything that interferes with schooling puts all of us at risk. Zero-tolerance policies are efficient responses to this crisis, and, by definition, they are fair—applied in the same way to each student.

Zero Tolerance and Rational Choice

Zero-tolerance policies do allow schools to remove students who endanger the safety and well-being of others, but they are even more important as deterrents. They are designed to persuade young people not to engage in dangerous, disruptive, or disrespectful behaviors. Like other crime prevention policies, they are meant to "head off trouble" before it begins (Casella, 2003, p. 875). These policies are based on the theory of "rational choice," which is rooted in understandings of human behavior developed by classical economists, including Jeremy Bentham. These theorists assume that humans act in their own best interests based on calculations they make about the costs and benefits inherent in a particular choice. People always choose the action that they believe will maximize their pleasure—and minimize their pain. Since punishment will result in increased pain, the perception that swift, severe consequences are inevitable deter individuals from choosing to behave in ways that violate the common good. If people do not fear being caught or punished for an act, there is little to deter them from engaging in whatever behavior enhances their own pleasure.

Zero-tolerance policies provide exactly the kind of punishment that acts as a deterrent. Young people are impetuous and often ill equipped to judge the potential of their actions to cause serious harm to themselves or others. Indeed, if causing such injury interferes with the pursuit of their own pleasure, it may not even reach their "radar screen." They need the external, counterbalancing forces of swift, severe, and certain punishment to rein in their impulsiveness. Zero-tolerance policies provide that counterweight. When the policies are followed consistently, students calculate their choices differently. When they perceive school authorities as serious about discipline—and when they understand that no one is exempt from taking responsibility for their actions—they make choices that better contribute to the order of the schools and ultimately to their own education (Crews, 2019).

The key component of zero-tolerance policies is the consistency with which the consequences are applied. Young people recognize that the only rules that really count are ones that apply equally to everyone. Many students regularly experience this kind of discipline outside of school. Children who play Little League baseball, for example, recognize that batters who swing and miss the ball three times are "out"— no matter whether they are the best or the worst player on the team. The "punishment" is immediate, can have serious implications for the outcome of the game, and is absolute. Consequently, players practice batting for hours, learning how to make good choices about when to swing and when not to do so. Although parents and coaches may protest a strikeout call, they never bring lawyers into the argument and rarely hold up the game for very long. The rules are the rules, the umpire is the interpreter of the rules, and, if you want to play baseball, you abide by them.

Similar consistency in schools provides students with the "certainty" that they will not be able to escape punishment for inappropriate behavior. Giving administrators or school boards discretion in applying consequences dilutes the power of zero-tolerance policies. "Many educators tend to bend over backwards to give students more breaks than they will ever receive out on the streets of our society and in the workplace where we are supposed to be preparing them to function" (National School Safety and Security Services, 2019). Punishment is no longer "swift, severe, and certain" and, therefore, it loses its efficacy in controlling students' choices. Such an atmosphere does not encourage young people to set aside their own interests. The consistent application of consequences for actions that jeopardize the safety and freedom of others does.

Benefits of Zero-Tolerance Policies

Zero-tolerance school disciplinary policies are beneficial to students, teachers, parents, administrators, and taxpayers in several important ways. They are fair, position public schools to compete effectively with private schools, turn the job of law enforcement over to professionals, minimize time spent on discipline, and—most importantly—are effective at creating and maintaining orderly learning environments.

The orderliness of a school has a tremendous impact on whether parents allow their children to attend it. In the past, parents believed that they were faced with choices between public schools that tolerate disruptive or disrespectful behavior and private schools that remove students whose actions endangers others' ability to learn. Parental satisfaction with discipline in private schools is 40% higher than of parents in regular public schools. However, zero-tolerance policies provide administrators of public schools with that same freedom and reassure taxpayers that their money is being well-spent. The fact that disciplinary policies of charter schools more closely resemble those of private schools is a factor that parents cite as a reason for choosing those schools and for their high degree of satisfaction with them (McQuiggan and Megra, 2017).

For example, the no-excuses policy and rigorous discipline at KIPP (Knowledge Is Power Program) schools provides evidence of what zero tolerance for inappropriate behaviors can do for schools that work with children who face significant challenges. A decade ago an observer noted that at KIPP schools, the "broken windows" theory, on which zero-tolerance policies are based, meant that no sign of disorder and not one rule violation was ignored—whether it be a piece of trash on the floor, a uniform violation, or the use of foul language (Livermore, 2008). A review of codes of conduct present in several parent and student handbooks of KIPP schools indicate that each unacceptable action has a highly structured and swift consequence. Uncommon Schools, another group of highly successful charter schools, also have zero tolerance for small infractions and, in doing so, ensure that more serious behaviors do not happen. The Code of Conduct at one Uncommon School in New York is typical. It states,

> Without a firm and consistent discipline policy, none of what we envision for the School can happen. We cannot overemphasize the importance of providing a strong discipline policy that every student and family knows and understands. Students and families have a right to attend a safe and orderly school. Therefore, for every infraction, there will be a consequence. This is the basis of our student Code of Conduct. (Brownsville Collegiate Charter School, 2019)

Another benefit of zero-tolerance policies is the increased presence of law enforcement officers in school. The COPS in Schools program has awarded grants to provide funding for over 14,000 "school resource officers" (SROs)—trained, sworn-in law enforcement officers. Generally, when a student's behavior requires arrest, the on-site SRO is able to act quickly. Because they are known to students, their presence as the arresting officer minimizes any danger or disruption inherent to the process. The presence of SROs is also a strong deterrent to inappropriate or dangerous student behaviors. A great deal of their time is spent on preventive duties, such as one-on-one counseling with students and coordinating extracurricular activities. They teach crime prevention in classes, help students deal with the presence of gangs in schools and neighborhoods, and help administrators develop policies and procedures that increase school safety (NASRO, 2019).

Civil Rights Protections under Zero-Tolerance Policies

Critics of zero-tolerance policies are quick to point out applications of the policy that they believe are fundamentally unfair. They argue that zero-tolerance policies result in punishment of "good" kids who made one "mistake." They also suggest that students with disabilities forfeit some of their rights, as protected by the Individuals with Disabilities Act (IDEA). However, federal and state laws require adherence to IDEA in disciplinary actions and allow modifications for mandated expulsions on a case-by-case basis. In those rare instances where real miscarriages of justice have taken place, students have been successful in using the courts for recourse (*Seal v. Morgan*, 2000; *Butler v. Rio Rancho Public School Board*, 2002). Critics also argue that a disproportionate number of students of color are suspended or expelled under zero-tolerance policies. However, since the policies are designed to treat all students who misbehave without bias, the cause of the discrepancy between exclusionary discipline rates and racial or ethnic representation in a school community cannot be blamed on zero tolerance. In fact, such policies were designed to address earlier findings of discretionary applications of discipline policies that were skewed by the biases of those administering them (Billitteri, 2008).

The most rigorous recent social science tells us that adult bias has played a major causal role in disparities in disciplinary rates among students from different racial or ethnic backgrounds. In fact, differences in disciplinary consequences are largely the result of differences in student behavior. Those differences are driven, not by race or ethnicity, but by social and economic factors.

> For example, students who come from a single-parent household are twice as likely to get suspended—and black students are nearly three times as likely to come from single-parent households. Similarly, controlling for student poverty or school and community characteristics dramatically shrinks disciplinary disparities by race, suggesting that those factors also play a large role. (Eden, 2019)

It is true that students who follow instructions, focus on their schoolwork, and observe school rules are less likely to be suspended and more likely to succeed academically than students who do not. However, students who engage in the type of behaviors that result in suspension often are doing so *instead of* taking an active part in academics. Research that focused on the causes of students' choice to limit their involvement in their schoolwork might provide better alternatives than eliminating disciplinary policies that contribute to the safety and order of schools (Eden, 2019; Glenn, 2019).

Students themselves report that relaxing zero-tolerance disciplinary policies have negative effects.

> In New York City, a majority of students at half of schools serving a high share of minority students said they saw more fights and that their peers were less respectful. In Chicago, peer respect deteriorated and teachers reported more disruptive behavior. In St. Paul, the district attorney declared school violence a "public-health crisis." In Syracuse, the district attorney ordered a restoration of discipline after violence surged and a teacher was stabbed. In East Baton Rouge, 60% of teachers say they've experienced an increase in violence or threats, and 41% say they don't feel safe in school. (Hess and Eden, 2017)

Providing protection for students with regard to the application of the most serious consequences makes good sense. Insisting on complex and time-consuming procedures that ostensibly protect students' rights to "due process" for minor infractions with less serious consequences do not. When justice is invoked only for those members of society who fail to carry out their obligations and the rights of the majority of students to attend safe and orderly schools are violated, something is seriously wrong. When making "exceptions" becomes discipline policy, rules become meaningless to students. Then learning does not happen, and taxpayers' hard-earned money is wasted. Justice for all demands the better solution offered by zero-tolerance policies.

Position 2: Discretionary Discipline Policies
Promote Justice in Public Schools

It is imperative that schools reconsider the way that they discipline students, and look to holistically develop them into positive, contributing members of society, rather than simply seek to deter them from crime. If this becomes the school's priority, then the student can be set on a better path and a more positive learning environment can be created within the school.

—Shared Justice (2018)

The Social Context of Zero-Tolerance Policies

Fear and love do strange things to people. When Americans became frightened by drug-related violent crime in the late 1980s, severe and nonnegotiable penalties for illegal acts seemed to make sense. The passage of the Violent Crime Control and Law Enforcement Act of 1994 was evidence of these concerns. The bill made it possible to invoke the death penalty for large-scale drug trafficking, required new and stiffer penalties for gang members found guilty of violent or drug-related crimes, and imposed mandatory minimum terms for some crimes and life sentences without possibility of parole for those convicted of a third federal felony. By 1999, responding to the incentive of increased federal aid to fight crime and build prisons, 42 states had passed similar laws. Research about the effectiveness of the laws produced surprising results. In California, for example, researchers found that there was no deterrent effect from the law and that counties that used the law most often actually had no lesser reductions in violent crimes than did counties that used the law the least (Males, 2011). Some reports indicated that an unintended consequence of the laws was the increase of violence in the crimes being committed, especially by offenders with two strikes (Iyengar, 2008; Males, 2011). Mandatory sentencing policies—ostensibly "color blind"—exacerbated racial disparities in the justice system. For example, African Americans accounted for 34% of arrests for drug-related crimes, while they constituted only 12% of the population. Disproportionality in arrests led to disparity in sentencing, with the result that 65% of people in prison for drug-related crimes were African Americans or Latinos (Mauer, 2011). The laws took away the discretionary power of judges who were meant to weigh the circumstances of a case; the age, intellectual capabilities, and emotional state of the accused; and the impact of the crime when deciding guilt and imposing consequences (Simons, 2010). The negative consequences of these laws have inspired reformers to work toward changing them for more than 20 years. Their work culminated in the First Step Act (2018), supported by both Republicans and Democrats. It increased judges' discretion in determining sentences.

Also during the 1990s, mandatory sentencing policies were adopted in the disciplinary policies of almost all school districts in the United States. They found their way into schools for seemingly valid reasons. Although incidents of gun violence in schools were relatively small in number, they prompted a desire to protect young people. The original zero-tolerance policy, the Gun-Free Schools Act, was clear-cut—if you brought a *gun* to school, you were expelled. Over time, however, the concept was applied to more and more infractions that were less and less serious. Harsh discipline codes tied the hands of caring school professionals as surely as mandatory sentences limited options for judges and resulted in serious consequences for students who had no intention of causing harm to anyone. They have a disproportionate impact on students of color and those with disabilities. They are costly in terms of money and time, taking both away from more pressing educational issues. They provide little return in deterring disruptive, disorderly, or disrespectful behavior in schools.

In addition, they violate a basic democratic norm—that punishment should fit the crime.

Disproportionate Impact on Students of Color

Mandatory sentencing policies have resulted in racial disparities in the justice system. Similarly, the expansion of zero-tolerance policies in schools to behavior that does not threaten the safety of students or staff has resulted in significant racial disparities in the rates of punishments for disciplinary infractions. For the last 40 years, researchers have consistently shown that students of color are suspended at significantly higher rates than their white counterparts, disproportionate to their presence in the schools (Gregory et al., 2010; Smith and Harper, 2015; Hines-Datiri and Andrews, 2017; U.S. Department of Education, Office of Civil Rights, 2019). During the 2015–2016 school year, African American male students were 8% of the public school population and 25% of students who received out of school suspensions. White male students were 25% of the population and the same percentage of students receiving an out of school suspension. African American female students, also 8% of the population, were 14% of students who received out of school suspensions (Onyeka-Crawford et al., 2017; U.S. Department of Education, Office of Civil Rights, 2019).

Students of color receive harsher penalties than their white counterparts for the same offense (Fenning and Rose, 2007; Losen and Skiba, 2010; Smith and Harper, 2015). For example, the number of suspensions in New York City public schools was reduced by 50% between 2012 and 2017. However, racial disparities in the number and length of suspensions remained. African American students received relatively longer suspensions on average for 80% of the infractions that most often resulted in suspension. The average length of suspension was almost double that students in other ethnic groups received for bullying, reckless behavior, and altercation (Cardichon and Darling-Hammond, 2019). In many schools, African American and Latino students are suspended most often for being "disrespectful," "defiant," or "loud" (Walsh, 2008; Wun, 2016; Hines-Datiri and Andrews, 2017; Basile et al., 2019).

Teachers and administrators are as susceptible as the rest of the population to stereotypes about people of color. These stereotypes can affect educators' perceptions of students, causing them to see children of color as more threatening or dangerous than their white counterparts. When disruptive events occur in a classroom, for example, teachers become fearful that they will not be able to manage the event. When that fear intersects with racial stereotypes, that concern often results in a student of color being identified, removed from class, and suspended. Often teachers and administrators fail to reflect on their contributions to students' behaviors. Zero-tolerance policies do not require such introspection. In fact, they cloak racial bias and cultural misunderstanding with the mantle of impartiality and contribute to its perpetuation (Brady et al., 2007; Fenning and Rose, 2007).

Discipline and Students with Disabilities

Most students come to school able to understand the rules and how to follow them. For students with disabilities, however, especially students with "behavioral disorders," coming to understand and being able to conform to expectations is a much more difficult task. The result is that students with disabilities are more likely to be excluded from schools. Students with disabilities represent about 12% of all public school students; however, they accounted for nearly 26% of students who were suspended, arrested, or referred to law enforcement. That is an overrepresentation of roughly 15.5 percentage points for referrals to law enforcement or arrests and 13 percentage points for out of school suspensions (General Accounting Office, 2018). In New Hampshire, an African American male student with disabilities attending an urban school has a one in three chance of being suspended (Gagnon et al., 2016).

The rate is higher for students with particular disabilities. Students with emotional disturbances are three times more likely to receive out of school suspensions and twice as likely to receive in school suspensions than students in any other disability category (U.S. Department of Education, Office of Special Education Programs, 2018). They are approximately five times as likely to be suspended as students who are not disabled. Some students whose disabilities make the academic tasks of school extremely difficult become disruptive or disorderly in response to work that is just too hard. All these behaviors make sense to children in light of what they "know" and feel about the world and their place within it. Since teachers and administrators do not perceive the world in the same way, the students are viewed as disrespectful, disorderly, disobedient, defiant, and disruptive. Their behaviors simply make no sense to adults who do not share their experiences and disabilities.

Students with disabilities often have trouble making sense of peer relationships as well. Interactions with their schoolmates become difficult. Disagreements break out over misunderstandings resulting from the "failure" (i.e., the inability) of students with disabilities to pick up on verbal and nonverbal cues. They continue talking when their classmates want to say something. They refuse to share toys, supplies, and materials they have taken without asking and are surprised by other children's anger. They fail to respect personal space and physically crowd, jostle, or bump others who resent the intrusion. Consequently, they are involved in more verbal and physical altercations with other students.

It is true that the original Individuals with Disabilities Act (1997) provided extensive procedure protection for students with disabilities with regard to school discipline. For example, if students' actions were found to be the result of their disabilities, they could receive "lighter sentences" than nondisabled students would. Objections to these protections were so strong, however, that when the bill was amended in 2004, the number of available modifications were reduced. This change was particularly true for behavior that fell into the "zero-tolerance" category for students without disabilities. In the revised bill, students with disabilities may be removed to an interim alternative educational setting for up to 45 school days not only for weapon- or drug-related violations, but also if they have inflicted serious bodily injury on another person at school or at a school function. The revised bill also eliminates the right of students with disabilities to remain in their current educational placements while they appeal a disciplinary decision if their violation of the school code would usually result in removal for more than 10 days. What is problematic about such provisions is that they undo decades of work to prevent students with disabilities from being excluded from schools. These policies allow school administrators to remove students with disabilities from classrooms—and even schools—for behavior that is a result of their disabling condition; that is, students are removed *because* they are disabled. A recent study revealed that, although administrators said that they were aware of their responsibility to protect the rights of students with disabilities, most were more likely to give priority to what they perceived as the safety of the larger school community. They argued that their primary responsibility was to preserve order for the good of the entire school, and "most, but not all, viewed their obligation to implement IDEA's disciplinary regulations as a deterrent to that goal" (McCarthy and Soodak, 2007, p. 463). Instead of providing students with disabilities with the needed supports to behave appropriately in the least restricted setting possible, it appears that the "safety" of some schools may be achieved through the sacrifice of those students' civil rights.

Effects of Zero-Tolerance Policies

We have increasing evidence that zero-tolerance policies have negative effects on students. Despite arguments that applying one-size-fits-all consequences is fair, the mandated consequences—especially those that exclude young people from classes or school—affect some students more than others. Students who already face other risk factors like poverty and neighborhood or family violence often find suspension or expulsion is one too many burdens. Researchers demonstrate that out of school suspension, the most commonly applied zero-tolerance consequence, is correlated with continued academic failure, grade retention, negative school attitudes, less participation in extracurricular activities, higher placement in special education programs, lower grades, poorer attendance, and continued disciplinary problems (Skiba et al., 2014; Steinberg and Lacoe, 2017). Students also drop out of school entirely.

These consequences should come as no surprise. When students are suspended, they obviously lose instructional time. They are usually at home, and most are provided with no access to their teachers or to the assignments on which their classmates are working. There are very few publicly funded alternatives to schools, and most places in those settings are reserved for students with disabilities. Delays in getting back into school are common even when students have "served their time" or been found "not guilty." In addition, they often feel ostracized and rejected by the adults to whom they had previously looked to for help. They often believe—sometimes correctly—that they have been unfairly singled out and lose faith in the integrity of teachers and administrators. Excluded students often become "transients," moving in and out of various educational settings, never feeling quite at home and never being able to establish the kind of relationships with other students that lead to academic success (Losen, 2011; Hemez et al., 2019).

In fact, the increase in dropouts that are connected to mandatory suspensions and expulsions may not be accidental at all. Students whose behavior is inappropriate are often young people who are struggling with academic tasks. They "act out" their frustration with schools' inability to meet their needs. In an era of high-stakes testing, poor performance on standardized assessments negatively impacts the school's "report card." It is plausible that administrators may use zero-tolerance policies to raise test scores by "pushing out" low-performing students. Certainly, that remedy is more affordable than providing students with small classes, tutoring, mentoring, and after-school programs that might actually help improve their academic performance and, in turn, decrease their inappropriate behavior.

In addition to increasing the number of students who drop out of school—or, perhaps more precisely, as a result of doing so—zero tolerance has also created a "school to prison pipeline." Suspension and expulsion are predictive of dropping out of high school and failing to earn a high school diploma is predictive of incarceration. Over 800,000 young people were arrested in 2017 in the United States—a 59% drop in 10 years (U.S. Department of Justice, 2019a). Approximately 44,000 are in correctional facilities (U.S. Department of Justice, 2019b). Of the 2.3 million people incarcerated in the United States, approximately 41% do not have a high school diploma, compared to 18% in the general population (Bender, 2018).

The "pipeline" is facilitated by an increased presence of police (SROs) in public schools, especially in urban areas. SROs are actually sworn members of the local police department and as such can and do overrule a school administrator in decisions about arresting students. Because not all their time is spent on law enforcement activities, SROs often provide mentoring or counseling services to students. However, those relationships can be dangerous to students who may not realize that the SRO is really a police officer. They may make statements to an SRO that they would not make to another police officer or underestimate the need to have a parent or attorney present when speaking to an SRO. More than 400,000 arrests are made in schools each year. Misbehaviors that would have been taken care of by school administrators in the past have been criminalized. The over-policing of schools interferes with instructional time, subjects students to intrusive searches with sexual overtones, and singles out students of color (Dohy and Banks, 2017; Glenn, 2019).

The school to prison pipeline is self-perpetuating. Zero-tolerance policies have a chilling effect on relationships between adults and young people. Those most in need of assistance, including the mentally ill, are discouraged by such policies from seeking it for fear that their concerns will be misinterpreted or misunderstood and will result in punishment in school or in prisons. Consequently, they receive no assistance in changing or dealing with the underlying causes of their behaviors. The acting out continues, harsh school penalties follow, and suspension leads to referrals to the criminal justice system or to behavior "on the street" that results in arrest and time in jail (Lustick, 2017; Mansfield et al., 2018).

Alternatives to Zero Tolerance

Admittedly, it is challenging to create disciplinary policies that exemplify the American ideal—protection of both individual rights and the common good. It is also necessary if young people are to believe that democratic values like fairness and justice are more than mere words. Initiatives to create disciplinary policies that support students while addressing inappropriate behavior have proven successful and are replacing zero-tolerance policies across the country. The federal government required all states to report suspensions, expulsions, school-related arrests, referrals to law enforcement, and incidences of school violence (including bullying and harassment) on their state and local report cards. The data from those reports are made public and provide opportunities for states to hold schools accountable (Musu et al., 2019). Some have incorporated the information to identify schools whose suspension and expulsion rates are indicative of larger problems that require improvement. At least 20 states and the District of Columbia make public how they are using information about suspension and expulsion rates to do so (Kostyo et al., 2018).

These research-based alternatives are often known as "restorative practices" (Passarella, 2017). They include teaching students skills to establish positive relationships and resolve conflicts. They also provide targeted behavioral supports, building community and student-school bonds. Programs that teach social and emotional skills have been found to improve students' attitudes about themselves and others, lower the levels of problem behaviors, reduce emotional distress, improve academic outcomes, and improve school safety. The programs increase high school and college graduation rates and have long-term benefits (Cardichon and Darling-Hammond, 2019; Fronius et al., 2019). Alternative disciplinary practices incorporate the best characteristics of the U.S. justice system. For example, schools act under the assumption that students are presumed innocent until their guilt is proven. Administrators have the right to consider the facts of each case—including the student's intent and the circumstances surrounding an incident—before applying consequences. School districts have established disciplinary codes that clearly spell out due process procedures.

In addition, schools have created disciplinary practices that identify "teachable moments" and use them to prevent problems. Teachers and staff help students develop the behaviors that are expected in school and society; instruction is intentional and not left to chance (Advocacy and Communications Solutions, 2015).

Schools are balancing students' need for structure and support models have clear rules that are enforced consistently—but the structure is less rigid than zero tolerance. When a rule is broken, teachers and administrators are able to decide how serious the infraction was and consider the student's intentions and the circumstances of the situation. Students see that they are respected as individuals, that their motivations and intentions are considered, and that consequences fit the seriousness of the act. Such practices support students' sense of justice and fairness—and reinforce their belief that those values are respected and lived out in the school. These models not only address problems that have already taken place but also go a long way in preventing future ones. They send students the message that public authority in the United States is fair and operates in the best interest of all its citizens. By creating and sustaining such beliefs, disciplinary policies that allow administrators discretion in determining consequences and that involve students, families, and communities in implementing them provide greater assurance than do policies that prescribe one-size-fits-all remedies.

In 2014, the federal government provided guidance, access to research, and resources to states and schools in their efforts to adopt alternatives to zero tolerance and held them accountable for doing so. In doing so, the Department of Education sent a clear message that zero-tolerance policies were ineffective at best and discriminatory and destructive at worst. It appears that the real purpose of such laws is not to help young people change their behaviors but to give adults reassurance that they are still "in charge." It turns out that the benefits of zero-tolerance policies were illusory and merely the stuff of good public relations campaigns.

However, the Department of Education rescinded the guidance in 2018 and pulled back the resources it was providing to schools to implement it. Even without federal support districts and states are continuing to explore and implement its spirit. "Generally, Restorative Justice practices are based on principles that establish a voice for victims, offenders, and community in order to address offender accountability for the harm caused (rather than the act itself) and to develop a plan to repair relationships" (Fronius et al., 2019, p. 35). In schools across the country students and adults are talking about the harm caused by a student's behavior. Young people are committing to take actions that will repair the damage they have done and accepting consequences that will eventually restore their status as a member of the school community (Fronius et al., 2019). They are not being excluded, but rather they are learning the skills that will ensure their participation in school and, ultimately, in all the communities they will become members of in the future. Our society will be safer and richer as a result.

FOR DISCUSSION

1. Opponents of zero tolerance argue that it is particularly harmful to students of color and that by giving administrators more discretion in disciplinary matters, the effects of prejudice could be lessened. However, administrators, like teachers, have biases. How can a district's disciplinary procedures protect students of color from racial prejudice without resorting to mandated consequences?

2. Are there some situations where zero tolerance is the correct or the only option? Discuss what they might be and why you think discretion is inappropriate in those cases.

3. Felons are allowed "three strikes" before mandatory life sentences are imposed. Would it be appropriate for schools to adopt a similar three-offense policy before imposing suspension or expulsion?

4. Interview a school administrator about his or her experiences with disciplining students with disabilities. Ask about the hardest situation that he or she has faced. Ask whether the administrator believes that making allowances for students with disabilities is appropriate. Discuss your findings in class. Drawing on class discussions and interviews, write an essay arguing for or against IDEA regulations regarding discipline.

REFERENCES

Advocacy and Communications Solutions (2015). Better Than Zero (advocacyandcommunication.org/tools-resources).

Basile, V., York, A., and Black, R. (2019). "Who Is the One Being Disrespectful? Understanding and Deconstructing the Criminalization of Elementary School Boys of Color." *Urban Education*. http://www.doi.org/10.1177/0042085919842627

Bender, K. (2018, March 2). Education Opportunities in Prison Are Key to Reducing Crime. Center for American Progress (americanprogress.org/issues/education-k-12/news/2018/03/02/447321/education-opportunities-prison-key-reducing-crime).

Billitteri, T. (2008). "Discipline in Schools." *Congressional Quarterly Researcher* 18(7):145–168.

Brady, K., Balmer, S., and Phenix, D. (2007). "School-Police Partnerships Effectiveness in Urban Schools." *Education and Urban Society* 39(4):455–478.

Brownstein, R. (2010, March, 23–27). "Pushed Out." *Education Digest*.

Brownsville Collegiate Charter School (2019). Code of Conduct. Uncommon Schools (nyc.uncommonschools.org/brownsville-collegiate).

Butler v. Rio Rancho Public School Board (2002). 245 F. Supp. 2d 1188 (U.S. Dist. Lexis 26238).

Cardichon, J., and Darling-Hammond, L. (2019). *Protecting Students' Civil Rights: The Federal Role in School Discipline*. Palo Alto, CA: Learning Policy Institute.

Casella, R. (2003). "Security, Schooling, and the Consumer's Choice to Segregate." *Urban Review* 35(2):129–148.

Common Good (2008). Overruled (commongood.org/burdenquestion-2.html).

Cornell, D. G., and Mayer, M. J. (2010). "Why Do School Order and Safety Matter?" *Educational Researcher* 39:7–15.

Crews, G. (2019). *Handbook of Research on School Violence in American K–12 Education*. Hershey, PA: IGI Global.

Dohy, J., and Banks, T. (2017). "The Impact of School Policing on Student Behaviors in Ohio Public Schools." *Journal of School Violence* 17(3):311–323.

Eden, M. (2019). *Safe and Orderly Schools: Updated Guidance on School Discipline*. New York: Manhattan Institute for Policy Research.

Education Commission of the States (2019, January). *The Status of School Discipline in State Policy*. Denver, CO: Education Commission of the States.

Fenning, P., and Rose, J. (2007). "Overrepresentation of African American Students in Exclusionary Discipline: The Role of School Policy." *Urban Education* 42(6):536–559.

Fissel, E., Wilcox, P., and Tillyer, M. (2019). "School Discipline Policies, Perceptions of Justice, and In-School Delinquency." *Crime & Delinquency* 65(10):1,343–1,370.

Fronius, T., Darling-Hammond, S., Persson, H., Guckenburg, S., Hurley, N., and Petrosino, A. (2019, March). *Restorative Justice in U.S. Schools: An Updated Research Review.* San Francisco: WestEd Justice and Prevention Research Center.

Gagnon, D., Jaffee, E., and Kennedy, R. (2016, Winter). *Exclusionary Discipline Highest in New Hampshire's Urban Schools* (Regional Issue Brief 46). Durham: University of New Hampshire, Carsey School of Public Policy.

General Accounting Office (2018, March). *Discipline Disparities for Black Students, Boys, and Students with Disabilities* (GAO-18-258). Washington, DC: General Accounting Office.

Glenn, J. (2019). "Resilience Matters: Examining the School to Prison Pipeline through the Lens of School-Based Problem Behaviors." *Justice Policy Journal* 16(1).

Gregory, A., Skiba, R., and Noguera, P. (2010). "The Achievement Gap and the Discipline Gap: Two Sides of the Same Coin?" *Educational Researcher* 39(1):59–68.

Hemez, P., Brent, J., and Mowen, T. (2019, October 31). "Exploring the School-to-Prison Pipeline: How School Suspensions Influence Incarceration During Young Adulthood." *Youth Violence and Juvenile Justice.* https://doi.org/ 10.1177/1541204019880945

Hess, F., and Eden, M. (2017, December 15). "When School-Discipline 'Reform' Makes Schools Less Safe." *National Review.*

Hines-Datiri, D., and Andrews, D. (2017). "The Effects of Zero Tolerance Policies on Black Girls: Using Critical Race Feminism and Figured Worlds to Examine School Discipline." *Urban Education.* https://doi.org/10.1177/0042085917690204

Iyengar, R. (2008). *I'd Rather Be Hanged for a Sheep Than a Lamb: The Unintended Consequences of "Three-Strikes" Laws.* (NBER Working Paper No. 13784). Cambridge, MA: National Bureau of Economic Research.

Kosciw, J. G., Greytak, E. A., Diaz, E. M., and Bartkiewicz, M. J. (2018). *2017 National School Climate Survey: The Experiences of Lesbian, Gay, Bisexual and Transgender Youth in Our Nation's Schools.* New York: GLSEN.

Kostyo, S., Cardichon, J., and Darling-Hammond, L. (2018, September). *Making ESSA's Equity Promise Real: State Strategies to Close the Opportunity Gap.* Palo Alto, CA: Learning Policy Institute.

Leff, S. S., Angelucci, J., Goldstein, A. B., Cardaciotto, L., Paskewich, B., and Grossman, M. B. (2007). Using a Participatory Action Research Model to Create a School-Based Intervention Program for Relationally Aggressive Girls—The Friend to Friend Program. In J. E. Zins, M. J. Elias, and C. A. Maher, eds., *Bullying, Victimization, and Peer Harassment.* New York: Haworth.

Livermore, C. (2008, Spring). "Unrelenting Expectations: A More Nuanced Understanding of the Broken Windows Theory of Cultural Management in Urban Education." *Penn GSE Perspectives on Urban Education* 5(2).

Losen, D. J. (2011). *Discipline Policies, Successful Schools, and Racial Justice.* Boulder, CO: National Education Policy Center.

Losen, D. J., and Skiba, R. (2010). Suspended Education: Urban Middle Schools in Crisis. University of California, Los Angeles, The Civil Rights Project (civilrightsproject.ucla.edu/ research/k-12-education/ school-discipline / suspended-education-urban-middle-schools-in-crisis/Suspended-Education_RNAL-2.pdf).

Lustick, H. (2017, November 14). "'Restorative Justice' or Restoring Order? Restorative School Discipline Practices in Urban Public Schools." *Urban Education.* https://doi.org/10.1177/ 0042085917741725

Males, M. (2011). *Striking Out: California's "Three Strikes and You're Out" Law Has Not Reduced Violent Crime.* San Francisco: Center on Juvenile and Criminal Justice.

Mansfield, K. C., Rainbolt, S., and Fowler, E. (2018). "Implementing Restorative Justice as a Step toward Racial Equity in School Discipline." *Teachers College Record* 120(14):1–24.

Mauer, M. (2011). "Addressing Racial Disparity in Incarceration." *The Prison Journal* 91(3, Supplement):87S–101S.

McCarthy, M., and Soodak, L. (2007). "The Politics of Discipline: Balancing School Safety and Rights of Students with Disabilities." *Exceptional Children* 73(4):456–474.

McQuiggan, M., and Megra, M. (2017). *Parent and Family Involvement in Education: Results from the National Household Education Surveys Program of 2016* (NCES 2017-102). Washington, DC: U.S. Department of Education, National Center for Education Statistics.

Musu, L., Zhang, A., Wang, K., Zhang, J., and Oudekerk, B. A. (2019). *Indicators of School Crime and Safety: 2018* (NCES 2019-047/NCJ 252571). Washington, DC: National Center for Education Statistics and Bureau of Justice Statistics, Office of Justice Programs.

NASRO (2019). NASRO Mission (nasro.org).

National School Safety and Security Services (2019). Zero Tolerance: School Safety and Discipline Policies (schoolsecurity.org/trends/zero_tolerance.html).

New York City Department of Education (2019). *Citywide Behavioral Expectations to Support Student Learning Grades 6–12.* New York: New York City Department of Education.

Olweus, D. (2008). *Bullying Is Not a Fact of Life.* Rockville, MD: U.S. Department of Health and Human Services.

Onyeka-Crawford, A., Patrick, K., and Chaudry, N. (2017). *Let Her Learn: Stopping School Pushout for Girls of Color.* Washington, DC: National Women's Law Center.

Passarella, A. (2017). Restorative Practices in Schools. Johns Hopkins, School of Education, Institute for Education Policy (edpolicy.education.jhu.edu/restorative-practices-in-schools).

Seal v. Morgan (2000). 229 F. 3rd 567 (6th Cir.).

Shared Justice (2018). Zero-Tolerance Policies and the School to Prison Pipeline (sharedjustice.org/domestic-justice/2017/12/21/zero-tolerance-policies-and-the-school-to-prison-pipeline).

Simons, M. (2010). "Symposium: Examining Modern Approaches to Prosecutorial Discretion: Prosecutorial Discretion in the Shadow of Advisory Guidelines and Mandatory Minimums." *Temple Political and Civil Rights Law Review* 19:377–389.

Skiba, R. (2000). *Zero Tolerance, Zero Evidence: An Analysis of School Disciplinary Practice* (Policy Research Report #SRS2). Bloomington: Indiana Education Policy Center.

Skiba, R., Arredondo, M., and Williams, N. (2014). "More Than a Metaphor: The Contribution of Exclusionary Discipline to a School-to-Prison Pipeline." *Equity & Excellence in Education* 47(4):546–564.

Smith, E. J., and Harper, S. R. (2015). *Disproportionate Impact of K–12 School Suspension and Expulsion on Black Students in Southern States.* Philadelphia: University of Pennsylvania, Center for the Study of Race and Equity in Education.

Steinberg, M., and Lacoe, J. (2017). "What Do We Know about School Discipline Reform?" *Education Next* 17(1):44–52.

U.S. Department of Education, Office of Civil Rights (2019, May). *School Climate and Safety: Data Highlights on School Climate and Safety in Our Nation's Public Schools.* Washington, DC: U.S. Department of Education.

U.S. Department of Education, Office of Special Education Programs (2018). *40th Annual Report to Congress on the Implementation of the Individuals with Disabilities Education Act, 2018.* Washington, DC: U.S. Department of Education.

U.S. Department of Health and Human Services (2019). Stop Bullying. Laws, Policies, and Regulations (stopbullying.gov/laws/index.html).

U.S. Department of Justice (2019a). *Juvenile Arrests, 2017* (NCJ 252713). Washington, DC: Office of Justice Programs.

——— (2019b). One Day Count of Juveniles in Residential Placement Facilities, 1997–2017. Statistical Briefing Book. Juveniles in Corrections. Office of Justice Programs (ojjdp.gov/ojstatbb/corrections/qa08201.asp?qaDate=2017).

Walsh, J. (2008, May 18). "Sent Home: The Suspension Gap." *Minneapolis Star Tribune.*

Wun, C. (2016). "Unaccounted Foundations: Black Girls, Anti-Black Racism, and Punishment in Schools." *Critical Sociology* 42(4–5): 737–750. https://doi.org/10.1177/0896920514560444

Violence in Schools

Preventable or Beyond School Control

13

Can schools deal effectively with violent or potentially violent students?

Position 1:   Schools Can and Should Prevent Violence

I believe that school is primarily a social institution. Education being a social process, the school is simply that form of community life in which all of those agencies are concentrated that will be most effective in bringing the child to share in the inherited resources of the race, and to use his own powers for social ends. . . . I believe that education, therefore, is a process of living and not a preparation for future living.

—Dewey (quoted in Dworkin, 1959, p. 22)

During the nineteenth century, John Dewey helped define the relationship between Americans and their public schools. Schools are extensions of the community in this country, he argued. Schools share in the burden of caring for the community's children and for equipping them with skills and habits necessary to survive and succeed. Schools take the community's highest ideals and translate them into academic and social programs for all children. Everyone is responsible for the education of the community's children. As Dewey wrote, "What the best and wisest parent wants for his own child, that must the community want for all its children" (quoted in Dworkin, 1959, p. 54).

Dewey recognized that social conditions constantly change and that schools always have to adjust to new demands placed on communities. When social problems overwhelm community resources, schools are expected to lend strength and assistance. In a speech delivered in 1899, he said, "It is useless to bemoan the departure of the good old days of children's modesty, reverence, and implicit obedience, if we expect merely by bemoaning and by exhortation to bring them back. It is radical conditions which have changed, and only an equally radical change in education suffices" (quoted in Dworkin, 1959, p. 37).

The Industrial Revolution upset the community's traditional structure and nature of work. Parents were working long hours, away from home, separated from their children. Many children also worked, at hard and often dangerous jobs. As a result, families had changed, and were not able to carry out the full range of their former functions. Schools were pressed to expand their role, to go beyond providing instruction in reading and arithmetic and help children adjust to the "radical conditions" of the day. Helping children adjust to the problems of a new industrial economy imposed a great burden on public education. Helping children understand and overcome the radical conditions of the twenty-first century may require even greater effort, but it is not a problem that schools can shirk. The community's problems are always the school's problems. We are concerned with violence here, a social problem with a long history and many causes.

The Violent Community

Violence is among the most "radical conditions" now confronting the nation and its school-age children. Violence increasingly affects the daily lives of children, and violence prevention and aggression management programs have become part of the common curriculum in schools. Society has changed in the past decades, and students' lives are filled with problems that were never before the concern of schools.

In some ways, school violence is a new American problem; in other ways, it is as old as the nation. American society is violent and has been so for a long time. You may recall that Andrew Jackson shot and killed a man who made insulting comments about his wife, and Aaron Burr killed political rival Alexander Hamilton in a New Jersey gun duel. The United States was born of revolution. It has made heroes of gunfighters and warriors. Americans have witnessed assassinations of national figures, racial lynchings, and riots by organized labor, farmers, and students. Violence is said to be as American as apple pie (Alvarez and Bachman, 2016). Until the 1930s, it was not possible to quantify the rate of violence, but since that time, the FBI's Uniform Crime Reporting Program has documented periods of increases in violent crime, including murder, forcible rape, robbery, and aggravated assault. The U.S. murder rate is the highest in the industrialized world, and we remain a leader in school violence and bullying.

Violence and the Media

Violence currently presents unprecedented dangers to school-age children. American films, music videos, and television are the most violent in the world. Messages about aggressive behavior enter the world of children no matter how hard families work to screen them out. These messages flow not only from children's direct experiences but also from news reports, film, music, and advertising. War toys line store shelves, cartoon heroes destroy villains on television and in films, music videos play darkly on themes of anger and destruction, and computer games encourage interactive simulations of murder and mayhem.

Television, movies, and the Internet bring a steady volume of vicarious violence into children's lives. Nearly 98% of U.S. households with children from 0 to 8 years old have at least one television set; 95% have a smartphone; and 75% have a tablet. In fact, 42% of these very young children have their own device. Children in this age group spend a little more than two hours a day with "screen media" (Rideout, 2017). Children 8 to 12 years old use screen media for almost five hours and teens use an average of seven and a half hours daily (Rideout and Robb, 2019). Children see over 100,000 fictional acts of violence and 8,000 murders before they finish elementary school. They can encounter "pretend" violence on video games. In addition, with increased access to social media, they also see real violence taking place, sometimes as it is happening. Among other things, researchers have found that viewing portrayals of violence leads to aggressive or violent behavior, and media violence is a significant correlate of real-world violence. Of course, no one risk factor leads to or explains violent actions; such behavior requires multiple risk factors and a lack of protective ones. However, research does show that watching on-screen violence is one of those factors and can be limited by limiting screen time. Doing so could be done at little cost (Anderson et al., 2017).

Violence is an increasingly familiar aspect of young people's school-age lives (see Figure 13.1). Each year approximately 1 million students are physically attacked or

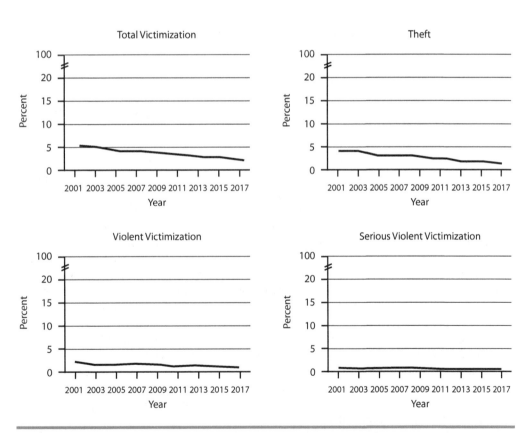

Figure 13.1   Percentage of Students Ages 12 to 18 Who Reported Criminal Victimization at School during the Previous Six Months by Type of Victimization (2001 to 2017) (Indicators of School Crime and Safety, 2019).

threatened with attack by people with and without firearms, explosives, and other weapons; out of the 23,000 who are robbed, 900 are robbed by people carrying weapons. Almost 1,000 are sexually assaulted or raped. There are over 200 school-related shootings on school grounds, at off-campus events, during transportation to and from school, or off-campus (but reported by school personnel) and homicides involving a student, faculty member, or staff member took place over 100 times (U.S. Department of Education, Office of Civil Rights, 2019). Although violence is more prevalent in urban areas and among poor and minorities, no one in any neighborhood is immune. School violence affects the suburbs and rural areas as well as cities. In fact, the number of students reporting the presence of gangs, one indicator of school violence, varies only slightly by the location of a school (Musu et al., 2019).

However, there is some good news in reports of school violence. Almost every indicator of school violence has been decreasing for the last 10 years (Musu et al., 2019). Violence may not be getting worse, but it is disturbing nonetheless. From the standpoint of any victim of school violence or the parents whose children have been victimized, there are no levels of acceptable violent behavior in schools.

School-Based Approaches to Violence Prevention

Too many children feel unsafe in schools, and too many schools have had to invest in metal detectors and guards instead of books and field trips. However, the most hopeful news is that schools can make a difference in preventing childhood aggressive behavior and future adult violence (David-Ferdon et al., 2016; Cuellar, 2018; Gaffney et al., 2019; Sivaraman et al., 2019).

Research shows that one of the most effective ways of preventing violence in schools is creating a community of trust in which rules are enforced consistently and fairly and students are treated with respect. Students perceive schools with positive relationships among young people and adults as "safe" (May, 2018). Students' sense of "school-connectedness," the perception that they are cared for and valued by school personnel and feel comfortable talking to them, reduces school violence. Students with strong relationships with some adults in the building, such as teachers, administrators, coaches, members of the custodial staff, or school nurses, "engage in fewer disruptive/oppositional behaviors, experience relatively more stable social-emotional well-being, and have higher academic achievement than their peers who report low levels of connectedness." They are also more likely to report their knowledge of a potential violent act by another student (Volungis and Goodman, 2017, pp. 2–3). School safety plans that include "connectedness" are plans with heart. They emphasize low-cost improvements including greeting students by name each day, promoting students' sense of ownership of school spaces, engaging them systematically in school safety planning, and ensuring that they have social and mental health supports in the building (Eith and Trump, 2019).

The Department of Homeland Security also recommends the development of a "threat assessment team," a group of adults in the building who have established criteria for concerning behaviors and ways of dealing with students who exhibit them before a tragedy occurs. These teams function as an early warning system and everyone in the school can report concerns to the team or an individual member. They also provide ongoing training for school personnel and serve as a liaison with law enforcement personnel (National Threat Assessment Center, 2018).

School personnel can also diminish violence in schools by preventing bullying or cyberbulling and addressing incidents decisively when they occur. Research suggests that whole-school interventions that include combinations of rules and punishment, teacher training, conflict resolution training, and individual counseling are more effective than programs that utilize only one type of response. By making changes to the total school environment one study showed that in 44 cases, there was an average decrease of 20% in bullying (Sivaraman et al., 2019).

Schools can also mitigate the threat of violence through disciplinary policies. Consistent disciplinary responses to inappropriate behavior, including the removal of disruptive students or those who present a danger to themselves or others are required. Schools that fail to exclude such students jeopardize the safety of others. However, while necessary, these measures are not sufficient to prevent violent acts in schools.

Schools can also draw on their expertise in teaching and learning to solve the problem of school violence. With appropriate instruction children can learn how to understand and control their anger. Schools can draw on existing curricula that teach students to recognize, name, and manage the feelings that most often trigger "acting out" or aggressive responses. Violence prevention programs include social and cognitive training for students and counseling support. Instruction in conflict resolution and management, attention to diversity issues, programs to reduce isolation and alienation, drug and alcohol education, antigang and antibullying programs, suicide prevention, special training for staff, and parent outreach are all within schools' power to create or implement (David-Ferdon et al., 2016; Sivaraman et al., 2019; Waschbusch et al., 2019).

"Hardening" Schools to Prevent Violence

Addressing school climate and ensuring that students feel connected and that their mental health needs are being met have been proven to be effective at preventing violent incidents. However, they do not exhaust the actions communities can take to ensure school safety. Stringent security measures in schools, including hiring school resource officers (SROs), installing security devices such as metal detectors, and even arming teachers with guns, are other reasonable deterrents. They serve as visible symbols of the school's commitment to security.

> While it is generally agreed that it is not possible to stop every potential act of violence in schools, schools can reduce the likelihood of a violent incident with significant casualties from occurring on their campuses by establishing a strong security team, completing a security assessment, and developing and implementing appropriate plans for security and emergency operations. (Federal Commission on School Safety, 2018, p. 120)

Schools' physical buildings and campuses should reflect a commitment to safety and deter potential attackers. Teachers or students should be able to lock classroom doors from the inside. The doors should have window blockers to prevent shooters from targeting victims inside the classroom. Doors and windows should be made of reinforced materials. There should be limited and controlled entry points. Classrooms should have secure spaces in which teachers and students can shelter if there is an active shooter event. The consistent, reliable use of security equipment adds an additional level of protection and reduces the possibility of human error that could prove tragic. Making the school's commitment to safety visible reduces the possibility that anyone could view the building and its inhabitants as soft targets (Sandy Hook Advisory Commission, 2015; Federal Commission on School Safety, 2018).

One additional, and admittedly controversial, action schools can take is to allow trained personnel to have weapons in school. In many cases, members of law enforcement, who already have preparation in responding to crisis situations and the use of weapons, can serve as school security staff. However, in some areas that is not possible. In those cases, allowing some members of school staff to be trained in crisis response and the use of arms is a viable option. The knowledge that there are people within a school building who are prepared to defend students and staff against violence would serve as a deterrent to someone contemplating doing harm (Federal Commission on School Safety, 2018). A number of state legislatures are considering laws that would allow arming teachers. Almost 500 school districts have already done so (Everytown for Gun Safety, 2019). Over 40% of the public support such measures (Sargent, 2018). "Allowing teachers and staff to carry concealed handguns is nothing new in the United States, and hasn't created any problems. Before the early 1990s, there were no state laws specifically restricting concealed carry on K–12 property so that teacher carry may have been common for much of our history" (Lott, 2019, p. 2). Correlation between armed staff and violence prevention is strong. There has been no mass shootings in any school that allows personnel to carry guns legally (Lott, 2019). While arming teachers or school staff may seem like a drastic measure, when it is part of an overall security plan, it appears to be an effective strategy for violence prevention.

While violence may seem to be irrational destruction or an explosion of spontaneous rage, it doesn't just happen. Violent acts are not without causes nor do they defy understanding. In addition to attending to individual students' family backgrounds and personal strengths and challenges, the best violence prevention efforts in schools are also based on an understanding of how history, economics, and culture are complicit in violent behavior. Violent acts cannot be prevented unless schools and communities attend to social and political forces producing them. The social and behavioral sciences have learned a lot about violence, and, if those insights are applied in schools, there is every reason to expect that schools can successfully stem the tide of violent behavior and protect children and society from the violent among us. If school personnel make schools more just and more satisfying places for all students and extend the power of schooling into students' daily lives, they can help reduce social conflicts and individual violence. The process likely will be slow and expensive, but if not begun in schools, future social and personal costs will be greater. Potentially violent children and their problems will not go away by themselves. To paraphrase John Dewey, what the best and wisest parents in the community want for their children should be made available to all children through the agency of the schools.

Position 2:	The Problem of School Violence Is Beyond School Control

Let's broaden the net. Let's bring in the juvenile and family court judge, let's bring in probation, let's bring in Social Services—a whole network of people that have got to start working together more carefully.

—Stevens (quoted in Hagerty, 2018)

American schools began with modest academic goals: teach children to read and write. Over the years, schools expanded their curricula to include academic instruction in content as well as skills and subject matter from art to social studies. The argument in this section is simple, direct, and straightforward: schools should teach academic content in the most compelling and academically legitimate ways possible. This is the primary job that schools are entrusted with and is what teachers are trained to do. Without academic skills, students are at a disadvantage and will be unable to compete for places in the best colleges, earn scholarships, land good jobs, or launch satisfying careers. Schooling is also about the mastery of skills necessary for success in life. Those skills include understanding and managing emotions, creating positive relationships, and making responsible decisions. The outcomes of such learning are not "happiness" or "self-esteem." They are the development of virtue, character, and self-discipline, all of which lessen the possibility of an individual engaging in violent acts. However, the case for such learning cannot be used as a reason to "diminish attention to academic skills or knowledge or deflect educators from the centrality of academic instruction" (Finn and Hess, 2019, p. 2).

The vast majority of students do not need special curriculum to teach them how to get along with others, settle disputes without violence, or manage aggression. They need academic content to succeed in life, and that's what schools should deliver. Schools must teach about our history and literature and instill in students a sense of civic responsibility if we are to survive as a nation. Schools must equip students with intellectual skills necessary to understand science, math, the arts, and humanities if they are to succeed individually. Beyond expecting educators to integrate their knowledge of social and emotional development to create educational experiences that are engaging, collaborative, and safe, asking them to prevent violent acts in schools goes beyond the scope of their expertise and the primary task of education. Schools cannot redistribute wealth or solve social problems. For better or worse, schools reflect society; they are not now—nor have they ever been—agents of social change. They have a mission to educate students and have little power and no authority to do anything else.

Concern about Violence in Schools Is Overblown

School violence is an overstated problem. Potentially violent students represent only 1% of children who enter school, and the rate of violence in school has not increased in 20 years. More than two-thirds of schools report no incidents of violent crimes and 90% reported no incidents of serious violent crimes (see Figure 13.2).

Despite widespread publicity depicting schools as dangerous places, rife with crime and violence, the conclusion drawn from reports of violence seems to say that school violence may be more of a media creation than a serious school problem. For the moment, at least, it seems fair to argue that schools are probably less dangerous for students and teachers than they have been in the past two decades.

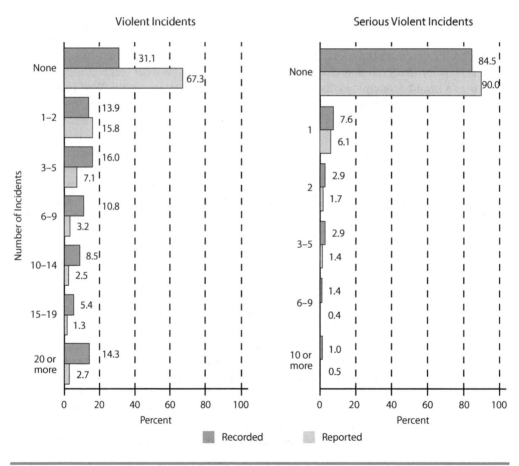

Figure 13.2   Percentage of Schools Recording and Reporting to the Police Violent and Serious Violent Incidents of Crime by Number of Incidents, School Year 2015 to 2016 (Indicators of School Crime and Safety, 2018)

Between 2001 and 2017, the percentage of students ages 12 to 18 who reported being afraid of attack or harm at school during the school year decreased from 6% to 4%, and the percentage who reported being afraid of attack or harm away from school during the school year decreased from 5% to 3%. (Musu et al., 2019, p. vi)

Which Students Are Potentially Violent?

Children do not show up for the first day of kindergarten as blank slates: the experiences of their early lives have etched on them many complex impressions, both good and bad. Most children are ready to begin school; their parents have invested tremendous amounts of time and energy in them. These children are self-controlled. They demonstrate mastery over their emotions, enthusiasm for learning, and respect for the teacher's authority. Others come from unstable, stressful family environments. They have experienced poor relationships and communications and were disciplined harshly or too laxly. Their parents were physically or verbally abusive. Victims of poor parenting or no parenting at all, they come to school with insufficient preparation for the academic side of school and inadequate control over their own behavior to get along with classmates. Still others come from healthier environments but suffer from mental illness that affects their ability to function in social and academic settings.

Teachers usually spot children from the last two groups quickly. The students are often overly impulsive, unable to express their feelings or control their behavior, have poor problem-solving skills, lack understanding of other people's feelings, and are sometimes even physically aggressive (David-Ferdon et al., 2016). However, despite the difficulties these students face, most of them do not become violent. Potentially violent students represent only 1% of children who enter school. Psychologists have developed profiles of school bullies and other potentially violent youth. Among other things, they tend to be loners who lack empathy for others, frequently are victims of violence at home, and have a great deal of pent-up anger, a low frustration tolerance, a record of involvement in substance abuse and other risky behaviors, and a lack of moral conscience (MacNeil, 2002). These troubled youth likely have average or above-average intelligence but are not likely to do well in school and threaten the educational quality and physical well-being of other children and themselves. They exhibit behaviors that should alert teachers and administrators to the danger they may pose to themselves and others (see Table 13.1).

Unfortunately, beyond identifying troubled students, research has not yet developed a strong knowledge base about the causes of violent behavior or the ways it can be prevented. No one knows how to prevent potentially violent children from becoming violent adults. Schools now embracing one violence management curriculum or another are doing so without adequate evidence of their long-term effectiveness. Many causes of violence are not within the schools' control. If children have not learned to control their aggression by the time they come to school, it may not be possible for them to disentangle the patterns of violence that took shape in their early years.

Developing and promoting ways in which these students can be identified as soon as possible can help ensure that they and their families gain access to appropriate treatment and services. In some cases, these services can even be school based and,

Table 13.1	Characteristics of Youths Who Have Caused School-Associated Deaths

1. Has a history of tantrums and uncontrollable angry outbursts.
2. Characteristically resorts to name-calling, cursing, or abusive language.
3. Habitually makes violent threats when angry.
4. Has previously brought a weapon to school.
5. Has a background of serious disciplinary problems at school and in the community.
6. Has a background of drug, alcohol, or substance abuse or dependency.
7. Is on the fringe of his or her peer group with few or no close friends.
8. Is preoccupied with weapons, explosives, or other incendiary devices.
9. Has previously been truant, suspended, or expelled from school.
10. Displays cruelty to animals.
11. Has little or no supervision and support from parents or a caring adult.
12. Has witnessed or been a victim of abuse or neglect in the home.
13. Has been bullied and/or bullies or intimidates peers or younger children.
14. Tends to blame others for difficulties and problems he or she causes him- or herself.
15. Consistently prefers television shows, movies, or music expressing violent themes or acts.
16. Prefers reading material dealing with violent themes, rituals, and abuse.
17. Reflects anger, frustration, and the dark side of life in school essays or writing projects.
18. Is on the fringe of or appears isolated from their peer social group.
19. Is often depressed and/or has significant mood swings.
20. Has threatened or attempted suicide.

Source: National School Safety Center (2019).

with such support, students who might otherwise have to be removed can remain in the building with their peers. In other cases, the young people's needs and their potential threat to themselves and others will require more dramatic remedies. However, once school personnel have alerted the appropriate authorities, they should be able to expect that state, local government, and law enforcement power will address students' needs. Child protective agencies can become involved in situations of abuse or neglect, including the failure of a parent to agree to or follow through on mental health treatment. Courts can appoint guardians. States can make it easier to commit young people who pose a danger to themselves or others to residential treatment facilities. Such actions are necessary if we are serious about reducing violence that takes place in school.

However, these actions are not within the power of school personnel, nor should they be. So schools' ability to control violence is limited. None of us wants to appear callous or indifferent to children, but schools are not social welfare agencies. Teachers are not social workers or psychiatrists. Educators are trained to teach children reading, math, social studies, and other important content and skills. We cannot reasonably expect schools and teachers to function in other capacities because we lack the political will to adequately pay the salaries of those with the appropriate preparation to deal with students who exhibit the potential for violence.

Alternative Schools for Potentially Violent Students

Some advocates, and even the federal government, have pressured school districts to keep unruly students in the building as a way of reducing racial discrimination in disciplinary policies. Schools cannot prevent violence if they are mandated to keep troubled students within the building, especially if there are inadequate social or mental health services to address their needs. However well intentioned these efforts are, they penalize well-behaving students, disempower teachers and administrators, and make schools more dangerous. Personnel cannot prevent violence if they cannot remove students who imperil everyone's safety (American Association of School Administrators, 2018; Federal Commission on School Safety, 2018).

Efforts to respond to the needs of the most troubled children and allowing them to stay in school not only are of doubtful benefit to them, they also negatively affect the academic progress of other children. Almost 6% of middle and high school students say they have avoided classes or school activities because they were afraid of being attacked or harmed. Students attending urban schools reported this behavior at higher rates than their counterparts in suburban or rural schools (Musu et al., 2019). Clearly a student cannot learn if they do not attend class. They are less likely to go to class if they fear for their safety. Creating and implementing violence prevention curricula and conducting school safety "drills," while leaving dangerous students in the building, distract from education's primary mission. Rather than acting as violence prevention these efforts unwittingly encourage students to accept and adapt to the presence of conflict and danger in school.

Schools should try every measure to help young children adapt to school and school discipline. But some children never will adjust to academic demands and or achieve the self-discipline required for success. Identifying those students and removing them to alternative settings deserve to be the focus of schools' efforts since they, unlike other options, are actually achievable. Educators have long recognized that alternatives in public education are sometimes necessary to serve special populations of students—teenage mothers, for example, or the physically disabled. The one-size-fits-all model of the comprehensive public high school does not serve everyone equally well, and some students rebel against the competition, perceived conformity, and order of traditional education. Many educators now acknowledge that the academic demands and social structure of traditional high schools may contribute to school violence. Students unaccustomed to impersonal rules governing school behavior and the emphasis that schools place on quiet compliance may lash out at teachers and other students. By the time they reach middle school, students learn the focus of schooling is on academic achievement and, unfortunately, students who do not achieve often develop indifferent or hostile attitudes. Sometimes they wave their hands and say "help" by acting out.

Alternative schools can siphon off the troubled, disaffected, potentially violent, and others for whom traditional schooling is not a good fit. Alternative schools often are better able to serve nonacademic students while allowing traditional schools to focus on the majority's academic needs. They are designed for students who, because of any number of problems—academic but more often behavioral or social—are not able to learn well in a traditional school environment. Today, all but three states have some form of alternative school program, sometimes as part of the school, other times as separate buildings with their own faculty and administrators. Alternative schools and programs serve students who are at risk of dropping out of school for any number of reasons. Slightly less than 1% of students (369,000) in the United States already attend alternative schools (Government Accountability Office, 2019).

Alternative schools are likely to be less formal than traditional schools and typically offer a lower student-to-teacher ratio. The record indicates these schools can go a long way toward ameliorating the anonymity and isolation some students experience in traditional schools. Many formerly disruptive students behave better when they work in a small, supportive setting. They are able to find a niche that eluded them in traditional schools and teachers willing to focus on personal and social problems that they bring with them to school (Kannam and Weiss, 2019).

Alternative schools can be very effective and should be viewed as appropriate educational options for disruptive students who have not responded to special curricular treatment and counseling in regular schools and classes. Unfortunately, although alternative schools try to accommodate students with a wide range of problems, they do not work for everyone. In fact, they may not work well for many of the most disruptive students. The same students who caused problems in traditional schools often continue to present problems when they transfer to alternative schools. For these students, more dramatic action is likely to be in order.

Schools should embrace all students equally when they first begin school. Special curriculum interventions—the so-called conflict and dispute resolution curricula—should be reserved exclusively for students who demonstrate behaviors associated with violence in adults (e.g., physical aggression and lack of self-control). Schools should use every technique at their disposal to curb disruptive behavior and bring the unruly child back into the fold. However, by middle school, students who impede the learning process of their classmates or threaten the welfare of other children should be considered as candidates for alternative schools. Students who are not likely to succeed in one kind of school should be given another chance in a different kind of school. These alternative schools have amassed a sound, though not perfect, record for educating the disaffected. For the small handful of very disruptive students who are unable to cooperate in an alternative school, expulsion is a harsh but sensible last resort. While segregating students from their peers is a serious limitation on their civil rights, it is a necessary option if society is intent on preventing the most dramatic and tragic types of violence in schools.

Gun-Free Schools and Student Safety

While shootings in schools make headlines and create heart break whenever they occur, they are mercifully infrequent relative to the number of schools in the United

States. The Department of Education reports that from 2000 to 2017, there were 37 active shooter incidents at elementary and secondary schools, resulting in 153 casualties (67 deaths and 86 wounded). Each of the incidents involved a single male shooter. Most of them were students or former students at the schools where the shooting took place. Twenty-two of them were apprehended by police, one was killed by law enforcement, and 14 took their own lives. Overall, however, youth homicides at schools, including those in school shootings, constitute less than 3% of the total number of youth homicides. Youth suicides at school are less than 1% of the total number of youth suicides (Musu et al., 2019). In fact, mass shootings that target children or adults are more likely to occur at home than at any other place (Center for American Progress, 2017).

For 30 years, the Gun-Free School Zones Act (GFSZA) has helped keep schools relatively safe from the most devastating kind of violence. The GFSZA prohibits carrying loaded or unlocked firearms within 1,000 feet of K–12 schools. The law provides an exception for law enforcement officers who are acting in their official capacity. A few states also provide exceptions for people who have permits to carry concealed firearms (Center for American Progress, 2017).

Not content to hold schools responsible for violence prevention through other methods, lawmakers and some members of the public are now telling school staff that they should carry weapons. This recent push to allow or require school personnel to have guns in schools should be examined closely before it is adopted across the country. The idea of an armed teacher, even a well-trained one, as the last line of defense in an active shooter situation is based neither on research nor experience.

The leaders of diverse groups, including the National Education Association, the American Federation of Teachers, the National Association of School Resource Officers, and the Major Cities Police Chiefs Association, have all expressed their opposition to allowing teachers to carry weapons into schools and expecting them to use them in case of a violent incident. Allowing adults to be armed at school creates safety risks with limited benefit in the effort to prevent mass shootings at schools. The laws that have been created do not require training comparable to that required by full-time law enforcement officers. Having guns in schools risks the possibility of students' obtaining those weapons. The risk of shootings actually increases when guns are present and the presence of armed staff will complicate law enforcement's response in an emergency (Everytown for Gun Safety, 2019).

Although they are outside of a school's ability to enact, alternatives to allowing or, in fact, requiring the presence of weapons in schools exist. They include passing "red flag" laws that allow family members and law enforcement officers to limit a person's access to weapons if he or she is presenting warning signs that they might resort to violence. Another option is requiring responsible firearm storage in homes with young people, which would also limit access without adult supervision. Raising the minimum age for the purchase of semiautomatic firearms to 21 and requiring background checks for all gun purchases are also commonsense actions that local, state, and federal governments could take. Experience and research indicates that the effectiveness of these laws will far outweigh the potential benefits of acting on the "myth" that an armed teacher will prevent deaths from school shootings. Even well-trained veteran police officers acknowledge that their shooting accuracy decreases when they exchange gunfire with a suspect. The idea that a teacher with less experience and training will be able to identify a perpetrator correctly, summon up the will to shoot a young person they know, and do so accurately is simply too doubtful to be the basis for policy (Everytown for Gun Safety, 2019).

What schools can do to control and prevent violence among students is to offer academic instruction that is rigorous and gives them hope that they will be prepared for the future. Students who have learning difficulties should be supported and helped to achieve success. Social and emotional learning should be incorporated into the curricula, with a focus on the tradition of virtue and character development that has characterized American society. Students should experience fair and consistent consequences when they violate rules and should be provided with opportunities and support to change inappropriate behavior. Schools should be expected and empowered to refer students and families to appropriate social and mental health agencies. And schools should be allowed to refer students to alternative settings or expel them from school if they pose a danger to themselves and others. Asking school personnel to take on other roles such as social workers, therapists, or law enforcement officers is futile and will increase, not decrease, the possibility of the very tragedies they hope to prevent.

FOR DISCUSSION

1. Research local school districts' policies regarding school personnel's ability to have guns in school buildings and to use them in violent situations. The Federal Commission on School Safety (2018) recommended that states and local governments consider the following when considering whether school personnel should be allowed to carry weapons:

    a. *Existing security measures*: What types of security measures already exist to ensure student safety? Is there a full-time SRO already present in case of an emergency?

    b. *Proximity of police*: How quickly can local police arrive in the event of an active shooter? How well do local police know the school (e.g., layout of the school, area around the school) in order to coordinate an effective response?

    c. *Acceptance of the school community*: Are school community stakeholders comfortable with arming school personnel? Are there staff members willing to voluntarily participate in such a program, particularly those with prior law enforcement or military training?

    d. *Preparedness*: What would initial and ongoing background checks and screening requirements entail? What initial and ongoing robust training requirements would be in place? How would firearms be properly secured yet made easily accessible when necessary?

    e. *Local policy and state law*: Does local policy and state law allow for the arming of school personnel? What infrastructure and resources exist for the creation of such a program? What potential liabilities exist for such a program (e.g., ability to maintain insurance coverage)?

    Do you find evidence that these items were considered in creating local policies about allowing guns on school grounds? If discussions about the topic are under way in other districts in your state, are these topics part of the conversation?

What arguments for and against allowing school personnel to bear weapons do you find most persuasive?

2. Researchers find that students and other youth express bullying in different ways according to gender. Boys tend to be physically aggressive, while girls are "relationally aggressive," that is, harming others through gossip, spreading rumors, and excluding them from social contact (Leff et al., 2007). Does this finding reflect your experiences with bullying and violence in elementary and secondary schools?

In your experience, did the schools handle bullying appropriately for both victim and bully? Did the schools respond differently to incidents involving the physical violence of boys and the relational violence of girls? Should they?

3. In Scandinavian countries, corporal punishment is prohibited by law in schools and in homes. All 50 of the United States allow corporal punishment at home. Nineteen allow it in schools. The Program Accreditation Criteria of the National Association for the Education of Young Children (2018) include the following statement about the interactions among teachers and children in preschools, kindergarten, and child care centers: "Teachers [should] abstain from corporal punishment or humiliating or frightening discipline techniques."

Is this a reasonable standard? Should parents have the right to determine whether corporal punishment can be used as a form of discipline on their own children at home or in the public schools they attend?

REFERENCES

Alvarez, A., and Bachman, R. (2016). *Violence: The Enduring Problem* (3rd ed.). Los Angeles: Sage.

American Association of School Administrators (2018). 2018 AASA Discipline Survey: An Analysis of How the 2014 Dear Colleague Letter on Nondiscriminatory Administration of School Discipline is Impacting District Practices and Policies (aasa.org/uploadedFiles/AASA_Blog(1)/AASASurveyDisciplineGuidance2014.pdf).

Anderson, C., Bushman, B., Bartholow, B., Cantor, J., Christakis, D., Coyne, S., Donnerstein, E., Funk Brockmyer, J., Gentile, D., Green, C., Huesmann, R., Hummer, T., Krahé, B., Strasburger, V., Warburton, W., Wilson, B., and Ybarra, M. (2017). "Screen Violence and Youth Behavior." *Pediatrics* 140(Supplement 2):140–148. https://doi.org/10.1542/peds.2016-1758T

Center for American Progress (2017). Keeping America's Schools Safe from Gun Violence (americanprogress.org/issues/guns-crime/reports/2017/04/07/430247/keeping-americas-schools-safe-gun-violence).

Cuellar, M. J. (2018). "School Safety Strategies and Their Effects on the Occurrence of School-Based Violence in U.S. High Schools: An Exploratory Study." *Journal of School Violence* 17(1):28–45. https://doi.org/10.1080/15388220.2016.1193742

David-Ferdon, C., Vivolo-Kantor, A., Dahlberg, L., Marshall, K., Rainford, N., and Hall, J. (2016). *A Comprehensive Technical Package for the Prevention of Youth Violence and Associated Risk Behaviors*. Atlanta, GA: National Center for Injury Prevention and Control, Centers for Disease Control and Prevention.

Dworkin, M. S. (1959). *Dewey on Education*. New York: Teachers College Press.

Eith, C., and Trump, K. (2019). "Why Social Bonding is a School-Safety Priority." *Educational Leadership* 77(2).

Everytown for Gun Safety (2019). Keeping our Schools Safe: A Plan to Stop Mass Shootings and End Gun Violence in American Schools (everytownresearch.org/reports/keeping-schools-safe-plan-stop-mass-shootings-end-gun-violence-american-schools).

Federal Commission on School Safety (2018). *Final Report of the Federal Commission on School Safety*. Washington, DC: Federal Commission on School Safety.

Finn, C., and Hess, F. (2019, April). *What Social and Emotional Learning Needs to Succeed and Survive*. Washington DC: American Enterprise Institute.

Gaffney, H., Ttofi, M. M., and Farrington, D. P. (2019). "Evaluating the Effectiveness of School-Bullying Prevention Programs: An Updated Meta-Analytical Review." *Aggression and Violent Behavior* (45):111–133. https://doi.org/10.1016/j.avb.2018.07.001

Government Accountability Office (2019). *Certain Groups of Students Attend Alternative Schools in Greater Proportions Than They Do Other Schools* (GAO-19-373). Washington, DC: Government Accountability Office.

Hagerty, B. (2018, May 21). "The Futility of Trying to Prevent More School Shootings in America." *The Atlantic*.

Indicators of School Crime and Safety (2018, March). Indicator 6: Violent and Other Criminal Incidents at Public Schools, and Those Reported to the Police. Institute of Education Sciences, National Center for Education Statistics (nces.ed.gov/programs/crimeindicators/ind_06.asp).

Indicators of School Crime and Safety (2019, April). Indicator 3: Prevalence of Victimization at School. Institute of Education Sciences, National Center for Education Statistics (nces.ed.gov/programs/crimeindicators/ind_03.asp).

Kannam, J., and Weiss, M. (2019). *Alternative Education in ESSA State Plans: A Review of 38 States*. Washington, DC: American Youth Policy Forum.

Leff, S. S., Angelucci, J., Goldstein, A. B., Cardacciotto, L., Paskewich, B., and Grossman, M. B. (2007). Using a Participatory Action Research Model to Create a School-Based Intervention Program for Relationally Aggressive Girls—The Friend to Friend Program. In J. E. Zins, M. J. Elias, and C. A. Maher, eds., *Bullying, Victimization, and Peer Harassment*. New York: Haworth.

Lott, J. (2019, April 25). Schools That Allow Teachers to Carry Guns Are Extremely Safe: Data on the Rate of Shootings and Accidents in Schools That Allow Teachers to Carry. http://dx.doi.org/10.2139/ssrn.3377801

MacNeil, G. (2002). School Bullying: An Overview. In L. A. Rapp-Paglicci, A. R. Roberts, and J. S. Wodarski, eds., *Handbook of Violence*. New York: Wiley.

May, D. (2018). "Introduction to the Special Issue on School Safety: Increasing Understanding/Decreasing Misunderstanding in the Realm of School Safety." *American Journal of Criminal Justice* 43(11):11–55.

Musu, L., Zhang, A., Wang, K., Zhang, J., and Oudekerk, B. (2019). *Indicators of School Crime and Safety: 2018* (NCES 2019-047/NCJ 252571). Washington, DC: National Center for Education Statistics and Bureau of Justice Statistics, Office of Justice Programs.

National Association for the Education of Young Children (2018). *Early Childhood Program Standards and Accreditation Criteria*. Washington, DC: National Association for the Education of Young Children.

National School Safety Center (2019). Checklist of Characteristics of Youth Who Have Caused School-Associated Violent Deaths (schoolsafety.us/media-resources/checklist-of-characteristics-of-youth-who-have-caused-school-associated-violent-deaths).

National Threat Assessment Center (2018). *Enhancing School Safety Using a Threat Assessment Model: An Operational Guide for Preventing Targeted School Violence*. Washington, DC: U.S. Secret Service, Department of Homeland Security.

Rideout, V. (2017). *The Common Sense Census: Media Use by Kids Age Zero to Eight*. San Francisco: Common Sense Media.

Rideout, V., and Robb, M. B. (2019). *The Common Sense Census: Media Use by Tweens and Teens, 2019*. San Francisco: Common Sense Media.

Sandy Hook Advisory Commission (2015). *Final Report of the Sandy Hook Advisory Commission* (shac.ct.gov/SHAC_Final_Report_3-6-2015.pdf).

Sargent, G. (2018, February 23). "A Frighteningly Large Number of Americans Support Arming Teachers." *Washington Post*.

Sivaraman, B., Nye, E., and Bowes, L. (2019). "School-Based Anti-Bullying Interventions for Adolescents in Low- and Middle-Income Countries: A Systematic Review." *Aggression and Violent Behavior* 45:154–162.

U.S. Department of Education, Office of Civil Rights (2019, May). *School Climate and Safety: Data Highlights on School Climate and Safety in Our Nation's Public Schools*. Washington, DC: U.S. Department of Education.

Volungis, A., and Goodman, K. (2017). "School Violence Prevention: Teachers Establishing Relationships with Students Using Counseling Strategies." *Psychology* 7(1). https://doi.org/10.1177/2158244017700460

Waschbusch, D. A., Breaux, R. P., and Babinski, D. E. (2019). "School-Based Interventions for Aggression and Defiance in Youth: A Framework for Evidence-Based Practice." *School Mental Health* 11:92–105. https://doi:10.1007/s12310-018-9269-0

Inclusion and Disability

Common or Special Education

14

Should selected children be included in regular school classes or separated into special education?

Position 1: For Inclusion

Normal was created, not discovered, by flawed, eccentric, self-interested, racist, ableist, homophobic, sexist humans. Normal is a statistical fiction, nothing more.

—Mooney (2019)

Disability studies in education holds the democratic promise of critically examining the social structures and processes that perpetuate injustice and inequality.

—Danforth (2016)

Democratic Purposes for Inclusion

Full inclusion of all children into school life is a fundamental social and educational principle in a free democracy. Students classified "special" or "exceptional" in physical or mental characteristics should not be isolated in separate schools or classes. An examination of the idea of disability is needed (Cluley et al., 2020). Inclusive schools recognize the richness in human diversity. Danforth (2008), using John Dewey's classic works on democracy, proposes the unification of individual and social interests in a "coherent democratic framework" (p. 61). That framework incorporates the positive individualized education ideas from traditional special education into a unified program of inclusion as part of a higher level of education for all students in civilized society.

Central to education in a democracy are concepts of equal opportunity and justice. Democracy requires citizens to have the opportunity to be fully educated. Equal opportunity and fairness underscore the idea of inclusion. Other important reasons

313

support inclusion of special students into regular school classes and activities, but the fundamental premise of democracy expects no less. Education is the primary means for realizing those premises. Isolating special education students not only labels and stigmatizes them but also limits their full interaction with others during their most formative years. This is detrimental to these students and it is also detrimental to the perceptions of nonexceptional students about life in the full society.

In addition to the obvious educational value of allowing all students to participate fully in the schools, inclusion is also a civil rights issue. Discrimination against persons with disabilities is illegal. The 1990 Americans with Disabilities Act barred such discrimination, as other laws barred discrimination based on race, gender, or age. Some institutions meet the access requirements of the Americans with Disabilities Act on purely physical grounds, providing ramps and elevators and modifying doors and bathrooms. This minimal approach is the equivalent of doing nothing more than removing "whites only" signs after the Civil Rights Act of 1964; it would not deal with underlying, pervasive instances of discrimination restricting access and opportunity. Education is primary for providing access to opportunities. Separate but equal education for African Americans was actually separate but not equal; similarly, separate special education is also separate but not equal.

In response to social and parental concerns and interests, early special education programs helped special needs students, but they also separated them. Today's programs are far superior to the historic ways of treating the mentally and physically disabled: institutionalized or imprisoned for life, ostracized or removed from public view, as well as physically mistreated or abused. The more recent policy of "mainstreaming" special needs students into regular classrooms sounds better than it actually is— some students with disabilities are placed in some regular art, music, physical education, and other classes depending on the disability, but they are still mainly separated from others during the school day.

The Legal Basis for Full Inclusion

During the past half century, the United States has declared that all children with disabilities be provided a free and appropriate education in public schools. Modifications in legislation, from 1975 to the present, have improved the educational rights of children with disabilities and their families. Full inclusion is the next logical step. Turnbull and Turnbull (1998) defined this evolving policy as "zero reject" and noted that an important effect was "to redefine the doctrine of equal educational opportunity as it applies to children with disabilities and to establish different meanings of equality as it applies to people with and without disabilities" (p. 92). Earlier laws interpreted equality as equal access to different resources—separate special education classes and schools. Newer laws assume that equal access means full access to regular resources— regular classes and schools but with special support to help students. As racism is discrimination because of race, ableism is discrimination because of disability.

The principle of inclusion goes well beyond the mainstreaming that developed since the 1975 landmark federal legislation, the Education of All Handicapped Children Act (Public Law 94-142). At the time Congress was considering this law, 1 million out of 8 million disabled children under age 21 were completely excluded from the U.S. public school system. They were outcasts. Mainstreaming grew out of an important clause of the law, offering the concept of the "least restrictive environment"—meaning that students with special needs who "demonstrate appropriate behavior and skills" should be in general classrooms rather than segregated programs. The law gave some children with special needs the educational, emotional, and social advantages offered to other students. It also gave parents the right to be advocates in fashioning an appropriate education for their differently abled children.

Changes in the law have led toward full inclusion. The 2004 Individuals with Disabilities Education Act (IDEA), as amended by parts of the Every Student Succeeds Act of 2015, requires schools to offer placement to meet the needs of students with disabilities and, to the maximum extent appropriate, to educate children with disabilities with other children. It recognizes disability as a "natural part of the human experience" that "in no way diminishes the right" to full social participation and contribution. The law expects schools to provide supplementary aids and services for disabled children as needed and requires that separation or removal from regular environments only occur when the child cannot learn in regular classes even with supplementary aids and services (IDEA, 2019). These rules set high standards that schools are expected to meet before excluding disabled students from regular classes. The purpose of this is to address ableism.

Court decisions are expansive in recognition of the individual and social benefits of inclusion. *Mills v. Board of Education of the District of Columbia* (1972) decided class-action litigation based on equal opportunity and due process—that children with physical or mental disabilities had a right to a suitable and free public education; lack of funds was not a defense for exclusion. Other cases supplement this (*Oberti v. Board of Education of the Borough of Clementon (NJ) School District,* 1993; see also Bateman and Cline, 2019).

Full inclusion is not limited to the United States. UNESCO (2015, 2020) sponsors the Global Education Monitoring Report, which includes a report on inclusion and education. In 2007, the United Nations Convention on the Rights of Persons with Disabilities reaffirmed that all persons with all types of disabilities enjoy all human rights and fundamental freedoms. The UN Programme on Disability reports on disability interests internationally. Moderate to severe disabilities affect about 5% of the world population. This figure includes almost 8% of populations of developed countries and over 4% of populations in less developed regions. The total number of disabled persons is estimated to reach over 300 million in the next few years (United Nations, 2018). Disparity between developed and less developed areas of the world reflects differences in measuring tools, in health practices, and in governmental policies on reporting disabilities. Health care improvements should cause an increase in numbers of disabled persons since children who previously might have died at birth or in infancy will survive but may have serious impairments (Mittler et al., 1993; Wedell, 1993; Sefa Dei et al., 2000; UNESCO, 2008; Gibson and Haynes, 2009).

Nationally, almost 61 million students, from ages 6 to 21, receive special education services. Their eligibility depends on a diagnosis of one or more of 13 disabilities, including autism, deafness, blindness, emotional disturbances, orthopedic limits, and intellectual or learning impairment (Young et al., 2019).

Language and Labels: Disabled, Exceptional, Average

Special education should mean the education of all students, because all are special in some form and education should provide for all individuals. But language is a social construct, dependent on time and place. Words convey intent, value, comparison, ideology, and a variety of nuances. They help identify, clarify, and unify, but they can also obscure and divide. Blue can mean a color; a blue moon is not a moon that is blue in color, but two full moons in one month; the blues can signal sad emotions or a musical style; and a blue state is where a majority vote for Democrats. Common definitions change in active languages. Words become labels for people and ideas, and sometimes these are misleading and unintended. Special education is such an example.

Normal and average are also examples. They can convey a modestly positive or negative sense, depending on the context: "The results of the blood test were normal" or "He is an average doctor." In school terms, a class grade of "C" is a normal or average grade, it is usually the mid-point of mental or physical measurements. Garrison Keillor, on the radio show *A Prairie Home Companion*, used to say about his fictional town "and all the children are above average," suggesting that as an ideal. However, if everyone scored exactly the same, there would be no above or below average: all are average.

Misleading ideas of "average" or" normal," and people's personal insecurities, fueled prejudice and discrimination against disabled children over a long period of history. Those who differ are labeled negatively to maintain the status of the favored. Although we often refer to an average, you will struggle to find a completely "average" person in physical, mental, and emotional characteristics. Who among us comes from a family of 2.3 children or is exactly average in human height, weight, IQ, and body measurements? Each of us differs from the average. Average suggests dullness and conformity; richness comes from diversity. Average is suitable as a broad guide for making tentative comparative judgments about many conditions, such as income tax deductions or the amount of sleep time needed, but should not be mindlessly used as a criterion to rank human qualities. Every child differs from average in some respect. Despite efforts in many schools to avoid negative views, separating students can cause some students to be perceived as deficient because of their labels, a form of ableism. Supreme Court Justice Sonia Sotomayor (2019) wrote a children's book to address the feelings she had as a child; the need to inject insulin for diabetes treatments gave her the sense that others saw her as different.

Identification of exceptionality varies by nation and time period (Taylor, 2003). In the United States, it usually refers to identifiable differences in physical, mental, emotional, or other abilities. Disabled or exceptional children differ from "average" ones based on school or test results in areas like reading, writing, listening, sitting attentively, seeing and hearing, and so on. Exceptionality includes both extremes of mental ability—the severely mentally or learning impaired and the gifted and talented. Both get special treatment and school support, but they bear different statuses in schools. Exceptional also includes those with a variety of physical differences from "average" children, including differences in sight, hearing, and use of limbs. Some exceptional children, on the gifted side, may also have learning or physical disabilities; a category now identified as twice exceptional (Kaufman, 2018).

Genetics, at-birth disabilities, improper medical practice, disease, parental irresponsibility, accidents, and inadequate health care are common causes of disabilities, but these are not self-inflicted. These chance happenings should not create a wall of separation from the rest of society; human variety is extraordinarily complex and incredibly wide ranging. Disability is identified as something that occurs at birth or through disease or some event, while handicaps are the secondary problems that occur because of discrimination, mistreatment, or help that is denied or delayed. Handicapped is a social problem of bias and discrimination, while disability is an individual problem. We may improve the measures, but human variability remains unknown and reflects cultural norms and prejudices.

Disability Studies in Education

Medical views are the basis of traditional definitions of and treatment for disabilities, based on how a person can function in particular settings. This presumes that we have a clear and precise definition of "ability" so that we can compare individuals and then identify the disabled person as deficient. But we all know that ability and functionality depend on situations and individuals. A person in one situation may have ability, but not in all. Are we not all disabled in some dimension of human existence? The newly emerging field of disability studies in education challenges the common view that disability means deficiency and requires social and educational separation (Danforth, 2016). For over 25 years, the Society for Disability Studies (disstudies.org) and its journal, *Disability Studies Quarterly*, provide thoughtful discussion of issues.

Disability studies is a broad-based interdisciplinary approach to understanding social, cultural, economic, political, and historic identification and treatment of people with disabilities. Critical study in the humanities, social sciences, education, and science, using questions about disability and society, leads to important analysis in literature, aesthetics, history, bioethics, critical theory, and human rights (Goffman, 1961; Batson and Bergman, 2002; Scully, 2008; Siebers, 2008, 2010; Garland Thomson, 2010; Smith, 2010; Baglieri, 2017; Valle and Connor, 2019). Disability studies look at cultural and social environments as determinants of disability and criticize negative social responses. It critiques social class and status, privilege and power, and ideologically limited views of disability. It also looks at minority status and disability through consideration of such factors as race, gender, age, ethnicity, sexual orientation, religion, national derivation, and language facility. Interest in disability studies sparked unsupportable fear among some advocates of special education, but disability studies offer many benefits to children with special needs (Connor, 2019).

Exclusion and Segregation: Racism and Ableism

The long effort to exclude some special needs students from regular school classes and activities has remarkable parallels with racial segregation efforts (Oakes, 2005; Stancil, 2018; DeMatthews, 2019). Ferri and Connor (2005) suggest: "As in the case of school desegregation, the movement from segregated placements toward more inclusive ones for students with disabilities has involved a long and often difficult struggle. . . ." Parallels also exist between the treatment of minorities and the treatment of disabled children in schools. Racism and ableism are both corrosive of our democracy and social values. A striking feature of school classification of children into special education classes, programs, or schools is that the students come disproportionately from minority ethnic and social class groups of society (Educational Testing Service, 1980; Anderson and Anderson, 1983; Ferri and Connor, 2005; Artiles and Bal, 2008; Valle and Connor, 2019). The combination of class, race, and classification as disabled becomes a recipe for discrimination. This is a civil rights issue on principle and a political issue in practice. Class and ethnicity have been used politically to limit the full participation of groups without wealth and power. Children with special needs have been subject to a similar political agenda restricting access, opportunity, and fulfillment of the democratic ideal (Harry et al., 2008).

Abnormality has historically been the basis for a variety of destructive actions by those in power, from infanticide to institutionalization. Poore (2007) documents the German treatment of children with disabilities over the twentieth century: hiding them as invalids, starving them to death in institutions, reducing them to street beggar or freak show status in the Weimar Republic; and sterilizing them during the Third Reich's eugenics effort. This history is similar to the United States and other parts of the world over the same period. Before 1910, the United States institutionalized many children with disabilities in isolation from society. Families of these children hid them, provided private care, or sent them off to live out their lives away from public view or participation. Winzer's (1993) comprehensive history summarizes: "A society's treatment of those who are weak and dependent is one critical indicator of its social progress. Social attitudes concerning the education and care of exceptional individuals reflect general cultural attitudes concerning the obligations of a society to its individual citizens" (p. 3). This, in the United States and in the civilized world, is a civil rights issue based on the most fundamental documents and foundational moral principles (Rotatori et al., 2011).

Social and Psychological Arguments for Inclusion

Persuasive arguments based on fundamental democratic principles and fair social policy favor full inclusion, and social and personal psychology offer other important arguments. Separation of exceptional children from the mainstream of children in schools has been recognized as traumatic for those separated, whether by race, gender, or abilities. In the landmark Supreme Court decision that declared racially segregated schools and the concept of "separate but equal" unconstitutional (*Brown v. Board of Education*, 1954), Chief Justice Earl Warren argued that separation in schools can cause children to "generate a feeling of inferiority as to . . . status in the community that may affect their hearts and minds in a way unlikely ever to be undone" (p. 493). Perceptions of special needs children are strongly influenced by their separation. Individual feelings of insecurity feed the concept that society values them less and prefers them out of sight (Shevin, 2007; Alur and Bach, 2010; Smith, 2010; Valle and Connor, 2019). As a matter of social policy, separation is inconsistent with the larger-scale interests of the United States (Sailor et al., 1991; Shevin, 2007; Danforth, 2008). A major benefit of full inclusion could be to dramatically change the current mass production, assembly line nature of many public schools to recognize the needs of all individual students.

Broad social policy goals underlie the tenets of inclusion for special needs youth in all society's activities and institutions. Full participation in the society requires full inclusion in the schools. Denying those rights to the disabled denies society the skills, the economic productivity, and the social and political values inherent in full participation of individuals with disabilities.

Changing public attitudes regarding our social responsibility for persons with disabilities, as well as a recognition of the general economic and social value in providing training for disadvantaged people, led to a variety of alterations in social policies and educational practices. This occurred at the same time as public schooling expanded in the early twentieth century. For the disabled, this meant segregation in separate schools and/or separate classes, teachers, and programs. The intent may have been benign, but segregation is inadequate as a social policy.

Inclusion Is More Than Mere Addition

Full inclusion expects far more of good education than merely adding classified students to general classes or mandating all students to run, climb, read, write, draw, or compute in only one way and at the same speed. Full inclusion assumes that schools will provide high-quality, individualized instruction, with well-prepared teachers, suitable and varied teaching materials, and appropriate schedules to support the idea that all students are capable of success. The principle of full inclusion merely extends the democratic principle of quality education for all to include children with special needs.

Federal policy guidelines specify that schools may not use lack of resources or personnel as an excuse for not providing free and appropriate education—in the least restrictive environments—to students with disabilities. School districts have been very slow to follow the law and the policies. Valle and Connor (2019) note that "inclusion remains more of an ideal than a widespread reality within public education." U.S. Department of Education (2019) data show that, after many years promoting inclusion, only about 60% of students labeled disabled are in regular classes 80% of school time. For students labeled with an intellectual disability the percentage is far lower. Schools are slow to change traditional patterns of separation. Common excuses used by schools are: "We don't provide inclusion," "This child is too disabled to be in a regular classroom," and "We give them special programs." These arguments don't meet the legal standard. Another main issue is inadequate teacher education for inclusive classrooms (Mader, 2017). Robert Slavin (2019) writes: "We put far too much effort into deciding what to call these students, far too little into teaching them." The law and court decisions require inclusion unless the severity of the disability precludes satisfactory education in regular classes. This high standard does not allow schools to ignore or dismiss the requirement to provide inclusion for the vast majority of students with disabilities (Kluth et al., 2001; Cigman, 2007).

Under IDEA, the Department of Education offers programs to implement quality education for children with disabilities. Response to Intervention (RTI) is a tiered instructional process to identify struggling students early, to provide research-based instruction, and to closely monitor progress for all students. The National Center for Learning Disabilities (ncld.org) supports the RTI Action Network (rtinetwork.org), with assistance to schools, teachers, parents, and officials in developing RTI in the schools. Success in this effort is dependent largely on effective implementation by well-prepared teachers in positive school settings, for which the research- and evidence-based approach offers grounded teacher practice and close monitoring (Jimerson et al., 2007; Glover and Vaughn, 2010; RTI Action Network, 2019).

Another area of interest to the Department of Education and to scholars in the area of disabilities education is the transition of disabled children into and through schools and from schools to postschool adult life in work, further education, integration into their communities, and related positive development of adult living skills. Positive behavior support is an ongoing theme for this work. One of the foci of federal interest is the Rehabilitation Services Administration, which oversees grants and activities to help individuals with physical and mental disabilities to gain employment, to live more independently, and to be successful in the community and in the labor market. The Rehabilitation Services Administration produces annual reviews and conducts state-by-state monitoring to judge progress, with agency report cards that rank states on several criteria related to success. This interest in the constructive, positive, and productive participation of disabled people is consistent with full inclusion approaches in schools.

Full inclusion does not mean that schools should bring in students with special needs only to insist on blind conformity to a single standard for all students, nor does it mean that nonconforming students should be ignored or mistreated in "regular" schools (Danforth and Smith, 2005). Inclusion assumes that the individual needs of every student, whether classified "special" or not, seriously must be considered to provide a quality education. This assumption undergirds the idea of full inclusion for students who are "special" or "exceptional."

Potential Problems

Full inclusion into the lives of schools is not an easy task. Fears of parents, teachers, administrators, and community members can be mitigated by developing strong programs of information, discussion, preparation, and positive interaction. Special education teachers fear loss of expert status and, perhaps, their jobs; and regular teachers are concerned about lack of preparation and support. Frequently cited causes of fears about inclusion are ineffective leadership, inadequate teacher preparation, ignorance of cultural factors, and inappropriate organization, policies, academic expectations and outdated curriculums, traditions related to social and teacher attitudes, testing, policies, regulations, corporate pressure, and behaviorist scholars.

These have a detrimental impact on efforts to develop full inclusion programs in schools. We need improved teacher education to better prepare teachers for educating diverse students and meeting individual student needs. Regular education teachers also need assistance in changing their teaching practices and working with special education teachers and parents on well-designed and well-implemented plans for individual students. We need to shake the lockstep curriculum, tracking, and teacher isolation common in the current school structure. We must seek involvement and support, provide high-quality assistance and incentives for improvement, and enlist school faculty and administrators in the process of full inclusion.

Mainstreaming failures have occurred where students with special needs were dumped into existing classes without adequate support—without preparing school staff or community or considering students' individual needs. Some special needs students were unable to demonstrate "appropriate behavior and skills" under school guidelines, and these schools made little effort to change programs or personnel to ensure students' success (Lombardi and Ludlow, 1996; Low, 2007). Mainstreaming became popular in the 1980s, but many schools and teachers were unprepared to handle special needs and faltered or were unnecessarily limited in their vision and operation. The most severely disabled students still are mainstreamed in only a few classes each day, usually classes such as art and physical education.

The individualized education plan (IEP) increases participation of general education teachers in planning for special needs students through membership on IEP teams and the development of a student's IEP. In addition, schools must consider how the student's disability affects involvement and performance in the school's general curriculum.

Inclusion, beyond mainstreaming, offers children with special needs the opportunity to be educated to "the maximum extent appropriate" in "the school or classroom he or she would otherwise have attended if he or she did not have a disability" (Rogers, 1993). Positive inclusion in schools depends on collaborative efforts by regular and special education teachers, parents, and administrators. Ill-prepared, poorly organized past efforts at mainstreaming must be avoided in inclusion. Teacher preparation and in-service programs should integrate the most useful knowledge from special education research and practice and should emphasize special methods for dealing with a wide range of students and for individualizing lessons (Cooley et al., 2008).

Not only are there serious detrimental consequences for the individual exceptional children who are placed in isolated or separated situations, but "average" children are likewise deprived of realistic social interaction and a more compassionate understanding of others' lives. Additionally, the community as a whole suffers from the suspicion, distrust, and misunderstanding created by separation (Risko and Bromley, 2001; Siebers, 2008, 2010). Justice requires that all citizens have equal opportunity to build fulfilling lives. We don't need forced separation and the stigmatization that results. It is ethically and practically inconsistent to continue separating children with special needs from other children in our schools.

Inclusion is consistent with fundamental principles of our society and with the law. The United States should do no less than provide full inclusion (Grossman, 1998; Vargas, 1999; Koenig and Bachman, 2004; Ferri and Connor, 2005; Oakes, 2005; Wolbrecht and Hero, 2005; Cameron, 2008; Smith, 2010; Salend, 2011; Baglieri,

2017). Not only is inclusion a matter of fundamental principles and law, but it is better educationally—for students and teachers (Kids Together, Inc., 2012; United Nations, 2016; Open Society Foundations, 2019).

Position 2:   Full Inclusion Is Not the Answer:
Special Programs Help Special Students

What school officials fail to mention is that full inclusion is primarily a cost-saving device and has long-term negative consequences for students, families, and society as a whole.

—Meyers (2019)

Being in every class together may actually alienate the student more than if they were separated for specific classes.

—Gerber (2018)

A central point of IDEA is that "to the maximum extent appropriate," disabled children will be educated with those who are not. Claims that this requires schools to place all disabled children in regular classrooms all day, all year are faulty. Full inclusion advocates ignore the significance of the term *maximum extent appropriate* in the law. Inclusion is not mandated by the law; the word is not even stated in those enactments.

For many disabled children, placement into regular classrooms is a physical, mental, and emotional challenge that should not be mandated and is not "appropriate." Special needs of individual students come in many varieties and regular teachers are often unprepared for all of them. Inclusion as an idea can mislead regular teachers into well-intentioned but inappropriate treatment of special students in their classes. School conditions may also be inappropriate. Bakken (2010) explains why general education classrooms are not the best place for all disabled students. He argues that schools need a continuum of educational placements for learners of a variety of special and diverse needs. Students with disabilities need special, individualized instructional programs with time for special work. The current climate in general education schools and classrooms does not lend itself easily or well to inclusive practices, and may actually be detrimental (Constantinescu and Samuels, 2016; Gilmour, 2018; Alphonso, 2019).

Thankfully, the bleak period when disabled children were considered less than human passed long ago. Children with disabilities have suffered, been reviled, ostracized, ridiculed, ignored, and destroyed. Some became members of circuses, some were hidden by their families, and others were placed in ill-funded and ill-supervised institutions with no chance for improvement. The families of disabled children also suffered social maligning. And society lost the contributions that it could have had from the many talents of people with disabilities. Fortunately, dramatic changes have occurred. We now recognize that the special needs of these children require special treatment, programs that offer support and hope. Special education schools, classes, and programs have been successful in enabling students. Disabled youngsters can benefit from special treatment by special people in special settings. The actual proportion of exceptional children is very small, in the range of 5% nationally; they deserve special financing, special treatment, special teachers, and special programs.

Special education provides more individualistic education, better prepared and specialized teachers, more appropriate teaching materials, superior facilities, and a setting better organized to help these children. Recognition of the special educational and emotional needs of disabled children is one of our finest modern traditions. These children need more than what we provide in regular classrooms, where they can be subject to ignorant or prejudiced schoolmates or ill-prepared school staff. As news reports show, regular schools leave much to be desired in the education of nondisabled students, how can they be expected to properly educate special students?

Special education, done properly, is more costly than regular instruction with all students together. Despite its value, special education funding is "insufficient, inefficient, and inequitable" (Fensterwald, 2018), and it is complex. Public school funds come mainly from state and local taxpayers; the federal government provides only about 8% of school budgets. Federal law mandates schools to provide special education services, stipulating that federal funds should cover 40% of average student costs. However, that percentage hasn't been achieved; federal funds for special needs actually cover about 15% of average costs, and the local district has to find extra funds or make accommodations (Understanding Special Education, 2019). Full inclusion could be a device to help school budgets in this area because it is cheaper to educate children with special needs in regular classes. That is unwise and, in the long run, economically foolish.

Limited school financing, coupled with academic requirements in the Every Student Succeeds Act and Common Core State Standards Initiative, classroom overcrowding and teacher stress, and district curricular or testing requirements, cause schools and teachers to standardize the school setting, student standards, teacher expectations, and classroom work. Teachers in regular programs, in general elementary school classes, and subject-based upper elementary and secondary classes are overworked and underappreciated. Placing special needs students in their classes, with minimal teacher preparation, scarce resources, and outsized expectations, adds to the predicament. Teachers have been found to spend less time on instruction and more time on classroom management when some special needs students are included (Fuchs et al., 2015). And teacher turnover is increasing (Gilmour, 2018). Conditions can restrict the amount and quality of important individualization and personal support expected for these deserving special needs students and for the nondisabled student population (Kabzems, 2003; Taylor, 2003; Koenig and Bachman, 2004; Meyers, 2019).

Full inclusion may not be the best choice for all (Cromwell, 2004). It can be detrimental to special and regular students, and potentially illegal. Full inclusion advocates ignore significant distinctions among children and the extra educational and emotional pressures on teachers and schools. Misdiagnosis of needs, inappropriate treatment, inadequate teacher preparation, and the increasing standardization in regular classes make full inclusion more complex, more stressful, and, worse, more likely to create more problems for special children and their nondisabled schoolmates (Kauffman et al., 2002; Buchman, 2006; Gilmour, 2018; Hettleman, 2019).

Humane and thoughtful treatment would not require a truly disabled child to undergo traumatic experiences to satisfy a stark, inflexible, and ill-informed interpretation of a law: the apparent position of those who press for full inclusion of children into standard classrooms. For mildly disabled children, placement in regular classes, along with specially trained teachers, special programs, and appropriate instruction and standards, will help and should be provided. But inflexible interpretation of laws and meeting some unsupported external standard for a percentage of special needs students in regular classes adds further to potential damage.

For Careful Inclusion of Individuals

Full inclusion is not necessary. Thoughtfully involving certain children with special needs in regular school classes and activities, on an individual basis and in suitable situations, does offer important benefits to schools and to those children. Careful inclusion of many students, offered by a well-prepared school district to parents of children whose academic work is likely to be enhanced and whose behavior is not likely to disrupt the education of others, is a positive step. But careful inclusion is not full inclusion. Some describe the difference as "hard versus soft" inclusion, the radical universalists versus the moderates (Low, 2007). Careful inclusion operates in many good schools. Expert diagnosis, classification, parental involvement, individually developed special programs, close evaluation of progress, and, for some, graduated access to regular classes have provided careful inclusion for individual students in many schools for many years. Disabled children and their families are provided excellent resources, fine tuned to the child's specific needs and carefully crafted to support the child's development. A focus on the child's highly individual needs and development is fundamental to this process.

Typical special education programs provide specially trained teachers and paraprofessionals, smaller class sizes, adjusted curricula, and fairer competition. Programs allow parents and teachers to jointly fashion an individualized program that maximizes the child's strengths and remediates areas of need. They are also able to access experts outside the school to assist children with special needs in preparing for the transition from school to work life.

Careful inclusion means providing different strokes for different folks if the criteria are sensible and consistent with individual capabilities and interests, family consultation, and social values. Putting all students into advanced Latin or into woodshop does not make sense; keeping disruptive or violent children in regular classes does not make sense. Beyond separate special education classes, access to education differs along several dimensions. Tracking or grouping students by ability testing or teacher evaluation separates students for most of their school careers (Urban and Waggoner, 1996; Spring, 1998; Meier, 2005; Oakes, 2005). Schools in different communities offer differing advantages as a result of funding differences. High school athletes are more costly to a school district than humanities students; only the best are selected for team membership. In elementary school classes, good readers are placed in one group and poor readers in another. Not all students are admitted to college preparatory or honors classes. We use various criteria to limit those who can drive cars, handle food, practice medicine, cut and style hair, be convicted of a crime, or run for president. These limits are not unfair unless they are abused, prejudicially applied, inconsistent with ethics, or not reasonable.

Special education and exceptional programs offer important benefits to the child: a low student-to-teacher ratio for increased individualized instruction and attention; teachers especially trained to educate and develop the skills of exceptional students; experts organized into study teams to provide diagnosis, treatment, and evaluation of student development; homogeneous grouping to permit the teacher to concentrate on common needs and characteristics; more opportunity for student success among peers and more realistic competition in academics and/or athletics; funds for facilities, special equipment, and specially designed student learning materials; and increased student self-esteem from individual attention and by limiting negative interaction with nondisabled students. In addition, special education programs offer opportunity for remedial education that could return mildly disabled children to the regular program. This is the substance and benefit of careful inclusion.

Regular School May Not Be Suitable

Special education benefits will be reduced with the advent of full inclusion. Regular schools are often unprepared to offer them in addition to their usual efforts, and initial extra funding will dry up or be absorbed into the ongoing operation of the schools. Fads and schools go hand in hand. The best place to find the newest fads in young people's language, music, dress, and manners is in schools. Not only are fads in popular culture highly noticeable, but schools are the birthplace of many other types of fads, often as a response to calls for school or social reform. Unfortunately, many of these educational fads are poorly thought out and counterproductive. Full inclusion is an example. The damage that full inclusion policies and practices may create for the very children they claim to help can be significant. Full inclusion carries negative implications for schools, teachers, parents, children, and the community (Petch-Hogan and Haggard, 1999; Cromwell, 2004; Constantinescu and Samuels, 2016; Meyers, 2019).

The mainstreaming movement thrust many disabled children into regular classrooms without adequate preparation for them and their new teachers and with excessive expectations. Reasonable people argued against large-scale mainstreaming; they were chastised, pilloried, or ignored. Full inclusion became another politically correct view. Effective special assistance programs were in our schools, after years of development. Many experts suggest full inclusion is an illusion because general classrooms and schools will never be capable of meeting the needs of all special or exceptional students (Kauffman and Hallahan, 1995; Kauffman et al., 2002; Bakken, 2010; Gilmour, 2018). These children require separate assistance and facilities. Variations among the types and severity of disabilities suggest how unlikely it is that any given school district will have general education teachers and courses that can accommodate and ade-quately fulfill the legal and social requirements to responsibly educate these children.

Regular classrooms and schools are designed to have nearly all students move more or less in unison to complete a diploma; they are not appropriate places to have the nec-essary interests, capabilities, and support for the special needs child. It will not be long before the early blush of full inclusion wears off for those teachers, students, and school staff—leaving the special needs child and family without proper attention and education (Ledoux et al., 2012). This is the fallout from the uncritical rush toward full inclusion.

Full Inclusion and Common Classroom Limits

Full inclusion limits regular classroom teachers by requiring them to allot extra time, materials, and energy to children who need extra support as well as requiring them to prepare and monitor individual education plans for each of these children. Full inclusion also limits nondisabled children by diverting time and energy from teachers to meet the special needs of a few students and by sometimes disrupting their schoolwork when the behaviors of a child with special needs are inappropriate in a general classroom. Finally, full inclusion limits the school's ability to make educa-tional decisions in the best interests of individual students. Full inclusion is a form of social engineering that cannot fulfill what it promises without serious repercussions for children and schools. Disruption and discipline problems can occur when some disabled students are mainstreamed or fully included in regular classes. Misconduct, of course, can be by regular or special students, but a situation of bullying, taunting, or disrespect against the special student in regular classes offers a supportable reason for a special student's misbehavior. Such situations are not always known or controllable by teachers and school staff and clearly do not provide the proper setting and special treatment that special youngsters deserve.

Regular schools discipline disabled students at a rate twice as high as nondis-abled. Suspension is common, but federal data show that restraint and seclusion were used almost 300,000 times in the 2012 school year. Teachers feel unprepared for this kind of disruption (Lewis, 2015). Wrightslaw (2019) notes that schools continue to suspend and expel disabled students "for behaviors caused by their disabilities." The National Center for Learning Disabilities (2017) data show a far higher rate of out-of-school suspensions for students of color who are disabled than for other students.

Bullying, for example, is an area of particular concern in regular classrooms and schools. Nearly 85% of special needs children experience bullying. Consistent research studies over 10 years show that students with disabilities are two to three times more likely than nondisabled students to be the victims of bullying and that the bullying of the disabled was more chronic (AbilityPath, 2011). Special needs students were also left out of the main social networks in regular classrooms by the actions of the other students (Carter and Spencer, 2006). Saylor and Leach (2009) examine this peer victimization issue in inclusion programs.

In addition, one in five principals reported that protective disciplinary procedures required for special students under the IDEA regulations are "burdensome and time consuming." Many students with behavioral problems are mistakenly classified as special for a number of reasons, including the additional school income from state and federal sources. As Navarrette (2002) indicates, "Thus the mischievous and the misdiagnosed are mixed with those who really need special education, those with mental retardation and other disabilities." Full inclusion needs full examination before implementation.

One Case Illustrates the Issue

Full inclusion of children with disabilities into regular classes runs some of the same risks of arousing overzealous legislation and activist court interpretation. Legislated mainstreaming has created significant problems—for schools, for teachers, for communities, and for both disabled and nondisabled children. A court case, *Oberti v. Board of Education of the Borough of Clementon (NJ) School District* (1993), illustrates problems associated with mainstreaming, the laws governing it, and court interpretations.

An eight-year-old Down syndrome child with impaired intellectual functioning and communication problems was tested by school experts and placed in a developmental kindergarten class in the morning to observe and socialize with peer children, but for academic work was in an afternoon separate special class. In the morning class, the child exhibited serious behavioral problems, including repeated toilet accidents, temper tantrums, crawling and hiding under furniture, and hitting and spitting on other children; and the child repeatedly hit the teacher and teacher's aide. Interestingly, the child did not exhibit disruptive behavior in the separate afternoon special education class. After study, the district wanted to place the child in a completely separate program, but the parents refused. After a hearing, an agreement placed him in a separate program for one year. His behavior improved, and he made academic progress. When the parents found, however, that the district did not plan to place him back into "regular" classes the following year, they objected, and an administrative law judge agreed with the district that: the separate special education class was the "least restrictive environment" under the IDEA law, the child's misbehavior in the developmental kindergarten class was extensive, and there was no meaningful educational benefit from that class. Unsatisfied, the parents went to court, and brought in a professor who claimed the child could be in regular classes provided that there were supplementary aids and special support. The district's expert witness claimed the child could not benefit from a regular class, his behavior could not be managed, the teacher could not communicate with him because of his communication problems, and the curriculum could not be modified enough to meet his needs. Other witnesses, who had worked with the child in different public and Catholic school settings, testified about his disruptive behavior, including hitting, throwing things, and running away. This judge held that the district had the burden of proof and had failed to meet the IDEA law's requirement for mainstreaming.

This case suggests a series of problems for schools, parents, communities, and children under full inclusion. The court directed that a disruptive and misbehaving child is to attend regular classes, where his actions are likely to be detrimental to other students' academic work and to the teacher's ongoing work. The disabled child's schoolwork, apparently satisfactory in separate special education classes, suffered significantly in the regular placement, even on a part-time basis, yet under the court's order, he now would be in regular classes full time. Parents of the nondisabled children do not have the same right to refuse placement for their children, require formal hearings on details they don't like, or protest in court when their children are subjected to a significantly modified curriculum or class disruption. School rules established for all children to provide order and safety are placed in jeopardy by a court order that makes the school ultrasensitive to the parents of a single student.

Full Inclusion and School Reality

Theoretically, inclusion could provide all the good things special education now provides—special teachers, individualization, and more self-esteem but with the added benefit of allowing exceptional children to participate fully in the school program. Long-term experience with school reforms suggests that any immediate, positive effects of inclusion are likely to be overcome by long-standing conformist standardization, bureaucracy, and funding requirements that make most schools dull and ineffective even for many regular students. The special needs child will be overlooked in these schools. The focus will shift from giving special attention to individual children's strengths and disabilities toward conforming to group standards imposed by federal or state officials, meeting community expectations in test scores, or facing other accountability measures of group success. Large class size will make it difficult for regular teachers to provide special assistance to exceptional children. Schools will not be able to fully control other students' disparaging or hurtful comments, and exceptional children again will suffer. School funds will decrease to a common standard, without special funds for special children. Exceptional students require exceptional effort, but schools will be stretched and unable to provide it (Noonan, 2008).

In addition, advocates of full inclusion are wrong when they argue that interaction with regular students in a regular program will benefit all who are disabled. A sorry history of bullying, taunting, labeling, ridicule, and exclusion by regular students is not likely to disappear because of some legislated program of interaction. There is no evidence that nondisabled children will suddenly develop appropriate classroom behavior when full inclusion takes place. Lectures and admonitions by school officials, no matter how well intentioned, are not likely to make a dent in the problem. Even if the majority of children are well behaved and nonprejudiced, it takes only a few to spoil the school setting for children with disabilities who already have been subjected to frequent stares and slights. School is tough enough for many regular students who happen to be different from the group. Life in many schools is not pleasant for children from poor families and for children who stutter, are noticeably shorter or taller or plump, are slower in speed or intellect, are from certain cultural backgrounds, or are not as gregarious or athletic or pretty as others. School subcultures create cauldrons of despair for many students who are not accepted because of minor differences (Palonsky, 1975); consider the problem that those with significant disabilities would face in regular schools. Buchman (2006) describes the benefits of a special education for her daughter; her daughter agrees and wishes that all children with learning disabilities could have that special treatment (Farber, 2006).

Laudable but Unrealistic Goals

The goal of inclusion may be laudable under some conditions and for some individuals. However, full inclusion for all students represents an ideal that does not mesh with day-to-day reality for large numbers of students. Many children now are participating successfully in effective special education classes and schools. Zigler and Hall (1986) noted a problem of excesses in the 1980s mainstreaming movement. Mainstreaming was a "normalization" idea; that more "normal" school settings would socialize disabled children. But normal school can constrict their choices and result in disservice to the very children the legislators sought to help by denying them their right to be different. Underlying normalization is homogeneity, which is unfair to those children whose special needs may come to be viewed as unacceptable. Bakken (2010) points out that inclusion is a topic that has "caused much debate, stirred emotions, and has received great attention" (p. 129), but that "inclusion" has no universally accepted definition and has changed over time. Instead, he argues strongly for "access to a high quality, effective, individualized educational environment" that is far more useful to students and "socially significant than mere placement and proximity to typically developing peers" (p. 129).

Full inclusion goes well beyond mainstreaming. It runs even greater risks of homogenizing our educational approach and causing a decline in special care and attention for children with exceptional needs. The political support for special programs and funds, support that took years to develop, will atrophy. Special education budgets will diminish. School administrators, with declining special education budgets, will be unlikely to champion the needs of this small and expensive proportion of their student populations. Regular class teachers, already overworked in large classes, will be unable to extend themselves even further for children who need more individualized help. Parents of nondisabled children may be sympathetic but are unlikely to support the diversion of general education funds, resources, and teacher time from the education of their own children.

We want as many disabled children as possible to be self-reliant, to be equipped for successful and productive lives, to participate constructively in the larger society, and to develop feelings of personal worth. We want no less for any child, but the child who is disabled needs special attention and support to reach these goals. One of the primary purposes of special education programs is to provide the setting and individualized attention these children need to develop self-reliance, success, productivity, and feelings of personal worth. These programs are jeopardized by the steamroller tactics of the full inclusionists.

Excessive mainstreaming caught schools unprepared, frustrated good teachers, diminished special services provided to individual children, and created confusion in schools. Well-prepared schools, specially trained teachers, clear guidelines for diagnosis and education, smaller classes, special materials to enhance learning, and a setting conducive to the best education now exist in many places: special education and gifted and talented programs offer these advantages. Full inclusion would overturn them in favor of a mandate for standardization and chaos beyond what occurred in excessive mainstreaming programs.

Schools vary significantly: it is impossible to define a "regular" school or classroom. Is a one-room school in rural Nevada "regular"? What about an urban school in Manhattan or a suburban school in Beverly Hills? Schools have some common patterns, but schooling occurs with separate groups of students in disparate locations. The Bronx High School of Science, vocational-technical high schools, tracking programs, honors programs, remedial courses, basic and advanced courses, reading groups, and selection for music and athletic programs illustrate the common practice of educating certain students separately for particular reasons. Full inclusion threatens these efforts to provide the best individual education for different students.

FOR DISCUSSION

1. *Dialectic Exercise*: Identify the best thesis and antithesis arguments about full inclusion. Evaluate the evidence you find for each argument. What additional evidence is needed; and where would you find it? What is your current view, and what would be the most convincing evidence for you to change your mind on full inclusion? What preliminary synthesis argument would you develop? How does it address social policy, school interests, and individual students and parents?

2. *Discussion*: How should the movement toward full inclusion influence teacher education programs? What would you propose for teacher preparation in this area? What should teachers know about and be able to do for special students included in general classrooms?

3. Data from the U.S. Department of Education show that the annual growth rate in children ages 3 to 21 who receive special education (over 3%) continues to exceed the annual growth rate in the general population between ages 3 to 21 (about 1%). The proportion of children evaluated as gifted and talented is about 3% of the student population. What reasons would explain an increase in proportion of children needing special education? What difference should this annual increase mean for school decisions on full inclusion? To critically examine this topic, what evidence would you need, and where would you expect to find that evidence?

4. How should gifted and talented programs be treated in terms of full inclusion policies? Should they be abolished, separated, enhanced, or diminished? On what grounds would you support your position? Who should decide and on what criteria? Are separate programs appropriate in public schools in a democracy? How is this issue similar to and different from treatment of special education students under IDEA law?

References

AbilityPath (2011). *Walk a Mile in Their Shoes: Bullying and the Child with Special Needs* (abilitypath.org).

Alphonso, C. (2019, January 7). "Educating Grayson: Are Inclusive Classrooms Failing Students?" *The Globe and Mail* (Toronto).

Alur, M., and Bach, M. (2010). *The Journey for Inclusive Education in the Indian Sub-Continent.* New York: Routledge.

Anderson, G. R., and Anderson, S. K. (1983). The Exceptional Native American. In L. Barton, ed., *The Politics of Special Education.* London: Falmer Press.

Artiles, A. J., and Bal, A. (2008). "The Next Generation of Disproportionality Research." *Journal of Special Education* 42(1):4–14.

Baglieri, S. (2017). *Disability Studies and the Inclusive Classroom* (2nd ed.). New York: Routledge.

Bakken, J. P. (2010). The General Education Classroom: This Is Not Where Students with Disabilities Should Be Placed. In F. E. Obiakor, J. P. Bakken, and A. F. Rotatori, eds., *Current Issues and Trends in Special Education* (Vol. 19). Bingley, United Kingdom: Emerald.

Bateman, D., and Cline, J. (2019). *Special Education Law Studies.* New York: Rowman & Littlefield.

Batson, T., and Bergman, E., eds. (2002). *Angels and Outcasts.* Washington, DC: Gallaudet University Press.

Brown v. Board of Education of Topeka, Shawnee County, Kansas, et al. (1954). 347 U.S. 483.

Buchman, D. (2006). *A Special Education.* Cambridge, MA: Da Capo Press.

Cameron, L. (2008). "The Maine Effect or How I Finally Embraced the Social Model of Disability." *Intellectual and Developmental Disabilities* 46(1):54–57.

Carter, B. B., and Spencer, V. G. (2006). "The Fear Factor: Bullying and Students with Disabilities." *International Journal of Special Education* 21(1):11–23.

Cigman, R., ed. (2007). *Included or Excluded?* New York: Routledge.

Cluley, V., Fyson, R., and Pilnick, A. (2020). "Theorizing Disability." *Disability and Society* 35(2).

Connor, D. J. (2019). "Why is Special Education so Afraid of Disability Studies?" *Journal of Curriculum Theorizing* 34(1) online.

Constantinescu, C., and Samuels, C. A. (2016, September 6). "Studies Flag Potential Downside to Inclusion." *Education Week.*

Cooley, S. M., Bicard, S., Bicard, D., and Casey, L. (2008). "A Field at Risk: The Teacher Shortage in Special Education." *Kappan* 89(8):597–600.

Cromwell, S. (2004). Inclusion: Has It Gone Too Far? (education-world.com).

Danforth, S. (2008). "John Dewey's Contributions to an Educational Philosophy of Intellectual Disability." *Educational Theory* 58(1):45–58.

——— (2016). Learning from Our Historical Evasions: Disability Studies and Schooling in a Liberal Democracy. In S. Danforth and S. Gabel, eds., *Vital Questions Facing Disability Studies in Education.* New York: Peter Lang.

Danforth, S., and Smith, T. J. (2005). *Engaging Troubled Students.* Thousand Oaks, CA: Corwin Press.

DeMatthews, D. (2019, December 4). "Addressing Racism and Ableism in Schools." *The Clearing House* 93(1).

Educational Testing Service (1980). "New Vistas in Special Education." *Focus* 8:1–20.

Farber, C. (2006). Afterword. In D. Buchman, ed., *A Special Education.* Cambridge, MA: Da Capo Press.

Fensterwald, J. (2018, March 8). Special Education Funding is a Morass; Straightening It Out May Not be Cheap or Easy. Ed Source (edsource.org).

Ferri, B. J., and Connor, D. J. (2005). "Tools of Exclusion: Race, Disability, and (Re)segregated Education." *Teachers College Record* 107(3):453–474.

Fuchs, L., Fuchs, D., Compton, D., Wehby, J., Schumacher, R., Gersten, R., and Jordan, N. (2015). "Inclusion versus Specialized Intervention for Very Low-Performing Students." *Exceptional Children* 8(2).

Garland Thomson, R. (2010). "Roosevelt's Sister: Why We Need Disability Studies in the Humanities." *Disabilities Studies Quarterly* 30(3/4).

Gerber, H. (2018, November 1). Problems with Inclusion in the Classroom. Blog, Sunbelt Staffing (sunbeltstaffing.com).

Gibson, S., and Haynes, J., eds. (2009). *Perspectives on Participation and Inclusion.* London: Continuum.

Gilmour, A. F. (2018, Fall). "Has Inclusion Gone Too Far?" *Education Next* 18(4).

Glover, T. A., and Vaughn, S., eds. (2010). *The Promise of Response to Intervention.* New York: Guilford Press.

Goffman, E. (1961). *Asylums.* Garden City, NY: Anchor Books.

Grossman, H. (1998). *Ending Discrimination in Special Education.* Springfield, IL: Charles C. Thomas.

Harry, B., Arnaiz, P., Klingner, J., and Sturges, K. (2008). "Schooling and the Construction of Identity among Minority Students in Spain and the United States." *Journal of Special Education* 42(1):15–25.

Hettleman, K. R., ed. (2019). *Mislabeled as Disabled.* New York: Radius Books.

IDEA (2019, December 18). Individuals with Disabilities Education Act website (sites.ed.gov).

Jimerson, S. R., Burns, M. K., and Vanderheyden, A. M., eds. (2007). *Handbook of Response to Intervention.* New York: Springer.

Kabzems, V. (2003). Labeling in the Name of Equality. In P. Devliger, ed., *Rethinking Disability.* Philadelphia: Garant.

Kauffman, J., Bantz, J., and McCullough, J. (2002). "Separate and Better." *Exceptionality* 10(3):149–170.

Kauffman, J., and Hallahan, D., eds. (1995). *The Illusion of Full Inclusion.* Austin TX: PRO-ED.

Kaufman, S. B., ed. (2018). *Twice Exceptional.* New York: Oxford University Press.

Kids Together, Inc. (2012, April). Benefits of Inclusive Education (kidstogether.org).

Kluth, P., Villa, R., and Thousand, J. (2001). "'Our School Doesn't Offer Inclusion' and Other Legal Blunders." *Educational Leadership* 50(4):24–27.

Koenig, J. A., and Bachman, L. F., eds. (2004). *Keeping Score for All.* Washington, DC: National Academies Press.

Ledoux, C., Graves, S. L., and Burt, W. (2012, Winter). "Meeting the Needs of Special Education Students in Inclusion Classrooms." *Journal of the American Academy of Special Education Professionals* 20–34.

Lewis, K. R. (2015, July 24). "Why Schools Overdiscipline Children with Disabilities." *The Atlantic.*

Lombardi, T. P., and Ludlow, B. L. (1996). *Trends Shaping the Future of Special Education.* Bloomington, IN: Phi Delta Kappa Educational Foundation.

Low, C. (2007). A Defense of Moderate Inclusion and the End of Ideology. In R. Cigman, ed., *Included or Excluded?* New York: Routledge.

Mader, J. (2017, March). "How Teacher Training Hinders Special Needs Students." *The Atlantic.*

Meier, K. J. (2005). School Boards and the Politics of Education Policy. In C. Wolbrecht and R. E. Hero, eds., *Politics of Democratic Inclusion.* Philadelphia: Temple University Press.

Meyers, M. (2019, December 4). What Is Full Inclusion and How Is It Damaging Our Public Schools? (wehavekids.com).

Mills v. Board of Education of the District of Columbia (1972). 348 F. Supp. 866.

Mittler, P., Brouillette, R., and Harris, D., eds. (1993). *Special Needs Education: World Yearbook of Education.* London: Kogan Page.

Mooney, J. (2019). *Normal Sucks.* New York: Henry Holt.

National Center for Learning Disabilities (2017, January 27). Social, Emotional, and Behavioral Challenges (ncld.org).

Navarrette, R. (2002, April 17). "The Special Ed Dumping Ground." *San Diego Union-Tribune.*

Noonan, M. A. (2008). "When Special Education As We Know It Ends—What, if Anything Will Replace It?" *Educational Horizons* 86(3):139–141.

Oakes, J. (2005). *Keeping Track: How Schools Structure Inequality* (2nd ed.). New Haven, CT: Yale University Press.

Oberti v. Board of Education of the Borough of Clementon (NJ) School District (1993). 995 F. 2d 1204 (3rd Cir.).

Open Society Foundations (2019, May). The Value of Inclusive Education (opensocietyfoundations.org).

Palonsky, S. (1975). "Hempies and Squeaks, Truckers and Cruisers: A Participant-Observer Investigation in a City High School." *Educational Administration Quarterly* 2:86–103.

Petch-Hogan, B., and Haggard, D. (1999). "The Inclusion Debate Continues." *Educational Forum* 35(3):128–140.

Poore, C. (2007). *Disability in Twentieth Century German Culture.* Ann Arbor: University of Michigan Press.

Risko, V., and Bromley, K. (2001). *Collaboration for Diverse Learners.* Newark, DE: International Reading Association.

Rogers, J. (1993). "The Inclusion Revolution." *Phi Delta Kappa Research Bulletin* 11:1–6.

Rotatori, A. F., Obiakor, F. E., and Bakken, J. P., eds. (2011). *History of Special Education.* Bingley: Emerald.

RTI Action Network (2019, December 19). What is RTI? (rtinetwork.org/learn/what/whatisrti).

Sailor, W., Gerry, M., and Wilson, W. C. (1991). Policy Implications of Emergent Full Inclusion Models. In M. C. Wang, M. Reynolds, and H. Walberg, eds., *Handbook of Special Education: Research and Practice* (Vol. 4). Oxford: Pergamon.

Salend, S. S. (2011). *Creating Inclusive Classrooms* (7th ed.). Columbus, OH: Pearson.

Saylor, C. F., and Leach, J. B. (2009). "Perceived Peer Victimization and Social Support in Students Accessing Special Inclusion Programming," *Journal of Developmental and Physical Disabilities* 21:69–80.

Scully, J. L. (2008). *Disability Bioethics.* Lanham, MD: Rowman & Littlefield.

Sefa Dei, G., James, I., Karumanchery, L., James Wilson, S., and Zine, J. (2000). *Removing the Margins.* Toronto: Canadian Scholars' Press.

Shevin, M. (2007). *Widening the Circle.* Boston: Beacon Press.

Siebers, T. (2008). *Disability Theory.* Ann Arbor: University of Michigan Press.

——— (2010). *Disability Ethics.* Ann Arbor: University of Michigan Press.

Slavin, R. E. (2019). Introduction. In K. R. Hettleman, ed., *Mislabeled as Disabled.* New York: Diversion.

Smith, P., ed. (2010). *Whatever Happened to Inclusion?* New York: Peter Lang.

Sotomayor, S. (2019) *Just Ask.* New York: Philomel Books.

Spring, J. (1998). *American Education* (8th ed.). New York: McGraw-Hill.

Stancil, W. (2018, March 14). "School Segregation is Not a Myth." *The Atlantic.*

Taylor, R. E. (2003). *Assessment of Exceptional Students* (6th ed.). Boston: Allyn and Bacon.

Turnbull, H. R., and Turnbull, A. P. (1998). *Free Appropriate Public Education: The Law and Children with Disabilities* (5th ed.). Denver: Love Publishing.

Understanding Special Education (2019). Understanding Special Education Funding (understandingspecialeducation.com).

UNESCO (2008, April). Inclusive Quality Education (portal.unesco.org).

——— (2015). *Education for All 2000–2015: Achievements and Challenges.* 2015 Global Monitoring Report. Paris: UNESCO.

——— (2020). 2020 Global Monitoring Report: Inclusion and Education. UNESCO (en.unesco.org/gem-report/report/2020/inclusion).

United Nations (2016). *Toolkit on Disability for Africa: Inclusive Education.* United Nations, Department of Economic Affairs.

——— (2018). *Realization of the Sustainable Development Goals by, for and with Persons with Disabilities.* United Nations Flagship Report on Disability and Development 2018. Department of Economic and Social Affairs.

Urban, W., and Waggoner, J. (1996). *American Education: A History.* New York: McGraw-Hill.

U.S. Department of Education (2019). IDEA Data Center. U.S. Department of Education, Office of Special Education Programs (ideadata.org/resources).

Valle, J. W., and Connor, D. J. (2019). *Rethinking Disability* (2nd ed.). New York: Routledge.

Vargas, S. R. L. (1999). "Democracy and Inclusion." *Maryland Law Review* 58(1):150–179.

Wedell, K. (1993). Varieties of School Integration. In P. Mittler, R. Brouillette, and D. Harris, eds., *Special Needs Education: World Yearbook of Education.* London: Kogan Page.

Winzer, M. A. (1993). *The History of Special Education: From Isolation to Integration.* Washington, DC: Gallaudet University Press.

Wolbrecht, C., and Hero, R. E. (2005). *The Politics of Democratic Inclusion.* Philadelphia: Temple University Press.

Wrightslaw (2019, December 21). Behavior Problems and Discipline (wrightslaw.com).

Young, N. D., Mumby, M. A., and Rice, M. F. (2019). *The Special Education Toolbox.* New York: Rowman & Littlefield.

Zigler, E., and Hall, N. (1986). Mainstreaming and the Philosophy of Normalization. In C. J. Meisel, ed., *Mainstreaming Handicapped Children.* Hillsdale, NJ: Lawrence Erlbaum.

Teachers, Unions, and the Profession

15

Do teacher professionalization and unions provide a positive influence on education?

Position 1:   The Teaching Profession and Teacher Unions: Champions of Good Teaching and School Improvement

---

People often ask me why I teach. My answer is simple: I want to live forever. Machines fall apart, money runs out and beauty fades. Our ideas, our lessons and our stories are all that can truly be passed down from one generation to the next.

—Kajitani (2017)

Anti-union myth making has a range of short-term and long-term costs. One insidious toll is the undermining of public confidence in teachers and schools, and another is discouraging people from entering the profession altogether.

—Ayers et al. (2018)

The Teaching Profession

Teaching has a long and usually distinguished history. Parent to child and elders to the young represent the earliest forms, with more structured and formally organized teaching arising as societies evolved and knowledge became more sophisticated and codified. Ancient Indian, Chinese, Greek, and Roman societies commonly revered teachers and depended on them to provide moral, intellectual, and civic education. Later, national systems of schooling, expanding scientific knowledge, and increasing requirements for educated populations accelerated the need for formally prepared teachers and encouraged their professionalization. In the United States, the

335

history of the teaching profession, however, is not straight and uplifting. In colonial times some teachers arrived as indentured servants; others were contractually required to assist ministers with religious duties on Sundays and in baptisms, funerals, and even grave digging (Smiley and Diekhoff, 1959); some were the community laughing stock à la Ichabod Crane; some were mothers instructing the children of others; some were scholars and mentors like Mr. Chips; and many were considered just low-level employees consuming tuition or taxpayer money. This mixed history is the background to current views of teachers, accounting for variability in social status, level of autonomy, educational and ethical requirements, and comparative financial rewards.

Strident public debate over the role and practice of teachers, their social and political status, professionalization, and associations signal the importance of education to society. Smiley and Diekhoff (1959) describe it: "Different cultures and other eras have viewed teachers with varying degrees of approbation, awe, or contempt. For the most part, however, the teacher seems to have occupied a peculiarly ambiguous position" (p. 23). Humanities scholar Gilbert Highet (1976) considered teaching "The Immortal Profession"; not all have shared that view.

In the nineteenth century, teaching was a temporary job. After a few years of teaching, often in schools where married teachers were not permitted, women often chose marriage and homemaking. Ambitious men expected to move from teaching to loftier, better paying occupations. Classroom teaching was seldom the chosen lifetime work of the more able. Teaching was considered as employment for workers who were "passing through" on their way to more serious pursuits (Holmes Group, 1986). At best, teaching was seen as a good short-term job, but people disparaged it as a career choice, and those who chose to stay in the classroom for more than a few years often encountered social derision. The sociologist Willard Waller (1932) observed that teachers were not treated like other workers and certainly not like professionals. He noted that in small towns, unmarried teachers were expected to live in a teacherage—a special boardinghouse—apart from other single adults who held nonteaching jobs. Defining a prejudice against teachers held by wealthier and better-educated members of the community, he wrote: "Teaching is quite generally regarded as a failure belt . . . the refuge of unmarriageable women and unsaleable men" (p. 61).

Early in the twentieth century, teachers were trained to believe that sacrifice was the essence of their profession. Teachers worked long hours, many classes had 50 or more students, salaries were low, and schools were poorly heated, poorly ventilated, and unsanitary. In many places, women teachers could not go out unescorted (except to attend church), or frequent places serving liquor. When married, they were forced to resign. Teachers lived truncated social lives, served at the whim of school boards, had no tenure, health, or retirement benefits. They could not select textbooks for their classes and were excluded from deliberations on curriculum. City school systems developed into large bureaucratic organizations where the powerlessness of teachers became institutionalized. School principals were once "main or principal teacher," but they became management and separate from teachers, sharing few teacher problems or perspectives.

Teacher associations began as programs to improve teaching practice; that led toward professionalization, and unionization followed much later. Teachers have been in nonunion organizations for over 100 years. The National Education Association

(NEA) was established in 1857 to represent the views of "practical" classroom teachers and administrators. Annual NEA conventions were for the exchange of teaching ideas. Discussion of labor issues, such as work conditions or wages, were avoided; the NEA was male dominated and led by school superintendents, professors of education, and school principals (Wesley, 1957). Eaton (1975), a critic of the NEA, said women teachers were "limited to listening" (p. 10).

Professions are a relatively modern development. In medieval times only the ministry, medicine, and law were called the learned professions. Since education is one prerequisite for all professions, each profession requires educators. But teaching itself was not recognized as a profession until states began to regulate it as a protection to parents, requiring more formal preparation and setting other conditions. Associations organized to protect and influence the field, and public recognition of teaching as more professional expanded. This pattern is similar to other professions that emerged after the Industrial Revolution and urbanization, like dentistry, engineering, and accounting. Those positions, however, are mainly in private enterprise. At one time teachers were privately employed, but now most are public employees and more subject to political waves and pressures. Teacher positions once were political spoils; the party in power gave out teacher jobs without restriction and a political change meant lots of turnover. State tenure laws in the 1920s intended to build stability with less teacher turnover and more district loyalty, stopping the practice of doling out teaching jobs as a political plum.

In these first two decades of the twenty-first century, teachers have broad respect, with blips of blame and demonizing. For almost 20 years, Gallup polls show that the public rates teachers among the most respected professions. In 2018, 60% rated teachers very high and only 10% rated them very low. This is just below medical specialists, whose very high scores range from 65 to 80%, and very low from 5 to 8%. Teachers are ranked above police (54% very high, 13% very low), clergy (37% very high, 15 very low), bankers (27% very high, 21% very low), lawyers (19% very high, 28% very low), telemarketers (8% very high, 44% very low), and members of Congress, who are at the bottom at 8% very high and 58% very low (Brenan, 2018b). Teachers are remembered with fondness, and seen as especially influential in life. That public and sentimental support, though, does not easily translate into better teacher income and working conditions. It is also inconsistent with political efforts which blame teachers for educational problems and taxpayer discontent. Teacher unions emerged to improve teachers' professional lives, but anti-union forces have held back the movement.

The Teacher Union Movement

Early courts held that all unions were illegal; workers who joined were guilty of entering into an illegal "conspiracy" to improve wages. That view changed (*Commonwealth v. Hunt*, 1842), but collective negotiations were fully legitimated with the Supreme Court's decision in *NLRB v. Jones and Laughlin Steel Company* (1937). The National Labor Relations Act (NLRA) of 1935 recognized the rights of workers in private industry to bargain collectively and elect a bargaining agent (a union) to negotiate with management. The NLRA is federal law and does not cover employees of state or local governments. Teachers could still be fired by school boards simply for joining a union (Kahlenberg, 2007). Public schools are extensions of the state and school boards are state employers excluded from federal labor legislation. States regulate employment relations in public education. The majority of state legislatures have taken action to recognize the rights of workers to organize and negotiate with employers. But some remain "right to work" states, and some states have recently limited rights to organize in response to anti-union views (Lovenheim and Willen, 2016; FindLaw, 2020).

Teacher unionism dates to the early twentieth century, when Chicago teachers organized the American Federation of Teachers (AFT) in 1916 as an affiliate of the American Federation of Labor. Initially, the NEA and AFT cooperated; NEA focused on profession and practice and AFT on improving teacher incomes and workplaces (Engel, 1976). With states allowing public employee bargaining, local affiliates of NEA and AFT became rivals. About 80% of U.S. teachers belong to the NEA or the AFT.

Initially, teachers were not eager to join unions; but the emerging culture of business-oriented school administrators was at odds with the culture of teachers (Jessup, 1978; Urban, 1982; Murphy, 1990). Unions and collective bargaining gave some balance against the business culture in the improvement of working conditions and education. Often the NEA functioned more like other professional associations (the American Bar Association or the American Medical Association) than labor organizations (the International Ladies' Garment Workers' Union or the United Auto Workers). AFT identified with unionized workers in other industries, believing common problems of workers could be addressed by cooperation and collective action; teacher organizations could benefit teachers by improving salaries and work conditions and assist the labor movement by improving education for working-class children. School administrators were openly hostile to organized labor in education. In the 1920s, fearing worker radicalism and union activity, school superintendents demanded teachers sign "yellow-dog contracts," agreements that they would not join a union. Despite organizing efforts, a workers' college, and special public schools for workers' children, AFT membership declined in the 1920s, remaining flat throughout most of the 1930s.

The NEA and AFT scrambled for members during the 1940s and 1950s. Teachers who joined unions were under severe pressure from school officials and from general public distrust resulting from McCarthyism investigations of suspected Communist influence in education and in unions. A watershed for public school unions occurred when the New York City affiliate of AFT declared the first strike in history in 1968. It was a brief but effective job action with teachers back in the classrooms the next day (Lieberman and Moscow, 1966; Eaton, 1975). The strike reverberated nationally, alerting the nation and teachers to the power of union advocacy for better teacher pay, more job security, and an audible voice in education. One labor historian states: "It essentially refined and broadened the concept of professionalism by assuring [teachers] more autonomy and less supervisory control" (Murphy, 1990, p. 209). Today, NEA represents about 3.2 million teachers, more than twice the number represented by the AFT.

Teachers are expected to convey cultural history and tradition, often tend toward socially conservative views, and may be first-generation college graduates who identify with management more than with labor or come from management-oriented family backgrounds. They are white-collar employees called "knowledge workers," paid for what they know and how they use their knowledge to produce value. Such workers are individualistic and difficult to unionize (Kerchner et al., 1997). Similar issues occur for physicians and others (Topol, 2019). Conservative anti-union criticism grew in the early twenty-first century, fueled by corporations and wealthy individuals. Coupled with taxpayer concern about public education costs, teacher unions were attacked and blamed for education issues. Several state governors, angered at teacher and other unions, succeed in passing anti-union legislation. Despite a decline in membership in other fields and continuing anti-union lobbying, most teachers belong to a union. NEA and AFT have more than 4 million members, and they vote at higher than average rates. The public strongly supports teachers and strikes for better pay and conditions (Galley, 2003; Ferguson, 2018; Weingarten, 2018).

Collective bargaining agreements usually cover all similar employees, but teachers are not required to join a union; school districts are not "union shops." Agency fees, charges to nonmembers to cover the costs of bargaining, are to limit free riding, where members pay dues but free riding nonmembers get the same benefits. In *Janus v. American Federation of State, County, and Municipal Employees, Council 31, et al.* (2018), the Supreme Court overturned 40 years of precedent in ruling agency fees illegal; this decision applied to almost 6 million public employees in 22 states. Janus was a state employee, not a teacher. He objected to the agency fee. His case was strongly supported by the National Right to Work Foundation, with significant resources from corporate billionaires (*Janus v. American Federation of State, County, and Municipal Employees, Council 31, et al.*, 2018). A similar case involved a California teacher whose personal story illustrates battles against unions, sex education, anti-Christian attitudes, and other matters over a long period of time (Friedrichs, 2018), but the Supreme Court deadlocked on her case. The *Janus* decision led to dire predictions on teacher union finances, members, and bargaining positions (Samuels, 2018; Miller, 2018). Teacher unions lost some fee money, but gained memberships. New state laws will limit consequences, making membership more attractive (DiSalvo, 2019). Harris (2019) argues that teacher unions may now be even more important. Unions are eager to see the education emphasis and criticism move from an obsession with test scores to a focus on developing teacher expertise and creativity.

Teachers in large numbers have engaged in protests and strikes in several states, including West Virginia, Oklahoma, Arizona, North Carolina, Kentucky, and Colorado, and in districts including Los Angeles, Denver, and others. Issues vary, but stagnant and unfair salaries, declining educational spending, and classroom conditions and expectations have been the impetus for most of them (Blanc, 2019; Jacobson, 2019). The public display of these issues has renewed teacher interest in collective action and increased public awareness of decades of neglect on teacher wages and workload. Public school teachers' average income now is just over $1,000 per week, an actual decline in inflation-adjusted money since 1996, while the average income of all college graduates now is over $1,400 per week. The Organisation for Economic Co-operation and Development (2018) worldwide data show that the lowest average teacher pay occurs in Estonia, Slovak Republic, and Hungary; the highest pay is in Luxembourg, Korea, Austria, Germany, and Canada. The United States is comparatively wealthy and a costly place to live, but it is only in the middle of pay comparisons, while U.S. teachers teach more hours (an average of 46.2 hours) than in many other nations (global average of 38.3 hours per week) (Organisation for Economic Co-operation and Development, 2018; Will, 2019).

Unions, Student Performance, and School Improvement

Among the main argument of anti-union forces is that teacher unions protect bad teachers, harm students because of union focus on teacher welfare and not students, take away from better business management of schools, and stifle education reform. These are erroneous, overblown, blatantly political, or fear-mongering views that are deliberately misleading.

Blaming unions for protecting weak teachers does not hold up to evidence or logic (Han, 2016). Before public school teachers are hired they are reviewed for proper academic and teaching credentials by school administrators and only offered jobs after administrative recommendation to and approval by a public board. Before being awarded tenure, new teachers are regularly and at least annually evaluated in their classrooms and in other school settings by school administrators for 2 to 5 years of probation, depending on state requirements. These evaluations are reviewed by administrators at the district level and must be approved by a board of local citizens. Unions play no part in these evaluations, except to try to assure fairness and due process. Weak teachers may make it through this system, but they do so because of management and board decisions, and not because of organized labor. And a fully tenured teacher can be fired for due cause. Contracts and state laws require the district to provide due process and the administration has to document the charge with evidence. Union contracts secure the accused teacher's rights to a fair proceeding, not a right to their job. No contract requires a district to keep a teacher no matter the evidence (Han, 2016). Districts with union contracts need to be even more careful about the quality of teachers hired and those retained and tenured; that is good for students and schools, and that is what happens (Singer, 2017). Bad teachers are an embarrassment to teachers' unions, just as the American Bar Association and the American Medical Association are embarrassed by lawyers and physicians found to be unethical, corrupt, or harmful to the public. No responsible union wants to protect incompetent workers, but they do want to be sure that any firing process is fair and equitable and teacher rights are protected.

Charges that unions cause decline in student achievement are another anti-union myth. Data show unions are responsible for increased school funding that actually reaches classrooms and helps students rather than administrators and their special interests (Barnum, 2019). A remarkable and very important point is that comparisons show that student performance tends to be better in states and districts that have strong teacher unions. Many of the states rated lowest in student achievement are also right to work states that do not allow unions. Globally, nations rated in the top 10 for student performance are ones with the strongest teachers' unions (Ravani, 2014; Wydra, 2018; Harris, 2019). This is strong evidence of the educational value of teacher unions.

Unions have been good for teachers. Research indicates unions have a positive effect on teachers' working conditions. Unlike the pre-union days, teachers cannot be dismissed simply because they are in the wrong political party, consume alcohol, change their marital status, or express unpopular political views. John Dewey believed that a union was necessary to protect teachers' intellectual and academic freedom (Kahlenberg, 2007). These are good conditions for students and for education. Much education "reform" in recent times has been led by the wealthy, corporations, and highly conservative organizations. Massive standardized testing requirements, less teacher participation in curricular and classroom decisions, digital learning to replace teachers, less academic freedom, increased class size, and restricted budgets have been the results. Reform is not always improvement. Unions have been good for students and for improved education. They have put faculty squarely in the front ranks of the battle for better schools and better education for children. It is in their interest to do so (Ravani, 2014; Barnum, 2019).

Unions and Education Reform

Teachers' unions support the evaluation of teachers, using academically appropriate assessment designs, but teachers and their unions recognize how difficult it is to measure teacher performance. As the late AFT president Albert Shanker argued, a used car salesman who sells 20 cars a month is probably twice as good as a salesman in the same dealership who sells 10 a month (Kahlenberg, 2007). This simple assessment formula cannot be applied to the evaluation of teachers, but it has not discouraged so-called education reformers from trying. Teacher quality cannot be measured solely by changes in student test scores. If it were that simple, students could be tested at point A. Teachers would provide instruction. Students would be retested at point B. We could then subtract A scores from B scores and attribute the difference between A and B solely to the teacher's skill. Simple and neat, but nothing in education works that way. Too much transpires between points A and B to make valid conclusions about a teacher's effectiveness based on gain scores alone.

Teachers know that how well students perform is a reflection of social factors and family environment at least as much as it indicates student learning or teacher skill. Garon (2011), a teacher, notes, "Of the five students who failed my senior advanced-placement English class last term, one was pregnant, one had just moved to a shelter, and one was bouncing between foster homes" (p. 97). Standardized testing never can account for student performance in the ways that teachers can. Among their many shortcomings, standardized testing systems typically fail to consider personal issues, test anxiety, and test preparation, and they do not tease out the differences between real learning and mere memorization (Perlstein, 2007; MET Project, 2013).

Teacher unions recognize that teacher evaluation processes need to be changed. For too long, the evaluation of teaching performance lacked rigor and consistency. Too few of the truly outstanding teachers received recognition, too few of the struggling teachers were given appropriate support, and too little effort was made to identify those teachers who should not be in the classroom at all. Teaching is complex, and any evaluation of teaching and teachers must be sensitive to its complexity. As the AFT (2011) notes,

> Any valid approach to evaluation necessarily will consider both outputs (test data and student work) and inputs (school environment, resources, professional development). . . . Student test scores based on valid assessments should be one of the performance criteria, as should classroom observations, portfolio reviews, appraisal of lesson plans, and student work. (p. 1)

Simple business solutions should not be applied to a multilayered education problem. Ravitch (2010) describes this as a "false analogy," and that putative school reformers, enamored of the private sector, "think they can fix education by applying the principles of business, organization, management, law, and marketing and by developing a good data collection system that provides the information necessary to incentivize the workforce—principals, teachers, and students—with appropriate rewards and sanctions" (p. 11). Walker (2019) identifies reform ideas that should be left behind, including: school vouchers, lunch-shaming of children getting federal lunch support, discriminatory dress codes, having computers and robots take over, and arming teachers rather than limiting guns. These ideas are mainly from corporate, wealthy class, and right-wing sources, often seeking to decimate public education.

An Increasing Teacher Shortage

Much of the information above explains a teacher shortage developing across the nation (Flannery, 2019; Garcia and Weiss, 2019). Teachers are burned out and exasperated because of: low comparative pay, slashed budgets with less supplies and books, school safety and suggestions that teachers carry guns, decreasing importance in educational decisions, and excessive testing and external school pressures, among others (Brenan, 2018a; Griggs, 2018). Teachers feel unappreciated and overworked. Half of them have seriously considered quitting because of unfair pay and low perceived value. Worse, for the long term, teachers are leaving positions and fewer students are enrolling in teacher education; in 2006, almost 10% of all first-year college students were interested in teaching, in 2016, it was less than 5% (McFeely, 2018). Fewer fully credentialed teachers are expected as schools try to fill gaps. Over 20% of teachers have 5 or fewer years experience, and are less tied to long career patterns. Unions want to develop a stronger, professional career and life for classroom teachers. Spurred by parents, students, teachers, teacher protests, and the poor results of previous test-driven, corporate-oriented school reform, states and school districts are increasingly recognizing the seriousness of this issue and are responding with more funds, better treatment of teachers, and improved work conditions.

Parents, legislators, and unions agree: the ultimate goal of schools is to help every student succeed. Unions use their collective strength to improve schools through appropriate policies and practices. Unionized teachers add their collective voice to debates about teacher accountability and school assessment programs, teacher education and development, school administration, and educational policy issues in a professional manner and with professional responsibilities. Nowhere is the union voice more necessary than in the support of teachers. What do classroom teachers need, and how can unions help? While salaries have always been a major issue for teachers, teachers themselves typically indicate that a "lack of support" is their top concern. Teacher unions want a voice in improving the status of teachers so that recruiting, sustaining, and retaining a high-quality teaching force is more likely. These are items of educational and social benefit—from attractive programs in teacher education to careful selection by schools, to strong district induction, to mentored and valuable early career development, to meaningful support and useful evaluation, to substantial participation in local educational decisions, to legitimate academic freedom, to educationally sound promotion opportunities. Teacher welfare is linked to quality schools and social development. Unions are not the only course for teacher and school progress; but they should have a major voice for teachers in that process.

There is broad and deep support for good schools. Too many schools are failing and too many districts and states are failing teachers. Unions support many school reform proposals and are properly suspicious of others. Unions are particularly wary of policies and procedures that are imposed on schools without the full consultation and participation of teachers. It is largely up to teachers to make schools successful; they deserve our focus.

Position 2:   Teacher Unions Stand in the Way of School Reform

Public sector unions should be illegal. They negotiate with elected officials who they help elect. . . . But the teachers' union is worse than all other public sector unions for one reason that eclipses all others: Their agenda is negatively affecting how we socialize and educate out children.

—Ring (2018)

A History of Self-Serving, Unsupported Union Claims

Teacher union officials say that when public monies are spent to improve working conditions for teachers, children are the ultimate beneficiaries. Their arguments are, no doubt, familiar. Public school students suffer because teachers are underpaid. Hardworking, devoted teachers deserve greater compensation. Unless teachers earn higher salaries, not only will the current crop of teachers become discouraged, but the most able college graduates will not consider a teaching career. Union leaders further argue that teachers need a stronger voice in school affairs. They claim that teachers will be more effective if allowed to join administrators in all areas of school leadership, including school improvement and supervision and evaluation of teaching.

The logic in these examples is simple: what is good for teachers is good for children. If the public wants better education for its children, the public should support union efforts to improve education through increased remuneration and greater authority for teachers. Collective bargaining practices, picket lines, work stoppages (strikes), and expansion of union control over schools should be considered beneficial to the community, parents, and students. Convincing? Not really. Making schools better places for teachers does not necessarily serve the students or public interest. The public's interest is measured not in teachers' job satisfaction but in the quality of learning provided to students. Despite the rhetoric of organized labor, teacher unions do not have a positive effect on student achievement. Researchers find negligible differences in achievement between public school students in union and nonunion schools. While research indicates evidence that collective bargaining improves teachers' salaries, benefits, and working conditions, it is more difficult to find a consistently positive influence of unions on student learning (Stone, 2000; Goldhaber, 2006; Buck, 2019). Unions cannot claim to make a difference where it counts most: students' academic performance. Despite failures of teacher unions to prove their worth in student achievement, the positive wage effect of unions—that is, their power to improve teachers' pay—clearly ensures that unions will remain players in education.

Less than 11% of American workers belong to a labor union (U.S. Bureau of Labor Statistics, 2019), the lowest number in recorded history, but teachers in America's schools are highly unionized. Over 70% of teachers belong to a union or similar organization (National Center for Education Statistics, 2020). The largest organizations are the NEA and the AFT, with millions of dues-paying members. Unions have great resources and great political power. Not only can teacher unions exert influence on the day-to-day workings of schools, but their political activities have given them unrivaled influence in the local, state, and federal governments as well. Terry Moe (2001) points out, "On education issues, the teacher unions are the 500-pound gorillas of legislative politics, and especially in legislatures where the Democrats are in control, they are in a better position than any other interest group to get what they want from government" (p. 175).

Teacher unions work for the benefit of teachers, not students. It is misleading when unions call for increased levels of training for teachers or stricter licensing standards. There is little evidence that such changes result in better education or improved student learning, but there is abundant evidence to indicate that these policies would primarily help increase income for teachers. Increased expectations for teacher certification and continuation, such as requiring teachers to have master's degrees, results in a smaller supply of teachers when demand is increasing. Unions hope that market forces will result in improved salaries.

It is hard to trust unions. Evidence does not support union advocacy of smaller class size, bigger automatic salary increases, more teacher free time, and more resources. It is not a clear effort to help children, but is simply a way to make teachers' work easier and increase the demand for teachers and union membership. One union recommendation is mentorship programs, where experienced classroom teachers help new teachers learn the ropes. This may sound reasonable, but it doubles the salaried teachers for a single class. Similarly, the call for more staff to support individual teachers in their classes means additional costs and no demonstrated student achievement results. The claim for such initiatives is benefits to students; the fact is higher costs and more union recruits from featherbedding—the addition of unnecessary workers (Ballou and Podgursky, 2000; *The Economist*, 2007; Sand, 2014).

Cowan and Strunk (2015) examined three decades of research on the effect of teacher unions on school districts and student outcomes, finding "teacher unionization and union strength are associated with increases in district expenditures and teacher salaries, particularly salaries for experienced teachers" and that evidence on student outcomes is "mixed, but suggestive of insignificant or modestly negative union effects." Lovenheim and Willen (2018), studying effects of collective bargaining for teachers since 1955, find that students spending 12 years in a collective bargaining school district earn almost $800 less per year in income, workers tend to be more unemployed than on average, and that collective bargaining locales have had a reduction in measured noncognitive skills in men.

Unions have extended their influence beyond bread-and-butter work issues and school management decisions into general politics. Past union efforts typically were limited to traditional labor concerns: wages and hours, working conditions, fringe benefits, grievance procedures, organization rights, and such specific work-related issues as extra pay for extra duty (e.g., athletic coaching or directing school plays). Over time, teacher unions began to demand a voice in school policy issues, including curriculum reform, class size, disciplinary practices, textbook selection procedures, in-service training, teacher transfer policies, and personnel matters—including hiring and awarding tenure (Kerchner, 1986; Kerchner and Koppich, 1993). Affiliates of the NEA and AFT want teachers to expand beyond their classroom activities and participate in discussions about school improvement, staff development, and student assessment. These demands go well beyond the traditional bargaining issues. Some union contracts give teachers the right to make decisions about how schools spend money, how teachers teach, and how students are to learn. In strongly unionized urban districts, union contracts can be hundreds of pages long. Under the familiar argument that collective negotiations will create a better education for children, union leaders claim that increased teacher participation in all the decision making and managerial aspects of education improves schools; there is no evidence to support this.

Unions are now heavily involved in political influence. Policies promoted by the unions are on the liberal side and often linked to the Democratic Party (Watson, 2017; Garris, 2017; Ring, 2018; Friedrichs, 2018). About $145 million was contributed to Democratic candidates and committees in 2019, and 90% of their political funding goes to Democrats, more than most other unions (Buck, 2019; Influence Watch, 2020). Izumi (2019), in an article wondering why teachers are predominantly liberal, describes the wave of teacher strikes as a device for killing real educational reform, like charter schools and vouchers. Some people have greeted the new union arguments with a healthy skepticism. Teachers' unions have used organizing and negotiating techniques borrowed from industrial unions in mining and manufacturing—collective bargaining and the threat of strikes—to improve their members' working conditions. There is every reason to be suspicious of the union idea that those tactics improve the quality of student learning.

Apologizing for Bad Teachers

The public is generally sympathetic to teachers, but not to teacher unions, and it is not hard to understand why. The sad fact remains that too many schools have teachers who are not able to do the work expected of them. Unfortunately, because of unions and tenure laws, even the poorest teachers will probably stay on the job until retirement. In many states, union opposition has brought actions against ineffective teachers to an absolute halt.

Unions are apologists for poor teaching and an obstacle to school reform. On one hand, unions praise the magical effect good teachers have on children's lives. On the other hand, they refuse to admit that weak teachers cause many of education's problems. In public schools, the quality of classroom instruction varies tremendously. Nestled among the great teachers, the good teachers, and the marginally adequate teachers are those who fail to convey enthusiasm for learning and, unfortunately, more than a few who have neither the personal qualities nor the skills and knowledge necessary to teach children. Good teachers whet students' appetites for academic achievement; bad teachers kill interest, leave students with enormous gaps of information, and tarnish the reputation of the profession. *Waiting for "Superman,"* the popular documentary film directed by Davis Guggenheim, notes that about one in every 51 physicians in America loses the license to practice medicine, and one in every 97 lawyers loses the license necessary to practice law. Yet only one in every 1,000 teachers is dismissed for incompetence.

Barnard (2019) states it: "Protecting bad teachers hurts kids." Joel Klein (2011), former chancellor of New York City's public schools, argues that in a school system with about 55,000 tenured teachers, "we were able to fire only a half dozen or so for incompetence in a given year" (p. 5). Tenure, lifetime job security unknown to most workers, is a privilege enjoyed by public school teachers, supported by unions, and destructive of education. Tenure is awarded to public school teachers following three to six years of teaching with satisfactory evaluations. The tenure hurdle is not a particularly high bar. Almost all teachers earn this sinecure for life. In New York City, 99% of all teachers win tenure, and are protected against dismissal. Tenure has outlived its usefulness as a protection from political patronage or despotic school administrators. Now there are other legal protections, and administrators are better trained. Unions have gone too far. Teachers should not be dismissed for personality disputes with an administrator, and teaching should not be a patronage position with wholesale changes of staff following every election. But teacher unions have made it all but impossible to remove even the least effective teachers from the classroom, and they serve as a roadblock to school reform (Moe, 2011).

Brill (2009) describes the workings of New York's Temporary Reassignment Centers, commonly known as "rubber rooms," where teachers were sent after being "accused of misconduct, such as hitting or molesting a student, or, in some cases, of incompetence, in a system that rarely calls anyone incompetent" (p. 2). With union protection, teachers in the rubber rooms were guaranteed a hearing by an arbitrator, a process that typically took three to five years and rarely resulted in dismissal. All the while, teachers in the rubber rooms around the city drew full salaries and added to their eventual pensions. It was possible for teachers assigned to the rubber rooms for years to retire at age 55, with an annual pension of $60,000, free from state taxes. The role of the union is to protect teachers; their role is not to educate children. As one school principal put it, the union president "would protect a dead body [teaching] in the classroom. That's her job" (p. 7).

You have all had good teachers and know from experience that good teachers can make a startling difference in student learning. Academic research demonstrates this as well. One team of researchers, for example, found that when low-income students have good teachers for four years in a row, their learning increases, and the gap between low-income students and the average-income student is eliminated (quoted in Moe, 2011, p. 4). Other research suggests that if we were to remove the bottom 5 to 8% of teachers and replace them with "average teachers," the United States would move close to the top of international student achievement in math and science (Hanushek, 2010).

Unions Fail to Support the Best Teachers

Public school students and their parents know that some teachers are far more effective than others, more able to promote academic achievement. Those teachers should be recognized and compensated for their superior results. Rewarding high levels of productivity is a cornerstone of the private sector, and it works to the benefit of the individual and the company. But this elegant compensation equation runs counter to the union-supported single-salary schedule. The salaries of most teachers reflect their years of service and the graduate credits they earned, not their contemporary performance in teaching. In most school districts, all first-year teachers, with baccalaureate degrees and no experience, are paid the same whether they work with disadvantaged or relatively advantaged students, whether they teach in subject areas with a shortage of teachers, such as math and science, or in a subject field with an abundant supply of candidates, or how difficult the specific position is in that school. Second-year teachers with the same credentials will receive the same salary increases independent of the achievements of their students or the teacher's contributions to student progress. This is not the best way to attract and reward high-quality teachers.

Consider the following approach to personnel decisions based on merit and quantifiable data. Most states require student testing in multiple grades every year. All students in a given grade level take the same standardized tests. Over the years, states have amassed lots of good achievement data, and it seems quite reasonable to use these data to measure how effective individual teachers are in promoting learning. Of course, to measure how much value a teacher has added, it is necessary to control for student demographics, class size, and teacher experience, but it can be done. Examining student gain scores on objective tests would provide useful data for making tenure decisions and awarding salary increases as well as considering teacher terminations. With objective data at hand, it would be possible to reward good results and penalize poor classroom performance.

Unfortunately, teacher unions object. As Joel Klein (2011) writes,

> I proposed that the City [of New York] use value-added numbers only for the top and bottom 20% of teachers: The top 20% would get positive credit; the bottom would lose credit. And even then, principals would take value-added data into account only as part of a much larger comprehensive tenure review. Even with these limitations, the [teacher union] said "No way." (pp. 3–4)

In November 2010, after eight years on the job, Joel Klein resigned, frustrated by union obstruction to school reform. On his last day on the job, Klein was told that he could withdraw the contributions he had made to the retirement system or leave the money in the system and receive a guaranteed annual rate of return of 8.25%. Klein was stunned and wondered how the system could be so generous at a time when banks were paying 1% interest. He was told that the union contract guaranteed the high rate and that if investments fell short, the city would make up the difference. "Who else," Klein asked rhetorically, "but Bernie Madoff guarantees 8.25% a year permanently?" (quoted in Brill, 2011, pp. 400–401).

Teacher Unions Have Outlived Their Usefulness

Garris (2017) lists five reasons why unions of teachers harm education:

1. They negotiate our public tax money;
2. They keep out or limit qualified teachers with state certification;
3. They stem teacher motivation with lock-step pay and tenure;
4. They advocate against alternate ideas—charter schools, vouchers, home schooling; and
5. They are strongly supportive of only the Democratic Party.

In the days when teachers had few rights and principals ran roughshod over them, unions helped to improve the working lives and benefits of teachers. But times have changed, and teacher unions are now harmful to teachers and education. The industrial age made unions attractive to teachers. In a postindustrial age, unions are an anachronism that restricts teachers and students and serves as an adversary to school reform. Reformers believe that improved student performance in academic work is the core purpose of education. That requires excellent teachers with appropriate rewards. Teacher unions oppose the reform agenda for schools, including pay for performance and other forms of accountability. Unions work to increase due-paying members, not the improvement of students and the community. Their considerable power and influence is on teacher support, but education should be about students. Unions become an obstacle to change and a political behemoth that stands in the way of what is good for students and society. A sound and rigorous education under the guidance of a skillful teacher requires opposition to the power of the unions.

FOR DISCUSSION

1. Is teaching a profession? Should it be? What defines a profession and which forms of work fit that definition? What difference should it make to the role and job of teaching whether or not it is generally perceived to be a profession? How do unions fit within the idea of professions? How do AFT and NEA fit?

2. A single-salary schedule for all teachers is common. There are vertical steps, rewarding teachers for longevity, and horizontal lanes, rewarding post-baccalaureate credit.

Pay-for-performance advocates argue that teachers' salaries should be based, in large part, on the performance of their students. Teacher unions argue that standardized test scores measure only a narrow range of student work and that performance pay could pit one teacher against another and undermine cooperation among teachers.

a. Is performance pay attractive to you? If so, how should it be measured? If not, what rewards should be available for better than average teaching?

b. Interview a collection of teachers; what motivates them to good teaching?

3. The next generation of teachers may hold views about their work that are different from the views of the teachers they will replace. What are your views, and how did you arrive at them? Interview others preparing to become teachers; what are their views and what support do they offer? How do they perceive the relative value of teacher unions? What do they think is the best way to make important educational decisions in schools?

4. Discuss teacher tenure. Is it a good policy for teachers and education? What should be done about weak and ineffective teachers?

References

American Federation of Teachers (2011). A Continuous Improvement Model for Teacher Development and Evaluation (aft.org).

Ayers, W., Laura, C., and Ayers, R. (2018). *You Can't Fire the Bad Ones*. Boston: Beacon Press.

Ballou, D., and Podgursky, M. (2000). Gaining Control of Professional Licensing and Advancement. In T. Loveless, ed., *Conflicting Missions?* Washington, DC: Brookings Institution.

Barnard, C. (2019, January 16). "Students Are Being Slowly Liberated from Teacher Unions." *Los Angeles Daily News*.

Barnum, M. (2019, April 15). Are Teachers Unions Helping or Hurting Schools? Chalkbeat (chalkbeat.org).

Blanc, E. (2019). *Red State Revolt*. New York: Verso.

Brenan, M. (2018a, March 5). Most U.S. Teachers Oppose Carrying Guns in School. Gallup (news.gallup.com/poll/229808/teachers-oppose-carrying-guns-schools.aspx).

Brenan, M. (2018b, December 20). Nurses Outpace Other Professions for Honesty, Ethics. Gallup (gallup.com/poll/245597/nurses-again-outpace-professions-honesty-ethics.aspx).

Brill, S. (2009, August 31). "The Rubber Room: Battle Over New York City's Worst Teachers." *The New Yorker*, pp. 1–15.

———— (2011). *Class Warfare: Inside the Fight to Fix America's Schools*. New York: Simon & Schuster.

Buck, D. (2019, January 2). 7 Reasons to Say Goodbye to Teachers Unions. Foundation for Economic Education (fee.org).

Commonwealth v. Hunt (1842). 445 Mass (4 met.) 111,38 Am. Dec 346.

Cowan, J. M., and Strunk, K. O. (2015, October). "The Impact of Teachers' Unions on Educational Outcomes." *Economics of Education Review* 48.

DiSalvo, D. (2019, February 13). "*Janus* Barely Dents Public-Sector Union Membership." *Wall Street Journal*.

Eaton, W. E. (1975). *The American Federation of Teachers, 1916–1961: A History of the Movement*. Carbondale: Southern Illinois University Press.

Engel, R. A. (1976). Teacher Negotiation: History and Comment. In E. M. Cresswell and M. J. Murphy, eds., *Education and Collective Bargaining*. Berkeley, CA: McCutchan.

Ferguson, M. (2018). "Washington View: Public Opinion on Teachers and Teaching." *Phi Delta Kappan* 100(1):40–41.

FindLaw (2020, January 4). Teacher Unions and Collective Bargaining (findlaw.com).

Flannery, M. E. (2019, December 9). "Teacher Shortage Sends Retired Teachers Back to the Classroom." *NEAToday*.

Friedrichs, R. (2018). *Standing Up To Goliath*. New York: Post Hill Press.

Galley, M. (2003, June 4). "Survey Finds Teachers Supportive of Unions." *Education Week*, pp. 1–3.

Garcia, E., and Weiss, E. (2019, March 26). The Teacher Shortage is Real, Large and Growing, and Worse Than We Thought. Economic Policy Institute (epi.org).

Garon, I. (2011). "Four Myths about Teachers." *Dissent* 58:97–98.

Garris, Z. (2017, February 10). Five Reasons Teacher Unions Are Harmful. Teach Diligently (teachdiligently.com).

Goldhaber, D. (2006). Are Teachers' Unions Good for Students? In J. Hannaway and A. J. Rotherman, eds., *Collective Bargaining in Education*. Cambridge, MA: Harvard University Press.

Griggs, B. (2018, May 3). These Charts Show Why America's Teachers Are Fired Up and Can't Take Any More. CNN (cnn.com).

Han, E. (2016, February 27). The Myth of Unions' Overprotection of Bad Teachers (scribd.com).

Hanushek, E. A. (2010). *The Economic Value of Higher Teacher Quality* (Working Paper No. 16606). National Bureau of Economic Research (nber.org/papers/w16606).

Harris, D. (2019, June 5). Teacher Unions May Be More Important Than Ever in 2020. Brown Center Chalkboard. The Brookings Institution (brookings.edu).

Highet, G. (1976). *The Immortal Profession*. New York: Weybright and Talley.

Holmes Group (1986). *Tomorrow's Teachers: A Report on the Holmes Group*. East Lansing, MI: Holmes Group.

Influence Watch (2020, January 15). National Education Association (influencewatch.org).

Izumi, L. (2019, April 3). Why Are Teachers Mostly Liberal? Pacific Research Institute (pacificresearch.org).

Jacobson, L. (2019, November 18). Tracker: Teachers on Strike. Education Dive (educationdive.com).

Janus v. American Federation of State, County, and Municipal Employees, Council 31, et al. (2018). 585 U.S. __.

Jessup, D. K. (1978). "Teacher Unionization: A Reassessment of Rank and File Education." *Sociology of Education* 51:44–55.

Kahlenberg, R. (2007). *Tough Liberal: Albert Shanker and the Battles over Schools, Unions, Race, and Democracy*. New York: Columbia University Press.

Kajitani, A. (2017). Introduction. In A. Newmark and A. Kajitani, eds., *Chicken Soup for the Soul: Inspiration for Teachers*. Cos Cob, CT: Chicken Soup for the Soul.

Kerchner, C. T. (1986). Union-Made Teaching: Effects of Labor Relations. In E. Z. Rothkopf, ed., *Review of Research in Education* (Vol. 13). Washington, DC: American Educational Research Association.

Kerchner, C. T., and Koppich, J. E. (1993). *A Union of Professionals: Labor Relations and Educational Reform*. New York: Teachers College Press.

Kerchner, C. T., Koppich, J. E., and Weeres, J. G. (1997). *United Mind Workers: Unions and Teaching in the Knowledge Society*. San Francisco: Jossey-Bass.

Klein, J. (2011, June). "The Failure of American Schools." *The Atlantic*, pp. 1–13.

Lieberman, M., and Moscow, M. H. (1966). *Collective Negotiations for Teachers: An Approach to School Administration*. Chicago: Rand McNally.

Lovenheim, M., and Willen, A. (2016, Winter). "Bad Bargain." *EducationNext* 16(1).

—— (2018, July). *The Long-Run Effects of Teacher Collective Bargaining* (Working Paper No. 24782). National Bureau of Economic Research (nber.org/papers/w24782).

McFeely, S. (2018, March 27). Why Your Best Teachers Are Leaving and 4 Ways to Keep Them. Gallup (gallup.com/education/237275/why-best-teachers-leaving-ways-keep.aspx).

MET Project (2013, January 8). Measures of Effective Teaching Project Releases Final Report. Bill and Melinda Gates Foundation (gatesfoundation.org/Media-Center/Press-Releases/2013/01/Measures-of-Effective-Teaching-Project-Releases-Final-Research-Report).

Miller, B. (2018, June 27). "Unpacking the *Janus* Decision" *Forbes.*

Moe, T. M. (2001). Teachers Unions. In T. M. Moe, ed., *A Primer on America's Schools.* Stanford, CA: Hoover Institution.

—— (2011). *Special Interest: Teachers Unions and America's Public Schools.* Washington, DC: Brookings Institution.

Murphy, M. (1990). *Blackboard Unions: The AFT and the NEA, 1900–1980.* Ithaca, NY: Cornell University Press.

National Center for Education Statistics (2020, January 12). National Teacher and Principal Survey (nces.gov).

NLRB v. Jones and Laughlin Steel Company (1937). 301 U.S. 1, 57 S. Ct. 615.

Organisation for Economic Co-operation and Development (2018, September 11). *Education at a Glance 2018* (oecd.org/education/education-at-a-glance).

Perlstein, L. (2007). *Tested: One American School Struggles to Make the Grade.* New York: Henry Holt.

Ravani, G. (2014, July 27). Why Public Education Needs Teachers Unions. EdSource (edsource.org).

Ravitch, D. (2010). *The Death and Life of the Great American School System.* New York: Basic Books.

Ring, E. (2018, August 1). Why Teachers Unions Are the Worst of the Worst. California Policy Center (californiapolicycenter.org).

Samuels, A. (2018, June 27). "Is This the End of Public-Sector Unions in America?" *The Atlantic.*

Sand, L. (2014, August 26). The Poor Teacher Canard Redux—Part II. California Policy Center (californiapolicycenter.org).

Singer, A. (2017, September 21). Teacher Unions Improve Teacher, Student, School Performance, Despite Rightwing Assault. HuffPost (huffpost.com/entry/teacher-unions-improve-teacher-student-and-school_b_59c38de1e4b0c87def883585).

Smiley, M. B., and Diekhoff, J. S. (1959). *Prologue to Teaching.* New York: Oxford University Press.

Stone, J. A. (2000). Collective Bargaining and Public Schools. In T. Loveless, ed., *Conflicting Missions?* Washington, DC: Brookings Institution.

The Economist (2007, February 22). "Do Unions Increase Productivity?"

Topol, E. (2019, August 5). "Why Doctors Should Organize." *The New Yorker.*

Urban, W. J. (1982). *Why Teachers Organized.* Detroit: Wayne State University Press.

U.S. Bureau of Labor Statistics (2019, January 18). Union Members Summary (bls.gov).

Walker, T. (2019, December, 16). 8 Education Trends and Ideas Worth Leaving Behind in 2020. NEAToday (neatoday.org).

Waller, W. (1932). *The Sociology of Teaching.* New York: Wiley.

Watson, M. (2017, June 21). Teacher Unions: Fighting the Bad Fight. Capital Research Center (capitalresearchcenter.org).

Weingarten, R. (2018, July 13). Hope in Darkness. Remarks at AFT Convention, Pittsburgh, PA.

Wesley, E. B. (1957). *NEA: The First Hundred Years.* New York: Harper and Brothers.

Will, M. (2019, December 17). The Teaching Profession in 2019. Blog, Teaching Now. *Education Week.*

Wydra, A. (2018, January 20). Teachers' Unions Improve Student Achievement. Chicago Policy Review (chicagopolicyreview.org).

Intellectual Freedom and Critical Thinking

Teachers, Students, and Society

16

How should we determine the balance and borders of freedom and responsibility for education?

Position 1:   For Increased Intellectual Freedom

Education International, a global association of education unions that represents 32.5 million educators in 170 countries, has just produced a new civic-education guide based on John Dewey's belief that "Democracy has to be born anew every generation, and education is its midwife."

—Gershman (2020)

This book's first chapter offered a focus on education for a democratic society and corollary advocacy for critical thinking about critical issues—in education and in other segments of life. America's basic ideals and principles require an educated populace, a necessary condition for a democratic system. Freedom is necessary for democracy and education. Critical thinking in and out of schools depends on intellectual freedom for teachers and students. In schools, this can be difficult because of the age and maturity of students, the capability of school administrators and teachers, a history of restrictive thinking, and contemporary social values and traditions. Controversies, large and small, surround our lives; some are highly sensitive nearly all of the time and some are sensitive at various times and places. Debates over religion, politics, morals, sex and sexual orientation, economics, racism, and a host of other social issues rise and fall. Education itself is a common controversial issue, with ferocious participants.

Important and pervasive social issues deserve critical study and that expectation requires intellectual freedom. Along with other organizations, the American Library Association (ALA) has a long, distinguished history defending intellectual freedom (Magi and Garnar, 2015; La Rue and Diaz, 2017; American Library Association, 2020). The ALA Office for Intellectual Freedom fights against censorship in libraries and schools and provides a passionate defense for the right to question. A highly successful ALA program is Banned Books Week, celebrated in libraries across the United States (Pekoll, 2019), as is their joint work with the Freedom to Read Foundation and the Media Coalition. The International Federation of Library Associations and Institutions (2018) strongly supports intellectual freedom among its international membership. Schools should help students understand issues through examination of evidence and reasoning in a free educational setting where questions can be raised and addressed. This is preparation for a thoughtful and reasoned life.

Academic freedom is the educational parallel term with intellectual freedom, used to support the free process of teaching and study. Schools are at the center of community life, as well as a proper location for thoughtful analysis and evaluation of social issues. In the context and heat of public debate over issues, some advocates on each side pursue efforts to censor or severely restrict teachers and students; this is a serious threat to academic freedom. Laws, professional associations, civil liberties organizations, and teacher tenure offer some defense. Nearly all teacher professional associations, including those representing teachers of English, social studies, science, and the arts, and the general teacher unions have basic statements in support of teacher and student rights. The National Council of Teachers of English (2019) statement includes: "the members of NCTE endorse and work to maintain academic freedom at all levels of public education." The National Council for the Social Studies (2016) policy statement asserts: "Academic freedom means both social studies educators and students have the opportunity to engage in intellectual debate without fear of censorship or retaliation."

Academic freedom is central to the purposes of education. Teacher competence and knowledge are crucial to its protection. Teaching, as Nieto (2006) and Sinha (2016) note, is a political act. Teacher neutrality is actually political, silently justifying the status quo and marginalizing some groups. Teaching is political in advocacy for education, learning, individual and social improvement, reasoning and rational decision making, informed knowledge, and, of course, critical thinking. Those conditions do not allow teachers to indoctrinate, to dominate despite evidence, or be unchallenged on reasoned grounds. Critical thinking, as identified in the first chapter, and academic freedom are necessary for education. Censorship and political restrictions diminish education and civilization (Mchangama, 2020; Yono, 2020).

The Evolution and Expansion of Academic Freedom

Socrates, charged with impiety and corruption of youth, defended himself by claiming the freedom for students and teachers to pursue truth. He argued against ignorance; freedom to teach and learn would uncover knowledge, eliminate ignorance, and improve society. His judges did not agree, and Socrates was sentenced to death. Academic freedom, over time, has fared better. Although it is regularly battered, it has survived and expanded. In early America it narrowly related to a few scholars in colleges, and not always successfully. We are closer now to the dual protections of intellectual freedom prescribed in Germany—*Lehrfreiheit* and *Lernfreiheit*—the freedom of teachers to teach and of learners to learn without institutional restriction (Hofstadter and Metzger, 1968; Daly et al., 2001). It is evolving in the United States and is now significantly more embedded in the culture of schools and educated society.

Unfortunately, state law differences and confusing court opinions produce mixed views on protection for specific actions and topics (O'Neil, 1981, 2008, 2010; Simpson, 2010; Worona and Shaw, 2018; American Library Association, 2020). The broad concept is generally understood, but specific application in classrooms and schools is sometimes contested. Court decisions can be murky (Worona and Shaw, 2018). Some support complete school board discretion over curriculum and student newspapers; others exhibit an expanding awareness of academic freedom and protection. Higher-level courts can be highly supportive of academic freedom for public school teachers. Justices Frankfurter and Douglas (*Wieman v. Updegraff*, 1952) argued that all teachers from primary grades to the university share a special role in developing good citizens, and all teachers should have the academic freedom necessary to be exemplars of open-mindedness and free inquiry. In *Cary v. Board of Education of Adams–Arapahoe School District* (1979), the decision specifically included public school teachers on the ground that all education requires that freedom. The Supreme Court decided in *Tinker v. Des Moines Independent School District* (1969) that teachers and students do not "shed their Constitutional rights at the schoolhouse gate."

Simpson (2010), noting the historic pattern of federal court decisions increasing teacher and student freedom in the 1960s and 1970s, summarizes court decision setbacks for K–12 teachers. In *Garcetti v. Ceballos* (2006), the Supreme Court ruled that public employees do not have First Amendment protection for speech issued during their public duties. In *Mayer v. Monroe County Community School Corp.* (2007), a court ruled that teacher speech can be determined and limited by the employer. Simpson, in light of "the harsh reality" of that decision, suggests teachers advocate for protective and clear "academic freedom" conditions in teacher contract language and in school board regulations. Restrictions on teacher speech show the significance of tenure protection, where firing can be only for due cause and requires due process. Teachers must continue to be active advocates for academic freedom in public discourse and political arenas. Academic freedom needs continual nurturing, expansion, and vigilance.

Educational Grounds for Academic Freedom

Where, if not in schools, will new generations explore and test divergent ideas, new concepts, and challenges to propaganda under the guidance of free and knowledgeable teachers? Students can test ideas and pursue intriguing possibilities in schools with less serious risks of social condemnation or ostracism. In a setting of critical thinking, students and teachers can engage more fully in intellectual development. There are two fundamental reasons for the advancement of academic freedom: (1) new ideas from new generations are basic to social progress, and (2) students who do not explore divergent ideas in school can be blinded to society's defects and imperfections and will be ill equipped to participate as citizens in improving democracy (Puddington et al., 2008).

Teaching can be conducted as simple indoctrination, with teachers presenting material and students memorizing it without thought or criticism. That is an incomplete and defective education. Teaching also can be chaotic, with no sense of organization or purpose—this, too, is incomplete and defective. Neither indoctrination nor chaos offers education. Education consists of knowledge, ideas, and challenges, increasingly sophisticated and complex. Indoctrination stunts the educational process, shrinking knowledge and constricting critical thinking. Chaotic schools confuse students, mix important and trivial ideas, and muddle critical thinking. Sound education is grounded in current knowledge and helps students use reason to challenge ideas.

The defining quality of academic freedom is freedom in the search for knowledge. That search is not limited to experts in ivory towers; it is the primary purpose of schooling at any level. Historic arguments against academic freedom for teachers were based on a mix of traditional ideas: "teachers are not scholars," "they have a captive audience," "they can influence impressionable minds," and "they are public employees subject to the will of boards and administrators." These arguments, based on ancient views of teachers, falter against the truth and the important necessity for teacher freedom in a democracy. Teachers have undergraduate degrees and most have graduate degrees; they exhibit scholarly qualities necessary for teachers. Students are expected to inquire and challenge, not be captive receptacles. Professional ethics do not countenance brainwashing. And public employees do not lose their rights. We are beyond the period of unprepared political hacks or rote memorization disciplinarians as teachers.

Learning occurs as people test new ideas against their own experiences and knowledge. Active learning does more than just help clear up student confusion. It offers intellectual involvement and ownership. Students can recognize flaws in existing knowledge or find new ways to understand. When only experts control knowledge or when censors limit ideas, we risk conformity, without challenges or conflicting opinions. We may feel uncomfortable with challenges to ideas we like, but they are the stuff of progress. Finocchio (personal communication, 2011), emeritus professor of biology, wrote a strong plea at his retirement: "Beware of those who interfere with the search for Truth, Beauty, Knowledge, and Wisdom. The road to freedom of inquiry must be free and clear." These words are equally applicable to elementary and secondary schools.

Young people encounter one-sided ideas in conversations with family, friends, in films, television, and other media. An educational setting offers more contemplative consideration and the opportunity to critically examine ideas. The real threat to society is students who can't examine controversial material in schools and who then distrust education and society as places for free exchange (Evans, 2007). Daly and Roach (1990) call for a renewed commitment to academic freedom to pursue these social and educational ends.

The Center of the Profession

Academic freedom is at the heart of the teaching profession (Encyclopedia Britannica, 2019; American Federation of Teachers, 2020). Professions are identified by the complex, purposeful nature of the work; educational requirements for admission;

and commonly held ethics and values. Medical professionals work to improve medical care, have specialized education in medical practice, and share a commitment to health. Attorneys work in law, have specialized training in its practice, and are dedicated to the value of justice. Teachers work to educate children, have knowledge of subjects and teaching practice, and share a devotion to enlightenment.

The nature of teachers' work and their shared devotion to enlightenment requires a special freedom to explore new ideas in the quest for knowledge. This freedom deserves protection beyond that provided to all citizens under the constitutional guarantee of free speech. Unlike other citizens, teachers have a professional obligation to search for truth and assist students in their search for truth (Zirkel, 1993; Meador, 2019). Teachers' jobs must not be at risk because they explore controversial material or consider ideas outside the mainstream. Professional and contractual responsibilities to educate require teachers to have freedom to examine issues.

Academic freedom, as all freedoms, has limits and conditions. Oliver Wendell Holmes famously claimed that rights to free speech would not protect "falsely shouting fire in a theater and causing a panic" (quoted in Budiansky, 2019, p. 384). But this view was overturned in a series of later cases leading to *Brandenburg v. Ohio* (1969) and others, which have narrowed the restrictions on free speech to "inciteful" speech—speech that intends to incite immediate illegal behavior in a setting where that is likely (Rotunda, 2019). Contemporary legal standards permit hate speech and other socially offensive communication unless intentionally meant to incite imminent lawless acts; common speech codes that restrict hateful words or signs are not in conformity. Free speech permits relatively unrestricted public expression.

Academic freedom presumes professional, content-based use of evidence and argument using "intellectual standards" (Simpson, 2020). Students and teachers are bound by law and legitimate regulation, and teachers are subject to professional ethics. Teacher competence is basic to academic freedom. Incompetent teachers do not deserve that extra protection; they should be suspended or dismissed if a fair and evidential evaluation finds them incompetent. A license to teach is not a license to practice incompetence (Bernard, 2008).

Academic Freedom and Teacher Competency: The Tenure Process

Competence is a mix of knowledge, skill, and judgment. For teachers it includes knowledge of the material and of the students in class, professional skill in teaching, and well-considered professional judgment. It depends on more than just accumulation of college credits, and includes practical demonstration of knowledge, skill, and judgment. As in other professions, competence should be measured by peers and wise supervisors; it continues to be refined as teachers gain experience. Initial competence is expected as the teaching credential program is fulfilled. That program of four or more years includes subject field and professional study and practice teaching under supervision. Then, depending on state law, teachers serve full-time for two to five years under school supervision before tenure is granted. This long test in actual teaching should determine competence; incompetent teachers should not get tenure.

The legal protection for academic freedom in schools is tenure, where teachers cannot be fired without due process and legitimate cause. Grounds for dismissal usually include moral turpitude, professional misconduct, and incompetence. Teachers should not be dismissed on the basis of personal or political disagreements with administrators or others. A tenured teacher has a right to know specific allegations, have a fair hearing, and an evidentially based decision by an appropriate body. The allegation must be clearly demonstrated and documented for the dismissal to be upheld. This protects tenured teachers from improper dismissal as a result of personality conflicts or local politics. There should be a high standard for becoming a teacher and for obtaining tenure; there also should be a high standard for dismissing a teacher.

Nontenured probationary teachers do not have the legal claims of tenure, but they deserve the general protection of academic freedom because they are expected to engage in enlightening education (Standler, 2000). Dismissal or nonrenewal of a probationary teacher can occur at the end of any given school term, without specifying a cause. Dismissal for dealing with controversial topics in a competent manner should, however, be prohibited by school policy as a condition for all teachers. Many excellent school districts honor this concept. Tenured faculty, protected from improper interference, need to ensure that nontenured teachers are not subjected to dismissal for performing their proper teaching function. It is a professional responsibility.

A general misunderstanding of the central role teachers play in a free society can cause them to be ignored or viewed as less than professional. Some people consider teachers to be low-level employees, hired to do what school managers ask. Excessive restrictions imposed on teachers can result. Legislatures, school boards, and administrators may censor teachers and teaching materials. Students are treated as nonpersons and expected to exhibit blind obedience. Outside of historic treatment, there are no grounds for restrictions that demean a teacher's work. Academic freedom, the essence of the teaching profession, deserves stronger advocacy as a necessary idea in our society. An educational effort would increase public awareness of the need for academic freedom and inform and inspire the people who go into teaching.

Obstacles to Academic Freedom

Notwithstanding the compelling reasons that support academic freedom, historical, political, and economic pressures develop (Wilson, 2008). Censorship, political restraint, anti-intellectualism, and illegitimate restrictions on teacher and student freedom have a long and sordid history in the United States. Under religious domination, early schools imposed moralistic requirements on teachers, such as firing them for impiety, for not attending religious services, or for not exhibiting sufficient religious zeal. In the nineteenth century, contracts required women teachers to be single, both genders to avoid drinking and smoking, to attend church each Sunday, to substitute for the minister on occasion, to not associate with "bad elements," and to avoid controversy. Communities required strict conformity. Teachers could be dismissed for dating, visiting pool halls, or simply disagreeing with local officials. A teacher stating political views could be summarily fired. No recourse could stop vigilante school boards or administrators.

Politics and economics added to earlier religious and moralistic restrictions on teachers (Pierce, 1933; Beale, 1936; Gellerman, 1938). Socialism and communism were visible targets in the 1920s, the 1960s, and surfacing again in the Reagan administration. Sexual topics and profanity are constant targets. Secular humanism—teachers and materials are anti-God, immoral, antifamily, and anti-American—is another. Current topics stimulating censors are drugs, politics, evolution, values education, self-esteem, economics, environmental issues, social activism, African American, feminist, or other minority literature, and entire courses in science, history, art, and English (Jenkinson, 1990; Horowitz, 2005; Lindorff, 2005; Seesholtz, 2005; American Library Association, 2020; National Coalition Against Censorship, 2020b). College teachers suffer as well, with many fired without due process (Sinclair, 1922; Veblen, 1957; Hofstadter and Metzger, 1968; Whittington, 2020). Academic freedom was an ideal, not common practice in early days. John Dewey and other scholars founded the American Association of University Professors (AAUP) in 1915 to protect academic freedom of college teachers, and Dewey recognized that all teachers, not just those in colleges, need academic freedom.

In the twenty-first century, teachers have gained in professional preparation and stature, but they are not fully free. Significant threats to academic freedom continue to limit education and place blinders on students. Textbook publishers shy away from controversial content. Texas State censors, for example, forced out a major American history textbook by highly respected historians because two paragraphs, out of 1,000 pages, suggested prostitution was rampant in the West in the nineteenth century (Stille, 2002). The Internet is the most recent focus of censors, with scare tactics used to block access to many legitimate Internet sites (O'Neil, 2008; Vandergrift, 2012; Hackernoon, 2019; Amnesty International, 2020; National Coalition Against Censorship, 2020a). Organized groups rise to protest "bad books." In 2011, Parents Against Bad Books in Schools (PABBIS) argued: "You might be shocked at the sensitive, controversial and inappropriate material that can be found in books in K–12 schools." PABBIS offered a list of 1,350 books and authors they consider suspicious—from Barbara Kingsolver and Toni Morrison to Leon Uris and Kurt Vonnegut, including major literary award winners and notable figures in literature, but to avoid reading the books, "shocking and inappropriate" segments were printed and available. Lists, like those from PABBIS, are used by parents and others to ask schools to ban books.

Websites that protest such censor intrusion into libraries include the Electronic Frontier Foundation (eff.org) and the Foundation for Individual Rights in Education (thefire.org). Publicized censorship and restraint actions have a chilling effect on other school boards, administrators, and teachers (Whitson, 1993; Ross, 2004; Patterson, 2010). The possibility of complaints creates fear. Daly (1991, 2010) found few school districts had policies to protect teacher and student rights to academic freedom. As a result, teacher self-censorship denies students and society the full exploration of ideas.

Sex, Politics, and Religion: Controversy and Censorship

Zealots on different sides of political, economic, and religious fences try to use schools as agents to impose their views and values on the young. They want indoctrination to make young people noncritical believers, inoculated and insulated from controversial ideas—ideas that differ from their own. Teachers are expected to force-feed students memorized material and avoid issues. Some avoid significant topics or neutralize and sterilize them to create student boredom. Efforts to censor or restrict teachers, schools, and students are manifold. Some examples include:

- A highly respected high school history teacher in the Denver Public Schools was dismissed because the newspaper published his views as a candidate for congress and the district thought he was too controversial. He had tenure, appealed, and won reinstatement, but the district limited him to teaching basic English and forbade his teaching history.

- Arizona Department of Education regulations don't require sex education. If it's offered, boys and girls must be separated, parents have to opt in, and it must stress abstinence.

- A Bakersfield, California, high school student paper was stopped from publishing a story about gender identity; after legal challenge, a county judge ruled students have the right to exercise freedom of speech and press without prior restraint.

- In Metuchen, New Jersey, the high school principal feared controversy and threatened a student-operated paper that used material from national news magazines, with those magazines' permission. After public protest, the school board refused to back the principal.

- The South Carolina legal code did not allow class discussion of LGBTQ or other alternatives to heterosexual lifestyles; teachers could not mention nonheterosexuals. A court decision in 2020 struck down the law.

- A student journalist in Virginia was censored for an accurate story about the son of a school board member who skipped classes.

- A Missouri state legislature bill in 2020 proposes "parental library review boards" to identify age-related public library material and then restrict access.

- The National Archives altered a photo of a protest march sign that was "unflattering" to the Trump administration; they later admitted it was a mistake.

- Words about puberty and homosexuality were cut by New York school administrators from a high school production of *A Chorus Line*; one student danced a part in silence.

- A tenured teacher in Colorado was dismissed for showing the publicly available Bernardo Bertolucci film *1900* as part of a class discussion about fascism. The tenured teacher appealed, the teachers' association provided an attorney, and the teacher was reinstated.

- Field trips at a Pennsylvania high school to see *MacBeth* and *Schindler's List* were canceled after some citizen complaints.

CENSORSHIP OF BOOKS IS A COMMON PROBLEM IN SCHOOLS AND LIBRARIES

Among the most frequently banned books are: *Harry Potter, Diary of Anne Frank, Catch-22, A Farewell to Arms, Deliverance, The Great Gatsby, The Adventures of Huckleberry Finn, To Kill a Mockingbird, The Chocolate War, Slaughterhouse Five, Catcher in the Rye, The*

Grapes of Wrath, Romeo and Juliet, The Color Purple, Beloved, Animal Farm, and *Invisible Man.* Recently banned or challenged books include ones dealing with homosexuality and transgender material: *Fun Home, A Day in the Life of Marlon Bundo, This One Summer, And Tango Makes Three,* and *George.* The main reasons for banning include profanity, obscenity, drinking and drug use, sexuality and sexual identity, racism, violence, antigovernment, and contempt for religions. The ALA reports that about 90% of book challenges are unreported and many of them are successful; censorship occurs without notice. Even comic books suffer censorship. Trombetta (2010) examines the history of very popular "horror" comics and a U.S. Senate committee hearing during the McCarthy period. They were essentially suppressed and the industry imposed a restrictive Comics Code (Comic Book Legal Defense Fund, 2020). A collection of those "banned" comics is available in the Young Adult section of some public libraries.

Included among the most censored book authors are Judy Blume, Mark Twain, Maya Angelou, John Steinbeck, J. D. Salinger, Toni Morrison, R. L. Stine, Maurice Sendak, William Golding, and Robert Cormier. Efforts to restrict or ban books, films, speakers, topics of study, magazines, speech, press, dress, art, drama, field trips, and other student and teacher activities permeate and undercut school life. If censorship is successful, education suffers. Teacher associations, the ALA and their Office for Intellectual Freedom, the American Civil Liberties Union, the AAUP, and the NCAC provide sources and assistance for teachers and students. NCAC also provides materials to understand and deal with censoring groups. (See Sherrow, 1996; Foerstel, 2002; Huff and Phillips, 2010; Trombetta, 2010; National Coalition Against Censorship, 2020b.)

A Necessity, Not a Frill

A society cannot be free when its schools are not. The need to provide strong support to academic freedom for teachers and their students is obvious. Ideas are the primary ingredients of democracy and education, and the realm of ideas is protected by academic freedom. This simple, elegant concept is not understood well enough by some of the public and even by some teachers. Academic freedom requires diligent effort, exercise, and expansion in schools. It is under constant threat. Academic freedom is the freedom of teachers to teach, of schools to determine educational policies and practices unfettered by political restraints or censorship, and the freedom of students to engage in study of ideas. It is essential to democracy. A society that professes freedom should demand no less freedom for its schools (Rorty, 1994; Wilson, 2008; American Library Association, 2020). The Supreme Court demonstrated its commitment to the principle of academic freedom in a 1967 decision, finding that a state law that demanded teachers take a loyalty oath was unconstitutional:

> Our nation is deeply committed to safeguarding academic freedom, which is of transcendent value to all of us and not merely to the teachers concerned. That freedom is, therefore, a special concern of the First Amendment, which does not tolerate laws that cast a pall of orthodoxy over the classroom. . . . The classroom is peculiarly the "marketplace of ideas." (*Keyishian v. Board of Regents,* 1967)

Propaganda and public deceit are practiced in all countries, including democracies, but citizens of a democracy are expected to have the right and the ability to question and examine propaganda and expose those deceits.

Despite the sometimes weak protection of academic freedom and often powerful political pressures brought to bear to stifle it, attaining freedom for teachers and students is worth the strenuous effort it demands. There are compelling democratic, educational, and professional grounds for expanding the protection of academic freedom to competent teachers and all students. And there are important social reasons why the public should support academic freedom in public education. Academic freedom is more than a set of platitudes, state regulations, and court decisions. It should be a fundamental expectation of schools in a free society. Academic freedom is a central truth for the profession of teaching.

Position 2:   For Teacher Responsibility: Freedom from Indoctrination

They must deliver the curriculum without attempting to indoctrinate students with their own personal beliefs, particularly on religious, political, and controversial topics. Simply put, K–12 teachers do not have the broad academic freedom that is usually accorded their counterparts in higher education.

—Underwood (2017)

This book is devoted to the consideration of critical issues in education. Academic freedom is one of those issues because of misunderstandings of its purposes and application to precollege level teachers and students. Academic freedom was developed for established scholars at the college and university level to provide the freedom to study topics in their specialty and report their results without political or institutional influence (Hofstadter and Metzger, 1968; Fisher, 2017; Dea, 2018). The purpose for this freedom is the advancement of knowledge, to further the work of recognized scholars. Below college level, the purpose of education is served by teachers providing and students acquiring basic and standard knowledge. This precollege purpose does not include teachers engaging in ideological indoctrination or deviation from the duly established curriculum. Teachers below college level have more impressionable students, in state-mandated settings, under parental purview. They bear special responsibilities.

Teaching is among the most influential positions in society. Teachers' influence goes well beyond the classroom doors, school grounds, and school terms; it can last for years, even a lifetime. Society organizes schools to educate the young in cultural traditions and accepted knowledge. Communities and parents deserve teachers who understand their significant role in that process and their necessary responsibilities. Teaching is next to parenting in its power to carry values and ideas from generation to generation. In some respects and circumstances, teachers exert more influence on children's views and values.

Power and Responsibility in Teaching

Rights and freedoms are not unlimited. Teacher rights and freedoms are necessarily tied to their responsibilities and are conditioned on their acceptance of those responsibilities. Teachers have responsibilities to the child, to the parents, to the community, to society, and to the profession. The child, being weaned from parental influence, looks to teachers for intellectual development, behavioral norms, and social guidance. This is a particularly important responsibility. Responsibilities to parents, for obvious reasons, are also very significant. The community is wisely concerned about the education of its young members; teachers have a responsibility to recognize and respect those values. Society gives teachers authority to develop sound knowledge and values in children. School is compulsory for that purpose and teachers bear that responsibility. Teachers also have duties to their profession, maintaining high standards of ethical conduct, academic quality, and sound practice. The power of teaching comes with responsibilities. These multiple responsibilities require accountability from teachers and schools.

TEACHER RESPONSIBILITIES TO CHILDREN

The paramount responsibility of teachers is to their students. Because precollegiate students are relatively immature and unformed, teachers must carefully exercise their influence and temper freedom with responsibility. The basic role of the teacher in elementary and secondary schools is to instruct students in traditional academic subjects, and to provide the tools and skills for students to become further educated in those subjects. This is a comprehensive responsibility and should be the main focus of the teacher's work. To the extent that teachers have students who need assistance in meeting norms of personal behavior, the teacher can provide guidance, contact the student's family, or refer special cases to appropriate authorities and counselors. Gjelten (2020) identifies the following responsibilities teachers have to their students:

- An education of quality;
- Appropriate supervision;
- Protection of student privacy;
- Respect and recognition of boundaries; and
- Limitations on discipline.

Teachers hold great potential power over children's lives, and teacher authority needs to be weighed heavily in teacher decisions on how to best convey their part of the school curriculum. Teachers derive power from maturity, knowledge, and position. Children are vulnerable. In forming and testing ideas, attitudes, and behaviors, children look to teachers for assistance and direction. Children naturally are curious and positive but cannot yet fully discern between good and bad, proper and improper.

In addition to helping students comprehend the content of a subject and develop learning skills, teachers can assist in improving their socially acceptable conduct. Teachers are not employed to challenge, threaten, or demean the religious, moral, or ethical beliefs of their students, and teachers should not attempt to impose their views of politics, economics, or social values on students.

Teacher Responsibilities to Parents

Schools, and teachers, have a special obligation to be responsive to parents' concerns for their children. This reasoning lies behind the legal concept that teachers act in loco parentis, or in place of the parent. That concept, with deep social and legal roots, protects teachers in handling student discipline and evaluation. It also requires teachers to remain sensitive to parental interests. Teachers, standing in place of the parents, take on similar responsibilities for children's development and protection. Teachers have responsibilities for providing a safe, healthy classroom environment, and they assume protective moral, ethical, and legal duties. In addition, they have educational responsibilities: they must teach children necessary knowledge and skills. Discharging these responsibilities demands responsiveness to parental concerns about the kinds of knowledge and values taught.

Parents have general, moral, and legal rights and obligations to and for their children—rights and obligations that teachers and schools must not undermine. Parents are expected to provide for the child's safety and welfare—physical, emotional, spiritual, and moral. Provision of food, clothing, and shelter is a parental obligation given up only when parents are incapable of providing them. Parents have moral obligations and rights, including instructing their children in determining right from wrong, good from bad. Parents instruct their children in ethical conduct by providing them with a set of socially acceptable behaviors, including integrity, honesty, courtesy, and respect. Under the law, parents can be held accountable for lack of adequate and appropriate care of their children; they can even be held legally responsible for their children's acts.

Because parents are presumed to have the child's interests at heart, they are given great latitude in providing care and upbringing. Parents are even permitted to exercise appropriate corporal punishment, more than any other person would be permitted to inflict on a child, under the legal idea that the parent has broad responsibilities and rights. At the root of laws regarding parents' rights and obligations is the idea that they are responsible for their children's upbringing, morality, and behaviors. Teachers, however, act as surrogate parents only in certain situations, with a number of limitations, and should not deviate from the norms of the good parent in the good society. Children are not put in schools as punishment or as a way to make up for family irresponsibility. Schools, therefore, must continue the cultural heritage by inculcating positive and supportive social and family values in the young.

Parents control much that their children see, hear, and do during the earliest years. Under state laws on schooling, parents extend that effort to include teachers, but they retain parental rights and interests. That is a good thing for the child and society as a child becomes more mature while studying under responsible, committed teachers. Parents retain strong interests in the learnings of their children long after primary school. Good schools and teachers give them nothing to fear in higher grades.

Teachers do not have license to do anything to students, physically or mentally. Teachers can require students to be attentive to lessons, be orderly, and be civil, but they are prohibited from abusive activities, such as striking students. Malevolent teacher behavior is outside the standards of professional conduct. Mental abuse of students is equally abhorrent but is less easy to detect. Mental abuse is no less harmful, however, to students, parents, or society. It can consist of vicious verbal personal attacks, indoctrination in antisocial values or behaviors, or manipulation of children's minds against parents or morality (Sowell, 2005; Stern, 2006). Parents have a right to insist teachers not subject their children to these tactics, but parents often are unaware of them until after the damage has been done.

Parents have a right to monitor what schools are teaching their children, hold the school accountable for it, and limit the potential for damage to their children. Beyond necessary limits on teachers, schools also must be subject to limits that conform to social mores. For example, book, video, and film purchases for school libraries should be continuously and vigilantly screened so that only the proper material is made available to our children. A parent review committee can be used to determine which books are suitable, with the opportunity for any parent to complain about library materials and have that complaint acted on effectively.

We need not only worry about what teaching materials are used in classrooms; we also must be vigilant about underage student access to media centers and the Internet. The Internet can be a valuable resource for children. There are many excellent websites for adding educational quality in such areas as science, history, the arts, literature, math, and other subjects. However, there exists a serious problem when websites containing inhumane, racist, sexual, or other inappropriate materials are available in schools. The Children's Internet Protection Act (2000) requires libraries to use filtering software on their devices to prevent obscenity, child pornography, or other harmful materials to be shown to children on their screens. Twenty-seven states also have Internet filtering laws that apply to publicly funded schools or libraries. Parents can exert control in their children's computer use at home to screen out inappropriate sites; schools have a greater responsibility in screening out any such sites from their computers since schools serve a broad cross section of children.

TEACHER RESPONSIBILITIES TO SOCIETY

Society, as well as parents, has a significant interest in children's education. Schools were established to pass on the cultural heritage and to provide the skills, attitudes, and knowledge needed to produce good citizens who meet their responsibilities in family, work, and social roles. Society has values, standards of behavior, and attitudes that schools must convey to children. These standards have evolved over a long period, and they represent our common culture. Society charges schools and teachers to ensure that social standards and the ideals that these standards represent are taught by example and by word.

Schools are social institutions, financed and regulated to fulfill social purposes. All states have laws and regulations that govern schools and reflect social interests; often these are among the longest sections of state law. Most state constitutions identify education as a required institution and schools consume the largest portion of state taxpayer funds. Attendance is mandated, and school boards are official state agencies that control hiring, curriculum, and expenditures. There is an extensive governmental investment in schools and teachers. Beyond formal government structures, education is a prime social function and interest. Schools do not exist as entities separate from society, able to chart their own courses as though they had no social responsibilities. They were not intended to instruct students in antisocial or immoral ideas or behaviors, nor will society allow them to do so. Society trusts teachers to develop the young into positive, productive citizens. Those few teachers who use their position to attempt to destroy social values or create social dissension are violating that trust. Those who sow the seeds of negativism, nihilism, or cynicism also are violating that trust. Society has the right to restrict, condemn, or exclude from teaching those who harm its interests.

TEACHER RESPONSIBILITIES TO THEIR PROFESSION

The teaching profession has an extensive and illustrious history; it is a history based on service to children and society. A teacher code of ethics recognizes teacher responsibilities as singularly important. The National Education Association (2020) Code of Ethics includes two principles: (1) commitment to the student and (2) commitment to the profession. The Association of American Educators (2020) shares these principles and also adds the commitment to professional colleagues. These convey teachers' responsibilities to student learning and to legal conduct as teachers in society. A basic responsibility of the teaching profession is to prepare young people for life in society, including social values and knowledge. Students look up to teachers; teacher professional conduct should exemplify society's ideals. This includes education on cultural heritage and social responsibility.

Teachers are the key to good education. They are also the key to poor education. When teachers are excellent, a school is excellent. But many schools are not excellent, and many teachers are weak and ineffective.

The false claim that academic freedom gives teachers the right to do what they wish does account for the real history of academic freedom. Even in the college setting, there are limits for researchers; they cannot do any research they might want, certainly none that knowingly harms people. We demand greater accountability from public school teachers than we do from teachers in colleges. Finn (2017) says: "too many . . . teachers are indoctrinating their students."

The teaching profession needs to change from protecting poor teachers to protecting children and society from those poor teachers. Unwise protections burden students, parents, and citizens, and pose a more serious threat to decency and social values (Limbaugh, 2005; Sowell, 2005). Teachers have a professional obligation to act to reject those who would tarnish the profession's reputation.

Academic freedom consists of the presentation of balanced views, with the teacher taking a neutral role to be sure there is fairness. This can't be done if schools hire teachers who think indoctrination is their right. We need a professional code of ethics for teachers that emphasizes the teaching of basic skills to help students achieve their educational goals. Freedom for teachers is directly linked to their responsibilities; a suitable code of ethics makes that clear.

Academic Freedom as License

A license to teach is not a license to impose one's views on others. Corruption of the young is at the least a moral crime; it is ethically reprehensible. The majority of teachers accept this and discharge their duties with integrity and care. For them, teaching is a calling to instruct the young in society's knowledge and values. This represents the best in the profession and is a great support to the well-being of the community and nation. Unfortunately, some teachers do not subscribe to the values of their profession. There is a difference between academic freedom and license, and no academic freedom should exist for those who indoctrinate others.

Some teachers are caught in drug raids, cheat on income taxes, and commit robbery—but these are exceptions. Teachers who engage in criminal conduct are subject to criminal penalties, and should not receive special treatment within the academic discipline. There is another form of crime, intellectual crime, that teachers can commit under the guise of academic freedom. Intellectual crimes include ridiculing student or family values, advocating antisocial attitudes, and influencing students to think or act in opposition to parent and community norms. These crimes can have an even greater, more devastating effect on children and society than legal transgressions because they tear at the nation's moral fiber. Perpetrators should not have special protection. There is nothing academic about confusing and confounding children about their families and society; teachers who commit such crimes deserve no consideration under the rubric of academic freedom. Distorting the minds of the young is misteaching and should be penalized (Olson, 2011; *Wall Street Journal*, 2012).

Some school teachers and their unions want to open a large umbrella of academic freedom to cover anything a teacher does or says. Their claims to protection are not justified, but can make school administrators wary. Thus, teachers with questionable expressions of viewpoints in the classroom often get away with it for years because the administration is afraid to reprimand them. Instead, the problem is hidden. Parents who protest are allowed to have their children transferred to other classes, but unsuspecting parents can fall prey to unprofessional classroom actions. It takes a courageous, persistent parent to thwart such a teacher. Often, public disclosure of the teacher's actions will rouse the community and force school officials to take action.

Teachers may have views that differ from community norms, but the classroom is not the place in which to express them. Teachers should not have the freedom to preach inappropriate ideas in schools. Schools are not meant to be forums for teachers whose viewpoints differ sharply from those of the community. Instead, schools are intended to express and affirm community values. Malleable students are a captive audience; teachers must not have the right to impose unfitting views on the young (Sowell, 2005).

Academic Freedom and Teacher Freedom

Within the limits of responsibility, teachers deserve respect and some freedom to determine how to teach. Teacher freedom can be separated from academic freedom, which is intended to protect university scholars. This does not denigrate teachers; teacher freedom is protected by community traditions and free speech in the law. The Constitution provides the right to make critical statements about the government, employers, or the state of the world provided that it is not slanderous, imminently dangerous, or obscene. We are free to speak, but we must accept the consequences for our statements (Standler, 2000). Expression of views, as in letters to a newspaper editor, is a right in the United States. However, these rights and freedoms do not guarantee job security (Harden, 2012). Teachers, more than most citizens, should be aware of the responsibilities surrounding public discourse. A teacher's imprudent comments can lead to public outrage. For public school teachers, the public is the employer; teachers should not expect refuge when they make malicious comments about schools, the community, or the nation. Teachers should not be in the classrooms if they use propaganda or inaccurate or misleading material. There is no special privilege granted to teachers merely because they close the classroom door.

Academic Freedom as a Function of Academic Position

Academic freedom protects scholars who recognize the academic responsibilities inherent in it. Scholars and other educators do not have the right to proselytize or indoctrinate students using the shield of special protection of academic freedom (Limbaugh, 2005). Buckley (1951), Hook (1953), and Kirk (1955) provide philosophic grounds for limiting teacher freedom to expert scholars engaged in publication of their research. Elementary and secondary school teachers differ from university scholars in their training, functions, employment status, and responsibilities. Elementary and secondary schools have broad responsibilities to parents, communities, and the state. Rhetoric about academic freedom does not diminish those significant responsibilities. Teachers deserve respect and appreciation for their contributions to society. They deserve the protection that the Bill of Rights gives to all U.S. citizens: freedom of speech, association, and assembly. All of us, including teachers, have these freedoms and responsibilities. Teacher responsibilities to students, parents, school officials, the teaching profession, and society make classroom teachers one of our most treasured resources.

FOR DISCUSSION

1. *Dialectic Exercise*: The idea that academic freedom is limited to university researchers in their field of study only can be considered a thesis. Propose a clear antithesis. Find evidence on each side, and evaluate it. What philosophic grounds and logic support each position? What would be a suitable synthesis? How would your synthesis affect the current situation for K–12 teachers in regard to the exercise of academic freedom?

2. Draft an example set of policies for a school district regarding teacher freedoms and student freedoms. Address the use of controversial materials in the classroom and the handling of complaints by parents or the community about selected teaching materials.

3. Should there be any restrictions on what a teacher can discuss in class? What set of principles should govern establishment of those limits? Should students have the same freedoms and limits? Is student age or teacher experience a significant factor in this determination? How should schools handle questions that arise about how a teacher handles controversy?

4. Which, if any, of the following topics should be banned from schoolbooks or class discussion?

Explicit sexual material	Violence
Sexism	Anti-American views
Racism	Antireligious ideas
Fascism	Socialism
Inhuman treatment of people	Animal, child, or spouse abuse

What justifies censorship of any of these topics? Who should decide? How would you construct a dialectic on censorship?

5. What role should teachers play in learning about and responding to efforts at censorship? Should censors be censored? How should a teacher be prepared to deal with censors and political restraint?

References

American Federation of Teachers (2020, January 30). Academic Freedom (aft.com).

American Library Association (2020). Intellectual Freedom News (ala.org/news/taxonomy/term/786).

Amnesty International (2020, January 24). Freedom of Expression and the Internet (amnestyusa.org).

Association of American Educators (2020, January 27). Code of Ethics for Educators (aaeteachers.org).

Beale, H. (1936). *Are American Teachers Free?* New York: Scribner's.

Bernard, S. (2008, March). "Should There Be Limits on Teachers' Freedom of Speech?" *Edutopia*.

Brandenburg v. Ohio (1969). 395 U.S. 444.

Buckley, W. F. (1951). *God and Man at Yale.* Chicago: Regnery.

Budiansky, S. (2019). *Oliver Wendell Holmes.* New York: W.W. Norton.

Cary v. Board of Education of Adams–Arapahoe School District (1979). 427 F. Supp. 945 (D. Colo. 1977), aff'd, 598 F. 2d 535 (10th Cir.).

Comic Book Legal Defense Fund (2020, January 20). History of Comics Censorship (cbldf.org).

Daly, J. K. (1991). "The Influence of Administrators on the Teaching of Social Studies." *Theory and Research in Social Education* 19:267–283.

Daly, J. K. (2010). "Learning about Teacher and Student Freedom." *Social Education* 74:306–309.

Daly, J. K., and Roach, P. B. (1990). "Reaffirming a Commitment to Academic Freedom." *Social Education* 54:342–345.

Daly, J. K., Schall, P., and Skeele, R. (2001). *Protecting the Right to Teach and Learn.* New York: Teachers College Press.

Dea, S. (2018, October 9). "A History of Academic Freedom." *University Affairs*.

Encyclopedia Britannica (2019, December 31). Academic Freedom (britannica.com).

Evans, R. W. (2007). *This Happened in America: Harold Rugg and the Censure of Social Studies.* Charlotte, NC: Information Age.

Finn, C. E. (2017, May 23). "The End of Teacher Tenure?" *Defining Ideas* (hoover.org).

Fisher, D. (2017, August 30). The Origin of Academic Freedom in the U.S. The Free Speech Center, Middle Tennessee State University (mtsu.edu/first-amendment).

Foerstel, H. N. (2002). *Banned in the USA.* Westport, CT: Greenwood Press.

Garcetti v. Ceballos (2006). 547 U.S. 410.

Gellerman, W. (1938). *The American Legion as Educator.* New York: Teachers College Press.

Gershman, C. (2020, January). "The Instinct for Freedom." *Journal of Democracy* 31(6).

Gjelten, E. A. (2020, January 26). What Are Teachers' Responsibilities to Their Students? (lawyers.com).

Hackernoon (2019, October 18). The Unsettling Rise of Internet Censorship Around the World (hackernoon.org).

Harden, N. (2012). "Academic Freedom, Terrorism, and the NYPD." *National Review* Online (nationalreview.com).

Hofstadter, R., and Metzger, W. (1968). *The Development of Academic Freedom in the United States.* New York: Columbia University Press.

Hook, S. (1953). *Heresy, Yes—Conspiracy, No.* New York: J. Day Co.

Horowitz, D. (2005, July 29). "Academic Freedom: David Horowitz vs. Russell Jacoby." *Frontpage.*

Huff, M., and Phillips, P. (2010). *Censored 2011.* New York: Seven Stories Press.

International Federation of Library Associations and Institutions (2018, November 20). Libraries and Intellectual Freedom (ifla.org).

Jenkinson, E. B. (1990). "Child Abuse in the Hate Factory." In A. Ochoa, ed., *Academic Freedom to Teach and to Learn.* Washington, DC: National Education Association.

Keyishian v. Board of Regents (1967). 385 U.S. 589.

Kirk, R. (1955). *Academic Freedom.* Chicago: Regnery.

La Rue, J., and Diaz, E. (2017, November 1). "50 Years of Intellectual Freedom." *American Libraries.*

Limbaugh, D. (2005). "False Promises of Academic Freedom." www.townhall.com/columnists.

Lindorff, D. (2005, February 10). Academic Freedom? What Academic Freedom?" Common Dreams (commondreams.org).

Magi, R., and Garnar, M. (2015). *A History of ALA Policy on Intellectual Freedom.* Chicago: American Library Association.

Mayer v. Monroe County Community School Corp. (2007). 474 F. 3rd 477,479–80 (7th Cir.), *cert. denied* 128 S. Ct. 160.

Mchangama, J. (2020, January 31). "Even Noxious Ideas Need Airing." *The Economist.*

Meador, D. (2019, October 23). The Importance of Maintaining Professionalism in Schools. ThoughtCo. (thoughtco.com).

National Coalition Against Censorship (2020a, January 24). Internet Free Expression Timeline (ncac.org).

——— (2020b, January 25). The First Amendment in Schools: Censorship (ncac.org).

National Council for the Social Studies (2016, May/June). "Academic Freedom and the Social Studies Teacher." *Social Education.*

National Council of Teachers of English (2019, November 7). Statement on Academic Freedom (ncte.org/statement/academic-freedom-copy).

National Education Association (2020, January 27). Code of Ethics (nea.org).

Nieto, S. (2006, Spring). Teaching as Political Work. Longfellow Lecture, Sarah Lawrence College.

O'Neil, R. M. (1981). *Classrooms in the Crossfire.* Bloomington: Indiana University Press.

——— (2008). *Academic Freedom in the Wired World.* Cambridge, MA: Harvard University Press.

——— (2010). "Legal Issues in the Protection of Student Freedoms." *Social Education* 74(6):322–325.

Olson, K. (2011). *Indoctrination: How "Useful Idiots" Are Using Our Schools to Subvert American Exceptionalism.* Bloomington, IN: AuthorHouse.

Parents Against Bad Books in Schools (2011). (pabbis.org).

Patterson, N. C. (2010). "What's Stopping You? Classroom Censorship for Better or Worse." *Social Education* 74(6):326–331.

Pekoll, K. (2019). *Beyond Banned Books.* Chicago: American Library Association.

Pierce, B. (1933). *Citizens' Organizations and the Civic Training of Youth.* New York: Scribner's.

Puddington, A., Melia, R. O., and Kelly, J. (2008). *Today's Americans: How Free?* Lanham, MD: Rowman & Littlefield.

Rorty, R. (1994). "Does Academic Freedom Have Philosophical Presuppositions?" *Academe* 80:52–63.

Ross, S. J. (2004, October 14). "21st Century Book-Burning." *Los Angeles Times.*

Rotunda, R. D. (2019, October 29). "The Right to Shout Fire in a Crowded Theatre: Hateful Speech and the First Amendment." *Chapman Law Review* 22(2):319–367.

Seesholtz, M. (2005, July 11). Diversity, Academic Freedom and Conservative T-Shirts (counterbias.org).

Sherrow, V. (1996). *Censorship in Schools.* Springfield, NJ: Enslow.

Simpson, M. D. (2010). "Defending Academic Freedom: Advice for Teachers." *Social Education* 74(6):310–315.

Simpson, R. M. (2020). "The Relation between Academic Freedom and Free Speech." *Ethics* (forthcoming).

Sinha, C. (2016, June). "Teaching as a Political Act." *Human Affairs* 26(3).

Sinclair, U. (1922). *The Goose-Step.* Pasadena, CA: Sinclair.

Sowell, T. (2005, February 15). Academic Freedom? Townhall (townhall.com).

Standler, R. B. (2000). Academic Freedom in the USA (rbs2.com/afree.htm).

Stern, S. (2006, March 12). "Pinko Teachers, Inc." *Frontpage.*

Stille, A. (2002, June 29). "Textbook Publishers Learn to Avoid Messing with Texas." *New York Times.*

Tinker v. Des Moines Independent School District (1969). 393 U.S. 503, 510–11.

Trombetta, J. (2010). *The Horror, The Horror!: Comic Books the Government Didn't Want You to Read.* New York: Abrams Comic Arts.

Underwood, J. (2017, December 4). "School Districts Control Teachers' Classroom Speech." *Phi Delta Kappan* 49(4).

United States v. American Library Association, Inc. (2003). 539 U.S. 194.

Vandergrift, K. (2012, April). Censorship, the Internet, Intellectual Freedom, and Youth. School of Communication and Information, Rutgers University (comminfo.rutgers.edu).

Veblen, T. (1957). *The Higher Learning in America: Memorandum on the Conduct of Universities by Businessmen.* New York: Sagamore.

Wall Street Journal (2012, March 26). "Tennessee Legislature Passes Landmark Academic Freedom on Evolution Bill."

Whitson, J. A. (1993). "After Hazelwood: The Role of School Officials in Conflicts Over the Curriculum." *ALAN Review* 20:2–6.

Whittington, K. E. (2020, Winter). "Academic Freedom Under Threat." Book Review, *Academe.*

Wieman v. Updegraff (1952). 244 U.S. 183.

Wilson, J. K. (2008). *Patriotic Correctness: Academic Freedom and Its Enemies.* Boulder, CO: Paradigm Press.

Worona, J., and Shaw, D. S. (2018, July 24). The Contours of First Amendment Free Speech Rights. Summer Law Conference, New York State School Boards.

Yono, K. (2020, February 4). "Not Quite Banned: Soft Censorship That Makes Stories Disappear." *School Library Journal.*

Zirkel, P. (1993). "Academic Freedom: Professional or Legal Right?" *Educational Leadership* 50:42–43.

Index